COMPARATIVE CONSTITUTIONAL LAW

CONTEMPORARY LEGAL EDUCATION SERIES

CONTEMPORARY LEGAL EDUCATION SERIES

ADVISORY COMMITTEE

Murray L. Schwartz, *Chairman*
Ralph S. Brown, Jr.
Alfred F. Conard
A. Kenneth Pye
Maurice Rosenberg
Jerre S. Williams

Comparative Constitutional Law

Cases and Materials

MAURO CAPPELLETTI

Professor of Law
University of Florence
European University Institute, Florence
Stanford Law School

WILLIAM COHEN

Professor of Law
Stanford Law School

THE BOBBS-MERRILL COMPANY, INC.
PUBLISHERS
INDIANAPOLIS • NEW YORK • CHARLOTTESVILLE, VIRGINIA

It is significant that most of the provisions of the Bill of Rights are procedural, for it is procedure that marks much of the difference between rule by law and rule by fiat. (Mr. Justice Douglas speaking for the U.S. Supreme Court in Wisconsin v. Constantineau, *400 U.S. 433, 436 (1971)).*

Preface

This book consists of two distinct parts. Part I is a structural analysis of constitutional adjudication in the contemporary world, without explicit reference to the content of the rules of higher law which are enforced. Chapter 1 traces the early history of judicial review, and outlines its contemporary expansion in the modern world. Chapter 2 briefly develops the distinctions between judicial and political review, while Chapter 3 traces in detail the tension between the French tradition of political review and current pressures for introduction of judicial review in France. Chapter 4 explores some important structural and functional differences among national systems of judicial review: centralized (or "European") versus decentralized (or "American") review; review "incidenter" versus review "principaliter"; decisions "inter partes" versus decisions "erga omnes"; and retroactive versus prospective decisions. Chapter 5 discusses the extraordinary recent phenomenon of the emergence of judicial review at a supranational level, the international sources of higher law and the organs — national and international — for adjudication of that law, with particular emphasis on the European Economic Community and its Court of Justice as well as the European Convention on Human Rights and its Commission and Court of Human Rights.

Part II is a picture of judicial review in action — a selection of materials illustrating the application of similar constitutional norms in the United States and continental Europe. We have not attempted, of course, to be encyclopedic in our selection of topics, nor have we tried to give up-to-date information of constitutional developments in any one of the countries discussed in this part of the book. With constitutional law casebooks in the United States — even those limited to issues of civil liberties — running to many hundreds, and even thousands, of pages, a comprehensive comparison of constitutional norms in force in many nations is beyond the reach of any single course.

Rather, in Chapters 6 through 11 we have chosen to concentrate on norms of fair procedure. Initially, and notwithstanding Justice Douglas' warning quoted above, most readers will probably find that choice to be surprising, given the wide range of substantive human rights which are emphasized in typical constitutional law courses both in America and in Europe. (Indeed, at least in the United States, most of the subject of these six chapters is not studied in constitutional law courses at all, but is scattered through courses in civil procedure, criminal procedure, federal jurisdiction, and administrative law.)

Our choice was the result of two factors. First, differences in procedural systems and institutions present the most marked contrast between common law and civil law countries. On the other hand, basic rules of fair procedure, such as judicial independence and impartiality and the parties' right to be heard, are essentially shared in common by western legal cultures. Hence, a comparative study of similar norms of fairness as they apply to considerably different procedural systems has provided a rich study in comparative law. Second, the European editor of this book has devoted much of his professional career to the comparative study of the problems of access to justice. From that work, there has developed naturally a concern for the *quality* of justice, as reflected in rules of procedure and especially in those rules which, by reason of their basic importance, have become part of the constitutions and even of international conventions binding for a large number of countries.

We have not, however, been unaware that much significant constitutional litigation deals with substantive, rather than procedural, constitutional rights. In these days of increased international concern for human rights, it would have been inappropriate to concentrate exclusively on rules of fair procedure. Chapter 11, which deals with the treatment of illegally seized evidence, combines concern for procedure with mechanisms for protection of basic human rights to dignity and privacy. And, finally, Chapter 12 represents the most striking comparison available in the comparative constitutional adjudication of substantive rights, with the almost contemporary, recent abortion decisions from the United States, France, Germany, Italy, and Austria, as well as the European Commission of Human Rights.

Some will initially find that the organization of Chapters 6 through 10 is unconventional and, perhaps, illogical. A more conventional organization, which was reflected in early, experimental editions of these materials, would have begun with the qualities of the decision makers who comprise the members of the tribunals (Chapter 8 on judicial independence and Chapter 9 on the natural judge), turning then to the right of access to those tribunals (Chapter 6), and finally to the quality of justice administered by those tribunals (Chapter 7 on notice and fair hearing and Chapter 10 on right to counsel). It will seem strange, especially to Europeans, that we have separated Chapters 7 and 10, which deal with different aspects of a fair hearing.

In teaching these materials in several law schools, however, the editors have become convinced that the fundamental dichotomy, which must be understood at the outset — a dichotomy which represents, originally, a basic divergence between civil law and common law, but which is also the point of a gradual, if slow, convergence — is that between the administrative courts of continental Europe and the administrative agencies of the United States. The materials in Chapter 6, dealing with plaintiffs' right of access to judicial review, illustrate that dichotomy and divergence, and it is here that we chose to begin. The materials in Chapter 7, which deal with the defendant's right of defense, continue to illustrate the same concept with reference to the defendant's access to court, but illustrate also the gradual convergence, *i.e.*, the continuing "judicialization" of administrative procedure in the United States. Chapters 8 and 9, dealing with constitutional guarantees of judges, complete the analysis of major differences dictated by reliance, on the one hand, on adjudication by administrative courts, and, on the other hand, on adjudication by quasi-judicial administrative agencies.

In the cases and materials which follow, translations from non-English sources are by the editors or under their direction, unless otherwise indicated. Numbered footnotes, with the original numbers retained, are from the excerpted materials, while asterisk footnotes are by the editors.

Finally, we wish to thank all those whose efforts have gone into the selection and editing of these materials and of prior experimental versions. There were three such unpublished, mimeographed versions prepared under the general editorship of Mr. Cappelletti. The first was prepared in 1969 with the assistance of R. Toothaker (Stanford), V. Vigoriti (Florence), D. Wilson (U.C. Berkeley), V. Grementieri (Florence), N. Trocker (Florence), R. Englehart (Oxford), and J. Epstein (Stanford). The second was prepared in 1970 with the additional assistance of S.P. Frankino (Harvard) and J. Weisner (Stanford). Finally, a third version was prepared in 1972 with the assistance of D. Goldstein (Stanford) as well as the continuing collaboration of Mr. Cappelletti's junior colleagues at the Florence Institute of Comparative Law; this third version was, in turn, subjected to a number of revisions between 1973 and 1976, in which T. Todd, S. Berke, and B. Hahn (Stanford) as well as G. Walter (Tübingen) and M. Heckly (Paris) were of much help. The first two versions were used by Mr. Cappelletti in courses he taught at Harvard Law School in 1969 and at Boalt Hall in 1970, whereas the third version was used in courses he taught at Stanford Law School in 1972 and 1973 and, jointly with Mr. Cohen, again at Stanford in 1975 and 1976, and at the European University Institute at Florence in 1977.

The present published version presents an entirely new book with a totally different structure and many new materials and approaches, for which Mr. Cohen's participation has been essential. Yet, the two present editors wish to acknowledge that the preparation of this book would have been impossible without the eight-year-long process of collection, revision, teaching and criticism — in sum, of trial and retrial — which has preceded its publication. In addition to those mentioned above, they want to express their gratitude to Dr. Jürgen Schwabe of Giessen, who read parts of the manuscript and made useful suggestions for its improvement.

As the long list of persons who participated in the finalization of this book may demonstrate, comparative law, while a fascinating tool to provide new, broader, enlightening perspectives and a deeper understanding of things and events, peoples and countries, is also a continuous exercise in intellectual patience and humility. Patience is necessary to pursue the continuing search for always new and often unexpected developments, to understand such developments, to place them in their connections — in other words, not to refuse them as "alien," "strange," "odd," or "bizarre." Humility, on the other hand, is imperative for at least two reasons: first, in order both to accept, indeed urge, criticism, even severe criticism, which is necessary to correct the many inevitable errors, gaps, and misunderstandings that readers will find in any comparative work of some dimension, and certainly in this one; and second, in order to maintain awareness of the fact that large comparative research can only be the collective product of the labor of many, even though someone has to bear individual responsibility for it. All those who helped — those named above and dozens of unnamed: students and colleagues, Europeans and Americans — are warmly thanked here by the present editors. Indeed, both of us are looking forward to further collaboration — to make of this book, through further revisions, a more valuable intellectual experience, a more valuable attempt to comprehend western societies' approaches to the problems of justice and human rights.

Florence   *Mauro Cappelletti*
Stanford   *William Cohen*
January, 1978*

---

* With only a few exceptions, this book does not include developments beyond this date.

Summary Table of Contents

Table of Contents

Table of Cases

UNITED STATES CASES

TABLE OF CASES

FOREIGN CASES

PART I
STRUCTURAL ANALYSIS OF CONSTITUTIONAL ADJUDICATION IN THE CONTEMPORARY WORLD

Chapter 1

THE HISTORY AND CONTEMPORARY EXPANSION OF JUDICIAL REVIEW

A. EARLY HISTORICAL ANTECEDENTS OF JUDICIAL REVIEW*

1. Judicial Review of Legislation: A Distinctively American Contribution to Political Theory?

While judicial review as a working method of subordinating state action to higher principles was first effectively implemented in the United States, clearly the idea did not spring new and fully developed from the head of John Marshall. Rather, the American version of judicial review was the logical result of centuries of European thought and colonial experiences, which had made western man in general willing to admit the theoretical primacy of certain kinds of law and had made Americans in particular ready to provide a *judicial* means of enforcing that primacy.

This is not to minimize the importance of the American contribution, since prior to the formation of the American system of judicial review, nothing similar had been created in other countries. The reason for this is readily understandable, as it was the Constitution of the United States which initiated the era of "constitutionalism," with the notion of the supremacy of the constitution over ordinary laws. The American Constitution represented the archetype of so-called "rigid" constitutions in contrast to "flexible" ones. That is to say that it was the model of those constitutions not subject to change or revision through the ordinary laws, but changeable, if at all, only by a special amending procedure. By way of contrast, the unwritten British Constitution is still flexible, as was the *Statuto Albertino,* the Italian Constitution of 1848, which has been replaced by the rigid Republican Constitution of 1948.

The American Constitution of 1789, on the other hand, expressly declared in article VI, paragraph 2: "This Constitution . . . shall be the supreme Law of the Land; and the Judges in every State shall be

---

* This section is adapted from M. CAPPELLETTI, JUDICIAL REVIEW IN THE CONTEMPORARY WORLD 25-32, 36-42 (1971).

3

bound thereby. . . ." This article, as it has been interpreted, especially through the work of John Marshall, has been of fundamental importance and has brought about radical innovations. On the one hand, it was the source of the supremacy of the Constitution; on the other hand, it led to the power and the duty of the judiciary to disregard laws contrary to the Constitution itself. In this context the judgment of the Supreme Court, rendered in 1803 by Chief Justice Marshall in *Marbury v. Madison,** is well-known. Here the differences between rigid and flexible constitutions and the necessity of choosing between one or the other were expounded with great logical clarity. It is evident, as the judgment declares, that either the constitution prevails over legislative enactments contrary to it, or the legislature is able to change the constitution by ordinary legislation. There is no middle road between these alternatives. Either the constitution is fundamental law, superior and unchangeable by ordinary means, or it is placed on the same level as ordinary legislative enactments and, as a result, can be altered at will by the legislative body. If the former alternative is accepted, then one must conclude that a legislative enactment contrary to the constitution is not law; if, on the other hand, the second alternative is chosen, written constitutions are no more than worthless attempts to limit a power which by its very nature is illimitable.

Marshall's decision, with its enunciation of the supremacy of the constitution over other laws and of the judicial power to disregard unconstitutional laws, has certainly been a grand innovation. Today almost all modern constitutions of the western world tend to be rigid rather than flexible; this fundamentally important world-wide movement was effectively begun by the American Constitution of 1789 and its courageous interpretation by the Supreme Court.

Yet these developments must be seen not as a denial, but as a fulfillment of the past. For, even without expressly and consciously envisaging "supremacy of the Constitution" over ordinary laws, other and earlier legal systems have provided various forms of supremacy of a certain law or of a given set of laws. These might, in modern terminology, justly be called constitutional or fundamental laws, "Grundgesetze," taking precedence over other laws which, again in modern terminology, might be called ordinary laws. Of course, while much of Western Europe has shared at one time or another in the desire to insure the supremacy of the fundamental law, local experiences have caused different states to look to different means for bringing about this goal. Some, for example, tended to look to the popular legislature to uphold higher principles, while others placed more faith in the judiciary. An examination of these historical similarities (*i.e.,* the common striving

---

* 5 U.S. (1 Cranch) 137 (1803).

toward the definition and enforcement of a higher law) and differences (*e.g.,* as to the faith to be placed in the legislature vis-à-vis the judiciary) would go far toward explaining present day contrasts between various systems of constitutional control.

2. "Higher Law" Conceptions in Classical Antiquity

The belief, then, in the need to subordinate certain acts of the law-making power to higher, more permanent principles is not confined to our own time. It may be traced, through the Enlightenment philosophers, the English courts of equity, the French *Parlements,* the medieval scholastics, and early Church fathers to its earliest direct origins in Greco-Roman civilization.

In Athenian law, for example, there was a distinction made between a *nómos,* corresponding to law in the strict sense, and a *pséphisma,* which in our times might be called a decree. In fact *nómoi* might in a certain sense be compared to modern constitutional laws, for they often concerned the organization of the State and could be amended only by a special procedure which would remind a modern lawyer of the procedure for revision of the Constitution. As a well known student of Attic law has written, there was "a notion common to all the Greek states" that the law or *nómos* ought to be something fixed and "withdrawn from the tumultuous vicissitudes of political life and from the headstrong impulses of the assemblies." Therefore, the procedure devised for amending the *nómoi* in Athens was very complex; revision of the laws was a matter of extreme seriousness and was surrounded by most carefully conceived and unusual guarantees. Heavy responsibility was placed on the person who proposed an amendment which was not eventually ratified or, even if ratified, subsequently appeared inadvisable. Thus the power to change the laws was withdrawn from the whims of a majority in the popular Assembly (the *ecclesía*). This idea is also reflected in the philosophy of the greatest thinkers of that era. Plato, for example, believed the laws should reflect the divine order of things, being superior and not adaptable to the changing interests of men or classes of men. For Aristotle, the laws were norms above human passions, and, significantly, he formulated a doctrine of the supremacy of the laws and of the illegality of the unjust law.

Nevertheless, the popular Assembly, or *ecclesía,* also had its own direct legislative power. The decisions of the Assembly did not, however, assume either the form or the weight of *nómoi* but rather of *psephísmata,* which might be termed decrees. The *pséphisma* could deal with a wide range of matters; it could even consist of norms of general effect, binding on all the citizens. In such a case it was "assimilated" to the law. One might also add that in certain of the more politically troubled times in the life of the Athenian *pólis,* the tendency to legislate by *psephísmata* became dominant. Nevertheless it remained a fundamental principle that the decree, whatever its content, had to be "legal both in form and in substance." As modern jurists would say, it had to be *constitutional;* it could not be contrary to the existing *nómoi.*

The results of illegality (or, as we would say, of unconstitutionality) on the part of decrees emanating from the *ecclesía* were two-fold. On the one hand there was a criminal liability incurred by the person who had proposed the decree; this liability gave rise to a public action called *graphè paranómon,* which had to be brought within one year. On the other hand, it seems that a decree contrary to a law was invalid following the principle — mentioned by Demosthenes — that the *nómos* was to prevail over a contrary *pséphisma.* The Athenian judges, who were bound to adjudicate "katá toùs nómous kaì katà psephísmata" (according to the laws and the decrees), were only bound to follow the *psephísmata* insofar as they were not in conflict with the *nómoi.*

This Greek distinction between ephemeral, man-made rules and the unchanging precepts of the "universal," "natural," or "divine" law has become a permanent feature of western thought. Sophocles, Plato, Aristotle, the Stoic philosophers, Cicero, and Roman jurisprudence as a whole with its distinction between the *jus gentium* and the *jus civile*, all tended to promote the idea of "one eternal and unchangeable law binding all nations through all time. . . ."

3. "Higher Law" Conceptions in Medieval Thought

Through Augustine, Isidore of Seville, Gratian and others, Greco-Roman conceptions of higher law assumed a prominent position in the thought of the Middle Ages, though such conceptions, to be sure, were given considerable theological content. In the writings of Thomas Aquinas, for example, natural law was conceived as a *lex superior* of divine origins to which all other norms were subjected. As one modern jurist writes, "the act of the sovereign which violated the limits placed by natural law was declared null and void. The judge, whose job it was to apply the law, was bound to consider as void (and therefore not binding) both administrative acts and laws contrary to [natural] law, even if they emanated from the Pope or the Emperor. According to some theories, even individual subjects were freed from the duty to obey, when faced with a commandment which did not conform with the [natural] law, to such an extent that the forceful imposition of an unjust law justified armed resistance and even tyrannicide." In place of the Roman or pseudo-Roman tenet that the sovereign is *not* subject to the laws (*Princeps legibus solutus*) some wished to substitute the opposite one: *Princeps legibus tenetur;* while others formulated a more moderate theory according to which the sovereign was not bound by civil law but was, however, bound by natural law.

Medieval theories, therefore, clearly distinguished between two types of norm: that of the *jus naturale,* which was superior and inviolable, and that of the *jus positivum*, which was bound to conform with the former. The same distinction, for that matter, was drawn by the theories of the natural law school of the 17th and 18th centuries, from the time of Grotius up to Rousseau. Although its secular and rational basis brought it into opposition with medieval thought, the natural law school of the 17th and 18th centuries affirmed the existence of "innate rights," intangible and inviolable, and, therefore, the existence of limitations and precepts binding on the legislator himself. This conception was so deeply rooted in the thought of that time that it is to be found even in the writings of the great theoretician of the English "Glorious Revolution" of 1688. John Locke, although asserting the absolute supremacy of Parliament — which, it has been said, "can do anything except transform a man into a woman and a woman into a man" — admitted that the legislative power could be limited by natural law.

It is true that this distinction between a natural law and a positive law was more suitable for exposition on a purely philosophical and theoretical level, separated from the facts of everyday life, than on the level of actual legal practice. What, it may be asked, was the actual position of the judge faced with an unjust law? What was his position when faced with a law which he adjudged to conflict with a superior norm of natural law? The answer of the philosophers was clear. One might recall some especially famous passages of Thomas Aquinas in the *Summa Theologica* in which he affirms that the law contrary to natural law is void and has no binding force whatever. However, despite such assertions from the philosophers, the fact remained that it was impossible to reconcile such theories with the realities of everyday life. On the one hand, there were the clear and precise rules of positive law, and on the other the imprecise and uncertain precepts of natural law. In effect, resolving a conflict between the two meant reconciling two distinct legal orders. A judge, faced with such a conflict, had to choose between applying the law of the state or the ill-defined principles of a legal system lacking both sanctions and institutions. Given this choice, it is not surprising that the judge would apply the positive law to concrete cases, leaving to the philosophers the airy formulations of natural law.

It was left to times nearer our own to provide the instruments whereby these two types of law could be assimilated within a unitary legal order. There was some divergence in the manner in which the natural law precepts evolved, were "positivized" and absorbed into the sphere of positive law of various states. But a cursory glance at

both French* and English legal developments, for example, will
show that the links between these early higher law theories and
modern conceptions of judicial review are close indeed.

  . . . .

4. England and Her Colonies

Like France — indeed a century before France — England stoutly
upheld the idea of parliamentary supremacy, though for different
reasons. While both countries were long exposed to higher law
theories, the English judiciary, unlike the French *Parlements,*
generally enjoyed the respect of all as a protector of individual
liberties against the government. These two traditions — a
consciousness of principles superior even to statutory law, and a
profound regard for the judiciary and for its independence — were
inherited by the American colonists, who were to find them most
useful in their own situation during the revolutionary period and
thereafter.

Pollock affirms the influence of natural law theories in England,
at the same time explaining the failure of the bench and bar to admit
such influence: "It is not credible that a doctrine which pervaded all
political speculation in Europe, and was assumed as a common
ground of authority by the opposing champions of the Empire and
the Papacy, should have been without influence among learned men
in England. If it be asked why the sages of the Common Law did not
expressly refer to the Law of Nature, the answer is that at no time
after, at latest, the Papal interference in the English politics of the
first half of the thirteenth century, was the citation of Roman
canonical authority acceptable in our country, save so far as it was
[strictly] necessary. . . . These considerations appear sufficient to
explain why 'it is not used among them that be learned in the laws
of England to reason what thing is commanded or prohibited by the
Law of Nature.' "

Prior to the 17th century, therefore, the English judicial tradition
had often tended to assign a subordinate role to the legislative
function of King and Parliament, holding that law was not created
but ascertained or declared. Common Law was fundamental law,
and, although it could be complemented by the legislator, it could
not be violated by him; hence law was largely withdrawn from
arbitrary interventions of King and Parliament. This was the tradition
Coke inherited and used as a weapon in his struggle against the
exercise of arbitrary power by King James I. The King claimed to be
endowed with reason equal to that of the judges, his "delegates," and
consequently claimed to be able to exercise the judicial power

---

* On France, *see* Ch. 3, § A, *infra.*

personally. Coke, however, replied that only judges could exercise that power, for only they were learned in the difficult science of law "which requires long study and experience, before that a man can attain to the cognizance of it." On the other hand, Coke affirmed "the traditional supremacy of the common law over the authority of Parliament." "It appears in our books," stated Coke in the famous *Bonham's Case* of 1610, "that in many cases, the common law will controul acts of parliament, and sometimes adjudge them to be utterly void: for when an act of parliament is against common right and reason, or repugnant, or impossible to be performed, the common law will controul it and adjudge such act to be void." Elsewhere Coke further asserted: "Fortescue and Littleton and all others agree that the law consists of three parts: first, common law; secondly, statute law; third, custom, which takes away the common law. But the common law corrects, allows and disallows both statute law and custom, for if there be repugnancy in statute or unreasonableness in custom, the common law disallows and rejects it."

But who ought to control and ascertain such "repugnancy or unreasonableness," and who ought to guarantee the supremacy of the common law against arbitrary decisions of the sovereign on the one hand and of Parliament on the other? This was the essential question, and Coke's answer, at this point in his life, was clear and precise: that control and that guarantee were the task of the judges. This was the function of the judges who, in the words of a modern scholar, "being the only authorized interpreters of that law which is independent of the legislator, constitute therefore ... a truly independent power." While the influence of Coke's doctrine in *Bonham's Case* is debatable, Coke unquestionably reflected the attitude of many common law judges. This attitude deified the common law and looked with a jaundiced eye on any statute in derogation of that law. While few denied that Parliament could change the law, most retained a residual feeling that the long established principles of the common law were in some way superior to statutory innovations. Hence, statutes were, if at all possible, construed so as to preserve "the previous policy of the law." "By the reign of Elizabeth, . . . many lawyers . . . gloried in the liberty which the courts enjoyed in playing fast and loose with statutes."

Though the Glorious Revolution of 1688 marked the triumph of legislative supremacy in England, the American colonies had nonetheless inherited both Coke's ideas regarding the subordination of Crown and Parliament to higher law and a judiciary accustomed to interpreting and at times ignoring legislative acts violating higher principles. This legacy proved useful. James Otis invoked *Bonham's Case* against the Writs of Assistance, and when, after independence, various state legislatures attempted to abolish debt collection, debase the currency and otherwise trample upon previously inviolable rights, the Federalists were quick to see the relevance of defining fundamental law in a national constitution and of using the judiciary to enforce that law.

Paradoxically, the "Glorious Revolution" not only did not hinder, but rather it spurred the development of the new doctrine of judicial review. Under English law every corporation from private companies to municipal corporations "is entitled to act only within the limits of its own charter or constitution." From that principle, the conclusion is derived that every act that exceeds the authority conferred on the corporation is null and void and cannot be enforced by the courts.

The English colonies, often founded as commercial enterprises, were managed under Crown charters. These "charters" may be considered as the first constitutions of the colonies, both because they had a binding effect on colonial legislation and also because they regulated the fundamental legal structure of the colonies themselves. Frequently these "constitutions" expressly provided that the colonies could pass their own laws only if these laws were "reasonable" and "not contrary to the laws of the Kingdom of England." Such provisions clearly imply that the laws should not be contrary to the sovereign will of the English Parliament. Thus it was by reason of this supremacy of the English law and Parliament that in numerous cases the Privy Council of the King held that the colonial laws could not stand if they were opposed to the colonial charters or to the laws of the Kingdom.

For these reasons the principle of *parliamentary supremacy* — and hence the supremacy of *positive law* — which was introduced in England following the "Glorious Revolution" of 1688, produced quite different results in America than in England. In England the result was to remove every control over the validity of legislation from the judges, despite the early successes of Lord Coke's doctrine. In America, on the contrary, the result was to empower the colonial judges to disregard local legislation not in conformity with the English law. Thus the apparent paradox has been explained: how the English principle of the uncontrolled supremacy of the legislature helped, rather than hindered, the formation in America of an opposite system — a system which allows the judges to control the validity of legislation. This explanation is confirmed by the experience of other ex-colonies, including Canada, Australia, and India, which likewise adopted judicial review upon attaining independence. . . .

When the English colonies in America proclaimed their independence in 1776, one of their first acts was to substitute for the old "charters" new constitutions consisting of the fundamental laws of the newly independent states. And, just as laws contrary to the "charters" and to the "laws of the Kingdom" had been considered null and void by the judges, so it is not surprising that laws contrary to the new constitutions of the independent states should also be held null and void in the same way. Though there is controversy over the authenticity of a number of precedents in this line of cases, several of them seem to be well verified.

It should be emphasized, therefore, that more than a century of American history and a strong line of precedents — to say nothing of contemporary writings — stood behind Chief Justice Marshall in 1803 when, interpreting the somewhat confused terms of article VI, paragraph 2 of the Federal Constitution of 1789, he enunciated "the principle, supposed to be essential to all written Constitutions, that a law repugnant to the Constitution is void; and that courts, as well as other departments, are bound by that instrument."

5. Conclusion: The Evolution of "Constitutional Justice"

So it is that judicial review, though it may come in varying forms to different countries at different times, is the result of an evolutionary pattern common to much of the West, in both civil and common law countries. First there was a period of "natural justice," when the acts of crown and parliament alike were said to be subject to a higher, though unwritten, law. Then, with the "Glorious Revolution" in England and the French Revolution a century later, came the era of "positive" or "legal justice," characterized by the primacy of the written statute and the popular legislature, and the relative powerlessness of both judges and natural law theory to control this primacy. This era carried a new flag to the citadel of justice: the "principle of legality." Institutions such as the French "Cour de cassation" and "Conseil d'Etat" were the instruments used to implement that principle.

Our own time has seen the burgeoning of "constitutional justice," which has in a sense combined the forms of legal justice and the substance of natural justice. Desirous of protecting the permanent will, rather than the temporary whims of the people, many modern states have reasserted higher law principles through written constitutions. Thus there has been a synthesis of three separate concepts: the supremacy of certain higher principles, the need to put even the higher law in written form, and the employment of the judiciary as a tool for enforcing the constitution against ordinary legislation. This union of concepts first occurred in the United States, but it has since come to be considered by many as essential to the rule of law (*Rechtsstaat*) anywhere.

B. THE EXPANSION OF JUDICIAL REVIEW SINCE 1803*

One of the essential legal developments of our time is, for a growing number of civil law countries, the introduction of judicial review of the constitutionality of legislation. Although this institution has ancient historical precedents, the matrix of its modern growth may certainly be seen, in part, in the American model. Developments in this field are cutting across the boundaries of legal families. . . .

Judicial review of legislation, a rarely encountered institution until recent times, has been introduced in the last few decades in various countries throughout the world. Since the last World War, the growth of this institution has experienced what could well be called a worldwide explosion. It almost appears as if no Western, or even Eastern, country purporting to be a modern democracy, can resist the temptation to adopt some form of control — judicial or otherwise — of the constitutionality of legislation. The phenomenon, of course, is particularly interesting where the power of control is entrusted to a judicial body, with the emergence of an interplay between two different and independent powers. Even the less radical phenomenon of a "political" — non-judicial — type of review, however, may be considered as a first step in the same direction.** With this proviso, we will limit our attention here to the judicial types of review. Let us first have a summary survey of the principal stages of this explosion.

1803. — *John Marshall* laid down, in *Marbury v. Madison*, the "sacred" principle, supposed to be essential to all written constitutions, that "an act of the legislature repugnant to the Constitution is void"; and that courts, as well as other departments, are bound by that instrument.

19th Century and first part of the 20th Century. — The idea that unconstitutional laws have no binding force for the judges began to make headway outside the United States: in Mexico with the institution of the "amparo contra leyes", in Switzerland (limited to cantonal laws) with that of the "recours de droit public" or "staatsrechtliche Beschwerde" as well as on the basis of the principle according to which "Bundesrecht bricht kantonales Recht"; in Norway since the end of the last century and in Denmark since the first part of our century; sporadically, and certainly without any chance of permanent success, in other countries such as Rumania, Greece, and Portugal. It seems correct to say, however, that these developments were, for the most part, of little practical or theoretical

---

* This section is adapted from Cappelletti, *The Significance of Judicial Review of Legislation in the Contemporary World*, 1 IUS PRIVATUM GENTIUM 147, 147-55 (1969).

** On the distinction between "political" and "judicial" review, *see* Ch. 2 *infra*.

significance, either within the nations in which they occurred, or as a manifestation of a more general need of that epoch.

After World War I. — In the small Austrian Republic, defeated in its imperial ambitions, *Hans Kelsen* and others elaborated a great Constitution — the Constitution of a new democratic state. "Verfassungsgerichtsbarkeit" and, in particular, judicial review of the constitutionality of legislation assumed a central position in that document. Although concentrated in a single judicial organ which was, at least until the Verfassungsnovelle of 1929,[1] isolated from the concrete needs of individuals and society, Austrian judicial review implied the affirmation of the principle that even legislation is subject to the limits and control of a higher legality. At the same time, even if without success, the same development occurred in Czechoslovakia with the Constitution of 1920, and was repeated a few years later in Spain through the Republican Constitution of 1931, a document soon torn to shreds by Spanish and foreign Fascism.

In Germany, judicial review of legislation emerged in the Weimar Republic, especially after a landmark decision of November 4, 1925, of the Reichsgericht. This occurred not by dint of a specific provision in the Constitution, but by the intrinsic force of the principle that, if the constitutional norm has to be granted the highest place in the hierachy of law sources, it has to prevail over unconstitutional ordinary norms (*"Verfassungsgesetz bricht einfaches Gesetz"*).

But constitutional justice does not suit dictatorial regimes. It immediately disappeared in Nazi Germany; and likewise it disappeared in the Austria of the "Anschluss", as well as in Franco's Spain. As for Italy, the "dangerous" idea of a judicial check of Fascist legislation was even more easily avoided. The constitution which was then in force — the Statuto albertino of 1848 — had always been construed as flexible and, therefore, not binding for ordinary legislation.

After World War II. — The explosive expansion of constitutional justice characterizes legal and political history of the last two decades.

---

[1] Constitutional reform of December 7, 1929. Until 1929, access to the Constitutional Court was limited to the Federal Executive (Bundesregierung) applying for judicial review of the constitutionality of state laws (Landesgesetze), and to the State Governments (Landesregierungen) applying for review of the constitutionality of federal laws. Private individuals had no access to the Court, nor could any issue of constitutionality of legislation be raised in a concrete litigation. Thus, with the exception of the Constitutional Court, all judges were (and are) forbidden to exercise any control on the constitutionality of legislation. The reform of 1929, however, introduced the possibility of raising issues of constitutionality of legislation in concrete cases pending before the "Oberster Gerichtshof" and the "Verwaltungsgerichtshof," the two superior organs of ordinary and administrative jurisdiction. In such cases, the issue has to be submitted to the Constitutional Court, whose decision is binding *erga omnes* as well as on the case at hand.

Italy, which had previously been outside this great phenomenon, soon became involved and took a leading role in it with its rigid Republican Constitution of January 1, 1948. It took, unfortunately, the catastrophe of external and civil war and occupation; it took the devastation of supreme values of man and society under Fascism, to sweep away the meaningless Albertine text and to impose upon the revived national conscience a cogent system of structures and values. The first phase — 1948 to 1956 — was still dominated by the strong resistance of those who could hardly adapt to a new conception of law and justice. The ordinary "career" judge, particularly the elderly judges of the Supreme Court of Cassation and the other appellate courts, did a very poor job in the implementation of a highly programmatic and progressive Constitution, strongly opposed to a stratification of either asocial or authoritarian legislation. But a new era was initiated with the creation in 1956 of the Constitutional Court, which for some years has been, even with its limitations, the most effective instrument for the implementation of that which in 1955 was incisively called "an unrealized Constitution."

As did Italy, so the other two defeated countries, Germany and Japan, saw in judicial review of legislation an effective instrument to prevent the return of autocratic government and to safeguard individual and societal values. So did the heavily American-oriented Japanese Constitution of May 3, 1947. And so did the Constitution of Bonn of May 23, 1949.

But the phenomenon did not remain limited to these three countries. It also occurred in Austria where the 1920 Constitution, as amended in 1929, was reenacted on May 1, 1945. It further spread to the Republic of Cyprus with the Constitution of August 16, 1960, and to the Republic of Turkey with the Constitution of July 9, 1961, each of them providing for the institution of a new Constitutional Court with the power of judicial review; a significant development in two more countries plagued by disorder and unrest, as if judicial review were to be considered a stabilizing factor after times of stress.

Judicial review of the constitutionality of legislation has even penetrated, for the first time, into a country of the Socialist legal family, Yugoslavia, with the Constitution of April 7, 1963, which provides for review by a Federal Constitutional Court and, on the regional level, by special Constitutional Courts in the six Federated Republics. This is a most important development because it seems to have peculiar implications for the Marxist-Leninist conception of state and law, with results that could become important in the evolution of the Communist legal ideology. Moreover, the Yugoslav development is not very likely to remain isolated in the Socialist world, if one can judge from certain institutions, even if more attenuated, introduced elsewhere, particularly in Rumania. The Constitution of 1965 of the Rumanian People's Republic has instituted a "Constitutional Commission," elected by Parliament and composed, in part, of specialists not members of Parliament. Its task is to advise on the constitutionality of legislative bills.

There are also suggestions of judicial review emerging in other Socialist countries, such as Poland and Czechoslovakia. An authoritative Polish jurist, *Rozmaryn,* wrote in 1966 that in the Socialist countries "among jurists and, sometimes, even within certain political parties," requests have been made "in favor of the introduction of judicial control" of the constitutionality of legislation. Professor *Rozmaryn's* personal opinion is that no ideological or political obstacle can be seen in the attribution of a function, similar to that of the Rumanian Constitutional Commission, to a *judicial* body such as a Supreme Court. Not even in such development would there be any attempt against "the sovereign position of the supreme representative organ." In the case of Czechoslovakia, a Constitutional Act of 1968 went so far as to order the establishment of a system similar to that of Yugoslavia. Due to well-known political circumstances, however, the legislation necessary to implement the system was never enacted.

Finally, another recent development has to be mentioned. Since a decision of the Swedish Supreme Court of November 13, 1964, Sweden, too, may be included among the countries that assert the courts' power of judicial review, even in the absence of any explicit constitutional provision or any specially constituted court.

The impressive geographic expansion of judicial review in the contemporary world emerges only in part from what has been said so far. To the above mentioned countries, almost all the former colonies of Great Britain ought to be added, from Canada to Australia, from India to Pakistan, etc. Also to be added are some Latin American countries, such as Uruguay, which concentrates the control of constitutionality of legislation in the ordinary Supreme Court — a solution analogous, in part, to that of Ireland, though apparently of limited success — or Brazil, where the "mandado de seguranca" has emerged, an institution somewhat similar to the Mexican "juicio de amparo".

The truly *universal* importance of judicial review today thus seems to be amply demonstrated.

A complete analysis of the influence in other countries of the American institution of judicial review — the oldest and, no doubt, still the most successful among the various developments mentioned above — will not be undertaken in this article. It seems fair to state, however, that its influence has been very great indeed.

In making such a statement, I do not embrace the thesis, suggested by some writers, that the American institution of judicial review of legislation brought about a completely new and unprecedented contribution to law and political science.

But notwithstanding historical precedents of control — including *judicial* — of the conformity of ordinary laws to a superior or constitutional law, the fact remains that the United States has clearly initiated a new era in the history of judicial review. Those historical precedents were either sporadic and unstable episodes, or the expression of theories (such as that of the prevalence of natural law over positive law) which lacked any effective judicial or political instrument for their realization. Only with the Supreme Court of *John Marshall* did a momentous theory attach itself to a powerful practical instrument of implementation. The theory was that, if the constitution is "a superior paramount law, unchangeable by ordinary means . . . , then a legislative act contrary to the constitution is not law." The instrument for implementation was the United States Supreme Court and, with it, the entire American court system, Federal and State. The courts, in accordance with *Marshall's* opinion that "it is emphatically the province and duty of the judicial department to say what the law is," had to reach the obvious result that, as a purematter of judicial interpretation of "what the law is," higher law had to be given prevalence over a conflicting lower law.

Thus the American system of judicial review became influential in other countries, both because of its theoretical clarity and its practical effectiveness. It certainly exerted influence on the Mexican "fathers" of the "Amparo," as well as on developments in other nations and continents before and, even more, after the last World War. In particular, the American system of judicial review was passively received by Japan through the Constitution of 1947. Much less bound to the American model were the Austrian, Italian, and German types of judicial review, where the reviewing power is concentrated in special Constitutional Courts; and this differentiation has been followed in other countries, including Cyprus, Turkey, and Yugoslavia. Yet it seems beyond discussion that the American precedent — together with that, highly original, of Austria — exercised a remarkable "persuasive authority" upon the members of the Constitutional Assemblies of Italy and Germany when they, after the war, introduced judicial review in the new Constitutions of their nations.

NOTES AND QUESTIONS

1. The major expansion of judicial review is not limited to the countries mentioned in the preceding excerpt. Further developments have occurred since the excerpted article was written in 1967, as exemplified by Israel (*infra*). In addition, a growing number of countries in the "developing world" have been attempting to introduce judicial review into their legal systems. *See, e.g.,* H. FIX ZAMUDIO, VEINTICINCO AÑOS DE EVOLUCIÓN DE LA

JUSTICIA CONSTITUCIONAL 1940-1965 (Mexico, UNAM-Instituto de Investigaciones Jurídicas, 1968) 51-63, 90-99. In particular for Latin America *see, e.g.,* E. VESCOVI, EL PROCESO DE INCONSTITUCIONALIDAD DE LA LEY (Montevideo, Facultad de Derecho y Ciencias Sociales, 1967); Rosenn, *Judicial Review in Latin America,* 35 OHIO ST. L.J. 785 (1974).

2. Israel has no written Constitution, but the Israeli legislature (Knesset) has enacted "Basic Laws" — dealing with "The Knesset," "Israel Lands," "The President of the State," "The Government," "Economic Organization of the State," and "The Army." * Section 4 of Basic Law: The Knesset, provides that "[t]he Knesset shall be elected by general, national, direct, equal, secret and proportional elections, in accordance with the Knesset Elections Law; this section shall not be varied save by a majority of the members of the Knesset." In 1969 the Knesset passed, with less than a "majority of its members," a Financing Law for governmental financing of election campaigns of political parties represented in the outgoing Knesset, but, in *Bergman v. Minister of Finance,*** the Israeli Supreme Court held that the law violated the equality requirements of Section 4 by discriminating against parties unrepresented in the outgoing Knesset. The Court thus ruled that the Minister of Finance could not proceed under the law, and the Knesset acquiesced by amending the law to conform with the Court's decision.***

As in most jurisdictions, Israel recognizes the maxim *lex posterior derogat legi priori.* How, then, can a prior act of the legislature serve as a source of higher law? In a nation of parliamentary supremacy, like Israel, or England, is it possible for the legislature to bind future legislatures by "entrenching" an enactment? Can parliament be "omnipotent" and yet be incapable of enacting laws restricting future parliaments? There has been strenuous debate in Israel concerning the question whether Israel's Knesset acts in an ordinary legislative capacity or as a "Constituent Assembly" in enacting Basic Laws. *See* Klein, *A New Era in Israel's Constitutional Law,* [1971] 6 Is. L. REV. 376; Compare LIKHOUSKI, ISRAEL'S PARLIAMENT (1971) *with* Nimmer, *The Uses of Judicial Review in Israel's Quest for a Constitution,* 70 COLUM. L. REV. 1217 (1970).

3. In addition to developments at the national level, Western Europe is experiencing the genesis of international sources of higher law.

---

* Proposals before the Knesset for other Basic Laws include one dealing with "The Rights of the Person."

** [1969] I 23 P.D. 693. An English Translation appears in [1969] 4 Is. L. REV. 559.

*** *See* Knesset and Local Authorities Elections (Financing, Limitation of Expenses and Audit) (Amendment) Law, 5729-1969, [23] Laws of the State of Israel [L.S.I.] 218 (1969).

See, e.g., Cappelletti, *Social and Political Aspects of Civil Procedure — Reforms and Trends in Western and Eastern Europe,* 69 MICH. L. REV. 847, 867-70 (1971).

Eighteen nations have ratified the European Convention on Human Rights,* which, *inter alia,* establishes minimum standards of due process for domestic civil and criminal proceedings. As yet the international institutions for judicial enforcement of the Convention — the European Commission on Human Rights, and the European Court of Human Rights — have been somewhat timid. Yet their potential for the future is clear. The most innovative feature is that an individual may attack action of a signatory nation before a transnational adjudicatory body.

Furthermore, the Convention has some force within the domestic legal order of the signatory nations. Its effect "ranges from states where the Convention is considered superior to the Constitution itself (*e.g.,* Netherlands), to those where it has constitutional force (*e.g.,* Austria), to those where it has the force of ordinary law (*e.g.,* Germany, Italy), and finally to those where it does not acquire the status of domestic law (*e.g.,* United Kingdom)." *Id.* at 869 n. 89.

Another international source of higher law is European Economic Community law. The highest national courts of the member states must refer issues of interpretation or validity of Community law to the Court of Justice of the European Communities for a binding decision. They are bound not to apply national law inconsistent with valid Community law.

For a discussion of the emergence of judicial review at the supranational level, *see* Ch. 5, *infra.*

4. Why was fascism incompatible with judicial review? Why was there an "explosive" expansion of judicial review after World War II, and why was it led by countries formerly governed by totalitarian regimes?

5. Why do all of the former English colonies have some system of judicial review, yet not England itself?

---

* Ratification is pending in two other nations which have recently become signatories to the Convention (Portugal and Spain).

Chapter 2

JUDICIAL REVIEW AND POLITICAL REVIEW*

A. POLITICAL CONTROL OF CONSTITUTIONALITY: GENERAL

Judicial review of the constitutionality of legislation presents an exciting and perplexing encounter between legislator and judge, between statute and judgment. However, judicial review is but a part of a much larger whole. If one defines "constitutional justice" as that condition in which citizens may trust their government to uphold certain rights considered inviolable, it is clear that judicial review of statutes is only one way of attaining this happy state. In fact, in a given country political factors may perhaps provide a better check than the courts on attempts to establish majoritarian tyranny. Even when speaking of strictly judicial protection of constitutionality (the *Verfassungsgerichtsbarkeit* of the Germans), one must grant that formal review of statutes for conformity with a written document is only one of the judicial means available for this end. This chapter will attempt to fit judicial review into this larger picture, showing the wide range of means, political and judicial, available to a country wishing to restrain the arbitrary exercise of governmental power. Later chapters will analyze judicial review: its history, the forms it has taken, and the trends in its evolution.

In certain countries a *political* review operates alongside or instead of *judicial* review. Usually under these systems the control is not exercised after the enactment of the law, but is *preventive;* it intervenes before the law comes into force. Sometimes the control is merely consultative, in that an opinion is given which does not have binding force upon the legislature and the executive.

Some of these political controls are indirect; without formally declaring statutes unconstitutional, they make it difficult for the legislature to change the accepted constitutional order. The American system of "checks and balances" does this by requiring that radical changes in the political order have the assent of nearly all major political groups in the country. Similarly, many would say that the combination of single member districts and strict party discipline in Great Britain has made it very difficult for minority groups intent upon extreme change to attain power.

---

*This chapter is adapted from M. CAPPELLETTI, JUDICIAL REVIEW IN THE CONTEMPORARY WORLD 1-2, 2-12, 16 (1971).

Other political controls are more explicit: elected representatives, or their appointees, are authorized to consider the conformity of proposed legislation with a written constitution. In the past, these bodies enjoyed only theoretical powers to annul legislation. Thus neither the *Supremo Poder Conservador* included in the Mexican Constitution of 1836, nor its model, the *Sénat Conservateur* of the French Constitution of the Year VIII (1799), was able to exercise its sweeping powers, though both served as precedents for twentieth century attempts at nonjudicial control of constitutionality. Two of these attempts will now be examined.*

B. POLITICAL CONTROL OF CONSTITUTIONALITY: ITALY

Italy furnishes a typical example of political control of legislation in a country where judicial review also exists. The Italian Constitution provides for at least two types of such control. First, there is that exercised by the central government over regional legislation under art. 127, paras. 1-3, of the Constitution. Second, there is the much more significant political control which rests with the President of the Republic. He has the duty of promulgating laws approved by Parliament, but he has discretion to suspend promulgation and ask the two Houses to subject the bill to further consideration. Under the Constitution (art. 74, para. 2), if the two Houses again approve the bill, the President is required to promulgate it. Some, however, interpret this provision restrictively. The primary duty of the President of the Republic under the Constitution (arts. 90 and 91) is to guarantee the observance of the Constitution. It is claimed therefore that, if the President considers a bill unconstitutional which has been reapproved by Parliament, he must refuse to promulgate it. Here we see the possibility of a conflict of competence between state authorities — in this example, between the President of the Republic and Parliament — which the Constitutional Court has ultimate authority to resolve; thus "political" control, exercised by the President of the Republic, might ultimately come under review by a body which, as we shall see, is judicial in character.

In the Federal Republic of Germany, too, the President in more than one case has asserted the power to refuse his signature to legislation he considers unconstitutional, though this power is not specifically granted him by the Constitution.

A similar power is vested in the President of the United States. His veto power, though not restricted to constitutional issues, may be employed when he considers a bill unconstitutional.

---

* On France, *see* Ch. 3, *infra.*

C. POLITICAL CONTROL OF CONSTITUTIONALITY: THE SOVIET UNION

Judicial review is lacking in the socialist legal systems, but for reasons very different from those which led to its rejection in France.* The French rejected the doctrine essentially because judicial interference in the legislative process was thought to conflict with proper separation of powers. In the Soviet Union and other socialist countries, on the other hand, judicial review was repudiated as one aspect of the "bourgeois doctrine" of the separation of powers. All powers are united in one supreme organ "drawn directly from the people," who are "the source of all power." Thus the laws which emanate from the supreme organ (Supreme Soviet, Popular Assembly), whose members are popularly elected, represent "the will of the whole sovereign people." Accordingly, from the principles of the unity of powers and the supremacy of the people flows the corollary that, under socialist systems, constitutional control may not be exercised by extra-parliamentary bodies nor modelled on the experience of West European countries and the United States.

Alongside this unitary orientation toward the exercise of state power there has existed in the socialist legal systems a concept of "constitution" which differs greatly from Western theory. In Western Europe the constitution is conceived as a body of more or less permanent rules and principles which express the fundamental value norms of the state and establish a program for their realization. In the U.S.S.R. and other socialist countries, the constitution has traditionally been conceived as a "superstructure" over the economy and a reflection of the actual socioeconomic results achieved.

Recent developments in socialist constitutional thought, however, indicate that this view is being replaced by a more "prescriptive," rather than strictly "descriptive" role of the constitution. Some prominent Soviet jurists now maintain that it is perfectly admissible to have rules which anticipate future stages of societal development. Under this approach, the constitution seeks to enunciate the guiding fundamental principles of the society, much as Western constitutions do.

This evolution can be seen in the Constitution of the U.S.S.R., enacted on October 7, 1977. This text, which replaces the Constitution of December 5, 1936, contains a new provision (art. 173) which declares:

> The Constitution of the U.S.S.R. has superior juridical power. All the laws and other acts of state organs are issued on the basis of and in conformity with the Constitution of the U.S.S.R.

---

* *See* Ch. 4, *infra.*

In addition to the new language of art. 173, the Constitution of 1977 improves upon the previous one by indicating which specific state organ will have the power to check state acts for their conformity with the Constitution.

> Art. 121. The Presidium of the Supreme Soviet of the U.S.S.R. . . . 4) exercises control over the observance of the Constitution and guarantees the conformity of the Constitutions and the laws of the Union Republics with the Constitution and the laws of the U.S.S.R.

It is important to remember that the Presidium is a body composed of 39 members elected from the Supreme Soviet.* Given its political nature, the Presidium clearly exercises control which is political, not judicial, in character. The scope of this control would be to guide the political organs and individuals along the paths set by the Constitution.**

The nonjudicial character of the control is not the only peculiarity which the Soviet constitutional system presents. There is another which seems to be of interest. Article 121 (4) of the 1977 Constitution does not limit the function of control to particular categories of acts. Thus, nothing prevents this control from being exercised over all law-creating acts. One should note a peculiar situation which, in this context, occurs in the Soviet Union. There is a multiplicity of bodies endowed with legislative powers, with the result that it is no easy task to draw a clear picture of the various sources of law, or of their relative hierarchical relationship which the Soviet commentators themselves often fail to clarify. For our purposes, it will suffice to observe that legislation in the Soviet State is drawn from three principal sources: (1) "Laws," ratified by the Supreme Soviet of the U.S.S.R.; (2) "Decrees," emanating from the Presidium of the Supreme Soviet; (3) "Orders," emanating from the Council of Ministers of the U.S.S.R. Laws have the highest position. Thus, we can see that the organ to which art. 121 (4) entrusts, among other tasks, the function of reviewing the constitutionality of law-creating acts, is one of the organs from which these acts emanate. Therefore, control of constitutionality in the Soviet Union is not

---

* The Supreme Soviet is a political organ roughly comparable to the Parliament of Western countries.

** Formal revision of the Constitution demands a particular procedure within the competence of the Supreme Soviet, so that even the Soviet Constitution may be said to be "rigid". However, in practice, since amongst the organs of control there are the Council of Ministers and individual ministers, in addition to the Presidium, these bodies may decide that the formal Constitution no longer accords with the economic situation of the moment; in such a case they can pass enactments contrary to the Constitution itself, and these enactments will later be submitted for approval — in practice never refused — to the Supreme Soviet. Revision of the Constitution in the formal sense will thus be effected by the Supreme Soviet after an adaptation effected by other bodies.

external, as is typical elsewhere, but internal to the major policy-making bodies of the state. The body controlled and the body controlling are either the same or, at least, very closely related (the Presidium is, as we have said, elected by the Supreme Soviet).

Such a situation may well be the only one compatible with the fundamental principles of a Communist system. Given that "the will of the people," expressed in the body which emanates from it (the Supreme Soviet in the U.S.S.R., the Popular Assembly or National Assembly elsewhere), represents "the supreme source of law," there is no body, except for this organ itself, which can be given the task of control over the constitutional legitimacy of its activities. This can explain why the same situation as in the U.S.S.R. arises in the other People's Republics, with the sole exception of Yugoslavia.

D. JUDICIAL CONTROL OF CONSTITUTIONALITY: GENERAL

Just as there are many possible political controls over arbitrary state action, so there are many different ways in which the judiciary might attain the same end. Even a court without the authority to annul unconstitutional legislation might, through rules of interpretation, application of "unwritten principles," and careful control of administrative acts, achieve a form of control of constitutionality. An example of such "implied" control would be that exercised by the French *Conseil d'Etat*.* Other courts, rather than focusing on the unconstitutional statute, will provide special forms of relief for individuals who complain of violations of "fundamental rights" by any branch of the government. These remedies may exist independently of any formal system of judicial review of statutes (one aspect of habeas corpus in Great Britain), or in conjunction with judicial review of legislation (one aspect of habeas corpus in the United States), or may specifically exclude the possibility of annulling a statute (one interpretation of *juicio de amparo* in Mexico). Yet, to the average citizen, these procedures might be a more meaningful guarantee of his rights than judicial review itself.

QUESTIONS

Why is there no judicial review in orthodox Marxian-socialist states? What is the real role of the socialist refutation of the "bourgeois" doctrine of separation of powers? How can you explain the fact that both the (strictly construed) French — and generally Civilian — doctrine of separation of powers and the opposite socialist doctrine of "democratic centralism" (or centralization of all powers) are seen as the theoretical justification for denying judicial review?

---

* *See* Ch. 3, *infra.*

Chapter 3

FROM POLITICAL TO JUDICIAL CONTROL: THE EXAMPLE OF FRANCE

A. INTRODUCTION

1. The Parlements and Popular Sovereignty*

The French have clung tenaciously to the idea that no judicial organ should be given the power to review statutes for conformity with a higher law. The Constitutions of the Year VIII (1799), 1852, 1946, and 1958 did admit the possibility of constitutional control of legislation, but until recently such control has been, at best, theoretical, and it has always been entrusted to specifically political bodies.

This rejection of judicial review does not mean that France has been immune to the attractions of higher law theory. There were, in fact, attempts during the *Ancien Régime* to affirm certain "fundamental" precepts. The *Parlements,* the higher courts set up in various French cities, came to assert in their relations with the French sovereign a power and duty "to examine all laws and decrees which come before us to see that there is in them nothing contrary . . . to the fundamental laws of the realm." Through the work of the French *Parlements,* a doctrine was formulated which had a great effect on Montesquieu and which shows a striking similarity to modern ideas of judicial review. This was the theory of the "heureuse impuissance" of the king to violate the fundamental laws, the "happy powerlessness" of the sovereign legislator to issue what we would call today unconstitutional laws.

But even as the judges proclaimed this limit on the royal power, the monarchs attempted to provide a means of insuring the supremacy of their own will. A *demande en cassation,* challenging a decision by a *Parlement,* could be brought before the sovereign's *Conseil des Parties* which could in turn annul the decision found to have been reached in violation of royal ordinances.

Despite the existence of this check on the *parlementaires,* these

* Adapted from M. CAPPELLETTI, JUDICIAL REVIEW IN THE CONTEMPORARY WORLD 32-36, 12-16 (1971).

judges of the higher courts acquired a reputation of interfering far too often with the activities of other state organs. Such interferences, though they might at times have been a salutary antidote to the absolutist tendencies of the monarchy, more frequently smacked of an arbitrary abuse of power. This was perhaps inherent in the attitude held by many judges toward their office. For them it was a "property right, a part of their estate," owned by them "by the same title they held their houses and lands." As with their own property, "they bought and sold judgeships, transmitted them by bequest, and rented them out when they wished to hold them for their minor children." Above all, they exploited their offices to the utmost — clearly at the expense of the litigants — just as a good landlord knows how best to exploit his lands. Not without reason were these judges almost always among the bitterest enemies of even the slightest liberal reform. They were the fiercest opponents of the Revolution, whose guillotine was soon to reap a rich harvest of their most honorable heads. Largely because of these abuses of the judicial function, the ideology of the Revolution, enshrined in the works of Rousseau and Montesquieu, stressed the omnipotence of statutory law, the equality of man before the law, and the rigid separation of powers in which the judge, the passive and "inanimate" *bouche de la loi,* performed the sole task of applying the letter of the law to individual cases — a task conceived as purely mechanical and in no way creative.

The legislature, therefore, as the voice of popular sovereignty, was seen as the best guarantor of fundamental rights. Concomitantly, and most significantly from the standpoint of the development of constitutional controls in continental Europe, there arose that "hostility which in France . . . has always been fostered against the notion that the acts of the superior organs and especially of the parliamentary assemblies, as representatives of national sovereignty, might be subjected to control" by the judiciary.

2. The *Cour de Cassation* *

This reaction against the pre-revoluntionary judges has led France to turn to political institutions to perform some functions more commonly assigned to judicial organs. However, before too sharp a line is drawn between political and judicial means of controlling the constitutionality of legislation, it should be noted that even political entities may evolve into something quite different than that intended by their founders. An example would be the development of the French *Cassation.* This institution, despite its modern purely judicial nature, was originally conceived as a nonjudicial organ of

---

* Adapted from CAPPELLETTI, *supra* 12-6.

control. Indeed, it was the result of a political philosophy which was radically opposed to any possibility of judicial review.

The *Tribunal de Cassation* was set up by the decree of Nov. 27 — Dec. 1, 1790, as a *nonjudicial* organ strictly connected with the legislative power. As the decree itself stated: "il y aura *près du Corps législatif* un Tribunal de Cassation." Its function was to prevent the judicial organs from interfering in the legislative sphere and to ensure that they applied only the letter of the law. This was a phase in the development of the concept which soon resulted in the great French codification, a concept that the entire body of law could and should be contained in written instruments. Despite the name *Tribunal,* which was later changed to "Court" (*Cour*), the *Tribunal de Cassation* originally had an essentially legislative character; it was a political, rather than a judicial body. In the words of the author of a leading work on *Cassation,* it was "an institution of a constitutional nature intended to preserve in its entirety that tenet of the separation of powers," which was held to be "the prime condition for the normal existence of the State." In view of its functions, there was a proposal to call it, instead of *Tribunal de Cassation, Conseil national pour la conservation des lois* — a name certainly more descriptive of its original task.

The *Tribunal de Cassation,* in short, was the offspring of the revolutionary legislators' profound distrust of the judges. In the first years of the Revolution, this distrust led them to emulate Justinian in attempting to deny the judges all power to interpret the laws out of fear that through interpretation the literal meaning of a law might be changed. The power of interpretation was reserved to the legislative body, by means of decrees issued at the request of the judges whenever they were in doubt as to the meaning of a legislative text. Only by the Napoleonic Code was this so-called *référé facultatif,* with its utopian prohibition of judicial interpretation, abolished.

The doctrine of the separation of powers was likewise strictly applied to prevent legislative interference with the judicial power. Thus the *Tribunal de Cassation,* although able to annul, at the request of a private citizen (or even, without such a request, "in the interest of the law"), judgments which contained "an express contravention of the text of the law," had to restrict itself rigidly to this task. It was "not to usurp judicial functions which are not its concern;" it had no power to "pronounce upon the interpretation of the laws or upon the decision in the dispute." For the new decision in the dispute, the *Tribunal de Cassation* remanded the case to the so-called "juridiction de renvoi," that is, to a different lower court which had complete freedom of decision and could even defy *Cassation* by reinstating the previous decision. The only limitation was that, if the second decision was again brought before the *Tribunal de Cassation* and again quashed by it, and if the second "juridiction de renvoi" persisted with the opinion held illegal by the *Cassation,* the so-called *référé obligatoire* before the *Corps législatif* became necessary. The legislative body then published a decree, declaratory of the law, which bound the courts on the third "renvoi."

Had *Cassation* not undergone profound changes during the nearly two centuries of its history, it would be difficult to imagine a more irreconcilable contrast between the ideas at the base of that institution and those which have inspired all systems of judicial review of legislation. For *Cassation* was, in a sense, the embodiment of the concept of the strictest separation of powers under which "law is law" and not what judges may think to be law. Judicial review, on the contrary, presupposes that the judiciary not only has the power of interpretation beyond the strict letter of the law, but, even more importantly, is entitled to rule upon the validity of ordinary legislation, deciding upon its conformity with the higher law. *Cassation* assumed the omnipotence of positive law as the manifestation of the supreme will of popular assemblies; judicial review requires the subjection of the ordinary law to a *lex superior* withdrawn from the vagaries of parliamentary majorities. Finally, the former institution presupposed a profound mistrust of the judiciary while the latter presumes a great confidence in it, if not even its "supremacy" in the constitutional organization of the State.

In fact, by the beginning of the 19th century the attenuation of strict revolutionary ideology was radically transforming the nature of the *Tribunal de Cassation,* by this time called *Cour de Cassation.* In this changed role *Cassation* penetrated to a number of countries, including Italy, Belgium, the Netherlands, Luxembourg, Greece, Spain, and Mexico. Once the judges' power to interpret the law had been recognized by the Napoleonic Code, the *Cour de Cassation* became the supreme *judicial* organ for the review of errors of law committed by inferior judges. The *référé obligatoire* was finally abolished by a law of April 1, 1837, and it was declared that in case of a difference on a point of law between the first *juridiction de renvoi* and the *Cour de Cassation,* the new judgment of the Court, sitting in joint session, should have not only the negative effect of annulment, but also the positive effect of binding the second *juridiction de renvoi.* After the law of April 1, 1837, "more and more decisively and consciously, the *Cour de Cassation* became what it is today, the Supreme Court for the judicial interpretation of the law." Thus it became the Court exercising that control of legality which, although not being by any means the same thing, yet is neither irreconcilable with, nor unrelated to, control of the constitutionality of legislation.

QUESTIONS

What are the basic similarities and differences between the French and American revolutions? What are the differences in the resulting approaches to constitutional government? Both the French and American systems have been called systems of "separation of powers," but the American approach is more accurately described as one of "checks and balances." As you read the remainder of this chapter, consider whether the legal history of France since the Revolution is characterized by gradual adaptation of their system of strict separation of powers into a system of checks and balances, and by emergence of the judicial branch as a real power.

3. The *Conseil Constitutionnel* **and** *Conseil d'Etat*

In France, two institutions review the constitutionality of acts by the State: the *Conseil Constitutionnel* and the *Conseil d'Etat.* The *Conseil Constitutionnel* is not a judicial body. It is a political institution, originally designed to define those areas that are the responsibility of the legislature and those that are the province of the executive. Until 1971, the Council was content merely to perform this function, generally with an anti-parliamentary bias. However, since 1971, the Council has begun to develop into an effective, independent organ for testing the constitutionality of parliamentary legislation.

The second institution, the *Conseil d'Etat,* is the only truly judicial body, and the only guarantor of the constitutional liberties of private litigants affected by state action. By case law, the *Conseil* has evolved a system of effective control over the constitutionality of administrative acts, regulations, and ordinances. An understanding of judicial review in France, therefore, requires a discussion not only of the officially recognized *Conseil Constitutionnel,* but also of the "case law" evolution of the *Conseil d'Etat.*

B. THE *CONSEIL D'ETAT*

1. Evolution Prior to the Constitution of 1958

Like the Cour de Cassation, the Conseil d'Etat was originally a political arm of another branch of government; however, it too has evolved into an independent judicial organ, as described in the following selection.*

Modern France was born in the Revolution of 1789. Much, however, that was apparently new was in fact a carry-over from the

---

* Excerpted from L. Brown & J. Garner, French Administrative Law 18-21 (1967). Reprinted with the permission of Butterworth Law Publishers, Ltd., London.

ancien régime. The Conseil d'Etat is itself in some measure an example.

In pre-Revolutionary France, the Conseil du Roi advised the King on legal and administrative matters; this had its origins, similar to those of the English Curia Regis, in the feudal system, but unlike its English counterpart it did not become the parent of many different courts of law. It remained primarily a political and arbitral body concerned with the determination of disputes and alleviation of tensions between the great nobles. The power of the lawyers was to be seen rather in the twelve regional royal courts or "parlements" (especially the Parlement of Paris) which in the eighteenth century in particular (under Louis XV and Louis XVI) not only interfered to a considerable degree in the executive government but also impeded such reforms as the monarchy sought to introduce. The parlements, in their zealous desire to keep a monopoly of all legal process, would also block a subject's appeal for justice to the Conseil du Roi. So with the coming of the Revolution a major break was made with tradition; the Conseil d'Etat had certain early resemblances to the Conseil du Roi of the ancien régime, but there is no direct link between the two.

The first step taken by the revolutionaries was to break the power of the parlements. This was done by the famous Law of 16-24 August 1790 which was in part inspired by the Montesquieu theory of the separation of powers, then recently applied in the United States Constitution of 1787. Article 12 of the Law, which is still in force, provides:

> "Judicial functions are distinct and will always remain separate from administrative functions. Judges in the civil courts may not, under pain of forfeiture of their offices, concern themselves in any manner whatsoever with the operation of the administration, nor shall they call administrators to account before them in respect of the exercise of their official functions."

This, of course, gave complete liberty to the administration; as the power of the King also was curbed and the Conseil du Roi was abolished, there was no one to whom the citizen could appeal for protection against the excesses of the executive. Napoleon, when he assumed power as First Consul, was conscious of the value, for administrative reform, of the information brought by individuals' complaints. In addition, he wanted expert advice on the drafting of laws and regulations, and in his constitution of "an VIII" (1799) he established a Conseil d'Etat, which was to operate under the direction of the three Consuls, but separate from them. The Conseil began its existence on Christmas Day, 1799. It was divided into five sections and presided over by the head of state, at first the First Consul, and then the Emperor. Initially the work of the five sections (each specializing in particular branches of administration) was to draft new laws and administrative regulations, and perhaps more important, in view of later development, to "resolve difficulties which might occur in the course of the administration." It is this last phrase which provided the constitutional basis for the subsequent growth of the judicial activity of the Conseil d'Etat. A Decree of the same year amplified somewhat these terms of reference by giving power to the Conseil to advise the head of state on the setting aside of improper acts of administrative authorities and on resolving the jurisdictional conflicts arising between the administration and the civil courts and between the various ministers.

The door being closed by the law of 1790 to redress in the ordinary courts, some outlet for the aggrieved citizen had obviously to be provided if the new régime were not to be one of administrative tyranny. The solution adopted in 1799 was that the citizen had first to lodge his complaint with the appropriate minister. If still unappeased, he should have a right of appeal from the minister to the Conseil d'Etat.

The Conseil d'Etat had, however, still to build its independence as a true court. This meant the elimination of two doctrines, that of the "justice retenue" and that of the "ministre-juge."

At this early date, although acting on appeal against the decision of the minister, the Conseil d'Etat had no power actually to decide nor to pronounce judgment; rather, its job was to advise the head of state as the minister's superior in the administrative hierarchy. But in practice its advice was invariably followed, although Napoleon did occasionally refer a case back to the Conseil for a second deliberation. One may compare the way in which a judgment of the Judicial Committee of the Privy Council is cast in the form of humble advice to Her Majesty but always followed. Nevertheless it was of great theoretical importance when the Conseil d'Etat was empowered by the Law of 24 May 1872 to reach decisions in suits against the administration without the formal pretence that it was merely advising the head of state on a decision which was legally his own. Thus, it is only since the beginning of the Third Republic (1870-1940) that the Conseil d'Etat has had the proper jurisdiction of a court, competent to deliver judgments, not in the name of the head of state, but (like the ordinary courts) in the name of the French people. In French parlance, this meant a shift of theory from "la justice retenue" to that of "la justice déléguée."*

---

* "In the following year the new Court of Conflicts (it too was established in 1872) decided what is still regarded as the most important case in French administrative law: *Blanco*, C.T. 8 Feb., 1873. That date marks the real beginning of the evolution of the Conseil d'Etat into 'one of the most systematic guarantees of the liberties of the individual against the state known at the present day.'

"In *Blanco* the jurisdiction of the Conseil d'Etat over administrative matters is confirmed as being exclusive and defined as coextensive with the field of public

On the other hand, a consequence of the principle according to which the administration should not be under the control of any court persisted in the doctrine of the ministre-juge. The Conseil d'Etat did not enjoy immediate jurisdiction in regard to the acts of the administration; complaints had to be brought before the appropriate minister, and only eventually, on appeal from his decision, to the Conseil d'Etat.

This is why, in 1889, the famous case of CADOT (C.E. 13 December 1889) marks a decisive stage of the Conseil's evolution. In this case the Conseil cast off the outworn practice that there had first to be a complaint by the aggrieved citizen to the minister. Since CADOT, in any matter involving a decision by the administration, a case can be carried directly before the Conseil. The plaintiff has only to state which decision has caused his grievance, or to provoke such a decision, to obtain access to the court. The administration lost its jurisdiction to receive the complaint, as it were, at first instance, and the Conseil d'Etat became, to adopt the French expression, "the juge de droit commun of the acts of the administration."

Meanwhile, there had occurred changes in the organisation of the Conseil which were no less significant of its development as an administrative court. In 1806 there was created within the Conseil a special body, the Commission du Contentieux, to deal with the judicial work of the Conseil as distinct from its advisory work for the various departments of government. This Commission in 1849 changed its name to that of the Section du Contentieux, under which style it has been known to the present day. As the "contentious section" it co-exists alongside the four other "administrative sections" into which the rest of the Conseil is sub-divided and which are concerned respectively with home affairs (section de l'intérieur), public works (section des travaux publics), social matters (section sociale) and finance (section de finance).

Another key date is 1831, in which year the Commission du Contentieux began to conduct its judicial business in public, at least to the extent of holding a public sitting at which the parties could be represented by counsel and after the close of which the Commission must publish a judgment containing reasons for its decisions.

---

service. Henceforth an action for damages against the state or one of its agencies could only be brought in the administrative court. Of even more importance, the decision read: 'the liability that the state incurs for damages caused to private individuals by the acts of persons employed by it in the public service cannot be governed by the principles laid down in the civil code for the regulation or relationship of private individuals. Such liability . . . has its own special rules, which may vary according to the needs of the administrative service and the necessity of reconciling the rights of the state with private rights.' " Cake, *The French Conseil d'Etat — An Essay on Administrative Jurisprudence,* 24 AD. L. REV. 315, 318-19 (1972).

The same year also saw the introduction into the procedural working of the Commission of a new and highly important officer, the Commissaire du Gouvernement. Intended originally to present the viewpoint of the government, this officer rapidly abrogated to himself an independent function and began to represent the general public interest rather than the policy of the administration.

The detachment of the Commission du Contentieux from the rest of the Conseil was underlined in 1849 when the decisions of the new-styled Section du Contentieux were no longer required to pass for formal approval through the general assembly of the Conseil d'Etat, as had been the previous practice (although the general assembly had long been in the habit of merely rubber-stamping whatever the Commission put before it).

In the result, the Conseil d'Etat emerges by the close of the nineteenth century as a court of first (and last) instance having a general jurisdiction to be seized directly of any complaint or suit against the administration.* And in its Section du Contentieux the Conseil d'Etat manifests all the features which the French associate with a court — a public hearing (however perfunctory), the representation of the parties by counsel, a spokesman for the public interest, a collegiate bench, and a published judgment supported by reasons.

It was this court, originating as an offshoot of the administration itself and staffed by high-ranking civil servants, that was to have the vital role of exercising judicial control over the administration as France entered the last decade of the nineteenth century. In the difficult transition from the laissez-faire liberalism of that century to the planned economy and collectivised society of the twentieth, the French were to bless the good fortune which had given them, almost by historical accident, this novel institution before which the humblest citizen could arraign and call to account the all-powerful and interfering state. Moreover, this institution was to be the prototype for other continental countries, such as Italy, Germany and Belgium. And once Dicey's distortions had been cleared away, it was to be looked upon with envy by English lawyers.

2. The Role of the *Conseil d'Etat* in Constitutional Adjudication

The evolution of the *Conseil d'Etat* into a court reviewing the constitutional validity of executive acts is in defiance of French tradition which, in reaction to the abuses of the judges of the *ancien régime,* denies French courts the power to invalidate state action. The *Conseil d'Etat,* clearly a judicial body, was required to decide if

---

* However, in 1953, due to a tremendous backlog of cases before the Conseil, most of its jurisdiction as a court of first instance was transferred to a system of lower administrative courts.

government actions challenged by private parties were authorized by an enabling statute (*loi d'habilitation*). If so authorized, the action would stand; if not, the aggrieved citizen could recover damages and the action would be declared *ultra vires (excès de pouvoir; détournement de pouvoir)*. Under no circumstances could the *Conseil d'Etat* invalidate an administrative act as unconstitutional, since the sole test of validity was the enabling statute. If the statute itself was unconstitutional, the *Conseil d'Etat* was helpless.

The Vichy regime with its bills of attainder (*lois d'exception*) and *ex post facto* legislation, forced reconsideration of the traditional French attitude towards judicial review. The *Conseil d'Etat* evolved a jurisprudence designed to suppress the Vichy abuses by narrowly construing statutes of the Vichy regime and rendering them unenforceable if at all possible. It began to enunciate "general principles of law," first as guides for the interpretation of statutes and later as unwritten principles of legislative — or higher — value. The right to judicial review of an administrative decision, the prohibition of *ex post facto* decrees, liberty of conscience, equality before the law: these are but a few examples of the principles which the *Conseil* derived from the Declaration of the Rights of Man (1789), the Preamble to the Constitution of 1946, or, simply, from "republican tradition."

The precise import of the general principles has been the subject of much debate. Some said that they were no more than guides for the interpretation of enabling statutes and that the critical question for the *Conseil* remained whether or not a challenged act was authorized by statute. Others were willing to admit that the principles have a validity independent of any written text and that all administrative acts must conflict with *neither* statutes *nor* general principles. Finally, a third group claimed that the principles were of constitutional value and would prevail even over a statute authorizing their violation.*

3. Impact of the Constitution of 1958

The new Constitution of 1958 rejected the traditional ideal of legislative supremacy and shifted significant power to the executive. This created an opportunity for the *Conseil d'Etat* to greatly expand

---

* Parallel to the administrative courts, the highest of which is the *Conseil d'Etat*, exist the ordinary civil courts, the decisions of which are subject to review by the *Cour de Cassation*. The latter has also developed a jurisprudence based upon "general principles of law." Since, however, the *Cour de Cassation* is specifically charged with interpreting a vast body of codified law, it has been easier for that Court to deny that it has assumed a normative role in "deducing" certain general principles for use in interpreting doubtful texts or in resolving disputes not covered by text. Rather the judges in *Cassation* have generally upheld, at least technically, the superiority of the written statute.

its jurisdiction. More important, it allowed the *Conseil d'Etat* to affirm the constitutional import of many of the "general principles of law."

Of particular importance are arts. 34-38 of the 1958 Constitution:

TITLE V

ON RELATIONS BETWEEN PARLIAMENT AND THE GOVERNMENT

Art. 34. All laws shall be passed by Parliament.

Laws shall establish the regulations concerning:

- civil rights and the fundamental guarantees granted to the citizens for the exercise of their public liberties; the obligations imposed by the national defense upon the persons and property of citizens;
- nationality, status and legal capacity of persons, marriage contracts, inheritance and gifts;
- determination of crimes and misdemeanors as well as the penalties imposed therefor; criminal procedure; amnesty; the creation of new judicial systems and the status of magistrates;
- the basis, the rate and the methods of collecting taxes of all types; the issuance of currency.

Laws shall likewise determine the regulations concerning:
- the electoral system of the Parliamentary assemblies and the local assemblies;
- the establishment of categories of public institutions;
- the fundamental guarantees granted to civil and military personnel employed by the State;
- the nationalization of enterprises and the transfer of the property of enterprises from the public to the private sector.

Laws shall determine the fundamental principles of:
- the general organization of national defense;
- the free administration of local communities, the extent of their jurisdiction and their resources;
- education;
- property rights, civil and commercial obligations;
- legislation pertaining to employment, unions and social security.

The financial laws shall determine the financial resources and obligations of the State under the conditions with the reservations to be provided for by an organic law.

Laws pertaining to national planning shall determine the objectives of the economic and social action of the State.

The provisions of the present article may be developed in detail and amplified by an organic law.

Art. 35. Parliament shall authorize the declaration of war.

Art. 36. Martial law shall be decreed in a meeting of the Council of Ministers.

Its prorogation beyond twelve days may be authorized only by Parliament.

Art. 37. Matters other than those that fall within the domain of law shall be of a regulatory character.

Legislative texts concerning these matters may be modified by decrees issued after consultation with the Council of State. Those legislative texts which may be passed after the present Constitution has become operative shall be modified by decree, only if the Constitutional Council has stated that they have a regulatory character as defined in the preceding paragraph.

Art. 38. The Government may, in order to carry out its program, ask Parliament to authorize it, for a limited period, to take through ordinances measures that are normally within the domain of law.

The ordinances shall be enacted in meetings of the Council of Ministers after consultation with the Council of State. They shall come into force upon their publication, but shall become null and void if the bill for their ratification is not submitted to Parliament before the date set by the enabling act.

At the expiration of the time limit referred to in the first paragraph of the present article, the ordinances may be modified only by law in those matters which are within the legislative domain.

Thus the power given to the executive under Arts. 37 and 38 of the new Constitution allowed it to promulgate regulations and ordinances clearly legislative in nature. If there were no check of the legality of these decrees, the "Government could do anything in its domain; its powers in its sphere would be unlimited." * Yet if these quasi-legislative enactments could be nullified by the *Conseil d'Etat* for failure to conform with the Constitution or "general principles," the *Conseil d'Etat* would have a power similar to that of invalidating statutes. Review of the legality of the ordinances and regulations promulgated by the executive pursuant to arts. 37 and 38 would require examining their conformity with the only enabling statute available — the Constitution. By declaring its power to nullify *all* government acts and decrees for noncompliance with statutes, the Constitution, or the general principles of law, the *Conseil d'Etat* was to become the most important organ of control in France of the constitutionality of state action.

---

* *Syndicat général des ingénieurs-conseils,* Decision of June 26, 1959, Conseil d'Etat, as reported in Recueil Dalloz 541 (1959) and in LONG, WEIL, & BRAIBANT, LES GRANDS ARRÉTS DE LA JURISPRUDENCE ADMINISTRATIVE 466 (1965).

4. The *Syndicat Général* Decision

SYNDICAT GÉNÉRAL DES INGÉNIEURS-CONSEILS

Decision of June 26, 1959, Conseil d'Etat
[1959] Dalloz, *Jurisprudence* [D. Jur.] 541
[1959] Sirey, *Jurisprudence* [S. Jur.] 202

[FACTS: Exercising his long-standing right to legislate for the colonies by decree, the French Minister for Overseas Territories ordered that certain types of building design and planning were to be done by licensed architects only. Various professional organizations protested that the edict gave an unjustified monopoly to the architects, thus violating an unwritten "general principle" of liberty of commerce.

[The edict had been published in no colony and rapidly appeared to be becoming a dead letter. There was a serious question whether the petitioning engineers and contractors were sufficiently threatened by the edict to seek a hearing as to its validity.

[The substantive questions were: (1) Are governmental decrees and ordinances issued under the authority of the Constitutions of 1946 and 1958 to be invalidated if they run counter to the Constitution or to other "general principles of law"? (2) If the decrees can be subjected to this sort of review, should the challenged decree be annulled?]

OPINION

Considering the appeal of the engineers' association . . . asking that the *Conseil d'Etat* overturn as an illegal exercise of power the decree of June 25, 1947 regulating the architects' profession in the territories subject to the Minister for Overseas Colonies . . . considering the French Constitution of October 27, 1946 (especially arts. 47, 71, 72, and 104) and considering the Constitution of October 4, 1958 . . . [we decide]:

With regard to the exceptions to the petition submitted by the Minister for Overseas Colonies: even though the challenged decree . . . had not, before the present appeal, been published in any of the territories subject to the Minister, there is still no reason why the decree cannot be attacked by those persons who would be harmed should the decree be so published. Considering that many members of the engineers' association would find their professional work in the colonies severely limited to the profit of the professional architects should the decree be applied, there is no question but that the *Syndicat* has standing to seek the invalidation of the decree.

. . .

With regard to the challenged decree: even though the Prime Minister . . . has, by virtue of art. 47 of the 1946 Constitution, the power to regulate by decree matters in the colonies which in the metropole could only be controlled by statute, nonetheless he must respect not only statutory provisions applicable in the colonies, but also the general principles of law, resulting notably from the Preamble of the Constitution, which will control all regulatory powers even in the absence of a legislative text. . . . Yet, considering that the challenged decree does not run counter to any statute applicable to the colonies and that in reserving to architects only the right to design the structures, proportions, and distribution of buildings . . . the decree does not go against any general principle of law, we decide: . . .

The appeal of the *Syndicat général* is rejected.

NOTE *

The significance of the above decision does not reside in the special question of the law of professions which is resolved, but rather in the position taken by the court with regard to a problem whose importance has greatly increased due to the redistribution of normative powers by the Constitution of 1958 (arts. 34 and 37): that is, the problem of judicial control of the constitutionality of regulations emanating from the government. . . D. Jur. 542.

. . . .

When the *Conseil d'Etat* decided. . . , the issue was no longer of practical importance. Since . . . the decree had never been promulgated in the colonies, and since the method of legislating for the territories had in the meantime changed . . . it was certain that the decree would never be enforced.

But it happens at times that questions of no practical importance to either appellants or government lead to issues of great juridical

---

*The following note by Professor Jean L'Huillier is excerpted from [1959] D.S. Jur. 542-45. Reprinted with permission.

The "notes" or "observations" which follow significant decisions of French courts are often by leading scholars, and are of great importance to the development of French jurisprudence. As may be clear, French decisions tend to be brief, stating the facts in the most general terms. The law is given in the form of conclusions. The common law practice of publishing the legal reasoning of each judge and the process by which a majority conclusion is reached is not followed. This exposition of the reasoning behind a decision, of the alternative approaches to a given case, and of the implications for the future development of the law is left to the scholars. Thus, an important decision, when published, is accompanied by an academic discussion whose importance to the reader may be as great as the text of the decision itself.

importance. The *Conseil d'Etat* has often seized upon minor litigations to entertain the most important questions. This was the case here. The appellants invoked, in order to overturn the decree, the principle of liberty of commerce and industry. The *Conseil* thus was led to decide the limits of the regulatory power, or, more generally, "if the autonomous regulatory power, which is not limited by statute, is or is not limited by certain unwritten principles."

The Constitution of October 4, 1958 gave special importance to the question insofar as art. 34 limits the domain of the legislature and art. 37 confers upon the executive an autonomous regulatory power in those areas no longer the province of the legislature . . . . It was now necessary to determine the limits of the regulatory power and the efficacy of judicial control of that power. Otherwise the government could do anything in its domain. In its sphere its powers would be unlimited: the risk of arbitrariness would be great and the role of the judge purely formal. The alternative would be to say that the executive must respect not only the Constitution but also certain general principles deduced by the Judiciary. In this case judicial control could be exercised over the validity of the autonomous regulatory power and the extension of executive power could be limited . . . .

The instant case can be better understood through the conclusions of the *Commissaire du gouvernement* * M. Fournier:

> (i) He reminds us first that the Judiciary has already applied certain "general principles" to the "legislator for the colonies." Since the latter had . . . legislative powers, this application can only be explained by giving to the "general principles" of law a constitutional or quasi-constitutional value.
>
> (ii) The *Commissaire* claims, moreover, that these unwritten rules are not all of the same nature: some have legislative or regulatory value only; other have a constitutional character. . . .
>
> The former are of a purely interpretative or supplementary value. "They only apply when there is no written text to the contrary . . . . depending on their content they will be subordinated to written rules and statutes. An example would

---

* The *Commissaire du gouvernement* plays an extremely important role in the decisions of the *Conseil d'Etat*. There are twelve *Commissaires* on the *Conseil*, appointed from among the senior civil servants there. The *Commissaire*'s original function was to defend the government's interests in litigation before the *Conseil*, but he has since become an advisor of the court, independent of either plaintiff or defendant. He is in fact, a member, without a vote, of the courts, and he addresses the latter after the parties have exhausted all opportunities to add to the record. The *Commissaire* may then argue for either party, citing case law, equity, and public policy. His influence over the development of the *Conseil's* jurisprudence has been considerable.

be the general rules of procedure applicable, even without specific text, before all administrative tribunals." We would put in this category the obligation to give grounds for all judgments, the requirement that the names of the deciding judges be published, the right to require that administrative remedies be exhausted before resorting to adversary proceedings, and the rules for determining what will be a quorum of any multi-membered body.

Among the latter principles, which have higher value, a distinction must be made between rules of procedure or jurisdiction and rules of substance.

The rules of jurisdiction fix the powers respectively of the legislature and of the executive. Before 1958 they were derived from the "tradition of republican constitutionalism" (as noted particularly by the opinion of the *Conseil d'Etat* dated February 6, 1953 [*Revue du Droit Public,* 1953, p. 170]). Today, they are to be found particularly in art. 34 of the Constitution . . . .

The rules of substance "are the general principles proper, i.e., those promulgated explicitly by the Declaration of Rights or deduced by the judge therefrom. Among these are the principle of the equality of all citizens, the guarantees of essential civil liberties, the idea of *res judicata,* the separation of powers, the prohibition of *ex post facto* laws, [etc.]."

(iii) The *Commissaire,* having made the above distinctions, adjudged that the recent evolution of the law showed that "liberty of commerce and industry" could no longer be considered a binding general principle and that the colonial legislator could limit this right at will.

The decision itself declares that the Government was bound to respect the general principles of law "which, resulting chiefly from the Preamble of the Constitution, control all regulations even in absence of legislative text . . . ."

In using such a broad formula the *Conseil d'Etat* showed its willingness to subject to the principles even the autonomous regulatory power granted by art. 37 of the 1958 Constitution as well as the ordinances promulgated by the executive under art. 38 . . . .

The government cannot, therefore, exercise its rule-making powers in such a way as to abridge the general principles of law . . . .

5. The Definition of General Principles

Syndicat général, rather than resolving the question of the value of the general principles, opened the door to further decades of speculation. It became necessary to examine the jurisprudence of a century and a half in order to determine which principles have enjoyed that degree of respect which would warrant their being given constitutional status.

The *Commissaire du gouvernement* in *Syndicat général,* etc., acknowledged the difference in value to be accorded various principles and labeled as *règles de fond* only those which had been mentioned in the Declaration of the Rights of Man.* Other rules, such as those dividing the legislative and executive competence, though having constitutional standing, will be less likely to excite the creative instincts of the *Conseil d'Etat* since they touch an essentially political area, one which, in any case, has been largely consigned to the *Conseil Constitutionnel.* Finally there are the rules of interpretation, *i.e.,* those that will be applied only if the *Conseil d'Etat* is faced with an unclear or incomplete law or regulation.

There are at least two "procedural" rights which have been upheld by the *Conseil d'Etat* even in the face of clear legislative or regulatory language to the contrary and even though neither is specifically mentioned in the Declaration of Rights. The importance of other rules of procedure would seem to vary according to their relevance to these "quasi-constitutional" rights, *i.e.,* the *droit de défense* and the right to judicial review of certain administrative decisions. As early as 1913 the *Conseil d'Etat* affirmed that "though the rules of procedure for disciplinary tribunals are not written in a code or text," the right to defend oneself is the "natural guarantee of all private persons accused of punishable infractions." ** The *Commissaire du gouvernement* went on to spell out various aspects of the right: the right to timely notice, the right to demand that all members of the tribunal be present at all times and that their names be affixed to the judgment, the right to be heard after the presentation of the charges and before the deliberation of the tribunal, and finally, the right to require that every judgment contain grounds.*** Though this early decision tended to consider all the above requirements as essential to a proper defense and appeal by the aggrieved party, later commentary has tended to distinguish among them. For example, while the right to present one's defense is of constitutional importance, the rule requiring that the relevant names be attached to the decision is interpretative only. The requirement that every decision contain an exposition of its grounds may be called constitutional, if considered as a means of detecting an erroneous application of the law, but some commentators have said this rule

---

* The "Declaration of the Rights of Man and the Citizen" is the French Bill of Rights, promulgated in 1789. The 1946 Constitution, in its Preamble, incorporated the Declaration by reference, as did the Constitution of 1958.

** Tery, Decision of June 20, 1913, Conseil d'Etat, in LONG, WEIL, & BRAIBANT, LES GRANDS ARRÊTS DE LA JURISPRUDENCE ADMINISTRATIVE 116, 118 (1965).

*** *Id.*

will yield before a legislative or administrative declaration to the contrary.

Intrinsic to the concept of the *droit de défense* is the idea that there should always be some form of judicial review of an administrative decision which takes the form of a serious sanction against an individual. This is the *droit de recours* before the *Conseil d'Etat* which, like the *droit de défense,* is not specifically mentioned by the Declaration of Rights or by the Preambles but which has nonetheless acquired constitutional import.

In the face of the clearest statutory language ("the decision of the jury of honor is not subject to judicial review";* "there will be no review whatsoever" **), the *Conseil d'Etat* has refused to find a legislative "intent" to deny aggrieved parties recourse before a judicial tribunal. Less important have been the principles whereby the courts have controlled the flow of the cases brought before them, *e.g.,* standing requirements, availability of *de novo* review of the facts.

There is still doubt whether various subordinate principles will prevail over executive *ordonnances,* or whether Herculean efforts will be made to read them into statutes. The rule forbidding judicial decisions based on the private knowledge of the judge or on arguments not raised in an adversary hearing would seem intimately linked to the *droit de défense.* The rule banning evidence gathered by illicit means might not, however, be so considered. Rules concerning private party access to administrative records, the right to be represented by an *avocat* before an oral hearing, the means of determining quorum rules for a given tribunal, the completeness necessary to the exposition of grounds for a decision: all are as yet of undetermined weight in the post-1958 jurisprudence of the *Conseil d'Etat.*

6. The *Dame David* Decision

DECISION OF OCTOBER 4, 1974

Conseil d'Etat
[1974] Recueil Lebon 464

The Conseil d'Etat; — Considering that, in the terms of Article 83 of the decree of July 20, 1972, establishing new provisions intended to be incorporated in the general part of a new Code of Civil Procedure, "proceedings are public, unless it follows from some

---

* *D'Aillieres,* Decision of Feb. 7, 1947, Conseil d'Etat, as reported in VON MEHREN, THE CIVIL LAW SYSTEM 278 (1957).

** *Lamotte,* Decision of Feb. 17, 1950, Conseil d'Etat, as reported in LONG, WEIL, & BRAIBANT, LES GRANDS ARRÊTS DE LA JURISPRUDENCE ADMINISTRATIVE 325 (1965).

provision that they must take place in camera. The presiding judge may, however, decide that the proceedings will take place or be continued in camera if an invasion of privacy will result from a public hearing, or if all the parties request it, or if disturbances likely to upset the calm of the proceedings arise"; — Considering that the publicity of judicial proceedings is a general principle of law; that only the legislature can thus decide, extend or restrict its limits; that the second paragraph of Article 83, which gives the presiding judge alone the right to decide that the proceedings will take place in camera if an invasion of privacy will result from a public hearing, or if all the parties request it, or if disturbances likely to upset the calm of the proceedings arise, restricts this principle and can not, therefore, be enacted by the executive; that Dame David, a journalist reporting on judicial proceedings, is thus entitled to request its annulment;

Decides: 1. Article 83, paragraph 2, of the decree of July 20, 1972 is annulled;

        2. The state will pay costs.

NOTES AND QUESTIONS

1. The *Dame David* decision is striking in its reversal of prior policy. Five months before, in *Barré et Honnet* ([1974] A.J.D.A. 545), the *Conseil d'Etat* had dealt with the problem of *astreinte*. *Astreinte* is a device aimed at securing compliance with court orders requiring specific performance, by adding to such orders a clause requiring payment of a specified amount of damages for delay in performance. While noting that the recognized power of judges to make an *astreinte* was "of the nature of a general principle of law," the *Conseil* had acknowledged that a decree could withdraw or regulate the power to issue an *astreinte* if no statute made express provision to the contrary. Can *Dame David* be distinguished from *Barré et Honnet*?

2. It is important to notice that *Dame David* is technically a separation of powers decision. The *Conseil d'Etat* did *not* hold that the principle of publicity of trials, as violated by the decree of July 20, 1972, was guaranteed by the Constitution. Rather, it held that "the publicity of judicial proceedings is a general principle of law" and thus in the legislative domain. Is this, in some sense, a retreat from *Syndicat général*? Does the approach expand or contract the power of the *Conseil d'Etat*?

3. What effect will this approach, if adopted generally by the *Conseil d'Etat,* have on the protection of fundamental rights in France? Suppose the legislature accepted the invitation of the *Conseil d'Etat,* and enacted a law equivalent to the decree of July 20, 1972. Would the decision of the *Conseil d'Etat* prevent Parliament from enacting a valid law with identical terms? Would the *Conseil Constitutionnel,* if the law were referred to it, be influenced by the decision of the *Conseil d'Etat?*

4. Notice that the plaintiff in *Dame David* was a journalist, asserting that she could not properly perform her job of reporting on judicial proceedings unless they were public. The *Conseil* specifically asserted that she was "entitled to request [the decree's] annulment."

Would she have had standing to challenge a similar regulation in an American court? The *Conseil* said only that publicity of judicial proceedings was a "general principle of law," without further elaboration. Would Dame David's standing in an American court depend upon whether she was asserting that the decree interfered with freedom of the press or that the decree denied litigants a fair trial? Is there also a ripeness problem?

5. What are the implications of *Dame David* for the balance of power between the executive and legislative branches? Article 34 reserves to Parliament the area of "fundamental guarantees," but the *Conseil d'Etat* eschewed this narrower basis for decision. Thus, rather than holding that publicity of trials was a "fundamental guarantee," and therefore in the legislative domain, the *Conseil* held that it fell within the broader category of "general principles," and was for that reason in the legislative domain. Now Parliament has exclusive jurisdiction over matters that concern "general principles," as defined by the *Conseil d'Etat,* whether or not a "fundamental guarantee" is involved.

Potential for conflict existed before the *Dame David* decision, as art. 34 explicitly reserves to Parliament regulations concerning "fundamental guarantees," but the decision has enlarged this potential considerably. For example, it is clear that the area of civil procedure is a matter for the executive. In fact, the administration published a new Code of Civil Procedure, effective January 1, 1976. Suppose that a provision of the code, or any other executive decree, restricted the right to judicial review of administrative decisions. In *Lamotte,* Decision of Feb. 17, 1950, Conseil d'Etat, [1950] D. Jur. 282; [1950] S. Jur. III 65, the *Conseil* declared that this right was a "general principle of law." *Canal et autres,* Decision of Oct. 19, 1962, Conseil d'Etat, [1962] Lebon 552, affirmed *Lamotte* and strongly implied that the right to judicial review was a fundamental guarantee. Is not all of civil procedure inseparably linked to the fundamental guarantee, or at least the general principle, of the right to be heard?

6. The *Conseil Constitutionnel* is clearly limited to reviewing statutes not yet promulgated. However, the *Conseil d'Etat* is not so limited, and, particularly with the dethronement of statutory law by the Constitution of 1958, there is no juridical reason why the *Conseil d'Etat* may not require that parliamentary legislation observe the same standards it has imposed on executive legislation. Still, while the *Conseil d'Etat* has openly assumed the power to refuse recognition to executive decisions, decrees, and ordinances running counter to the Constitution or general principles, it has opposed unconstitutional statutes, if at all, in a much more subtle way. It has "reinterpreted" statutes so as to avoid conflict with higher principles, ignored or narrowly construed clearly expressed legislative intent to violate such principles, and even, in some cases, awarded money damages to private individuals harmed by statutes authorizing unconstitutional acts. (*See Lacombe,* Decision of Dec. 1, 1961, Conseil d'Etat, [1962] D. Jur. 89.)

Despite the existence of subtle techniques for protecting higher principles against legislative encroachment, the *Conseil d'Etat* has been reluctant to declare legislation invalid. There are cases where challenged administrative action was admitted to violate the Constitution or "general principles of law," but the challenged action was found to be authorized by a broadly worded enabling statute. For example, in *Union fédérale des magistrats et Sieur Reliquet,** the enabling statute authorized the executive "to take any exceptional measure required under the circumstances to restore order."

Still, there is a line of decisions, represented by *Lamotte, supra* Note 5, where similarly broad statutes were ignored and the challenged actions invalidated. *Lamotte,* where the statute (a holdover from the Vichy regime) specifically forbade "any administrative or judicial recourse," is probably the one case where the *Conseil d'Etat* in fact refused to apply a parliamentary act because of its unconstitutionality. If the *Conseil* ever openly assumes the power to review the constitutionality of legislation, *Lamotte* will be the precedent.

C. THE *CONSEIL CONSTITUTIONNEL*

1. Historical Background

The *Conseil Constitutionnel* is not the first body to be charged with the review of the constitutionality of French legislation, but it is the first to assume a meaningful role. The *Sénat Conservateur* (Constitution of the year VIII, December 13, 1799), had been labeled "completely useless," and a similar body established by the Constitution of 1852 had likewise been called "sterile." ** Similarly, the "Constitutional Committee" of the 1946 Constitution "had

---

* L'ACTUALITÉ JURIDIQUE 590-91 (1965). *See also Syndicat des propriétaires de forêts de chênes-lièges d'Algérie,* L'ACTUALITÉ JURIDIQUE 130 (1958).

** *See* FRANCINE BATAILLER, LE CONSEIL D'ETAT: JUGE CONSTITUTIONNEL, 28-32 (1966).

nothing judicial about it, neither in its composition, nor in its manner of convocation, nor in its powers. . . . Its task was to 'examine laws voted by the Assembly which might require a revision of the Constitution.' " * It could not examine laws for conformity with the Preamble (*i.e.,* civil liberties questions). The authorities persistently refused to convene the Committee and it rendered only one decision.

Thus, from 1789 (the date of the Revolutionary Declaration of Human Rights) to 1958 there existed no real institution in France with the right to invalidate unconstitutional statutes. This was due partly to the lack of a bill of rights in the 1875 Constitutional Laws, but mainly to the commitment of both the 1875 Constitutional Laws and the 1946 Constitution (as well as previous French Constitutions after the Revolution) to the supremacy of the legislature.

2. Phase I: 1958-1971

a. *The Constitution of 1958*

The 1958 Constitution marked the end of parliamentary supremacy. It divided the legislative power between Parliament and the executive. Article 34 enumerated the powers of the former, to be exercised by formal statutes (*lois*), and art. 37 gave the latter authority to regulate "all matters other than those which are the domain of the *loi.*" This fragmentation of the lawmaking power between executive and Parliament required a body to arbitrate and decide jurisdictional conflicts, just as the American division of legislative power between the federal and state governments encouraged the assumption of the same role by the United States Supreme Court. Articles 61 and 62, therefore, allow for the submission of statutes, before their promulgation, to the *Conseil Constitutionnel,* "which will pronounce upon their conformity to the Constitution. . . . A provision declared unconstitutional will not be promulgated or enforced."

The Preamble of the 1946 Constitution incorporated by reference the 1789 "Declaration of the Rights of Man and of the Citizen." Article 92 of the 1946 Constitution provided, however, that the "Constitutional Committee" could not examine conformity of a law with the Preamble. The 1958 Constitution, in its Preamble, likewise explicitly incorporated the 1789 Declaration. Significantly, nothing in the 1958 Constitution forbade the *Conseil* to apply declarations of civil liberties, unlike the 1946 Constitution.

---

* *Id.* at 29.

b. Structural Characteristics of the Conseil Constitutionnel

The text above seems broad enough, but an examination of the *Conseil Constitutionnel,* its composition, jurisdiction and methods shows that it was not originally intended to be a judicial organ of review.

Consider the following "congenital defects":

(i) "Preview," Not Review

The *Conseil* may only review legislation between the times of its enactment and promulgation. After promulgation, the *Conseil* is without jurisdiction (except for the jurisdiction conferred by the final sentence of art. 37; *see* § C.3.b., *infra*).

(ii) Standing

Until 1974, the *Conseil* could only act if summoned by one of four political officials — the President of the Republic, the Prime Minister, or the president of either house of the legislature. In 1974, art. 61 of the Constitution was amended to extend standing to any group of 60 members of either legislative chamber. Still, clearly "if the legislature and the executive *together* attempt to violate the Constitution, the *Conseil Constitutionnel* is helpless" * since no private parties have standing.

(iii) Jurisdiction

Only parliamentary legislation is subject to the *Conseil*'s control. The validity of executive legislation is determined exclusively by the *Conseil d'Etat.*

(iv) Personnel

In addition to *ex officio* members (all former Presidents of the Republic) there are nine appointees, three of whom are appointed by the President of the Republic, three by the President of the Senate and three by the President of the National Assembly. Appointees serve for a non-renewable term of nine years. Very few have distinguished themselves as legal scholars. This in marked contrast to other high French courts, whose members are senior career judges rather than politicians.

c. Decisions of the Conseil Constitutionnel Prior to 1971

In addition to these structural infirmities, the decisions of the *Conseil Constitutionnel* during the years 1958-71 tended to limit its already circumscribed jurisdiction. Unlike the *Conseil d'Etat,* which has seized opportunities to expand its influence (*see* § B., *supra*), the

---

* BATAILLER, *supra* at 35.

Conseil Constitutionnel until 1971, acted merely as an auxiliary of the executive *vis-à-vis* Parliament, assiduously restricting Parliament to its limited role under art. 34.

(i) The Decision of December 23, 1960 *

Article 60 of the 1958 Constitution grants the *Conseil Constitutionnel* the power to "oversee the regularity of referenda and proclaim their results." This, along with the ordinance which gave effect to it, seemed to give the *Conseil* full power to hear complaints of election irregularities and to annul proceedings found illegal or fraudulent. It seemed to Jacques Soustelle, whose party had been prevented by the Government from using the national communications media for campaign propaganda, that the *Conseil* would be empowered to rectify his grievance. The *Conseil* decided otherwise, saying that since the enabling texts had not specifically granted it authority to hear complaints made before the election, it must confine itself to post-election hearings and sanctions.

The decision, in addition to denying Soustelle a meaningful remedy, had several important results. (1) The *Conseil* gave further evidence of its "textualism." Unless a power was explicitly granted by an enabling text, it would not be assumed by the *Conseil*. "We regret the *Conseil Constitutionnel* did not find a different answer in the very generous terms of art. 60 of the Constitution itself, terms which, naturally, ought to control its interpretation."** (2) By limiting itself to one remedy — complete invalidation of an election already held — the *Conseil* denied itself the power that would have allowed effective control of election irregularities. It is unlikely that a national referendum will be annulled because Jacques Soustelle or any other opposition candidate has been forbidden to speak on the RTF (*Radiodiffusion-Télévision Française*). The grievance could have been remedied only if the *Conseil* could intervene in specific matters before the election was held.

(ii) The Decision of January 20, 1961 ***

Article 61 of the Constitution allows the *Conseil Constitutionnel* to be convened only by certain specified authorities. No private party initiative is permitted. The power of the *Conseil* was further restricted by its decision that it would consider no issue unless it had been raised by the convening authority. This in essence would allow the ruling political party to pass a law and submit to the *Conseil* only the provisions introduced as minority amendments.**** Although

---

* [1962] Recueil Dalloz 467, note by Léo Hamon.
** DUVERGER, INSTITUTIONS POLITIQUES ET DROIT CONSTITUTIONNEL 469 (1968).
*** [1962] D. Jur. 177, note by Léo Hamon.
**** Recall that, until 1974, a parliamentary minority had no standing to invoke the jurisdiction of the *Conseil*.

art. 61 seems to authorize the *Conseil* to consider all issues concerning the validity of the law placed before it, the *Conseil* again took the narrowest possible view of its jurisdiction.

(iii) The Decisions of July 18, 1961, and February 9, 1965*

Article 34 of the Constitution states that: "Laws [*lois*] shall establish the regulations concerning: . . . the creation of new systems of courts and the status of magistrates." Although these decisions concluded that the legislature has exclusive competence to create new courts under art. 34, they nonetheless limited the scope of that power: only the executive could determine the number, physical location, or competence of any newly created court. Again the *Conseil Constitutionnel* had restricted its own competence.

(iv) The Consistent Refusal to Declare a Law Violative of Any Provisions Other Than Those Concerning Separation of Powers

There is no indication in art. 61 that the *Conseil Constitutionnel* cannot declare a law unconstitutional because it violates individual liberties. Those liberties are given constitutional status by the Preamble of the Constitution of 1946 which is incorporated by reference in the Preamble of the Constitution of 1958. Moreover, the 1958 Constitution, unlike the Constitution of 1946, does not specifically forbid the *Conseil* to examine conformity of a law with the Preamble. During the 1958-71 period, however, the *Conseil* only declared unconstitutional those laws which impinged upon the powers of the executive. One commentator summed up the situation prior to 1971: "Never has the *Conseil Constitutionnel* tested a law by any article other than 34, 37, or 38. As a practical matter the right to censure a law as violative of any constitutional guarantee, or of the Preamble, has fallen into desuetude. This abstention is logical from the standpoint of the authorities who convene the *Conseil* and who are, above all, concerned with keeping Parliament under control. . . . The *Conseil*, therefore, exists to bar legislation in areas reserved to the executive power. It does not protect the rights of the citizens, but rather the prerogatives of the Government." **

QUESTIONS

1. What conception of law is reflected in the structure and procedures of the *Conseil Constitutionnel*? How does this compare with the common law view?

2. Human institutions are generally observed to attempt to enlarge their spheres of authority. Why did the *Conseil Constitutionnel,* at least until 1971, act differently?

---

* [1961] D. Jur. 541; [1967] D.S. Jur. 405.
** BATAILLER, LE CONSEIL D'ETAT: JUDGE CONSTITUTIONNEL 38f. (1966).

3. Phase II: Post-1971

a. *The Decision of July 16, 1971*

DECISION OF JULY 16, 1971

Conseil Constitutionnel
[1971] J.O. July 18, 1971

[FACTS: The *Conseil Constitutionnel* was summoned on July 1, 1971 at the request of the President of the Senate to decide upon the constitutionality of an unpromulgated bill. The bill, discussed by the National Assembly and the Senate, and then passed by the National Assembly, amended arts. 5 and 7 of the law of July 1, 1901 concerning the *contrat d'association* (freedom of association), placing prior restraints on that right. Passage of this bill was motivated by contemporary political controversy, since its provisions were essentially aimed against leftists (*gauchistes*).]

OPINION

Considering the Constitution and in particular its Preamble:

Considering the *ordonnance* of November 7, 1958 concerning the organic law on the *Conseil Constitutionnel* and in particular chapter II of Title II of the above-mentioned *ordonnance* ; Considering the law of January 1, 1901 relating to the *contrat d'association,* as amended:

. . .*.*

Considering that the bill under examination before this *Conseil Constitutionnel* has been submitted to the vote of the two Assemblies, according to the procedure required by the Constitution during the parliamentary session that began on April 2, 1971;

Considering that among the fundamental principles recognized by the laws of the Republic and solemnly reaffirmed by the Preamble of the Constitution, we also find the principle of freedom of association; that this principle is at the basis of the general provisions of the law of July 1, 1901, concerning the *contrat d'association*; according to this principle, associations [including political, religious and commercial groups] can be created freely and they can be "incorporated" upon completion of the sole requirement that they make a preliminary declaration which is to be deposited with the competent authority [the *Préfet*]; that, therefore, except for provisions applying to special categories of associations, the creation of the associations cannot be challenged by the preliminary intervention of either the judicial or the administrative authority even if they seem defective or even if they have an illicit object for their purposes.

. . . The subject of the provisions of art. 3 of the bill under examination which is coming under the scrutiny of this *Conseil Constitutionnel* before its promulgation, is the institution of a procedure according to which the acquisition of the legal capacity of "incorporated" associations will depend upon a preliminary check of the association's conformity to law, carried out by the judicial authority.

Considering, therefore, that there are grounds to declare the provisions of art. 3 of the bill under examination, which amends art. 7 of the law of July 1, 1901, unconstitutional. Consequently, the last sentence of para. 2 of art. 1 of the bill under examination must also be declared unconstitutional because it makes reference to the above-mentioned art. 3.

Considering that it does not appear either from the text of the bill, as it was drafted and passed [by the Assembly], or from the parliamentary debate that the above-mentioned provisions are indivisible from the whole of the bill submitted to the *Conseil Constitutionnel*;

Considering, finally that the other provisions of this text do not violate the Constitution,

[This *Conseil* therefore decides]:

Those provisions of art. 3 of the bill submitted for the examination of the *Conseil Constitutionnel* amending the law of July 1, 1901, as well as the provisions of art. 1 of the bill under examination which made reference to those provisions of art. 3, are unconstitutional;

The other provisions of the above-mentioned bill are declared constitutional;

This decision will be published in the *Journal Officiel* of the French Republic.

NOTES AND QUESTIONS

1. This was the first time that the *Conseil Constitutionnel* went beyond separation of powers considerations to invalidate a law on civil liberties grounds. Moreover, the decision is striking because no constitutional text — neither the 1789 Declaration of the Rights of Man nor the Preambles to the 1946 and 1958 Constitutions — explicitly mentions "freedom of association." (The Preamble of 1946, however, does guarantee, *inter alia,* "the fundamental principles recognized by the laws of the republic." At least since 1901, freedom of association has been recognized as a fundamental principle of the French "republican tradition.") The *Conseil*'s reliance on an unwritten Constitutional value was especially significant, because a narrower decision reaching the same result had been possible. The *Conseil* could have relied on art. 4 of the 1958

Constitution, which guarantees the freedom to form political parties. Even that would have been a bold, new development. Yet the *Conseil* reached out for a broader basis for decision.

Why do you suppose the *Conseil* effected such a drastic alteration of its policies in 1971?

2. Maurice Duverger, a leading authority and professor of public law, commented extensively on the decision. Portions of his commentary follow.*

The decision of the Conseil Constitutionnel of July 16, 1971, upholding the freedom to form associations without preliminary controls: will it provoke new case law or will it be left without effect?

Two contradictory elements of evaluation ought to be underlined. On the one hand, the audacious achievement of the Council corresponds to the general evolutionary pattern of western political systems. Constitutional courts exercising judicial review now exist in other countries: in Germany and Italy, notably, they play an increasing role in the protection of human rights. On the other hand, the congenital infirmities of our *Conseil Constitutionnel* make it a very difficult task for it to assume a similar function. Its judges are not selected on the basis of independent recruitment. Direct appeals cannot be brought before it by citizens.

Another aspect of the problem that ought not to be forgotten is the one to be developed here. In extending the power of constitutional review from relations between public powers to the rights and liberties of citizens, the *Conseil Constitutionnel* may provoke a change in the case law of ordinary courts in this field. It makes it easier for them to take the path opened by the Supreme Court of the United States in 1803 in the famous decision *Marbury v. Madison*: that of judicial review of laws through ordinary proceedings. Such review is no more inscribed in the American Constitution than in ours. The Supreme Court deduced it from the general principle that the Constitution is superior to ordinary laws and that those laws thus ought to conform to it. The citizen to whom a court is to apply an unconstitutional law is entitled to invoke an objection of unconstitutionality. The Supreme Court settles the question in the last resort by means of the appellate system.

The Constitution superior to Statutory law

Until now, the French judges have refused to take the same road even though the principle of the superiority of the

---
*Le Monde, August 7, 1971. Reprinted with permission.

Constitution over ordinary laws has always existed in our legal system. Under the Third Republic, two major arguments were invoked to justify the judges' attitude. On the one hand, the Parliament was then considered the supreme organ of the State; its decisions could not be reviewed by the courts. The law was held to be an "expression of the general will" which was binding on everyone. Such reasoning had faults: for it logically implied that the Constitution was not superior to the law and that it could thus be modified by ordinary legislative procedure, as in Great Britain. The latter conclusion was however refused; and this, therefore, led to a logical contradiction, or more exactly, to a hypocritical situation: the superiority of the Constitution was purely theoretical, because it was deprived of any sanction.

The second argument was more solid. The Constitution of 1875 defined only the organizational procedures of the branches of government. There were no provisions concerning the rights and liberties of citizens. Legislation could not violate constitutional principles in this field because none existed. Unconstitutionality could only be based on the fact that the rules of legislative procedure had been ignored. To sanction such unconstitutionality, the courts would have had to involve themselves in the internal functioning of the Parliament, an involvement contrary to the principle of the separation of powers. It is natural that they refused to do it.

The Preambles of 1946 and 1958

The situation is radically different under the Fifth Republic. On the one hand, Parliament is no longer the supreme organ of the State. Legislative power is strictly defined and held in check. Legislation does not have any special majesty; moreover because of the narrow limit assigned to it (art. 34), it has even lost universal jurisdiction. Now legislation is but one juridical act among others on the hierarchical ladder; it no longer occupies a privileged position. It is superior to governmental decrees, but inferior to the Constitution which is the more authentic expression of the general will since it is based on popular referendum. It is second nature for the courts to impose respect for the Constitution over the ordinary law, as they impose their respect for the superiority of legislation over executive action.

On the other hand, the Constitution is no longer limited to defining the procedural rules concerning the branches of government. It also states the basic principles concerning the rights and liberties of citizens. The Preamble of 1946 had already solemnly reaffirmed the rules consecrated by the Declaration of Rights of 1789 and the "fundamental principles recognized by the laws of the Republic," adding to them new principles "particularly necessary in our time." Article 92 of the Constitution [of 1946], however, then excluded the Preamble from the judicial review exercised by the *Comité Constitutionnel,* precursor of the present *Conseil Constitutionnel.* This meant that the Preamble had a juridical value inferior to that of the Constitution and it was an implication that the courts did not have to assure its strict application.

The Preamble of 1958 does not suffer this infirmity. It affirms exactly the same rights and liberties as the Preamble of 1946, to which it makes express reference. But it no longer has second class juridical value. A difference no longer exists between it and the Constitution, insofar as the review exercised by the *Conseil Constitutionnel* is concerned. The rights and liberties proclaimed by the Preamble are made integral parts of the Constitution and impose themselves with the same force on the legislature.

The timidity of the Judiciary

Legal obstacles to judicial review of the constitutionality of legislation by ordinary courts have thus disappeared. Even more: a specific text now tells them to follow that path; *i.e.,* the constitutional law of June 3, 1958, which defines the basic principles that the new Constitution ought to be putting to work. It says: "The judicial authority must remain independent in order to be able to guarantee respect for essential liberties such as those defined in the Preamble of the Constitution of 1946 and by the Declaration of Human Rights to which it refers." The Constitution of the United States contains no provision making it so clear that the courts do exercise review over the constitutionality of legislation. If the French judges exercised such review, their action would be more solidly grounded in law than that of their American colleagues.

Only a long tradition of timidity and dependence still holds the French judges back; some desire to abandon it. The decision of the *Conseil Constitutionnel* reinforces the latter's position by putting forth an interpretation of "the fundamental principles recognized by the laws of the Republic" and furnishes the judges with a solid basis for exercising judicial review over legislation.

. . . .

Some sufficient bases

Thus the judges have at their command sufficiently precise bases for reviewing the constitutionality of the laws. They can readily compare the laws passed by the Parliament to a group of clear rules to which they ought to conform. They have no legal excuse to maintain a tradition developed under a different system of law, which no longer corresponds to the present system. The boldness and courage which the *Conseil Constitutionnel* has shown can aid them in a change as necessary as it is difficult. If tomorrow the President of the Senate fails to submit to the *Conseil* a law unconstitutional on grounds analogous to those of the text passed on June 7, it will be scandalous if the courts apply it. It will be scarcely less scandalous from now on, if they continue to apply texts so equally non-conforming to the Preamble of the Constitution although they have escaped the vigilance of M. Poher [the President of the Senate]. Conditions are now ripe for a "*Marbury v. Madison*" decision to be rendered by the French judges.

3. Is Duverger correct when he asserts that only the "timidity of the judiciary" prevents a French *Marbury* v. *Madison* decision? Recall that the *Marbury* doctrine means that every court, no matter how low, has the power and the obligation to determine the constitutional validity of legislation. Consider the following: (a) In France there is no formal rule of *stare decisis.* (b) France has two almost entirely autonomous court systems — the ordinary civil and criminal courts, and the administrative courts — with no higher court to resolve conflicts of decisions between them. Would conflicts on constitutional issues cause more problems than may occur on other kinds of issues? (c) Even the highest courts in France are really groups of panels of judges. For example, there are almost 100 judges in the *Cour de Cassation.* Is this lack of organizational continuity more serious when constitutional issues are involved? (d) France has a bureaucratic career judiciary. Is that judiciary suited to the task of deciding issues of basic values, often represented by vague expressions like "fairness," "equality," or "due process"?

b. The Decision of November 28, 1973

In addition to its jurisdiction under art. 61 to annul legislation prior to promulgation, the jurisdiction of the *Conseil Constitutionnel* may be invoked under art. 41 or art. 37 of the Constitution of 1958.

Article 41 deals with bills under discussion in Parliament. If the administration believes that proposed legislation originating from Parliament (as distinguished from legislation presented by the government) is not within legislative powers defined by art. 34, or is inconsistent with executive powers under art. 38, the government may request that the proposed legislation be dismissed. If the government and the President of either house of the legislature disagree, the *Conseil Constitutionnel* is required to resolve the disagreement within eight days, upon the request of the government or the President.

Article 37, second paragraph, concerns pre-existing parliamentary legislation which deals with an area reserved to the executive by art. 37, first paragraph. If the legislation was enacted before the Constitution became operative in 1958, the government may modify it by decree, with the advice of the *Conseil d'Etat.* (The final text of the decree must be identical to the one submitted to the *Conseil d'Etat* or adopted by it.)

If legislation is enacted after the Constitution became operative, the government can modify it by decree only if the *Conseil Constitutionnel* declares that the legislation has a "regulatory character" and thus is reserved to the executive by art. 37, first paragraph.

This was the setting of the decision of November 28, 1973.*

This is an extremely important decision which belongs in spirit, and as a measure of the Conseil's new activism, to the short line of decisions which have established the Conseil's role as a guardian of individual constitutional rights against legislative infringement.

Acting under the provisions of Article 37 (¶ 2) the Prime Minister asked the Conseil constitutionnel to rule that certain provisions of a statute relating to the concentration of agricultural holdings were of regulatory character and therefore subject to amendment or abrogation by decree. The Conseil ruled as requested, but as to Article 188-9, 1° of the Rural Code which imposed penal sanctions for failure to file required declarations or obtain necessary authorizations, the Conseil observed:

> Considering that above-mentioned provisions impose a penalty of 500 to 2,000F for failure to obtain prior authorization or to file a prior declaration in the case of concentration of agricultural holdings. . . . *Considering that the provisions of the Preamble, of paragraphs 3 and 5 of art. 34 and of art. 66 of the Constitution, taken together, indicate that the determination of contraventions and of the punishments which are applicable to them is a regulatory matter when such penalties do not involve deprivation of liberty;* Considering that it appears from the provisions of arts. 1 and 466 of the penal code that fines which do not exceed a maximum of 2,000F are police penalties applicable to contraventions; that, consequently, the above-mentioned provisions of the Rural Code which provide only for a fine not exceeding 2,000F, are within the competence of the regulatory power [of the government].

This decision brought the Conseil constitutionnel into conflict with the Conseil d'Etat and has had significant repercussions before the

---

*The remainder of this section is excerpted from Beardsley, *Constitutional Review in France,* 1975 SUP. CT. REV. 189, 227-29.

All excerpts from this article are reprinted with permission.

judicial tribunals. It also brought both the substantive constitutional limitations contained in the Preamble and the terms of Article 66 (forbidding arbitrary detention) to bear on the interpretation of the competence granted Parliament by Article 34.

The problem before the Conseil involved the allocation to Parliament by Article 34 of the exclusive power to make "rules concerning: — the determination of crimes and delicts — as well as the punishments applicable thereto." "Crime" (*crime*) and "delict" (*délit*) are technical terms of French criminal law, defined by the Penal Code, which group offenses on the basis of the punishments applicable to them. At the time of the 28 November 1973 decision the Penal Code classified as delicts those offenses punishable by a fine in excess of 2,000F or imprisonment for more than two months. Crimes were those offenses for which considerably more rigorous punishments were imposed. Beneath the delict threshold there is a third category of offense known as the contravention de police. At the time of the adoption of the Constitution in October 1958, the delict threshold had been even lower: 360F or ten days' imprisonment. These limits were increased to the 1973 levels by an ordinance adopted under Article 92 of the Constitution in December 1958.

In the drafting of the 1958 Constitution, the words "crime and delict" had been substituted for the more inclusive term "infractions" which had appeared in an earlier draft. On the basis of that substitution, the Conseil d'Etat had concluded in 1960 that the draftsmen intended to include only the determination of crimes and delicts (in the Penal Code sense) in Article 34 and to leave the Government free to prescribe "contraventions" and their punishments. The Conseil constitutionnel had taken the same position in several earlier decisions. All of these decisions were open to question — not for their interpretation of the purpose of the modification in Article 34 — but because they failed to grapple with the problems flowing from legislative definition (by the 1958 Ordinance) of the operative terms. If "crime and delict" possesses a constitutional meaning capable of limiting Parliament and conferring lawmaking power on the Government through Article 37, one would expect it to be the meaning attached to those terms by the legislation in effect when the Constitution came into force, and not that which resulted from subsequent legislative modification. The legislative definition of those terms did not rise to the level either of an organic law explicitly and properly defining the terms of Article 34 nor to a delegation of legislative authority under Article 38. But both Conseils had assumed that the subsequent legislative definitions of "crime," "delict" and "contravention" sufficed to shift lawmaking power from Parliament to Government under Articles 34 and 37, while simultaneously treating the Government's power as an autonomous one deriving directly from the Constitution.

The Conseil constitutionnel's 1973 decision still relies on statutory definitions of the domain reserved to Parliament to confirm that the Government can establish contraventions subject to a fine not in excess of 2,000F, but rejects those definitions in relation to imprisonment, insisting that "deprivation of liberty" can only be constitutionally prescribed by specific legislation, citing the Preamble, Article 66 and Article 34 (¶¶ 3 and 5). There is no basis in Article 34 for distinguishing between fines and imprisonment, although there is ample basis to dispute the existence of any autonomous regulatory power to define offenses if the system, as the decisions of both Conseils imply, extends to Parliament broad powers of definition whose exercise necessarily defines the upper limit of the "contravention."

But difficulties with the rationale of the decision are not of crucial importance for present purposes. What matters is that the Conseil went out of its way to issue what amounted to an advisory opinion on how far the Government might go in the exercise of its regulatory authority and did so on the basis of the same broadly libertarian approach to the Constitution as had inspired the 1971 decision. The Conseil's observations on the scope of the Government's authority in penal matters were strictly obiter. Perhaps they were more disturbing for that reason.

NOTES AND QUESTIONS

1. The decision of November 28, 1973 is important for a variety of reasons. Consider the following:

(a) The *Conseil Constitutionnel* reconfirmed the implications of the 1971 decision — that it would continue to function as protector of individual rights.

(b) In the past the *Conseil* had, at most, answered the specific question asked. Yet here it reached out, in dictum, to protect a basic right of French citizens. Like the Supreme Court in *Marbury* v. *Madison,* the *Conseil* did not interfere with the executive acts which were challenged, but it restricted the executive in a dictum that could not be disobeyed. Furthermore, the precise restriction was a departure from prior policy. Earlier decisions on the issue had said only that petty offenses were in the executive domain. There had been no indication that offenses punished by imprisonment were all within the legislative domain.

(c) The authority for the decision was the Preamble and Arts. 34 and 66 of the Constitution, "taken together." Does this indicate that the *Conseil* is likely to indulge in creative constitutional interpretation to safeguard civil liberties?

(d) The *Conseil*'s history had been marked by a distinct bias toward the executive. In this case its dictum restricted executive power in favor of the legislature. Does this represent a shift in the ideology of the *Conseil*? If so, what social and historical factors might have contributed to the shift?

2. Consider the following reaction by a leading French scholar: Georges Vedel.*

> Not even a sentence, but a subordinate clause. And its author is not a politician, but the *Conseil Constitutionnel.*
>
> In a long decision of November 28, 1973, the high court was called upon to pass on the question of whether the various provisions concerning agriculture came under the legislative or regulatory sphere, in other words within the competence of Parliament or the executive. With regard to the penalties applicable to certain infractions, the Council made a statement which must be reported word for word:
>
> "Considering that it follows from the combined provisions of the Preamble, paragraphs 3 and 5 of Article 34 and Article 66 of the Constitution that the determination of petty offences and the penalties applicable to them belongs to the regulatory sphere, when the said penalties do not involve the loss of liberty. . ."
>
> . . . .
>
> Now according to the penal code, infractions with penalties not exceeding a fine of two thousand francs or two months' imprisonment do not constitute either felonies (*crimes*) or misdemeanors (*délits*), but only petty offenses (*contraventions*). Since, in accordance with Article 37 of the Constitution, all matters except those within the domain of the law are of a regulatory character, it seemed to follow that the executive could, by means of simple decrees and thus without the intervention of Parliament, create infractions and the corresponding penalties for them, providing that these did not go beyond fines of 2000F or two months' imprisonment.
>
> This is the thesis adopted by the Conseil d'Etat in a decision of February 12, 1960 (Société EKY). With regard to this decision, I myself considered that legally it was in conformity with the reverential favor accorded by the constitutional text to the regulatory power of the executive, while deploring that we had come to the point where a "constitutional aberration" permitted the administration and the executive to "fabricate any number of sealed orders for ordinary Frenchmen guilty of disobedience."

---

* *Au Conseil Constitutionnel: Encore une petite phrase,* Le Monde, Dec. 5, 1973, at 11, Col. 1. Reprinted with permission.

But the *Conseil Constitutionnel* did not resign itself to this observation. In its reasoning it refused to isolate the part of Article 34 of the Constitution cited above. First, it compared it with the Preamble to the Constitution which incorporates in our positive law the principles of 1789, including the rule formulated by Article 7 of the Declaration of the Rights of Man and of the Citizen:

"No man can be accused, arrested or detained except in the cases determined by law."

The decision also looks to paragraph 3 of Article 34 of the Constitution which places under the protection of the legislature "the fundamental guarantees granted to the citizens for the exercise of their public liberties."

Finally, the Constitutional Council refers to Article 66 of the Constitution — too often forgotten:

"No-one may be arbitarily detained.

The judicial authority, guardian of individual liberty, shall ensure respect for this principle under the conditions stipulated by law."

One must bear in mind all of these provisions, and the legal scholars are guilty for not having done so before. . . .

From the viewpoint of juridical practice, the "little sentence" is not negligible. A number of regulatory texts, accepted for fifteen years, punish various petty offences with imprisonment, as is shown for example by reading the regulatory part of the highway code. Now, however old the regulation, any litigant may raise before the repressive jurisdiction called upon to judge him the illegality — and a fortiori the unconstitutionality — of this regulation serving as the grounds for the proceedings. The sanction for the irregularity of the regulation is the fact that the repressive judge must refuse to apply the penalty.

Of course, the repressive jurisdictions, at the head of which is the criminal division of the *Cour de Cassation* are not bound by the "doctrine" which the *Conseil Constitutionnel* has just stated. If, as stated in Article 62 of the Constitution, its decisions "are binding on the public powers and all the administrative and jurisdictional authorities," this is only effective for the object of each decision (in this case the juridical or regulatory nature of a particular provision of the rural code). Otherwise, there is no binding authority concerning res judicata.

But it is hard to see how the repressive judge could henceforward dismiss the principles which the *Conseil Constitutionnel* has just formulated all the more strikingly because the "little sentence" was not necessary for the solution of the concrete question that it had to decide in regard to the rural code.

In the first place, the juridical reasoning of the *Conseil Constitutionnel* is convincing, even if nobody had thought of it before.

Secondly, how could the judicial authority, which is reminded by the high court's decision citing Article 66 that it is the "guardian of individual liberty" and that in this matter it must obey only the law, appear to be less concerned about the rights of the citizens than the constitutional judge?

. . . .

Finally, the *Conseil Constitutionnel* is progressively affirming its own status. For a long time — without this being its own fault — its image in the eyes of the public was that of an auxiliary to the executive, charged with keeping Parliament within its limits, without being able to oppose undertakings originating elsewhere. But, after having said no in 1971 to the law threatening the freedom of association, and again in 1972 to certain provisions of the organic law on incompatibilities, it is continuing upon the course of a liberal and republican interpretation of our Constitution. It is proving that it is not merely the arbiter of conflicts between princes but, like the Supreme Court of the United States, the protector of the rights of the citizens.

[W]e learn that the Constitution of 1958 did not intend to deny the republican tradition which reserves all matters concerning individual liberty to the national representatives. We find evidence of the fact that, for the first time since the Revolution, France has a real constitutional judge capable of guaranteeing not only the correct interplay of the mechanics of the public powers but also respect for the rights of the citizens, whereas the derisory constitutional court of the Fourth Republic had found itself forbidden (as we too easily forget) from ruling on the violation of these same rights. (Article 92 in fine of the 1946 Constitution). Of course, there is still some progress to be made, which does not depend on the *Conseil Constitutionnel*, notably to extend the control of the judges to the acts of the executive and to broaden the standing requirements for referrals to it. But if I were the government, as they say in the cafés, I wouldn't argue with the decision of November 28, 1973. I would rather salute it as a consecration and (who knows?) as a reason for soon giving to the French a rule of law which, in the full sense of the term, they have never known.

c. The Decision of the Cour de Cassation in the Schiavon Case, February 26, 1974

[Would the *Conseil Constitutionnel's* "little sentence" be authoritative in cases arising in the *Cour de Cassation* and the *Conseil d'Etat*?]*

From the constitutional lawyer's point of view, one of the more serious defects of the institutional mechanism for the adjudication of substantive constitutional issues in the Fifth Republic is its inability to deal with divergent interpretations of the basic law. Despite the unwillingness of the judicial and administrative tribunals to pass upon the constitutionality of acts of Parliament, both must inevitably take account of the Constitution in dealing with their respective adjudicative tasks. The Conseil d'Etat is equally bound to look to the Constitution in the exercise of its advisory functions. There have been a number of manifestations of concern over the maintenance of a unified interpretation of the Constitution as between the Conseil constitutionnel and the Conseil d'Etat. There are multiple possibilities for conflict, not only in the process of defining the boundary between the legislative and regulatory domains identified by Articles 34 and 37, but also in substantive matters. As for the judicial tribunals, the strength of their commitment to the traditional refusal to review will be sorely tested in any case in which they are called upon to give effect to a statute which — not having been subject to review by the Conseil constitutionnel — plainly violates in principle or in detail a constitutional rule consecrated by a decision of the Conseil constitutionnel. Events subsequent to the Conseil's decisions of 27 November 1973 and 15 January 1975 illustrate the difficulty and raise the question whether France is to have one constitution or three — depending upon which and how many of its three highest jurisdictions are called upon to deal with a given issue.

The decision of the Conseil constitutionnel of 27 November 1973 created a dilemma which the system has only been able to resolve by denying the authority of the Conseil's pronouncement in that decision on the scope of the Government's rule-making powers in penal matters. The principle announced by the Conseil — that imprisonment may be imposed only in virtue of a statute adopted by Parliament — calls into question the validity of existing regulations which had been adopted by decree and which punish "contraventions," such as violations of the Highway Code, with short terms of imprisonment. There was an immediate reaction in the lower courts. At least two lower courts refused to enforce such regulations in the weeks following the Conseil's decision on the

---

* This section is excerpted from Beardsley, *Constitutional Review in France,* 1975 SUP. CT. REV. 189, 245-51.

ground of unconstitutionality. The problem arose in two other cases before the Court of Cassation in February 1974. In the meantime, the Government had submitted a draft decree modifying the Highway Code to the administrative sections of the Conseil d'Etat for an advisory opinion. The opinion rendered by the Conseil squarely confronted the Conseil constitutionnel's position and rejected it. Technically, these developments put the question of the authority of the decisions of the Conseil constitutionnel and the extent to which that authority attaches to an utterance like the troublesome "petite phrase" of the November 1973 decision. More broadly, they challenge the integrity of the curiously compartmentalized system for the legal resolution of constitutional questions which has grown out of the 1958 constitutional arrangements. The response to the technical question has formed the basis for dealing with the problem in the Conseil d'Etat and the Court of Cassation and must receive attention here.

The authority of the decisions of the Conseil constitutionnel is determined by Article 62 of the 1958 Constitution which provides:

> The decisions of the Conseil constitutionnel are not subject to any appeal. They are binding on the public authorities [*pouvoirs publics*] and on all administrative and judicial adjudicative authorities.

This provision, which would appear to give wide and final authority to the decisions of the Conseil constitutionnel and to oblige every organ of the state, including the courts, to conform its own decisions to those of the Conseil, in fact exercises only the weakest sort of unifying influence upon the decisions of the Conseil d'Etat and Court of Cassation. Article 62 is without sanction. The Conseil constitutionnel has no means of reversing or modifying judgments which are inconsistent with its own decisions. Moreover, the rule of Article 62 has been assimilated to the rule of the civil law which attributes *la force de la chose jugée* (to be called *"res judicata"* hereinafter for convenience without suggesting more than gross analogy between the French and Common Law concepts) to final civil judgments. Normally, in civil matters, the *res judicata* effect attaches only to the *dispositif* of the judgment (*i.e.,* that part of the judgment which fixes the rights of the parties) and not the reasoning which supports the decision. The Conseil constitutionnel has claimed a somewhat broader *res judicata* effect in its decisions in asserting that the force conferred by Article 62 extends both to the *dispositif* and to the reasons which are its "essential support." The Conseil's decision of 28 November 1973 put the question of the effect of Article 62 before the Conseil d'Etat and the Court of Cassation, and it was on the basis of restrictive interpretation of that article that both bodies denied legal effect to the *petite phrase.*

In the *Schiavon* decision of 26 February 1974 the Court of Cassation had to grapple with the claim that Schiavon's conviction for involuntary homicide was bad in law because it was founded on certain provisions of the Highway Code which had been established by decree and were sanctioned by imprisonment, a sanction which the Conseil constitutionnel had held could not constitutionally be prescribed by decree. The problem was examined at length by Procureur-general Touffait in his argument before the Court. The Conseil constitutionnel, like other adjudicative organs, Touffait maintained, is subject to the "fundamental principles of adjudicative procedure" which prohibit such bodies from deciding any issue other than that which is placed before them by the parties. It decides that issue. It does not establish general principles. In an important passage in his argument Touffait evokes the classic prohibitions on the rendition of *arrêts de règlement:*

> ... [I]t is obvious that the Conseil constitutionnel cannot issue general regulatory orders [*arrêts de règlement*], an act which would be contrary to the principle of French public law set out in art. 5 of the Civil Code: "Judges are forbidden to pronounce by way of general disposition on the causes submitted to them." It cannot therefore announce rules which are binding in all analogous cases, for *it would thus overstep its role of review of laws and regulations in conformity with the Constitution in order to fulfill a legislative role and would seriously disturb the balance of powers established by the Constitution* with all of the consequences difficult to measure which such an interference by one power with another may produce. (Emphasis in original.)

The argument, it will immediately be recognized, goes far beyond the issue of judicial review and raises that of judicial precedent. . . . While it is to be expected that the Conseil constitutionnel will also seek to adhere over time to the principles and reasoning announced in its decisions, its isolation from the hierarchies of the judicial and administrative courts gives the denial of a more general law declaring force to the Conseil's decision, a far greater negative impact on the unity of the system. . . .

The absence of an obligation to apply the principle announced by the Conseil constitutionnel did not settle the matter for the Court of Cassation, since there was no doubt about that Court's power to test the "legality" or constitutionality of a regulation or about the propriety of Schiavon's challenge to the regulation, quite apart from any question of the effect to be attributed to the Conseil's decision. The competence of the judicial courts in this regard in criminal proceedings constitutes one of the most important exceptions to the principle of the exclusive jurisdiction of the administrative courts in respect of any challenge to the validity of acts of the administration. The Court of Cassation thus had to deal with Schiavon's claim. If it were to deal with the substantive constitutional issue, it would remain difficult to avoid confronting the position of the Conseil constitutionnel.

The Court [of Cassation] resolved the problem by falling back on the position [that] judicial tribunals are incompetent to test the constitutionality of a statute. The regulation challenged by Schiavon imposed penalties which fell within the limits described by the Penal Code definition of the "contravention" and its punishments. Because those definitions have statutory force, the court could not examine their constitutional validity. The statutory definitions in turn shielded the regulations from constitutional challenge. The difficulty, of course, is that the Government's regulatory powers in respect of "contraventions" had been thought to be autonomous powers deriving directly from Articles 34 and 37 of the Constitution (also cited by the Court of Cassation in its decision.) Nonetheless, a decision dealing with the constitutionality of the regulations as an exercise of autonomous regulatory power would necessarily have called into question the validity of the statutory definitions. By focusing on the statutory character of the definitions, the Court was thus able to invoke its traditional position in respect of the constitutionality of legislation, and avoid tackling a difficult constitutional question.

Just over one month earlier, the Conseil d'Etat had rendered its advisory opinion to the Government on new draft Highway Code provisions which imposed sanctions impliedly involving a deprivation of liberty. The Conseil addressed itself to the November 1973 decision of the Conseil constitutionnel and rejected the notion that a punishment involving a deprivation of liberty could only be imposed by statute. The Conseil d'Etat relied on its own prior decisions and on a 1963 decision of the Conseil constitutionnel and made no effort to resolve the problem of the autonomous or delegated character of Government authority in the matter. The opinion delicately avoided any reaffirmation of constitutional autonomy for the Government in this area.

In the result, the state of the law on the prescription by decree of punishments involving deprivation of liberty is roughly as follows: The country's highest adjudicative body charged explicitly with the interpretation of the Constitution, the Conseil constitutionnel, has declared that such punishments can only be constitutionally prescribed by statute. The prescription of such punishments by decree is, however, not a matter which is subject to review by the Conseil constitutionnel. The Conseil d'Etat, charged both with advising the Government in the drafting of decrees and with the adjudication of claims that decrees adopted by the Government are in excess of its constitutional powers, has taken the position that the prescription of such punishments for "contraventions" is within the powers of the Government. The Court of Cassation has declared that it will not inquire into the constitutionality of such decrees because they are shielded by a statutory definition of "contravention" which includes offenses punishable by a brief term of imprisonment. That definition was, of course, considered by the Conseil constitutionnel. There is no possibility of resolving this difficulty by recourse to a higher tribunal having jurisdiction over all three. The Frenchman who, knowing of the decision of the Conseil constitutionnel, goes to jail for violation of a regulation adopted by the Government in the exercise of its autonomous decree power under Article 37 would seem to have the right (nonconstitutional) to be more than a little perplexed.

NOTES AND QUESTIONS

1. Unlike illegal *lois,* illegal regulations may be denied effect by the ordinary French courts. However, the regulation involved in *Schiavon* was based on a definition of "petty offense" contained in the Penal Code. Are you convinced that this attenuated connection to *loi* should have precluded the *Cour de Cassation* from refusing to apply the regulation? Under this approach, do you suppose that there are many regulations that *Cassation* will find amenable to review?

2. Under art. 37, the advisory section of the *Conseil d'Etat* counseled the executive that the *Conseil Constitutionnel's* "petite phrase" was mere dictum and need not be followed. Suppose, in another case, it becomes a "holding" of the *Conseil.* What should the *Conseil d'Etat* do in that event?

d. The Decision of December 27, 1973*

An increasingly important weapon in the arsenal of the *Direction générale des impôts* is Article 180 of the General Tax Code. . . . In effect the taxpayer may be taxed on his consumption — expenditures plus revenues in kind — rather than on his income. Once the tax administration is able to show that the taxpayer's "open or notorious personal expenditures" and his revenues in kind exceed his declared income and exempt revenue, he is subject to administrative assessment under Article 180, and can attack the assessment only by showing that the administration has erred in applying the relatively simple prescriptions of Article 180.

This is strong medicine for the understatement of income, and, given the very limited rights of defense, the Conseil d'Etat has tended to interpret Article 180 rigorously against the government mainly through narrow, literal construction of the requirement that the expenses considered be "personal" and "open" (*ostensible)* or "notorious" (*notoire).* The Government, sensitive to criticism of the

*This section is excerpted from Beardsley, *Constitutional Review in France,* 1975 SUP. CT. REV. 189, 230-33.

use and potential abuse of Article 180, has been at pains over the years to assure Parliament that it was and would be applied only with all of the judgment and discretion that might be thought desirable. Nonetheless, during the parliamentary debates on the Finance Law for 1974 (a grand annual exercise dealing mainly with the budget, appropriations, and tax law revision), the Government found itself confronted with a proposal to amend Article 180 by substituting for the notion of open or notorious personal expenditures a set of relatively concrete standards for the determination of taxable income in cases in which the taxpayer's declared revenues were less than his expenditures.

The Government countered with an amendment of its own which would merely have added the following paragraph to the existing Article 180:

> The taxpayer to whom the provisions of the present article are applied may obtain the discharge of the assessment against him hereunder if he establishes before the tax court [*juge d'impôt*] that the circumstances do not permit one to presume the existence of hidden or illegal resources or of an attempt to avoid the normal payment of tax, and if his taxable income does not exceed 50 per cent of the upper limit of the amounts included in the highest income tax bracket.

The amended text proposed by the Government was approved, and the Finance Law for 1974, including the amendment to Article 180 was adopted by Parliament on 18 December 1973.

The amendment to Article 180 was referred to the Conseil constitutionnel on 20 December 1973 by Alain Poher, President of the Senate. The possibility of referring the amendment — which had become Article 62 of the Finance Law for 1974 — to the Conseil had been mooted in the Senate debates and Senator Dailly had noted that it would be necessary to be very prudent in that regard, referring only the offending last phrase to the Conseil, for otherwise the attempt to limit the discretion of the Fisc under Article 180 would fail altogether. M. Poher's letter to M. Palewski, then the President of the Conseil constitutionnel, following Dailly's advice, asked only that Conseil consider the conformity to the Constitution "and its Preamble" of the last phrase of the amending article, *i.e.,* that which limited the benefit of the right to contest the assessment to lower-bracket taxpayers. The President of the Senate contended in his letter to M. Palewski that "discrimination based on the real or supposed wealth of a certain category of citizens" violates the principle of "equality before the law."

The Conseil's decision, rendered on 27 December 1973, rejected the amendment to Article 180 as unconstitutional in its entirety. In the result, the original Article 180 and the extravagant powers of tax collection which it embodies were left intact and unamended to the satisfaction of the Government, while the President of the Senate was also upheld — in principle at least — in his view of the unconstitutionality of the reservation to lower-bracket taxpayers only of the right to contest an Article 180 assessment.

The Conseil again founded its decision on the Preamble, holding that the provisions in question would "discriminate against citizens in respect of the possibility of attacking an administrative tax assessment affecting them; that the said disposition thus infringes the principle of equality before the law contained in the Declaration of Rights of 1789 and solemnly reaffirmed by the Preamble of the Constitution." For good measure the Council also invoked the provisions of the organic law on Finance Acts which prohibits amendments to the Government's Finance Bill whose effect would be other than a reduction of expense or an increase in revenues. Despite this seemingly adequate independent ground, the decision was cast in terms which left no doubt that the substantive constitutional restriction was dispositive.

NOTE

While less remarkable than the November 28 decision, the Decision of December 27, 1973 is another strong confirmation of the 1971 turning point in the jurisprudence of the *Conseil Constitutionnel*. Also, for the first time, the *Conseil* struck the entire enactment referred to it, not just the part specifically attacked.

e. The Decision of January 15, 1975*

The decision of 15 January 1975 was the second decision taken upon reference by a parliamentary minority under the 1974 amendment to Article 61. Eighty-one deputies joined in referring to the Conseil the statute which was to become the Law of 17 January 1975 relative to the interruption of pregnancy. Adopted on 20 December 1974, over substantial Gaullist opposition, the statute recited the law's "guaranty" of respect for every human being "from the beginning of life" and affirmed that this principle might be infringed only in "cases of necessity" and under the conditions prescribed by the new statute and the Code of Public Health was amended to provide that:

> A pregnant woman whose condition places her in a situation of distress may request that a doctor interrupt the pregnancy. This interruption may only be effected prior to the end of the tenth week of pregnancy.

The statute contains a number of additional provisions assuring the right of doctors and private hospitals to refuse to perform abortions,

---

*The following is excerpted from Beardsley, *Constitutional Review in France*, 1975 SUP. CT. REV. 189, 233-36.

imposing certain counseling requirements before and after the performance of the operation and otherwise regulating the medical and administrative application of the statute. There is, however, no elaboration of the basic criteria of the availability of an abortion: "distress" and "necessity." That aspect of the matter is left entirely in the hands of doctor and patient.

Jean Foyer, one of the most vocal parliamentary opponents of the abortion bill, offered a statement of the views of the deputies who had referred the law to the Conseil in *Le Monde* of 24-25 December 1974. Two principal substantive arguments were advanced, one founded on the Preamble of the 1958 Constitution, and the other based on the European Convention on Human Rights, ratified by France in 1973. . . .

The Conseil sustained the constitutionality of the abortion law, holding itself incompetent to rule on the conformity of a statute to a treaty and ruling that the statute did not violate the "principle of liberty posed by art. 2 of the Declaration of the Rights of Man and of the Citizen," nor any of "fundamental principles recognized by the laws of the Republic," nor the principle of the 1946 Preamble pursuant to which "the nation guarantees to the infant the protection of his health." The Conseil relied heavily on the statutory language purporting to limit the availability of abortion to "situations of distress" in which therapeutic motives are presumed operative. The statute, the Conseil concluded, does not violate "the principle of the respect of every human being from the beginning of his life, recited in Article 1 [of the statute], except in cases of necessity and in accordance with the conditions and restrictions which it defines; and thus does not infringe the principle of liberty set out in Article 2 of the Declaration of Rights" nor any other principle having constitutional force contained in the Preamble. As in the prior decisions of July 1971 and December 1973, the Conseil adhered to the laconic style typical of the decisions of the Conseil d'Etat and of the Court of Cassation, and merely recited the constitutional sources without explaining or elaborating the principle it drew from them.*

f. The Decisions of July 23, 1975**

One of these decisions invalidated a statute authorizing the presiding judge of the *tribunal correctionnel* to determine whether a case would be tried before a single judge or a three-judge panel (the latter being obligatory under prior law). The Conseil held that this provision violated the principle of equality before the law affirmed by the 1789 Declaration of Rights in that it would permit "citizens finding themselves in similar situations and prosecuted for

---

* The text of the decision appears *infra* Ch. 5, § C.1. and Ch. 12, § B.

** The following is excerpted from Beardsley, *Constitutional Review in France,* 1975 Sup. Ct. Rev. 189, 225-26 n. 152.

the same offenses to be judged by courts of different composition"
at the sole discretion of the judge. Such distinctions would have to
be established by legislation and could not constitutionally be left
to judicial discretion. The other decision upheld the institution of
a new business tax replacing the old *patente* (a kind of business
license tax). The constitutional issue concerned the proper
application of Art. 40 . . . in the legislative process leading to the
adoption of the challenged legislation.

NOTES

In the United States, the question in equal protection cases is
whether the reason for treating people unequally (as most laws do)
is sufficient to withstand constitutional scrutiny, and a discussion of
this issue is ordinarily the subject of an opinion of considerable
length. Both the decision of December 27, 1973 and the "single
judge" decision of July 23, 1975 were based on the "principle of
equality." The terse opinions of the *Conseil Constitutionnel* (as well
as those of other supreme courts in France), however, provide no
indication of how this principle will be applied in the future. This
highlights the importance of the authoritative notes attached to the
decisions by leading scholars, and of the statements of the Procureur
général (for the *Conseil Constitutionnel*) or the Commissaire du
gouvernement (for the *Conseil d'Etat*).

g. *The Decision of January 12, 1977*

The Decision of January 12, 1977, reprinted below, involved
proposed legislation giving to the French police broad powers to
search vehicles. The two police organizations mentioned in the
decision — the *officiers de police judiciaire* and the *agents de police
judiciaire* — share responsibility for reporting on criminal infractions, gathering evidence, and apprehending those suspected of
crimes. (The *agents,* however, have lesser powers than the *officiers,*
whom they assist.)

The decision also refers to the French theory of *pouvoirs
exceptionnels* ("exceptional powers," or, as it is sometimes called,
"circonstances exceptionnelles," or "exceptional circumstances"),
a theory developed by the case law of the *Conseil d'Etat* but also
utilized by nonadministrative courts. According to this judge-made
doctrine, normally unlawful administrative decisions and acts,
including those of the police, become legal if they are necessary to
insure maintenance of "public order" and functioning of "public
services."

DECISION OF JANUARY 12, 1977

Conseil Constitutionnel
[1977] J.O. January 13, 1977

The *Conseil Constitutionnel* ... "Considering that individual liberty constitutes one of the fundamental principles guaranteed by the Laws of the Republic and proclaimed by the Preamble of the Constitution of 1946 affirmed by the Preamble of the Constitution of 1958; Considering that Article 66 of the Constitution by reasserting that principle assigns its protection to the judiciary; Considering that the purpose of the text submitted to the examination of the *Conseil Constitutionnel* is to give to the *officiers de police judiciaire* or, upon the request of the latter, to the *agents de police judiciaire,* the power to search any vehicle or its contents merely if this vehicle is on a public road and the search is made in the presence of the owner or the driver of the vehicle. Considering that if the two above-mentioned conditions are fulfilled, the powers attributed by this provision to the *officiers de police judiciaire* and the *agents* acting upon the request of the latter could be exercised, without restriction, in all circumstances, even without a lawful regime of *pouvoirs exceptionnels,* and although no infraction has been committed and with no requirement of a threat to the public order. Considering that in view of the extension of powers, not otherwise limited, conferred upon the *officiers de police judiciaire* and to the *agents,* of the very general character of the situations in which these powers could be exercised and of the imprecision of the scope of the controls to which they could lead, this text infringes the essential principles upon which is founded the protection of individual liberty and that, consequently, it does not conform to the Constitution.

The provisions of the single article of the law authorizing the search of vehicles for the investigation and the prevention of criminal infractions are therefore declared not to conform to the Constitution."

NOTES AND QUESTIONS

1. Do the jurisdictions of the *Conseil Constitutionnel* and the *Conseil d'Etat* overlap? Consider the division of lawmaking powers between the legislature and the executive under arts. 34 and 37. A *Conseil Constitutionnel* decision could, for example, invalidate a bill encroaching upon executive power under arts. 34 and 37. The executive accordingly might issue a decree on that same subject. A private party could then ask the *Conseil d'Etat* to annul the decree as outside the executive power under art. 37. A similar situation would occur if the *Conseil d'Etat* declared an executive regulation unauthorized by art. 37, only to have the *Conseil Constitutionnel* declare a legislative bill on the same subject to be unauthorized by art. 34.

2. Along with the constitutional amendment to art. 61 that passed in 1974 (conferring standing on 60 members of either house), it was proposed by Giscard d'Estaing's cabinet that the *Conseil Constitutionnel* itself have power to initiate, *ex officio,* pre-promulgation review of statutes; however, this amendment was rejected by Parliament. Was it a good idea? Would it have overly accentuated the political nature of the *Conseil*?

Why did the French government in 1974 propose expansion of constitutional review? Since 1972, further expansion has been proposed by left-wing parties, although they had vigorously opposed judicial review in the past — notably in the Constituent Assembly of 1946. Why have they changed their position?

3. Would you characterize the *Conseil Constitutionnel* now as a "quasi-judicial" institution? What are the characteristics of a "judicial," rather than "political," organ of government?

4. Now that the *Conseil Constitutionnel* has gone beyond separation of power issues to render opinions on the fundamental rights of French citizens, does it make sense to continue to limit its jurisdiction to unpromulgated laws?

5. A rejected 1972 proposal would have established a Constitutional Court, along the lines of Italy and Germany, with jurisdiction over all constitutional questions — legislative and executive — and with standing by individuals to invoke the Court's jurisdiction. Do you think the French will ultimately turn to such an institution, or will they follow the American model, where all courts must pass on the conformity of statutes to the Constitution? What obstacles are there to transplanting the American system in France?

Chapter 4

THE MODERN SYSTEMS OF JUDICIAL REVIEW

A. THE ORGANS OF CONTROL *

1. Introduction

Though the events of the 20th century brought the West as a whole to see the value of judicial review of the constitutionality of legislation, the historical and philosophical differences between the states of the West prevented their adopting identical systems of such control. Deep-seated suspicions of the judicial office, commitments to legal positivism, and other more practical considerations have meant that judicial review in various countries is conducted by different *organs* of review, which employ different *methods,* and whose decisions may have differing *effects.* It is this array of organs, methods, and effects which will be discussed in this chapter.

2. Judicial Review: Centralized or Decentralized

One might distinguish two broad types of judicial control over the constitutionality of legislation:

a) The "decentralized" type gives the power of control to *all the judicial organs* of a given legal system. This has also been called the "American" system of control. The beginnings of this type of control may be found in the United States, where judicial review remains the most characteristic and "unique" institution.

b) The "centralized" type of control confines the power of review to *one single judicial organ.* By analogy, the "centralized" type might be referred to as "Austrian," for the archetype is contained in the Austrian Constitution of October 1, 1920 (the so-called *Oktoberverfassung*). This Constitution, based on proposals formulated by the Austrian jurist Hans Kelsen, was re-enacted in Austria after World War II, as amended by the *Novelle* of 1929.

Both of these systems have been introduced, even very recently, in several countries, and thus have served as models outside their country of origin.

---

* Adapted from M. CAPPELLETTI, JUDICIAL REVIEW IN THE CONTEMPORARY WORLD 45-68 (1971).

There are also what might be called "mixed" or "intermediate" systems: *e.g.,* in Mexico, where because of a prima facie divergence between articles 103 and 133 of the Constitution, it would be difficult to put the system into one or the other of the categories given in the text. This is true not only from the point of view of the *organs* of control, but also from that of the *method* by which questions of constitutional legitimacy are resolved. Even in the latter respect the Mexican system has a place somewhere between the systems working "by way of direct action" and those working "by way of defense." The Irish system is another example of a mixed system in that review power is concentrated, as a rule, in the one "High Court," which is not, however, a special constitutional court. Rather, it is one of Ireland's ordinary courts.

The "American," or North American, system of judicial review is found primarily in many of Britain's former colonies, including Canada, Australia, and India. In Chapter 1 we tried to explain the apparent paradox which led to the establishment of judicial review in the colonies, despite its rejection in England where the principle of parliamentary supremacy prevailed.

The American system of control has also been introduced in Japan under the current Japanese Constitution of May 3, 1947. In Europe as well, the American system has had and still has its analogues. A certain parallel can be found, for example, in Swiss law, where, alongside a direct action before the Federal Tribunal (*staatsrechtliche Beschwerde* or *recours de droit public*), there exists a general right of review (*richterliches Prüfungsrecht*) in the ordinary courts. Although this judicial review is limited to the laws of the cantons and has much less practical importance than the direct action just mentioned, the Swiss judges have a general power to disregard laws of the cantons in conflict with the Federal Constitution. This power has been derived from the principle that federal law "breaks" cantonal law (*Bundesrecht bricht kantonales Recht*). However, there is no judicial control over the constitutionality of federal laws; this limitation has been criticized by modern writers, although it is a traditional feature of the Swiss legal system.

Norwegian law (since the end of the last century) and Danish law (from the beginning of this century) have also asserted the "incontestable" power of the courts to review the conformity of legislation with the constitution and to disregard, in the concrete case, a law held unconstitutional, although admittedly this power has been used with extreme moderation and fairly infrequently. A similar power has also been asserted in Sweden in the last few years.

Germany and Italy, where today we find the centralized rather than the decentralized system, also experimented briefly with the American type of control: Germany under the Weimar Constitution and Italy from 1948 to 1956, that is to say from the adoption of the "rigid" Constitution until the Constitutional Court began to function.

But however widespread has been the acceptance of the older, decentralized system of control of constitutionality, also remarkable has been the expansion, especially in recent years, of the centralized or Austrian system. Unsuccessful attempts were made to adopt it in Czechoslovakia in 1920 and in Spain in 1931, but they were not very significant largely due to the short and stormy lives of these two Republics. The centralized system was adopted by the Constitution of the Italian Republic of January 1, 1948 and by the Bonn Constitution of May 23, 1949, both still in force. This system was also established by the Constitution of the Republic of Cyprus of August 16, 1960; by the Constitution of the Turkish Republic of July 9, 1961; and finally by the Constitution of the Federal Socialist Republic of Yugoslavia of April 7, 1963. This latter is the first and, up to now, the only Constitution of a country under a Communist regime to adopt a system of judicial review, though, significantly, a recent [1968] Czechoslovakian constitutional law has contemplated the establishment of constitutional courts, both on a federal and on a state level. In Yugoslavia, the review is exercised by a special Federal Constitutional Court and, on the regional level, by special Constitutional Courts in the six Federate Republics. One cannot fail to notice that this new element in constitutional law may profoundly transform Communist theories of state and law.

3. The Rationale of the Decentralized Form of Judicial Review

The theory behind giving the entire judiciary the duty of constitutional control is, on its face, logical and simple, as is apparent from Marshall's judgment in *Marbury* v. *Madison* and earlier from the writings of Alexander Hamilton.

Substantially, the argument is as follows:

a) The function of all judges is to interpret the laws, in order to apply them to the concrete cases which come before them.

b) One of the more obvious canons of interpretation of legislation is that when two legislative enactments conflict with each other, the judge must apply the prevailing one.

c) Given two enactments of equal normative force, the prevailing one will be determined by the traditional criteria of "lex posterior derogat legi priori," "lex specialis derogat legi generali," etc.

d) But, clearly, these criteria are no longer valid when the conflict is between enactments of different normative force. In this case they are replaced by the obvious criterion of "lex superior derogat legi inferiori:" a constitutional norm, if the constitution is rigid, prevails over an ordinary legislative norm in conflict with it, just as ordinary legislation prevails over subordinate legislation, or, as the Germans would say, *Gesetze* prevail over *Verordnungen.*

e) Hence, one must conclude that *any* judge, having to decide a case where an applicable ordinary legislative norm conflicts with the Constitution, must disregard the former and apply the latter.

4. The Rationale of Centralized Judicial Review

This reasoning is so coherent and simple that one might well ask for what strange reason the Austrian Constitution of 1920-1929 preferred to establish a centralized system of judicial review; and why this system has been adopted by the constitutions of several countries (all of the civil law tradition), including Czechoslovakia, Spain, Italy, Germany, Cyprus, Turkey and Yugoslavia.

But, despite possible logical inconsistencies, the solution adopted by the Austrian and then by the other constitutions mentioned above was not without its reasons. The following seem to be the most important.

a) The centralized system reflects a different conception of the separation of powers, and is based on a radically different doctrine from that upon which decentralized review is founded.

Under a centralized system one can no longer uphold the classic reasoning of Hamilton and Marshall, which tried to resolve the problem of unconstitutional laws and of judicial review purely in terms of statutory interpretation.

The civil law countries tend to adhere more rigidly to the doctrines of the separation of powers and the supremacy of statutory law. Originally these doctrines meant, to Montesquieu, Rousseau, and others haunted by fears of a self-seeking, anti-democratic judiciary, that any judicial interpretation or, a fortiori, invalidation of statutes was a *political* act, and therefore an encroachment on the exclusive power of the legislative branch to make law. Even today, although the advisability of some sort of control over the constitutionality of legislation is admitted, the essentially political aspects of this function are recognized. Thus the centralized systems refuse to grant the judiciary in general the power to review legislation; in fact, the ordinary judges must accept and apply the law as they find it. Several scholars have even, not without some justification, spoken of a genuine presumption of legislative validity. The only attenuation of these notions lies in the power of the ordinary judges to suspend concrete litigation pending a reference to the Constitutional Court of a constitutional issue which has been raised. In Austria even this power is severely curtailed.

This recognition of the political character of judicial review is reflected both in the manner of appointing the members of the special constitutional courts and in the sort of questions entertained by such courts. The agencies appointing the judges are usually prescribed by the constitution itself and an effort is made to ensure that the courts' membership reflects all major political groupings, so that the courts are "not the prolonged arm of some other state organ or of the political parties." Similarly, the centralized constitutional courts do not shy away from considering issues which the Supreme Court of the United States would reject as essentially "political." The American Court has often avoided questions which it has called "political."

This policy, grounded both in the conviction that some questions are better answered by other branches of the government and in a realistic desire to avoid provoking a direct clash with the other branches of government, is facilitated by several doctrines: those of "ripeness," "case or controversy," "standing," "political question," etc.

In contrast, the continental courts, consistent with their admitted quasi-political function, may at times entertain such dangerous questions. Thus the European constitutional courts and the French *Conseil Constitutionnel* may be specifically charged with determining the constitutionality of political parties (art. 21, para. 2, of the German Basic Law of 1949) and the validity of elections (art. 41 of the German Basic Law and arts. 58-60 of the French Constitution of 1958), with deciding the most delicate conflicts of jurisdiction between legislature and executive (arts. 34, 37 and 61 of the 1958 French Constitution; art. 134 of the 1948 Italian Constitution; art. 93, paras. 1 and 3 of the German Basic Law), with deciding the validity of treaties, etc. Also to be considered is the fact that the continental constitutional courts do not confine their deliberations to the facts of the specific case but rather tend to treat issues in the abstract, since they are obliged to make a final decision, regarding a given law, which will be valid *erga omnes.*

Nonetheless, such functions remain barred to the judiciary as a whole in these systems; in this way, they attempt to remain true to strict concepts of separation of powers.

b) The centralized system reflects the absence of the principle of stare decisis in civil law jurisdictions.

In the decentralized or American type of control all the judicial organs, federal and state, superior and inferior, have the power and duty to disregard unconstitutional legislation in the concrete cases which come before them. Yet the American system makes no explicit provision for decisions with *erga omnes* effects or formal declarations of invalidity of unconstitutional statutes. Since even in American courts, state and federal, there may be differences of opinion as to the constitutionality of a law, it might be asked how the citizenry can ever be sure what attitude a particular court will take toward a particular law. The answer is that the serious consequences of conflicts and uncertainty have been avoided in the United States, and in the other common law countries where the decentralized system of judicial review operates, through the basic principle of stare decisis, by force of which a decision by the highest court in any jurisdiction is binding on all lower courts in the same jurisdiction. The exceptions to this general rule do not substantially affect the validity of our present argument, since the final result of the principle of binding precedents is that through the system of appeals the question of constitutionality can eventually be decided by the superior judicial organs and, in particular, by the Supreme Court, whose decision will be binding on all other courts. Thus the principle of stare decisis means that a judgment of unconstitutionality will become effective, practically speaking, *erga omnes.*

It is true that the rule of stare decisis is generally less strictly observed in America than in England, and less strictly adhered to in constitutional cases than in others. Yet, it is interesting to note that the fundamentally important result of changing what would be a mere *cognitio incidentalis* of unconstitutionality, valid only for the particular case, into a statement of the law with validity *erga omnes,* has been achieved through the rule of stare decisis. It is difficult to agree with certain attempts, both old and recent, to deny or modify excessively the importance of stare decisis as one of the elements differentiating the so-called Anglo-Saxon systems from the continental ones. When one asserts, as many have done, that "in the field of constitutional law the principle of stare decisis has been practically suppressed," this is only half the truth. It is true that the Supreme Court has been assuming the right to change its own legal doctrines and hence to go against previous decisions. But, on the other hand, there can be no doubt that the decisions of the Supreme Court itself are considered as fully binding and are followed by the lower courts and other public organs.

A decision is thus not limited to the case at hand and bars a contrary decision in other cases. Through the instrument of stare decisis, "non-application" in the particular case becomes in practice a genuine quashing of the unconstitutional law which is definitive for future cases. In short, it becomes a true annulment of the law with, at least in theory, retroactive effects, although there are rare cases where a law previously held invalid by the Supreme Court has been revived by a change in constitutional doctrine.* (Much more frequent has been the reverse situation, with the Supreme Court holding unconstitutional a law previously held to be constitutional.)

Although judicial decisions in civil law countries are important informal sources of law, the principle of stare decisis is foreign to civil law judges. A system which allowed each judge to decide on the constitutionality of statutes could therefore result in a law being disregarded as unconstitutional by some judges, while being held constitutional and applied by others. Furthermore, the same judicial organ, which had one day disregarded a given law, might uphold it

---

* On retroactivity, *see* § C., *infra.*

the next day, having changed its mind about the law's constitutional legitimacy. Differences could arise between judicial bodies of different type or degree, for example between ordinary courts and administrative tribunals, or between the younger, more radical judges of the inferior courts and the older, more tradition conscious judges of the higher courts. This is notoriously what happened in Italy from 1948 to 1956 and what continues to happen on a large scale in Japan. The extremely dangerous result could be a serious conflict between the judicial organs and grave uncertainty as to the law. Moreover, even though a given law has been held unconstitutional with regard to one party, nevertheless other affected parties would have to raise the issue of constitutionality *de novo*. A Japanese writer offers a typical example, Japan being precisely one of the countries where, it appears, the gravity of these disadvantages is becoming increasingly evident. A plaintiff files suit claiming that a certain tax law is unconstitutional and obtains a judgment to that effect; but, the writer continues, "according to the individual-effect theory, the law per se remains in force and binding on taxation offices." As a result, every other interested party must initiate a separate action to escape the effects of the law.

And so, though the "American" system has been introduced in several civil law countries, it has not been an unqualified success. Weimar Germany, and post-war Italy prior to the institution of its Constitutional Court, fully revealed the unsuitability of the decentralized method for civil law countries; and the same may be said for Japan. In Norway, Denmark, and Sweden, on the other hand, the problem is not acute, but only because decentralized judicial review is relatively unimportant and the judges exercise the power with extreme prudence and moderation. In other civil law countries, this type of judicial review has not been successful, with the possible exception of Switzerland where the type of judicial review adopted is much more of a compromise between the two systems.

Accordingly, in establishing a system of judicial review, the countries to whom the notion of stare decisis was foreign had to work with legal instruments very different from those of the United States and other common law countries. In the former countries it was thought essential to find an adequate substitute for the American Supreme Court. The need was felt for a judicial body capable of giving decisions of general binding effect in cases dealing with the constitutionality of legislation. It was hoped that such special bodies could avoid the conflicts and chaotic uncertainties of which we have spoken above.

Faced with this need, the "Fathers" of the Austrian Constitution decided to establish the *Verfassungsgerichtshof*, a special

Constitutional Court. The same solution was chosen at the same time in Czechoslovakia and subsequently in Spain, Italy, Germany, and in the three previously mentioned states — Cyprus, Turkey, and Yugoslavia — which have only recently adopted centralized judicial review where the controlling power is confined to one judicial organ specifically created for this function.

c) The centralized system reflects the unsuitability of traditional civil law courts for judicial review.

The American Supreme Court, and, for example, its Japanese counterpart under the Constitution of 1947 are far from being the equivalents of the European constitutional courts. While the latter concern themselves solely with constitutional questions, the jurisdiction of the Supreme Court in the United States is not so confined, since most cases arise through the normal appellate system and not through any ad hoc procedure.* Even for constitutional questions no special procedure is used; to view such writs as habeas corpus, certiorari, or the writ of error as the basis of judicial review is a fundamental, though rather frequent, error. Thus the Supreme Court should be compared not to the special constitutional courts, but rather to the highest courts of appeal on the continent, such as the Austrian *Oberster Gerichtshof,* the German *Bundesgerichtshof,* or the Italian *Corte di cassazione.* However, it is important to note that in practice the American Supreme Court has increasingly assumed a position not very dissimilar from that occupied by the European constitutional courts. The proportion of the Supreme Court's cases which deal with important constitutional matters and the resolution of federal-state conflicts continues to grow, and now comprises the most significant part of the docket of its decided cases.

At this point one might inquire why those countries which decided to have a centralized system of judicial review wanted to create special constitutional courts, and did not grant jurisdiction over constitutional matters to the existing highest courts of appeal. Constitutional jurisdiction might have been granted to these courts alone, without authorizing all judges to review legislation. Furthermore, one of the inherent difficulties of judicial review in a civil law country might have been overcome by making decisions of constitutional questions by these courts binding on all inferior courts. The Swiss Federal Tribunal could have provided a useful precedent for such a scheme.

But despite their theoretical suitability, the traditional highest courts of most civil law countries were found to lack the structure, procedures, and mentality required for an effective control over the constitutionality of legislation.

---

* For development of this, *see* § B., *infra.*

The European "supreme courts" lack the compact, manageable structure of the United States Supreme Court. Germany is typical. There are no less than five high courts, one each for ordinary civil and criminal questions, administrative matters, tax disputes, labor problems, and controversies involving social legislation. Even within a given high court there are several different divisions (*Senate*), each with many members who sit and decide cases independently of the other divisions. Furthermore, since more judges belong to a division than are required to decide a single case, the individual judges called to take part in decisions by the division may vary from case to case. For example, a few hundred judges belong to the Italian Court of Cassation. It is difficult to imagine how, amidst such a welter of judges and jurisdictions, a consistent and carefully considered constitutional jurisprudence could ever be devised.

Procedurally these courts of last instance are also handicapped by their frequent lack of a device similar to the certiorari of the United States Supreme Court, and thus have no discretionary power to refuse jurisdiction. To illustrate, the Italian Court of Cassation must hear every case brought before it, an average of three to four thousand civil cases per year, while the Italian Constitutional Court delivers fewer than two hundred judgments annually. Thus, if the Court of Cassation were to have jurisdiction over constitutional cases as well, such cases would represent a fairly insignificant portion of its workload. Thus submerged, these cases would receive neither the time nor the consideration that they require. The situation is very similar for the supreme courts of other civil law countries, such as Germany.

Lastly, the bulk of Europe's judiciary seems psychologically incapable of the value-oriented, quasi-political functions involved in judicial review. It should be borne in mind that continental judges usually are "career judges," who enter the judiciary at a very early age and are promoted to the higher courts largely on the basis of seniority. Their professional training develops skills in technical rather than policy-oriented application of statutes. The exercise of judicial review, however, is rather different from the usual judicial function of applying the law. Modern constitutions do not limit themselves to a fixed definition of what the law is, but contain broad programs for future action. Therefore the task of fulfilling the constitution often demands a higher sense of discretion than the task of interpreting ordinary statutes. That is certainly one reason why Kelsen, Calamandrei, and others have considered it to be a legislative rather than a purely judicial activity.

To impose the function of judicial review on European superior courts, to whom such an activity would be unfamiliar and foreign to their traditions, was not considered suitable. In fact, these considerations had been amply borne out in practice. Both Weimar

Germany, and Italy from 1948 to 1956, experimented with the decentralized system of judicial review. Since the power was exercised by all the courts, cases came in the last instance before the *Reichsgericht* or the *Corte di cassazione*, the highest ordinary courts in the respective countries. In Germany, however, the system certainly did not produce satisfactory results. In Italy, the Court of Cassation, often with the acquiescence of the *Consiglio di Stato*, used its powers of interpretation much more in the sense of "unfulfilling" the Constitution than of fulfilling it. During these eight years, the Court of Cassation, even more than other courts, gave the best possible proof of its unsuitability to judge constitutional questions. Apparently the long traditions of this Court, with the professional deformation of its elderly career judges, instead of being of benefit were much more of a handicap to the Court in its new role.

Nor are such practical confirmations of the unsuitability of decentralized review in civil law countries confined to Germany and Italy. In the Scandinavian countries, the modest role of the Supreme Court, and of the judiciary in general, in matters of judicial review is generally recognized. In Japan in the first twenty years after the promulgation of the Constitution, the Japanese Supreme Court found statutes unconstitutional in, at best, two cases; and in only one of these situations was the statute in question still in effect at the time of the decision. This may be attributable to the way of thinking of the career judges in that Court. Finally, in Switzerland the success of the *Tribunal fédéral* in matters of judicial review confirms, rather than denies, this observation, if one remembers that that court is composed of twenty-six judges who are not career judges but elected by the Federal Assembly.

The Justices of the Supreme Court of the United States, on the other hand, in the light of almost two centuries of experience, have demonstrated, on the whole, their suitability for their delicate task. While the Court has often reached results that many would condemn, it has not suffered from the hesitancy and unfamiliarity with constitutional adjudication of European decentralized systems. Indeed, some of the greatest names in American history have been those of Justices of the Supreme Court. This fact is, of course, due to various circumstances, but one that deserves emphasizing is that judicial review was a product of the Supreme Court itself. It may be said that the Court has necessarily had to achieve a high level of performance, in order to fulfill a function with which the courage of its early Justices had endowed it. Furthermore, there is the fact that the members of that Court — and the same applies to the other federal courts — are not "career" judges, as is the usual case with the ordinary European judges. They are politically appointed, not necessarily from the ranks of the lower courts.

These, then, seem to be the most important reasons why, when adopting judicial review, several civil law countries (Austria, Germany, Italy, etc.) chose not to use existing judicial organs and the members of the professional judiciary. Rather, they preferred to introduce entirely new and special judicial bodies, despite the serious problems of coordination arising from this choice. Naturally these special courts, as all the other judicial organs, have full independence and autonomy. However, their members (or at least the majority of them) are not career judges, but, following the analogy of the American Supreme Court, are selected from diverse backgrounds and appointed by the highest legislative or executive organs of the State. For example, the Austrian *Verfassungsgerichtshof* is composed of 14 judges (plus 6 substitutes), 8 of these (plus 3 substitutes) being nominated by the President of the Republic after proposals by the Cabinet; the other 6 (plus 3 substitutes) are also nominated by the President of the Republic but selected from a list submitted by both Houses of Parliament. The Italian *Corte costituzionale* is composed of 15 judges, one third of whom are nominated by the President of the Republic, one third by Parliament and one third by the highest civil, penal and administrative courts. The German *Bundesverfassungsgericht* is composed of 16 judges nominated by Parliament, half being chosen by the *Bundestag* and half by the *Bundesrat*. In all three countries the choice must be made from lawyers, that is to say from persons who, apart from other requirements such as age, etc., have completed regular studies in law.

5. Converging Trends

For the sake of clarity a dichotomy has been drawn between "centralized" and "decentralized" forms of judicial review, a dichotomy which in fact exaggerates the differences between the two systems. For the sake of balance, several points of convergence between the two approaches should now be re-emphasized. The twentieth century has blurred long-standing distinctions between the natural law and the positive law, between precedent-oriented and statute-oriented courts, and between varying separation of powers theories, distinctions which lay at the bottom of the assumed differences in attitude toward judicial review.

The very establishment of special constitutional courts with the power to review and invalidate statutes for failure to conform with the constitution was, of course, a considerable compromise with that conception of the separation of powers which would deny such a power to all judicial organs. True, the ordinary courts remain barred from judicial review in countries with a centralized system of control. However, even in these countries the ordinary courts have a role to play in this task. They often must make the initial judgment as to whether a constitutional issue ought to be referred to the special court.* This duty, as well as the obligation to recognize the binding effects of constitutional court decisions,** may help to stimulate a "constitutional consciousness" in the European judiciary similar to that which has been found for nearly two centuries in its American counterpart.

Nor is the movement toward convergence confined to the European side of the Atlantic. Through the use of certiorari, the United States Supreme Court, with the growing numbers of cases in which review is sought each year, confines itself more to the most significant — mostly constitutionally grounded — questions. This is, of course, the exact role of the European constitutional courts which have no jurisdiction at all in "ordinary" cases. Likewise, the role of the American Supreme Court is now openly admitted to be partly political. Its membership has always been specially appointed by a popularly elected president, and recent confirmation hearings by the Senate show an increasing recognition of the highly political functions of the high court.

Judicial review in the world today is, therefore, a continuum ranging from those countries, like the Soviet Union, whose only control of constitutionality is nonjudicial, to those states where this control is pre-eminently judicial, as in the United States. The other states, searching for forms which accord with their philosophies and yet answer the demands of our time, give the best evidence that judicial review is not only a viable but also a most flexible institution.

B. THE PROCESS OF CONTROL***

1. Two Methods of Reviewing a Constitutional Question: "Incidenter" and "Principaliter"

The differences between the centralized and decentralized systems clearly are more than historical. Largely due to a lack of confidence in the suitability of the traditional judiciary for the new task and to the conviction that judicial review is to a certain extent political in nature, the civil law countries have tended to confine constitutional control to specially created bodies of primarily political appointees. For similar reasons they have also developed different methods of raising and deciding questions of the constitutionality of legislation. Essentially, while the decentralized system encourages private parties to introduce constitutional issues before ordinary tribunals

---

* *See* § B., *infra.*
** *See* § C., *infra.*
*** Adapted from M. Cappelletti, *supra* at 22-23, 69-84.

in connection with regular judicial proceedings (review "incidenter"), the centralized approach tends, at least in its archetypal form, to emphasize presentation of constitutional issues before the special constitutional courts via special actions initiated by various government authorities (review "principaliter"). The United States is the country where review "incidenter" is most typical; the Austrian Constitution of 1920, on the other hand, devised a system of review classically "principaliter."

2. The American System as the Prototype of Decentralized Review "Incidenter"

In the United States and the other countries — such as Australia, Canada, Japan, Norway, Denmark, and now also Sweden — where similar systems are in force, the question of a law's constitutionality cannot be placed before the court "as a principal issue," that is to say in a separate constitutional case instituted ad hoc by a special action. (Legislative or executive organs may request advisory opinions on questions of constitutionality from the supreme courts in Canada, India, Norway, Finland and at least ten of the fifty states of the United States. This does not, however, constitute a genuine exercise of judicial review but rather one of constitutional consultation.) Constitutional questions must form part of a concrete case or controversy (whether civil, penal or any other type), and only arise to the extent that the law under consideration is *relevant* to the decision in the particular case. Thus the court competent to try the case that raises the question of constitutionality will be the very same court which is competent to decide the question itself. Hence, just as matters of constitutional legitimacy of legislation are not decided by special constitutional courts, so they are not decided by special constitutional procedures. They are *merely incidental* to the case at hand, although sometimes, in view of the general importance of the issue, certain federal or state authorities may intervene in the proceedings and address to the court what is aptly called an amicus curiae brief, presenting their views on the matter of constitutionality, not as real parties to the action, but rather as interested third parties. American courts, including the Supreme Court, encounter and decide matters of legislative constitutionality only within the context of concrete adversary litigation and only as necessary to the disposition of the case. And, in the American system, which is undoubtedly the most typical of the systems in which the constitutional jurisdiction is incidental, the matter of constitutionality can be raised in the course of any type of judicial proceeding.

3. The Austrian System of 1920-1929 as the Prototype of Centralized Review "Principaliter"

The Austrian system of judicial review in its original form under the *Bundesverfassung* of October 1, 1920, was a direct contrast to the American one, even though it has subsequently been modified. This Constitution not only created a special Constitutional Court — the *Verfassungsgerichtshof* — which had the exclusive competence over matters of constitutionality, but also gave this Court a power of control which could only be exercised after a special plea ("Antrag"). In this way judicial review in Austria, in contrast to the American system, came to be *entirely disassociated from concrete cases* whether civil, penal or administrative. Therefore, while in America judicial review can only be exercised "as an incidental issue" or (as has also been said, even though not entirely accurately) "by way of defense," in Austria it had to be exercised "as a principal issue" or "by way of action" in a special ad hoc proceeding.

The judges, therefore, under the original Austrian system, with the exception of those in the single Constitutional Court, had no power to review legislation, nor did they have the consequent power not to apply laws which they considered unconstitutional. In effect, this principle was and still is expressly declared by the words of art. 89, para. 1, of the Austrian Constitution: "Review of the validity of duly promulgated laws is not within the powers of the courts." Furthermore, the Austrian judges did not even have the right to ask the Constitutional Court to exercise that review which was forbidden to them. Questions of the constitutionality of laws could be brought before the Constitutional Court only by way of a direct plea by certain political, not judicial, organs mentioned in the Constitution. These organs were the Federal Executive (*Bundesregierung*) for judicial review of laws of the Länder (*Landesgesetze*) and the Governments of the Länder (*Landesregierungen*) for review of Federal legislation. There was no time limit fixed for the exercise of this right of action by these political organs, which alone possessed the right of access to the Constitutional Court.

4. Modifications of the Austrian Prototype

A glance at the original Austrian system, set up by the 1920 Constitution, shows immediately that it was entirely insufficient. As we have just seen, only the *Länder* and Federal Executives had the right to initiate proceedings for judicial review before the Constitutional Court as a principal issue against federal or *Länder* legislation respectively. Accordingly, review of constitutionality had only limited significance. It came, in practice, to be restricted to providing a defense against unconstitutional trespasses on the part of the federal legislature in the sphere of authority reserved to the *Länder* legislatures, and vice-versa. Thus it guaranteed between the federal authorities and the *Länder* a mutual respect for their "constitutional division of competences" (*verfassungsrechtliche Kompetenzverteilung*). On the other hand, laws which curtailed individual liberties remained, practically speaking, outside the ambit of control. Neither the Federal nor the *Länder* Governments were bound to initiate an action for judicial review against laws which they considered unconstitutional. The power was entirely discretionary. And so, inevitably, these political organs were interested in initiating the action only in fairly rare and exceptional cases. In this way the Constitutional Court could in practice be prevented from the consideration of many unconstitutional laws; and we have already seen how, by virtue of a specific provision of the Constitution, laws, even if manifestly unconstitutional, had to be blindly applied by all the judges as if they were perfectly valid.

An amendment to the Austrian Constitution (*Bundes-Verfassungsnovelle*) in 1929 modified somewhat this system of judicial review exercisable exclusively "by way of action." The current system in Austria is the result of that *Novelle* of 1929, which, though suppressed under the dictatorship, was revived after the last war with but a few variations, which are of no concern for our purposes.

This important constitutional reform of 1929 amended art. 140 of the Austrian Constitution by granting the right held by certain political organs to two ordinary *judicial* organs as well. Thus, the right to initiate proceedings for judicial review before the Constitutional Court was given not only to the Federal and *Länder* Governments, but now also to the *Oberster Gerichtshof* (the highest civil and criminal Court) and to the *Verwaltungsgerichtshof* (the central administrative Court).

There is, however, a difference between the rights of the Federal and *Länder* Governments, and those of these two judicial organs. The latter cannot raise the question of constitutionality before the Constitutional Court "principaliter," *i.e.* by way of direct action. Rather, they do so "incidenter," *i.e.* by way of defense, in the course and on the occasion of a normal case (civil, penal, or administrative) pending before them, where the decision depends on the federal or state law whose constitutionality is in doubt.

The *Novelle* of 1929 thus brought the Austrian system of review a little closer to the American model. The most obvious improvements over the 1920 Constitution are immediately apparent. While the two highest ordinary courts in Austria are still not themselves allowed to perform any functions of control over constitutional legitimacy, they are given the right to ask the Constitutional Court to exercise this control over laws relevant to the decisions in the concrete cases pending before them. This power is no longer discretionary but imposes a real obligation upon the two highest organs of ordinary and administrative justice not to apply laws whose constitutionality is in doubt, without having first heard the binding judgment of the Constitutional Court. Consequently, no law is excluded from the practical possibility of review. It may also be noted that, similar to the amicus curiae, third parties as well as the litigants in the concrete case may intervene before the Constitutional Court. Such an intervention can be made by the interested governments, *i.e.,* the Federal Government in questions concerning the constitutionality of federal laws, or the Government of the *Land* when its law is at issue.

Hence the reform of 1929 notably moderated the most serious defects of the 1920 system, without, however, entirely removing them. It must be emphasized that of all the civil, criminal, and administrative courts, only the two superior Courts have access to the *Verfassungsgerichtshof.* All the other judges must unquestioningly apply the laws to cases coming before them, even those laws which appear manifestly unconstitutional. Hence the serious disadvantage results that only in the last stages of a civil, criminal, or administrative case can a law finally be voided, by being referred to the Constitutional Court by the *Oberster Gerichtshof* or the *Verwaltungsgerichtshof.* Until that stage, inferior judges, as well as governmental agencies, are necessarily bound to apply the law.

This most apparent defect of the Austrian system has been avoided both by that of Italy, in effect since 1956, and by that of Germany, adopted by the Bonn Constitution of 1949. This is not, however, to deny the great influence deservedly exercised on both these systems by the ingenious Austrian precedent.

We have already mentioned that both in Germany and Italy, as in Austria, the ordinary judges (civil, criminal, and administrative) are forbidden to review the constitutionality of legislation. This function is reserved exclusively to the Constitutional Courts of the respective countries. But in Italy and Germany, contrary to Austria, all the ordinary judges, even the inferior ones, are not passively bound to apply any law which they consider unconstitutional. Rather, they have the power and the duty to place issues of constitutionality before the Constitutional Court so as to obtain a binding decision from that body. Thus, all the judges, and not only those of the superior courts, have the right to invoke the jurisdiction of the Constitutional Court, provided that the law is relevant to the concrete case before them. The case is then suspended until such time as the Constitutional Court shall have decided the preliminary issue of constitutionality.

It is thus apparent that, from the standpoint of the manner in which constitutional issues are presented, the Italian and German systems have drawn considerably closer to the Anerican system of judicial review. It is not the case for Italy and Germany (as it is in the United States) that all the judges are competent to *perform* the function of judicial review. However, they all at least have the right to *require* the Constitutional Court to exercise its powers of review.

Nevertheless, this "incidental" way is not the only method of raising a constitutional issue before the German and Italian Constitutional Courts. Certain political organs have the right to bring a direct action, independent of any concrete case, by instituting an ad hoc proceeding before the Constitutional court. From this point of view, we see a divergence from the American system on the part of these two European countries, and an approximation to the Austrian system of control of constitutionality.

In Italy, the Court can be convened through direct action by the executive organs of the regions (*giunte regionali*) in matters of national or regional laws which a region contends have infringed the area of competence reserved to it by the Constitution (constitutional law of February 9, 1948, No. 1, art. 2). Conversely, this right belongs to the central Executive in disputes over the constitutionality of regional laws (art. 127, para. 4, of the Constitution). In Germany, a still larger selection of institutions and individuals has the right to invoke, "by way of action," the procedures of the Federal Constitutional Court or the Constitutional Courts of the *Länder* for control of legislation. In particular, the Constitution guarantees this right to the Federal Government, to the Governments of the *Länder*, and to one third of the members of the *Bundestag*. Furthermore, the ordinary law of March 12, 1951 on the *Bundesverfassungsgericht,* established the *Verfassungsbeschwerde,* an extraordinary recourse available to the individual whose fundamental rights have been directly denied by any statute, judicial decision, or administrative act. It allows him to obtain an expeditious hearing before the Federal Constitutional Court (*Bundesverfassungsgericht*) if he alleges a violation of a *Grundrecht* or other constitutional right of equivalent importance. Since 1969, the *Verfassungsbeschwerde* is guaranteed by the Constitution.*

The effects of a decision by the Federal Constitutional Court in response to a constitutional petition may be far-reaching. A statute found unconstitutional is declared null. This declaration binds all inferior courts and administrative agencies.

Accordingly, *Verfassungsbeschwerde* allows one to have his constitutionally grounded complaint heard speedily by the Constitutional Court in a direct action concerned solely with the constitutional issue raised. Though there is a requirement of exhaustion of ordinary remedies (unless a self-executing statute is

---

* Article 93, para. 4a GG.

challenged), a party may avoid these often costly and time-consuming procedures by showing that the alleged grievance is of "general importance" or that "grave and irreparable damage" may result from denying an immediate hearing. It must be remembered that many civil law systems do not provide for the immediate equitable relief available in the common law. The Mexican *amparo*, for example, attacks the problem by suspending the effects of state action while the federal court's decision is pending. *Verfassungsbeschwerde* accomplishes much the same result both by allowing an allegation of "grave and irreparable damage" and by permitting the Constitutional Court to adopt provisional remedies, with the added advantage that a favorable decision by the Court will annul the invalid act or law not only with regard to the complaining party but also vis-à-vis all others in the same situation.

To sum up, one can say that there was originally a clear distinction between the so-called American approach to judicial review, exercised solely incidentally, and the Austrian system of control exercised solely by way of direct action. This distinction was, however, attenuated in Austria in 1929 and still further in the systems of control adopted in Italy and Germany after the last World War, and recently imitated in certain other countries — *e.g.*, in Turkey in 1961. Here questions of legislative constitutionality can be brought before the Constitutional Courts in two ways. Firstly, this can be done "incidenter" as a result of the dispute in a concrete case whether civil, criminal, or administrative. Secondly, it can be done "principaliter" by means of a direct action brought, unrelated to any concrete case, solely to test the constitutionality of a given law before the Constitutional Court. Here, the initiative will rest either with certain nonjudicial organs, or even with a parliamentary minority or an individual person.

5. Ordinary and Extraordinary Means of Raising Constitutional Issues in Both Systems

An examination of the way in which a private party raises a constitutional question in both the centralized and decentralized systems would show both the divergent outlooks as well as the common problems of judicial review in each of the two major western legal families.

In the United States, a private party may raise a constitutional question before any court of first instance, civil or criminal. The court will decide the question along with all others posed by the case. The losing party may then appeal the decisions of first instance and the record of the case will gradually work its way up the judicial hierarchy, the most important issues, including the constitutional, being susceptible to ultimate resolution by the Supreme Court. The constitutional issue is seldom if ever considered apart from the fact situation which gave rise to it.

The process by which a similar constitutional question would be resolved in the civil law countries is quite different. In Italy, for example, the private party — or, for that matter, the court itself *ex officio* — may raise the issue in any stage of any judicial proceeding, but the court is powerless to decide it. Rather, the court simply determines if the issue is relevant to the case and if it is not "manifestly unfounded" (this determination is not appealable, though it may be raised again when the entire case goes before the courts of later instance). Relevance and prima facie foundation being determined, the issue is referred to the Constitutional Court. However, since the latter cannot decide the other factual and legal issues of the case, these must remain below, to be decided in proceedings which are stayed pending the decision on the constitutional question. This question thus tends to be considered in the abstract and the decision is addressed rather to the statute challenged than to the facts of the case at hand.

A major problem faced by both systems is the avoidance of irreparable injury to the party pending an ultimate decision on the challenged statute. For example, when a person is arbitrarily denied a passport by an administrative agency or when labor union picketers are illegally arrested, the rights denied them are fundamental. If these rights continue to be denied pending vindication in the courts, the harm caused may not be compensable, and the possibility of money damages will be of little comfort. What is needed, then, are special remedies for violations of special rights — remedies which are at once expeditious and which avoid irreparable harm to the aggrieved petitioner pending a final decision.

Both systems have devised such recourses for violations of particularly important rights. The traditional battery of writs and injunctions available to common law judges has proven effective in precipitating early, if tentative, decisions on constitutional questions. Some of the civil law countries have devised similar statutory remedies for higher law violations; Germany's *Verfassungsbeschwerde* is especially effective in that the Constitutional Court may suspend the application of challenged state actions pending final decision regarding their constitutionality. Italy as yet lacks a similar remedy; the criminal accused must await the making of a formal charge before he may advance his constitutional defense. Similarly, the person denied a fundamental right by an administrative agency must often exhaust irrelevant administrative remedies or build an artificial case (*fictio litis*) before he may go to court and present the ultimately important constitutional question. All of this hearkens back to the old truth that a right without an adequate remedy is no right at all, and it is to be expected that there will be an increasing recognition in some civil law countries of the inadequacy of the remedial aspect of their new systems of judicial review.

6. Conclusion

The distinguishing mark of the centralized systems of constitutional control is the lack of a single judicial organ which may consider and resolve all the issues of a particular case. The special constitutional courts are barred from deciding factual disputes, ordinary legal questions, and issues of statutory interpretation; the ordinary courts, in turn, may not decide constitutional challenges. Thus, the typical continental court structure does not resemble the American structure where all courts are subject to the unifying influence of the Supreme Court. Rather, on issues of federal law, there are three or more separate structures, each with its high court. None of the high courts (Cassation, Council of State, Constitutional Court, etc.) is subject to control by any other court with regard to decisions within its field.

The results of this lack of any court with complete jurisdiction are profound. First, the ordinary courts are not greatly encouraged to develop a "constitutional consciousness" which would lead them to perform their regular duties (judicial investigations, factual determinations, statutory interpretation, etc.) with an eye to avoiding violations of constitutional rights. The ordinary judge is directly controlled not by the Constitutional Court but by one of the other high courts of his country. None of these latter courts has the formal duty of concerning itself with defining constitutional norms, and the pressures for constitutional awareness are correspondingly less. Speaking of the Italian situation, Professors Merryman and Vigoriti have said: *

> An example is afforded by the interpretations given by the ordinary courts, led by the Court of Cassation, in Italy, to various statutes dealing with the criminal accused's right to counsel. These interpretations have "seemed to place a higher value on judicial convenience, economy and expedition than on expansion of the scope of legal protection afforded criminal defendants .... One suspects that there may be something self-fulfilling about this. ... It becomes the primary obligation of the Constitutional Court to translate the precepts of that document [*i.e.* the Constitution] into specific decisions on the constitutionality of statutes. Since that obligation lies principally with the Constitutional Court, other courts can feel free to pursue other principal objectives."

---

* Merryman & Vigoriti, *When Courts Collide: Constitution and Cassation in Italy,* 15 AM. J. COMP. L. 665, 681 (1967).

Second, the special constitutional courts inevitably tend to focus not on the particular fact situation in which a given individual was denied a certain right, but rather on the constitutionality of a specified, abstract, statutory proposition. After all, the primary duty of the special constitutional court is not so much to decide a particular case as it is to give a formal declaration of a statute's constitutionality or lack thereof. Since this declaration will bind *erga omnes,* the statute is the matter of concern, not the fact situation which resulted in its being challenged.

Thus, while on the face of it some might say that the centralized system, with review both *incidenter* and by way of direct action, is more complete than its decentralized counterpart, others might claim that the newer form of review suffers from a serious lack of judicial flexibility, largely because of the separation of constitutional questions from specific fact situations. The result may be that the constitutional courts will be unable to avoid deciding questions that would be better postponed, or, worse, they will be unable to perform their duty of protecting individual rights without provoking dangerous conflicts with other branches of government.

The ability to say not "yes" or "no," but rather "maybe" to a constitutional question is a hallmark of the American Supreme Court, which has evolved an impressive array of means of avoiding delicate constitutional questions. The Court, to insure that it is not flooded with questions to which it cannot give adequate attention, or to put off a decision of great delicacy, will require that the question posed arise from a real, not a feigned, dispute, that it have been timely put and debated in the lower courts, and that the interest of the parties involved be such as to insure an adequate presentation of all points of view.

The Court may not always apply these and similar doctrines neutrally. It may in fact use them to tip the judicial scales for or against the constitutional challenge, *without* a formal declaration of constitutionality or unconstitutionality. Perhaps because of their youth, or perhaps due to the structural features outlined above, the European courts have not yet gone as far in developing methods of blocking the legislature without provoking dangerous reactions.

What is this "mediating way between the ultimates of legitimation and invalidation"? One aspect is the use of the Court's power to interpret statutes so as to avoid any construction which could be conceived of as unconstitutional. Or the Court might say that a given statute, if it is to limit a certain right, must do so explicitly or be voided for vagueness. Another technique is to affirm that while Congress might be able to legislate in a given field, it must not delegate this power to non-elective administrative bodies.

Thus in all these cases — the reinterpreted statute, the statute voided for vagueness, and the law struck down for having improperly delegated a particular power — the Court effectively protects the right of the person challenging the law, but does so without formally declaring that a given norm may not be established by the legislature. In all of these cases the legislature is not barred from reconsidering the statute and re-enacting it in such a way as to make clear its desire to pass the law, but political reality being what it is, the legislature often finds it impracticable to do so.

Whether the special constitutional courts may be able to evolve similar weapons of limited warfare against unconstitutionality is open to question. What is clear is the difficulty of doing so, in light of their lack of the formal power to interpret statutes. When a constitutional court takes it upon itself to interpret a statute so as to avoid a conflict with higher constitutional standards, it runs a serious risk of conflict with the highest ordinary courts, which, as a rule, claim complete independence from the constitutional court in matters of statutory interpretation. Further, the constitutional courts lack power to refuse jurisdiction for purely discretionary reasons, and tend to consider constitutional issues in the abstract. Nevertheless, there are signs of attempts by the constitutional courts in the civil law countries to develop their own sort of flexibility. The German Constitutional Court, for example, has its own version of the "political question" doctrine. The Italian Constitutional Court may have an efficacious tool in its ability to uphold, without *erga omnes* effect, the constitutionality of a law. Thus a statute, upheld in one case, may be reconsidered later without any prejudice to the Court's ability to find it invalid.

The advisability of conferring such broad powers on the constitutional courts is quite another matter. The United States Supreme Court has often used its "political question," "case and controversy" and "standing" doctrines to delay decisions on statutes which may, in the meantime, cause great hardship to those affected. Indeed the cost and inconvenience of mounting a constitutional case may be such that decades may pass before a plaintiff is found who is willing, for example, to violate the statute, submit to arrest, and then go through the long process of litigation which leads to a hearing before the Supreme Court. A classic example is the Connecticut birth control statute which was not declared unconstitutional until 1965 though there had been challenges made as early as 1943. Each time before 1965, when the question was brought before the Court, it was avoided through the invocation of devices similar to those described.

Indeed, the latitude given the American Supreme Court is at once an expression of confidence in the judiciary and a realization that judicial review is at least potentially a deviant institution in a democratic society. On the one hand there is faith that the judiciary will not use its tools unscrupulously to deny hearings indefinitely to those who deserve them. At the same time, the courts have seen that since their effectiveness rests on the esteem in which they are held by the electorate, they must always keep in mind the attitudes of that electorate. Certain questions are too explosive to be decided by any judicial body. Other questions should be delayed, or referred back to the legislature for a more considered opinion. It is paradoxical that judicial review in Europe, where there has always been an extreme concern with the political implications of judicial control of legislation, seems to encourage politically dangerous decisions by the judges called upon to administer it.

7. Converging Trends

Yet it again behooves us, after contrasting the two systems of judicial review, to emphasize their growing similarities. The European prototype — one single court vested with the power to entertain constitutional questions brought *principaliter* and abstracted from concrete cases — is, as has been shown, far removed from the systems now in force in Italy and Germany, and, to an extent, in Austria itself, where the lower courts may play a real part in judicial review, incidental to their function of adjudicating ordinary cases.

Similarly in the United States, Chief Justice Marshall's rationale in *Marbury* v. *Madison*, with its emphasis on the incidental nature of judicial review, seems somewhat at variance with the recent evolution of the institution. The old maxims of judicial restraint — "case and controversy," "justiciability," "standing," etc. — have been diluted by new procedural devices — class actions, requests for declaratory relief, and other means of raising abstract constitutional issues. The Supreme Court is only in some ways an ordinary court of appeals; in others it is, like the European constitutional courts, "a special organ of constitutional review."

C. THE EFFECTS OF CONTROL *

1. Effects of Control: Theory and Reality

The dilemmas posed by judicial review in a democracy are perhaps nowhere more apparent than when one speaks of the effects of a decision that a statute is unconstitutional. Is the statute involved to be voided in part or in its entirety? Is the decision to bind all future litigants or only those immediately before the court? Is the newly defined constitutional right to be applied retroactively or prospectively? Behind the terse questions lies a mass of issues, subtle

---

* Sections 1-3 of this part are adapted from M. CAPPELLETTI, *supra* 85-96.

and complicated, for which all attempts at broad theoretical explanations have been inadequate. So while both the centralized and decentralized systems of review offer, in their theoretical bases, widely divergent answers to the questions posed, practical considerations in each system have caused a striking convergence between them.

2. Decisions: "Inter Partes" or "Erga Omnes"?

Austria's Constitutional Court, again the archetype of the centralized systems, makes its decisions binding not only on the parties to the case, but also on all others finding themselves similarly situated in the future. Thus, a decision of unconstitutionality gives rise to an annulment which, although not retroactive, yet operates *erga omnes.* Hence one speaks appropriately of an "Allgemeinwirkung" or general efficacy. The law, in other words, once a judgment of unconstitutionality has been given, is invalidated for everyone, just as if it had been abrogated by a subsequent statute; and the legislative enactments which preceded the unconstitutional one return into force (art. 140, § 4, of the Austrian Constitution), unless the Constitutional Court decrees otherwise.

The American system is based on a quite opposite theory, as are those systems, such as the Japanese one, which have modeled themselves upon it. The same can be said even for some more original systems, such as the Mexican one where the "principio de la relatividad," corresponding to the so-called "fórmula de Otero," prevails. The fundamental rule in all these systems is that the judge must not go beyond nonapplication of the law in the particular case. Thus judicial review does not have, as in Austria, Italy, Germany and elsewhere, general *erga omnes* efficacy, but only a special *inter partes* validity, related solely to the concrete case ("Individualwirkung"). This element, however, has largely been eliminated in the United States by force of the principle of stare decisis, especially where there is a decision of the Supreme Court. Even in Mexico, it has been considerably attenuated, if not eliminated, through the limited binding force accorded to the "jurisprudencia" of the *Suprema Corte de Justicia,* as well as through the institution of the *suplencia de la queja deficiente* introduced in 1951, and infrequently used so far, by which a Mexican court may draw the parties' attention to the fact that the state action which is the subject of plaintiff's claim has already been declared unconstitutional in prior decisions of the *Suprema Corte.*

The refusal of the United States Supreme Court to make formal, permanently binding decrees of unconstitutionality is partly based on myth, and partly on a deeply felt need to relate judicial decisions to present realities and not to future possibilities. On one hand, it is felt that open declarations of permanent nullity, declarations at times accompanied by a revival of previous laws, once superseded but given new force, smack far too much of judicial law-making. It is certainly a myth that judges never make law, but only declare it, yet this myth is at the basis of popular acceptance of judicial review in the United States and, according to many, it should not be lightly disregarded. On a more practical plane, there is a realization that no judge can foresee all the possible applications of a given statute, and that no judge, therefore, should be asked to do so.

But all this says more about past attitudes than about present reality. The judges of the centralized courts appear more and more to share with their American counterparts a realization of the frequent need to limit the future effects of their decisions. They often try to evade sweeping declarations of constitutionality both by interpreting statutes to avoid constitutional problems, and, if this proves impossible, by excising from the statute only the most offensive parts and leaving the rest as an effective statement of the legislative will. The choices made by the judges — whether to reinterpret, to totally invalidate, or to save part of the law — are often made in both systems not only by reference to plain texts, but also to "motives of political or social seasonableness."

However, note that in Italy, at least, the device of interpreting the statute so as to avoid the constitutional question (*i.e.* supplying an *interpretazione adeguatrice*) is weakened by the fact that the interpretations, as opposed to decisions of unconstitutionality, of the law by the Constitutional Court are not binding on the ordinary courts which look rather to the Court of Cassation for guidance on such questions. The problem is somewhat less pressing in Germany due to the existence of a statute saying that pronouncements of the Constitutional Court, *including* interpretations, which grow out of constitutional cases, bind the lower courts.

The United States Supreme Court has, in turn, been forced, by the very weightiness of recent questions brought before it, to take account of the legislative implications of its function, and to frame its decrees with regard for their *erga omnes* effects. The school segregation and voter reapportionment cases were, for example, class actions, *i.e.*, they asked relief not only for the individual plaintiffs concerned, but for "all others similarly situated." By its nature the class action asks for more than *inter partes* relief; it takes away the cushioning effects provided by the fact that the significance of traditional constitutional cases was felt only gradually as successive individual litigants sought to vindicate their newly defined rights. There were few areas where the Court sensed greater dangers than in those of racial integration and legislative redistricting. Once having decided to reach these constitutional questions, therefore, the Court had little choice but to frame decrees strikingly legislative in nature. The original segregation cases were given future applicability only; the schools were to be desegregated not forthwith, but "with all deliberate speed." Reapportionment cases are often similarly legislative and future oriented. This is far beyond mere settlement of disputes between private parties.

3. Decisions: Retroactive or Prospective?

Here again both systems of judicial review have moved far beyond their original premises.

In the decentralized systems, according to more traditional concepts, an unconstitutional law, being contrary to a superior norm, is held to be absolutely null and void. Hence, we can see that the judge, in the exercise of his power of review, does not annul but merely declares the pre-existing nullity of the unconstitutional law.

In the Austrian system, on the other hand, an unconstitutional law is not void, but merely voidable; even if unconstitutional, such a law is valid and effective up to the moment when the decision of the Constitutional Court is published. The Austrian Constitutional Court, therefore, does not merely declare a pre-existing nullity, but it annuls and quashes ("aufhebt") the unconstitutional law. And this is not all. What is even more remarkable is that the Austrian Constitutional Court has a discretionary power to order that the annulment of the law shall only operate from a fixed date subsequent to the publication ("Kundmachung") of its judgment, provided that the deferment of the constitutive (*i.e.,* annulling) effect of the judgment should not be for more than one year. However, even when the Austrian Constitutional Court chooses to defer the general effect of a decision of unconstitutionality, the parties to the original case in which the issue was raised and decided *will* have the benefits of the declaration of unconstitutionality. The Turkish Constitution also provides for deferring the effect of decisions that laws are unconstitutional, but with the limitation that the effective date of the Constitutional Court's decision shall be deferred for no more than six months. A similar provision is also to be found in the Yugoslav system adopted in 1963.

To sum up, the American system of judicial review has the character of a merely "declaratory" review. At any rate this is the traditional view, although lately it has been the subject of much discussion and modification as we shall see. The Austrian system, on the other hand, has taken the form of review "constitutive" of the invalidity and hence of the ineffectiveness of the law in opposition to the Constitution. As a logical result, in the former system the judgment operates *ex tunc,* retroactively, for it is a simple ascertainment of a pre-existing nullity. In the Austrian system, on the contrary, the judgment of unconstitutionality, being constitutive, operates *ex nunc* or even *pro futuro,* without any retroactive effect.

Italy and Germany are again, in a sense, half-way between the more "concrete," pragmatic American approach, tied to the immediate requirements of individual cases, and that more theoretical, abstract and "general" one followed in Kelsen's Austrian system. Both in Italy and in Germany the judgment, in which the Constitutional Court pronounces the unconstitutionality of a law, has validity *erga omnes,* "Allgemeinwirkung," just as in Austria. Hence the unconstitutional law is invalidated for everyone and for always, and not merely denied application in the concrete case. However, both in Italy and in Germany — and in the latter country even more definitely than in the former — the judgment of unconstitutionality is not effective only *ex nunc* or *pro futuro.* Rather, the efficacy in principle operates retroactively (*ex tunc*).

In other words, both in Italy and Germany — as in the United States — the mere fact of unconstitutionality is a ground of absolute nullity and therefore of ineffectiveness *ipso jure* of the laws, even before the actual unconstitutionality has been solemnly declared in the binding judgment of the Constitutional Court.

The Italian and German departures from the original Austrian model may give some indication of the abandonment, by both systems of review, of a purely theoretical approach to the retroactivity problem. Instead, judicial review everywhere is influenced by practical considerations, among which are:

a) *The need to reward the plaintiff who brings his constitutional complaint before the courts:* As previously noted, the Austrian *Bundes-Verfassungsnovelle* of 1929 amended the Constitution and gave the two Austrian superior courts, the *Oberster Gerichtshof* and the *Verwaltungsgerichtshof,* the right to raise constitutional issues before the Constitutional Court, limited to the laws relevant to the particular case being heard by them. But how could this new right be reconciled with the notion that the Constitutional Court's judgment operated, not retroactively, but only *ex nunc* or *pro futuro?*

The question needs clarification. One should consider that in lawsuits (civil, criminal, or administrative) coming before the courts, the issue is always one of rights, duties, status, and responsibilities arising from facts having occurred in the past. These facts — contracts, torts, transfers of land, etc. — are governed by a legal norm valid at the moment they arise (and therefore at a time anterior to the judicial proceeding). Let us now assume the unconstitutionality of that legal norm. Under the American system (according to the traditional interpretation) and likewise in modern Italy and Germany, that norm, being unconstitutional, was invalid even before it was actually declared unconstitutional through the instrument of judicial review. Therefore it was invalid even in respect to facts taking place before the judicial control of constitutionality was exercised. Under the Austrian system, on the other hand, the unconstitutional norm is held perfectly valid and effective at least up to the moment when the decision of the Constitutional Court, lacking retroactive force, is published. In this way, the events, which are the object of the case pending before the *Oberster Gerichtshof* or the *Verwaltungsgerichtshof,* were — at the time of their occurrence — validly and effectively governed by the unconstitutional norm. The following result would therefore be perfectly logical and coherent in theory, although just as absurd and unacceptable in practice: the decision of the Constitutional Court would not have any effect upon the very case pending before the *Oberster Gerichtshof* or the *Verwaltungsgerichtshof* in the course of which the question of constitutionality arose.

Precisely in order to avoid this absurd consequence, the Austrian system, as it was after the reform of 1929 and as it is today, has partially modified the idea rigorously adhered to in 1920, which denied any retroactivity at all to the decisions of the Constitutional Court. The reformed system of 1929 has in fact accepted that — limited to the concrete case in which the issue of constitutionality has arisen "incidenter" — the law declared unconstitutional by the Constitutional Court should not be applied to events taking place prior to the judgment itself. Kelsen himself, writing in 1929, had to recognize that "the retroactive effect of the annulment is a technical necessity since, without it, the [judicial] authorities having to apply the law would have no immediate and therefore no sufficiently strong interest to put the machinery of the Constitutional Court in motion. ... They must be encouraged to submit these claims by giving a retroactive effect to the annulment in the concrete case." However, the retroactive application of the decision to only the parties of the case at hand and not to all others similarly situated can obviously result in serious inequality.

b) *The reliance factor:* As practical necessity in Austria required the modification of the strict theory of nonretroactivity in 1929, similarly in the United States, as in Germany and Italy, a parallel necessity has compelled considerable modification of the opposite doctrine of *ex tunc* efficacy, or retroactivity. This doctrine presupposes that the unconstitutional law is null and void *ab origine.* This means that every act — whether private, *e.g.,* a contract, or public, *e.g.,* an administrative act or judicial decision — will have no valid legal basis if it is performed on the strength of the unconstitutional law. It can happen, however, that an unconstitutional law may have been generally and unquestioningly applied by public bodies and private citizens for a considerable time. For example, an office-holder, elected or nominated on the basis of a law declared unconstitutional at a much later date, may have held that office for a long period; the state may have levied a tax for many years, or a private citizen drawn a pension or performed certain contractual obligations, on the basis of a law which subsequently turns out to be unconstitutional; and so one might go on with endless examples. What then happens with a law which, after being unquestioningly applied for many years, is at some time held unconstitutional in a judgment having retroactive effects according to the doctrine presented here? Is it possible to abolish all the effects which have resulted, without any valid legal basis, from those public and private acts which formerly were done in accordance with such a law?

The answer to these questions has been inspired, especially in the case law of the American courts, by the development of a pragmatic and broad-minded way of thinking. A similar philosophy prevails in Italy and Germany, where the tendency has been to respect certain "consolidated effects," due to acts based on laws later declared contrary to the constitution.

This topic of the effects of judgments on the constitutionality of laws brings with it a host of complex problems, both theoretical and practical. For example, there is the problem of which law is applicable in place of the one declared unconstitutional; the problem of the effect of a judgment upholding the constitutionality of a law; the problem of the effect of the reasons given for constitutional decisions, for instance when a law is upheld by the Constitutional Court due to a certain interpretation; the problem of the retroactivity of a judgment contrary to previous decisions; and so on. On the whole, these problems are treated with such variations from country to country, that it would be impossible to give a useful synthesis in comparative terms.

c) *The criminal defendant:* In both systems of review there is one case which argues most strongly for the retroactive application of a constitutional decision. It is that of the person who is serving a criminal sentence after being convicted of violating a law subsequently declared unconstitutional. Italy and Germany, by statute, and the United States, by case law, have all looked favorably on petitions for release in such cases. Nevertheless, in criminal, as well as civil cases, Austria still stands by the strict rule of nonretroactivity, save as regards the parties to the case in which the law is found unconstitutional. Perhaps it is in the Austrian criminal case that one sees most clearly the competition between values which characterizes all decisions regarding retroactivity. On the one hand, there is the argument for "equal protection" for all persons convicted under the same criminal statute ("it does not seem that the mere time factor, the somewhat accidental moment of the judgment, should thus determine rights and duties"). On the other, there is the

Austrian emphasis on the "stability of the legal order and the faith people place in it." It hardly seems, however, that "legal stability" is sufficient justification for the continued imprisonment of a person convicted under an unconstitutional statute.

But what of the prisoner whose *crime* remains on the books, but whose conviction was brought about through *procedures* subsequently found to violate his basic rights (to an attorney, to immunity from arbitrary searches, against self-incrimination, etc.)? The conviction may be "final," but the execution of the sentence continues; nor, with the availability of remedies like habeas corpus, can it be said that the proceeding is immune from judicial attack.

For example, Germany has by specific statutory provision extended an already existing statutory device to allow a prisoner to reopen his trial *(Wiederaufnahme)*, though his conviction may have long before become "final," if the statute under which he was convicted is later declared unconstitutional. *See* § 79(1) of the *Bundesverfassungsgerichtsgesetz*. Whether one can avail himself of the *Wiederaufnahme* if the *procedures* used to convict are later declared unconstitutional, is a question which has been debated by legal scholars but which has been decided negatively by the Federal Constitutional Court. *See* Decision of July 7, 1960, Bundesverfassungsgericht [BVerfG], W. Ger., 11 Entscheidungen des Bundesverfassungsgerichts [BVerfGE] 263.

Italy presents a similar situation. Art. 30, para. 4, of the law of March 11, 1953, No. 87, on the Constitutional Court provides that the execution of a criminal judgment, though final, based on a law later held to be unconstitutional, ceases immediately upon the declaration of unconstitutionality. This provision has been interpreted as applying only to substantive law. *See, e.g.,* Decision of Dec. 29, 1966, No. 127, Corte cost., Italy, [1966] 24 Raccolta ufficiale delle sentenze e ordinanze delle Corte costituzionale [Rac. uff. corte cost.] 483; [1967] Foro Italiano [Foro It.] I 1; [1967] Giurisprudenza Italiana [Giur. Ital.] I 275; [1966] Giurisprudenza costituzionale [Giur. cost.] 1697. The spectre of thousands of prisoners, convicted under old procedures, asking for their liberty, is one which haunts, perhaps needlessly, law enforcement officials and public alike. The debate continues on both sides of the Atlantic.

4. Prospectivity in Austrian Constitutional Adjudication

X v. Austria

Decision of February 5, 1971

European Commission of Human Rights
1971 Y.B. Eur. Conv. on Human Rights 168

[THE FACTS:

[An Austrian tax law declared that compensation paid to a holder, or the spouse of a holder, of 25 percent of the stock of a company would be considered profits of the company. The law also required that the stock holdings of a person's relatives be considered in determining whether he owned 25 percent. On October 14, 1964, the Austrian Constitutional Court decided that the last-mentioned provision was unconstitutional. The decision, however, did not take effect until December 31, 1964.

[In 1965 and 1966, appellant company was assessed taxes, based on the unconstitutional law, for the years 1960-64. Having exhausted its appeals on the assessments in Austria, the company appealed to the European Commission of Human Rights, alleging a violation of the European Convention on Human Rights.]

THE LAW

Whereas the applicant company considers that the decisions . . . infringe its property rights as safeguarded by Article I of the First Protocol; whereas it relies in particular on paragraph (2) of Article I of the First Protocol, which provides that the right of every natural or legal person to the peaceful enjoyment of his possessions as guaranteed by paragraph (1) shall not impair "the right of a State to enforce such laws as it deems necessary . . . to secure the payment of taxes";

It follows from this provision that taxation may only be levied by virtue of a law and that the collection of taxes without such statutory basis is arbitrary and amounts to a violation of the right to the peaceful enjoyment of one's possessions within the meaning of the provision in question;
 . . . .

This raises the question whether a statutory provision which had been annulled as unconstitutional by the Constitutional Court could legally be applied by the Austrian courts after the annulment had taken effect, and accordingly whether application in the present case of an annulled law amounted to a violation of the Convention and in particular of the First Protocol, as the applicant maintains;

The Commission finds that the Constitutional Court, in rejecting the applicant's constitutional appeal relied on Article 140 of the Federal Constitution, which provides that unconstitutional laws remain in force until annulled by that Court as unconstitutional; the

Court has in most cases adopted the same view, holding that decisions of annulment take effect only *ex nunc*;

The Commission observes that in its decisions on this subject, the Constitutional Court has taken the view that, even after the annulment of a statutory provision takes effect, the provision in question remains applicable to matters prior to that date (in accordance with the "*Konkretisierungstheorie*");

The Commission is of the opinion that the Constitutional Court, when annulling a statute as unconstitutional but restricting the effects of such annulment to matters subsequent to the entry into force of the annulment, cannot be considered as acting contrary to Article 1 of the First Protocol except insofar as the statute annulled was itself contrary to that article;

There is no provision in the Convention forbidding the High Contracting Parties to annul a statute *ex nunc* and nevertheless continue to apply it to matters prior to the annulment;

The Commission finds that application of such a statute does not amount to a violation of the Convention, in particular of Article 1 of the First Protocol; it follows that the application is manifestly ill-founded and must be rejected by virtue of Article 27 (2) of the Convention;

Now therefore the Commission,

DECLARES THIS APPLICATION INADMISSIBLE.

NOTES AND QUESTIONS

1. Would the argument of the applicant before the Commission have been stronger if it had been based on denial of the right to "equality" ? While it is true that most taxpayers were required to pay taxes on the basis of the unconstitutional law through December 31, 1964, the party to the 1964 Austrian Constitutional Court decision was excused from prior taxes. Note that, unlike the constitutions of Austria, Germany and Italy, the European Convention contains no general protection of a right of equality. Rather, art. 14 provides that "rights . . . shall be secured without discrimination on any ground such as sex, race, colour, language, religion, political or other opinion, national or social origin, association with a national minority, property, birth or other status."

2. Suppose the Austrian Constitutional Court were to invalidate a criminal statute under the Austrian constitution. Does the Commission's decision mean that a person languishing in prison for violation of that same statute has been denied no rights under the Convention? Consider art. 7(1), which provides that: "No one shall be held guilty of any criminal offence on account of any act or omission which did not constitute a criminal offence under national

or international law *at the time when it was committed.* " (Emphasis added.)

3. Suppose that the Austrian Constitutional Court had concluded that the tax law in question violated both the Austrian Constitution and the European Convention. Would its decision of invalidity still be entirely prospective? If so, would an application to the Commission, by a person compelled to pay taxes by the invalid law, still be "manifestly ill-founded" ?

5. Prospectivity in American Constitutional Adjudication

a. Linkletter v. Walker

In *Linkletter* v. *Walker,* 381 U.S. 618 (1965), the Supreme Court, for the first time, applied a new rule of constitutional law prospectively. The *Linkletter* decision was modest and tentative — the Court refused to apply the rule of *Mapp* v. *Ohio,* 367 U.S. 643 (1961) (requiring exclusion of illegally seized evidence in State criminal trials), to cases in which convictions had become final before *Mapp* was decided. In more than a decade since *Linkletter,* the prospectivity doctrine has been greatly expanded. Indeed, the law of prospectivity itself has become a complex and debated field of law.

b. The Timing Issue — The Starting Point for Prospective Application

One major issue arising since *Linkletter* has been selection of the appropriate point of time from which a decision will be applied prospectively. Under *Linkletter, Mapp* applied retroactively to all cases where the time for final direct appellate review had not expired. *Johnson* v. *New Jersey,* 384 U.S. 719 (1966), held the doctrine of *Miranda* v. *Arizona,* 384 U.S. 436 (1966) (requiring elaborate warnings to criminal suspects during police interrogation), inapplicable to *trials* which had commenced prior to the *Miranda* decision. The next predictable step was to apply a new decision prospectively only to *violations* of the new rule which occurred after the decision. *Stovall* v. *Denno,* 388 U.S. 293 (1967), held that the rule of *United States* v. *Wade,* 388 U.S. 218 (1967), and *Gilbert* v. *California,* 388 U.S. 263 (1967) (right to counsel in post-indictment lineup), was applicable only to lineups which took place after those decisions. Since *Stovall,* prospective decisions have only been applied to cases where the constitutional violation occurred after the decision. (*See, e.g., Desist* v. *United States,* 394 U.S. 244 (1969); *Morrissey* v. *Brewer,* 408 U.S. 471, 490 (1972).)

c. Retroactive Application in the Case
Announcing the Rule

Despite the fact that new constitutional rules of criminal procedure are often applied only to events which occur after the new decision, the Court has continued to apply the new rule in the very case which announced the rule. Two reasons have been given for that practice: it is necessary to reward the litigant who raises the issue, and prevails, to provide an incentive for raising the issue in the first place; refusing to apply the new rule in the case announcing it would amount to an advisory opinion, violating the case or controversy requirement of Article III of the Constitution. Whether or not those reasons are sound, the common practice of applying the rule retroactively in the decision which announces it, while refusing to apply the rule to other pending cases, has raised serious arguments about discrimination. Often, for example, a number of cases pending before the Supreme Court will raise the identical issue. The Court will hear argument in one, or a few, of those cases. The newly-announced rule will apply in those cases, and convictions will be reversed. But, in scores of pending cases which are indistinguishable, convictions will be affirmed. (Just how much a matter of chance is the question of who will be a beneficiary of a new rule is illustrated by the cases of Jessie James Gilbert. Identifications of Gilbert at a single lineup produced witnesses who testified against him in both federal and state criminal trials. On June 12, 1967, his state conviction was reversed. *Gilbert* v. *California, supra.* But, on the same day, it was decided that the rule in Gilbert's case would not be applied to other cases then pending before the Court. *Stovall* v. *Denno, supra.* Among those pending cases was Gilbert's federal conviction, involving the same lineup as well as the same constitutional argument. Thus, on the same day that Jessie James Gilbert was the "chance beneficiary" of the rule announced in his state criminal case, certiorari was denied in his federal criminal case! *Gilbert* v. *United States,* 388 U.S. 922 (1967).)

Applying the new rule retroactively in the case before the Court, while applying it only prospectively in other cases, has produced a further anomaly. Consider this problem. The Court announces a new constitutional rule of criminal procedure, and decides that it will apply only prospectively. A lower federal court is considering a case involving a different rule of law. The government seeks affirmance of the conviction on the basis of an old Supreme Court decision. The defendant argues that the new Supreme Court decision, although it deals with a different issue, logically requires the court to overrule the earlier decision. Assuming that the relevant events transpired before the more recent decision, does prospective application require the lower court to ignore even the reasoning of the new decision until it is confronted with a case where the events transpired after that decision? On the one hand, it is anomalous to apply a new decision prospectively only to cases exactly like it, but apply it retroactively to issues which are related, but different. On the other hand, applying the new decision with rigorous prospectivity requires lower courts to follow old decisions of the Supreme Court, even in cases where the lower court can predict with 100 percent accuracy that the Supreme Court itself would no longer follow them. (In other words, can it be error for the lower court to follow the "correct" constitutional rule?)

The problem just mentioned was before the Court in *United States v. White,* 401 U.S. 745 (1971). In 1952, over the dissents of Justices Douglas and Black, the Court had sustained the admissibility of evidence obtained by wiring a government informant for sound with a concealed radio transmitter. *On Lee* v. *United States,* 343 U.S. 747 (1952). In *White,* the United States Court of Appeals refused to follow *On Lee* because it had been undermined by later cases, among them *Katz* v. *United States,* 389 U.S. 347 (1967). It had been decided previously, however, that *Katz* (which held electronic eavesdropping within the Fourth Amendment's regulation of unreasonable searches and seizures) was applicable only prospectively. *Desist* v. *United States,* 394 U.S. 244 (1969). And the conversations monitored in *White* had occurred before the *Katz* decision. For that reason, a majority of the Court in *White* held that it was necessary for the Court of Appeals to judge the case by the law prior to *Katz* ! (The lineup of judges in *White* was peculiarly confusing. A plurality of four Justices also believed that *On Lee* was right and should be reaffirmed in any event. Justice Brennan concurred only on the retroactivity point, making a majority on that issue alone. Justice Black, who had dissented in *On Lee,* and who had consistently argued that new decisions should be retroactively applied, concurred in *White* on the ground that *Katz,* where he also dissented, had been wrongly decided! Because of Justice Black's cryptic concurrence, the authority of the *On Lee* decision remains a debatable point.)

The injustice of applying new constitutional rules to "chance beneficiaries" and the anomalies of such decisions as *United States v. White* have led some advocates of prospectivity to argue for "pure" prospective application — including prospective application in the case announcing the new rule. Professor Beytagh has argued that public defenders and civil liberties organizations would continue to raise constitutional issues of criminal procedure even if the defendant in the particular case was not "rewarded" by having the rule applied to his case. He argues that the advisory opinion problem could be solved by deciding cases in two stages — first deciding the appropriate rule and then, if a new rule is announced, deciding whether it is to be applied only prospectively. Professor Beytagh further argues that since, for the foreseeable future, there will be few precedent-shattering decisions announcing new rights for criminal defendants, the issue of prospective application will wane in importance. Beytagh, *Ten Years of Retroactivity: A Critique and a Proposal,* 61 VA. L. REV. 1557 (1975).

The same factors which Professor Beytagh has urged for expansion of prospective application have, however, led others to call for retrenchment or abandonment of the practice of prospective application of new constitutional decisions.

d. Criticism of Prospectivity

From *Linkletter* to the present, much discussion of prospectivity of constitutional adjudication has been tied intimately to the merits of the new rules being announced. The avowed purpose of the *Linkletter* decision was to avoid the wholesale jail delivery which might occur if all state prisoners could demand new trials where illegally seized evidence had played a part in their conviction. Thus, Justices who had disagreed with *Mapp* were more than content to limit the impact of that decision. But, as the Court expanded prospective application to apply new rules only from the date of the alleged constitutional violation, a major restraint on rapid change in the constitutional law of criminal procedure was removed. It can be argued that the activism of the Warren Court in the field of criminal procedure was due in part to the growth of the principle of prospective application. Freed from concern about the impact upon pending serious criminal cases, the Court was less reluctant to announce sweeping and revolutionary new rules governing criminal procedure. Thus, it is not surprising that some Justices who disagreed with the substantive developments began to have second thoughts about the value of prospective application. At the same time, Justices who fully supported the substantive developments could be shocked at the prospect of persons languishing in prison, despite violation of their fundamental constitutional rights. Particular decisions on prospectivity have accordingly produced unlikely voting patterns—with "conservative" Justices Brennan and Rehnquist agreeing on prospectivity, while Justices Douglas and Harlan were arguing for retroactivity.

Both Justices Douglas and Harlan have argued that prospective application of constitutional decisions strikes at the heart of the basic rationale of *Marbury* v. *Madison,* since it requires lower courts to treat statutes and overruled decisions as "law," even if they have been held to violate the Constitution. Professor Mishkin has made a similar argument:

> Despite (and perhaps also because of) its shortcomings as a description of reality, the "declaratory theory" expresses a symbolic concept of the judicial process on which much of courts' prestige and power depend. This is the strongly held and deeply

felt belief that judges are bound by a body of fixed, overriding law, that they apply that law impersonally as well as impartially, that they exercise no individual choice and have no program of their own to advance. It is easy enough for the sophisticated to show elements of naivete in this view — and no more difficult to scoff at symbols generally. But the fact remains that symbols constitute an important element in any societal structure — and that this symbolic view of courts is a major factor in securing respect for, and obedience to, judicial decisions. If the view be in part myth, it is a myth by which we live and which can be sacrificed only at substantial cost; consider, for example, the loss involved if judges could not appeal to the idea that it is "the law" or "the Constitution" — and not they personally — who command a given result.

Moreover, this symbol embodies substantial elements of truth. This is most evident in the context of routine judicial operation in the mine-run of cases. But its validity is not confined to that setting; even the highest courts, in the most novel cases, may properly be viewed as subject to the law, if "the law" is seen not simply as composed of rules and doctrines but in terms of institutions and processes of which rules and doctrines are merely a part. Judges — including Supreme Court Justices — in fact do not have completely unfettered choice, even as to issues clearly within their province. The choices they do have, though substantial and important, are still necessarily conditioned by traditions, processes, and institutions of law.

. . . .

Prospective limitation of judicial decisions wars with this symbol. . . . Prospective lawmaking is generally equated with legislation. Indeed, the conscious confrontation of the question of an effective date — even if only in the form of providing explicit affirmative justification for retroactive operation — smacks of the legislative process; for it is ordinarily taken for granted (particularly under the Blackstonian symbolic conception) that judicial decisions operate with inevitable retroactive effect. Beyond that, explicit treatment of that question, particularly if a definite time is set for transition from one rule to another, highlights the fact that the court has changed the law. And heightened consciousness of such change inevitably brings to the fore the element of judicial choice inherent in a decision to reject an old rule and establish a new one.

Mishkin, *The High Court, The Great Writ, and the Due Process of Time and Law*, 79 HARV. L. REV. 56, 62-66 (1965).*

---

e. The Criteria for Prospectivity in Criminal Procedure Cases

If for no other reason, administrative impracticality rules out prospective application for all Supreme Court decisions on issues of criminal procedure. *Mapp* v. *Ohio, Miranda* v. *Arizona* and the *Wade* and *Gilbert* cases all announced rules which broke sharply with the past — overruling past decisions or developing novel and unprecedented constitutional standards. A decision will be applied prospectively only if it establishes "a new principle of law, either by overruling clear past precedent on which litigants may have relied ... or by deciding an issue of first impression whose resolution was not clearly foreshadowed." (*Chevron Oil Co.* v. *Huson,* 404 U.S. 97, 106 (1971).) That criterion was sharply at issue in *United States* v. *Peltier,* 422 U.S. 531 (1975). Two years earlier, *Almeida-Sanchez* v. *United States,* 413 U.S. 266 (1973), had invalidated roving warrantless searches by border patrol agents. No Supreme Court cases prior to *Almeida-Sanchez* had sustained the challenged search practice, but the agents had relied upon statute and administrative regulation. The Court in *Peltier,* per Mr. Justice Rehnquist, decided nevertheless that *Almeida-Sanchez* was a "new decision" which should be applied only prospectively. The four dissenters argued strenuously that *Almeida-Sanchez* was not a "sharp break" with past precedent. Justice Brennan argued that cases like *Peltier* encouraged police to "rely" on the validity of practices of dubious constitutionality, since they had little to lose if the Court should eventually rule against them.

When will a "new decision" on constitutional issues of criminal procedure be applied retroactively? In *Linkletter,* the Court emphasized that introduction of illegally-seized physical evidence did not compromise the fact-finding process for determining guilt or innocence. The Court stated that "new decisions" which went to the fairness of the trial or the integrity of the fact-finding process would be applied retroactively. (The Court cited *Griffin* v. *Illinois,* 351 U.S. 12 (1956) (free trial transcript for indigents); *Gideon* v. *Wainwright,* 372 U.S. 355 (1963) (appointed counsel for indigent criminal defendants); *Jackson* v. *Denno,* 378 U.S. 368 (1964) (trial judge must make preliminary factual determination of voluntariness of confession).) Later cases have shown that the distinction is not so simple. A "three-pronged test" has developed: "(a) the purpose to be served by the new standards, (b) the extent of the reliance by law enforcement authorities on the old standards, and (c) the effect on the administration of justice of a retroactive application of the new standards." *Stovall* v. *Denno,* 388 U.S. 293, 297 (1967). In more recent cases, dissenters have complained that the three-pronged test is a charade and all new rules of criminal procedure will be applied prospectively if they favor criminal defendants and are not central to the integrity of the process of determining guilt or innocence at the trial. (*See Michigan* v. *Payne,* 412 U.S. 47, 61-62 (1973) (Marshall, J., dissenting) (prospectivity of rule that defendant may not be given a heavier sentence on retrial after a successful appeal merely to punish him for his successful appeal).)

Parenthetically, it should be noted that "new decisions" on issues of criminal procedure which are favorable to the prosecution have been applied retroactively. (*See Stone* v. *Powell,* 428 U.S. 465, 502, 533 (1976) (Brennan, J., dissenting) (overruling previous decisions that claims of illegal search and seizure were cognizable in federal habeas corpus).)

f. Prospectivity Beyond Issues of Constitutional Criminal Procedure

As indicated, prospectivity began as a device to prevent evacuating the jails upon announcement of a new rule of criminal procedure. And, as the cases discussed above demonstrate, most prospectivity decisions have involved decisions on constitutional criminal procedure. New decisions on other kinds of constitutional issues relating to the criminal law have been given fully retroactive application. Most prominent is the rule that a new decision holding a criminal statute unconstitutional will be applied retroactively. The government has no legitimate claim to continue to incarcerate a prisoner for violation of a law which is "void." *United States* v. *United States Coin & Currency,* 401 U.S. 715 (1971). Similar results have been reached when it is decided that the Constitution prevents imposing a particular form of punishment on the defendant (*Moore* v. *Illinois,* 408 U.S. 786 (1972) (death penalty)), or deprives the court of jurisdiction to sentence the defendant (*Robinson* v. *Neil,* 409 U.S. 505 (1973) (double jeopardy).) (*But cf. Gosa* v. *Mayden,* 413 U.S. 665 (1973) (rule forbidding military court martial for non-service-connected crimes is prospective only).)

The prospectivity doctrine has not, however, been completely confined to decisions concerning constitutional rules of criminal procedure. It has been applied to a "new decision" construing the federal rules of criminal procedure. (*Halliday* v. *United States,* 394 U.S. 831 (1969).) In constitutional law cases, prospectivity has been applied in cases involving voting rights (*Cipriano* v. *City of Houma,* 395 U.S. 701 (1969) (state law limiting participation in revenue bond elections to property owners)) and expenditures for church-related schools which violate the Establishment Clause (*Lemon* v. *Kurtzman,* 411 U.S. 192 (1973) (permitting compensation of sectarian schools for services performed prior to decisions invalidating state aid program)). Prospectivity has been applied, finally, in one private civil action involving only issues of statutory law. (*Chevron Oil Co.* v.

Huson, 404 U.S. 97 (1971) (statute of limitations in personal injury action under federal statute).)

QUESTIONS

1. Suppose four persons in different sections of the country are charged with, and convicted of, federal crimes. In all four cases, evidence is introduced against them which was discovered in the course of an airport search. All four defendants appeal on the ground that the airport search was a violation of the Fourth Amendment. United States Courts of Appeals in the First and Third Circuits affirm the convictions on the ground that the particular practice complained of does not violate the Fourth Amendment. The Second and Fourth Circuits disagree, and reverse the convictions. Defendants seek a writ of certiorari in the First and Third Circuit cases; the government applies for certiorari in the Second and Fourth Circuit cases. The United States Supreme Court grants certiorari in the First and Second Circuit cases, holding the Third and Fourth Circuit cases on its docket pending disposition of the other two cases. Eventually, the Supreme Court decides that the Second and Fourth Circuits were right — the particular practice does violate the Fourth Amendment. Accordingly, it reverses the First Circuit and affirms the Second Circuit decision. What should it now do with the Third and Fourth Circuit decisions? Should it let the Third Circuit decision, which is "wrong," stand, while it reverses the Fourth Circuit decision which is "right"?

2. Do you agree with Professor Beytagh that it would be feasible to employ "pure" prospectivity, even in the case announcing a new rule?

3. Do you agree with Professor Mishkin that rules of prospective application, particularly when applied in more than a few, exceptional cases, are destructive of the symbolic meaning of the rule of law? Are they also inconsistent with the "higher law" premise of *Marbury* v. *Madison*? In the field of constitutional law, has the United States become "more Austrian than the Germans"?

Chapter 5

INTERNATIONAL SOURCES OF HIGHER LAW

A. THE EUROPEAN COMMUNITIES

1. Introduction

a. The Structure of the EEC

European Community law is based upon three treaties, which formed the European Coal and Steel Community (ECSC) (1951), the European Economic Community (EEC) (1957), and the European Atomic Energy Community (EURATOM) (1957).

Clearly the most important of these is the EEC, which aims at the coordination of the economic, social and foreign policies of the nine members. Not merely a "free customs," commercial exchange treaty, it seeks the creation of a new community or federation of states. It also has civil liberties goals; for example, art. 119 of the treaty establishes that it is the obligation of each member state to assure "the application of the principle that men and women should receive equal pay for equal work."

Until 1973, the members of the EEC were France, West Germany, Italy, Belgium, the Netherlands, and Luxembourg. In 1973, the original six were joined by the United Kingdom, Ireland, and Denmark.

The governmental organs of the EEC (which are also, at the same time, the governmental organs of the other two Communities) are the Assembly, the Commission, the Council of Ministers, and the Court of Justice.

The Assembly, composed of members of the national parliaments elected by those parliaments, has an advisory and supervisory role with respect to the other EEC organs. It meets only a few times a year and, so far, has not assumed an important role. However, in 1979, pursuant to art. 138 (3) of the Treaty, the Assembly will become directly elected and may then begin to realize its full potential as a "European Parliament." (*See* the German Constitutional Court decision of May 29, 1974, *infra* § D.2. and the decision of the French *Conseil Constitutionnel* of December 30, 1976, *infra* § D.3.)

The Commission and the Council of Ministers possess the legislative and executive power of the EEC. The Commission has 13 members — two from each of the four major countries (France, Germany, Great Britain, and Italy), and one from each of the five

113

other members. Once appointed, the commissioners are to function as representatives of the EEC, rather than as representatives of their native countries.

The Council of Ministers is composed of nine ministers, one from each member nation, their identity depending on the issue before the Council. For example, on an agricultural issue, the nine national Ministers of Agriculture comprise the Council. The ministers act as delegates of their governments.

The Commission and Council can make and enforce regulations, directives, decisions, opinions, and recommendations. A "regulation" is a generally binding law in each member state; there is no requirement of national action for it to take effect. A "directive" is a mandatory guideline; its objective is binding on the member states, but the national governments decide how to implement it. "Decisions" are binding on the parties involved. Finally, "opinions" and "recommendations" have no binding force, but are merely advisory.

The adjudicatory organ of the EEC is the Court of Justice, composed of nine judges, who are completely independent once appointed for a term of six years "by mutual agreement between the governments of the nine member states." Under the EEC Treaty, the Court has three major areas of jurisdiction:

(1) actions brought by the Commission, or by any member state, against another member for violations of Community law (arts. 169 and 170);

(2) (a) actions by any member, the Commission, or the Council, or by any individual directly interested, against illegal actions of the Council or Commission (art. 173); or (b) similar actions for illegal omissions of the Council or Commission (art. 175);

(3) reference to the Court by a national court for an interpretation of Community law (art. 177).

Our interest in the EEC is as a source of higher law for purposes of judicial review. As you read the materials in this section, keep in mind the following potential conflicts:

(1) EEC law versus prior ordinary national law (Community law has prevailed in all member countries so far. There is no real problem here, with the possible exception of Great Britain).

(2) EEC law versus subsequent national law.

(3) EEC law versus constitutional national law.

Also, consider whether the issue of conformity of national law with Community law is a "constitutional" issue which can be decided in much of Continental Europe only by the special tribunal set up for constitutional questions, and not by the ordinary courts.

b. Overview of the Issue of Conflicts Between Community Law and National Law *

The primary question still troubling the two legal systems — Community and national — is the resolution of substantive conflicts between Community law and national law. Problems arise (a) when subsequently enacted Community law is inconsistent with national law; (b) when subsequently enacted national law conflicts with existing Community law; and (c) when a national constitutional court determines that Community law conflicts with prevailing national constitutional law. . . . There is no corollary in the Community Treaties to the Supremacy Clause of the United States Constitution. Thus, while the Court of Justice has consistently adopted the view of the supremacy of Community law, such a doctrine also requires acceptance by the national legal systems.

The Court views supremacy as the legal foundation of the Communities "without which its legal order could not function effectively." This judicial assertion of the supremacy of Community law is responsive to the unique legal and political order created by the Treaties and to the mutual submission to the rule of Community law that is implicit in the Treaties. The Court has advanced the doctrine of the supremacy of Community law primarily on the ground that Community law exists as an independent legal order created by the limitation of the sovereignty of the Member States and by a limited transfer of sovereignty to the Community. A national court, according to the Court of Justice, participates simultaneously in two separate legal orders — the Community legal system and its own national legal systems.

In the Court's view, the legal order created by the Treaties is unlike any other legal order and requires a different manner of assimilation into the national legal system than either traditional international law or foreign law. Thus, although the domestic law of a Member State governs its manner of applying foreign law in its decisions (for example, when national conflicts law requires the court to apply the law of a foreign jurisdiction) such rules would not govern the application of Community law within the national legal system. Similarly, national law may govern the application of international law within a member state, determining the rank of international law in relation to national law, without, however, limiting in any way the sovereignty of the national legal order. Community law should not, under the doctrine of supremacy formulated by the Court of Justice, be assimilated into international law. Unlike international law, Community law is to be applied within the Member States as a

---

* Excerpted from Hay & Thompson, *The Community Court and Supremacy of Community Law: A Progress Report,* 8 VAND. J. OF TRANSNAT'L L. 651, 659-64, 667-68 (1975). Reprinted with permission.

superior legal order over which unilateral national law *cannot* prevail. Although the Court more frequently upholds the supremacy of Community law on the basis that Community law is a separate and superior legal order created by the transfer of certain powers to the Community from the member states, the Court also considers the supremacy of Community law when it declares provisions of Community law to be directly applicable in the Member States since the direct applicability of the Community law confers on private parties direct rights or obligations under Community law, which can be litigated in national courts.

...The Court has ruled that Community law prevails over subsequently enacted national law, and in a decision under article 169 the Court reaffirmed its position that Community law prevails over national law under all circumstances. The case law of the Court and its formulation of the doctrine of supremacy has been embraced by some national courts and resisted by others. Setting aside for the moment situations in which Community law conflicts with prior national constitutional law, a conflict between national law and subsequently enacted Community law, whether primary or secondary, has generally been resolved by national courts in favor of Community law. Unfortunately, these decisions have been resolved too frequently on the traditional ground that subsequently enacted law impliedly repeals a prior inconsistent law, which results in a correct solution but for the wrong reasons. This resolution and the accompanying rationale ignore the Community Court's theory of separate legal orders since it places Community law and national law on an equal plane; logically extended, it would obviously mandate supremacy of subsequently enacted national law over prior Community law, in derogation of the doctrine of supremacy.

. . . .

Conflicts between Community law and national law can also arise when Community law is inconsistent with *subsequently* enacted national law, as mentioned earlier. Again, "supremacy" and the Court's view require that the application of Community law should not depend on any priority of time, but rather should result from the nature of Community law as a separate, and higher, legal order.

. . . .

In another context supremacy has become a major problem in Italy and Germany, the two Member States that have constitutional courts empowered to review legislative acts for their conformity with constitutional standards. The issue of how national constitutional guarantees should fit into the Community legal framework or, indeed, be protected against intrusion by Community law has been keenly debated in both countries.

... The Community legal process is admittedly not democratic in the accepted sense of the term. Community law, other than the original Treaty provisions, which *were* examined by national parliaments as part of the ratification procedure, emanates either from the Council (cabinet ministers of the Member States), the Commission (consisting of independent international civil servants), or a combination of the two. The European Parliament, composed of national parliamentarians not directly elected to the European Parliament, enjoys only an advisory role in law-making. "Law" thus emanates from a technocracy, and the German [Constitutional Court's] decision * is the first official articulation of concern over what this kind of law-making may mean for individual citizens who enjoy the protection of national constitutional guarantees when national law-making is involved.

At the same time, it must be remembered that the Communities act mainly in the economic, social and technical spheres, all areas in which the infringement of fundamental rights seemingly would occur only rarely.

2. *Costa v. ENEL*

a. *In the Italian Corte Costituzionale* **

CASE 6/64

COSTA v. ENEL

Court of Justice of the European Communities
10 Rec. 1143 (1964); [1964] C.M.L.R. 425 [144]

Under Law No. 1643 of 6 December 1962 and subsequent decrees, the Italian Republic nationalized the production and distribution of electric energy and created an organization, the Ente Nazionale per l'Energia Elettrica (or ENEL), to which was transferred the property of the electricity [companies].

Sig. Flaminio Costa, an advocate in Milan and a shareholder of Edisonvolta, a firm which had been affected by the nationalization, claimed that he was not liable for a bill amounting to 1,925 lire (roughly $3.08) sent to him for electricity supplied to him by ENEL. In proceedings before the Giudice Conciliatore (Justice of the Peace) of Milan . . . Avv. Costa claimed that the Nationalization Law of 6 December 1962 was contrary to the Italian Constitution and also contrary to a number of provisions of the EEC Treaty. In particular, he alleged: . . . .

---

* *Internationale Handelsgesellschaft mbH v. Einfuhr- & Vorratsstelle für Getreide & Futtermittel,* [1974] 2 C.M.L.R. 540, reprinted § D.2., *infra.*

** From STEIN, HAY & WAELBROECK, EUROPEAN COMMUNITY LAW AND INSTITUTIONS IN PERSPECTIVE 202-06 (1976). Reprinted with permission.

[144] Revised and reprinted with permission of Common Law Reports, Limited, London.

(b) that as an Italian national, and in addition as a shareholder of Edisonvolta, he had an interest in the payment for the supply of electricity being made to the latter company;

(c) that he did not [intend] to pay the sum to ENEL because the Law that created it, and the regulations issued under delegated authority relating to the transfer of other electricity companies to it, were [unconstitutional].

He thereupon successfully requested the judge to refer the case, for preliminary opinions, to both the Italian Constitutional Court and, under Article 177 of the EEC Treaty, to the European Court.

Reference to the Constitutional Court

By order of 10 September 1963, the Milan judge, after remarking that Edisonvolta had not entered an appearance and that the only questions of constitutional importance liable to affect the proceedings before him were those regarding the lawful [establishment] of ENEL, put five questions to the Constitutional Court. These related to five different grounds for alleging the constitutional invalidity of the Law of 6 December 1962; [the Law had been alleged to violate]:

. . . .

(5) Article 11 [145] of the Constitution, in that the whole of the Law conflicts with the following provisions of the EEC Treaty: Article 102, inasmuch as the Law, before being passed, should have been submitted for examination by the EEC Commission; Article 93(3), inasmuch as the Law considers as lawful the aids which the Treaty forbids, and in particular because in Article 4(11) it envisages a more favorable treatment for the Acciaierie di Terni; Article 53, inasmuch as that Article prevents the introduction of new restrictions on the principle of freedom of establishment; and Article 37(2), inasmuch as the Law created a national monopoly.

The order of the Milan judge was notified to the parties, to the President of the Council of Ministers and to the Presidents of both Chambers of Parliament on various dates between 23rd September and 3rd October and was published in the Official Gazette of the Republic on 2 November 1963.

Reference to the European Court

By order of 16 January 1964, the Milan judge decided as follows:

"In view of Article 177 of the Treaty of 25 March 1957 instituting the EEC, incorporated in Italian law by Law No. 1203

---

[145] Art. 11 provides: "Italy agrees, on conditions of equality with other States, to the limitations of sovereignty necessary for an order which is to insure peace and justice among nations and promotes and encourages international organizations directed toward this purpose."

of 14 October 1957, and in view of the allegation that Law No. 1643 of 6 December 1962 and the presidential decrees issued in execution of this Law (No. 1679 of 15 December 1962, No. 36 of 4 February 1963, No. 138 of 25 February 1963 and No. 219 of 14 March 1963) violate Articles 102, 93, 53, and 37 of the aforementioned Treaty, the proceedings are suspended and a certified copy of the file is ordered to be transmitted to the Court of Justice of the EEC at Luxembourg.''

JUDGMENT OF THE CORTE COSTITUZIONALE (March 7, 1964) [146]

. . . . [Reliance is placed on the provision of] Article 11 that Italy agrees, under conditions of parity with other States, to such limitations of sovereignty as are necessary for the establishment of an order that will ensure peace and justice amongst nations; and [that] it will promote and favor international organizations for this purpose.

This means that, given certain circumstances, it is possible to stipulate treaties as a result of which we accept certain limitations [upon] our sovereignty and it is quite lawful to give effect to such treaties by means of an ordinary law; but this does not result in any deviation from the existing rule relating to the efficacy, within national law, of the obligations undertaken by the State in connection with its relations with other States, since Article 11 did not confer a greater effect upon the ordinary Law that gives effect to a treaty. Nor can we agree with the view according to which any Law containing provisions differing from those of international treaties is unlawful . . . [under] Article 11. . . .

Quite often this Court has declared unlawful certain provisions of legislative decrees that did not correspond with the Law that granted delegated powers to issue them, relating the cause of illegality to a violation of Article 76 of the Constitution.

But the situation is quite different as regards that part of Article 11 [which contains] the provision [under consideration here]. Article 76 lays down certain rules regarding the exercise of a delegated legislative function and for this reason non-compliance with the principles of the delegating Law results in [a] violation of Article 76. Article 11, on the other hand, inasmuch as it is considered as a permissive provision, ascribes no particular significance to a Law giving execution to an international treaty as opposed to any other Law.

Nor is there any validity in the other argument, according to which the State, once it has agreed to limitations [upon] its own sovereignty, could not pass [a] Law withdrawing such limitations and

[146] 87 FORO ITALIANO I, 465 (1964); 116 GIUR. ITAL. I, 516 (1964); SENTENZE E ORDINANZE DELLA CORTE COSTITUZIONALE 82 (1964).

restoring its freedom of action, without [violating] the Constitution. Against this can be set our foregoing remarks . . . that the violation of a treaty, even if it results in [liability of the State under international law] does not detract from the [internal] validity of [the] conflicting Law.

There is no doubt that the State is bound to honor its obligations, just as there is no doubt that an international treaty is fully effective in so far as a Law has given execution to it. But with regard to such Law . . . [it is also true that] subsequent laws [must prevail] in accordance with the principles governing the succession of laws in time; it follows that any conflict between the one and the other cannot give rise to [a] constitutional [question].

From the foregoing we reach the conclusion that for present purposes there is no point [in] dealing with the character of the EEC and with the consequences that derive from the Law giving effect to the Treaty creating the EEC; nor is it necessary to question whether the Law that is being attacked before us has violated the obligations undertaken by virtue of the Treaty aforesaid. It follows from this that the question regarding the remission of the file to the Court of Justice of the European Community, and the relevant question of jurisdiction, do not even arise.

For all these reasons this Court declares that any question [of] the constitutional legality of the Law of 6 December 1962 No. 1643 (creating ENEL), raised by the order before it in connection with Article 3, Article 4, Article 41, Article 43, and Article 67 of the Constitution, is unfounded.

NOTE AND QUESTION

Whether an ordinary treaty is received into a nation's domestic law without the need for enabling legislation, and whether a treaty prevails over subsequently-enacted domestic law, are, themselves, questions of domestic law. From country to country, that domestic law is not uniform. In the United States, a treaty which is by its terms self-executing becomes the law of the land without the necessity of a separate enabling statute. This is pursuant to Art. VI, section 2, of the Constitution, which provides that the "Constitution, and the Laws of the United States which shall be made in Pursuance thereof; and all Treaties made, or which shall be made, under the Authority of the United States, shall be the supreme Law of the Land . . . ." Chief Justice Marshall explained the legal significance of the Supremacy Clause in 1829 as follows: *

A treaty is in its nature a contract between two nations, not a

---

* *Foster* v. *Neilson,* 27 U.S. (2 Pet.) 253, 313-14 (1829).

legislative act. It does not generally effect, of itself, the object
to be accomplished . . . .

In the United States a different principle is established. Our
constitution declares a treaty to be the law of the land. It is,
consequently, to be regarded in courts of justice as equivalent
to an act of the legislature, whenever it operates of itself without
the aid of any legislative provision.

On the other hand, a treaty and an Act of Congress stand on equal
footing in the internal law of the United States. Accordingly, if the
treaty conflicts with a federal statute, the last in time prevails.*

Without amendment to the Constitution, would it be possible in
the United States to subordinate later statutes to a treaty obligation?

b. In the European Court of Justice: **

. . . .

Regarding the application of Article 177
Plea based on the wording of the question
There is a complaint to the effect that the question involved seeks
a judgment, by virtue of Article 177, as to whether a law is in
accordance with the Treaty.

Under that article, however, national courts whose decisions are,
as in the instant case, unappealable, must refer to the Court of Justice
for a preliminary ruling on the interpretation of the Treaty when such
a question is raised before them. Under this provision, the Court of
Justice may neither apply the Treaty to a specific case nor rule on
the validity of an internal measure in relation to the Treaty, as it could
do within the framework of Article 169. It can, however, sift out from
a request that has been improperly formulated by a national court
those questions only that concern the application of the Treaty. Thus
the Court need not rule on the validity of an Italian law in relation
to the Treaty, but need only interpret the above-mentioned articles
in the light of the legal data submitted by the Giudice Conciliatore.

Plea based on the absence of any need for interpretation
There is a complaint to the effect that the Milan court requested
an interpretation of the Treaty that is not needed to settle the action
brought before it. Article 177, however, based as it is on a clear
separation of functions between the national courts and the Court
of Justice, does not authorize the latter either to consider the facts

---

* *Whitney* v. *Robertson*, 124 U.S. 190, 194 (1888); *The Chinese Exclusion Case*,
130 U.S. 581, 600 (1889).

** The following is from [1961-1966 Transfer Binder] COMM. MKT. REP. (CCH)
§ 8023, at 7390-98. Reproduced with permission from the translation appearing in
COMMON MARKET REPORTS, published and copyrighted by Commerce Clearing
House, Inc., Chicago, Illinois.

in the case or to judge the reasons or objectives of the request for interpretation.

Plea based on the judge's duty to apply internal law

The *Italian Government* claims that the request of the Giudice Conciliatore is "absolutely inadmissible" because the national court cannot make use of Article 177, since it is bound to apply an internal law.

Unlike ordinary international treaties, the EEC Treaty established its own legal order, which was incorporated into the legal systems of the Member States at the time the Treaty came into force and to which the courts of the Member States are bound. In fact, by establishing a Community of unlimited duration, having its own institutions, personality and legal capacity, the ability to be represented on the international level and, particularly, real powers resulting from a limitation of the jurisdiction of the States or from a transfer of their powers to the Community, the States relinquished, albeit in limited areas, their sovereign rights and thus created a body of law applicable to their nationals and to themselves.

This incorporation into the law of each member country of provisions of a Community origin, and the letter and spirit of the Treaty in general, have as a corollary the impossibility for the States to assert as against a legal order accepted by them on a reciprocal basis a subsequent unilateral measure which could not be challenged by it. The executory power of Community law cannot, in fact, vary from one State to another because of subsequent internal laws without jeopardizing fulfillment of the Treaty objectives set forth in Article 5, paragraph 2, and without bringing about a discrimination prohibited by Article 7. The obligations agreed to in the Treaty establishing the EEC would not be unconditional, only contingent, if they could be challenged by future legislative acts of the signatories. Wherever a right to act unilaterally is given to the States it is by virtue of a specific special clause (for example, Articles 15, 93(3), and 223-225). On the other hand, requests by the States for exceptions are subject to authorization procedures (for example, Articles 8(4), 17(4), 25, 26, 73, 93(2), third subparagraph, and 226) that would be purposeless if it were possible for the States to side-step their obligations through a mere law.

The preeminence of Community law is confirmed by Article 189, under which regulations are "binding" and "directly applicable in each Member State." This provision, which contains no reservation, would be meaningless if a Member State could unilaterally nullify its effects through a legislative act that could be asserted as against the Community texts.

As a result of all these factors, it would be impossible legally to assert any internal text whatsoever against the law created by the Treaty and originating from an independent source, considering the specific original nature of that law, without robbing it of its Community nature and without jeopardizing the legal foundation of the Community itself. The transfer by the States from their internal legal systems over to the Community legal order, of rights and obligations to reflect those set forth in the Treaty, therefore entails a definitive limitation of their sovereign rights, against which a subsequent unilateral act that would be incompatible with the Community concept cannot be asserted. Thus Article 177 may be applied, notwithstanding any national law, where there is a question of Treaty interpretation.

The questions submitted by the Giudice Conciliatore regarding Articles 102, 93, 53 and 37 seek, to begin with, an answer to whether these provisions have an immediate effect or create for those subject to a State's laws rights which the domestic courts must safeguard and if so, what these rights are.

Regarding the interpretation of Article 102

Under Article 102, where "there is reason to fear" that the introduction of a legislative provision may cause a "distortion," the Member State wishing to introduce such provision "shall consult the Commission," which may then recommend to the States such measures as may be appropriate to avoid such distortion.

This article, which belongs to the chapter on "approximation of laws," seeks to avoid an increase in the divergencies between the national laws with regard to the Treaty objectives. Through this provision, the Member States have limited their freedom of initiative by agreeing to comply with a suitable consultation procedure. By clearly putting themselves under the obligation to consult the Commission, for preventive purposes, whenever the proposed legislation might create even a minor risk of possible distortion, the States have thus entered into an agreement with the Community that binds them as States, but does not give rise to rights for those subject to their laws which the domestic courts must safeguard.

The Commission, for its part, is bound to see to it that the provisions of this article are respected, but this duty does not give individuals a possibility to allege, within the framework of Community law and through Article 177, either a default of the State concerned, or a failure on the part of the Commission.

Regarding the interpretation of Article 93

Under paragraphs 1 and 2 of Article 93, the Commission shall, in conjunction with the Member States, "submit to constant examination all systems of aids existing in those States" so as to put into operation the appropriate measures required by the functioning of the Common Market. Under paragraph 3 of Article 93, the Commission must be informed, in sufficient time, of any plans to grant or modify grants of aids, and the Member State concerned may not put the proposed measures into effect before completion of the

Community procedure and, where applicable, of the proceedings before the Court of Justice.

The purpose of these provisions, which belong under the section of the Treaty devoted to "aids granted by the States," is, on the one hand, gradually to do away with existing aids and, on the other hand, to prevent the introduction in any form of new aids likely to favor, directly or indirectly, to a significant extent, either enterprises or products and their constituting even a possible risk of distortion of competition. In Article 92, the States recognized that the aids in question were incompatible with the Common Market and thus implicitly agreed not to introduce any such aids except for derogations provided by the Treaty, whereas under Article 93 they merely agreed to submit to suitable procedures for the abolition of existing aids or for the introduction of new aids. By thus formally agreeing to inform the Commission "in sufficient time" regarding proposed aids, and by agreeing to submit to the procedures provided in Article 93, the States entered into an agreement with the Community which binds them as States but grants no rights to those subject to their laws, except in the last provision of paragraph 3 of that article, which has nothing to do with the instant case.

The Commission, for its part, is bound to see to it that the provisions of this article are respected, and under this article it must even, in conjunction with the States, submit existing systems of aids to constant examination, but this duty does not confer upon individuals the right to allege, within the framework of Article 177, either a default of the State concerned or a failure on the part of the Commission.

Regarding the interpretation of Article 53

Under Article 53, the Member States agree, without prejudice to other Treaty provisions, not to introduce any new restrictions on the establishment in their territories of nationals of other Member States. The duty thus subscribed to by the States amounts legally to a simple abstention. It is not subject to any condition, and neither its execution nor its effects require the enactment of any legislation either by the States or by the Commission. It is, therefore, complete, legally perfect, and consequently capable of producing direct effects in relations between the Member States and the persons under their jurisdiction.

A prohibition so clearly expressed, which came into force with the Treaty throughout the Community and was thus incorporated into the legal systems of the Member States, is law in these States and is of direct concern to their nationals, for whose benefit it has created individual rights which the domestic courts must safeguard.

The requested interpretation of Article 53 makes it imperative that it be considered within the context of the chapter relating to the right of establishment in which it is located. After having ordered, in

Article 52, the gradual abolition of "restrictions on the freedom of establishment of nationals of a Member State in the territory of another Member State," the chapter in question provides in Article 53 that these States shall not introduce any "new restrictions on the establishment, in their territories, of nationals of the other Member States." The question, therefore, is under what conditions the nationals of the other Member States enjoy freedom of establishment. Article 52, paragraph 2, is explicit on this point in that it stipulates that freedom of establishment shall include the right to engage in non-wage-earning activities, to set up and manage enterprises "under the conditions laid down for its own nationals by the law of the country where such establishment is effected." In order for Article 53 to be respected, it is therefore sufficient that no new measure make the establishment of nationals of other Member States subject to stricter rules than those laid down for a State's own nationals, regardless of the legal make-up of the enterprises.

Regarding the interpretation of Article 37

Under Article 37, paragraph 1, the Member States shall gradually adjust any "State trading monopolies" so as to ensure that no discrimination exists between the nationals of the Member States with regard to supply and marketing. In addition, it provides, in paragraph 2, a duty for these States to abstain from introducing any new measure which is contrary to this provision.

Thus the States have agreed to two obligations: the one, active, to adjust their State monopolies, and the other, passive, to avoid taking any new measure. This latter obligation is the one for which an interpretation is requested, as is an interpretation of the factors of the first obligation that are necessary for this interpretation.

Article 37, paragraph 2, lays down an unconditional prohibition which constitutes, not an obligation to do, but an obligation not to do. This obligation is not accompanied by any reservation that its execution depends on a positive act of internal law. By its very nature, this prohibition can produce direct effects in the legal relationship between the Member States and the persons under their jurisdiction.

A prohibition so clearly expressed, that has come into force with the Treaty throughout the entire Community and has therefore been incorporated into the legal systems of the Member States, is the very law of these States and is of direct concern to their nationals, for whose benefit it entails individual rights which the national courts must safeguard.

The requested interpretation of Article 37, because of the complex nature of the text and the interrelationship between paragraphs 1 and 2, makes it imperative that the latter be considered within the framework of the entire chapter of which they are a part. This chapter is devoted to the "elimination of quantitative restrictions between the Member States."

Thus the purpose of the reference in Article 37, paragraph 2, to the "principles laid down in paragraph 1" is to prevent the introduction of any new "discrimination between the nationals of Member States as regards the supply or marketing of goods." This purpose having been specified, Article 37, paragraph 1, describes and prohibits the means by which this purpose might be thwarted. Thus all new monopolies or organizations referred to in Article 37, paragraph 1, are prohibited by the reference in Article 37, paragraph 2, in so far as they tend to introduce new discriminations as to supply and marketing. The judge in the original action must therefore first investigate whether this purpose is actually thwarted, i.e., whether the measure at issue itself results in a new discrimination between the nationals of the Member States as to supply and marketing, or whether this will be a consequence of the measure.

In addition, there is reason to consider the means referred to in Article 37, paragraph 1. This article prohibits the introduction, not of all State monopolies, but of "trading" monopolies, in so far as they tend to introduce the above-mentioned discriminations. In order to come within the prohibition of this provision, the State monopolies and the organizations in question must, on the one hand, have as their purpose transactions in a commercial product that is likely to be the object of competition and of trade between the Member States and, on the other hand, play an active part in such trade. It is for the judge in the original action to decide in each case whether the economic activity concerned involves a certain product which, by its nature and because of technical or international requirements, to which it is subject, can play an active part in imports or exports between the nationals of the Member States.

As to costs

The costs incurred by the Commission and by the Italian Government, which submitted their comments to the Court, cannot be reimbursed. In this instance, with respect to the parties in the action pending before the Giudice Conciliatore of Milan, the proceedings are in the nature of an incidental matter raised before that judge.

[Ruling]

FOR THESE REASONS,

. . . .

THE COURT, ruling on the plea of inadmissibility based on Article 177, declares and decrees:

The questions submitted by the Giudice Conciliatore of Milan by virtue of Article 177 are admissible in so far as they concern, in this case, an interpretation of the provisions of the EEC Treaty, since no subsequent unilateral act can be asserted against the rules of the Community;

rules as follows:

(1) Article 102 contains no provisions capable of entailing for those subject to the law rights which the domestic courts must safeguard;

(2) Likewise, those portions of Article 93 relating to the question posed contain no such provisions;

(3) Article 53 constitutes a Community rule capable of entailing for those subject to the law rights which the domestic courts must safeguard.

These provisions prohibit any new measure whose object is to make the establishment of nationals of other Member States subject to stricter rules than those reserved for those subject to the law, regardless of the legal make-up of the enterprises.

(4) All of the provisions of Article 37, paragraph 2, constitute a Community rule capable of entailing for those subject to the law rights which the domestic courts must safeguard.

Within the framework of the question presented, the object of these provisions is to prohibit any new measure that is contrary to the principles of Article 37, paragraph 1, i.e., any measure, the object or effect of which is a new discrimination between the nationals of the Member States as to supply and marketing, through monopolies or organizations that must, on the one hand, have as their object transactions in a commercial product that can involve competition and trade between Member States and, on the other hand, play an active part in such trade;

and decides:

It is for the Giudice Conciliatore of Milan to rule on the costs of this action.

Thus ruled at Luxembourg, July 15, 1964.

Read in open court at Luxembourg, July 15, 1964.

<table>
<tr><td>The Registrar</td><td>The President</td></tr>
<tr><td>A. VAN HOUTTE</td><td>A. M. DONNER</td></tr>
</table>

CONCLUSIONS

of Advocate General Maurice Lagrange

Hearing of June 25, 1964.

. . . .

[Conflict between National and Community Law]

[T]he problem is that of the *co-existence of two (hypothetically) contradictory legal norms that are equally applicable in the internal legal system,* the one originating from the Treaty or the Community institutions, and the other from national authorities: which one shall prevail as long as the conflict has not been eliminated? That is the question.

Without wishing to fall back on doctrinary concepts, which are far too controversial, on the nature of the European Communities, or to take sides between a "federal Europe" and a "Europe of nations," or between "supranational" and "international," the judge (this is his function) can only consider the Treaty as it is. The Treaty establishing the EEC — this is simply a statement of fact — like the other two European treaties, creates its own *legal order,* separate from the legal order of each of the Member States, but which takes its place to some extent according to exact rules laid down by the Treaty itself — rules that consist in *transfers of jurisdiction,* which have been agreed to, to common institutions.

[Ways of Giving Effect to EEC Law]

In order to keep to the question of norms, it is universally conceded that the EEC Treaty, albeit to a far lesser extent than the ECSC Treaty, contains a number of provisions whose nature and purpose makes them directly applicable in the internal legal order into which they have been "received" as a result of the ratification (a procedure which, in any case, is not limited to the European treaties). Thus you yourselves have recognized this "self-executing" character, to use the accepted expression, with regard to Article 12 and Article 31, when specifying that those were provisions that *had immediate effects and created individual rights which the domestic courts must safeguard.* As for provisions that do not have such a direct effect, these become part of the internal legal order in two different ways, depending on whether or not the Community's executive institutions (the Council or the Commission or, as is more often the case, the two acting as a unit with the intervention of the European Parliament) have or have not been given the power to issue a regulation. When such is not the case, then there is an obligation to be carried out by a Member State, either spontaneously or pursuant to recommendations or directives of the executives, and the Treaty becomes part of the internal legal order only through internal measures taken by the competent bodies of the State in question. When, on the other hand, the Community executives have the power to issue a regulation, and they use this power, incorporation into the internal order takes place automatically as a result of the publication of the regulation: this is due most obviously to the combined provisions of Article 189, paragraph 2, and of Article 191. Under Article 189, paragraph 2, "regulations shall have general application. They shall be binding in all their parts and *directly applicable in each*

Member State." Under Article 191, "the regulations shall be published in the Official Journal of the Community. *They shall come into force* on the date provided for in them or, failing this, on the twentieth day following their publication."

[Directly Applicable Provisions]

Thus two types of provisions are considered directly applicable:
(1) those Treaty provisions that are considered "self-executing;" and
(2) those that have become the subject of implementing regulations.

. . . .

It is thus impossible to escape the problem resulting from the coexistence, in each Member State, of two legal orders — the internal order and the Community order — each one operating in its own jurisdictional sphere, or, therefore, the question of how far the jurisdiction of one might encroach on the other.

For encroachments arising out of actions of Community institutions, there is no problem: they would be sanctioned by the Court through one of the procedures provided in the Treaty for the benefit of the Member States as well as for the benefit of individuals, particularly through the appeal for annulment (Article 173) and the exception of illegality (Article 184).

As for encroachments arising out of actions of the national authorities, *they too must be sanctioned,* not only for the benefit of the Member States, but also for the benefit of individuals when they have individual rights derived from the Treaty or from the Community regulations. As the Court has pointed out, it is for the domestic courts to safeguard these rights.

. . . .

[Decision of Italian Constitutional Court]

. . . .

It is, of course, not for us to analyze this decision. We shall say only (even though we say it rather emphatically) that the Constitutional Court concerns itself with the conflict between the law in question and the ratification *law,* whereas it is really a matter of conflict between the law and the *Treaty* (ratified by an ordinary law). But what we wish to emphasize is the disastrous — the term is not too strong — consequences that such a decision, if it were upheld, might have on the operation of the institutional system established by the Treaty and, therefore, on the very future of the Common Market.

In fact, we believe that we have proved that this system is based on the establishment of a legal order that is separate from that of the Member States, but closely, even organically, related to it, so that consistent mutual respect between the respective authorities of the Community institutions and the national institutions is one of the basic conditions for an operation of the system that is in keeping with the Treaty and therefore for the realization of the Community objectives. We have seen, in particular, that this mutual respect demands that the self-executing provisions of the Treaty and the regulations properly adopted by the Community executives be applied immediately in the Member States. Such is the legal order set up by the Treaty of Rome and it is for the Court of Justice, and for it alone, to state this in its decisions where necessary.

If it should happen that a constitutional judge of one of the Member States, in the exercise of his full jurisdiction, should come to recognize that such a result cannot be reached within the framework of the constitutional norms of his country, for instance with respect to ordinary laws in conflict with the Treaty, that are allegedly superior to the Treaty itself, without any judge (not even a constitutional judge) having the power to stay their application as long as they had not been abrogated or modified by Parliament, such a decision would create a conflict between the two legal orders that would be absolutely impossible to settle and that would shake the very foundations of the Treaty. Not only would it be impossible to apply the Treaty, under the conditions it has provided, in the country concerned, but, through a chain reaction, it would most likely not be any more possible to apply it in the other countries of the Community. This would, in any event, be the case in those countries (such as France) where international agreements have priority only "on condition of reciprocity."

Under the circumstances, there appear to be only two possible solutions for the State in question: either to amend the Constitution to make it compatible with the Treaty, or to denounce the latter. In fact, that State, in signing the Treaty, in ratifying it and in depositing its instruments of ratification, has committed itself vis-à-vis its partners and could not remain inactive without being derelict in its international obligations. Hence, one can understand why the Commission which, by virtue of Article 155, has been given the task of seeing to the application of the Treaty, informed the Court in its comments of the "strong apprehension" it feels with respect to the decree of February 24, 1964.

. . . .

NOTES AND QUESTIONS

1. After the decision of the European Court of Justice, the Milan Justice of the Peace held Law No. 1643 to be in conflict with art. 37 of the EEC Treaty. The judgment decreed that plaintiff did not owe the defendant 1,925 lire, and held the defendant liable for 620,000 lire in costs. [1966] Foro It. I, 938, [1968] 7 C.M.L.R. 267. The decision was reversed by the Court of Cassation on the ground that plaintiff lacked standing under Italian law. [1970] Foro It. I, 765-71.

(Notice that the European Court in *Costa* stated that referral to it was mandatory under art. 177 because the Conciliatore of Milan was a court of last resort. This was incorrect. While true under the Italian Code of Civil Procedure, this had been superseded by the Italian Constitution, which provided for recourse in Cassation as a matter of right.)

2. The precise controversy in the *Costa* case was not important. The amount in controversy was about three dollars and the Court of Justice decided only an abstract question of principle without saying whether or not the Italian nationalization statute of 1962 was in conflict with the treaty. The Milan Justice of the Peace was unable to do more than decide the three dollar controversy, with no effect whatsoever on the real issue at stake — the validity of the 1962 statute.

Yet the *Costa* decision is extremely significant with reference to the status of EEC law:

(a) It indicated that, in addition to questions of constitutionality — reserved to the exclusive jurisdiction of the Constitutional Court — there was a new type of higher law question emerging from Community law.

(b) The Court of Justice clearly affirmed the superiority of Community law *vis-à-vis* national legislation, including posterior legislation.

3. If the Milan Court was convinced that Italian law did conflict with EEC law, should it have followed the direction of the Italian *Corte Costituzionale* or the instructions of the European Court? Notice that the *Corte Costituzionale* held that conflict of the statute with EEC law was not a constitutional question (and thus not to be decided by that court), and then in dictum stated that EEC law should not be treated as superior law. However, it was the holding of the European Court that EEC law must prevail.

4. Is there a *Marbury* doctrine emerging in Europe, with decentralized review of legislation for conformity with Community law? Since the *Corte Costituzionale* held that such conformity was not a constitutional issue and thus not for that court to decide, must the question then be decided by ordinary courts? This was, in fact, the conclusion reached by the Court of Cassation in the Decision of October 6, 1972, No. 2896, following a precedent of May 21, 1971 by the Belgian Court of Cassation. (Compare the later development in France represented by the *Cafés Jacques Vabre* decision, § C.2., *infra*.)

5. We have seen that the difficulty of implementing decentralized judicial review in continental Europe stemmed from such problems as a lack of *stare decisis,* the composite structure of the ordinary supreme courts, and the nature of the career judiciary. Are these problems mitigated in the case of Community Law? An interpretation by the European Court of Justice, although rendered in an abstract way, is binding on all domestic courts. The accepted doctrine is that the national courts must accept such an interpretation or request a new ruling by the European Court. Only the Court of Justice can overrule itself. Moreover, the Court of Justice is not a composite court, but is composed of nine judges, who are not career judges but are appointed by the national governments.

Similar arguments could be made in Italy, Germany, and Austria with respect to constitutional issues and their Constitutional Courts. Yet, ordinary courts are not permitted to decide constitutional issues, even in the first instance and subject to review by the constitutional courts. Why not?

6. What will the effect of the *Costa* developments be in Great Britain, with its strong tradition of parliamentary supremacy? That issue is considered in the next section of this chapter.

3. Community Law and Great Britain

a. An Initial View by a British Scholar *

We are now to enter a new sort of international club where the rules require more than mere restraint: they require the integration of two legal systems which may conflict at many points. Our obligation is to ensure that community law is paramount. But how can it be paramount when, like the rest of our law, it is at the mercy of any future Act of Parliament which must, under the fundamental rule of our constitution, prevail over any pre-existing law whatsoever? It is unrealistic to suppose that conflicts will not occur — one need only look at the many cases already in the Common Market Law Reports.

. . . .

[A]s we rehearse our part for the concert of Europe we comfort ourselves by saying "it will all be all right on the night."

. . . .

If we are to be good Europeans, we must surely offer some security against undermining the European legal order ourselves. It would be quite unreasonable to leave it to our judiciary to refuse to apply future Acts of Parliament, when in conflict with Community law, by

---

* Excerpted from Wade, *Sovereignty and the European Communities,* 88 L.Q. REV. 1, 3-5 (1972). Reprinted with permission of Sweet and Maxwell Ltd., London.

some spontaneous constitutional volte-face of their own. Nor is there any necessity to do so, since there are several ways in which we can give pre-eminence to Community law within the constitution as it stands. The problem ought therefore to be attacked at the technical level: how can we most suitably adjust our existing system so as to secure full respect for the new legal order which in principle we accept?

One expedient would be a European Communities (Annual) Act, by which Parliament would once a year assert the supremacy of Community law and so resolve intervening conflicts at regular intervals. It might even be justifiable to give such Acts retrospective effect, so that litigants would know that it would be useless to disregard Community law even during the yearly interval. Alternatively, and preferably, some small change should be made in the format of every Act of Parliament passed after our own Act of Accession, so as to give to each one the stamp of the new legal order. The conventional words of enactment might be altered, or some short formula added at the end such as "this Act conforms to the European Communities." The Act of Accession would provide that this form of words would be taken to mean that the Act was subject to Community law. Most major Acts now include the provision that regulations under the Act shall be made by statutory instrument. Just as that provision incorporates the machinery of the Statutory Instruments Act 1946, so the new words would signify Parliament's intention to respect Community law as a matter of course. Then in truth there would be no constitutional innovation: Parliament would be able to revert to the old form at any time if it wished, in legal theory if not in political reality. Nor ought objection to be made to a small change in the mode of legislation. It is only natural that a new legal order should require new legal forms.

There are indeed some who suggest that Parliament has, or can acquire, power to bind its successors, so that the Act of Accession could effectively safeguard Community law against subsequent statutes. The weakness of all such theories is that they are merely predictions of what judges might decide in unprecedented future situations, and that they assume that judges will then say something quite different from what they have clearly and consistently said hitherto: that the latest expression of Parliament's will is supreme. In a country which has no overriding constitutional legislation, a change in this *grundnorm* can be achieved only by a legal revolution and only if the judges elect to abandon their deeply rooted allegiance to the ruling Parliament of the day.

b. The Bulmer Decision

H. P. BULMER LTD. v. J. BOLLINGER S.A.

Court of Appeal
[1974] 2 All E.R. 1226

LORD DENNING M.R. 1. In France the name champagne is well protected by law. It denotes a sparkling wine produced in a well favoured district of France, called the Champagne district. The vineyards are about 100 miles east of Paris, around Rheims and Epernay. The wine has a high reputation all the world over.

In England, too, the name champagne is well protected by law when used for wine. As far back as 1956 some intruders brought into England a somewhat similar wine. It had been produced in the Costa Brava district of Spain. They marketed it under the name "Spanish champagne." The French growers and shippers brought an action to stop it. They succeeded. Danckwerts J. held that the French growers had a goodwill connected with the word champagne: and that the Spanish intruders had been guilty of dishonest trading: see *J. Bollinger* v. *Costa Brava Wine Co. Ltd.* [1960] Ch. 262; *J. Bollinger* v. *Costa Brava Wine Co. Ltd. (No. 2)* [1961] 1 W.L.R. 277. That case opened up a new field of English law. It gave a remedy for unfair competition. It was applied in the sherry case, *Vine Products Ltd.* v. *Mackenzie & Co. Ltd.* [1969] R.P.C. 1, when Cross J. said, at p. 23: ". . . the decision went beyond the well-trodden paths of passing off into the unmapped area of 'unfair trading' or 'unlawful competition.'" It was followed recently by Foster J. in the Scotch whisky case, *Walker (John) & Sons Ltd.* v. *Henry Ost & Co. Ltd.* [1970] 1 W.L.R. 917.

That case in 1960 concerned wine — wine made from grapes — for which the French are so famous. Now we are concerned with cider and perry. Cider from apples. Perry from pears. We English do know something about these. At any rate, those who come from Somerset or Herefordshire.

For many years now some producers of cider in England have been marketing some of their drinks as "champagne cider" and "champagne perry." When it started the French producers of champagne took no steps to stop it. It went on for a long time. But in 1970 the French producers brought an action against an English firm, claiming an injunction. They sought to stop the use of the name champagne on these drinks. To counter this, two of the biggest producers of cider in England on October 8, 1970, brought an action against the French producers. They claimed declarations that they were entitled to use the expression "champagne cider" and "champagne perry." They said that they had used those expressions for 70 or 80 years in England; that many millions of bottles had been marketed under those descriptions; and that the Government of the United Kingdom had recognised it in the various regulations. They said further that the French producers had acquiesced in the use and were estopped from complaining.

In answer the French producers of champagne claimed that the use of the word "champagne" in connection with any beverage other than champagne was likely to lead to the belief that such beverage was or resembled champagne, or was a substitute for it, or was in some way connected with champagne. They claimed an injunction to stop the English producers from using the word "champagne" in connection with any beverage not being a wine produced in the Champagne district of France.

2. *After England joined the common market*

Thus far it was a straightforward action for passing-off. It was to be determined by well known principles of English law. But on January 1, 1973, England joined the common market. On March 26, 1973, the French producers amended their pleading so as to add these claims:

> "9A. Following the adhesion of the United Kingdom to the European Economic Community the use of the word 'champagne' in connection with any beverage other than champagne will contravene European community law."

They relied on Regulation 816/70, article 30 and Regulation 817/70, articles 12 and 13. By a further amendment they counterclaimed for:

> "A declaration that the use by the plaintiffs of the expressions 'champagne cider' and 'champagne perry' in relation to beverages other than wine produced in the Champagne district of France is contrary to European community law."

3. *Reference to Luxembourg*

Now the French producers ask that two points of European community law should be referred to the European Court of Justice at Luxembourg. Shortened they are: "(A) whether . . . the use of the word 'champagne' in connection with any beverage other than champagne is a contravention of . . . the provisions of European community law; (B) whether . . . a national court of a member state should . . . refer to the Court of Justice of the European community such a question as has been raised herein. . . ."

The judge at first instance refused to refer either question at this stage. He said that he would try the whole case out before he came to a decision on it.

The French producers appeal to this court.

4. *The Regulations*

The community Regulations relied upon by the French producers are these: Regulation 816/70, article 30:

> "2. Member states may subject the use of a geographical mark for describing a table wine to the condition, in particular, that that wine is obtained wholly from certain vine-producing areas expressly designated and that it comes exclusively from the territory marked out in an exact manner, whose name it bears."

"Wine" means "the product obtained exclusively from whole or partial alcoholic fermentation of fresh grapes, whether or not crushed, or of grape must." Regulation 817/70, article 12:

> "1. The community reference q.w.p.s.r." [quality wine produced in a specific region] "or a traditional specific reference used in member states to describe certain wines, may only be used for wines complying with the provisions of this Regulation and with those adopted in application of this Regulation. . . ."

The specific traditional reference for France is: *"Appellation d' origine controlée ... Champagne et Vin délimité de qualité supérieure."* Article 13: "Each member state shall ensure the inspection and protection of q.w.p.s.r. marketed in accordance with this Regulation."

The French producers claim that, under those regulations, the name champagne is their own special property. It must not be applied to any *wine* which is not produced in the Champagne district of France. So much the English producers concede. But the French producers go further. They say that the name champagne must not be applied to any *beverage* other than their champagne. It must not, therefore, be applied to cider or perry, even though they are not wines at all. The English producers deny this. They say that the Regulations apply only to *wines* — the product of grapes — and not to cider or perry — the product of apples and pears.

This is obviously a point of the first importance to the French wine trade and to the English cider trade. It depends no doubt on the true interpretation of the Regulations. It seems that three points of principle arise:

First: by which court should these Regulations be interpreted? By the European Court at Luxembourg? or by the national courts of England?

Second: at what stage should the task of interpretation be done? Should it be done *now before* the case is tried out in the English court or at a later stage *after* the other issues have been determined?

Third: in any case, whichever be the court to interpret them, *what are the principles* to be applied in the interpretation of the Regulations? If we were to interpret the Regulations as if they were

an English statute, I should think they would apply only to wines, not
to cider or perry. But if other principles were to be applied, the result
might be different. That is indeed what the French producers say.
They contend that the European court can fill in any gaps in the
Regulations. So that the words can be extended so as to forbid the
use of the word "champagne" for cider or perry. That is, no doubt,
the reason why the French producers want the point to be referred
here and now to the European court.

To answer these questions, we must consider several points of
fundamental importance.

To make the discussion easier to understand, I will speak only of
the interpretation of "the Treaty," but this must be regarded as
including the Regulations and directives under it. I will make
reference to the English courts because I am specially concerned with
them: but this must be regarded as including the national courts of
any member state.

5. *The impact of the Treaty on English law*

The first and fundamental point is that the Treaty concerns only
those matters which have a European element, that is to say, matters
which affect people or property in the nine countries of the common
market besides ourselves. The Treaty does not touch any of the
matters which concern solely England and the people in it. These
are still governed by English law. They are not affected by the Treaty.
But when we come to matters with a European element, the Treaty
is like an incoming tide. It flows into the estuaries and up the rivers.
It cannot be held back, Parliament has decreed that the Treaty is
henceforward to be part of our law. It is equal in force to any statute.
The governing provision is section 2 (1) of the European
Communities Act 1972. It says:

> "All such rights, powers, liabilities, obligations and restrictions
> from time to time created or arising by or under the Treaties,
> and all such remedies and procedures from time to time provided
> for by or under the Treaties, as in accordance with the Treaties
> are without further enactment to be given legal effect or used
> in the United Kingdom shall be recognised and available in law,
> and be enforced, allowed and followed accordingly; and the
> expression 'enforceable community right' and similar
> expressions shall be read as referring to one to which this
> subsection applies."

The statute is expressed in forthright terms which are absolute and
all-embracing. Any rights or obligations created by the Treaty are
to be given legal effect in England without more ado. Any remedies
or procedures provided by the Treaty are to be made available here
without being open to question. In [the] future, in transactions which

cross the frontiers, we must no longer speak or think of English law as something on its own. We must speak and think of community law, of community rights and obligations, and we must give effect to them. This means a great effort for the lawyers. We have to learn a new system. The Treaty, with the regulations and directives, covers many volumes. The case law is contained in hundreds of reported cases both in the European Court of Justice and in the national courts of the nine. Many must be studied before the right result can be reached. We must get down to it.

6. *By what courts is the treaty to be interpreted?*

It is important to distinguish between the task of interpreting the Treaty — to see what it means — and the task of *applying* it — to apply its provisions to the case in hand. Let me put on one side the task of *applying* the Treaty. On this matter in our courts, the English judges have the final word. They are the only judges who are empowered to decide the case itself. They have to find the facts, to state the issues, to give judgment for one side or the other, and to see that the judgment is enforced.

Before the English judges can apply the Treaty, they have to see what it means and what is its effect. In the task of *interpreting* the Treaty, the English judges are no longer the final authority. They no longer carry the law in their breasts. They are no longer in a position to give rulings which are of binding force. The supreme tribunal for *interpreting* the Treaty is the European Court of Justice, at Luxembourg. Our Parliament has so decreed. Section 3 of the European Communities Act 1972 says:

> "(1) For the purposes of all legal proceedings any question as to the meaning or effect of any of the Treaties, or as to the validity, meaning or effect of any community instrument, shall be treated as a question of law (and, if not referred to the European court, be for determination as such in accordance with the principles laid down by and any relevant decision of the European court). (2) Judicial notice shall be taken of the Treaties, of the Official Journal of the Communities and of any decision of, or expression of opinion by, the European court on any such question as aforesaid; . . . ."

Coupled with that section, we must read article 177 of the Treaty. It says:

> (1) "The Court of Justice" (i.e. the European Court of Justice) "shall have jurisdiction to give preliminary rulings concerning: *(a)* the interpretation of this Treaty; *(b)* the validity and interpretation of acts of the institutions of the community; *(c)* the interpretation of the statutes of bodies established by an act of the Council, where those statutes so provide."

(2) "Where such a question is raised before any court or tribunal of a member state, that court or tribunal may, if it considers that a decision on the question is necessary to enable it to give judgment, request the Court of Justice to give a ruling thereon."
(3) "Where any such question is raised in a case pending before a court or tribunal of a member state, against whose decisions there is no judicial remedy under national law, that court or tribunal shall bring the matter before the Court of Justice."

That article shows that, if a question of interpretation or validity is raised, the European court is supreme. It is the ultimate authority. Even the House of Lords has to bow down to it. If a question is raised before the House of Lords on the interpretation of the Treaty — on which it is necessary to give a ruling — the House of Lords is bound to refer it to the European court. Article 177 (3) uses that emphatic word "shall." The House has no option. It must refer the matter to the European court, and, having done so, it is bound to follow the ruling in that *particular* case in which the point arises. But the ruling in that case does not bind *other* cases. The European court is not absolutely bound by its previous decisions: see *Da Costa en Schaake N. V.* v. *Nederlandse Belastingsadministratie,* [1963] C.M.L.R. 224. It has no doctrine of stare decisis. Its decisions are much influenced by considerations of policy and economics: and, as these change, so may their rulings change. It follows from this that, if the House of Lords in a *subsequent* case thinks that a previous ruling of the European court was wrong — or should not be followed — it can refer the point again to the European court: and the European court can reconsider it. On reconsideration it can make a ruling which will bind that *particular* case. But not subsequent cases. And so on.

7. *The discretion to refer or not to refer*

But short of the House of Lords, no other English court is bound to refer a question to the European court at Luxembourg. Not even a question on the *interpretation* of the Treaty. Article 177 (2) uses the permissive word "may" in contrast to "shall" in article 177 (3). In England the trial judge has complete *discretion.* If a question arises on the interpretation of the Treaty, an English judge can decide it for himself. He need not refer it to the court at Luxembourg unless he wishes. He can say: "It will be too costly," or "it will take too long to get an answer," or "I am well able to decide it myself." If he does decide it himself, the European court cannot interfere. None of the parties can go off to the European court and complain. The European court would not listen to any party who went moaning to them. The European court take the view that the trial judge has a complete discretion to refer or not to refer: see *Rheinmühlen, Düsseldorf, Düsseldorf-Holthausen (Firma)* v. *Einfuhr und Vorratsstelle für Getreide und Futtermittel, Frankfurt-am-Main,*

January 16, 1974 — with which they cannot interfere: see *Milchwerke Heinz Wöhrmann & Sohn K.G.* v. *Commission of the European Economic Community* [1963] C.M.L.R. 152. If a party wishes to challenge the decision of the trial judge in England — to refer or not to refer — he must appeal to the Court of Appeal in England. (If the judge makes an order referring the question to Luxembourg, the party can appeal *without leave:* see R.S.C., Ord. 114. If the judge refuses to make an order, he needs leave, because it is an interlocutory order: section 31 of the Supreme Court of Judicature (Consolidation) Act 1925, the judges of the Court of Appeal, in their turn, have complete discretion. They can interpret the Treaty themselves if they think fit.) If the Court of Appeal do interpret it themselves, the European court will not rebuke them for doing so. If a party wishes to challenge the decision of the Court of Appeal — to refer or not to refer — he must get leave to go to the House of Lords and go there. It is only in that august place that there is no discretion. If the point of interpretation is one which is "necessary" to give a ruling, the House must refer it to the European court at Luxembourg. The reason behind this imperative is this: the cases which get to the House of Lords are substantial cases of the first importance. If a point of interpretation arises there, it is assumed to be worthy of reference to the European court at Luxembourg. Whereas the points in the lower courts may not be worth troubling the European court about: see the judgment of the German Court of Appeal at Frankfurt in *In re Export of Oat Flakes* [1969] C.M.L.R. 85, 97.

[Furthermore, no national court should refer an issue unless a decision on that issue is "necessary." An issue is "necessary" when (1) it is conclusive of the case; (2) there is no convincing previous ruling on it by the European court; and (3) the point is sufficiently unclear that the Treaty of Rome must be "interpreted" rather than merely "applied." Additionally, the facts of the case must first be ascertained to ensure that there is not an alternative basis for decision.

[If the issue is truly "necessary," then the lower courts, in deciding whether or not to refer it to the European court, should consider (1) possible delay, (2) the workload of the European court, (3) the ability to phrase the question clearly, (4) the difficulty and importance of the point, (5) expense, and (6) the wishes of the parties.]

10. *The principles of interpretation*

In view of these considerations, it is apparent that in very many cases the English courts will interpret the Treaty themselves. They will not refer the question to the European court at Luxembourg. What then are the principles of interpretation to be applied? Beyond doubt the English courts must follow the same principles as the

European court. Otherwise there would be differences between the countries of the nine. That would never do. All the courts of all nine countries should interpret the Treaty in the same way. They should all apply the same principles. It is enjoined on the English courts by section 3 of the European Community Act 1972, which I have read.

What a task is thus set before us! The Treaty is quite unlike any of the enactments to which we have become accustomed. The draftsmen of our statutes have striven to express themselves with the utmost exactness. They have tried to foresee all possible circumstances that may arise and to provide for them. They have sacrificed style and simplicity. They have foregone brevity. They have become long and involved. In consequence, the judges have followed suit. They interpret a statute as applying only to the circumstances covered by the very words. They give them a literal interpretation. If the words of the statute do not cover a new situation — which was not foreseen — the judges hold that they have no power to fill the gap. To do so would be a "naked usurpation of the legislative function": see *Magor and St. Mellons Rural District Council* v. *Newport Borough Council* [1952] A.C. 189, 191. The gap must remain open until Parliament finds time to fill it.

How different is this Treaty? It lays down general principles. It expresses its aims and purposes. All in sentences of moderate length and commendable style. But it lacks precision. It uses words and phrases without defining what they mean. An English lawyer would look for an interpretation clause, but he would look in vain. There is none. All the way through the Treaty there are gaps and lacunae. These have to be filled in by the judges, or by Regulations or directives. It is the European way. That appears from the decision of the Hamburg court in *In re Tax on Imported Lemons* [1968] C.M.L.R. 1.

Likewise the Regulations and directives. They are enacted by the Council sitting in Brussels for everyone to obey. They are quite unlike our statutory instruments. They have to give the reasons on which they are based: article 190. So they start off with pages of preambles, "whereas" and "whereas" and "whereas." These show the purpose and intent of the Regulations and directives. Then follow the provisions which are to be obeyed. Here again words and phrases are used without defining their import. Such as "personal conduct" in the Directive 64/221, article 3 (E.E.C.) which was considered by Pennycuick V.-C. in *Van Duyn* v. *Home Office* [1974] 1 W.L.R. 1107. In case of difficulty, recourse is had to the preambles. These are useful to show the purpose and intent behind it all. But much is left to the judges. The enactments give only an outline plan. The details are to be filled in by the judges.

Seeing these differences, what are the English courts to do when they are faced with a problem of interpretation? They must follow the European pattern. No longer must they examine the words in meticulous detail. No longer must they argue about the precise grammatical sense. They must look to the purpose or intent. To quote the words of the European court in the *Da Costa* case [1963] C.M.L.R. 224, 237, they must deduce "from the wording and the spirit of the Treaty the meaning of the community rules." They must not confine themselves to the English text. They must consider, if need be, all the authentic texts, of which there are now eight: see *Sociale Verzekeringsbank* v. *Van der Vecht* [1968] C.M.L.R. 151. They must divine the spirit of the Treaty and gain inspiration from it. If they find a gap, they must fill it as best they can. They must do what the framers of the instrument would have done if they had thought about it. So we must do the same. Those are the principles, as I understand it, on which the European court acts.

11. *Applied to the present case*

To return to the three questions I asked at the beginning.

First: I think these Regulations should be interpreted by the High Court and the Court of Appeal in England. But if the cases should reach the House of Lords they must be interpreted by the European Court.

Second: the task of interpretation should be done at the time of the trial or the appeal, together with the other issues in the case.

Third: the English court should apply the same principles of interpretation as the European court would do if it had to decide the point.

I come now to the two specific questions sought to be referred. The first question raised is: "Whether . . . the use of the word 'champagne' in connection with any beverage other than champagne is a contravention of the provisions of European community law." I do not think it is *necessary* at this stage to decide that question. Take the claim in passing off. If the French growers succeeded in this claim for passing off in English law — for an injunction and damages — it would not be necessary to decide the point under the Regulations. So the facts must be found before it can be said that a reference is "necessary."

Next take the claim of the French growers for a declaration that the use of the expression "champagne cider" and "champagne perry" was contrary to European community law. Mr. Sparrow said that it would be necessary on this issue to decide the point on the Regulations. I do not agree. It is always a matter for the discretion of the judge whether to grant a declaration or not. He could very properly say in the present case: "Whatever the true interpretation of the Regulations, it is not a case in which I would make any declaration on the point." Taking that view, it would not be necessary to decide the point.

Even if it could be said to be necessary to decide the point, I think that an English court (short of the House of Lords) should not, as [a] matter of discretion, refer it to the European court. It should decide the point itself. It would take much time and money to get a ruling from the European court. Meanwhile, the whole action would be held up. It is, no doubt, an important point, but not a difficult one to decide. I think it would be better to deal with it as part of the whole case, both by the trial judge and by the Court of Appeal. If it should then go to the House of Lords, it will by that time have become clear whether it is a "necessary" point or not. If it is, then the House of Lords will refer it.

The second point is: "Whether a national court should . . . refer to the Court of Justice such a question as has been raised herein." The object of this question is to get a ruling from the European court as to the circumstances in which a national court should refer a question of interpretation to the European court. I am quite clear that it is unnecessary to ask this question. The answer is clear. It is not the province of the European court to give any guidance or advice to the national court as to when it should, or should not, refer a question. That is a matter for the national court itself. It is no concern of the European court.

In my opinion Whitford, J. was right in refusing to refer either of the questions. I would dismiss the appeal.

[Concurring opinions of Stamp, L.J. and Stephenson, L.J. omitted.]

NOTES AND QUESTIONS

1. The special problem with superiority of Community law in Great Britain is its strong tradition of Parliamentary supremacy. Did the conflict in *Bulmer* raise this issue? What were the sources of English law in potential conflict with EEC law in the case?

2. Lord Denning stated that the EEC Treaty "is equal in force to any statute." Was this merely the narrowest view required to decide the *Bulmer* case, or does this foreshadow another *Costa* decision? Notice that Lord Denning does go beyond the Italian Constitutional Court in *Costa* by recognizing that Community law is directly applicable in British courts, without the necessity for a British statute to incorporate it.

3. Lord Denning recognizes that new "European" methods of interpretation must be learned. Is it correct that continental statutory interpretation is a "naked usurpation of the legislative function"?

The continental theory is that all law is contained in the national codes. Thus, since no judge-made law, in theory, exists, all of the creative work of continental judges must be "statutory interpretation." While English common law judges tend to interpret statutes with more literalness than American judges, historically English judges have exercised considerable creativity in the "development of the common law." Note for example, that the tort of "unlawful competition," which was the original basis for the action in *Bulmer* itself, was an "unmarred area" of common law. Would continental judges view creation of law without *any* statutory authority as a "naked usurpation of the legislative function"?

4. *Bulmer,* as far as it goes, was followed in another decision written by Lord Denning, *Schorsh Meir* v. *Hennin,* [1975] All E.R. 152. In that case a German plaintiff sued an English defendant in a British court, yet demanded that the judgment be rendered in German marks, the currency of the contract, rather than in sterling; sterling had been devalued since the time at which the sterling exchange value of the debt would have to be calculated. The British common law rule, dating back to 1605, was that a British court could render judgment only in sterling. The Court of Appeal, however, held for the German plaintiff. Lord Denning's opinion, with which Foster, J., agreed, rested on two grounds. First, the reasons for the common law rule had ceased to exist, and there was no longer any prohibition in English law from giving judgment enforcing a contract to pay in a foreign currency. Second, the common law rule in any event was superseded by art. 106 of the Treaty of Rome. Lord Denning's opinion concluded:

> This is the first case in which we have had actually to apply the Treaty of Rome in these courts. It shows its great effect. It has brought about a fundamental change. Hitherto our English courts have only been able to give judgment in sterling. In future when a debt is incurred by an English debtor to a creditor in one of the Member States — payable in the currency of that State — the English courts can give judgment for the amount in that money. This change will have effects, too, beyond the Common Market. It has already made us think again about our own laws. As a result, it is my opinion, that, whatever the foreign currency, be it United States dollars or Japanese yen, or any other, the English courts can give judgment in that money where it is the currency of the contract.

Lawton, J., disagreed with the majority's conclusion that the common law rule, although it was "legalistic nonsense," had been superseded. He said: "It is . . . my duty to apply the law, not to reform it." Significantly, however, he concurred in the result on the basis of art. 106 of the Treaty of Rome.

5. The Court of Appeal is the highest British court below the House of Lords. Since the House of Lords usually decides only 50 or 60 cases each year, a decision by the Court of Appeal is a significant one.

Lord Denning states that only the House of Lords is a "court of last resort" under art. 177, and thus referral to the European Court by the Court of Appeal is discretionary. His argument is that the reason for making referral mandatory only for courts of last resort is to ensure that important issues are referred.

Is the real reason for art. 177 the impact of a decision by a court of last resort, even on less important issues? Although there is no formal *stare decisis* in civil law countries, the decisions of the highest courts are persuasive in a way that decisions of lower courts are not. In Britain, of course, if the House of Lords does not review a decision of the Court of Appeal, lower courts must follow the decision because there is a formal rule of *stare decisis*. From this perspective, is the British Court of Appeal *more* of a "court of last resort" than the European Courts of Cassation?

B. INTRODUCTION TO THE EUROPEAN CONVENTION ON HUMAN RIGHTS*

The Convention for the Protection of Human Rights and Fundamental Freedoms was signed in Rome, November 4, 1950, by the member states of the Council of Europe, and entered into effect September 3, 1953, with the deposit of the tenth instrument of ratification (as prescribed in art. 66). At the present time eighteen of the twenty states of the Council of Europe have ratified the Convention: Austria, Belgium, Cyprus, Denmark, France, the Federal Republic of Germany, Greece, Iceland, Ireland, Italy, Luxembourg, Malta, the Netherlands, Norway, Sweden, Switzerland, Turkey, and the United Kingdom.**

In several states, the Convention became incorporated into domestic law by its ratification, while in others, the Convention has not become an integral part of the domestic legal structure, but does extrinsically establish rules to which that domestic system must conform. A spectrum of force may be seen ranging from those states where the Convention is superior to the Constitution (e.g., the Netherlands), to those in which it is not a source of domestic law under which claims may be brought or defenses asserted (e.g., the United Kingdom and the Scandinavian countries). Intermediate points may be found in those states where it has constitutional law force (e.g., Austria) and in those where it has the force of ordinary statutes (e.g., the Federal Republic of Germany and Italy).

The organs of control under the Convention are three: the European Commission of Human Rights, the Committee of

---

* This section is adapted from M. CAPPELLETTI, J. GORDLEY, & E. JOHNSON, JR., TOWARD EQUAL JUSTICE: A COMPARATIVE STUDY OF LEGAL AID IN MODERN SOCIETIES 657-60 (1975).

** Ratification is pending in the last two states to sign, Portugal and Spain.

Ministers of the Council of Europe, and the European Court of Human Rights. The first two bodies exercise a dual judicial-political role. Only the Court is occupied with solely a judicial function.

Petitions asserting violations of the principles of the Convention are made to the Commission. Application may be made by a member state or, where the respondent state has indicated its acceptance of the additional competence of the Commission to receive individual applications (in accordance with art. 25), by an individual on his own behalf. Thirteen states presently accept the right of individual application: Austria, Belgium, Denmark, the Federal Republic of Germany, Iceland, Ireland, Italy, Luxembourg, the Netherlands, Norway, Sweden, Switzerland, and the United Kingdom.

Upon receipt of the application, the Commission proceeds to an examination as to its admissibility. This examination is particularly interesting in that it is not limited to formal elements but extends even to the merits to the extent necessary to determine whether or not the petition is manifestly ill-founded.

The decision as to admissibility has a definitive character and concludes the strictly judicial phase of the Commission's activities. Once the application has been declared admissible a new phase opens.

The Commission attempts to achieve an amicable settlement of the dispute (art. 30) after making an examination of the petition and, if need be, an investigation together with the representatives of the parties (arts. 28 and 29). If this phase cannot be concluded in a "political" fashion through a friendly settlement, it will result in a "judicial" conclusion with a report in which the Commission will state its opinion as to whether the facts found disclose a violation by the state concerning its obligations under the Convention (art. 31). It is interesting to note that of 8,113 cases brought before the Commission by individual application from 1955 to December 31, 1977, only 174 have been declared admissible by the Commission. The great majority, to be specific 6,664, were declared inadmissible, without even being communicated to the government concerned, as clearly not acceptable. COUNCIL OF EUROPE, EUROPEAN COMMISSION OF HUMAN RIGHTS, ANNUAL REVIEW 1977, at 40 (Strasbourg, January 1978).

Once the activities of the Commission are concluded, i.e., the petition has been declared admissible and no friendly settlement has been effected, the case is decided in one of two fashions: politically, by the Committee of Ministers, or judicially by the European Court. A rather complicated system is employed in determining to which of the two organs the case will be submitted. In general, the decision depends on the state itself. Parties to the Convention may accept the general jurisdiction of the Court, or may accede to its jurisdiction in specific cases only. Even if the particular state has accepted the general jurisdiction of the Court, a case may be decided by the Committee of Ministers in instances where neither the state involved nor the Commission chooses to submit the question to the Court.

Whichever course is taken the effects are analogous. The decision of both the Committee of Ministers or of the Court is equally binding and definitive. When a state's law is found to conflict with the Convention, the state is bound to conform its law to the Court's decision. Supervision of this duty is left to the Committee of Ministers. Moreover, where domestic law of the offending state does not permit total or partial reparation to the individual who brought the case, the Court has power to accord "just satisfaction to the injured party." Legal scholars believe that the Court has the power to accord a monetary award for either material or mental damages suffered.

It should be stressed that the decisions of the Court of Human Rights are not enforceable in national law. The judgment can only be satisfied through action by the state government, under the supervision of the Committee of Ministers. Judgments of the European Economic Community's Court of Justice, by contrast, are treated as though rendered by a national court and may be executed in the same way as any normal domestic court judgment.

The Convention itself, which is in English and French texts of equal authenticity, consists of five sections and a separate protocol (concluded in Paris in 1952). The first eighteen articles comprise Section I.

Arts. 2 through 14 set forth the fundamental rights and freedoms which are to be protected by the Convention (e.g., life, liberty and security of person, freedom of thought and expression, peaceful assembly, association) and provide for nondiscrimination in their enjoyment as well as for recourse to the courts for their protection. Arts. 15 through 18 establish a limited number of instances where the state may qualify or restrict those rights provided for in the preceding 13 articles (e.g., time of war or public emergency provided there is no inconsistency with general principles of international law, and free restriction on alien political activity). Section II consists simply of art. 19 which establishes the Commission and the Court. Section III deals with the workings of the Commission, which consists of a number of members equal to that of the High Contracting Parties, with no more than one member from the same state, who serve a six year term and who may be re-elected. The members of the Commission are elected by the Committee of Ministers by an absolute majority of votes, from a list of names drawn up by the Bureau of the Consultative Assembly of the Council of Europe. This Assembly consists of Representatives of each Member, elected by its Parliament or appointed in such manner as Parliament shall decide.

Each member of the Commission sits in his individual capacity, rather than as a representative of his state. Art. 26 requires that all domestic remedies be exhausted prior to access to the Commission. Section IV deals with the European Court of Human Rights. It is composed of a number of judges equal to that of the members of the Council of Europe, with a provision similar to that of the Commission that no two judges may be nationals of the same state. The judges are elected by the Consultative Assembly of the Council of Europe from a list of persons nominated by the Member States. Section V deals with administrative and other miscellaneous matters. The protocol of March 1952 guarantees peaceful enjoyment of possession, the right to education, and requires that its signatories hold free elections at reasonable intervals.

NOTES AND QUESTIONS

1. What does it mean to say that, in a particular country, "the Convention has not become an integral part of the domestic legal structure, but does extrinsically establish rules to which that domestic system must conform" ? What is the status of the Convention in the United Kingdom, where it is not a source of domestic law yet the right of individual petition is recognized?

2. In the *Phansopkar* case (*R* v. *Secretary of State,* [1975] All E.R. 497, 511), Lord Justice Scarman said that the delay involved in the case infringed "at least two human rights recognized, and therefore protected, by English law" — the right to prompt justice, asserted in the Magna Carta, and the right to respect for the family, asserted in art. 8 of the European Convention.

> [I]t is now the duty of our public authorities in administering the law, . . . and of our courts in interpreting the law . . . to have regard [for the European Convention]. . . . It may, of course, happen that [these] basic rights . . . have to yield to express requirements of a statute. But in my judgment it is the duty of the courts, so long as they do not defy or disregard clear unequivocal provisions, to construe statutes in a manner which promotes, not endangers, those rights. Problems of ambiguity or omission, if they arise under the language of an Act, should be resolved so as to give effect to, or at the very least so as not to derogate from, the rights recognised by Magna Carta and the European Convention.

In the *Salamat Bibi* case (*R* v. *Chief Immigration Officer,* [1976] All E.R. 843, 847-48), however, Lord Denning said:

> The position, as I understand it, is that if there is any ambiguity in our statutes or uncertainty in our law, then these courts can

look to the convention as an aid to clear up the ambiguity and uncertainty, seeking always to bring them into harmony with it. Furthermore, when Parliament is enacting a statute or the Secretary of State is framing rules, the courts will assume that they had regard to the provisions of the convention and intended to make the enactment accord with the convention, and will interpret them accordingly. But I would dispute altogether that the convention is part of our law. Treaties and declarations do not become part of our law until they are made law by Parliament. [Also, it would be too much to expect ordinary public officials to know or apply the convention in the performance of their administrative duties.] So it is much better for us to stick to our own statutes and principles, and only look to the convention for guidance in case of doubt.

What is the difference between these two approaches?

C. INTERNATIONAL HIGHER LAW IN FRANCE

1. The European Convention on Human Rights in the French *Conseil Constitutionnel*

DECISION OF JANUARY 15, 1975

Conseil Constitutionnel
[1975] A.J.D.A. 134

The *Conseil Constitutionnel* seized the 20th of December, 1974, by M.M. . . . under the terms provided by Article 61 of the Constitution, with the issue concerning the constitutionality of the text of the law adopted by Parliament relative to the voluntary interruption of pregnancy;

Considering the observations produced in support of this issue;

Considering the Constitution and notably its Preamble;

Considering the *ordonnance* of November 7, 1958 (the organic law of the Constitutional Council), in particular Chapter II of Title II of the *ordonnance;*

Having heard the Reporter's report;

Considering that Article 61 of the Constitution does not confer on the *Conseil Constitutionnel* a general power of evaluation and decision identical to that of Parliament, but rather gives it competence solely to pronounce the conformity to the Constitution of the laws referred to its scrutiny;

Considering in the first place, that, according to the terms of Article 55 of the Constitution, "The treaties or [international] accords regularly ratified or approved have, from their publication, an authority superior to that of the laws, upon the reservation, for each accord or treaty, of its application by the other party";

Considering that, even though these provisions, under the conditions which they define, confer on treaties superiority over the laws, they neither prescribe nor imply that the respect of this superiority principle must be enforced within the framework of the control of the conformity of laws to the Constitution provided by Article 61;

Considering that, in effect, the decisions taken on the basis of Article 61 of the Constitution assume an absolute and definitive character, as is made clear by Article 62, which prevents the promulgation and application of all provisions once declared unconstitutional [by this *Conseil Constitutionnel*]; that, in contrast, the superiority of the treaties over the laws, which principle is posed by the aforementioned Article 55, has a character at the same time relative and contingent, since such superiority is limited to the scope of the application of the treaty and is subordinated to a condition of reciprocity, and the realization of this condition may vary according to the behavior of one or more of the signatory States at the time when one must judge the respect of the condition;

Considering that a law contrary to a treaty would thus not be, for that reason only, contrary to the Constitution;

Considering that, therefore, the control of the respect of the principle of Article 55 of the Constitution would not be exercisable under the framework of review provided by Article 61, by reason of the difference in nature of the two controls;

Considering that, under these conditions, it is not the task of this *Conseil Constitutionnel*, when it is seized [with issues of constitutionality] under the terms of Article 61 of the Constitution, to examine the conformity of a law to the provisions of a treaty or an international accord;

[The *Conseil* also held that the law did not violate any of the guarantees of the French Constitution. *See* Ch. 12, § B. *infra.*]

NOTE *

. . . .

The decision in which the *Conseil [Constitutionnel]* has affirmed the constitutionality of the law concerning the voluntary termination of pregnancy, published in the Official Journal of January 18, has already aroused by its caution as much criticism as the previous ones by their boldness, even from those who basically approve the solution adopted. From a juridical point of view — the only one we should consider here — caution is revealed in regard to the two series of arguments put forward by the authors of the recourse. Asked to

---

* [1975] A.J.D.A. II Jur. 134, note by Professor J. Rivero of the University of Paris. Reprinted with permission of L'Actualité Juridique du Droit Administratif.

affirm the nonconformity of the law to Article 2 of the European Convention on Human Rights, the *Conseil* declared itself incompetent to give a ruling in this capacity. As for the confrontation between the law and the constitutional texts placed in opposition to it, it remained strictly literal, excluding any interpretation liable to be imputed to the personal opinions of the members of the *Conseil* in an issue which engaged and divided consciences at their deepest level.

It is this double caution — in regard to international law (I) and to the constitutional texts (II) — that we should like to analyse, and try to understand (III).

Is the European Convention safeguarding human rights and fundamental freedoms, the ratification of which, authorized by the law of December 31, 1973, became effective with the order of publication in the Official Journal of May 4, 1974, binding on national legislation, and is the *Conseil Constitutionnel* competent to declare unconstitutional a law contrary to one of the articles of the Convention?

From the juridical point of view, this was the essential question asked by Parliament, who had referred the law to the *Conseil* pursuant to the reform effected by the constitutional law of October 29, 1974. As we know, the question was answered negatively.

The argument of the plaintiffs was based on the famous formula of Article 55 of the Constitution which gives "treaties or agreements duly ratified or approved, upon their publication, an authority superior to that of legislation. . . ." Since the Constitution affirms the superiority of a treaty over a law, a law contrary to a treaty disregards the hierarchy of norms imposed by Article 55 and, therefore, that provision itself: it is thus contrary to the Constitution.

. . . .

In reality, the first part of the text [of Article 55], which appears to give the *absolute* primacy of a treaty over a law, is inseparable from the second: "with the reservation, for each accord or treaty, of its application by the other party"; and this reservation transforms the absolute primacy, which would make a law contrary to the treaty an equally absolute nullity, into a *relative* primacy. Furthermore, the reservation supposes, and then accepts, the existence of laws contrary to the treaties, since it authorizes the application of such laws with regard to the States which avoid their [reciprocal] obligations. Article 55, therefore, does not proclaim, against the legislature, the interdiction of the enactment of laws not conforming to treaties. It anticipates, in contrast, the eventuality of such a situation, and it regulates it by means of a distinction: if the conflict between the two acts affects one State which is in conformity to the treaty, it is this [conforming] State which may prevail over the contrary law; if the condition of reciprocity is not met, the law retains its authority.

Article 55 does not then permit consideration of a law as vitiated *ab initio* by its nonconformity to a treaty. The nullity which taints it is not absolute but relative: not enforceable against the State which conforms itself to the treaty, enforceable against those [States] which avoid their [reciprocal] obligations.

One sees, therefore, the difference that separates the subordination of the laws to the Constitution, on the one hand, and to treaties, on the other hand: in the first case, absolute subordination sanctioned by an absolute nullity; in the second, relative subordination sanctioned by a relative nullity. This is the analysis which the *Conseil Constitutionnel* followed, and it has two consequences:

— As a main point, "a law contrary to a treaty would not, for that reason alone, be contrary to the Constitution," since it [the Constitution] in Article 55, admits the application, and thus the existence, of such a law to the advantage of the nonreciprocity.

— With respect to procedure, the control of constitutionality under Article 61, which tends to a decision absolute and definitive, is not able to serve as a framework of control of the conformity of a law to a treaty.

The final conclusion necessarily derives from these premises: "It is not the concern of the *Conseil Constitutionnel,* in reference to the application of Article 61 of the Constitution, to examine the conformity of a law to the stipulations of a treaty." Some have deplored this timidity. Nevertheless, it is hard to find fault with the precise reasoning from which it derives.

However, the reasoning is affected with a certain threshold error: for the European Convention is manifestly distinguished from the treaties which the Assembly had in view in drafting Article 55. The State which ratifies it assumes, *vis-à-vis* the other Parties to the Convention, a group of obligations with regard not only to themselves and their nationals, but also to its own nationals: it promises all nations to respect the liberties of all — domestic or foreign — who come under the exercise of its sovereignty, and if it fails to honor this promise, the other Parties to the Convention may summon it to the international institutions created by the Convention. The European Commission of the Rights of Man, in its decision *Fall,* of January 11, 1961, cited by Charles Rousseau (*Droit International public* t. II p. 723), expressed itself this way:

> In concluding the Convention, the States did not wish to concede some reciprocal rights and obligations useful to the pursuit of their national interests, but to realize the objectives of the Council of Europe which the statute announces, and to install public community order.

Therefore,

> the obligations subscribed to by the States under the Convention have essentially an objective character which aims to protect the fundamental rights of individuals against the encroachments of the contracting States, rather than aiming to create the subjective and reciprocal rights between two States.

Beginning from this analysis, the principle of reciprocity of Article 55 changes complexion. It is possible to be applied — with the reservation, if it comes into force, of the eventual role of Article 60 of the Convention of Vienna excluding all reciprocity in that which concerns "the provisions relative to the protection of the human person contained in the humanitarian treaties" — to the *international sanction of the obligation.* Thus, France would be able to oppose that principle to a State which purported to petition the European Commission at the same time that that State itself would not respect the norm the violation of which it denounced. It is without effect on the obligation, which is "objective" according to the formula of the decision *Fall,* and absolute, with the consequence that the "superior authority" that Article 55 confers to treaties is not made relative by the effect of the principle of reciprocity, insofar as by means of these treaties France has accepted some obligations toward its own nationals.

On the terrain bearing on the relationship between the law and a treaty in general, the reasoning of the *Conseil* follows Article 55, and the conclusion appears incontestable. A practical consideration, moreover, has been able to lead in the same direction: to elevate all the treaties concluded by France to constitutional supra-legality for which the *Conseil* is the guardian, would have been to give to such concept of supra-legal constitutionality a content, not only excessive, but very difficult to define. The solution could have been different if pushing the analysis further, the *Conseil* after having announced, as it did, the general rule, had shown its inapplicability to the particular case of the Convention by which the State assumes obligations *vis-à-vis,* not the coparties, guarantors and not beneficiaries of the promise made, but to those under its jurisdiction [its nationals]. In this case, the law which fails to recognize the obligation is tainted by an initial and absolute vice which seems to call also for "absolute and definite" censure.

But was the *Conseil* unable to go on this terrain? It is here that the caution appears. It is evident that Article 55 has had in view only the most frequent and classic case: that of treaties by which one State contracts some obligations and on the other side are several other States. It would be wrong to find there a basis for a positive solution, to introduce there a distinction foreign to the text and without doubt to the thought of the authors. The route was possible, but bold. In the sense of the prudence, an equal part was played, moreover, by the doubt that could exist with regard to the place assigned to treaties in the hierarchy of judicial norms by the 1958 Constitution. Article 55 places them above the law. But Article 54 subordinates them to the Constitution: since if it contains a clause contrary to the Constitution, the authorization to ratify it is impossible without constitutional revision.

Thus, in order to situate [treaties] in the legal order, one can transpose the formula applied by René Chapus to general principles of law: "supralegislative" certainly, but "infraconstitutional." Now the *Conseil,* according to Article 61, is the watchdog of conformity *to the Constitution,* and this, according to Article 54, in regard to treaties themselves. One can understand its hesitancy to include among those texts, the respect of which it supervises, other texts which are submitted to its control for comparison with them.

One can object that it is not the contradiction between the law and the treaty which causes the censure of the former, but its nonconformity to Article 55. In reality, the disregard of Article 55, or unconstitutionality, is indirect here: it is only established inasmuch as the law is contrary to the treaty. The conformity of the law to the treaty, in relation to the main question of the conformity of the law to the Constitution, constitutes a sort of preliminary question — not even as an application of the rule "le juge de l'action est juge de l'exception," which would have permitted it to enlarge its scope of action — to which the *Conseil* did not see fit to extend its competence, in a strict interpretation of its mission as judge of "conformity to the Constitution."

Caution prevailed over boldness on all these points. As we have seen, it is not without juridical justifications. Yet it still results, in practice, in a paradoxical situation. The decision of January 15 implicitly admits the need to "guarantee respect for the principle expressed in Article 55," it being understood that this guarantee cannnot be exercised "within the examination provided for in Article 61." A substitute must still be found, which can only be that of judicial and administrative jurisdictions. We thus come back to the classical problem of the attitude of the judge when confronted with a law in opposition to a treaty. The problem is easily solved in the case of a prior law, because of the rule 'lex posterior derogat priori,' which operates here in favor of the treaty. But the real problem is that of a subsequent law. Both *jurisprudences* try to evade it by interpreting the law in the light of the treaty, so as to efface the contradiction. This is only a palliative. What would they do when confronted with a manifest conflict, particularly with a law disregarding a freedom sanctioned by the European Declaration?

There is no doubt with regard to administrative authority: Pres. Odent has expounded at length (*Cours de contentieux administratif,* I p. 127ff): to evaluate the conformity of a subsequent law to treaties would be, for the administrative judge "to verify the internal validity of the law, which exceeds his authority." The eminent writer deplores the existence of this imperfection in our jurisdictional order, but he rules out the possibility of an evolution in *jurisprudence.* As for judicial authority, even if its position seems less categorical, the advocate general Blondeau, evoking the hypothesis of a manifest conflict between a treaty and a law, nevertheless writes: "I am convinced that, however explicit Article 55 of the Constitution may be, both civil and criminal courts would apply the law" (Blondeau, *L'Application du Droit Conventionnel par les Juridictions Françaises de l'Ordre Judiciaire,* in L'APPLICATION DU DROIT INTERNATIONAL PAR LE JUGE FRANÇAIS 61 (1972)).

. . . .

Thus we have reached an impasse. No framework is found in which to "guarantee respect for the principle expressed in Article 55," the need for which is stated in the decision of January 15: because a treaty is infraconstitutional, the judge charged with ascertaining the conformity of a law to the Constitution refuses to examine the conformity of a law to a treaty; because a treaty is supralegislative, the ordinary judges do not consider themselves authorized to "verify the internal validity of the law" in respect to it. So that, in the event of Parliament's passing a law contrary to the European Convention on Human Rights, the French citizen could, paradoxically, only rely for his defense on a foreign signatory of the Convention referring the matter to the Commission!

The risk is indeed limited, inasmuch as it is difficult to envision fundamental freedoms guaranteed on the European level but not in the internal order, by the Preamble and the "texts to which it refers." So that the disputed law could be deferred on this basis to the *Conseil Constitutionnel,* namely by a parliamentary minority, pursuant to the constitutional reform of October 29, 1974, as was the case in the present instance. But the fact remains that this situation is unfortunate. Public opinion today is only too apt to refuse to believe in the protection that the law claims to afford everyone. A constitutional rule deprived of sanction because of a defect in our juridical system can only confirm it in this skepticism. Perhaps it could not be otherwise: but it is regrettable that this is so, and that on this point the constitutional judge seems to match the traditional reticence of the judicial judge and the administrative judge confronted with an international rule.

. . . .

NOTES AND QUESTIONS

1. Do you agree with Professor Rivero's distinction between absolute primacy (of the Constitution) and relative primacy (of treaties)?

2. Professor Rivero also distinguishes between treaties which impose only obligations between states, and treaties (like the European Convention) which aim at creating obligations of the states to their own citizens. He then concludes that the reciprocity principle of art. 55 concerns only the first type of treaty. Do you agree? In light of that distinction, why did Rivero nevertheless accept the decision of the *Conseil Constitutionnel*?

3. In the latter part of his note, Rivero says that "we have reached an impasse." Does this impasse still exist after the *Cafès Jacques Vabre* decision of the *Cour de Cassation* (reprinted below) and after the decision of the *Conseil Constitutionnel* of December 30, 1976 on the election of the European Parliament at the universal suffrage (*see infra* § C.3. and Notes and Questions after § C.4.)?

2. The European Economic Community Treaty in the French Court of Cassation

ADMINISTRATION DES DOUANES v. LA SOCIÉTÉ "CAFÈS JACQUES VABRE," S.A.

Cour de Cassation,* Chambre Mixte
May 24, 1975
[1975] 2 C.M.L.R. 336**

[Under French tax regulations, plaintiff, an importer of soluble coffee extract from Holland, was subjected to a higher internal consumption tax than that charged users of comparable national products. Plaintiff sued the Customs Administration alleging, *inter alia*, that the unequal tax rate was a violation of art. 95 of the EEC

---

* The Court of Cassation is comprised of numerous chambers, which usually function independently. However, under certain circumstances a *Chambre Mixte* may be convened — when the case raises an important question of principle, or the question falls within the jurisdiction of various chambers, or the resolution of the issue may result in inconsistent judgments. A Mixed Chamber is also mandatory in certain situations, as when the *Procureur général* or the First President (of the Court) orders it.

Such a chamber is presided over by the First President and normally contains the Presidents and a senior judge and two other judges of several chambers. The *Procureur général* must address the Court when it sits as a Mixed Chamber.

Here the First President had ordered a hearing before a Mixed Chamber representing all of the chambers of the Court of Cassation. Thus, among the judges present were the presidents of all the civil and criminal chambers of the Court; the enhanced effect of a decision by such a Court is apparent.

** Reprinted with permission of Common Law Reports, Ltd., London.

Treaty. The lower court held in favor of plaintiff, and the government appealed.]

. . . .

On the second ground

[4] It is also complained against the judgment that it held illegal the internal consumption tax laid down by section 265 of the Customs Code as a consequence of its incompatibility with the provisions of **Article 95** of the Treaty of 25 March 1957 on the ground that, by virtue of Article 55 of the Constitution, the latter has an authority higher than that of internal statute, even if the statute be later in time; whereas, according to the appeal, it is for the fiscal court to judge the legality of regulations laying down a tax which is challenged, but it could not without exceeding its powers discard the application of an internal statute on the pretext that it is unconstitutional. The provisions of section 265 of the Customs Code taken together were enacted by the Act of 14 December 1966 which conferred on them the absolute authority which belongs to legislative provisions and which are binding on all French courts.

[5] But the Treaty of 25 March 1957, which by virtue of the above-mentioned Article of the Constitution has an authority greater than that of statutes, institutes a separate legal order integrated with that of the member-States. Because of that separateness, the legal order which it has created is directly applicable to the nationals of those States and is binding on their courts. Therefore the Cour d'Appel was correct and did not exceed its powers in deciding that **Article 95** of the Treaty was to be applied in the instant case, and not section 265 of the Customs Code, even though the latter was later in date. Whence it follows that the ground must be dismissed.

On the third ground

[6] It is also complained that the judgment applied **Article 95** of the Treaty of 25 March 1957 when, according to the appeal, Article 55 of the Constitution expressly subjects the authority which it gives to treaties ratified by France to the condition that they should be applied by the other party. The judge at first instance was not therefore able validly to apply this constitutional provision without investigating whether the State (Holland) from which the product in question was imported has met this condition of reciprocity.

[7] But in the Community legal order the failings of a member-State of the European Economic Community to comply with the obligations falling on it by virute of the Treaty of 25 March 1957 are subject to the procedure laid down by **Article 170** of that Treaty and so the plea of lack of reciprocity cannot be made before the

national courts. Whence it follows that this ground must be dismissed.

. . . .

THE COURT, for these reasons,
Dismisses the appeal.

Submissions of the Procureur Général (M. Adolphe Touffait)

I

The Customs Administration has raised six grounds of appeal in the case which is before you, only the second raising the basic issue of conflict between the Treaty instituting the European Community and a subsequent domestic statute (*loi*), an issue which is so important that in order to reply to it you were led to sit *en banc* in a 'mixed chamber' comprising all the divisions of the Cour de Cassation, for all the divisions are affected by the solution which you will reach.

. . . .

V

It only remains to examine the second ground, a crucial ground which poses the problem of the conflict between a subsequent statute the terms of which are in contradiction with those of the EEC Treaty. For this it is necessary that section 265 of the Customs Code should be statutory in nature and not subordinate legislation.

. . . .

Consequently, you are obliged to examine the question of the primacy of the Treaty over a subsequent statute. . . .

VI

Let us then examine in the light of this analysis the substance of the second ground, which merits a re-reading. What does it say? Infringement of Article 55 of the Constitution, of section 265 of the Customs Code, of the principle of separation of powers, of section 102 of the decree of 20 July 1972, lack of reasoning, lack of statutory basis, in that the judgment under appeal holds to be *illegal* the internal consumption tax because of its incompatibility with the provisions of **Article 95** of the Rome Treaty, on the ground that those Community provisions have an authority which is superior to that of internal statute even if the latter is subsequent to the Treaty, that all the same, a fiscal court could not without exceeding its powers refrain from applying an internal statute on the pretext of its being unconstitutional.

Allow me to say that this second ground of appeal is imprecise in its formulation, for never, either at first or at second instance does the judgment declare 'illegal' the internal consumption tax laid down by section 265 of the Customs Code and at no time did either of those judicial decisions say that section 265 was unconstitutional.

While the statement of claim (*mémoire ampliatif*) thus inaccurately interprets the decisions of the lower courts, the defence (*mémoire en réplique*) of the Customs Administration raises, impliedly if not expressly, the question of conflict between the Treaty instituting the European Community and a subsequent statute which is contrary to the said Treaty. Really, and in a precise manner, there is raised before you the question of how to resolve the conflict between two parties, one of whom relies on **Article 95 (2)** of the Rome Treaty, dating from 25 March 1957, which forbids any member-State to impose on the products from another member-State internal taxes of a nature to protect indirectly other products, and the other of whom calls for the application of section 265 of the Customs Code which institutes an internal consumption tax on coffee (head 21.02 of the Customs Tariff), which is a text of a statutory character and is subsequent to the Rome Treaty.

This is a fundamental question which has never been raised so clearly before your Court.

For although, *inter alia,* your Criminal Chamber in a judgment of 22 October 1970. . . held Community law to be superior to national law — it was a conflict between a Community Regulation 24 and the French statutes of 1 August 1905 and 13 October 1941, and so prior to the Rome Treaty — that judgment, as well as another of 7 January 1972, cannot serve us directly as precedents, for it was by applying the case law of the administrative courts as well as of the ordinary courts that the prior statute was held to be repealed by a treaty having provisions contrary to the said statute.

What is therefore the argument of the Customs Administration which calls for the application of the subsequent statute?

We find it set out especially in the defence, and M. Boré has expounded it before you with his customary skill.

He began by raising his hat to the primacy of Community law, with a limitation however expressed to the effect that 'that primacy cannot apply absolutely.'

. . . .

VII

However that may be, in its defence the Customs Administration, citing a judgment of the Conseil d'Etat of 1 March 1968, SYNDICAT GENERAL DE FABRICANTS DE SEMOULES DE FRANCE, submits that that Court refused to exercise a power of *'censure'* against a French statutory provision promulgated subsequent to the Community provisions which were incompatible with it, '. . . for a judge,' it said, 'cannot engage in any assessment of the constitutionality of a statute by excluding the application of it in favour of a Community provision.'

. . . .

However, while the judgment of the Conseil d'Etat keeps to a prudent wording, the conclusions of the Commissaire du Gouvernement are very clear and they constitute the basis of the argument of the Customs Administration here. What do they say?

. . . .

[M. Touffait then makes reference to the arguments raised by Madame Questiaux, Commissaire du Gouvernement, in the case of *Syndicat Général de Fabricants de Semoules de France,* before the *Conseil d'Etat.*]

> 'You cannot,' she said, 'control the conformity of [statute] with the Treaty,' [for] 'the administrative court cannot make the effort which is asked of it without altering, by its mere will, its institutional position.
>
> It may neither criticise nor misconstrue a statute. That consideration has always led it to refuse to examine grounds based on the constitutional invalidity of a statute [all the more so now that] the Constitution has specifically dealt with the judicial review of legislation by adopting a restrictive view and conferring such review upon the Constitutional Council.'

This argument is taken up in the *mémorire ampliatif* which says: 'No French court, with the exception of the Constitutional Council (Conseil Constitutionnel) has the power to declare a statute unconstitutional.'

> ' Under Article 55 of the Constitution, which gives primacy to a treaty over internal law, Madame Questiaux recommends the judge to make an effort at reconciliation when he is interpreting a statute which is subsequent to the Treaty. He can say, where the statute is silent or ambiguous, that it did not intend to infringe the international rule. But if the legislator has expressed a clear will, Article 55 does not excuse the judge from respecting that will and the judge should therefore apply the subsequent statute.'

Faced with that argument, which has been urged before you, what did the ordinary courts (*juges judiciaires*) reply: 'It is,' they said,

> 'in no way a matter of confronting internal law with the Constitution, but to the contrary under that Constitution of comparing the internal provision with the treaty; but according to Article 55 of the Constitution, treaties have an authority superior to that of statute; it follows that the provisions of the Rome Treaty, directly applicable in the internal legal order of

each member-State, have priority over statutory provisions, even if subsequent to the treaty.'

'And far from making itself judge of the constitutionality of statute, the court is called upon only to find that the national statute has had its effects stopped in so far as they are incompatible with the provisions of the Treaty, it being remarked that the scope of the statute remains unrestricted as regards foreign States other than the member-States of the Community.'

'In sum, it is a conflict between two legal norms of differing hierarchical value conflicting one with the other and is to be resolved by applying the superior rule.'

This manner of reasoning of the judges in this case is indeed not an isolated instance, and it is to be found in several judgments of courts of appeal.

. . . .

X

But in order to adopt this argument without reservation we have to examine whether by ruling to that effect we may not be reproached with having dealt with a problem of constitutionality of statute *i.e.,* does examining whether a statute is in conformity with a treaty not amount to review of the constitutionality of statutes?

I have already set out the view on this point of Madame Questiaux, commissaire du governement, in the SEMOULES case which answered the question in the affirmative.

The contrary view of the judge of the 1st arrondissement is expressed in the following paragraph: 'It is in no way a question of a confrontation of the internal statute with the Constitution but, on the contrary, of a comparison, by virtue of that Constitution, of that provisions with the treaty. . . . It is thus not a matter of judging the constitutionality of a statute. . . .'

. . . .

We are thus faced with two categorical statements. Which are we to adopt?

Fortunately, I can refrain from engaging in a long legal reasoning and try to show you that it is not a question of constitutionality, for since the filing of this appeal there occurred a decision of the Conseil Constitutionnel dated 15 January 1975.

. . . .

May I express here one regret, that this major decision, necessarily terse because of the drafting technique of decisions of the Conseil Constitutionnel borrowed from that of the Conseil d'Etat, was not illuminated by the publication of the report of the Councillor rapporteur or by any other internal measure of the Conseil Constitutionnel.

However that may be, it is I think permissible to interpret without fear of mistake the concise paragraphs of the Conseil Constitutionnel.

. . . .

What did the Conseil Constitutionnel say?

> 'Article 61 of the Constitution only gives it power to give a ruling on the conformity with the Constitution of statutes submitted to it. While the provisions of Article 55 of the Constitution confer on treaties an authority which is superior to that of statutes, they do not imply that compliance with that principle is to be enforced by the Conseil Constitutionnel.'

It can then be concluded from this position taken by the Conseil Constitutionnel that compliance should be enforced by the courts to which the problem is submitted, and it is for them, on pain of denial of justice, to reply.

Then follows this paragraph, which clarifies the doctrine of the Conseil Constitutionnel: 'Decisions taken under Article 61 of the Constitution are absolute and definitive in character and that bars promulgation and application of any provision which has been declared unconstitutional. On the contrary, the superiority of treaties over statute is both relative and contingent' — *relative* because limited to the field of application of the treaty and not applying therefore to non-signatory States, *contingent* because subject to a condition of reciprocity of application by the other party.

It follows that a statute contrary to a treaty cannot be taxed with being unconstitutional and the enforcement of compliance with the principle set out in Article 55 could not be applied within the field laid down in Article 61 of the Constitution because of the difference in nature between these two enforcement devices. Consequently, it is not for the Conseil Constitutionnel to examine the conformity of a statute with the requirements of an international agreement. The Conseil Constitutionnel thus lays down a criterion of jurisdiction which is very important, for the principal argument put forward by the proponents of the argument that the courts have no jurisdiction to provide a sanction against violation of Article 55 was based on the concept that involvement in the enforcement of the primacy of the treaty over subsequent statute would mean ineluctably moving into the review of constitutionality of statute. But the Conseil Constitutionnel has decided that that is not so.

According to this decision of 15 January 1975 it is thus not for the judge, when faced with a conflict between treaty and subsequent statute, to review the constitutionality of a statute but to examine a conflict between an internal statute and an international act which, once duly ratified and published, penetrates into our internal legal order and the Constitution does not get involved except to fix the rule which permits the conflict to be resolved by giving the treaty a superior authority.

That is the decision of the Constitutional Council and that, by virtue of Article 62 of the Constitution, is binding on the public authorities and on all administrative and judicial agencies. This constitutional text is made explicit by a decision of the Conseil Constitutionnel of 16 January 1962 which added to it: 'with the very scope that is given to it by the grounds which are its necessary support.'

Writers without exception and the case law of the Conseil d'Etat have deduced from this that the obligatory force of the decisions of the Conseil Constitutionnel applied not only to the order of the Conseil (the *dispositif*) but also to the body of the judgment (the *motifs*) which formed one with it and led very directly to the solution in that case. We can then conclude from that that the conflict between subsequent statute and treaty does not raise a question of constitutionality of that statute and so the argument of the ordinary courts is supported by the decision of the Conseil Constitutionnel.

XI

I could almost bring my legal discussion to an end at this point, but in view of the importance of this question I should like now — as quickly as possible — to justify the solution which I have proposed to you on the basis of public international law, leading up to the Treaty instituting the European Economic Community.

The relations between international law and internal law have been constructed, thought out and set out in the framework of systems classified under the headings of dualism and monism, each of these being the expression of a measure of historical truth, according to the dominant ideas on the national level and the evolution of international society.

To give form to that idea it is not without usefulness to cite the opinion of my eminent predecessor, M. Matter, who on 22 December 1931 in this room, expressed the almost unanimous case law of the time as follows: 'Suppose', he said, 'that there be conflict between statute and a treaty, what ought the judge to do? There is no doubt on that: you do not and cannot have cognizance of any other will than that of statute. That is the very principle upon which rest our judicial institutions.'

But at that time, apart from certain treaties concerning the Postal Union, industrial and literary property, railways, the international conventions related only to the law of war, the freedom of the sea, the safety of the state; and the dualist doctrine prevailed, refusing to recognise the superiority of treaties with regard to statute which is still considered sacred.

But since then the world has been shaken by war and by many dramatic events, and men nourished on the ideas of Duguit and Georges Scelle, have during the dark hours of the occupation ripened the vision of an independent world.

International law as contained in treaties has become considerably enlarged and bears on trade, industry, telecommunications, culture, public health, labour law, human rights, fundamental liberties, etc. International life is organising and institutionalising itself in numerous organs prime among which is the United Nations Organisation.

The idea emerges irresistibly that there can be no international relations if the diplomatic agreements can be put in balk by unilateral decisions of the contracting powers and the duty of the State to respect its international obligations becomes a fundamental principle, and on the morrow of the liberation politicians who were often lawyers realised that their ideas — which might fall under the weight of legal and judicial tradition — would have to be incorporated solemnly in the Constitution if they were to triumph.

That is how for the first time in France the Constitution of 27 October 1946, in its Articles 26 and 28, expressly and in general form incorporated the principle of the primacy of international treaties over internal laws.

Article 26 relates to laws prior to the Treaty. *Article 28 relates to laws subsequent to the Treaty.*

It took the following form:

> 'Diplomatic treaties duly ratified and published have an authority superior to that of internal laws and their provisions may not be *repealed, altered or suspended* except following proper denunciation, notified through diplomatic channels. When it is one of the treaties covered by Article 27 [*i.e.,* a treaty whose ratification must be by statute] the denunciation must be authorised by the National Assembly, except for treaties of commerce.'

There is thus no ambiguity about this wording.

The fact that the equivalent of these two Articles of the 1946 Constitution is a single Article 55 in that of 1958 does not represent a change in will in the constitution-makers.

It is only necessary to read the analytic record of the Constitutional Consultative Committee, whose discussion was concerned only with the notion of reciprocity in the application of the treaty, to realise this.

Besides, how is one to understand Article 55 otherwise? The concept of superiority only has sense with regard to subsequent laws.

If article 55 had been intended to refer only to laws prior to the treaty it would have been sufficient for it to provide that 'a treaty has statutory force,' since it is an absolute principle that subsequent statute prevails over a prior statute.

An analysis of the texts, in accord with the international ethic intended by the makers of the Constitutions of 1946 and 1958, thus ineluctably leads to the consideration that the concept of superiority of treaties over statutes only has sense with regard to statutes subsequent to the treaty, as it is clear that the international legal order can only be realised and developed if the States loyally apply the treaties they have signed, ratified and published.

XII

... [S]ince I have — I hope — succeeded in demonstrating the superiority of the provisions of international treaty law over the provisions of internal law, we now have to develop our analysis of the same conflict, but where the conflict is with the Treaty instituting the European Economic Community whose ideas and obligations differ and go beyond those deriving from classic treaties.

This is an ambitious task, for the Treaty has the aim of establishing and providing the foundations for an ever closer union between the people of Europe, of ensuring by common action the economic and social progress of their countries by eliminating the barriers which divide them, of seeking together stability in expansion, balance in trade, fairness in competition, of abolishing obstacles to international trade.

In order to attain these ends, the Treaty confirms the preeminence of Community law in its **Article 5** and gives it expression in **Article 189** under which regulations are 'binding' and 'directly applicable in all member-States' and takes from the signatory governments the power which they have in classic international law to determine the meaning or the scope of an obscure or ambiguous clause in a diplomatic act to give it to a joint European tribunal which is to ensure a uniform interpretation of the Treaty, lays down organs which have their own powers, particularly that of producing sources of law and procedures which have the effect of determining a corresponding limitation of the powers of the member-States.

This principle of the preeminence of Community law over internal law has been taken up several times by the Court of Justice of the European Communities and particularly demonstrated in its judgment in COSTA V. ENEL (6/64):

. . . .

The force of Community law cannot in fact vary from one State to another in favour of subsequent internal laws without imperilling the realisation of the aims of the Treaty.

From all these indisputable principles, I think that you must draw a conclusion for the reasoning of your judgment.

It would be possible for you to give precedence to the application of **Article 95** of the Rome Treaty over the subsequent statute by relying on Article 55 of our Constitution, but personally I would ask you not to mention it and instead base your reasoning on the very nature of the legal order instituted by the Rome Treaty.

Indeed, in so far as you restricted yourselves to deriving from Article 55 of our Constitution the primacy in the French internal system of Community law over national law you would be explaining and justifying that action as regards our country, but such reasoning would let it be accepted that it is on our Constitution and on it alone that depends the ranking of Community law in our internal legal system.

In doing so you would impliedly be supplying a far from negligible argument to the courts of the member-States which, lacking any affirmation in their constitutions of the primacy of the Treaty, would be tempted to deduce therefrom the opposite solution, as the Italian Constitutional court did in 1962 when it claimed that it was for internal constitutional law to fix the ranking of Community law in the internal order of each member-State.

Those are the reasons, Gentlemen, why I ask you not to base your reasoning on Article 55 of our Constitution; you will thus recognise that the transfer made by the States from their internal legal order to the Community legal order, *within the limits of the rights and obligations corresponding to the provisions of the Treaty,* involves a definitive limitation of their sovereign rights against which a subsequent unilateral act which is incompatible with the notion of Community cannot prevail.

Besides, that is the method which you are already applying in all your divisions when you refer to the Court of Justice at Luxembourg under **Article 177,** relying solely on that **Article** of the Treaty without making reference to any Article of the Constitution or French legislative text, thus recognising that the national judge is the common law judge of the application of Community law.[48]

---

[48] The Cour de Cassation has not wholly followed this suggestion of the Ministère Public and, while affirming the separateness of the EEC Treaty, also relied on Article 55 in proclaiming the superior authority of the Treaty over even subsequent statutes.... This position of the Cour de Cassation can apparently be explained by two reasons:

(a) in referring to the wording of Article 55 in its judgment the Court let it be known that the principle it was laying down applied to *all* treaties which had been duly ratified or approved;

(b) our country can pride itself on possessing such a constitutional text: Has not Niboyet written ([1946] Dalloz 89), in commenting on Articles 26 and 28 of the Constitution of 27 October 1946: 'France can be truly proud of affirming the

In this great but difficult and delicate task of building Europe, *difficult* because it often comes up against national economic differences which have to be eliminated, *delicate* because all the institutions of the country are involved, Parliament, Government, Conseil Constitutionnel, Conseil d'Etat, Cour de Cassation, it is indispensable that all the decisions of these various organs should be compatible with the objectives of the Community, as it is necessary that the finalities of the Rome Treaty should inspire the interpretative law of all the member-States. It would not be without utility, I think, to run through them rapidly.

XIII

Our problem *does not arise in Holland,* for the relations between international law and internal law have been settled by the Constitutional amendments of 1953 and 1956; Article 66 expressly affirms the pre-eminence of treaties over even subsequent statute and Article 67 does the same for derived Community law.

Nor does it arise in Luxembourg where the case law is based on a judgment of the Cour Supérieure de Justice of 14 July 1954 (PAGANI) which gives primacy without dispute to the international legal order over subsequent internal legal provisions. In view of this well established case law the question of the primacy of Community law has never come before the courts in the Grand Duchy.

But the problem has arisen and very sharply so in Belgium, in Germany and in Italy and all the more sharply in those three countries because the judgments proclaiming the primacy of Community law over subsequent internal statute have come outside any constitutional support.

In Belgium, after equivocal and hesitant decisions by lower courts, the question arose in a typical case in which the Belgian Government had been condemned by the Court of Justice of the European Communities for having created in 1958 a tax contrary to **Article 12** of the Treaty.

. . . .

[T]he Belgian Cour de Cassation, in its judgment of 27 May 1971, [held] as follows:

> 'In the event of a conflict between a norm of domestic law and a norm of international law which produces direct effects in the internal legal system, the rule established by the treaty shall prevail. The primacy of the treaty results from the very nature of international treaty law.

---

primacy of the international order over the internal order, an affirmation which is in accordance with international ethics. In that respect our Constitution could serve as a model for many foreign countries.'

This is *a fortiori* the case when a conflict exists, as in the present case, between a norm of internal law and a norm of Community law.

The reason is that the treaties which have created Community law have instituted a new legal system in whose favour the member-States have restricted the exercise of their sovereign powers in the areas determined by those treaties.'

In Germany, after a large number of contradictory decisions by courts of first instance or appeal, the Federal Constitutional Court (Bundesverfassungsgericht) by a judgment of 9 June 1971 saw no objections of a constitutional nature to the Federal Finance Court (Bundesfinanzhof) giving to **Article 95** of the EEC Treaty primacy over subsequent German tax law on the basis of a preliminary ruling of the European Court of Justice.

. . . .

In Italy where the teachings of the dualist doctrine by the great internationalist Anzilotti, President of the Permanent Court of International Justice, have impregnated many generations of lawyers, the resistance to the doctrine of primacy of the Rome Treaty over subsequent internal statute has been longer, but in a long judgment of 18 December 1973 (FRONTINI V. AMMINISTRAZIONE DELLE FINANZE DELLO STATO)* lengthily reasoned, the Italian Constitutional Court has adopted it with éclat. . . .

It is in this context that the judgment you are to deliver will be read and commented upon; its audience will extend beyond the frontiers of our country and spread over the whole of the member-States of the Community.

XIV

This panoramic survey of the case law of the member-States of the European Economic Community suffices to demonstrate that after some years of groping and hesitation there has been created under the guidance of the Court of Justice of the European Communities, that attentive guardian of the will of the authors of the Treaty, by demonstrating, but avoiding the reefs of government by the judiciary — a European legal consciousness within all the national courts concerned to recognise the primacy of Community law without which there could not be created that unity of the market which is desired by the signatory governments and approved by their national sovereignty, reaffirmed at the conferences in The Hague on 2 December 1969 and Paris on 20-21 October 1972; and it is for all these reasons that I conclude very firmly that the second ground of appeal should be dismissed.

---

* The *Frontini* case is reproduced at § D.1., *infra.*

NOTES AND QUESTIONS

1. Under the Supremacy Clause of the United States Constitution, Art. VI, cl. 2, treaties and federal statutes prevail over inconsistent state laws. Since the result stems from the Supremacy Clause, if a state law is held invalid because it is in conflict with a federal law, is the state law "unconstitutional"? In many cases, there are strong similarities in the process of deciding whether state laws are "unconstitutional" in the strict sense and deciding whether state laws have been preempted by federal legislation. Note, *Pre-Emption as a Preferential Ground: A New Canon of Construction,* 12 STAN. L. REV. 208 (1959). Some statutes dealing with the jurisdiction of federal courts turn on the issue whether a state law is claimed to be invalid on grounds that it is unconstitutional. Claims under the Supremacy Clause have generally been held not to be "constitutional" issues for those purposes. *See, e.g., Swift & Co.* v. *Wickham,* 382 U.S. 111 (1965). Those decisions may rest, however, on the context in which the term was used in the particular jurisdictional statute, or on a general policy of narrowly construing the jurisdiction of federal courts. How would one approach the question whether, as an abstract matter, a claim that a state law is invalidated by a federal statute or treaty is a "constitutional" claim? Is there any point in asking that question? Is the question similar to the issue in *Cafès Jacques Vabre* as to whether invalidation of a statute because of conflict with a treaty is a "constitutional" decision?

2. Notice the clear argument by *Commissaire du Gouvernement Questiaux* in the 1968 *Semoules* case that conflict between a treaty and a subsequent statute requires the judges to respect the "clear will" of the legislature in enacting the subsequent statute. Her argument was premised on the conclusion that to do otherwise would be to engage in the forbidden process of "judicial review of legislation." Does Procureur Général Touffait meet that argument by quoting the statement of the *judges judiciaires* that what was proposed was not judicial review but merely resolution of "a conflict between two legal norms of hierarchical values conflicting one with the other"? Is that not the rationale of *Marbury* v. *Madison,* previously so assiduously avoided by French courts? Touffait himself argues that the Constitution is not involved except in establishing the "rule which permits the conflict to be resolved by giving the treaty a superior authority." Does that really distinguish cases where the Constitution itself is the "superior authority"?

3. Touffait relied heavily on the *Conseil Constitutionnel*'s decision in the abortion case for his argument that the issue of conformity of laws with treaties is not "constitutional." It is likely that the abortion decision, coupled with *Cassation*'s decision in *Cafès Jacques Vabre,* will induce the *Conseil d'Etat* to retreat from its contrary decision of 1968 in the *Semoules* case?

4. Note, finally, that the *Cour de Cassation* rejected Touffait's suggestion that it rely only on the special nature of the EEC, and instead also based its decision on Art. 55. Will ordinary French courts, including courts of first instance, now be required to entertain claims of inconsistency of statutes with other treaties? Particularly, what about conformity of French law with the provisions of the European Convention on Human Rights? You will recall that France has not accepted that part of the Convention which provides for individual application. Thus a French citizen cannot file a claim with the Commission of Human Rights that French law is in conflict with the Convention. Can that claim now be litigated in the ordinary courts? (Note that the *Conseil Constitutionnel*'s abortion decision, so heavily relied upon by Touffait, involved the European Convention and not the EEC Treaty.) And, if so, does France now have a transnational bill of rights that must be applied by ordinary courts in concrete cases? Is it simply too anomalous that ordinary judges would have the power to declare a statute invalid under a transnational bill of rights but would be powerless to enforce the French bill of rights? Recall the functional problems which would be faced if French judges followed the reasoning of *Marbury* v. *Madison* and refused to apply unconstitutional laws. Would those problems be absent if a French judge were to refuse to apply a law in conflict with the European Convention on Human Rights?

D. COMMUNITY LAW AND NATIONAL CONSTITUTIONAL LAW

1. Italy

SOCIETÀ ACCIAIERIE SAN MICHELE v. HIGH AUTHORITY

Corte Costituzionale, Decision of December 27, 1965, No. 98
[1967] 6 C.M.L.R. 160 *

[Appellant, an Italian steel firm, was ordered by the High Authority of the European Coal and Steel Community to pay a fine. Appellant challenged the constitutionality of the E.C.S.C. Treaty, and the Turin Tribunale referred the issue to the Italian *Corte Costituzionale.*] The basis for this reference is to be found in the fact that **Articles 33, 41** and **92** of the E.C.S.C. Treaty are stated to be contrary to the provisions of Articles 102 and 113 of the Italian Constitution. The Turin Court points out in its judgment that the provisions of the E.C.S.C. Treaty previously referred to, ascribe exclusive jurisdiction to the European Court on all appeals against the decisions of the High Authority, as well as power to suspend the effect of decisions already issued. Furthermore, the protection against such decisions

---

* Reprinted with permission of Common Law Reports, Ltd., London.

is limited to cases of *détournement de pouvoir.* Therefore, these provisions of the E.C.S.C. Treaty clash with certain fundamental principles of the Italian Constitution, namely, those that assign jurisdictional protection to ordinary judges created in accordance with and controlled by, the provisions on the judiciary, as well as with those which do not allow the creation of extraordinary or special judges, at the same time ensuring to every citizen full protection of his rights and other lawful interests against the executive.

. . . .

2. These three provisions are clearly outside the framework of Articles 102 and 113 of the Constitution. In the view of this Court, such Articles relate only to the protection of the rights and other lawful interests which are assigned to each subject by virtue of his position within the internal legal system; they do not concern the rights and lawful interests which the subject derives from his position in a foreign system such as that of the E.C.S.C. In so far as the E.C.S.C. has as its task the co-ordination of certain economic activities taking place within the territory of several States, it makes up a system which is entirely distinct from the internal one.

In recognising the Community order the State was endeavouring not so much to insert the same in its own system, but rather to make way within such system for that international co-operation which the State has as its aim. Thus, there were circumscribed the instances where the activity which the bodies of the Community are entitled to exercise within their respective spheres of operation may have effect within the internal system.

It cannot be denied, however, that these effects must be established without prejudice to the right of the individual to his jurisdictional protection. Such right is amongst the inviolable attributes of man which our Constitution guarantees in Article 2; indeed it can also be derived from the consideration given to it in Article 6 of the European Convention on Human Rights to which execution was given by our Law No. 808 of 4 August 1955. Nevertheless, the Community order does ensure jurisdictional protection against the conduct of its organs as regards individual subjects (and this, after all, is the only point which the Turin Court considered relevant). As a matter of fact, the protection is expressed by way of appeal to a Court of Justice which, as **Article 31** of the Treaty literally dictates, has a duty to ensure compliance with the law both in the interpretation and in the application of the provisions that make up the Community system; a Court moreover which is established and operates in accordance with rules that, in substance, correspond to those of our own system, even if they do not blindly follow certain regulations of the same, which are not wholly suitable for a body of such an international character. The European Court of Justice can unanimously be described as exercising jurisdictional functions; and one may add that its members are duty bound to exercise such function independently and impartially (see **Article 32 (2)** and **32 (3)** of the Treaty and Articles 2 and 19 of the Statute of the Court). It is quite irrelevant, as far as the effect of Articles 102 and 106 are concerned, to embark upon a discussion as to whether the Court can be described as an organ exercising special jurisdiction *vis-à-vis* certain ordinary tribunals within the jurisdiction of the Italian State, because the relationship between ordinary and extraordinary judicial function (to which the previously mentioned provisions of our Constitution refer) must be sought within the framework of the internal legal system and does not apply to any comparison between the Italian and the Community jurisdiction, whose organs are admittedly placed in separate juridical spheres.

It follows that the organs of our internal jurisdiction are not qualified to criticise acts by organs of the E.C.S.C. because the latter are not subject to the sovereign power of the member-States of the Community, and cannot be found within the framework of any such State: Therefore, their acts can only be subject to a legislative qualification on the part of individual member-States albeit within the limits where there may exist an obligation not to refuse to acknowledge their effects.

. . . .

5. In this Court's judgment, therefore, the question of constitutional legality raised by the reference from the Turin Court must be declared unfounded.

FRONTINI v. MINISTERO DELLE FINANZE

Corte Costituzionale, Decision of December 27, 1973, No. 183
[1974] 2 C.M.L.R. 372 *

FACTS

In the course of civil proceedings brought by Franco Frontini and the company Commercio Prodotti Alimentari Srl against the Minister for Finance and against Vincenzo Duplicato, Guido Tommasoni and Angelo Manganello relating to the amount, fixed in certain EEC regulations, of the agricultural levies on certain imports, the Tribunale of Turin raised the question of the constitutional validity of section 2 of the EEC Treaty Ratification Act 1957, which made effective in Italy **Article 189** of the EEC Treaty, as against Articles 23 and 70-75 of the Italian Constitution.

. . . .

---

* Reprinted with permission of Common Law Reports, Ltd., London.

JUDGMENT

[1] By reference order of the Tribunale of Turin the question is raised of the constitutional validity of section 2 of the EEC Treaty Ratification Act 1957 which made effective in Italy **Article 189** of the Treaty instituting the European Economic Community, signed in Rome on 25 March 1957, in the light of Articles 70, 71, 72, 73, 74, 75 and 23 of the Constitution; by three identical orders of the Tribunale of Genoa the same question is raised in the light of Articles 70, 76 and 77 of the Constitution.

[2] The orders contain exhaustive reasoning on the relevance of the question of constitutional validity to the ultimate decision on the merits of the respective cases.

[3] The proceedings can be joined and answered with a single judgment of this Court.

[4] 2. The admissibility of questioning the constitutional validity of the ordinary statute ratifying and implementing an international treaty with regard to specific provisions of the treaty itself, has already been recognised by this Court in SOC. ACCIAIERIE SAN MICHELE V. HIGH AUTHORITY (1965).

[5] 3. The Treaty instituting the EEC provides in **Article 189 (1)** that 'in order to carry out their task the Council and the Commission shall, in accordance with the provisions of this Treaty, make regulations, issue directives, take decisions, make recommendations or deliver opinions.' The effect of these various acts is then defined, and in paragraph **(2)** of **Article 189** it is stated: 'A regulation shall have general application. It shall be binding in its entirety and directly applicable in all member-States.'

[6] The constitutional validity of this provision of the Treaty is being questioned under various aspects by means of an impugning of the implementation statute which adapted our internal law to it. It is noted in the reference orders that by **Article 189** the binding effect and immediate applicability as against the state and Italian citizens of acts which have the force and power of ordinary statutes, issued from organs other than those to which the Constitution attributes the exercise of the legislative function; that thereby is introduced into our system a new source of primary legislative process, with the resultant removal of legislative power from the normal constitutionally authorised organs of the state, in matters of wide and generically characterised content; that as against Community regulations there are lacking the guarantees laid down by the Constitution for the ordinary statutes of the state (forms of promulgation and publication, possibility to promote repeal referendum, admissibility of control by this Court to protect the fundamental rights of the citizens); that, finally, via these regulations financial obligations (*prestazioni patrimoniali*) can be imposed on

Italian citizens in violation of the statute monopoly (*riserva di legge*) laid down by Article 23 of the Constitution. **Article 189** of the Rome Treaty would involve not only limitations on sovereignty but also 'an inadmissible surrender of sovereignty, or an alteration of the fundamental constitutional structure itself of our state,' and Article 11 of the Constitution would not remove the envisaged constitutional doubt 'either because, apart from its value as a statement of guiding policy, it does not exclude the need of a constitutional statute for limitations of national sovereignty or because it would seem directed to ends other than the typically economic ends pursued by the setting up of the EEC.'

[7] The question must be dismissed. The EEC Treaty Ratification Act 1957, whereby the Italian Parliament gave full and complete execution to the Treaty instituting the EEC, has a sure basis of validity in Article 11 of the Constitution, whereby Italy 'consents, on condition of reciprocity with other States, to limitations of sovereignty necessary for an arrangement which may ensure peace and justice between the nations' and then 'promotes and favours the international organisations directed to such an aim.' That provision, which not by chance is included in the 'fundamental principles' of the Constitution, indicates a clear and precise political aim: the makers of the Constitution referred, in the preamble, to the adherence of Italy to the United Nations Organisation, but were inspired by policy principles of general validity, of which the Economic Community and the other European regional organisations constitute a concrete actualisation. It is sufficient to consider the solemn recitals contained in the preamble to the Treaty and the rules concerning the principles (**Articles 1** *et seq.*), the foundations (**Articles 9** *et seq.*) and the policy of the Community (**Articles 85** *et seq.*) to see how the setting up of the EEC was made by the common will of the member-States to 'lay the foundations of an ever closer union among the peoples of Europe,' in order to 'ensure the economic and social progress of their countries by common action to eliminate the barriers which divide Europe,' all this with the precise aim to 'preserve and strengthen peace and liberty, and calling upon the other peoples of Europe who share their ideal to join in their efforts' and to 'confirm the solidarity which binds Europe and the overseas countries and desiring to ensure the development of their prosperity, in accordance with the principles of the Charter of the United Nations.' There is therefore no possible doubt of the full concordance of the Rome Treaty with the aims indicated in Article 11 of the Constitution.

. . . .

Fundamental requirements of equality and legal certainty demand that the Community norms, which cannot be characterised as a source of international law, nor of foreign law, nor of internal law of the individual States, ought to have full compulsory efficacy and direct application in all the member-States, without the necessity of reception and implementation statutes, as acts having the force and value of statute in every country of the Community, to the extent of entering into force everywhere simultaneously and receiving equal and uniform application to all their addressees. It is also in accordance with the logic of the Community system that EEC regulations, provided that they are complete in themselves, which as a rule characterises norms governing inter-citizen relations as the immediate source of rights and obligations both for the States and for their citizens in their capacity as subjects of the Community, should not be the subject of state-issued provisions which reproduce them, either in full or in an executory manner, and which could differ from them or subject their entry into force to conditions, even less which take their place, derogate from them or abrogate them, even in part. And where one of these regulations involves the necessity for the state to issue norms creating the organisation for the restructuring or new constitution of administrative agencies or services, or else to provide for new or increased expenditure, outside the financial ceiling required by Article 81 of the Constitution, through appropriate variations in the budget, it is obvious that compliance with these obligations on the part of the state could not constitute a condition or ground for suspending the applicability of the Community legislation, which, at least in its inter-citizen content, enters immediately into force.

[13] 8. The system of relationship between Community order and internal order, as set out above, provides a sure solution for the doubts expressed in the reference order about the absence, in relation to the EEC regulations, of the guarantees which our Constitution has regarding state legislation, the enactment and publication of statutes, the admissibility of the repeal referendum and the judicial review of constitutionality. The constitutional provisions govern solely the legislative activity of the organs of the Italian State, and by their nature are not referable or applicable to the activity of the Community organs, which are governed by the Rome Treaty, which constitutes the constitution (*lo statuto fondamentale*) of the Community.

. . . .

[17] In this same perspective too the question should be judged of the constitutional legitimacy of **Article 189** of the EEC Treaty, in so far as it permits the issue of regulations involving the levy of monetary obligations. That does not involve a derogation from the statute monopoly (*riserva di legge*) laid down in Article 23 of the Constitution, since that provision is not formally applicable to the Community legislation, which comes out of an autonomous

production source, part of an order which is distinct from the internal order. . . .

[18] 9. Equally unfounded appear the doubts as to the lack of control by this court in protection of the fundamental rights guaranteed by our Constitution to the citizens.

[19] It should be remembered particularly that the order of the European Economic Community contains a special system of court supervision, characterised by the fullness of jurisdiction attributed to the Court of Justice by **Articles 164** *et seq.* of the Treaty. The Court of Justice of the Community, apart from ensuring 'that in the interpretation and application of this Treaty the law is observed' **(Article 164),** carries out review of the legality of the legislative acts of the Council and the Commission, with jurisdiction to receive actions 'on grounds of lack of competence, infringement of an essential procedural requirement (*violazione delle forme sostanziali*), infringement of this Treaty or of any rule of law relating to its application, or misuse of powers' brought by a member-State or by any natural or legal person **(Articles 173 (1) and (2)),** and has power to declare void acts which have been attacked and found unlawful, and to state which of the effects of the regulation which it has declared void shall be considered as binding **(Article 174).** The Court of Justice is also competent to give preliminary rulings, upon the conditions set out in **Article 177,** on the interpretation of the Treaty, on the validity and interpretation of acts of the institutions of the Community, and on the interpretation of the statutes of bodies established by an act of the Council when such questions are raised 'before any court or tribunal of a member-State.'

[20] The amplitude of the judicial protection which the Community order assures against the acts of its organs which may harm the rights or interests of individual citizens has already been recognised by this Court in SOC. ACCIAIERIE SAN MICHELE *V.* HIGH AUTHORITY (1965), which declared unfounded the question of constitutionality raised in connection with **Articles 102** and **113** of the Constitution with regard to the alleged special nature of the Court of Justice as a judicial organ and to the content of the judicial protection guaranteed by it.

[21] It should, on the other hand, be mentioned that the legislative competence of the organs of the EEC is laid down by **Article 189** of the Rome Treaty as limited to matter concerning economic relations, *i.e.* matter with regard to which our Constitution lays down the statute monopoly (*riserva di legge*) or the reference to statute (*rinvio alla legge*), but the precise and exact provisions of the Treaty provide a safe guarantee, so that it appears difficult to form even abstractly the hypothesis that a Community regulation can have an effect in civil, ethico-social, or political relations through which provisions conflict with the Italian Constitution. It is hardly necessary

to add that by Article 11 of the Constitution limitations of sovereignty are allowed solely for the purpose of the ends indicated therein, and it should therefore be excluded that such limitations of sovereignty, concretely set out in the Rome Treaty, signed by countries whose systems are based on the principle of the rule of law and guarantee the essential liberties of citizens, can nevertheless give the organs of the EEC an unacceptable power to violate the fundamental principles of our constitutional order or the inalienable rights of man. And it is obvious that if ever **Article 189** had to be given such an aberrant interpretation, in such a case the guarantee would always be assured that this Court would control the continuing compatibility of the Treaty with the above-mentioned fundamental principles. But it should be excluded that this Court can control individual regulations, given that Article 134 of the Constitution relates solely to the review of constitutionality of statutes and acts having statutory force of the state and of the regions, and Community regulations, in the present context, are not such.

[22] For these reasons, the Court declares not founded the question of constitutionality of section 2 of the EEC Treaty Ratification Act 1957 (no. 1203 of 14 October 1957), in the part in which it implemented **Article 189** of the Treaty of 25 March 1957 instituting the European Economic Community, raised in the orders above mentioned with regard to Articles 70-77 and 23 of the Constitution.

NOTES AND QUESTIONS

1. What effect does the *Frontini* decision have on the *Corte Costituzionale*'s prior decision in *Costa?*

2. In the debate over ratification of the United States Constitution, the absence of a Bill of Rights was a major issue. Among the arguments for ratification, Hamilton argued in The Federalist # 84 that a Bill of Rights was not necessary, since the limited powers of the federal government made a guarantee of rights unnecessary. James Madison, who was instrumental in the First Congress of the United States in producing the proposed Constitutional Amendments, which became the Bill of Rights, was himself of the view that it was unnecessary. In a 1788 letter to Thomas Jefferson, he explained that a Bill of Rights was unimportant because, among other reasons "the limited powers of the federal Government and the jealousy of the subordinate Governments, afford a security which had not existed in the case of the State Governments." 5 WRITINGS OF JAMES MADISON 269 (G. Hunt ed. 1904). The United States Bill of Rights was of little significance in the constitutional adjudication of the United States Supreme Court until well into the Twentieth Century. Does that suggest that a Bill of Rights may be important even if it is difficult to "form even abstractly the hypothesis that a Community regulation can have an effect" on civil rights?

2. Germany

INTERNATIONALE HANDELSGESELLSCHAFT mbH v. EINFUHR- & VORRATSSTELLE FÜR GETREIDE & FUTTERMITTEL *

German Constitutional Court, May 29, 1974
[1974] 2 C.M.L.R. 540, 547-52, 554

[After a preliminary ruling of validity by the European Court of Justice, the Administrative Court of Frankfurt (*Verwaltungsgericht*)] stayed the proceedings by a decision of 24 November 1971 and requested the ruling of the Bundesverfassungsgericht under Article 100 (1) of the Constitution as to whether the obligation to export existing under European Community law and the associated duty to make an export deposit are compatible with the Constitution and, if so, whether the rule that the deposit is to be released only in a case of *force majeure* is compatible with the Constitution.

. . . .

[17] I. The reference is admissible.

[18] 1. An essential preliminary for this ruling is the closer, though not yet conclusive, determination of the relationship between the constitutional law of the Federal Republic of Germany and European Community law, which has come into being on the basis of the Treaty establishing the European Economic Community (hereinafter referred to as 'Community law'). The present case demands only the clarification of the relationship between the guarantees of fundamental rights in the Constitution and the rules of secondary Community law of the EEC, the execution of which is in the hands of administrative authorities in the Federal Republic of Germany. For there is at the moment nothing to support the view that rules of the Treaty establishing the EEC, that is, primary Community law, could be in conflict with provisions of the Constitution of the Federal Republic of Germany. It can equally remain open whether the same considerations apply to the relationship between the law of the Constitution *outside* its catalogue of fundamental rights, and Community law, as apply, according to the following reasoning, to the relationship between the guarantees of fundamental rights in the Constitution and secondary Community law.

[19] 2. This Court — in this respect in agreement with the law developed by the European Court of Justice — adheres to its settled

---

* Reprinted with permission of Common Law Reports, Ltd., London.

view that Community law is neither a component part of the national legal system nor international law, but forms an independent system of law flowing from an autonomous legal source; for the Community is not a State, in particular not a federal State, but 'a *sui generis* community in the process of progressive integration,' an 'inter-State institution' within the meaning of Article 24 (1) of the Constitution.

[20] It follows from this that, in principle, the two legal spheres stand independent of and side by side one another in their validity, and that, in particular, the competent Community organs, including the European Court of Justice, have to rule on the binding force, construction and observance of Community law, and the competent national organs on the binding force, construction and observance of the constitutional law of the Federal Republic of Germany. The European Court of Justice cannot with binding effect rule on whether a rule of Community law is compatible with the Constitution, nor can the Bundesverfassungsgericht rule on whether, and with what implications, a rule of secondary Community law is compatible with primary Community law. This does not lead to any difficulties as long as the two systems of law do not come into conflict with one another in their substance. There therefore grows forth from the special relationship which has arisen between the Community and its members by the establishment of the Community first and foremost the duty for the competent organs, in particular for the two courts charged with reviewing law — the European Court of Justice and the Bundesverfassungsgericht — to concern themselves in their decisions with the concordance of the two systems of law. Only in so far as this is unsuccessful can there arise the conflict which demands the drawing of conclusions from the relationship of principle between the two legal spheres set out above.

[21] For, in this case, it is not enough simply to speak of the 'precedence' of Community law over national constitutional law, in order to justify the conclusion that Community law must always prevail over national constitutional law because, otherwise, the Community would be put in question. Community law is just as little put in question when, exceptionally, Community law is not permitted to prevail over entrenched (*zwingende*) constitutional law, as international law is put in question by Article 25 of the Constitution when it provides that the general rules of international law only take precedence over simple federal law, and as another (foreign) system of law is put in question when it is ousted by the public policy of the Federal Republic of Germany. The binding of the Federal Republic of Germany (and of all member-States) by the Treaty is not, according to the meaning and spirit of the Treaties, one-sided, but also binds the Community which they establish to carry out its part in order to resolve the conflict here assumed, that is, to seek a system which is compatible with an entrenched precept of the constitutional

law of the Federal Republic of Germany. Invoking such a conflict is therefore not in itself a violation of the Treaty, but sets in motion inside the European organs the Treaty mechanism which resolves the conflict on a political level.

[22] 3. Article 24 of the Constitution deals with the transfer of sovereign rights to inter-State institutions. This cannot be taken literally. Like every constitutional provision of a similar fundamental nature, Article 24 of the Constitution must be understood and construed in the overall context of the whole Constitution. That is, it does not open the way to amending the basic structure of the Constitution, which forms the basis of its identity, without a formal amendment to the Constitution, that is, it does not open any such way through the legislation of the inter-State institution. Certainly, the competent Community organs can make law which the competent German constitutional organs could not make under the law of the Constitution and which is nonetheless valid and is to be applied directly in the Federal Republic of Germany. But Article 24 of the Constitution limits this possibility in that it nullifies any amendment of the Treaty which would destroy the identity of the valid constitution of the Federal Republic of Germany by encroaching on the structures which go to make it up. And the same would apply to rules of secondary Community law made on the basis of a corresponding interpretation of the valid Treaty and in the same way affecting the structures essential to the Constitution. Article 24 does not actually give authority to transfer sovereign rights, but opens up the national legal system (within the limitations indicated) in such a way that the Federal Republic of Germany's exclusive claim to rule is taken back in the sphere of validity of the Constitution and room is given, within the State's sphere of rule, to the direct effect and applicability of law from another source.

[23] 4. The part of the Constitution dealing with fundamental rights is an inalienable essential feature of the valid Constitution of the Federal Republic of Germany and one which forms part of the constitutional structure of the Constitution. Article 24 of the Constitution does not without reservation allow it to be subjected to qualifications. In this, the present state of integration of the Community is of crucial importance. The Community still lacks a democratically legitimated parliament directly elected by general suffrage which possesses legislative powers and to which the Community organs empowered to legislate are fully responsible on a political level; it still lacks in particular a codified catalogue of fundamental rights, the substance of which is reliably and unambiguously fixed for the future in the same way as the substance of the Constitution and therefore allows a comparison and a decision as to whether, at the time in question, the Community law standard with regard to fundamental rights generally binding in the

Community is adequate in the long term measured by the standard of the Constitution with regard to fundamental rights (without prejudice to possible amendments) in such a way that there is no exceeding the limitation indicated, set by Article 24 of the Constitution. As long as this legal certainty, which is not guaranteed merely by the decisions of the European Court of Justice, favourable though these have been to fundamental rights, is not achieved in the course of the further integration of the Community, the reservation derived from Article 24 of the Constitution applies. What is involved is, therefore, a legal difficulty arising exclusively from the Community's continuing integration process, which is still in flux and which will end with the present transitional phase.

[24] Provisionally, therefore, in the hypothetical case of a conflict between Community law and a part of national constitutional law or, more precisely, of the guarantees of fundamental rights in the Constitution, there arises the question of which system of law takes precedence, that is, ousts the other. In this conflict of norms, the guarantee of fundamental rights in the Constitution prevails as long as the competent organs of the Community have not removed the conflict of norms in accordance with the Treaty mechanism.

[25] 5. From the relationship between Constitution and Community law outlined above, the following conclusions emerge with regard to the jurisdiction of the European Court of Justice and of the Bundesverfassungsgericht.

[26] (a) In accordance with the Treaty rules on jurisdiction, the European Court of Justice has jurisdiction to rule on the legal validity of the norms of Community law (including the unwritten norms of Community law which it considers exist) and on their construction. It does not, however, decide incidental questions of national law of the Federal Republic of Germany (or in any other member-State) with binding force for this State. Statements in the reasoning of its judgments that a particular aspect of a Community norm accords or is compatible in its substance with a constitutional rule of national law — here, with a guarantee of fundamental rights in the Constitution — constitute non-binding obiter dicta.

[27] In the framework of this jurisdiction, the European Court determines the content of Community law with binding effect for all the member-States. Accordingly, under the terms of **Article 177** of the Treaty, the courts of the Federal Republic of Germany have to obtain the ruling of the European Court before they raise the question of the compatibility of the norm of Community law which is relevant to their decision with guarantees of fundamental rights in the Constitution.

[28] (b) As emerges from the foregoing outline, the Bundesverfassungsgericht never rules on the validity or invalidity of a rule of Community law. At most, it can come to the conclusion that

such a rule cannot be applied by the authorities or courts of the Federal Republic of Germany in so far as it conflicts with a rule of the Constitution relating to fundamental rights. It can (just like, vice versa, the European Court) itself decide incidental questions of Community law in so far as the requirements of **Article 177** of the Treaty, which are also binding on the Bundesverfassungsgericht, are not present or a ruling of the European Court, binding under Community law on the Bundesverfassungsgericht, does not supervene.

[29] 6. Fundamental rights can be guaranteed by law in numerous ways and may accordingly enjoy numerous types of judicial protection. As its previous decisions show, the European Court also considers that it has jurisdiction by its decisions to protect fundamental rights in accordance with Community law. On the other hand, only the Bundesverfassungsgericht is entitled, within the framework of the powers granted to it in the Constitution, to protect the fundamental rights guaranteed in the Constitution. No other court can deprive it of this duty imposed by constitutional law. Thus, accordingly, in so far as citizens of the Federal Republic of Germany have a claim to judicial protection of their fundamental rights guaranteed in the Constitution, their status cannot suffer any impairment merely because they are directly affected by legal acts of authorities or courts of the Federal Republic of Germany which are based on Community law. Otherwise, a perceptible gap in judicial protection might arise precisely for the most elementary status rights of the citizen. Moreover, no different considerations apply to the constitution of a community of States with a constitution based on freedom and democracy which is called in question than apply to a federal State with a constitution based on freedom and democracy: It does not harm the Community and its constitution based on freedom (and democracy) if and in so far as its members in their constitutions give stronger guarantees of the liberties of their citizens than does the Community.

. . . .

[35] The result is: As long as the integration process has not progressed so far that Community law also receives a catalogue of fundamental rights decided on by a parliament and of settled validity, which is adequate in comparison with the catalogue of fundamental rights contained in the Constitution, a reference by a court in the Federal Republic of Germany to the Bundesverfassungsgericht in judicial review proceedings, following the obtaining of a ruling of the European Court under **Article 177** of the Treaty, is admissible and necessary if the German court regards the rule of Community law which is relevant to its decision as inapplicable in the interpretation given by the European Court, because and in so far as it conflicts with one of the fundamental rights in the Constitution.

[The court held, on the merits, that the challenged rule of Community law did not violate the German Constitution.]

DISSENTING OPINION (Rupp, Hirsch and Wand JJ.)

[47] We regard the reference as inadmissible and therefore cannot concur in the judgment under sections B I and II.

I

[48] Rules of law which have been issued by organs of the European Communities on the basis of powers transferred to them (secondary Community law) cannot be examined for their compatibility with the norms on fundamental rights in the Constitution.

[49] 1. In Article 24 (1) of the Constitution, the constitution of the Federal Republic of Germany provides that the federation can by statute transfer sovereign rights to inter-State institutions. It made use of this power in ratifying the EEC Treaty (*cf.,* section 1 of the EEC Treaty Ratification Act 1957). Therefore, on a limited sector (**Articles 2** and **3** of the EEC Treaty), there has arisen an autonomous system of law which has at its disposal organs of its own, a collection of norms of its own and its own system for legal protection. Community organs are equipped with law-making powers. The rules of law issued by them, which belong neither to the national system of law nor to international law, form — together with the provisions of the Treaty and unwritten principles of law — the Community's fund of legal norms. In interpreting and applying the Treaty, the European Court of Justice ensures that the law is upheld. This system of Community law is autonomous and independent of the national legal sphere.

[50] 2. Both legal spheres recognise — each for its own sector — norms dealing with fundamental rights and a legal protection system calculated to enforce these rights.

[51] (a) Fundamental rights are guaranteed not only by the Constitution within the national system of law of the Federal Republic of Germany, but also by the system of law of the European Communities.

[52] Apart from isolated provisions with a content approaching that of provisions on fundamental rights (*e.g.,* **Articles 7 (1)** and **119**), the EEC Treaty contains in **Article 215 (2)** a reference to the general legal principles which are common to the legal systems of the member-States. Above all, the essential elements of the principle of the rule of law and fundamental rights are guaranteed at Community level in the case law of the European Court. The principle of proportionality has been recognised by the European Court from the very beginning of its case law as the criterion for the

legality of actions of the Community organs. In the preliminary ruling obtained by the Verwaltungsgericht in the original proceedings, the European Court not only examined whether the security deposit prescribed in the EEC regulations now before the Bundesverfassungsgericht for examination is a 'necessary and appropriate means' of achieving the desired end, but also discusses whether commerce is excessively burdened by the security deposit.

[53] The demand for legality of administration also finds expression in the decisions given by the European Court.

[54] The requirement of certainty of law and of protection of confidence has been time and again recognised by the European Court. The observance of the principle of the fair hearing and of the prohibition on double jeopary is guaranteed by the decisions of the European Court.

[55] While, from the start, great importance attached, in the decisions of the European Court, to the ban on discrimination, it is only in the last few years that the protection of liberties has come to make itself felt. On this point too, however, there is enough case law to permit the statement that fundamental rights are adequately protected at Community level. The European Court has repeatedly emphasised that the observance of fundamental rights belongs to the general legal principles, the upholding of which it is the European Court's duty to ensure. The criteria for this are first and foremost the constitutional traditions of the member-States. That means, as the European Court states in its judgment of 14 May 1974, that no measure can be recognised as lawful which is incompatible with the fundamental rights recognised and protected by the constitutions of the member-States. Apart from this, the European Court made it clear in the same judgment that restrictions of fundamental rights for the achievement of the aims of the European Communities serving the common weal reach their limit where the fundamental rights would be affected in their very essence. Thus, despite the lack of a catalogue of fundamental rights, the protection of the fundamental rights guaranteed in the Constitution is also guaranteed in the legal system of the European Communities — though to some extent in modified form — through the case law of the European Court of Justice. Additionally, after the ratification by France of the European Human Rights Convention and the Supplementary Protocol of 20 March 1952, all member-States of the Communities are now contracting parties to the Convention. It is therefore to be reckoned that the European Court will make use of the provisions, contained in the Convention and the Supplementary Protocol, on the protection of human rights and fundamental freedoms in order to establish what are the general legal principles which are common to the legal systems of the member-States, as is already indicated in the judgment of 14 May 1974.

. . . .

. . . On an objective interpretation, Article 24 (1) of the Constitution says not only that the transfer of sovereign rights to inter-State institutions is admissible, but also that the sovereign acts of the inter-State institutions are to be recognised by the Federal Republic of Germany. This precludes any subjection of these acts to national review. For this is precisely what the Federal Republic of Germany has relinquished by its entry into the EEC, its consent to the establishment of Community organs, and its collaboration in the foundation of an autonomous sovereign power. The sovereign acts which are to be recognised and which are not subject to any national review include the law-making of the European Community organs. The rules of law issued by them cannot therefore be dependent in their validity and applicability on whether they match the criteria of national law. In content, Community law takes precedence over divergent provisions of national law. This applies not only in relation to norms of simple national law, but also *vis-à-vis* norms of the national constitution dealing with fundamental rights.

. . . .

The protection of fundamental rights guaranteed inside the Community does not differ in essence and structure from the fundamental rights system of the national Constitution. In both systems, the central nucleus of fundamental rights is recognised and protected. The fundamental rights which apply within the legal sphere of the European Communities are identical to those guaranteed by the Constitution; their basis is formed by the common constitutional traditions of the member-States — their recognition rests on the same conceptions of value and order. That is enough. No member-State can demand a guarantee of fundamental rights at Community level in precisely the same form as is known to the national Constitution. Article 24 (1) of the Constitution permits the handover of fundamental rights to a Community which, while it does not consider itself bound by the fundamental rights guaranteed at national level, nonetheless guarantees inside its system of law a protection of fundamental rights which corresponds in its basic features to the standard of the Constitution. It follows from this that rules of Community law are only bound by the fundamental rights norms which apply at Community level, and do not additionally have to satisfy the fundamental rights norms of the national Constitution.

[62] The 'basic structure of the Constitution, on which its identity rests' is not at stake in this process. The question of whether Article 24 (1) of the Constitution permits a transfer of sovereign rights which gives Community organs the opportunity to make law binding nationally, entirely untrammelled by being bound by fundamental rights, no longer poses itself today. It is therefore mistaken from the start for the majority of the Court to believe that it has to ward off some 'encroachment' on the structures which go to make up the

Constitution, and in particular its section dealing with fundamental rights, by binding Community law to the fundamental rights norms of the national Constitution. Nor can such an assumption be founded by reference to the fact that the European Communities do not yet possess any codified catalogue of fundamental rights. In this context, the mode of guaranteeing the fundamental rights is irrelevant, and the assertion that only a codification offers adequate certainty of law does not bear examination. It is not obvious why — as the majority of the Court holds — 'the present state of integration of the Community' should be relevant to the relationship between Community law and the Constitution. The argument that the fundamental rights of the Constitution must also prevail over secondary Community law because the Community still lacks a directly legitimated parliament is not in itself conclusive. The protection of fundamental rights and the democratic principle are not interchangeable inside a democratically constituted Community based on the idea of freedom; they complement one another. While the achievement of the democratic principle in the EEC would cause the legislator and the executive to be more deeply concerned with fundamental rights, this would not make the judicial protection of fundamental rights superfluous.

[63] The view of the law adopted by the majority of the Court leads, moreover, to unacceptable results. If the applicability of secondary Community law were dependent on its satisfying the fundamental rights norms of the national Constitution, then — since the member-States guarantee fundamental rights to differing extents — the situation could arise where legal rules of the Communities are applicable in some member-States, but not in others. This would result, precisely on the field of Community law, in a fragmentation of law. To open up this possibility means exposing a part of European legal unity, endangering the existence of the Community, and negating the basic idea of European unification.

[64] By taking the view it has adopted, the majority of the Court also puts itself in conflict with the settled case law of the European Court. The European Court has concluded from the text and spirit of the Treaty that no national rules of law of the member-States of any kind whatsoever — not even provisions of national constitutional law — can take precedence over Community law, which flows from an autonomous legal source. The European Parliament has also repeatedly expressed the same view. In addition, the Italian Corte Costituzionale has made clear in its judgment of [27] December 1973 that regulations of Community law are not subject to review for their compatibility with Italian constitutional law.

[65] The Bundesverfassungsgericht possesses no jurisdiction to examine rules of Community law against the criteria of the Constitution, in particular of its section on fundamental rights, in

order, on this basis, to answer the question of their validity. It is true that the majority of the Court concedes that the Bundesverfassungsgericht should not rule on the validity or invalidity of a norm of Community law, but retracts this finding in the end by adding that the Bundesverfassungsgericht can declare such a norm inapplicable in the sphere of the Federal Republic of Germany. But this distinction between invalidity and inapplicability of a norm exhausts itself in the use of different words. If a court declares a legal norm generally inapplicable because of violation of superior law, it is thereby stating, on a commonsense view, that the norm does not apply, that is, that it is invalid. The Bundesverfassungsgericht does not possess this power in respect of the legal rules of the Community organs. The fact that the majority of the Court nonetheless claims this power is an inadmissible trespass on the jurisdiction reserved to the European Court, the recognition of which is dictated by Article 24 (1) of the Constitution; this trespass creates a special status for the Federal Republic of Germany and exposes it to the justified reproach of violating the EEC Treaty and jeopardising the legal system of the Community.

. . . .

NOTES AND QUESTIONS

1. The decision of the German Constitutional Court agrees with that of the Italian Constitutional Court on the general point that there is a limit to the supremacy of Community law. Is there, however, a significant difference between the approach of the two decisions? Critics of the German approach have cited the *Frontini* approach as the preferred alternative. The EEC Commission has filed a protest with Germany over the decision of its Constitutional Court, but has filed no similar protest with Italy.

2. Consider the following statements in the EEC Commission's protest filed with Germany:

By claiming the power to verify the compatibility of Community secondary legislation with the fundamental rights in the Basic Law, the [German] Constitutional Court is impugning the exclusive jurisdiction of the Court of Justice to ensure that in the interpretation and application of the treaties the law is observed (Article 164 of the EEC Treaty).

The Commission has informed the German Government of its grave concern. Commission of the European Communities, Eighth General Report on the Activities of the European Communities in 1974 at 270 (1975).

Also, consider the position of the EEC Court of Justice in its preliminary ruling in the *Internationale Handelsgesellschaft* decision:

> *As to the protection of fundamental rights in the Community legal system*
>
> [3] Recourse to legal rules or concepts of national law to judge the validity of instruments promulgated by Community institutions would have the effect of harming the unity and efficacity of Community law. The validity of such instruments can only be judged in the light of Community law. In fact, the law born from the Treaty, the issue of an autonomous source, could not, by its very nature, have the courts opposing to it rules of national law of any nature whatever without losing its Community character and without the legal basis of the Community itself being put in question. Therefore the validity of a Community instrument or its effect within a member-State cannot be affected by allegations that it strikes at either the fundamental rights as formulated in that State's constitution or the principles of a national constitutional structure.
>
> [4] An examination should however be made as to whether some analogous guarantee, inherent in Community law, has not been infringed. For respect for fundamental rights has an integral part in the general principles of law of which the Court of Justice ensures respect. The protection of such rights, while inspired by the constitutional principles common to the member-States must be ensured within the framework of the Community's structure and objectives. We should therefore examine in the light of the doubts expressed by the Administrative Court whether the deposit system did infringe fundamental rights respect for which must be ensured in the Community legal order. [1972] C.M.L.R. 255, 283.

Do these statements fully resolve the issues raised by the German and the Italian Constitutional Courts?

3. The German Constitutional Court stated in § 23 of the *Internationale Handelsgesellschaft* decision, *supra,* that "the Community still lacks a democratically legitimated Parliament directly elected by general suffrage which possesses legislative powers and to which the Community organs empowered to legislate are fully responsible on a political level."

The existing "European Parliament," the Assembly, lacks the attributes indicated by the Court in several respects. First, its representatives are still elected by the national legislatures of the member countries. Second, despite the fact that its powers were recently expanded to include control over the budget of the European Communities, the Assembly generally acts only in an advisory capacity.

Articles 137 and 138 of the Treaty of Rome contain as a goal for the future the direct election by universal suffrage of representatives of a European Parliament; * however, the Council of Europe has encountered many roadblocks in trying to achieve this goal. The Council did, in December of 1974, recommend that an election be held as soon as possible. After two years of negotiations, an agreement was reached on the following points:

1. Apportionment of seats between member states;
2. Approximate date of the elections (May-June 1978);
3. The necessity to employ different election procedures in the various countries until uniform procedures can be formulated which comply with art. 138.3 of the Treaty.

These agreements were formalized in the act of the Council of Ministers of September 20, 1976. It is this Act which was referred by the President of the French Republic to the *Conseil Constitutionnel.* The *Conseil*'s decision regarding the constitutionality of the Act follows.

3. France

DECISION OF DECEMBER 30, 1976

Conseil Constitutionnel

[1976] J.O. 7651

The *Conseil Constitutionnel,* seized on December 3, 1976 by the President of the Republic under the terms provided by Article 54 of the Constitution with the issue concerning the constitutionality of the decision of the Council of the European Communities of September 20, 1976 pertaining to the election of the Assembly by direct universal suffrage;

. . . .

Considering that the decision of the Council of Ministers of the European Communities of September 20th, 1976 and the Act which is annexed only purport to stipulate that the representatives to the peoples Assembly of the states united in the Community are elected by direct universal suffrage and to fix some conditions of this election;

Considering that although the Preamble of the 1946 Constitution, reaffirmed by the Preamble of the 1958 Constitution, provides that, under condition of reciprocity, France accepts the limitations of sovereignty which are necessary to the organization and the defense of peace — no provision of a constitutional nature authorizes transfers of the whole or a part of the national sovereignty to any international organization;

---

* For a discussion of the structure of the EEC, *see* § A.1.a., *supra.*

Considering that the Act submitted to the *Conseil Constitutionnel* does not contain any provision modifying the jurisdiction and powers specifically assigned in the text of the Treaties to the European Communities and, particularly, to their Assembly by the member states, or modifying the nature of that Assembly, which remains composed of the representatives of each of the peoples of these states;

Considering that the election by direct universal suffrage of the representatives of the peoples of the member states to the Assembly of the European Communities does not create a sovereignty or institutions the nature of which would be incompatible with the respect of the national sovereignty, nor does it infringe upon the jurisdiction and powers of the institutions of the Republic and, notably, of the Parliament; that any transformation or derogation could only result in a modification of the treaties, subject to the constraints of the articles of Title VI * as well as of Article 61 of the Constitution.

Considering that the international agreement of September 20, 1976 does not include any stipulation fixing, for the election of the French representatives to the Assembly of the European Communities, conditions of such a nature as to question the indivisibility of the Republic, the principle of which is restated in Article 2 of the Constitution; that the wording of "uniform electoral procedure" which is mentioned in Article 7 of the Act submitted to the *Conseil Constitutionnel* should not be construed as allowing an exception to this principle; that, in a general way, the implementation texts of this Act will have to abide by the principles stated above as well as with all the other principles of a constitutional value;

Considering that the sovereignty which is defined in Article 3 of the Constitution of the French Republic, whether in its foundation or in its exercise, can only be national and that only the representative of the French people elected in the framework of the institutions of the Republic can be viewed as participating in the exercise of this sovereignty;

Considering that it follows from the above that the Act of September 20, 1976 pertains to the election of the members of an Assembly which does not belong to the constitutional order of the French Republic and which does not participate in the exercise of the national sovereignty; that consequently, the conformity to the Constitution of the international commitment submitted to the *Conseil Constitutionnel* must not be reviewed with respect to

---

* Title VI of the French Constitution deals with treaties and international agreements.

Articles 23 and 34 of the Constitution, * which are relative to the allocation of the competency and the procedures pertaining to the institutions which participate in the exercise of the French sovereignty.

Declares:

. . . [that, in] view of the above considerations, the decision of the Council of the European Communities of September 20, 1976 and the Act which is annexed do not contain any provision contrary to the Constitution.

NOTES AND QUESTIONS

1. This opinion marks the first time that the *Conseil*'s jurisdiction was invoked by the President of the Republic under arts. 54 and 61 of the French Constitution. This referral was provoked by the fact that the question of the conformity of the September 1976 agreement with the Constitution arts. 2 and 3 was raised by the traditional line of the Gaullist movement under the leadership of Michel Debré under art. 54.

Article 2: France is an indivisible, secular, democratic and social republic. . . .

Article 3: The national sovereignty belongs to the people which exercises it by its representatives and by referendum.

No section of the people nor any individual can attribute to itself the exercise of the national sovereignty.

Suffrage can be direct or indirect in the conditions provided by the Constitution. It is always universal and secret.

Article 54: If the Constitutional Council, seized by the President of the Republic, by the Prime Minister or by the President of one or the other of the assemblies, has declared that a provision of an international agreement is contrary to the Constitution, the authorization to ratify or to approve it can only occur after the Constitution has been amended.

2. As some commentators have pointed out (Favoreu et Philip, *Jurisprudence du Conseil Constitutionnel — Election ou suffrage Universel Direct des Membres de l'Assemblée Européenne,* [1977] REVUE DU DROIT PUBLIC ET DE LA SCIENCE POLITIQUE EN FRANCE ET A L'ETRANGER 129-67), the "international character" of the September 1976 agreement — constituted by a decision of the Council of Ministers of the EEC and attached Act — and the necessity to have it ratified or approved was questionable and one could argue that the issue was more one of interpretation and enforcement of a provision of an already ratified treaty (Art. 138 of the Rome Treaty)

* Article 23 deals with the incompatibility of governmental and parliamentary functions. Article 34 defines the scope of the law-making power of the Parliament.

falling within the jurisdiction of the European Court of Justice than one of internal constitutional law.. The Constitutional Council did not discuss the matter but implicitly answered the question by accepting to review the agreement. In so doing, does it appear to you more ready to risk itself in an international legal environment than it was at the time of the Abortion Decision of January 15, 1975?

Remember, however, that the issues in the two cases were radically different. Whereas in the abortion decision the conflict was one between *a ratified international agreement* and *a non-promulgated law,* in the *European Parliament* decision it was one between a *non-ratified international agreement* and the *Constitution.*

Whereas the abortion decision dealt with a fundamental right, the right to life, of utmost moral and practical interest, the *European Parliament* decision concerned the area of allocation of sovereignty. Thus, not only was it less directly sensitive to moral pressures, but its scope was also more general than the Italian, German and European Court decisions.

3. Can the *European Parliament* decision of the *Conseil Constitutionnel* be reconciled with the *Cafès Jacques Vabre* decision of the *Cour de Cassation?* With the submissions of Procureur Général Touffait about this decision?

4. The Court of Justice of the European Communities

FIRMA J. NOLD KG v. E.C. COMMISSION

Court of Justice of the European Communities
Decision of May 14, 1974
[1974] 2 C.M.L.R. 338, 351-52, 354-55 *

JUDGMENT (Drafting judge, Pescatore J.)

[1] By application filed on 31 January 1973, the undertaking J. Nold KG, which carries on in Darmstadt a wholesale trade in coal and construction materials, requested — according to the final version of its submissions — annulment of the Commission's decision of 21 December 1972 relating to the authorisation of new sales rules of Ruhrkohle AG and, in the alternative, a declaration that that decision is void and not applicable in so far as it concerns the applicant. The latter complains in essence that the decision authorised the Ruhr coal sales agency to make the direct supply of coal conditional on the conclusion of firm two-year contracts, providing for a minimum purchase of 6,000 tonnes annually for the supply of domestic homes and small industry, a tonnage which considerably exceeds its annual sales in that sector, and had thus excluded it from its position as direct wholesaler.

---

* Reprinted with permission of Common Law Reports, Ltd., London.

2. *On the plaint of an alleged violation of fundamental rights*

[12] The applicant finally claims a violation of certain of its fundamental rights by reason of the fact that the restrictions imposed by the new trading rules authorised by the Commission have the effect, by eliminating it from direct supply, of attacking the profitability of its undertaking and the free management of its affairs, to the point of threatening its existence. Thus, under this heading a quasi-property right is infringed, as well as the right of free exercise of its commercial activities, which are protected by the Constitution of the Federal Republic of Germany, as also by the constitutions of other member-States, and various international instruments, particularly the European Convention for the Protection of Human Rights of 4 November 1950, including the additional Protocol of 20 March 1952.

[13] As this Court has already held, fundamental rights form an integral part of the general principles of law which it enforces. In assuring the protection of such rights, this Court is required to base itself on the constitutional traditions common to the member-States and therefore could not allow measures which are incompatible with the fundamental rights recognised and guaranteed by the constitutions of such States. The international treaties on the protection of human rights in which the member-States have co-operated or to which they have adhered can also supply indications which may be taken into account within the framework of Community law. It is in the light of these principles that the plaints raised by the applicant should be assessed.

[14] While protection may be ensured for the right of property by the constitutional order of all the member-States and while similar guarantees are given to the free exercise of trade, labour and other commercial activities, the rights thus guaranteed, far from appearing as absolute prerogatives, should be considered in the light of the social function of the property and activities which are protected. For that reason, rights of that type are usually guaranteed only subject to limitations relating to the public interest. In the Community legal order, it thus appears legitimate, as regards these rights, to maintain certain limits justified by the general objectives pursued by the Community, so long as the substance of the rights is not impaired. As concerns the guarantees given to undertakings in particular, they could in no case be extended to the protection of mere commercial interests or prospects, the contingent character of which is inherent in the very essence of economic activity.

[15] The disadvantages put forward by the applicant are in reality the consequence of economic change and not of the decision in issue. It is for the applicant, confronted by the economic change caused by the recession in coal production, to face the new situation and itself to make the necessary adaptation.

[16] For all these reasons the ground must be dismissed.

[17] Therefore the application must be dismissed.

. . . .

NOTES AND QUESTIONS

1. Can any nation with a written constitution subordinate its own constitutional guarantees of liberty to treaty membership in an international organization? In the United States, the treaty power is independent of other Congressional powers. For example, in implementing a treaty, Congress can pass substantive legislation which would otherwise not be within its enumerated powers and thus reserved to the states. *Missouri* v. *Holland,* 252 U.S. 416 (1920). Justice Holmes' opinion in *Missouri* v. *Holland* also contained a dictum, however, which could be read to mean that treaties were not subject to the limitations of the Bill of Rights. *Id.* at 433. The controversy was concluded in 1957, when Justice Black wrote:

> . . .no agreement with a foreign nation can confer power on Congress, or on any other branch of the Government, which is free from the restraints of the Constitution. . . . The prohibitions of the Constitution were designed to apply to all branches of the National Government and they cannot be nullified by the Executive or by the Executive and the Senate combined. [*Reid* v. *Covert,* 354 U.S. 1, 16-17 (1957).]

Note, however, that in the United States, as a matter of internal law, treaties are subordinated to subsequent legislation.

> It would be completely anomalous to say that a treaty need not comply with the Constitution when such an agreement can be overridden by a statute that must conform to that instrument. [*Id.*]

Would Justice Black's conclusion, that a treaty contrary to the Bill of Rights is invalid, be different if it were possible in the United States to ratify a treaty superior to subsequent legislation?

After *Reid* v. *Covert,* the Supreme Court entertained on the merits a claim that the Japanese Security Treaty was contrary to the Bill of Rights. The argument was rejected on the merits. *Wilson* v. *Gerard,* 354 U.S. 524 (1957). No provision in any treaty has been held unconstitutional by the Supreme Court. HENKIN, FOREIGN AFFAIRS AND THE CONSTITUTION 137 (1972).

2. Based on the decisions of the constitutional courts of France, Germany and Italy and on the decision of the European Court in the *Nold* case, what is the status of the "United Europe" as a legal entity? Do you agree with the following comments by Professors Favoreu and Philip?

There are only national sovereignties; there is no European sovereignty: so could be roughly presented the position of the Constitutional Council. . . . The position of the Constitutional Council on the legal nature of the Communities and on their evolution surely puts an end to some of the broad interpretations of the Community agreements. But it is not so distant from the one of the German and Italian Constitutional Courts and one can even say that it is not in flagrant conflict with the one of the European Court of Justice. . . .

[The position of the Council] does not exclude the possibility of a Community legal order nor of a definitive limitation of sovereignty. What the decision of the Constitutional Council does exclude is a transfer of all or part of the national sovereignty and thus the recognition of a new sovereignty without a preliminary revision of the Constitution; but the Court of Justice has never, so far, attributed to the European Communities the quality and the powers of a sovereign entity to which the whole or a part of the national sovereignty could be transferred.*

Can a distinction be made between "transfers" and "limitations," whether "definitive" or not, of sovereignty? Between a "national or European legal order" and a "national or European sovereignty"?

Did the European Court in the *Nold* decision indirectly attribute "to the European Communities the quality and the powers of a sovereign entity" when it stated that there is a Community public interest in the ambit of the general objectives pursued by the Community and that such public interest can justify certain limits regarding fundamental rights?

3. There is no formal "Bill of Rights" in Community law; rather it has been emerging through the decisions of the Court of Justice. This began in 1969, in *Stauder* v. *City of Ulm,* [1970] 9 C.M.L.R. 112, where the Court stated that EEC law must not "jeopardize the fundamental rights of the individual contained in the general principles of the law of the Community." *Id.* at 119. This was reaffirmed in 1970, when the Court issued its preliminary ruling in the *Internationale Handelsgesellschaft* case. [1972] 11 C.M.L.R. 177. The final such decision is *Nold,* reprinted above.

Notice that Community rights are not the sum of all national rights; rather, they are deduced from the "constitutional traditions common to the member-States." Thus, the Court will consider individual national systems and common agreements, like the European Convention on Human Rights. Clearly these common elements are

---

* L. Favoreu & L. Philip, *Chronique Constitutionnelle,* [1977] Revue du Droit Public et de la Science Politique en France et a l'Etranger no. 1, 129, 158, 161, 163.

not readily ascertainable, particularly after the entry of two common law countries — Great Britian and Ireland — in 1973.

4. Would it be an acceptable solution for the EEC to adopt the European Convention on Human Rights? Would it then have to accept the jurisdiction of the European Commission and Court of Human Rights? Are there other possible problems?

5. If there is a higher Community law, it means that ordinary Community law which violates it is not to be applied. What, then, is the role of the national courts in deciding such a question?

PART II
CONSTITUTIONAL ADJUDICATION IN PRACTICE: SELECTED TOPICS

INTRODUCTION *

It is a matter of common observation that, historically, certain rights and guarantees emerged as "fundamental," or, particularly in modern times, as "constitutionally" or "internationally" proclaimed, and so became differentiated from other rights and guarantees.

This phenomenon is not alien to the law of procedure. For millennia a number of basic principles have developed to represent the "fundamental" rights of the parties *vis-à-vis* the judge, the adversary, and third persons: such as the ancient principles of (a) the party's exclusive right to initiate an action and to determine its subject matter (*"nemo judex sine actore," "ne eat judex ultra petita et allegata a partibus"*), (b) judicial impartiality (*"nemo judex in re sua"*), and (c) the right of defense (*"audiatur et altera pars"*). Other principles have a somewhat less ancient history, such as the great liberal guarantee of judicial independence from the executive; still others such as the right to a "natural" or "lawful" judge (that is, a judge predetermined by law), and the guarantee of an open and public proceeding, can be considered a conquest, or an aspiration, of modern times.

Intrinsic to the consideration of those principles as "basic" (*"Grundsätze"* in German terminology was the belief that they represented both an essential minimum for any civilized system of administration of justice and also permanent, immutable ingredients of such administration. Significantly, the English have been known to speak of rules of "natural" justice. The tendency was to consider them valid beyond limits of space and time — universal and eternal. Clearly this was a Utopian belief, since experience should have made it clear that no principles, institutions, or values live empyreally and abstractly *per se,* alienated from the mutable circumstances of history and society.

With the decline of natural law conceptions, even "basic" principles of judicial administration have usually found their "positivization" in statutes and codes. Yet, recent experience has tragically brought many peoples to the new belief that certain values, rules, and guarantees, although themselves susceptible to the general destiny of mutability of all that is humanly designed, should be insulated from an excessively easy possibility of violation and change. Special legislative procedures should be prescribed for their amendment; special sanctions and remedies should be adopted for their infringement. Hence, their "constitutionalization": in other

---

* The following is adapted from Cappelletti, *General Report to the 1971 Conference of the International Association of Legal Science,* in Fundamental Guarantees of the Parties in Civil Litigation 664-67 (M. Cappelletti & D. Tallon eds. 1973).

words, their incorporation into a newer type of positive law, a "higher" law that binds, to a certain degree, even the legislature.

Particularly after World War II this development took on universal dimensions as a reaction against abhorred violation and abuse; it was especially marked in countries emerging from the nightmare of dictatorship and defeat such as Germany, Italy, and Japan. This growing phenomenon is a major aspect of what has been called "modern constitutionalism." Less pronounced, yet parallel, is another development, the "internationalization" of certain similar guarantees and rights. From the point of view of strictly positive law, however, this latter development has not yet grown to major proportions. To be sure, an increasing number of international documents do proclaim procedural rights and guarantees, such as the Universal Declaration of Human Rights of 1948 (especially Arts. 8 and 10) and the covenants later enacted for its implementation. Unfortunately, however, these texts still bear little juridical significance since no effective tools have been yet devised for their enforcement. The only remarkable exception to this unhappy situation is the European Convention for the Protection of Human Rights and Fundamental Freedoms, signed in Rome on November 4, 1950.

Chapter 6

THE RIGHT OF ACTION

A. INTRODUCTION *

Is there a right of access to court for the resolution of civil litigation? Two opposite solutions have emerged.

The first solution is one which allows entrusting adjudicatory functions to nonjudicial bodies — whether they be called administrative agencies, special tribunals, compulsory arbitrators, state arbitrators, or whatnot. Although from their decisions some more or less limited possibility of appeal to courts may exist, this is by no means a constitutional law requirement. Indeed, such possibility does not always exist; decisions of nonjudicial adjudicatory bodies may be final and unreviewable in court.

The second solution is one which rigorously and constitutionally forbids entrusting adjudicatory powers to nonjudicial bodies, unless "full" court review of their decisions — i.e., *de novo* review of both fact and law — is open.

(i) *The Anglo-American and socialist solution, and its rationale*

Generally speaking, the first solution can be found in Common Law as well as in socialist nations; apparently, it also is the prevailing solution in Scandinavian and African countries. There are noteworthy limitations to this general principle, however. One example of such limitations is the U.S. Constitution's guarantee of trial by jury, which can stand in the way of legislative freedom to assign the adjudication of certain categories of cases to bodies other than the normal "trial courts." Such a shifting of cases is not possible whenever they are covered by the trial by jury requirements of the Sixth Amendment (Federal criminal cases) or the Seventh Amendment ("suits at common law, where the value in controversy shall exceed twenty dollars") or corresponding constitutional guarantees under state constitutions. Another example is illustrated by the British and the Canadian courts' practice of interpreting in a most restrictive manner — sometimes even wholly contravening —

---

* Adapted from Cappelletti, *General Report of the 1971 Conference of the International Association of Legal Science,* in Fundamental Guarantees of the Parties in Civil Litigation 702-18, 720-21 (M. Cappelletti & D. Tallon eds. 1973).

the so-called "finality" or "privative" clauses granting finality to the decisions of certain nonjudicial adjudicative bodies, which would have been nonreviewable in court.

It should be stressed that all of this turns around a most important practice which has grown to striking proportions in the last fifty years or so in countries such as the U.S.A., Great Britain, Canada, and the Soviet Union. This is the practice — central to this Part of our study — of taking away civil (that is, noncriminal) disputes from the courts and entrusting them to decision by administrative agencies, state arbitration bodies, and the like.

The policy underlying this practice is a very pervasive one. In contrast to the laissez-faire state of the last century, the 20th-century governments are involved in newer and growing tasks, most of them of a social nature. The central philosophy of the 19th-century state was a "negative" one, that is, one of noninterference: individual rights were protected in that the public organs guaranteed that they would neither interfere, nor permit interference, with the citizen's life, property, and enterprise. The 20th-century state, on the contrary, has increasingly become a "social state." Its philosophy can no longer be predominantly negative; rather, it has taken on an essentially "positive" character — one of increasingly frequent intervention in the economy, regulation of property, and control over enterprise. Hence the growing need to effectuate such interventions through a vast number of bodies entrusted with economic and social functions, in order to perform that "social revolution" which is the central feature of our century.

"New Deal" America is but one striking example of such a development, which had substantial analogies in Great Britain, especially under the Labour governments, and was preceded by basically similar developments — although, of course, extremely different in tension, abruptness, and degree — in the Soviet Union. "New Deal" America experienced both the sudden deluge of new administrative agencies, and the threatened explosion of the courts. Faced with the new tasks of the "social state," the traditional courts were physically and philosophically unable to match such a new challenge. Judges were too few; their formalistic and burdensome procedures were not flexible enough to deal rapidly, efficiently, and economically with new social and economic demands; their political and cultural outlook as well as their sociological background made them incapable of coping with certain issues in a socially desirable way; indeed, they were hardly adaptable to understanding the newly emerging philosophy of the 20th-century state.

Hence the need was felt to entrust adjudicative functions to different "judges," taking such functions away from the courts of law, and limiting, or even excluding, court review of these "judges'" decisions. Far from being a socially desirable or even a "fundamental" value, a general right of access to court or court review appeared to hamper social progress and favor economic stagnation; because it costs much money and takes much time, such a right appeared to be more frequently an advantage to the economically strong than to the needy.

Thus, the new development was generally found not only possible, but highly desirable; constitutional obstacles, if any, were obliterated and overcome. Today, civil procedure "proper," that is, procedure in the civil "courts," is but a relatively small portion of a gigantic mass phenomenon. In this phenomenon, along with the courts, myriads of other bodies — in some way integrated with the active administration, hence politically answerable to the people rather than shielded, as the traditional judges, from democratic pressures — act as nonjudicial, quasi-judicial, or para-judicial agencies adjudicating matters which indeed are "civil," and making decisions which only infrequently are subject to "full" review in court.

(ii) *The opposing solution affirmed by the newer Constitutions of Japan, Italy, and the Federal Republic of Germany: its historical background*

Both the Japanese Constitution of 1946 and the Italian Constitution of 1947 are explicit in guaranteeing a general right of access to court. In the words of the Japanese Constitution, "No person shall be denied the right of access to the courts"; in the words of the Italian Constitution, "everyone has the right to sue in court for the protection of his rights and legitimate interests."

Most explicitly, the Constitution of Japan also adds that "the *whole* judicial power" is vested in the courts established by law, and that "no organ or agency of the executive shall be given final judicial power." Almost as explicit is the Constitution of Italy which adds to the general proclamation of the "right to sue in court" (Art. 24) that "No one shall be denied the right to be tried by his natural judge pre-established by law," that the judicial function is vested in the courts described in Arts. 102 and 103, that all the persons acting as judges of such courts enjoy independence and impartiality safeguards as established in Arts. 101-110, and that "Judicial protection of rights and legitimate interests against acts of the public administration will always be admitted before the ordinary or administrative courts. Such judicial protection cannot be abolished or limited to specified categories of acts or to particular forms of judicial review."

Equally stringent is the 1949 Constitution of the Federal Republic of Germany. To be sure, unlike the two Constitutions mentioned before, it does not contain an explicit affirmation of a general "right of action" in court. Art. 19(4) of the German Basic Law, however, is similar to the Italian Constitution's Art. 113; it establishes that

"Should any person's right be violated by the public authority, recourse to court shall be open to him. If no other court has jurisdiction, recourse shall be to the ordinary court." Moreover, Arts. 92, 97, and 101 establish that the judicial function shall be vested in the federal and *Länder* courts; that all judges — including, as in Italy, the administrative court judges — shall be assured a full range of independence and impartiality safeguards; and that "No one may be removed from the jurisdiction of his judge established by law" (*gesetzlicher Richter*).

Thus, it is now clear in all three countries that it would be unconstitutional to entrust adjudicatory functions to nonjudicial bodies, unless these bodies' decisions were subject to full review in court. Judicial interpretations have confirmed time and again that this is the rigorous solution adopted by the three countries' fundamental law.

. . . .

One may ask, then, why such a profound divergence exists between the approach adopted by this group of nations and that adopted, instead, by Anglo-American and socialist nations.

One first and very conclusive reason is that the Japanese, German, and Italian Constitutions were the immediate reaction against a tragic experience of state abuse, particularly by the executive. Because of sad past experiences in those countries, broad control powers vested in independent courts are preferred to perhaps more efficient but unreviewable action by administrative agencies. As for Italy, suffice it to recall those times when, by ordinary act of Parliament or even by delegated legislation of the Cabinet, administrative decisions such as those taken against "non-Aryans" by the fascist Minister of the Interior could be declared final and unreviewable in court.

This forceful historical background, then, can explain the rigorous, even rigid reaction of the newer democratic Constitutions of those three nations. It is probable that in countries where a due process tradition is deeply rooted among both the people and the public administration, a solution like the one examined in Section (i) can prove acceptable or even desirable; it is undoubtedly a more flexible solution and allows state intervention to adapt itself more easily to the impetus of changing and newly emerging needs of modern societies. Yet, the dangers can outweigh the advantages in those countries which are not similarly trained in such a tradition. Here, *Kabinettsjustiz*, that is, a system of adjudicating bodies subservient to the executive, could once again prove to be the easiest instrument for tyranny and abuse.

There is, however, a second aspect which must be taken into account, at least insofar as Germany and Italy are concerned. It seems clear that one additional reason why these two countries have so rigidly adopted and so far maintained the solution just examined is that, since the second half of the last century, both of them have introduced a comprehensive system of "administrative courts," substantially patterned after the French. These administrative courts have affirmed themselves as truly independent and impartial bodies, endowed with real courts' prestige and maintaining fundamental standards of procedural fairness; and yet they are sufficiently different from the "ordinary" courts, sufficiently specialized in the subject matters with which they have to deal, and sufficiently closed, both organically and culturally, to the active administration whose acts they have to review. It must also be noted that in Germany — and perhaps again on the French pattern — the network of courts does not ramify, as in Italy, into the dichotomy "ordinary" and "administrative" courts only. The Constitution establishes "tax," "labor," and "social" courts alongside both the administrative courts and the ordinary courts for civil and criminal matters (Art. 95, paragraph 1); the Constitution also allows the establishment of a court for industrial property rights (Art. 96, paragraph 1) and of other "courts for special fields" (Art. 101, paragraph 2). Needless to say, the judges of these courts will be selected in a manner assuring such special qualifications as deemed desirable for the particular fields in which they are called to act. For instance, the German Constitution itself prescribes that the judges of the Supreme Courts in the fields of ordinary civil and criminal, administrative, tax, labor, and social jurisdiction ". . . shall be selected jointly by the Ministers competent for the particular matter and a committee for judicial selection consisting of the *Land* Ministers competent for the particular matter and an equal number of members elected by the *Bundestag*."

Admittedly, the dichotomy of the court system in Italy and, even more so, the pluralism of the hierarchy of courts in Germany, may be — and indeed are — the source of a great number of problems and complications, as one can easily imagine. On the other hand, if judicial review is to be maintained, only a network of specialized courts, sympathetic with, yet sufficiently independent from, the public administration, can favorably match such a new role without being doomed to explosion.

Divergencies, then, do exist. Indeed, a deep contrast has come to light together with the pervasive policies and *raisons d'être* behind each of the opposing solutions adopted in the two groups of nations mentioned in the preceding Sections.

And yet, even very strong converging trends emerge; they are clearly aimed at finding a correct balance between two apparently irreconcilable opposites: (a) the citizens' right to have all his grievances heard by the courts, and (b) the speedy and efficient functioning of administrative bodies, whose task could be made difficult or impossible to accomplish if their every decision were subject to challenge in court.

We have, on the one hand, very clear indications in the first group of nations of a trend — confirmed even at the European Convention's level — toward "judicialization" of nonjudicial adjudicating bodies. This means that certain guarantees of impartiality, as well as certain minimum standards of procedure turning around the "right to be heard," are more and more emerging as imperative even for those bodies, and that judicial review of such bodies' decisions tends more and more to be admitted, at least in case of violations of these minimum standards and guarantees. We can clearly see this trend at work in the U.S.A., Great Britain, and Canada. Even in socialist nations, a trend to introduce a "court model" into the nonjudicial adjudicatory agencies has been apparent during the last two decades.

On the other hand, there is a growing consciousness in the second group of nations that the reaction of their post-World War II constitutions, as justified as it could be historically, has led nevertheless to just another extreme, and that this overreaction might weigh heavily upon the efficiency and flexibility of state interventions. One realizes that the judicial administration itself might severely suffer from an excessive expansion of its role and a growing flood of cases to decide; that traditional "judges" and "courts" might not be the right persons and bodies for newer challenging tasks, and it would be wrong to assume that they, and their complex procedures, have an inherent vocation to settle all problems of modern life; that, indeed, in technologically advanced societies there is a growing need for expert assistance in civil litigation, and even in ordinary courts the role of the experts in influencing judicial decisions has become so great that it has been asked whether we are witnessing, in part, a transfer of the judicial function from the court to the expert; that, generally, contemporary societies are more concerned with "social justice" and conciliation than with "droits subjectifs" and adversary proceedings, the latter being the traditional fields of the courts' action; and, finally, that a new generation has grown since the old authoritarianism's downfall, a generation educated in a new constitutional atmosphere and hopefully able to impose "due process" standards without and beyond the barbed wires of a rigid system of review by the "courts."

Thus, the first group of nations is perhaps taking a similar road as have a number of Continental European nations, led by France and including Germany and Italy, in the past century — namely, toward a slow but progressive transformation of nonjudicial adjudicating bodies into real administrative "courts," although such courts will undoubtedly be much more varied and diversified, both in their structures and procedures, than the European model. On the other hand, the second group of nations is visibly moving toward a similarly greater articulation and variation. Not only have these nations tried time and again to design specialized and simplified procedures to be followed before the normal courts, but they have also increasingly allowed the creation of "specialized courts" or "special divisions" of ordinary courts to deal with special matters in a more flexible, speedy, informal, as well as socially and technically conscious way. In these courts, or divisions of courts, the professional and traditional judges are frequently substituted by, or sit together with, other judges, most often lay judges, who are more acutely aware of the technical and economic peculiarities of a given subject matter, and more sympathetic with its social implications and special needs.

B. JUDICIAL REVIEW OF ADMINISTRATIVE ACTION

1. The Existence of a Right of Action in Continental Europe

The "right of action" is the right to have legal disputes resolved by a court. The most important aspect of this is the right to judicial review of administrative action.

In Germany and Italy the right of action is constitutionally guaranteed. Article 19, para. 4, of the German Constitution provides:

> Should any person's right be violated by public authority, recourse to the court shall be open to him. If no other court has jurisdiction, recourse shall be to the ordinary courts.

The analogous provision of the Italian Constitution is Art. 113:

> Judicial protection of rights and legitimate interests against acts of the public administration will always be admitted before ordinary or administrative courts.
>
> Such judicial protection cannot be abolished or limited to specified categories of acts or to particular forms of procedure for challenging them.
>
> The law will determine what judicial organs can annul acts of the public administration in those cases and with those effects provided for by the law.

Also, Art. 24, para. 1, provides that "Everyone may proceed at law for the protection of his rights and legitimate interests."

There is no equivalent article in the Constitution of France. Consider, however, the following decision by the *Conseil d'Etat.*

MINISTER OF AGRICULTURE v. DAME LAMOTTE
Decision of February 17, 1950, Conseil d'Etat
[1950] D. Jur. 282; [1950] S. Jur. III 65*

The *Conseil d'Etat* (CE), ruling in its adjudicative capacity.

On the report of the first sub-division of the Adjudicative Division;

Having seen the appeal and the explanatory memorandum submitted on behalf of the Minister of Agriculture, registered with the Secretariat for the Adjudicative Division of the CE on 28 October 1946 and 23 February 1948 praying the CE to annul a decision dated 4 October 1946 by which the Council of the Prefecture of Lyon (CPL) annulled a decision dated 10 August 1944, by which the Prefect of Ain, by virtue of Art. 4 of the statute of 23 May 1943, had granted Sieur de Testa the property known as "du Sauberthier," situated in the commune of Montluel belonging to Dame Lamotte (née Vial);

Having seen the statutes of 19 February 1942 and 23 May 1943;

Having seen the order of 9 August 1944;

Having seen the order of 31 July 1945;

Having heard the report of Sieur Després, "Maître des Requêtes";

Having heard the arguments of Maître Rousseau, counsel for the Minister of Agriculture, and of Maître Galland, counsel for Dame Lamotte;

Having heard the submissions of Sieur Delvolvé, "Maître des Requétes," "Commissaire du Gouvernement";

Considering that, by a decision of 29 January 1941, taken under the statute of 27 August 1940, the prefect of Ain granted the property known as "du Sauberthier" (in the commune of Montluel), belonging to Dame Lamotte, née Vial, to Sieur de Testa "for a period of nine years entire and consecutive which shall begin to run from 1 February 1941";

That by a decision of 24 July 1942, the CE annulled this grant on the grounds that the property "had not lain abandoned and uncultivated for more than two years"; that by a later decision of 9 April 1943, the CE annulled a second decision of the Prefect of Ain, made on 20 August 1941, which granted to Sieur de Testa three further pieces of land adjoining the property;

Considering finally that, by a decision of 29 December 1944, the CE annulled a third decision dated 2 November 1943, as being an abuse of authority. By this decision the Prefect of Ain "in order to delay execution of the aforementioned decisions of 24 July 1942 and

---

* 57 REVUE DU DROIT PUBLIQUE ET DE LA SCIENCE POLITIQUE EN FRANCE ET A L'ETRANGER 487 (1951).

of 9 April 1943," had "requisitioned" the property "du Sauberthier," to the benefit of the same Sieur de Testa;

Considering that the Minister of Agriculture has referred to the CE a decision dated 4 October 1946 by which the council of the inter-departmental prefecture of Lyon, seized of a claim by Dame Lamotte against a fourth decision of the Prefect of Ain, dated 10 August 1944, granting once again the property of "Sauberthier" to Sieur de Testa, annulled the said grant; that the Minister argues that the council of the prefecture ought to have rejected that claim as inadmissible by virtue of Art. 4 of the statute of 23 May 1943;

Considering that art. 4, paragraph 2 of the act called the Statute of 23 May 1943 provides that "the grant of the concession cannot be made the object of any judicial or administrative recourse"; that — even though this prior provision, insofar as it has not been declared void in conformity with the order of 9 August 1944 relative to the re-establishment of the Republican legal system, has the effect of abolishing the recourse before the council of the prefecture which had been made available to the proprietor by Art. 29 of the statute of 19 February 1942 to allow her to contest, in particular, the regularity of the grant — it did not exclude the recourse of "excess of authority" [excès de pouvoir or "ultra vires"] before the CE against the grant, a recourse which is available, even without textual authority, against any administrative act, and which ensures according to general principles of law, respect for the law; that it follows from this, on the one hand, that the Minister of Agriculture is entitled to demand the annulment of the decision of the Prefect of Ain of 10 August 1944; but that, on the other hand, the CE is entitled to review, as judge of "excess of authority," the request for annulment of the decision of the Prefect of Ain of 10 August 1944 presented by Dame Lamotte.

Considering that the documents in the file establish that the said decision purely and simply affirmed the earlier grant, made to the benefit of Sieur de Testa, for a period of 9 years "to count from 1 February 1941," as has been said above; that the said decision had no other object but deliberately to oppose the above-mentioned decisions of the CE ruling in its adjudicative capacity; and that thus the said decision is tainted by an abuse of authority;

Decides

Article 1 — the above-mentioned decision of the CPL of 4 October 1946 is annulled;

Article 2 — the decision of the Prefect of Ain of 10 August 1944 is annulled.

COMMENTARY BY PROFESSOR MARCEL WALINE *

The case reported [above] provides a particularly striking example of the rebellion of the administration against decisions of the CE. . . . The . . . decision is characteristic of the will of the CE to force the administration to comply [with its decisions]. In this case the CE encountered a provision of a statute of the Vichy government which excluded all "administrative or judicial recourse" in cases of concessions of uncultivated or abandoned land. By an inexplicable oversight, this provision, clearly contrary to the most elementary principles of our public law, was not declared void by the order of 9 August 1944, nor by the texts which expanded it. It must then be considered "provisionally applicable." The preclusion of any judicial remedy, however, seemed so shocking to the CE, that it did not hesitate to interpret it as being inapplicable to the remedy for excess of authority. We shall see, in the interesting findings of M. Delvolvé, Commissaire du Gouvernement, what ingenious, indeed subtle reasoning he proposed to reach an even more radical solution:

Findings of M. Delvolvé, Commissaire du Gouvernement:

I. The appeal of the Minister of Agriculture against the decision of the conseil de Préfecture de Lyon of 19 July 1946, is the latest episode in a conflict between a stubborn administration and the CE. Simply from the point of view of the respect due to your own decisions, the judgment that you will have to give is highly important.

However, you will have to examine questions of an even greater importance, since the case involves nothing less than the upholding of the principle of the rule of law (*principe de légalité*). What is most serious is that, in order to ignore the authority of decided cases, the administration has finally found support and arguments in a statute of 1943, which at least on its face seems purely and simply to abolish any judicial remedy in order to avoid the possibility of a judicial control which is inconvenient to the exercise of arbitrary power.

The Act called the Statute of 23 May 1943, "ensuring the utilization of uncultivated or abandoned land," is at issue.

Dame Lamotte is the owner of a large property called "du Sauberthier," in the commune of Montluel, in the département of Ain.

A first text, having force of law, the Act called the Statute of 27 April 1940, authorized the concession of uncultivated and abandoned lands by prefectural decision; by virtue of this, the

* Waline, *Notes de Jurisprudence,* 67 Revue du Droit Publique et de la Science Politique en France et a l'Etranger 478, 478-80, 482-86 (1951).
Reprinted with permission.

property was the subject of a concession by the Prefect of Ain dated 29 January 1941, for the benefit of one Sieur de Testa. Dame Lamotte attacked this decision before the CE.

When the CE took cognizance of this case, a body of case law had already established a complete and precise definition of the state of "abandonment and lack of cultivation" sufficient to justify the grant of a concession. In applying this case law the CE by a decision of 24 July 1942 annulled the prefectural decision of 29 January 1941: the property "du Sauberthier" could not be held to be uncultivated or abandoned.

. . . .

In order to keep Sieur de Testa in possession despite these decisions, the administration then invoked the Statute of 11 July 1938 on the organization of the nation in time of war. A prefectural decision of 2 November 1943 ordered no longer the concession, but rather a "requisition" of the property "du Sauberthier" for the benefit of Sieur de Testa.

This requisition was attacked before you, and you annulled it by a decision of 29 December 1944, on the grounds that the requisition was only made in order to obstruct the execution of your earlier decisions.

But meanwhile the text which, according to the administration, has abolished without exception any possibility of judicial recourse against decisions of concession, had intervened.

Uncertain as to the fate of his requisition order, but with the support of this new text, on the 10th of August 1944 the Prefect made two decisions: the first brought the requisition to an end, which by the way did not eliminate its importance in the suit then under way; the second once again granted a concession of that property to Sieur de Testa; more precisely it reactivated the initial concession, as we shall see in a moment.

It was before the CPL that Dame Lamotte attacked this new decision. . . .

Before the CPL, the administration pleaded that the Act called the Statute of 23 May 1943, precluded any judicial remedy.

The CPL nonetheless annulled the prefectural decision of 10 August 1944. It stated in its decision . . . that the wording of the Statute of 23 May 1943 "does not imply any intent of the legislature to deprive the proprietor of a remedy which had been made available to him by the earlier Statute and which, in any case, is only a particular application of the general rule of public law according to which any administrative act, whatever the organ from which it emanates, is subject to the control of the administrative courts."

It is this decision [of the CPL] which the Minister of Agriculture had appealed [before the CE].

II. We should first re-read carefully the text cited. The second paragraph of [Art. 4 of] the Act called the Statute of 23 May 1943 is drafted as follows: The grant of the concession cannot be subject to any administrative or judicial recourse by the proprietor.

. . . .

III.A. However, this appeal raises a much more serious question which it would be useful to deal with for the sake of the reputation of public law, and which you could not avoid in any case. . . .

This question, assuming that the legislation of 1943 had really intended to exclude all remedies (which is debatable), is whether such an intention can still be effective after the re-establishment of the republican legal system by the order of 9 August 1944.

The question is a serious one because neither this order, nor any subsequent order or Statute, has expressly established the nullity of the Act called the Statute of 23 May 1943.

Not that the Republican legislature had completely neglected this Statute: it even established in the Statute of 9 August 1947 the nullity of three articles of it (Arts. 7, 8 and 9). . . .

However, it went no further and has never made a ruling on the provision of Art. 4, which, the Minister alleges, abolished all recourse.

Logically, we ought first to see whether this interpretation is correct and whether the authors of the text of 1943 really intended to abolish all judicial control.

However, we shall not follow this logical line of reckoning because the intention of the legislature in 1943 matters little; today its enactment only has the legal force which the legislature of the Fourth Republic has allowed. It is thus the intention of this latter legislature which must be interpreted. This intention, as far as it is shown by the order of 9 August 1944, must lead you to control the legality of the Act of 23 May 1943 and to conclude that, even assuming that the 1943 legislature had wished to abolish all judicial check, paragraph 2 of Article 4 of that Act has no effect today and that the review power entrusted to the Conseil de Préfecture by the earlier texts must be upheld.

This solution may appear daring. In fact it recalls the notorious judicial control of the constitutionality of laws which has been rejected by the whole of French case law in terms which are extremely firm and clear and which are politically, if not legally, fully justified.

But this is only an appearance. It is not a judicial control of constitutionality of legislation which we are proposing to you; it is merely the application of legislative texts relative to the re-establishment of the republican legal order and, so far as it is necessary, their interpretation.

B. The terms of the order of 9 August 1944 and the expressions which were used subsequently and consistently by the legislature to describe the legislation of the Vichy government leave no doubt as to the worth of this legislation and as to the source of its present force.

If the legislature of August 1944 had intended to strike only those of these Acts [of the Vichy government] which were contrary to the principles of freedom and equality which are the basis of our legal order, it would have said so. . . . It did not so limit itself. It declared that in general all the Acts of the Vichy government were void and of no effect. And it gave the explicit reason for this in its statement of reasons: no obligatory force can be derived from the intent of a mere *de facto* authority.

These expressions indicate that the Vichy legislation can derive no obligatory force except within the intention of the legislature of August 1944.

The last paragraph of Art. 2 of the order of 9 August 1944 provides, it is true, that the nullity of Vichy Acts must be expressly declared and that these Acts remain valid in so far as this nullity has not been declared.

The legislature of August 1944 thus expressed its intention, at least provisionally, to maintain a certain number of the earlier texts in order to avoid, as stated in the reasoning, judicial disorder or uncertainty.

But these texts only draw their legal force from the order of August 1944, like a sort of a posteriori delegation; they are thus deprived of their legislative character: the administration, the legislator and the CE itself all take care to call them not "Statutes" but "Acts called Statutes" (*actes dits lois*).

Thenceforth, they are subject to review for legality. . . .

To be sure, . . . you will have authority to declare the nullity of a provision of an "Act called Statute" only if it is clearly contrary to the intention of the legislature of the Fourth Republic.

. . . .

In a field very close to that of the racial laws, that of the reinstatement of civil servants, you did not hesitate to require the reinstatement of those who had been affected by the Act called the Statute of 17 July 1940, which forbade the sons of foreigners to work in the public sector (decision of 16 May 1945, the *Rocamora Case*). And yet, the nullity of the text had not been declared [by the legislature of the Fourth Republic]. . . .

The Act called the Law of 23 May 1943, with which we are concerned, . . . repudiated perhaps the most important principle of our public law, a principle prior to the republican legislation itself and for which all of your case law for 150 years tended to instill respect on the part of all administrative authorities, however highly placed they be and whatever their character, including the President of the Republic himself acting by authority of a fully enabling Statute or as a Colonial Legislator.

This principle, so basic that no regulatory provision can escape it, is the principle of the "rule of law" (*principe de légalité*).

It is the essential guarantee of the citizens and of the state.

It binds the legislature itself because a law which ignores it would contain an inherent contradiction, since it would permit the administrative authorities to act arbitrarily, in contempt of the substantive or procedural rules established by the law. . . .

What becomes of these provisions and guarantees upheld by the new text if it abolishes judicial control?

Such a law destroys itself: the example which you have before you today shows the importance of this principle, which is the foundation of legality itself or of the "légalité républicaine," whose re-establishment was the object of the order of 9 August 1944.

The legislature of August 1944 could not, at the same time as it was solemnly re-establishing this principle of the rule of law, have been able to legalize the denial of such an essential principle.

Thus you can decide, without disregarding either the intentions of our legal system, or the principle which excludes constitutional control of the laws by the judges:

— that the "Acts called Statutes" still in force are subject to review for legality;

— that the re-establishment both of the principle of legality and of the judicial control which is the essential guarantee of that principle is the necessary consequence of the re-establishment of the republican legal order;

— that the provisions of the Acts called Statutes which derogate from these principles can no longer be applied.

Thus paragraph 2 of Article 4 of the Act called the Statute of 23 May 1943 must be deemed not to have been written.

. . . .

Article 18 bis of the order of 21 April 1944, complemented by that of 6 April 1945, made the decisions of the "Jury d'Honneur" "not subject to any appeal," and you decided in the case of "Aillières and others" of 7 February 1947, that in the absence of a clearly shown intention on the part of the authors of this provision, this expression could not be interpreted as precluding the appeal to "cassation" which is, by the way, only a form of appeal for excess of authority.

The principle thus affirmed in 1947 is even more certain for decisions of administrative authorities. Even in the absence of a [legislative] text, the appeal for excess of authority is available against any executive act in order to ensure respect for the law. This appeal remains available even if all other recourse has been excluded by the legislature.

NOTES AND QUESTION

1. The *Conseil d'Etat* has affirmed its decision in *Lamotte* in a number of subsequent cases, and specifically with reference to laws passed after the exceptional period of the war. *See,* for example, *Conseil d'Etat* Decision of April 17, 1953, [1953] Recueil Lebon 175, and Decision of May 17, 1957, [1957] Recueil Lebon 314.

2. If contemporary French parliamentary legislation were to preclude judicial review of an administrative decision, does the *Lamotte* decision require the *Conseil d'Etat* to entertain an action for judicial recourse?

3. For a further discussion of *Lamotte, see* Ch. 3, § B.6., n. 5, *supra.*

2. Limitations of the Right of Action in Continental Europe

It is clear that the Italian and German Constitutions guarantee a right of action against acts of public authorities. Hence the decisions of the Constitutional Courts deal not with the existence of the right, but rather with its contours. The essential question is whether certain limitations on access to court are constitutional.

a. Italy

STROPPA v. PRESIDENTE CONSIGLIO DEI MINISTRI

Corte costituzionale, Decision of March 31, 1961, No. 21
[1961] 6 Giur. Cost. 138; [1961] 11 Rac. uff. corte cost. 191;
[1961] Foro. It. I, 561

[FACTS: The *ordinanza* which submitted the question of constitutionality to the Court does not state the particular fact situation. The case involved *"solve et repete."* This Latin formula — first pay and then request repayment — expressed a well-known concept of taxation law. The taxpayer was obliged to pay the amount of the tax established by the Administration before being allowed to challenge the assessment in court.]

OPINION

The question presented in this proceeding has given rise to a great amount of doctrinal discussion and occasioned numerous decisions resulting in the proposal of various ways to limit the doctrine of *solve et repete*. The task of the *Corte costituzionale* is not that of placing the institution in one or another dogmatic category, but of resolving the question of whether it is constitutional with respect to the principles contained in arts. 3, 24 and 113 of the Constitution, as has been requested by the *Pretore* * of Pavia.

It seems necessary, first of all, to point out that reference to the principle of the immediate executory force of administrative acts does not contribute to the solution of the question in the sense asserted by the Finance Administration. That principle, which enables the administration to proceed in an executive fashion against the delinquent taxpayer notwithstanding his appeal, assuming that the ordinary judge is not authorized to suspend the execution of measures of administrative authority, is independent of the institution of *solve et repete*. It may be said, rather, that the existence of the immediate executory force reduces, in a certain sense, the importance of the principle [of *solve et repete*], both theoretically and practically.

Solve et repete is undoubtedly a particularly energetic and efficacious measure in the collection of taxes in the public interest. It was for this reason that it was introduced and has been retained for so long in Italian legislation, notwithstanding numerous governmental and parliamentary projects for its abolition. For an equally long period it has survived notwithstanding severe scholarly criticism as well as correcting and limiting interpretation by the courts to the effect that it should not be applied where the tax claim involved is *prima facie* absolutely unfounded.

All this confirms that, even independent of the principles contained in the Constitution and before its approval, the institution underwent an observable evolution in the public sensibility which can be seen in the interpretation and application of the existing norms. This evolution was provoked by the excessiveness of the measure which does not conform to the principles of a modern legal system in terms of the relation between the citizen and the state.

It seems difficult to imagine that the constituent legislature has ignored a problem which has been so much debated. It is even more difficult to think that it has not considered the problem implicitly resolved through the formulation of those general principles which

---

* The *Pretura* is a single-judge court of first instance in civil matters between 50,000 and 750,000 lire, petty criminal offences, and specific matters designated by statute. For civil matters under 50,000 lire, the competent court is the *Conciliatore*. The *Pretore* is the judge of the *Pretura*.

are directed to the regulation of the relationships between the citizens and the state. These principles are intended to reconcile the exigencies of tax collection to the rights of the citizen establishing in each case the necessary conditions to make these rights equally enforceable by all.

The imposition of the burden of payment of the tax, as an indispensable prerequisite to the assertion by the taxpayer of his right to initiate a legal proceeding to ascertain its legitimacy, is contrary, in the opinion of the Court, to the principles contained in the articles of the Constitution specified in the *ordinanza* of the *pretore.*

It is contrary to the norm contained in art. 3 [the equality principle]. Dissimilarity of treatment is evident between a taxpayer who is in a position to pay the entire tax immediately and one who does not have sufficient means to make the payment and is not able to obtain such in the form of a loan. . . . The former is accorded, in consequence of his economic condition, the power to demand justice and obtain it where he can prove the justness of his case; in the case of the latter this faculty is made difficult, and often impossible, not only by the practical requirements but also on the basis of the law because of the procedural prerequisites which require the payment of what may well be a very large sum.

The same considerations also justify the reference to the principle contained in art. 24, para. 1, and art. 113 of the Constitution, in which the use of the words "everyone" and "always" clearly confirms the equal right of all citizens to request and obtain judicial protection, whether concerning private causes, or against the state and its subordinate public departments.

The Court, therefore, finds that the institution of *solve et repete* is contrary to the principles of the Constitution, and holds that the rule which provides for it must be declared unconstitutional.

NOTES AND QUESTIONS

1. In the United States, nineteenth century cases establish the proposition that one may be required to pay a disputed tax without a judicial hearing, so long as a subsequent suit for refund is permitted. *E.g., Cary* v. *Curtis,* 44 U.S. 265 (1845). It is thought that those decisions are still valid, on the ground that "history and the necessities of revenue alike make it clear that the government must have constitutional power to make people pay their taxes first and litigate afterward." P. BATOR, P. MISHKIN, D. SHAPIRO, & H. WECHSLER, HART & WECHSLER'S THE FEDERAL COURTS AND THE FEDERAL SYSTEM 334 (2d ed. 1973). It is, however, unusual to require payment of taxes as a precondition to litigation of the legality of a tax. What if the government does require people to pay their taxes first and litigate afterward, and the taxpayer "does not have sufficient means to make the payment and is unable to obtain such in the form of a loan"? In Italy, is the principle of the *Stroppa* decision limited to taxpayers who are too poor to pay or borrow the tax?

2. For a discussion of the related constitutional problem of the impact of fee requirements imposed in litigation, *see Carabba and Marcellusi* v. *Presidente Consiglio dei Ministri, infra* § C.1., and the notes following that decision.

SONAGLIA v. ISTITUTO NAZIONALE DELLA PREVIDENZA SOCIALE

Corte costituzionale, Decision of June 16, 1964, No. 47
[1964] 9 Giur. Cost. 586; [1964] 19 Rac. uff.
corte cost. 427; [1964] Foro It. I, 1334

FACTS

The Court of Appeal of Turin in deciding the case between Maria Sonaglia and the *Istituto Nazionale della Previdenza Sociale* (the Bureau of Social Assistance), has raised doubts concerning the constitutionality of art. 460 of the Code of Civil Procedure and of the fourth para. of art. 97 of the Royal Decree of October 4, 1935, No. 1827 which deal with matters of social assistance.

Art. 460 C.C.P. provides * that an action concerning social assistance cannot be brought unless certain administrative proceedings before the Bureau of Social Assistance prescribed by the law have been exhausted, or unless the Bureau fails to provide an answer in such a proceeding within a statutory time limitation. Para. 4 of art. 97 of the Royal Decree provides that no suit may be brought against the Bureau of Social Assistance before the timely conclusion of an administrative proceeding.

The Court of Appeal of Turin found some inconsistency between these provisions and art. 113 of the Constitution because if the administrative proceeding is not initiated within a short period of time, the individual loses his right of action in court. That court thought that it could not be said that the expiration of the time period in which the aggrieved party may file an administrative recourse is a voluntary waiver of the right of action because the nonactivity of the interested individual can be caused by ignorance or negligence. Although interpreting those rules as an attempt to promote, whenever possible, an administrative resolution for this type of dispute, the court was doubtful of their constitutionality. In reality the sanctions for the nonfulfillment of the burdens imposed, that court thought, go too far in that they do not consist of procedural

---

* This article was subsequently modified by law of August 11, 1973, No. 553, which reformed the procedure in labor and social assistance disputes.

consequences such as increased litigation expenses, and, in fact, can deprive the litigant of his right of action.

. . . .

OPINION

No doubt the concept embodied in art. 113 of the Constitution, according to which the courts "always" have jurisdiction to hear a challenge to acts of the public administration, prohibits any violation of the right of action in court. That article, however, does not require that citizens must always obtain this judicial protection in the same way and with the same effect (see decision of July 3, 1962, No. 87); nor does it forbid the regulation of this right by ordinary legislation, in order to render it concrete, so long as that regulation does not make its exercise impossible or even too difficult.

The law which assures first an administrative recourse, and then a judicial remedy intended either to obtain damages or to block execution of the acts in question, has already been held by this court not to run afoul of art. 113 of the Constitution. In fact, that law is not substantially different from the rules challenged here which condition the initiation of judicial action concerning social assistance matters on a prior, timely application for administrative relief with an agency constituted for that purpose.

The challenged rules impose the burden of administrative recourse before any judicial proceedings on the supposition (a) that the Bureau of Social Assistance will, since it is part of the public administration, conform its behavior to the law and therefore, will not refuse assistance where it is due, and (b) that it will give such assistance without judicial coercion. Thus, these rules operate to eliminate many of these disputes, at the administrative level, leaving for the courts only those that are not resolvable by recourse. Such regulation is not an exclusion or a limitation of the right of action in court.

The right of action, guaranteed by the Constitution, does not mean that access to the courts must be available "immediately" after the right arises. Therefore, it is not persuasive to object that the preconditioning of the action upon the exhaustion of an administrative recourse unduly postpones the exercise of the right of action. This Court has always held constitutional those rules which impose upon the litigants burdens directed towards avoiding abuses of the right of action. . . . The rules challenged here are but another example of an attempt to avoid abuses and excesses by subordinating the right of action to the exercise of a prior administrative remedy.

Rather than subordinate the right of action to the interest of the public administration this system serves judicial economy and, therefore, the efficiency of the right of action itself. . . .

The Court of Appeal of Turin suggests that the applicant's right of action is compromised because the challenged rules provide that the expiration of the time period provided for administrative recourse without any such recourse having been made, will forfeit the right to action in court. Moreover, such a time period is particularly short — ninety days — in comparison to the statute of limitations provided for the right of action (five years).

It must be held, however, that the time period in question attempts to safeguard the principle of obligatory administrative recourse; and the same purpose explains the forfeiture of the rights provided for inobservance of the time period. In numerous other cases, individual's rights are subject to forfeiture if they are not exercised within a prescribed time. In applying such a system here, the law has made a value judgment to the effect that it is appropriate to eliminate, in the shortest possible time, all uncertainties regarding the right to receive social assistance. It would be absurd to contend that art. 113 of the Constitution insures a "perpetual" right of action — the impossibility of subjecting it to forfeiture or statutory limitation. . . .

As far as the time period established for recourse to the Executive Committee is concerned, it was 30 days . . . and it was increased to 90 days in order to make it possible for the individual to evaluate better those reasons advanced by the Bureau against the original application. This ninety-day time period is greater than that generally provided for recourse to the *Consiglio di Stato* * and must be considered adequate for the needs of the applicant. . . .

Another prejudicial aspect of the right of action, presented by the Court of Appeal of Turin, derives from the asserted limitation that the ordinary judge has in evaluating matters already subjected to review at the administrative level; in other words, the ordinary judge should be bound by the factual findings of the administrative proceeding.

It does not follow, however, from any of the challenged rules that the judge must base his decision exclusively on the evidence gathered in the administrative proceeding. In fact, the *Corte di Cassazione* ** in its decisions has explicitly denied that the judge is so constrained. The judicial proceeding is not merely a review of the legality of the decision of the Executive Committee, but is an examination *de novo* of the facts which determine eligibility for social assistance. . . .

---

* The *Consiglio di Stato* (Council of State) is the highest and by far the most important of the administrative courts, in some cases acting as a court of first instance and in most cases as an appellate court.

** The *Corte di Cassazione* is the supreme court in civil and criminal cases. It is at the peak of the pyramidal structure of the ordinary courts. It reviews only questions of law and usually decides in five-judge panels.

b. *Germany*
DECISION OF JANUARY 12, 1960

Bundesverfassungsgericht
[1960] 10 BVerfGE 264

FACTS

In an administrative proceeding concerning the payment of outstanding land tax the plaintiff's demand had been rejected. Upon bringing an appeal against this judgment to the Superior Administrative Court of Bavaria, the appellant was required to pay, within a prescribed period of time, the judicial costs in advance, according to art. 24 * in connection with arts. 23 and 15 of the Bavarian *Kostengesetz* (Fiscal Law). The request of the appellant for legal aid had been rejected,** since it was determined that the appeal did not have a sufficient probability of success. Since the advance payment was not made, the Administrative Court limited itself to deciding, after the expiration of the period provided for in art. 24, § 3, that the appellant must bear the costs of appeal. . . .

[On last appeal the] Federal Administrative Court suspended the proceeding in accordance with art. 100, para. 1, of the Basic Law and asked for a determination of the Constitutional Court as to whether art. 24 is contrary to the Basic Law. . . . The Federal Administrative Court was of the opinion that art. 24 was unconstitutional; *Rechtsweg* (access to the courts) is denied an individual lacking adequate means, whose request for legal aid is rejected because of a lack of sufficient probability of success, if advance payment of costs is required, since liability for such costs is only determined after the proceeding is finally adjudicated. Further, the Court stated, he is placed at an unjust disadvantage in comparison to those possessing adequate means, since the presumption of withdrawal also applies in instances where it is clear that the petitioner desires to continue with his claim but lacks the funds to make the required advance payment. This rule was therefore said to be contrary to art. 19, para. 4, as well as art. 3, para. 1, of the Basic Law.***

. . . .

---

* Article 24 states that: "(1) The court may order that the applicant pay security for costs within a certain period. Whether the security is to be imposed is determined by the court at the request of the representative of the public interest [the public prosecutor]. (2) If the security for costs is not paid in the specified time the application is considered to have been withdrawn. If the applicant requests legal aid before the expiration of the period, this period is extended until two weeks after the decision wholly or partly rejecting legal aid becomes final."

** If legal aid is awarded, the plaintiff does not have to pay a security for judicial costs.

*** Art. 3 (1) of the Basic Law states that "all persons are equal before the law."

Opinion

[The Bavarian Superior Administrative Court in various decisions has held art. 24 to be constitutional. Similar opinions were expressed supporting the constitutionality of the article by the Minister-President of Bavaria, the Bavarian Parliament, and the Federal Minister of Justice.]

III

The request is admissible.

The constitutional doubts of the Federal Administrative Court are directed not simply to the presumption of withdrawal by failure to make the advance payment (art. 24, para. 2) but to the principle of requiring advance payment in administrative court proceedings (art. 24, para. 1). Therefore the substantial content of art. 24 must be examined as relevant to the decision of the Federal Administrative Court. . . .

IV

1. The significance of art. 19, para. 4, of the Basic Law lies in the removal of the "authoritarianism" of the executive power in relation to the citizen. No act of the executive which interferes with the rights of the citizen can be excluded from control in the courts. The *Rechtsweg* [*i.e.,* the right to go to court], however, is not without limits. Though art. 19, para. 4, concedes to the citizen general judicial protection against the public power, this does not mean that all traditional rules of procedural law which legally or factually make admittance to the courts difficult are no longer in force. Most of these principles guarantee the certainty of the law and the orderly process of the administration of justice and also serve in a larger sense to insure the legal protection of the citizen. Therefore there has never been any doubt that art. 19, para. 4, guarantees recourse to the courts only within the limits of the procedural law existing at a given time and that it is possible that recourse to the courts can be conditioned on the fulfillment of certain formal requirements, such as the observance of certain time limitations, lawful representation by counsel, etc. . . . Only if through these norms recourse to the courts is made unreasonably exacting or difficult in a way which cannot be justified on objective grounds would they no longer be consistent with art. 19, para. 4, of the Basic Law.

On the basis of the foregoing it is obviously still permissible that the State establish court costs. Constitutional doubts cannot be raised as to the traditional form of legal aid, in particular, insofar as its granting is made dependent on an examination of the probability of success.

For the same reasons it follows that no challenge is possible if according to art. 24 in connection with arts. 23 and 15 the applicant in an administrative court proceeding is required to make an advance payment. Rules of this type, which apply also in other proceedings, are justified in that, on the one hand, by making the applicant aware of the costs involved in the proceeding, they help to avoid frivolous litigation; on the other, they simplify the collection of costs and serve to insure the claim of the State to court costs. For those who lack adequate means and who feel that they have been injured in their rights by the public authority, admittance to the courts is not thereby made unreasonably onerous. They can request legal aid and if it is granted they are freed from the obligation of advance payment. If it is refused (despite their poverty) the rejection itself presupposes that the Court has ascertained, on the basis of an examination of their applications, which, though not exhaustive, is extensive, that they lack sufficient probability of success. In this case the requirement of prior payment of costs by the applicant is justified since it dissuades him from continuing with the proceeding and saves the State from probable expense. It cannot be the purpose of art. 19, para. 4, of the Basic Law that those lacking adequate means be allowed to pursue fruitless litigation at the expense of the general public.

The Federal Administrative Court is particularly disturbed by the fact that according to art. 24, para. 2, nonpayment of security for costs results in withdrawal of the petition by force of law. In fact it implies a marked disadvantage to the rights of the petitioner. Nevertheless such a rule cannot be constitutionally challenged in the case of administrative court proceedings. If, as shown, the requirement of security for costs is admissible, sanctions must be permissible in the case of nonpayment on the premise that they are both appropriate and reasonable. The usual consequence, that the proceeding is, in effect, held in abeyance, could not for valid reasons seem sufficient to the legislature, since in an administrative court proceeding the action generally has the effect of suspending the enforcement of the challenged administrative act (§ 51, Administrative Court Rules). Therefore, the applicant could as a rule achieve, in fact, nullification of the challenged administrative act by simply suspending the proceeding. It cannot be challenged that the legislature took this hypothesis as the principal basis for the application of art. 24 and regulated the consequence of nonpayment of security for costs in a manner appropriate thereto. Moreover, this rule is not without parallel in federal law. The practical result is no different when it is prescribed that the court must consider the application inadmissible if payment is not made within the prescribed time period.

The severity of the sanction of the fiction of withdrawal of the application is substantially attenuated both through the structure of the rule as well as its practical application, as the Bavarian Administrative Court has reported. There do not seem to be unequivocal precedents as yet; it is not certain if in every proceeding security for costs *must* be paid, or if the wording of art. 24 ("may") in connection with the correspondingly applicable art. 15, para. 2, makes it possible for the court to avoid its imposition in appropriate cases, such as those in which there is no suspending effect as a result of the application. The latter opinion is upheld by different senates of the Bavarian Superior Administrative Court and one of the senates has even reported that from the time the law came into force until Aug. 1, 1959, in only about 20% of all of its proceedings has security for costs been required. In any case the decisions of the Administrative Court subject the Court which orders the payment of security for costs, and which alone can cause the fiction of withdrawal of the application, to severe requirements: the period of time and amount of the security required must be appropriate, and the applicant must be explicitly informed of the legal consequences of nonpayment and of the possibility of legal aid. Further, according to the decisions of the Administrative Court the period for payment can be extended more than once, and, where failure to make payment does not depend on the fault of the applicant, the period may be reinstated. In this way it is in large measure assured that access to the administrative courts is not made excessively difficult or unreasonable. Art. 24 is therefore not contrary to the guarantee of access to justice (*Rechtsweg*) of art. 19, para. 4, first sentence, of the Basic Law.

2. The preceding considerations show further that the rule is not contradictory to the principle of equality nor to the principle of the welfare state (*Sozialstaat*).* These rules require a broad assimilation of the situation of those who possess means and those who do not in the sphere of judicial protection. This requirement is satisfied by the legislator when he makes the position of the poor person equal to that of the individual of means who would not reasonably pursue a similar action after taking the costs involved into consideration. Insofar as herein there is a *de facto* difficulty in obtaining access to the courts, it does not *de jure* concern an unequal treatment.

Therefore, there do not exist decisive constitutional doubts regarding art. 24.

Art. 24 is not contrary to the Basic Law.

---

* Art. 20 (1) of the Basic Law states: "The German Federal Republic is a democratic and social federal state."

NOTES

1. Are there common themes in the decision in the principal case and the decisions of the Italian Constitutional Court in the *Stroppa* and *Sonaglia* cases? What is the role played by the rule, prevailing in Germany but not in Italy, that the commencement of a judicial proceeding has the effect of suspending the enforcement of the challenged administrative act? The German Constitutional Court has held that this rule is an essential part of the basic right of action in administrative cases. 35 BVerfGE 401. Under what circumstances may the right of action be attenuated by precluding judicial review of administrative action?

2. When judicial review of administrative action is available, how are administrative findings of fact treated? The German Constitutional Court has held that:

> To restrict the court to a review of the law, and to require or allow it to base its decision on unreviewed administrative findings of fact, would be irreconcilable with Art. 19, para. 4 of the Basic Law. 21 BVerfGE 191, 194-95.

See also the *Sonaglia* case, *supra* § B.2.a., the *Miraglia* case, *infra* at Ch. 7, § A.1.a., as well as the instant case.

3. Are you convinced by the German Court's reliance on the legal aid system, in view of the fact that the decision on eligibility for legal aid is made in summary proceedings? Should the right of action require judicial review even of decisions denying legal aid? (Note that such review is in fact granted under German law.) Compare the decision of the Italian Constitutional Court in *Carabba and Marcellusi v. Presidente Consiglio dei Ministri, infra* § C.1.

3. Judicial Review of Administrative Action in the United States

No explicit provision of the United States Constitution guarantees an individual a general right to resort to the courts for authoritative resolution of disputes. (One exception is contained in Article I, Section 9, forbidding the suspension of the writ of habeas corpus. At the least, this requires access to some court to test the legality of detention of the individual by officials of the federal government.) Can a general right to access to court be derived from the language of the Due Process Clauses of the Fifth and Fourteenth Amendments, which forbid denials of life, liberty, or property "without due process of law"?

The Due Process Clauses require that a number of disputes between government and the individual be resolved by fundamentally fair procedures. (The issue of the kinds of governmental decisions which invoke the requirement of a fair hearing will be considered in Ch. 7 *infra.*) In many situations, however, the fair hearing required by due process can be a quasi-judicial hearing before an administrative agency. The issue of access to court then becomes the question of the extent to which the decisions of administrative officials are subject to review by courts. Does due process require that there be judicial review of administrative decisions? Putting the question another way, if "due" process is not always "judicial" process, do individuals still have a constitutional right to test the lawfulness of governmental decisions in the ordinary courts?

In brief, there is no authoritative answer to the question just put. Probably, there is no constitutional right to have judicial redetermination of facts found by administrative agencies in a fair hearing. Ordinarily, courts are limited to deciding whether administrative findings of fact are supported by "substantial evidence." Some older cases described a category of "constitutional facts" to which the individual was entitled to *de novo* judicial review. *Ohio Valley Water Co.* v. *Ben Avon Borough,* 253 U.S. 287 (1920), held that a public utility was entitled to judicial review *de novo* of administrative findings as to the valuation of its property in a rate-making proceeding. *Ng Fung Ho* v. *White,* 259 U.S. 276 (1922), decided on similar reasoning that an "alien" ordered to be deported was entitled to *de novo* review by the court of the claim that he was a citizen. One analytical problem with both cases is the difficulty of distinguishing "constitutional" facts from ordinary facts. As a result, most commentators believe that the doctrine of constitutional fact is no longer viable.* Another related concept, equally doubtful today, is the notion that the Constitution required judicial review of facts that went to the administrative agency's "jurisdiction." *Crowell* v. *Benson,* 285 U.S. 22 (1932).

QUESTIONS

Under present law, if a person is excluded from the United States, as an alien, he has a right to a fair administrative hearing on his claim to be an American citizen. He has, in addition, a statutory right to a judicial trial *de novo* on his rejected claim of citizenship. Could Congress validly amend the law to make an administrative finding of noncitizenship binding on the courts if supported by substantial evidence?

Aside from the dubious doctrines of "constitutional fact" and "jurisdictional fact," any due process right to judicial review of

---

* K. DAVIS, 4 ADMINISTRATIVE LAW TREATISE § 29.09 (1958). *Compare,* however, L. JAFFE, JUDICIAL CONTROL OF ADMINISTRATIVE ACTION 651-52 (1965) *and* Strong, *The Persistent Doctrine of "Constitutional Fact,"* 46 N.C.L. REV. 223 (1968).

administrative decisions is probably limited to review of issues of law. Does the following famous dictum state a reliable principle?

> The supremacy of law demands that there shall be opportunity to have some court decide whether an erroneous rule of law was applied; and whether the proceeding in which the facts were adjudicated was conducted regularly.*

JOHNSON v. ROBISON

Supreme Court of the United States
415 U.S. 361, 94 S. Ct. 1160, 39 L. Ed. 2d 389 (1974)

[Johnson was a conscientious objector who had been exempted from military service, but who had performed the required alternative civilian service. He brought this class action against the Administrator of Veterans' Affairs, seeking a declaratory judgment that the federal statute providing for veterans' educational benefits was unconstitutional in denying benefits to conscientious objectors. The government argued that the action should be dismissed for lack of jurisdiction under 38 U.S.C. § 211(a), which provides that

> ... the decisions of the Administrator on any question of law or fact under any law administered by the Veterans' Administration providing benefits for veterans and their dependents or survivors shall be final and conclusive and no other official or any court of the United States shall have power or jurisdiction to review any such decision by an action in the nature of mandamus or otherwise.]

MR. JUSTICE BRENNAN delivered the opinion of the Court.

. . . .

We consider first appellants' contention that § 211(a) bars federal courts from deciding the constitutionality of veterans' benefits legislation. Such a construction would, of course, raise serious questions concerning the constitutionality of § 211 (a),[8] and in such case "it is a cardinal principle that this Court will first ascertain whether a construction of the statute is fairly possible by which the [constitutional] question[s] may be avoided."

Plainly, no explicit provision of § 211(a) bars judicial consideration of appellee's constitutional claims. That section provides

---

* *St. Joseph Stockyards Co.* v. *United States,* 298 U.S. 38, 84 (1936) (Brandeis, J., concurring).

[8] Compare *Ex parte McCardle,* 7 Wall. 506 (1869); *Sheldon* v. *Sill,* 8 How. 441 (1850), with *Martin* v. *Hunter's Lessee,* 1 Wheat. 304 (1816); *St. Joseph Stock Yards Co.* v. *United States,* 298 U. S. 38, 84 (1936) (Brandeis, J., concurring). See Hart, *The Power of Congress to Limit the Jurisdiction of Federal Courts: An Exercise in Dialectic,* 66 HARV. L. REV. 1362 (1953).

that "the *decisions* of the Administrator on any question of law or fact *under* any law administered by the Veterans' Administration providing benefits for veterans . . . shall be final and conclusive and no . . . court of the United States shall have power or jurisdiction to review any such decision. . . ." (Emphasis added.) The prohibitions would appear to be aimed at review only of those decisions of law or fact that arise in the *administration* by the Veterans' Administration of a *statute* providing benefits for veterans. A decision of law or fact "under" a statute is made by the Administrator in the interpretation or application of a particular provision of the statute to a particular set of facts. Appellee's constitutional challenge is not to any such decision of the *Administrator,* but rather to a decision of *Congress* to create a statutory class entitled to benefits that does not include . . . conscientious objectors who performed alternative civilian service. Thus, as the District Court stated: "The questions of law presented in these proceedings arise under the Constitution, not under the statute whose validity is challenged." 352 F. Supp., at 853.

. . . .

Nor does the legislative history accompanying the 1970 amendment of § 211 (a) demonstrate a congressional intention to bar judicial review even of constitutional questions. No-review clauses similar to § 211 (a) have been a part of veterans' benefits legislation since 1933. While the legislative history accompanying these precursor no-review clauses is almost nonexistent, the Administrator, in a letter written in 1952 in connection with a revision of the clause under consideration by the Subcommittee of the House Committee on Veterans' Affairs, comprehensively explained the policies necessitating the no-review clause and identified two primary purposes: (1) to insure that veterans' benefits claims will not burden the courts and the Veterans' Administration with expensive and time-consuming litigation, and (2) to insure that the technical and complex determinations and applications of Veterans' Administration policy connected with veterans' benefits decisions will be adequately and uniformly made.

The legislative history of the 1970 amendment indicates nothing more than a congressional intent to preserve these two primary purposes. Before amendment, the no-review clause made final "the decisions of the Administrator on any question of law or fact *concerning a claim for benefits or payments* under [certain] law[s] administered by the Veterans' Administration" (emphasis added), 38 U. S. C. § 211 (a) (1964 ed.), 71 Stat. 92. In a series of decisions . . . the Court of Appeals for the District of Columbia Circuit interpreted the term "claim" as a limitation upon the reach of § 211 (a), and as a consequence held that judicial review of actions by the Administrator *subsequent* to an original grant of benefits was not barred.

Congress perceived this judicial interpretation as a threat to the dual purposes of the no-review clause. First, the interpretation would lead to an inevitable increase in litigation with consequent burdens upon the courts and the Veterans' Administration. In its House Report, the Committee on Veterans' Affairs stated that . . . suits in constantly increasing numbers have been filed in the U. S. District Court for the District of Columbia by plaintiffs seeking a resumption of terminated benefits." H. R. Rep. No. 91-1166, p. 10 (1970). This same concern over the rising number of court cases was expressed by the Administrator in a letter to the Committee:

> "The [District of Columbia] decisions have not been followed in any of the other 10 Federal judicial circuits throughout the country. Nevertheless, soon after the *Tracy* decision, suits in the nature of mandamus or for declaratory judgment commenced to be filed in the U. S. District Court for the District of Columbia in constantly increasing numbers by plaintiffs seeking resumption of terminated benefits. As of March 8, 1970, 353 suits of this type had been filed in the District of Columbia circuit.
>
> . . . .
>
> "The scope of the . . . decisions . . . is so broad that it could well afford a basis for judicial review of millions of decisions terminating or reducing many types of benefits provided under laws administered by the Veterans' Administration. Such review might even extend to the decisions of predecessor agencies made many years ago." *Id.*, at 21, 24.

Second, Congress was concerned that the judicial interpretation of § 211 (a) would involve the courts in day-to-day determination and interpretation of Veterans' Administration policy. The House Report states that the cases already filed in the courts in response to [the District of Columbia decisions]

> "involve a large variety of matters — a 1930's termination of a widow's pension payments under a statute then extant, because of her open and notorious adulterous cohabitation; invalid marriage to a veteran; severance of a veteran's service connection for disability compensation; reduction of such compensation because of lessened disability . . . [and] suits . . . brought by [Filipino] widows of World War II servicemen seeking restoration of death compensation or pension benefits terminated after the Administrator raised a presumption of their remarriage on the basis of evidence gathered through field examination. Notwithstanding the 1962 endorsement by the

Congress of the Veterans' Administrations [*sic*] administrative presumption of remarriage rule, most of [the suits brought by Filipino widows] have resulted in judgments adverse to the Government." *Id.*, at 10.

The Administrator voiced similar concerns, stating that "it seems obvious that suits similar to the several hundred already filed can — and undoubtedly will — subject nearly every aspect of our benefit determinations to judicial review, including rating decisions, related Veterans' Administration regulations, Administrator's decisions, and various adjudication procedures." Letter to the Committee on Veterans' Affairs 23-24.

Thus, the 1970 amendment was enacted to overrule the interpretation of the Court of Appeals for the District of Columbia Circuit, and thereby restore vitality to the two primary purposes to be served by the no-review clause. Nothing whatever in the legislative history of the 1970 amendment, or predecessor no-review clauses, suggests any congressional intent to preclude judicial cognizance of constitutional challenges to veterans' benefits legislation. Such challenges obviously do not contravene the purposes of the no-review clause, for they cannot be expected to burden the courts by their volume, nor do they involve technical considerations of Veterans' Administration policy. We therefore conclude, in agreement with the District Court, that a construction of § 211 (a) that does not extend the prohibitions of that section to actions challenging the constitutionality of laws providing benefits for veterans is not only "fairly possible" but is the most reasonable construction, for neither the text nor the scant legislative history of § 211 (a) provides the "clear and convincing" evidence of congressional intent required by this Court before a statute will be construed to restrict access to judicial review. See *Abbott Laboratories* v. *Gardner,* 387 U. S. 136, 141 (1967).

[On the merits, the Court upheld the constitutionality of the legislation. Justice Douglas dissented.]

NOTES AND QUESTIONS

1. One reason that there is no clear answer to the question whether there is a constitutional right to judicial review of administrative decisions is that it is commonplace for the courts in the United States to strain to interpret federal laws which restrict judicial review as inapplicable to the particular case before them.

In that sense, the *Johnson* case is typical. Notice, however, that judicial review is available in the *Johnson* case on the argument that the pragmatic factors which influenced Congress to deny judicial review to routine determinations of veterans' benefits were inapplicable. Suppose that a veteran's educational benefits are terminated because, under a debatable interpretation of the law applicable to the particular facts, the Veterans' Administration decided that he was ineligible for benefits. If the disappointed veteran brings suit for his benefits, claiming that the V.A. has misinterpreted the law, would § 211 (a) now be applicable? If so, would § 211 (a) be unconstitutional on the ground that it denied the plaintiff "an opportunity to have some court decide whether an erroneous rule of law was applied"? Should it matter if the alleged misinterpretation of the law was also claimed to violate constitutional rights?

2. Suppose § 211 (a) were amended to make it clear that judicial review was precluded in cases like *Johnson.* Would § 211 (a) then be unconstitutional? Notice the various pragmatic factors which the legislative history of § 211 (a) demonstrates were relied upon by Congress in precluding judicial review of questions of law. If those pragmatic considerations are sound, could they be accommodated in a general rule that an individual has a constitutional right to judicial review of questions of law? Professor Rabin suggests that Congress and the V.A. had exaggerated the costs of judicial review, and had given too little weight to the "constraints and loyalties generated in a bureaucratic system" which "create a potential problem of arbitrariness in the handling of individual cases." * If the constitutional right to judicial review of questions of law turns on a balance between the pragmatic costs and benefits of judicial review in particular cases, what deference should be given to Congress' decision on how the balance should be struck? Does it make a difference whether an administrative decision takes away a person's "rights," revokes a preexisting government "benefit," or merely refuses to give a new "benefit"?

3. *Ortwein* v. *Schwab,* 410 U.S. 656 (1973), involved the constitutionality of a law which required a $25 filing fee to be paid to a state appellate court when a welfare recipient, whose benefits were terminated, sought judicial review of the administrative decision denying the benefits. The Court's brief *per curiam* opinion held that the filing fee did not violate due process on the ground that the applicant's interest in benefits was not sufficiently "funda-mental." There was, however, an alternative ground of decision.

> The Court has held that procedural due process requires that a welfare recipient be given a pre-termination evidentiary hearing. . . . These appellants have had hearings. The hearings provide a procedure, not conditioned on payment of any fee,

---

* Rabin, *Preclusion of Judicial Review in the Processing of Claims for Veterans' Benefits: A Preliminary Analysis,* 27 STAN. L. REV. 905, 922 (1975).

through which appellants have been able to seek redress. This Court has long recognized that, even in criminal cases, due process does not require a State to provide an appellate system. . . . Under the facts of this case, appellants were not denied due process.

On this point, Justice Marshall's dissent said:

We are concerned in this case not with appellate review of a judicial determination, but with initial access to the courts for review of an adverse administrative determination. By analogizing these two situations the majority *sub silentio* answers a question this Court studiously has avoided — whether there is a due process right to judicial review. . . . Access to the courts before a person is deprived of valuable interests, at least with respect to questions of law, seems to me to be the essence of due process. . . .

Should *Ortwein* be read as deciding that potential recipients of government benefits have no constitutional right to judicial review on questions of law even if they can afford to pay a filing fee? (The issues in the *Ortwein* case are discussed further, at Ch. 10, § B.2.a., *infra.*)

4. How do you explain the fact that in the United States, "due process" has not required "judicial process" for the resolution of *all* disputed questions of law and fact arising in the administration of the laws?

C. RIGHT OF ACTION IN PRIVATE DISPUTES

1. Italy

CARABBA AND MARCELLUSI v. PRESIDENTE CONSIGLIO DEI MINISTRI

Corte costituzionale, Decision of November 29, 1960, No. 67;
[1960] 5 Giur. Cost. 1195; [1960] 10 Rac. uff. corte cost. 289
[1960] Foro It. I, 1873

[FACTS: The *ordinanza* of the *Tribunale* * of Chieti which submitted the question of constitutionality to the Court does not state the particular fact situation. The issue concerns the validity of a requirement of posting security for costs (*cautio pro expensis*). In Italy, as in most countries, including Great Britain, the rule is that the loser must pay the litigation costs — court costs and attorney's fees — of both sides. Article 98 of the Italian Code of Civil Procedure provided that the judge could order any plaintiff, who was not a recipient of legal aid, to post an indemnification bond for litigation

---

* The *Tribunale* is the normal court of first instance. Its decisions are taken by a three-judge panel. The *Tribunale* is also the court of second instance for cases decided by the *Pretore.*

costs if it appeared that those costs might not be paid in the event of an adverse judgment.]

OPINION

. . . .

. . . [T]he Court holds, according to its established practice, that it must examine the question of the constitutionality of art. 98 of the Code of Civil Procedure with reference to art. 3 [the equality principle] as well as to art. 24 [the right of action and defense] of the Constitution, and that these must be jointly interpreted in the determination of the present proceeding.

From these two provisions one may derive the principle that both the right to commence a legal proceeding for the protection of one's rights and legitimate interests and the right of defense at every phase and stage of legal proceedings are inviolable, and that these rules apply equally to all, regardless of personal and social conditions. There appears to be no doubt that art. 98 of the Code Civ. Proc., which provides for the posting of a bond by those who are not recipients of legal aid whenever it appears that the expenses of the proceeding may not be recoverable, links the application of this bond (*cautio pro expensis*) to the economic status of the party. Consequently, it is not required from one who possesses an estate of some size.

Furthermore, the nonapplicability of this bond procedure when the plaintiff is a recipient of legal aid does not eliminate the disparity since attainment of that status is dependent upon a demonstration of the individual's state of poverty and must be refused to those who do not meet the requisite criteria. Furthermore, the preliminary proceedings for the determination of the applicability of legal aid are not always as rapid as is desirable.

Recalling various doctrinal approaches, counsel have widely discussed the extent of the examination power entrusted to the *giudice istruttore* (examining judge) * in order to decide upon the request of the defendant to impose this bond on the plaintiff. According to some, such an examination extends even to the merits of the controversy and to the probability that one or another litigant will prevail as well as to the frivolous character of the litigation. The Court feels that it does not have the power to pronounce on these

---

* The *giudice istruttore* is assigned by the chief judge of the tribunal at the close of the introductory stage. He is in charge of the proof-taking stage and after the conclusion of that stage he reports to an adjudicating panel consisting of himself and two other judges.

arguments, which directly concern the content and the extent of a power attributed to the ordinary judge.

This limits the Court to the observation that the text of the existing statute is consistently interpreted by the courts to mean that the requirement of *cautio pro expensis* should be held to be applicable even in the appellate courts, where it may be required of the appellant, whether he was plaintiff or defendant in the court of first instance.* It may be imposed as well in summary ex parte proceedings. Such interpretation, together with the exclusion of all possibility of a recourse [to challenge the decision of the *giudice istruttore*], makes the imposition of the bond and, if the bond is not posted either in money or in the form of Italian Treasury Securities within the time established, the consequent termination of the proceeding, capable of provoking extremely serious consequences respecting the exercise of the rights which art. 24 of the Constitution proclaims inviolable.

The counsel for the defendant in the lower court proceeding and the *Avvocatura dello Stato* ** have mentioned, by analogy, other procedural institutions which provide for the imposition of a financial burden and which are nevertheless presumed constitutional — such as deposits to guarantee payment in the event of an adverse holding, the principle of *solve et repete* in fiscal matters, and others.

In the judgment of the court, these institutions and that which is in question are different in many ways, and certainly with regard to the present problem. First of all, it is evident that for the most part the other institutions cited serve functions of particular public interest, which the legislature wishes to safeguard, whereas the *cautio pro expensis* serves no definite public end, not even one inherent in the proceeding. It is simply a procedural obstacle. In the second place the other institutions imply a judicial or administrative act, issued, therefore, by a public authority. This can be considered sufficient reason to justify the imposition of a bond, even if it is susceptible to challenge and reform. Finally, it must be noted that in all the cases presented as analogous to the institution under examination the burden is imposed on the basis of definitely established objective standards, whereas in the case of the *cautio pro expensis* it is concerned with, even though not exclusively, those conditions both personal and social which art. 3 precludes from consideration in the exercise of the equal protection of the law.

The foregoing considerations require the Court to hold art. 98 of

---

* The Court alludes to the fact that, if an appellate proceeding is terminated, under the Italian law that lower court's decision becomes final and is no longer subject to appeals.

** The *Avvocatura dello Stato* is a salaried body of attorneys. They represent and provide legal advice to the State and most state agencies.

the Code of Civil Procedure to be contrary to the principles of arts. 3 and 24 of the Constitution.

For these reasons, art. 98 of the Code of Civil Procedure is declared unconstitutional on the basis of the norms contained in arts. 3 and 24 of the Constitution.

NOTES AND QUESTIONS

1. Notice that the German decision of January 12, 1960, *supra* § B.2.b., interpreted the right of action together with the guarantee of equality in art. 3 of the German Constitution. Article 3 of the Italian Constitution has a similar guarantee of equality. The decision of the Italian Constitutional Court both in the principal case and in *Stroppa, supra* § B.2.a., relied in part on the guarantee of equality in art. 3 of the Constitution. Indeed, in determining the contours of the right of action in private disputes, it has become common to read the constitutional guarantee of equality in conjunction with the guarantee of a right of action.

2. Other forms of security bonds in civil litigation have been upheld by the Italian Constitutional Court. These include: the requirement of a bond to suspend a contested enforcement proceeding (Decision of April 26, 1962, Corte cost., [1962] 7 Giur, Cost. 318; [1962] 14 Rac. uff. corte cost. 33; [1962] Foro It. I, 851); the requirement of a bond for issuance of an attachment (Decision of July 3, 1967, Corte cost., [1967] 12 Giur. Cost. 1001; [1967] 26 Rac. uff. corte cost. 5; [1967] Foro It. I, 1683); deposits to discourage unfounded appeals (*e.g.,* Decision of May 3, 1963, Corte cost., [1963] 8 Giur. Cost. 498; [1963] 16 Rac. uff. corte cost. 373; [1963] Foro It. I, 855). In each of the preceding cases, the Court has examined the effect of the bond or deposit, and distinguished it from *cautio pro expensis* on 3 grounds: objective, rather than subjective, criteria determine whether the bond or deposit is required; failure to pay the bond or deposit does not forfeit the right of action; the interest protected by the bond or deposit is efficient operation of judicial functions, rather than the private interest of the opposing party. As to the last ground, in the case of deposits for appeal, the Court explained that they were not designed to protect the appellee from harassment, but to protect the courts from unjustified appeals. Would similar arguments have sustained *solve et repete*? (Notice the Court's discussion of the issue in *Carabba.* Did it change its mind the next year in *Stroppa? See* § B.2.a., *supra.*) Should it make a difference that the amount of these appeal deposits is so small (from three to five dollars) that they have become quite formal and do not, except in theory, serve the function of discouraging frivolous appeals?

3. The Constitutional Court has upheld requirements that documents subject to registration fees may not be introduced into evidence if the fee was not paid. If a document subject to an unpaid registration fee is offered into evidence, the proceeding is suspended until the fee and penalties are paid. Decision of April 9, 1963, Corte cost., [1963] 8 Giur. Cost. 170; [1963] 16 Rac. uff. corte cost. 285; [1963] Foro It. I, 646. *See* Phillips, *The Italian Registration Tax,* 20 STAN. L. REV. 811, 813 (1968). Registration fees on documents have been upheld even in the case of registration fees required to be paid only when and if the documents are to be used in litigation. Decision of Dec. 22, 1969, Corte cost., [1969] 14 Giur. Cost. 2359; [1969] 30 Rac. uff. corte cost. 607; [1969] Foro It. I, 386. Can these decisions be distinguished from *Carabba* on the ground that the financial burden of the document fee serves a purpose — collection of revenue — which is extrinsic to the litigation in which the document is sought to be introduced? Or does that make those decisions even more difficult to understand? Suppose that the document which is refused admission into evidence is essential to decision in the case, and the litigant lacks the funds to pay the fee. *Cf. D'Agostino* v. *Ministero Trasporti,* Ch. 7 § A.1.a., *infra.*

4. In Germany there is no explicit provision of the Constitution guaranteeing a right of action for private disputes. However, it has been asserted that a right of action for private disputes can be based on arts. 101 (right to a lawful judge) and 103 (right to a hearing in accordance with law) of the Constitution. *See,* for example, Baur, *Les Garanties Fondamentales des Parties dans le Procès Civil en République Fédérale d'Allemagne,* in FUNDAMENTAL GUARANTEES OF THE PARTIES IN CIVIL LITIGATION 13 (M Cappelletti & D. Tallon eds. 1973).

5. Compare the *Carabba* decision with the German decision on posting security, *supra* § B.2.b. What were the differences between the two systems of security? Both decisions also considered the effect of a rule that security is not required for those admitted to legal aid. The Italian legal aid system operates much less effectively than that of Germany. Does that explain the differences between the reasoning in the German and Italian cases?

6. When the Italian court annulled *cautio pro expensis,* it did so for everyone, rich or poor. That was also the result in *Stroppa* (*supra* § B.2.a.), which annulled *solve et repete.* Are the rich then the real beneficiaries of decisions, based, in part, on equal access for the poor? Compare the American result in *Boddie* v. *Connecticut, infra* § C.3.

7. In a recent decision of the Italian *Corte Costituzionale,* a statutory requirement that a dispute be submitted to binding arbitration was held to be unconstitutional. The Court stated that "the source of arbitration cannot be a law" as "the foundation of all arbitration must be grounded in the goodwill of the parties." The

Court combined the provisions of art. 24, para. 1 (right of action), and art. 102, para. 1 (monopoly on judicial functions by ordinary judges), in reaching its decision. While acknowledging that parties could waive their "right of action" through contractual arbitration clauses, it noted that it "would be a contradiction to require a constitutional amendment in order to create new special tribunals and at the same time to allow entire sets of controversies to be taken away from ordinary judges by means of mandatory arbitration." *Sacchetti* v. *Ditta Seriscreen,* Decision of July 14, 1977, Corte cost., [1977] Foro It. I, 1849.

8. Would the rationale of the *Sacchetti* decision raise doubts about the validity of some contractual provisions requiring mandatory arbitration? A challenge to a contractual arbitration clause was rejected by the European Commission of Human Rights in its Decision of March 5, 1962, [1962] Y.B. EUR. CONV. ON HUMAN RIGHTS 88.

In a proceeding before the European Commission, the applicant had claimed that binding arbitration denied him the right to a "fair and public hearing" under art. 6(1) of the Convention. (*See* the *Golder* and *Knechtl* cases, which follow *infra* § C.2., on the relationship of art. 6(1) to the concept of right of action.) While the Commission stated that the application might be admissible if a contract to arbitrate was signed under constraint, or if the arbitration was conducted in an unfair manner, it concluded that the arbitration clause in the contract amounted to renunciation of any right of access to court guaranteed by art. 6(1). If the right of access to court is seen as a fundamental right, should it be so easy to waive that right in the text of a private contract? Should it make a difference whether the arbitration clause was part of a form contract prepared by one party to the contract? Would a less troublesome explanation of the 1962 decision be that the applicant had received a "fair and public hearing" in the arbitration proceeding? Would the alternative explanation just propounded be inconsistent with the European concept of a right of action? Consider the last question further in connection with the *Knechtl* and *Golder* cases which follow.

2. The European Convention on Human Rights

The principal provision of the European Convention that is relevant to the right of action is art. 6(1):

> In the determination of his civil rights and obligations or of any criminal charge against him, everyone is entitled to a fair and public hearing within a reasonable time by an independent and impartial tribunal established by law. Judgment shall be pronounced publicly but the press and public may be excluded from all or part of the trial in the interests of morals, public order

or national security in a democratic society, where the interests of juveniles or the protection of the private life of the parties so require, or to the extent strictly necessary in the opinion of the court in special circumstances where publicity would prejudice the interests of justice.

Consider, also, art. 5(4):

Everyone who is deprived of his liberty by arrest or detention shall be entitled to take proceedings by which the lawfulness of his detention shall be decided speedily by a court and his release ordered if the detention is not lawful.

and art. 13:

Everyone whose rights and freedoms as set forth in this Convention are violated shall have an effective remedy before a national authority notwithstanding that the violation has been committed by persons acting in an official capacity.

Application No. 4115/69

(KNECHTL v. UNITED KINGDOM)

European Commission of Human Rights, Decision of December 16, 1970 [1970] Y.B. Eur. Conv. on Human Rights 730; 36 Collection of Decisions 43

THE FACTS

. . . .

The Applicant was born in Hungary in 1939. He left Hungary during the uprising in 1956 and came to England early in 1957. He has been resident in England since that time and is described as stateless.

In 1967 his left leg was amputated while he was serving a prison sentence. He alleges that he lost his leg through the negligence of the prison authorities and of certain doctors, and the object of his present application is that he was refused permission while in prison to consult a solicitor with a view to bringing legal proceedings against them. The Application has been considered under art. 6 (1) of the Convention which provides that in the determination of his civil rights, everyone is entitled to a hearing within a reasonable time by a tribunal established by law; and under art. 8 which guarantees the right to respect for correspondence.

. . . .

The Law

. . . .

Whereas the Applicant alleged that, by the refusal of the United Kingdom authorities to allow him to consult a solicitor, he was denied access to a court as guaranteed by the above provision; whereas the Respondent Government has submitted that art. 6 (1) does not guarantee any right to institute proceedings before a court of law but only lays down certain procedural safeguards where proceedings have once been instituted;

Whereas the Commission observes that the question whether art. 6 (1) of the Convention guarantees the right of access to the courts has never been expressly decided; whereas, in the light of the submissions of the parties, the Commission considers that the Application raises an important issue concerning the interpretation of the Convention whose determination should depend upon an examination of the merits of the Application; whereas therefore the Application cannot in this respect be considered as being manifestly ill-founded within the meaning of art. 27 (2) of the Convention;

Whereas the Respondent Government has further submitted that, even if art. 6 (1) does guarantee the right to institute proceedings before a court, that right must be subject to certain limitations in the case of persons lawfully detained in prison in accordance with art. 5 of the Convention; and whereas the Respondent Government contended on this ground that the refusal to allow the Applicant to consult a solicitor, with a view to bringing legal proceedings, was in any event consistent with art. 6;

Whereas the Applicant's representative has submitted that all restrictions on the rights guaranteed by the Convention are expressly provided for, and that there are no such restrictions on the rights guaranteed by art. 6 as might have been applicable in the present case;

. . . .

Whereas, therefore, the Application, insofar as it raises questions under art. 6 (1), cannot be declared inadmissible as being manifestly ill-founded in accordance with art. 27 (2) of the Convention; and whereas no other ground for declaring this aspect of the Application inadmissible has been found;

. . . .

Now therefore the Commission
DECLARES THIS APPLICATION ADMISSIBLE.

NOTE

Ultimately, the *Knechtl* Case was settled when the United Kingdom, without admitting that the Applicant's rights under the Convention had been violated, offered to make an *ex gratia* payment of ₤750 sterling to the Applicant; he accepted and withdrew his Application without prejudicing his right to continue his action in the English courts.

Further, it should be noted that the United Kingdom has made changes in its practice of allowing prisoners to seek legal advise: In a White Paper, "Legal Advice to Prisoners," laid before Parliament on December 10, 1971, it is provided that a prisoner who has suffered some physical injury or disablement, or impairment of his physical condition and who claims damages based on the alleged negligence of prison authorities may consult a solicitor and give instructions for the institution of proceedings in accordance with the latter's advice, without restriction, unless there are overriding considerations of security.

The *Knechtl* case was referred to in the above-mentioned paper.

Application No. 4451/70

GOLDER v. THE UNITED KINGDOM

European Court of Human Rights, Decision of February 21, 1975
Collection of Decisions (separate cover)

[FACTS: While serving a prison sentence for robbery, Golder was accused by a prison officer (Mr. Laird) of having participated in a prison disturbance. Letters by Golder to his Member of Parliament and to a Chief Constable, complaining of the problems caused by the accusation, were stopped by the prison governor because the issue had not yet been raised through authorized prison channels. Laird subsequently admitted some doubt in his identification, and another prison officer reported that Golder had actually been with him during the disturbance. However, the accusation remained on Golder's record, and, suspecting that this jeopardized his opportunity for parole, he petitioned the Home Secretary for permission to contact a solicitor to discuss a possible civil action for libel against Laird. This petition was denied, and Golder appealed to the European Commission on Human Rights.]

21. In their report, the Commission expressed the opinion:
- unanimously, that Article 6 § 1 guarantees a right of access to the courts;
- unanimously, that in Article 6 § 1, whether read alone or together with other Articles of the Convention, there are no inherent limitations on the right of a convicted prisoner to institute proceedings and for this purpose to have unrestricted access to a

lawyer; and that consequently the restrictions imposed by the present practice of the United Kingdom authorities are inconsistent with Article 6 § 1;

by seven votes to two, that Article 8 § 1 is applicable to the facts of the present case;

that the same facts which constitute a violation of Article 6 § 1 constitute also a violation of Article 8 (by eight votes to one, as explained to the Court by the Principal Delegate on 12 October 1974).

The Commission furthermore expressed the opinion that the right of access to the courts guaranteed by Article 6 § 1 is not qualified by the requirement "within a reasonable time." In the application bringing the case before the Court, the Government made objection to this opinion of the Commission but stated in their memorial that they no longer wished to argue the issue. . . .

AS TO THE LAW

. . . .

25. In the present case the Court is called upon to decide two distinct questions arising on the text cited above.

(i) Is Article 6 § 1 limited to guaranteeing in substance the right to a fair trial in legal proceedings which are already pending, or does it in addition secure a right of access to the courts for every person wishing to commence an action in order to have his civil rights and obligations determined?

(ii) In the latter eventuality, are there any implied limitations on the right of access or on the exercise of that right which are applicable in the present case?

A. *ON THE "RIGHT OF ACCESS"*

26. . . . Golder had made it most clear that he intended "taking civil action for libel"; it was for this purpose that he wished to contact a solicitor, which was a normal preliminary step in itself and in Golder's case probably essential on account of his imprisonment. By forbidding Golder to make such contact, the Home Secretary actually impeded the launching of the contemplated action. Without formally denying Golder his right to institute proceedings before a court, the Home Secretary did in fact prevent him from commencing an action at that time, 1970. Hindrance in fact can contravene the Convention just like a legal impediment.

. . . .

The Court accordingly has to examine whether the hindrance thus established violated a right guaranteed by the Convention and more particularly by Article 6, on which Golder relied in this respect.

27. One point has not been put in issue and the Court takes it for granted: the "right" which Golder wished, rightly or wrongly, to invoke against Laird before an English court was a "civil right" within the meaning of Article 6 § 1.

28. Again, Article 6 § 1 does not state a right of access to the courts or tribunals in express terms. It enunciates rights which are distinct but stem from the same basic idea and which, taken together, make up a single right not specifically defined in the narrower sense of the term. It is the duty of the Court to ascertain, by means of interpretation, whether access to the courts constitutes one factor or aspect of this right.

29. The submissions made to the Court were in the first place directed to the manner in which the Convention, and particularly Article 6 § 1, should be interpreted. The Court is prepared to consider, as do the Government and the Commission, that it should be guided by Articles 31 to 33 of the Vienna Convention of 23 May 1969 on the Law of Treaties. That Convention has not yet entered into force and it specifies, at Article 4, that it will not be retroactive, but its Articles 31 to 33 enunciate in essence generally accepted principles of international law to which the Court has already referred on occasion. In this respect, for the interpretation of the European Convention account is to be taken of those Articles subject, where appropriate, to "any relevant rules of the organization" — the Council of Europe — within which it has been adopted (Article 5 of the Vienna Convention).

30. In the way in which it is presented in the "general rule" in Article 31 of the Vienna Convention, the process of interpretation of a treaty is a unity, a single combined operation; this rule, closely integrated, places on the same footing the various elements enumerated in the four paragraphs of the Article.

31. The terms of Article 6 § 1 of the European Convention, taken in their context, provide reason to think that this right is included among the guarantees set forth.

32. The clearest indications are to be found in the French text, first sentence. In the field of *contestations civiles* (civil claims) everyone has a right to proceedings instituted by or against him being conducted in a certain way — *"équitablement"* (fairly), *"publiquement"* (publicly), *"dans un délai raisonnable"* (within a reasonable time), etc. — but also and primarily *"à ce que sa cause soit entendue"* (that his case be heard) not by any authority whatever but *"par un tribunal"* (by a court or tribunal) within the meaning of Article 6 § 1 (Ringeisen judgment of 16 July 1971, Series A no. 13, p. 39, § 95). The Government have emphasised rightly that in French *"cause"* may mean *"procès qui se plaide"* (Littré, *Dictionnaire de la langue française, tome* 1, p. 509, 5°). This, however, is not the sole ordinary sense of this noun; it serves also

to indicate by extension *"l'ensemble des intérêts à soutenir, à faire prévaloir"* (Paul Robert, *Dictionnaire alphabétique et analogique de la langue française, tome* 1, p. 666, II-2°). Similarly, the *"contestation"* (claim) generally exists prior to the legal proceedings and is a concept independent of them. As regard the phrase *"tribunal indépendent et impartial établi par la loi"* (independent and impartial tribunal established by law), it conjures up the idea of organisation rather than that of functioning, of institutions rather than of procedure.

The English text, for its part, speaks of an "independent and impartial tribunal established by law." Moreover, the phrase "in the determination of his civil rights and obligations," on which the Government have relied in support of their contention, does not necessarily refer only to judicial proceedings already pending: as the Commission have observed, it may be taken as synonymous with "wherever his civil rights and obligations are being determined" (paragraph 52 of the report). It too would then imply the right to have the determination of disputes relating to civil rights and obligations made by a court or "tribunal."

The Government have submitted that the expressions "fair and public hearing" and "within a reasonable time," the second sentence in paragraph 1 ("judgment," "trial"), and paragraph 3 of Article 6 clearly presuppose proceedings pending before a court.

While the right to a fair, public and expeditious judicial procedure can assuredly apply only to proceedings in being, it does not, however, necessarily follow that a right to the very institution of such proceedings is thereby excluded; the Delegates of the Commission rightly underlined this at paragraph 21 of their memorial. Besides, in criminal matters, the "reasonable time" may start to run from a date prior to the seisin of the trial court, of the "tribunal" competent for the "determination ... of (the) criminal charge" ... (Wemhoff judgment of 27 June 1968, Series A no. 7, pp. 26-27, § 19; Neumeister judgment of 27 June 1968, Series A no. 8, p. 41, § 18; Ringeisen judgment of 16 July 1971, Series A no. 13, p. 45, § 110). It is conceivable also that in civil matters the reasonable time may begin to run, in certain circumstances, even before the issue of the writ commencing proceedings before the court to which the plaintiff submits the dispute.

33. The Government have furthermore argued the necessity of relating Article 6 § 1 to Articles 5 § 4 and 13. They have observed that the latter provide expressly for a right of access to the courts; the omission of any corresponding clause in Article 6 § 1 seems to them to be only the more striking. The Government have also submitted that if Article 6 § 1 were interpreted as providing such a right of access, Articles 5 § 4 and 13 would become superfluous.

The Commission's Delegates replied in substance that Articles 5

§ 4 and 13, as opposed to Article 6 § 1, are "accessory" to other provisions. Those Articles, they say, do not state a specific right but are designed to afford procedural guarantees, "based on recourse," the former for the "right to liberty," as stated in Article 5 § 1, the second for the whole of the "rights and freedoms as set forth in this Convention." Article 6 § 1, they continue, is intended to protect "in itself" the "right to a good administration of justice," of which "the right that justice should be administered" constitutes "an essential and inherent element." This would serve to explain the contrast between the wording of Article 6 § 1 and that of Articles 5 § 4 and 13.

This reasoning is not without force even though the expression "right to a fair (or good) administration of justice," which sometimes is used on account of its conciseness and convenience (for example, in the Delcourt judgment of 17 January 1970, [see Ch. 7, § A.4., *infra*] does not appear in the text of Article 6 § 1, and can also be understood as referring only to working and not to the organisation of justice.

The Court finds in particular that the interpretation which the Government has contested does not lead to confounding Article 6 § 1 with Articles 5 § 4 and 13, nor making these latter provisions superfluous. Article 13 speaks of an effective remedy before a "national authority" ("*instance nationale*") which may not be a "tribunal" or "court" within the meaning of Articles 6 § 1 and 5 § 4. Furthermore, the effective remedy deals with the violation of a right guaranteed by the Convention, while Articles 6 § 1 and 5 § 4 cover claims relating in the first case to the existence or scope of civil rights and in the second to the lawfulness of arrest or detention. What is more, the three provisions do not operate in the same field. The concept of "civil rights and obligations" (Article 6 § 1) is not co-extensive with that of "rights and freedoms as set forth in this Convention" (Article 13), even if there may be some overlapping. As to the "right to liberty" (Article 5), its "civil" character is at any rate open to argument. . . . Besides, the requirements of Article 5 § 4 in certain respects appear stricter than those of Article 6 § 1, particularly as regards the element of "time."

34. As stated in Article 31 § 2 of the Vienna Convention, the preamble to a treaty forms an integral part of the context. Furthermore, the preamble is generally very useful for the determination of the "object" and "purpose" of the instrument to be construed.

In the present case, the most significant passage in the Preamble to the European Convention is the signatory Governments declaring that they are "resolved, as the Governments of European countries which are like-minded and have a common heritage of political traditions, ideals, freedom and the rule of law, to take the first steps for the collective enforcement of certain of the Rights stated in the Universal Declaration" of 10 December 1948.

. . . .

And in civil matters one can scarcely conceive of the rule of law without there being a possibility of having access to the courts.

35. Article 31 § 3 (c) of the Vienna Convention indicates that account is to be taken, together with the context, of "any relevant rules of international law applicable in the relations between the parties." Among those rules are general principles of law and especially "general principles of law recognized by civilized nations" (Article 38 § 1 (c) of the Statute of the International Court of Justice). Incidentally, the Legal Committee of the Consultative Assembly of the Council of Europe foresaw in August 1950 that "the Commission and the Court must necessarily apply such principles" in the execution of their duties and thus considered it to be "unnecessary" to insert a specific clause to this effect in the Convention . . . .

The principle whereby a civil claim must be capable of being submitted to a judge ranks as one of the universally "recognised" fundamental principles of law; the same is true of the principle of international law which forbids the denial of justice. Article 6 § 1 must be read in the light of these principles.

Were Article 6 § 1 to be understood as concerning exclusively the conduct of an action which had already been initiated before a court, a Contracting State could, without acting in breach of that text, do away with its courts, or take away their jurisdiction to determine certain classes of civil actions and entrust it to organs dependent on the Government. Such assumptions, indissociable from a danger of arbitrary power, would have serious consequences which are repugnant to the aforementioned principles and which the Court cannot overlook . . . .

It would be inconceivable, in the opinion of the Court, that Article 6 § 1 should describe in detail the procedural guarantees afforded to parties in a pending lawsuit and should not first protect that which alone makes it in fact possible to benefit from such guarantees, that is, access to a court. The fair, public and expeditious characteristics of judicial proceedings are of no value at all if there are no judicial proceedings.

36. Taking all the preceding considerations together, it follows that the right of access constitutes an element which is inherent in the right stated by Article 6 § 1. This is not an extensive interpretation forcing new obligations on the Contracting States: it is based on the very terms of the first sentence of Article 6 § 1 read in its context and having regard to the object and purpose of the Convention, a lawmaking treaty . . . , and to general principles of law.

The Court thus reaches the conclusion, without needing to resort to "supplementary means of interpretation" as envisaged at Article 32 of the Vienna Convention, that Article 6 § 1 secures to everyone the right to have any claim relating to his civil rights and obligations brought before a court or tribunal. In this way the Article embodies the "right to a court," of which the right of access, that is the right to institute proceedings before courts in civil matters, constitutes one aspect only. To this are added the guarantees laid down by Article 6 § 1 as regards both the organisation and composition of the court, and the conduct of the proceedings. In sum, the whole makes up the right to a fair hearing. The Court has no need to ascertain in the present case whether and to what extent Article 6 § 1 further requires a decision on the very substance of the dispute (English "determination," French "*décidera*").

B. *ON THE "IMPLIED LIMITATIONS"*

37. Since the impediment to access to the courts, mentioned in paragraph 26 above, affected a right guaranteed by Article 6 § 1, it remains to determine whether it was nonetheless justifiable by virtue of some legitimate limitation on the enjoyment or exercise of that right.
38. The Court considers, accepting the views of the Commission and the alternative submission of the Government, that the right of access to the courts is not absolute. As this is a right which the Convention sets forth (see Articles 13, 14, 17 and 25) without, in the narrower sense of the term, defining, there is room, apart from the bounds delimiting the very content of any right, for limitations permitted by implication.

. . . .

It is not the function of the Court to elaborate a general theory of the limitations admissible in the case of convicted prisoners, nor even to rule *in abstracto* on the compatibility of Rules 33 § 2, 34 § 8 and 37 § 2 of the Prison Rules 1964 with the Convention. Seised of a case which has its origin in a petition presented by an individual, the Court is called upon to pronounce itself only on the point whether or not the application of those Rules in the present case violated the Convention to the prejudice of Golder. . . .
40. In this connection, the Court confines itself to noting what follows.

In petitioning the Home Secretary for leave to consult a solicitor with a view to suing Laird for libel, Golder was seeking to exculpate himself of the charge made against him by that prison officer on 25 October 1969 and which had entailed for him unpleasant consequences, some of which still subsisted by 20 March 1970 (paragraphs 12, 15 and 16 above). Furthermore, the contemplated legal proceedings would have concerned an incident which was connected with prison life and had occurred while the applicant was imprisoned. Finally, those proceedings would have been directed against a member of the prison staff who had made the charge in the course of his duties and who was subject to the Home Secretary's authority.

In these circumstances, Golder could justifiably wish to consult a solicitor with a view to instituting legal proceedings. It was not for the Home Secretary himself to appraise the prospects of the action contemplated; it was for an independent and impartial court to rule on any claim that might be brought. In declining to accord the leave which had been requested, the Home Secretary failed to respect, in the person of Golder, the right to go before a court as guaranteed by Article 6 § 1.

. . . .

FOR THESE REASONS, THE COURT,

1. *Holds* by nine votes to three that there has been a breach of Article 6 § 1;

. . . .

[Dissenting opinions of Judges Verdross, Zekia, and Fitzmaurice* omitted.]

NOTES AND QUESTIONS

1. The Court states that "in civil matters one can scarcely conceive of the rule of law without there being a possibility of having access to the courts." Does the rejected argument of the British Government embody just such a conception? Does the *Golder* case illustrate a lack of mutual understanding by English and Continental European lawyers and judges of the different conceptions of the rule of law in Anglo-American and Continental European law? *See* § A., *supra.* Why did the British Government contest the case so actively?

2. Both *Knechtl* and *Golder* were concerned with private tort litigation although the allegedly tortious acts were committed by government employees. What is the effect of the *Golder* decision on a right of action with respect to administrative acts? Does the *Golder* decision require that judicial review be made available in Great Britain for all administrative acts? Does it require that there be *de novo* review of facts as well as law in the courts?

3. Do you think Great Britain thought that it was agreeing to a right of action when it ratified the European Convention? Consider

---

* Extensive passages from Judge Fitzmaurice's long dissent are contained in the notes which follow.

the following selection from the dissent of Judge Fitzmaurice (the British member of the Court):

> 38. In my view, the correct approach to the interpretation of Article 6.1 is to bear in mind not only that it is a provision embodied in an instrument depending for its force upon the agreement — and indeed the *continuing* support — of governments, but also that it is an instrument of a very special kind, emulated in the field of human rights only by the Inter-American Convention on Human Rights signed at San José nearly twenty years later. This was in considerable measure founded on the European one, particularly as regards its "enforcement" machinery. But it has not been brought into force. Such machinery is not to be found in the United Nations Covenants on Human Rights, which in any case also do not seem to be in force. Speaking generally, the various conventions and covenants on human rights, but more particularly the European Convention, have broken entirely new ground internationally, making heavy inroads on some of the most cherished preserves of governments in the sphere of their domestic jurisdiction or *domaine réservé.* Most especially, and most strikingly, is this the case as regards what is often known as the "right of individual petition," whereby private persons or entities are enabled to (in effect) sue their own governments before an international commission or tribunal, — something that, even as recently as thirty years ago, would have been regarded as internationally inconceivable. For these reasons governments have been hesitant to become parties to instruments most of which, apart from the European Convention, have apparently not so far attracted a sufficient number of ratifications to bring them into force. Other governments, that have ratified the European Convention, have hesitated long before accepting the compulsory jurisdiction of the Court of Human Rights set up under it. Similar delays have occurred in subscribing to the right of individual petition which, like the jurisdiction of the Court, has to be separately accepted. This right moreover, may require not only an initial, but a continuing acceptance, since it may be, and in several instances has been given only for a fixed, though renewable, period. It is indeed solely by reason of an acceptance of this kind that it has been possible for the present (*Golder*) case to be brought before the European Commission and Court of Human Rights at all.
>
> 39. These various factors could justify even a somewhat restrictive interpretation of the Convention but, without going as far as that, they must be said, unquestionably, not only to justify, but positively to demand, a cautious and conservative

interpretation, particularly as regards any provisions the meaning of which may be uncertain, and where extensive constructions might have the effect of imposing upon the contracting States obligations they had not really meant to assume, or would not have understood themselves to be assuming. (In this connexion the passage quoted in the footnote below (24) from the oral argument of Counsel for the United Kingdom before the Commission should be carefully noted.) Any serious doubt must therefore be resolved in favour of, rather than against, the government concerned, — and if it were true, as the Judgment of the Court seeks to suggest, that there *is* no serious doubt in the present case, then one must wonder what it is the participants have been arguing about over approximately the last five years!

4. The American Convention of Human Rights, referred to by Judge Fitzmaurice, was convened in San José, Costa Rica in 1969. It was signed by delegates of 12 States — El Salvador, Colombia, Ecuador, Honduras, Paraguay, Panama, Chile, Uruguay, Guatemala, Nicaragua, Venezuela, and Costa Rica — and will enter into force upon ratification by 11 States. Like the European Convention, the American Convention provides for individual petitions (art. 44); furthermore, art. 8, para. 1, provides:

> Every person has the right to a hearing, with due guarantees and within a reasonable time, by a competent, independent, and impartial tribunal, previously established by law, in the substantiation of any accusation of a criminal nature made against him or for the determination of his rights and obligations of a civil, labor, fiscal, or any other nature.

This bears a rather obvious resemblance to art. 6, § 1 of the European Convention. In the unlikely event that the United States were to become a party to the American Convention, would it require the United States to accept the *Golder* case's conception of a right of action?

---

(24) "As regards the question of access to the courts, this is not a case of a Government trying to repudiate obligations freely undertaken. That much is quite clear. If one thing has emerged from all the discussion in the case of Mr. Knechtl and the pleadings so far in the case of Mr. Golder, it is that the Government of the United Kingdom had no idea when it was accepting Art. 6 of the Convention that it was accepting an obligation to accord a right of access to the courts without qualification. Whether we are right on the interpretation or whether we are wrong, I submit that that much is absolutely clear. I am not going to review in detail all the evidence or the views of the United Kingdom in this respect which have been placed before the Commission. But I submit that it is perfectly clear from all the constitutional material that has been submitted, from its part in the drafting of the European Establishment Convention, that the United Kingdom had no intention of assuming, and did not know that it was expected to assume, any such obligation."

3. United States

BODDIE v. CONNECTICUT

Supreme Court of the United States

401 U.S. 371, 91 S. Ct. 780, 28 L. Ed. 2d 113 (1971)

[This was a class action by welfare recipients challenging a requirement of prepayment of court fees and costs averaging $60 in order to maintain an action for divorce. The District Court upheld the filing fee requirement. The Supreme Court reversed.]

MR. JUSTICE HARLAN delivered the opinion of the Court.

. . . Our conclusion is that, given the basic position of the marriage relationship in this society's hierarchy of values and the concomitant state monopolization of the means for legally dissolving this relationship, due process does prohibit a State from denying, solely because of inability to pay, access to its courts to individuals who seek judicial dissolution of their marriages.

I

At its core, the right to due process reflects a fundamental value in our American constitutional system. Our understanding of that value is the basis upon which we have resolved this case.

Perhaps no characteristic of an organized and cohesive society is more fundamental than its erection and enforcement of a system of rules defining the various rights and duties of its members, enabling them to govern their affairs and definitively settle their differences in an orderly, predictable manner. Without such a "legal system," social organization and cohesion are virtually impossible; with the ability to seek regularized resolution of conflicts individuals are capable of interdependent action that enables them to strive for achievements without the anxieties that would beset them in a disorganized society. Put more succinctly, it is this injection of the rule of law that allows society to reap the benefits of rejecting what political theorists call the "state of nature."

American society, of course, bottoms its systematic definition of individual rights and duties, as well as its machinery for dispute settlement, not on custom or the will of strategically placed individuals, but on the common-law model. It is to courts, or other quasi-judicial official bodies, that we ultimately look for the implementation of a regularized, orderly process of dispute settlement. Within this framework, those who wrote our original Constitution, in the Fifth Amendment, and later those who drafted the Fourteenth Amendment, recognized the centrality of the concept of due process in the operation of this system. Without this guarantee that one may not be deprived of his rights, neither liberty nor property, without due process of law, the State's monopoly over techniques for binding conflict resolution could hardly be said to be acceptable under our scheme of things. Only by providing that the social enforcement mechanism must function strictly within these bounds can we hope to maintain an ordered society that is also just. It is upon this premise that this Court has through years of adjudication put flesh upon the due process principle.

Such litigation has, however, typically involved rights of defendants — not, as here, persons seeking access to the judicial process in the first instance. This is because our society has been so structured that resort to the courts is not usually the only available, legitimate means of resolving private disputes. Indeed, private structuring of individual relationships and repair of their breach is largely encouraged in American life, subject only to the caveat that the formal judicial process, if resorted to, is paramount. Thus, this Court has seldom been asked to view access to the courts as an element of due process. The legitimacy of the State's monopoly over techniques of final dispute settlement, even where some are denied access to its use, stands unimpaired where recognized, effective alternatives for the adjustment of differences remain. But the successful invocation of this governmental power by plaintiffs has often created serious problems for defendants' rights. For at that point, the judicial proceeding becomes the only effective means of resolving the dispute at hand and denial of a defendant's full access to that process raises grave problems for its legitimacy.

Recognition of this theoretical framework illuminates the precise issue presented in this case. As this Court on more than one occasion has recognized, marriage involves interests of basic importance in our society. See, *e. g., Loving* v. *Virginia,* 388 U. S. 1 (1967); *Skinner* v. *Oklahoma,* 316 U. S. 535 (1942); *Meyer* v. *Nebraska,* 262 U. S. 390 (1923). It is not surprising, then, that the States have seen fit to oversee many aspects of that institution. Without a prior judicial imprimatur, individuals may freely enter into and rescind commercial contracts, for example, but we are unaware of any jurisdiction where private citizens may covenant for or dissolve marriages without state approval. Even where all substantive requirements are concededly met, we know of no instance where two consenting adults may divorce and mutually liberate themselves from the constraints of legal obligations that go with marriage, and more fundamentally the prohibition against remarriage, without invoking the State's judicial machinery.

Thus, although they assert here due process rights as would-be plaintiffs, we think appellants' plight, because resort to the state courts is the only avenue to dissolution of their marriages, is akin to that of defendants faced with exclusion from the only forum effectively empowered to settle their disputes. Resort to the judicial process by these plaintiffs is no more voluntary in a realistic sense than that of the defendant called upon to defend his interests in court. For both groups this process is not only the paramount dispute-settlement technique, but, in fact, the only available one. In this posture we think that this appeal is properly to be resolved in light of the principles enunciated in our due process decisions that delimit rights of defendants compelled to litigate their differences in the judicial forum.

II

These due process decisions, representing over a hundred years of effort by this Court to give concrete embodiment to this concept, provide, we think, complete vindication for appellants' contentions. In particular, precedent has firmly embedded in our due process jurisprudence two important principles upon whose application we rest our decision in the case before us.

A

Prior cases establish, first, that due process requires, at a minimum, that absent a countervailing state interest of overriding significance, persons forced to settle their claims of right and duty through the judicial process must be given a meaningful opportunity to be heard. Early in our jurisprudence, this Court voiced the doctrine that "[w]herever one is assailed in his person or his property, there he may defend," . . . .

B

Our cases further establish that a statute or a rule may be held constitutionally invalid as applied when it operates to deprive an individual of a protected right although its general validity as a measure enacted in the legitimate exercise of state power is beyond question. Thus, in cases involving religious freedom, free speech or assembly, this Court has often held that a valid statute was unconstitutionally applied in particular circumstances because it interfered with an individual's exercise of those rights.

No less than these rights, the right to a meaningful opportunity to be heard within the limits of practicality, must be protected against denial by particular laws that operate to jeopardize it for particular individuals.

. . . .

III

Drawing upon the principles established by the cases just canvassed, we conclude that the State's refusal to admit these appellants to its courts, the sole means in Connecticut for obtaining a divorce, must be regarded as the equivalent of denying them an opportunity to be heard upon their claimed right to a dissolution of their marriages, and, in the absence of a sufficient countervailing justification for the State's action, a denial of due process.

The arguments for this kind of fee and cost requirement are that the State's interest in the prevention of frivolous litigation is substantial, its use of court fees and process costs to allocate scarce resources is rational, and its balance between the defendant's right to notice and the plaintiff's right to access is reasonable.

In our opinion, none of these considerations is sufficient to override the interest of these plaintiff-appellants in having access to the only avenue open for dissolving their allegedly untenable marriages. Not only is there no necessary connection between a litigant's assets and the seriousness of his motives in bringing suit, but it is here beyond present dispute that appellants bring these actions in good faith. Moreover, other alternatives exist to fees and cost requirements as a means for conserving the time of courts and protecting parties from frivolous litigation, such as penalties for false pleadings or affidavits, and actions for malicious prosecution or abuse of process, to mention only a few. In the same vein we think that reliable alternatives exist to service of process by a state-paid sheriff if the State is unwilling to assume the cost of official service. . . .

. . . .

IV

In concluding that the Due Process Clause of the Fourteenth Amendment requires that these appellants be afforded an opportunity to go into court to obtain a divorce, we wish to re-emphasize that we go no further than necessary to dispose of the case before us, a case where the *bona fides* of both appellants' indigency and desire for divorce are here beyond dispute. We do not decide that access for all individuals to the courts is a right that is, in all circumstances, guaranteed by the Due Process Clause of the Fourteenth Amendment so that its exercise may not be placed beyond the reach of any individual, for, as we have already noted, in the case before us this right is the exclusive precondition to the adjustment of a fundamental human relationship. The requirement that these appellants resort to the judicial process is entirely a state-created matter. Thus we hold only that a State may not, consistent with the obligations imposed on it by the Due Process Clause of the Fourteenth Amendment, pre-empt the right to dissolve this legal relationship without affording all citizens access to the means it has prescribed for doing so.

Reversed.

MR. JUSTICE DOUGLAS, concurring in the result.

. . . "Our decisions for more than a decade now have made clear that differences in access to the instruments needed to vindicate legal rights, when based upon the financial situation of the defendant are repugnant to the Constitution." *Roberts* v. *LaVallee,* 389 U. S. 40, 42. . . .

. . . .

Thus, under Connecticut law divorces may be denied or granted solely on the basis of wealth. Just as denying further judicial review in *Burns* and *Smith,* appellate counsel in *Douglas,* and a transcript in *Griffin* created an invidious distinction based on wealth, so, too, does making the grant or denial of a divorce to turn on the wealth of the parties. Affluence does not pass muster under the Equal Protection Clause for determining who must remain married and who shall be allowed to separate.

MR. JUSTICE BRENNAN, concurring in part.

. . . I cannot join the Court's opinion insofar as today's holding is made to depend upon the factor that only the State can grant a divorce and that an indigent would be locked into a marriage if unable to pay the fees required to obtain a divorce. A State has an ultimate monopoly of all judicial process and attendant enforcement machinery. As a practical matter, if disputes cannot be successfully settled between the parties, the court system is usually "the only forum effectively empowered to settle their disputes. Resort to the judicial process by these plaintiffs is no more voluntary in a realistic sense than that of the defendant called upon to defend his interests in court." . . . I see no constitutional distinction between appellants' attempt to enforce this state statutory right and an attempt to vindicate any other right arising under federal or state law. If fee requirements close the courts to an indigent he can no more invoke the aid of the courts for other forms of relief than he can escape the legal incidents of a marriage. The right to be heard in some way at some time extends to all proceedings entertained by courts. The possible distinctions suggested by the Court today will not withstand analysis.

In addition, this case presents a classic problem of equal protection of the laws. . . .

MR. JUSTICE BLACK, dissenting.

. . . .

Criminal defendants are brought into court by the State or Federal

Government to defend themselves against charges of crime. They go into court knowing that they may be convicted, and condemned to lose their lives, their liberty, or their property, as a penalty for their crimes. Because of this great governmental power the United States Constitution has provided special protections for people charged with crime. . . .

Civil lawsuits, however, are not like government prosecutions for crime. Civil courts are set up by government to give people who have quarrels with their neighbors the chance to use a neutral governmental agency to adjust their differences. In such cases the government is not usually involved as a party, and there is no deprivation of life, liberty, or property as punishment for crime. Our Federal Constitution, therefore, does not place such private disputes on the same high level as it places criminal trials and punishment. There is consequently no necessity, no reason, why government should in civil trials be hampered or handicapped by the strict and rigid due process rules the Constitution has provided to protect people charged with crime.

This distinction between civil and criminal proceedings is implicit in *Cohen* v. *Beneficial Loan Corp.,* 337 U. S. 541 (1949), where we held that a statute requiring some, but not all, plaintiffs in stockholder derivative actions to post a bond did not violate the Due Process or the Equal Protection Clause. The *Cohen* case is indistinguishable from the one before us. In *Cohen,* as here, the statute applied to plaintiffs. In both situations the legal relationships involved are creatures of the State, extensively governed by state law. The effect of both statutes may be to deter frivolous or ill-considered suits, and in both instances the State has a considerable interest in the prevention of such suits, which might harm the very relationship the State created and fostered. Finally, the effect of both statutes may be to close the state courts entirely to certain plaintiffs, a result the Court explicitly accepted in *Cohen.* See *id.,* at 552. I believe the present case should be controlled by the Court's thorough opinion in *Cohen.*

. . . *Cohen* can only be distinguished on the ground that it involved a stockholders' suit, while this case involves marriage, an interest "of basic importance in our society." Thus the Court's opinion appears to rest solely on a philosophy that any law violates due process if it is unreasonable, arbitrary, indecent, deviates from the fundamental, is shocking to the conscience, or fails to meet other tests composed of similar words or phrases equally lacking in any possible constitutional precision. These concepts, of course, mark no constitutional boundaries and cannot possibly depend upon anything but the belief of particular judges, at particular times, concerning particular interests which those judges have divined to be of "basic importance."

NOTES AND QUESTIONS

1. Given the doubt which surrounds the question, in the United States, whether there is a constitutional right of access to the courts to resolve disputes between the individual and government, one should not be surprised that the question of the right to court access to resolve disputes between individuals is even more in doubt. Despite the rationale of Justice Harlan's opinion in the *Boddie* case, does the case have anything to do with that question? Does the decision preclude a requirement of payment of fees by persons who have the means to pay them? Should the case then be viewed, as Justices Douglas and Brennan see it, as part of the general question of equal justice for the poor? (That question will be examined at more length in Ch. 10 §§ A.4. and B.2.a., *infra*.) Can you think of any practical situation, beyond waiver of fees and other costs of litigation for those too poor to pay, where a constitutional right of access to court for resolution of private disputes would be important?

2. Does any case other than divorce meet Justice Harlan's twofold test for a constitutional right of access to court? Two later cases suggest that the answer to that question may be "no." In *United States* v. *Kras,* 409 U.S. 434 (1973), involving a filing fee in bankruptcy cases, Justice Blackmun's opinion for the Court distinguished *Boddie* on two grounds: courts were not the only avenue for resolution of the debtor's plight since he could, in theory, come to a negotiated agreement with his creditors; bankruptcy was not a fundamental right as was marriage. Notice, particularly, the first distinction. How many private legal disputes are there that cannot be resolved, in theory, by a negotiated settlement? And, in *Ortwein* v. *Schwab,* 410 U.S. 656 (1973) (previously mentioned, *supra* § B.3., Note 3), the Court relied on *Kras* to hold that indigent welfare recipients had no constitutional right to waiver of court fees required to obtain judicial review of termination or reduction of their welfare benefits. Is it anomalous to limit a constitutional right of access to court for settlement of disputes to those cases where, in theory as well as fact, the dispute cannot be settled any other way?

3. Again putting to one side issues of inequality in access to the courts, does it make sense to have a constitutional right to judicial resolution of private disputes? In most cases where the legislature decides to curtail particular forms of litigation or the assertion of particular kinds of defenses, it can simply change the substantive law involved, effectively precluding the assertion of plaintiffs' claims or defendants' defenses. *Boddie* does not hold that people have a substantive constitutional right to a divorce. Why then, once divorce is permitted, is there a due process right to court access in divorce cases? Consider, for example, the case of so-called "heart balm" laws widely enacted decades ago. It was widely believed that the cause of action for breach of promise of marriage was more often used for extortion by unworthy plaintiffs than do redress real injuries by worthy plaintiffs. The solution was to abolish the substantive cause of action. If there was a broad right of access to courts in civil cases, would abolition of substantive causes of action violate that right? If not, could the legislature leave the cause of action for breach of promise of marriage intact *in theory* while banning its enforcement in court by *all* persons? Is the distinction between abolishing the right and abolishing the remedy mere formalism?

4. Returning, momentarily, to issues of inequality of the poor in access to court, is it important to decide, as a preliminary question, whether there is a "fundamental" right of access to court which is independent of the constitutional guarantee of equal protection of the laws? Consider the following:

> It is not the province of this Court to create substantive Constitutional rights in the name of guaranteeing equal protection of the laws. . . . [T]he answer lies in assessing whether there is a right . . . explicitly or implicitly guaranteed by the Constitution. [*San Antonio School District* v. *Rodriguez,* 411 U.S. 1, 33-34 (1973).]

As indicated, we will return to this issue in connection with the discussion of questions of equal justice for the poor. (*See* Ch. 10 §§ A.4. and B.2.a., *infra.*)

Chapter 7

NOTICE AND FAIR HEARING

With respect to legal proceedings, the rights to notice and a fair hearing are basic in both Europe and the United States. In Italy and Germany, the relevant constitutional provisions are:
a) Italian Constitution, art. 24, para. 2:
   Everyone shall have the inviolable right of defense in every phase and stage of any legal proceedings.
b) German Constitution, art. 103(1):
   In the courts everyone shall be entitled to a hearing on all legal matters.
Moreover, art. 6 of the European Convention on Human Rights provides:
   (1) In the determination of his civil rights and obligations or of any criminal charge against him, everyone is entitled to a fair and public hearing within a reasonable time by an independent and impartial tribunal established by law. . . .
   . . . .
   (3) Everyone charged with a criminal offence has the following minimum rights:
   . . . .
   (c) to defend himself in person or through legal assistance of his own choosing . . . .
Inherent in legal systems of the United States and the Continent are the notions that, for a hearing to be fair: (1) prior notice of the hearing is essential, (2) both parties must have the right to produce and contest evidence, and (3) whenever feasible, the hearing should precede a decision on the merits. In reading the remainder of this chapter, consider why these shared ideas often lead to divergent results on the two continents.

A. FAIR HEARING

1. Right to Produce and Contest Evidence

a. Italy

MIRAGLIA AND SACCONE v. PRESIDENTE CONSIGLIO DEI MINISTRI

Corte costituzionale, Decision of December 22, 1961, No. 70
[1961] 6 Guir. Cost. 1282; [1961] Rac. uff. corte cost. 319
[1962] 85 Foro It. I, 13

[FACTS: In the course of an action for the discontinuance of a lease extended by law under a post-war rent control provision, the *Pretore* of Palermo submitted to the Constitutional Court the question of the constitutionality of art. 10 of the Law of May 23, 1950, No. 253. This article provided that the *Genio Civile* (Public Works Office) alone could ascertain the technical conditions necessitating condemnation of dwellings. Such condemnation was a valid reason for ending the lease. The findings of the *Genio Civile* were binding upon the judge.

[According to the *ordinanza* of the *Pretore,* this statute denied the right of the citizen to obtain the judicial protection guaranteed by art. 24 of the Constitution because it took from the judge the power to choose an expert witness other than the *Genio Civile* and prevented him from supervising, controlling, or even replacing the *Genio Civile* if he thought it necessary.]

OPINION

Although the *ordinanza* seems to refer to the article in its entirety, the challenge is evidently restricted to that part of the article in which the *Genio Civile* is required to make a determination of the condition of the dwelling and of the requirement that it be abandoned; that is, to the second parts of paras. 1 and 2.

These provisions are interpreted similarly by most of the judicial and doctrinal opinion of the day. It has been, and is presently held that the determination of the *Genio Civile* binds the judge who has control only over its legitimacy. He can point out violations of the law, contradictions, and patent errors of opinion, as well as request clarification, or if the need exists, order the entire determination done again. But the judge is precluded from naming a different consultant or resorting to other sources.

If this is the proper interpretation of these provisions, and there is no reason to doubt that it is, the Court holds them to be contrary to art. 24 of the Constitution. In fact, the peculiarity of the proceeding established by these rules does not fully guarantee the right of defense which is insured by art. 24. . . . The right of defense is denied in that the challenged norms take away from the judge the power to freely evaluate the principal issue of the controversy. In this way, the decision of the case is taken from the ordinary judge and placed in the hands of an administrative organ.

... The consequence is that, since the termination of the lease depends entirely on a determination which cannot be controlled by the court, the substantive rights involved are not properly protected. The determination of the *Genio Civile,* although constituting a stage of the proceeding, is enacted as an administrative measure, such that the lessor and lessee would not have a right to evidence. ... This does not merely represent an anomaly, but imparts a fatal defect in the protection afforded by arts. 24 and 3 of the Constitution. In effect, it impedes the interested parties from availing themselves of the means of proof guaranteed to them in a proceeding.

Finally, among the reasons which require that the challenged provisions be declared unconstitutional is the fact that a fair hearing is not allowed. According to the statute, the *Genio Civile* must consult the parties, but this can be, and is done, separately, these separate declarations not being transcribed or made known to the judge. Even if the *Genio Civile* establishes a true and proper dialogue between the interested parties (which, in truth, is not done) it remains that the judge is not a part of it. Moreover, these provisions allow, and it often happens, that the determination of the *Genio Civile* is concluded even before judicial action has commenced. Once the proceeding comes before the judge, the parties can defend themselves on everything except the most crucial issue of the case. They can in other words, point out contradictions or patent errors made, but they are not allowed to challenge the content of the determination. In sum, they do not participate actively and in open argument in the essential development of the proceeding. The challenged norms therefore are contrary to art. 24, para. 2, of the Constitution, since the right of defense is compromised when open debate is not insured and procedural obstacles limit the presentation of evidence by the parties. ...

NOTES AND QUESTIONS

1. Are there any differences between the scope of the right of action, discussed in Ch. 6, and the right of defense discussed in the *Miraglia* case? It is a denial of the right of action [art. 24, para. 1] to make the decision of an administrator on issues of fact or law binding on the *plaintiff* in a court action. (*See* the *Sonaglia* case, Ch. 6, § B.2.a., *supra.*) Is it quite simply a denial of the right of defense [art. 24, para. 2] if the decision of an administrator on issues of fact or law is made binding on the *defendant* in a court action? The court in *Miraglia* points out that, while the *Genio Civile* consults the adversary parties, he does not conduct an adversary hearing. Would the constitutionality of the rent control law have been established if the *Genio Civile* had been required to conduct a fair adversary hearing, but his conclusions of fact and law drawn from that hearing had still been made binding on the courts?

2. Are there any differences between the right of action and the right of defense, on the one hand, and the right to present evidence, on the other? Recall the *Stroppa* case, Ch. 6, § B.2.a., *supra,* which held it to be a denial of the right of action to require the taxpayer to pay a disputed tax before he could contest the legality of the tax in court. Consider the case of *Agostini* v. *Malquori,* Decision of Apr. 9, 1963, Corte cost., [1963] 8 Giur. Cost. 170; [1963] 16 Rac. uff. corte cost. 285; [1963] 86 Foro It., I 646, previously discussed in the notes to the *Carabba* case. That case upheld the registration fees on documents to be used in litigation. If the fee is not paid, the document cannot be used in the proceeding and the proceeding itself is suspended until the tax and penalties are paid. In upholding the registration fees, the *Corte Costituzionale* reasoned that the registration fees involved the right to evidence and not the right to defense or the right of action. The opinion, bitterly criticized by several commentators, implicitly indicated that the fee requirement was analogous to rules of admissibility of testimony, and rules dealing with formal procedures for admission of evidence.

3. Does it make sense to conclude that the right of defense is not involved when a fee requirement precludes the introduction of evidence crucial to the decisions? Are the registration fee cases different from *Miraglia* in that they do not involve the transfer of adjudication functions to an administrative agency? Consider whether the *D'Agostino* case, which follows, rejects the rationale of the *Agostini* case.

D'AGOSTINO v. MINISTERO TRASPORTI

Corte costituzionale, Decision of June 3, 1966, No. 53
[1966] 11 Giur. Cost. 858; [1966] 23 Rac. uff. corte cost. 498
[1966] 89 Foro It. I, 991

[FACTS: The *ordinanze* which submitted the question of constitutionality to the Court do not state the facts.]

OPINION

These two *ordinanze* propose substantially the same question of constitutionality. Therefore they may be dealt with in a single proceeding.

We hold that art. 4 of the Law of June 25, 1909, No. 372 concerning the regulation of railroads, is unconstitutional in that part in which the state railroad company * is given a general and discretionary power to withhold from the court the factual findings of inquests made after an accident.

We do recognize that the company's discretionary power to withhold reports containing only appraisals concerning results of the inquest is not in conflict with constitutional principles. Those appraisals are evaluations, with which the company may not even agree, and do not contain any factual findings. However, the documents which give the elements of evidence on which the appraisals are based, cannot be withheld from the proceeding without violating the right of defense. . . .

According to the previous holdings of this Court, the right of defense, at least, guarantees the right to technical-professional assistance and a full hearing in the course of the proceeding, but this is not all. . . . In fact, if the procedural right to present to the judge evidence of favorable facts is denied or limited, or if the right to exhibit evidence concerning those facts is denied or limited, then it is the right of defense itself which is being denied or limited.

Therefore, it is extremely significant that the rule in question may be applied in such a way that the judge is prevented from examining all the evidence gathered in the inquest. Specifically we refer to those elements which are susceptible to change or dispersion if not registered immediately, elements which only a prompt and diligent inquest of the railroad company can ascertain, by virtue of its unique technical experience. . . .

Moreover, we cannot forget that by giving the company the discretionary power to withhold factual findings from the judge, those liable may be exonerated and questionable findings of fact will remain unquestioned. . . .

The right of defense does not grant only the right to appear in the courtroom, just as the right of action does not only grant the right to initiate a suit. The power of the judge to inquire into the elements of proof he considers necessary to the formation of his opinion must not be limited, because if it is limited the party's right to a full hearing is denied. . . .

For these reasons the *Corte Costituzionale* . . . holds that art. 4 of the Law of June 25, 1909, No. 372 (concerning the regulation of the state railroad company) is unconstitutional in that part in which it grants the company a general and discretionary power to withhold from the courts transcripts and reports containing the factual findings of the railroad's inquest. . . .

---

* The state railroad company is a government agency.

NOTES AND QUESTIONS

1. Despite the rationale of the *D'Agostino* decision, the *Corte Costituzionale* again decided that it was constitutional to exclude documents for which registration fees had not been paid. *Frusca Co.* v. *Corruti,* Corte cost., Decision of Dec. 22, 1969, No. 157, [1969] 14 Giur. Cost. 2359; [1969] 30 Rac. uff. corte cost. 615; [1970] 93 Foro It. I, 386.

2. On the other hand, in the Decision of July 23, 1974, No. 248, *Pavone* v. *Vescovo et al.,* [1974] 97 Foro It. I, 2220, the *Corte Costituzionale* struck down art. 247 of the Code of Civil Procedure which excluded the testimony of the wife and close relatives of the parties in civil cases. The Court held this centuries-old exclusion to be violative of art. 24 of the Constitution since "it results in an unjustifiable compression of both the right of action and the right of defense." *Id.* at 2221. The Court repeated the phrase which is central in the *D'Agostino* case that the right of action and defense is violated "if the procedural right to present to the judge evidence of favorable facts is denied or limited, or if the right to exhibit evidence concerning those facts is denied or limited." *Id.* at 2221.

3. How is the problem of *D'Agostino* — availability of accident reports — handled in the United States? *See* Federal Rules of Civil Procedure 34(b) and Official Comment thereto.

b. Germany
DECISION OF JULY 24, 1963

Bundesverfassungsgericht
[1965] 17 BVerfGE 86

[FACTS: Petitioner, a storekeeper, was inducted into the German defense forces in 1945 at the age of 60. He was hospitalized for grenade fragment wounds, and when he returned home, his wife was killed in a bombing raid. In 1949, he had unsuccessfully sought a pension based on his military disability, which was denied because he was found to have only a 20 percent disability. In 1951, his application was successful, on a finding that his disability reduced his earning capacity by 30 percent, the minimum then required for pensions for military service connected disabilities. In 1952, his further request for a widower's pension, for survivors of persons dead as a result of military action, was denied on the ground that it required that he have sustained permanent reduction of his earning capacity exceeding 50 percent. The decision was upheld in the social courts. This petition to the Constitutional Court is presented by the deceased petitioner's son, who contends that petitioner was denied a fair hearing in the Social Court, since it based its decision that he had not suffered sufficient disability on the expert opinion of Dr. S.

employed by the administrative agency to determine the extent of his disability.]

OPINION

. . . .

The determination that at the time of the death of his wife the petitioner was more than fifty percent disabled with regard to his capacity to earn a living and that this condition was not merely temporary was important to the decisions which rejected his claim to a widower's pension. In this connection it must be determined whether he received a fair hearing.

. . . .

The Social Court denied the widower's pension [*inter alia,* on the basis of the fact that] in 1949 he was found by Dr. S. to be only 20 percent disabled; he was not therefore lacking in the capacity to work in the sense of the statute. . . .

On appeal to the Federal Social Court the petitioner pointed out that he had not known of the expert opinion of Dr. S. and that neither he nor his counsel . . . had seen it. In 1949 when the expert opinion was made, and even later, he had had no cause to examine the pension documents since no judicial proceeding had been initiated at that time. In the proceeding concerning the widower's pension the expert opinion . . . was neither mentioned nor called upon. He asserts that had he had the opportunity to take a position against the statement of the expert witness, the judgment of his incapacity to earn a living would have been otherwise.

The Federal Social Court has found this claim to be "inadmissible" since the right to a fair hearing concerns only "judicial" (as opposed to administrative) proceedings. It is therefore not violated "if a Court of Social Justice bases its decision completely or partially on expert opinion, taken in an administrative proceeding under the War Victims Assistance Act, of which . . . [the party] had no knowledge."

We cannot agree with that.

1. Consistent with previous decisions of the Federal Constitutional Court, art. 103, para. 1, of the Bonn Constitution does not allow, as a basis of judicial decision, facts or evidence on which the parties have not had the opportunity to be heard. . . . This prohibition includes all facts and evidence regardless of origin. There is no objective ground by which we can see that a party should, on the one hand, have the right to be heard on evidence taken in the proceeding itself, while on the other, the Court should have the right to use evidence taken by prior administrative measures, of which the party has had no knowledge and was not forewarned, and on which he did not have the opportunity to be heard.

The use of the expert opinion of Dr. S., which was unknown to the petitioner, in the decision of the [Social Court] is contrary to art. 103, para. 1, of the Basic Law.

2. Of course, we could not annul the decisions if the evidence taken in violation of the right to be heard would have been used only in an auxiliary fashion, or if the hearing of the interested party would clearly not have resulted in a more favorable decision from his point of view, because then the challenged decisions would not be based on the denial of a fair hearing and the party would not have been injured.

But here an injury exists. It deals with the use of the expert opinion of Dr. S. . . . not merely as an auxiliary argument which could be dismissed without affecting the basis of the decision. [On the contrary] . . . the determination of the Social Court was based substantially on the expert testimony of Dr. S. . . .

. . . The decisions of the Social Court and the Federal Social Court are annulled as being in violation of art. 103, para. 1, of the Basic Law.

NOTES AND QUESTIONS

1. Would it have been more appropriate to base this decision on art. 19 (4) of the German Constitution, which provides a right of action for persons whose rights are violated by public authority? (*See* Ch. 6, § B., *supra*.) Note the position of the Federal Social Court that no provision of the German Constitution guaranteed a fair hearing in the administrative proceeding itself. Does the Constitutional Court disagree with that?

2. As previously indicated, while the German Constitution contains an explicit provision for a right of action in review of administrative decisions, there is no explicit provision which provides a right of action in private disputes. Nevertheless, the right might be found in a combination of the right to a lawful judge (art. 101) and the right to a fair hearing (art. 103). (Ch. 6, § C.1., *supra*.)

DECISION OF FEBRUARY 1, 1967

Bundesverfassungsgericht
[1967] 21 BVerfGE 132

[FACTS]: Petitioner's marriage had been dissolved in 1960. There was a child born in 1956 during the marriage. After the divorce the petitioner went to the U.S., while his ex-wife and child remained in the Federal Republic.

In 1961 the public prosecutor challenged the legitimacy of the child through a special procedure [in which the only parties are the public prosecutor and the child]. The youth welfare office — as representative of the child — gave the petitioner's lawyers notice of the beginning of the proceeding. The petitioner, however, was not sent the petition nor was he requested to attend the oral proceedings. Based on the evidence, without the participation of the petitioner, the court declared in its decision of August 12, 1967, that the child was not the petitioner's. A copy of the decision was sent to the parties and the child's mother. Neither notification nor consignment [a formal means of notification] was carried out as to the petitioner.

Petitioner brings *Verfassungsbeschwerde* against this decision, asserting the violation of art. 103 of the Constitution (right to be heard).

Opinion

The decision under attack violates the petitioner's basic right under art. 103.

The successful challenge of the child's legitimacy which has effect for and against everyone, abolishes the rights of the father, particularly the right, protected by the Constitution (art. 6 para. 2), to the guardianship and education of the child. Because of the immediate effect that the decision would have upon the petitioner, even though he was not a party to the proceeding, he should have been granted a right to be heard. This right, guaranteed by art. 103, belongs to everyone whose rights are directly affected by a judicial decision. It is of no importance that the code of civil procedure did not provide for the participation of the father in the proceeding initiated by the public prosecutor against the child.... When procedural rules insufficiently guarantee the constitutionally granted minimum of a right to be heard, the Constitutional Court has derived directly from art. 103 the duty to hear a person.... In this proceeding, the court should have given the petitioner at least a chance to participate by sending him the petitions and notifying him of his right to attend.

NOTE AND QUESTIONS

It is often difficult to distinguish the right to fair procedure from substantive constitutional rights. Consider *Stanley* v. *Illinois*, 405 U.S. 645 (1972). Stanley was an unwed father whose children, on their mother's death, were declared wards of the state. Stanley was not permitted to prove that he was a fit parent and should have custody of the children. The Court held that the Illinois law established an unconstitutional conclusive presumption, and denied Stanley procedural due process. That is, the constitutional violation was in denying Stanley the right to a hearing on his fitness as a parent. It has been argued that what was really at issue in the *Stanley* case was not an issue of fair procedure, but the substantive constitutional right of the male parent of an illegitimate child to custody of the child. *Compare* Note, *Irrebuttable Presumptions: An Illusory Analysis,* 27 STAN. L. REV. 449 (1975) *with* Note, *The Irrebuttable Presumption Doctrine in the Supreme Court,* 87 HARV. L. REV. 1543 (1974). In other words, if, as a matter of *substantive* due process the father can be denied custody of his illegitimate children even if he is a fit parent, then Illinois need not give him a hearing on the question whether he is a fit parent.

Do you think that the German decision, too, inevitably involves constitutional issues going beyond the constitutional right to a fair hearing — questions of the substantive rights of children and their parents? Suppose that Stanley had been denied a hearing on a claim that the children were legitimate. Would the case then have involved a "pure" question of fair procedure?

2. Right to a Prior Hearing

DECISION OF JANUARY 8, 1959

Bundesverfassungsgericht
[1959] 9 BVerfGE 89

[FACTS]: The petitioner was ordered placed in temporary confinement by the *Amtsgericht** of Schwäbisch Hall during the course of the court's investigation into repeated instances of fraud and defamation alleged to have been commited by her. The action was taken to prevent her from prejudicing the ultimate decision by the concealment or destruction of evidence. On petitioner's appeal, the *Landgericht*** of Heilbronn annulled the confinement order on the grounds that no real probability existed that evidence remained to be concealed. The state attorney then appealed to the *Oberlandesgericht* of Stuttgart which overturned the prior appellate decision and reinstated the order on the basis that the accused could still attempt to impede the determination of the truth. Neither the petitioner nor her attorneys were notified of the appeal of the state attorney to the *Oberlandesgericht.* Only the decision was communicated to the petitioner's attorneys. The petitioner then requested that the *Oberlandesgericht* reverse its decision. The new appeal was rejected.

---

   * This is a single-judge court of first instance in civil matters under 3,000 DM and specific matters designated by statute. It is also the court of first instance for petty criminal offenses, for which the professional judge is sometimes assisted by two lay judges.
   ** The *Landgerichte* are the normal courts of first instance for major criminal offenses and for civil cases where the amount in controversy exceeds 3,000 DM. Their decisions are made by three-judge panels in civil cases, and by five-judge panels (3 professional judges and 2 lay persons) in criminal cases. They are also the courts of second instance for appeals from the *Amtsgericht.*

[To review this decision, a *Verfassungsbeschwerde* was brought asserting violation of the right to a fair hearing under art. 103 of the Basic Law.]

OPINION

The *Verfassungsbeschwerde* is admissible.
. . . .

1. The principle of the fair hearing, elevated to a fundamental right in art. 103, para. 1, of the Basic Law, is a result of the concept of *Rechtsstaat* [rule of law] in the area of judicial proceedings. The task of the courts, to achieve a definitive decision in a concrete factual situation, cannot generally be accomplished without hearing the parties. This hearing is therefore the principal requisite of a just decision. Moreover, the dignity of the person requires that his rights are not disposed of in a peremptorily arbitrary fashion. The individual must not become merely the object of the decision, but must, where the decision will affect his rights, have the possibility to speak, to influence the proceeding and its result.

The right of the accused to be heard has for a long time been substantially recognized and respected in procedural law. The various procedural systems have "concretized" the principle. At the same time this principle had to be harmonized with other principles resulting from the peculiar exigencies of the various modes of procedure. The elevation of this principle to a fundamental right has not affected the legitimacy of such contrary interests and the importance of harmonizing them with the right of the party to be heard. Its inclusion in the Basic Law was to make abuses in judicial proceedings, such as took place during the National Socialist regime, impossible and to reestablish the confidence of the people in the impartiality of the administration of justice. But art. 103, para. 1, of the Basic Law cannot have been intended to eliminate the carefully reasoned adjustments between the different interests which must be respected in the various proceedings nor the limitations of the fair hearing based on these adjustments.

Article 103, para. 1, of the Basic Law thus takes as its starting point the idea that the more precise formulation of the fair hearing should be left to the various procedural systems. Since the procedural systems existent at the time the Basic Law entered into effect satisfied, as a rule, the exigencies of the fair hearing, an interpretation of art. 103, para. 1, of the Basic Law should be made principally on the basis of the contruction of procedural law which antedated this Constitution.

The Bavarian Constitutional Court reached the conclusion that the inclusion of the principle of the fair hearing in the Basic Law merely confers constitutional status on existing procedural formulations.

The Federal Constitutional Court goes further. It recognizes that existing procedural law and its application in judicial practice certainly assure a fair hearing, but it does not always do so in a sufficient way. The Federal Constitutional Court, therefore, uses art. 103, para. 1, of the Basic Law in the interpretation of the existing procedural law as well as to *establish new principles* regarding a fair hearing.

2. Since a fair hearing should give the interested party the opportunity to influence the future judicial decision, as a rule only a hearing *prior* to the decision is meaningful. In particular, the finality and immutability which is customarily associated with judicial decisions requires that the interested party be heard before a definitive decision is made . . . .

However, traditionally the courts are also assigned tasks which do not deal with the pronouncement of definitive decisions involving a fact situation, but with provisional measures regulating a temporary situation, or with temporary protection of private or public rights. Such provisional measures are recognized, for example, in the *ZPO* * in the form of writ of attachment (*Arrest*) and of temporary injunction (*einstweilige Verfügung*), and in the constitutional and administrative courts in the form of temporary injunction (*einstweilige Anordnung*). In the area of criminal proceedings temporary confinement orders, seizures and searches are to be considered. In these cases it is, therefore, particularly difficult to proceed in a proper way since interferences in the rights of the parties occur on the basis of summary investigations of the fact situation and often with the consultation of only one party. Therefore, these measures are as a rule assigned to the courts. The presence of the judge insures that the interests of the party who has either not been heard or had insufficient opportunity to be heard are duly protected and, in particular, that the legal requisites of such interferences are strictly observed. . . .

The presence of the judge is to insure the application of the guarantees of the judicial proceeding. The reasons which require a hearing of the parties before the issuance of a judicial decision are here also decisive. Article 103, para. 1, of the Basic Law is, as a rule, applicable also in this type of case.

However, the protection of endangered interests can make immediate measures necessary not only without a complete clarification of the factual situation, but also without allowing a hearing of the interested party prior to their effectuation. When very

---

* Code of Civil Procedure.

important interests are affected it may be necessary to forego the
envisioned prior hearing to avoid giving the party involved warning
of the impending measure. The presence of the judge makes the
application of such measures, without hearing the adverse party,
sustainable. Since in such cases there is an interference in the rights
of the parties, an *exception* to the principle of a prior hearing is
*admissible only when it is imperative to achieve the objective of the
measure.* For the legislator, the requirement exists that interference
without prior hearing be subjected to strict requisites. Moreover, the
principle of *Rechtsstaat* requires that the party involved at least be
given the opportunity to be heard after the measures are taken in
order to refute their propriety. . . . In the above examples this
principle is regularly observed. In the case of an attachment or
temporary injunction [*i.e.,* in civil cases] the *ZPO* entitles the adverse
party to file an objection which entails a formal hearing. Similar
objection is also possible in constitutional or administrative matters.

[In this case, the Constitutional Court concluded that the
constitutional challenge was unfounded. The first decision of the
Oberlandesgericht had not recognized petitioner's right to a fair
hearing, insofar as it did not inform petitioner of her right to contest
the decision. This error, however, was harmless, since petitioner's
attorney did present arguments contesting the decision, which were
taken into consideration in the second decision of the *Oberlandesgericht.*]

NOTE AND QUESTIONS

As will become apparent in the next section of this chapter, the
standards applied by the Constitutional Court in determining
whether a hearing must precede the challenged decision, or may
follow it, are not dissimilar from standards applied by the United
States Supreme Court. Notice, however, that the issue in the
preceding case concerns the question whether *a court* may act first
and satisfy the fair hearing requirement with a later hearing. One
problem in the United States cases which follow is whether *an
administrative agency* may take action prior to holding an adversary
hearing. In cases involving decisions by administrative agencies,
would the German Constitution require, in some cases, that there
be a fair administrative hearing prior to administrative action? For
example, could an administrator constitutionally terminate an
indigent's welfare benefits without a prior hearing? *Compare
Goldberg* v. *Kelly, infra* § A.3.

3. Right to Fair Administrative Hearings in the United States

WISCONSIN v. CONSTANTINEAU

Supreme Court of the United States
400 U.S. 433, 91 S. Ct. 507, 27 L. Ed. 2d 515 (1971)

Mr. Justice Douglas delivered the opinion of the Court.

Appellee is an adult resident of Hartford, Wis. She brought suit in a federal district court in Wisconsin to have a Wisconsin statute declared unconstitutional.

The Act, Wis. Stat. § 176.26 (1967), provides that designated persons may in writing forbid the sale or gift of intoxicating liquors to one who "by excessive drinking" produces described conditions or exhibits specified traits, such as exposing himself or family "to want" or becoming "dangerous to the peace" of the community.

The chief of police of Hartford, without notice or hearing to appellee, caused to be posted a notice in all retail liquor outlets in Hartford that sales or gifts or liquors to appellee were forbidden for one year. Thereupon this suit was brought against the chief of police claiming damages and asking for injunctive relief. The State of Wisconsin intervened as a defendant on the injunctive phase of the case and that was the only issue tried and decided, the . . . court holding the Act unconstitutional on its face and enjoining its enforcement. The court said:

> "In 'posting' an individual, the particular city official or spouse is doing more than denying him the ability to purchase alcoholic beverages within the city limits. In essence, he is giving notice to the public that he has found the particular individual's behavior to fall within one of the categories enumerated in the statutes. It would be naive not to recognize that such 'posting' or characterization of an individual will expose him to public embarrassment and ridicule, and it is our opinion that procedural due process requires that before one acting pursuant to State statute can make such a quasi-judicial determination, the individual involved must be given notice of the intent to post and an opportunity to present his side of the matter." 302 F. Supp., at 864.

We have no doubt as to the power of a State to deal with the evils described in the Act. The police power of the States over intoxicating liquors was extremely broad even prior to the Twenty-first Amendment. *Crane* v. *Campbell,* 245 U. S. 304. The only issue present here is whether the label or characterization given a person by "posting," though a mark of serious illness to some, is to others such a stigma or badge of disgrace that procedural due process requires notice and an opportunity to be heard. We agree with the District Court that the private interest is such that those requirements of procedural due process must be met.

It is significant that most of the provisions of the Bill of Rights are procedural, for it is procedure that marks much of the difference between rule by law and rule by fiat.

We reviewed in *Cafeteria Workers* v. *McElroy,* 367 U. S. 886, 895, the nature of the various "private interest[s]" that have fallen on one side or the other of the line. See also *Sniadach* v. *Family Finance Corp.,* 395 U. S. 337, 339-342. Generalizations are hazardous as some state and federal administrative procedures are summary by reason of necessity or history. Yet certainly where the State attaches "a badge of infamy" to the citizen, due process comes into play. *Wieman* v. *Updegraff,* 344 U. S. 183, 191. "[T]he right to be heard before being condemned to suffer grievous loss of any kind, even though it may not involve the stigma and hardships of a criminal conviction, is a principle basic to our society." *Anti-Fascist Committee* v. *McGrath,* 341 U. S. 123, 168 (Frankfurter, J., concurring).

Where a person's good name, reputation, honor, or integrity is at stake because of what the government is doing to him, notice and an opportunity to be heard are essential. "Posting" under the Wisconsin Act may to some be merely the mark of illness, to others it is a stigma, an official branding of a person. The label is a degrading one. Under the Wisconsin Act, a resident of Hartford is given no process at all. This appellee was not afforded a chance to defend herself. She may have been the victim of an official's caprice. Only when the whole proceedings leading to the pinning of an unsavory label on a person are aired can oppressive results be prevented.

. . . .

Affirmed.

MR. CHIEF JUSTICE BURGER, with whom MR. JUSTICE BLACKMUM joins, dissenting.

The Court today strikes down, as unconstitutional, a Wisconsin statute that has never been challenged or tested in the Wisconsin state courts. The judges of Wisconsin probably will be taken by surprise by our summary action since few, if any, have ever heard of this case.

Very likely we reach a correct result since the Wisconsin statute appears, on its face and in its application, to be in conflict with accepted concepts of due process.

The reason for my dissent is that it seems to me a very odd business to strike down a state statute, on the books for almost 40 years, without any opportunity for the state courts to dispose of the problem either under the Wisconsin Constitution or the U. S. Constitution.

. . . .

MR. JUSTICE BLACK, with whom MR. JUSTICE BLACKMUM joins, dissenting.

I agree substantially with the dissent of THE CHIEF JUSTICE. I would vacate the District Court's judgment and remand with directions to withhold its proceedings to enable appellee to file a declaratory judgment or other state court action challenging the police chief's posting of notices in all Hartford retail liquor outlets forbidding sales or gifts of liquors to appellee for one year. As the Court's opinion, the cases there cited, and THE CHIEF JUSTICE's dissent point out, such a course of action is justified "where the issue of state law is uncertain" and where the state court might confine the state law's meaning so "as not to have any constitutional infirmity." The Wisconsin Act appears on its face to grant authority to a man's wife, a mayor, a town's supervisors, the county superintendent of the poor, a sheriff, or a district attorney to post notices forbidding liquor establishments from giving or selling any alcoholic beverages to the person so posted. The effect of such sweeping powers, if there is nothing else in the State's law to limit them, is practically the same as that of an old common-law bill of attainder, against which our forebears [sic] had such an abhorrence that they forbade it in Art. I, § 9, of the Constitution. See, *e.g., United States* v. *Lovett,* 328 U. S. 303 (1946). And here the Wisconsin law purports on its face to place such arbitrary and tyrannical power in the hands of minor officers and others that these modern bills of attainder can be issued *ex parte,* without notice or hearing of any kind or character. It is impossible for me to believe that the Supreme Court of Wisconsin would uphold any such boundless power over the lives and liberties of its citizens. . . .

NOTES AND QUESTIONS

1. What is the principle in *Constantineau*? Must all government actions which do positive harm to discrete individuals be accompanied by some form of hearing? Even with reference to harm to reputation, does the Constitution require that all official acts of government officials which harm an individual's reputation be accompanied by a hearing?

2. The Chief of Police of Louisville, Ky., distributed a five-page circular, alerting merchants to possible shoplifters. In the circular were five pages of mug shot photos, arranged alphabetically, of persons identified as "active shoplifters." Davis, a photographer employed by a Louisville newspaper, had been arrested for shoplifting, and his name and mug shot appeared on the circular. (Shortly after the flyer was circulated, charges against him were dismissed.) Davis brought an action in federal court, seeking damages under 42 U.S.C. § 1983, on the theory that official conduct

branding him as a criminal, without a hearing, was a violation of his constitutional rights. The Supreme Court, in an opinion by Justice Rehnquist, concluded that Davis had been denied no constitutional rights since a person's reputation was neither "liberty" nor "property." *Constantineau* was distinguished on the ground that "posting" had done more than injure Ms. Constantineau's reputation. It had taken away her right to buy a drink! *Paul* v. *Davis,* 424 U.S. 693 (1976). Does it make sense to require fair procedures for official action that alters one's capacity to buy liquor, but to require no procedures for official action which publicly brands a person to be a criminal? Can *Paul* v. *Davis* be explained on the ground that Davis had a practical means for obtaining a hearing by suing Paul for defamation of character? What if Paul's misidentification of Davis as a shoplifter is the result of a good faith mistake? Would Continental European law have required a hearing before a police official issued a defamatory circular?

3. *Paul* v. *Davis* underscores that the requirement of a fair hearing, under both the Fifth and Fourteenth Amendments, is premised on an initial decision that the government has taken an individual's "life, liberty or property." Until recently, that foreclosed any constitutional requirement of fair procedure in connection with denial of government benefits. Benefits the individual received from government were characterized as "privilges" rather than "rights." Since people had no constitutional right to a government job, a government subsidy, a public education, and the like, the Constitution required no particular procedures before these benefits were withdrawn. It is clear enough now that the right-privilege distinction has been repudiated, and that procedural due process prohibits withdrawing some government benefits without a hearing. What is not so clear is the shape of the structure that has replaced the ancient wisdom about government benefits.

GOLDBERG v. KELLY

Supreme Court of the United States
397 U.S. 254, 90 S. Ct. 1011, 25 L. Ed. 2d 287 (1970)

MR. JUSTICE BRENNAN delivered the opinion of the Court.

The question for decision is whether a State that terminates public assistance payments to a particular recipient without affording him the opportunity for an evidentiary hearing prior to termination denies the recipient procedural due process in violation of the Due Process Clause of the Fourteenth Amendment.

This action was brought in the District Court for the Southern District of New York by residents of New York City receiving financial aid under the federally assisted program of Aid to Familes with Dependent Children (AFDC) or under New York State's general

Home Relief program. Their complaint alleged that the New York State and New York City officials administering these programs terminated, or were about to terminate, such aid without prior notice and hearing, thereby denying them due process of law. At the time the suits were filed there was no requirement of prior notice or hearing of any kind before termination of financial aid. However, the State and city adopted procedures for notice and hearing after the suits were brought, and the plaintiffs, appellees here, then challenged the constitutional adequacy of those procedures.

. . . . .

I

The constitutional issue to be decided, therefore, is the narrow one whether the Due Process Clause requires that the recipient be afforded an evidentiary hearing *before* the termination of benefits.[7] The District Court held that only a pre-termination evidentiary hearing would satisfy the constitutional command, and rejected the argument of the state and city officials that the combination of the post-termination "fair hearing" with the informal pre-termination review disposed of all due process claims. The court said: "While post-termination review is relevant, there is one overpowering fact which controls here. By hypothesis, a welfare recipient is destitute, without funds or assets. . . . Suffice it to say that to cut off a welfare recipient in the face of . . . 'brutal need' without a prior hearing of some sort is unconscionable, unless overwhelming considerations justify it." *Kelly* v. *Wyman,* 294 F. Supp. 893, 899, 900 (1968). The court rejected the argument that the need to protect the public's tax revenues supplied the requisite "overwhelming consideration." "Against the justified desire to protect public funds must be weighed the individual's overpowering need in this unique situation not to be wrongfully deprived of assistance. . . . While the problem of additional expense must be kept in mind, it does not justify denying a hearing meeting the ordinary standards of due process. Under all the circumstances, we hold that due process requires an adequate hearing before termination of welfare benefits, and the fact that there is a later constitutionally fair proceeding does not alter the result." *Id.,* at 901. Although state officials were party defendants in the action, only the Commissioner of Social Services of the City of New York appealed. . . . We affirm.

Appellant does not contend that procedural due process is not

---

[7] Appellant does not question the recipient's due process right to evidentiary review *after* termination. For a general discussion of the provision of an evidentiary hearing prior to termination, see Comment, The Constitutional Minimum for the Termination of Welfare Benefits: The Need for and Requirements of a Prior Hearing, 68 Mich. L. Rev. 112 (1969).

applicable to the termination of welfare benefits. Such benefits are a matter of statutory entitlement for persons qualified to receive them.[8] Their termination involves state action that adjudicates important rights. The constitutional challenge cannot be answered by an argument that public assistance benefits are "a 'privilege' and not a 'right.' " *Shapiro* v. *Thompson,* 394 U. S. 618, 627 n. 6 (1969). Relevant constitutional restraints apply as much to the withdrawal of public assistance benefits as to disqualification for unemployment compensation, *Sherbert* v. *Verner,* 374 U. S. 398 (1963); or to denial of a tax exemption, *Speiser* v. *Randall,* 357 U. S. 513 (1958); or to discharge from public employment, *Slochower* v. *Board of Higher Education,* 350 U. S. 551 (1956). The extent to which procedural due process must be afforded the recipient is influenced by the extent to which he may be "condemned to suffer grievous loss," *Joint Anti-Fascist Refuge Committee* v. *McGrath,* 341 U. S. 123, 168 (1951) (Frankfurter, J., concurring), and depends upon whether the recipient's interest in avoiding that loss outweighs the governmental interest in summary adjudication. Accordingly, as we said in *Cafeteria & Restaurant Workers Union* v. *McElroy,* 367 U. S. 886, 895 (1961), "consideration of what procedures due process may require under any given set of circumstances must begin with a determination of the precise nature of the government function involved as well as of the private interest that has been affected by governmental action." See also *Hannah* v. *Larche,* 363 U. S. 420, 440, 442 (1960).

It is true, of course, that some governmental benefits may be administratively terminated without affording the recipient a pre-termination evidentiary hearing. But we agree with the District Court that when welfare is discontinued, only a pre-termination evidentiary hearing provides the recipient with procedural due process. Cf. *Sniadach* v. *Family Finance Corp.,* 395 U. S. 337 (1969).

---

[8] It may be realistic today to regard welfare entitlements as more like "property" than a "gratuity." Much of the existing wealth in this country takes the form of rights that do not fall within traditional common-law concepts of property. It has been aptly noted that "[s]ociety today is built around entitlement. The automobile dealer has his franchise, the doctor and lawyer their professional licenses, the worker his union membership, contract, and pension rights, the executive his contract and stock options; all are devices to aid security and independence. Many of the most important of these entitlements now flow from governments: subsidies to farmers and businessmen, routes for airlines and channels for television stations; long term contracts for defense, space, and education; social security pensions for individuals. Such sources of security, whether private or public, are no longer regarded as luxuries or gratuities; to the recipients they are essentials, fully deserved, and in no sense a form of charity. It is only the poor whose entitlements, although recognized by public policy, have not been effectively enforced." Reich, Individual Rights and Social Welfare: The Emerging Legal Issues, 74 Yale L.J. 1245, 1255 (1965). See also Reich, The New Property, 73 Yale L.J. 733 (1964).

For qualified recipients, welfare provides the means to obtain essential food, clothing, housing, and medical care. Cf. *Nash* v. *Florida Industrial Commission,* 389 U. S. 235, 239 (1967). Thus the crucial factor in this context — a factor not present in the case of the blacklisted government contractor, the discharged government employee, the taxpayer denied a tax exemption, or virtually anyone else whose governmental entitlements are ended — is that termination of aid pending resolution of a controversy over eligibility may deprive an *eligible* recipient of the very means by which to live while he waits. Since he lacks independent resources, his situation becomes immediately desperate. His need to concentrate upon finding the means for daily subsistence, in turn, adversely affects his ability to seek redress from the welfare bureaucracy.

Moreover, important governmental interests are promoted by affording recipients a pre-termination evidentiary hearing. From its founding the Nation's basic commitment has been to foster the dignity and well-being of all persons within its borders. We have come to recognize that forces not within the control of the poor contribute to their poverty. This perception, against the background of our traditions, has significantly influenced the development of the contemporary public assistance system. Welfare, by meeting the basic demands of subsistence, can help bring within the reach of the poor the same opportunities that are available to others to participate meaningfully in the life of the community. At the same time, welfare guards against the societal malaise that may flow from a widespread sense of unjustified frustration and insecurity. Public assistance, then, is not mere charity, but a means to "promote the general Welfare, and secure the Blessings of Liberty to ourselves and our Posterity." The same governmental interests that counsel the provision of welfare, counsel as well its uninterrupted provision to those eligible to receive it; pre-termination evidentiary hearings are indispensable to that end.

Appellant does not challenge the force of these considerations but argues that they are outweighed by countervailing governmental interests in conserving fiscal and administrative resources. These interests, the argument goes, justify the delay of any evidentiary hearing until after discontinuance of the grants. Summary adjudication protects the public fisc by stopping payments promptly upon discovery of reason to believe that a recipient is no longer eligible. Since most terminations are accepted without challenge, summary adjudication also conserves both the fisc and administrative time and energy by reducing the number of evidentiary hearings actually held.

We agree with the District Court, however, that these governmental interests are not overriding in the welfare context. The requirement of a prior hearing doubtless involves some greater expense, and the benefits paid to ineligible recipients pending decision at the hearing probably cannot be recouped, since these recipients are likely to be judgment-proof. But the State is not without weapons to minimize these increased costs. Much of the drain on fiscal and administrative resources can be reduced by developing procedures for prompt pre-termination hearings and by skillful use of personnel and facilities. Indeed, the very provision for a post-termination evidentiary hearing in New York's Home Relief program is itself cogent evidence that the State recognizes the primacy of the public interest in correct eligibility determinations and therefore in the provision of procedural safeguards. Thus, the interest of the eligible recipient in uninterrupted receipt of public assistance, coupled with the State's interest that his payments not be erroneously terminated, clearly outweighs the State's competing concern to prevent any increase in its fiscal and administrative burdens. As the District Court correctly concluded, "[t]he stakes are simply too high for the welfare recipient, and the possibility for honest error or irritable misjudgment too great, to allow termination of aid without giving the recipient a chance, if he so desires, to be fully informed of the case against him so that he may contest its basis and produce evidence in rebuttal." 294 F. Supp., at 904-905.

II

We also agree with the District Court, however, that the pre-termination hearing need not take the form of a judicial or quasi-judicial trial. We bear in mind that the statutory "fair hearing" will provide the recipient with a full administrative review. Accordingly, the pre-termination hearing has one function only: to produce an initial determination of the validity of the welfare department's grounds for discontinuance of payments in order to protect a recipient against an erroneous termination of his benefits. Cf. *Sniadach* v. *Family Finance Corp.,* 395 U. S. 337, 343 (1969) (HARLAN, J., concurring). Thus, a complete record and a comprehensive opinion, which would serve primarily to facilitate judicial review and to guide future decisions, need not be provided at the pre-termination stage. We recognize, too, that both welfare authorities and recipients have an interest in relatively speedy resolution of questions of eligibility, that they are used to dealing with one another informally, and that some welfare departments have very burdensome caseloads. These considerations justify the limitation of the pre-termination hearing to minimum procedural safeguards, adapted to the particular characteristics of welfare recipients, and to the limited nature of the controversies to be resolved. We wish to add that we, no less than the dissenters, recognize the importance of not imposing upon the States or the

Federal Government in this developing field of law any procedural requirements beyond those demanded by rudimentary due process.

"The fundamental requisite of due process of law is the opportunity to be heard." *Grannis* v. *Ordean,* 234 U. S. 385, 394 (1914). The hearing must be "at a meaningful time and in a meaningful manner." *Armstrong* v. *Manzo,* 380 U. S. 545, 552 (1965). In the present context these principles require that a recipient have timely and adequate notice detailing the reasons for a proposed termination, and an effective opportunity to defend by confronting any adverse witnesses and by presenting his own arguments and evidence orally. These rights are important in cases such as those before us, where recipients have challenged proposed terminations as resting on incorrect or misleading factual premises or on misapplication of rules or policies to the facts of particular cases.

. . . .

The city's procedures presently do not permit recipients to appear personally with or without counsel before the official who finally determines continued eligibility. Thus a recipient is not permitted to present evidence to that official orally, or to confront or cross-examine adverse witnesses. These omissions are fatal to the constitutional adequacy of the procedures.

The opportunity to be heard must be tailored to the capacities and circumstances of those who are to be heard. It is not enough that a welfare recipient may present his position to the decision maker in writing or secondhand through his caseworker. Written submissions are an unrealistic option for most recipients, who lack the educational attainment necessary to write effectively and who cannot obtain professional assistance. Moreover, written submissions do not afford the flexibility of oral presentations; they do not permit the recipient to mold his argument to the issues the decision maker appears to regard as important. Particularly where credibility and veracity are at issue, as they must be in many termination proceedings, written submissions are a wholly unsatisfactory basis for decision. The secondhand presentation to the decision maker by the caseworker has its own deficiencies; since the caseworker usually gathers the facts upon which the charge of ineligibility rests, the presentation of the recipient's side of the controversy cannot safely be left to him. Therefore a recipient must be allowed to state his position orally. Informal procedures will suffice; in this context due process does not require a particular order of proof or mode of offering evidence.

In almost every setting where important decisions turn on questions of fact, due process requires an opportunity to confront and cross-examine adverse witnesses. *E.g., ICC* v. *Louisville & N. R. Co.,* 227 U. S. 88, 93-94 (1913); *Willner* v. *Committee on Character & Fitness,* 373 U. S. 96, 103-104 (1963). What we said in *Greene* v.

McElroy, 360 U. S. 474, 496-497 (1959), is particularly pertinent here:

> "Certain principles have remained relatively immutable in our jurisprudence. One of these is that where governmental action seriously injures an individual, and the reasonableness of the action depends on fact findings, the evidence used to prove the Government's case must be disclosed to the individual so that he has an opportunity to show that it is untrue. While this is important in the case of documentary evidence, it is even more important where the evidence consists of the testimony of individuals whose memory might be faulty or who, in fact, might be perjurers or persons motivated by malice, vindictiveness, intolerance, prejudice, or jealousy. We have formalized these protections in the requirements of confrontation and cross-examination. They have ancient roots. They find expression in the Sixth Amendment.... This Court has been zealous to protect these rights from erosion. It has spoken out not only in criminal cases, ... but also in all types of cases where administrative ... actions were under scrutiny."

Welfare recipients must therefore be given an opportunity to confront and cross-examine the witnesses relied on by the department.

"The right to be heard would be, in many cases, of little avail if it did not comprehend the right to be heard by counsel." *Powell* v. *Alabama,* 287 U. S. 45, 68-69 (1932). We do not say that counsel must be provided at the pre-termination hearing, but only that the recipient must be allowed to retain an attorney if he so desires. Counsel can help delineate the issues, present the factual contentions in an orderly manner, conduct cross-examination, and generally safeguard the interests of the recipient. We do not anticipate that this assistance will unduly prolong or otherwise encumber the hearing.

Finally, the decision maker's conclusion as to a recipient's eligibility must rest solely on the legal rules and evidence adduced at the hearing. *Ohio Bell Tel. Co.* v. *PUC,* 301 U. S. 292 (1937); *United States* v. *Abilene & S. R. Co.,* 265 U. S. 274, 288-289 (1924). To demonstrate compliance with this elementary requirement, the decision maker should state the reasons for his determination and indicate the evidence he relied on, cf. *Wichita R. & Light Co.* v. *PUC,* 260 U. S. 48, 57-59 (1922), though his statement need not amount to a full opinion or even formal findings of fact and conclusions of law. And, of course, an impartial decision maker is essential. Cf. *In re Murchison,* 349 U. S. 133 (1955); *Wong Yang Sung* v. *McGrath,* 339 U. S. 33, 45-46 (1950). We agree with the District Court that prior involvement in some aspects of a case will not necessarily bar a welfare official from acting as a decision maker. He should not, however, have participated in making the determination under review.

Affirmed.

Mr. Justice Black, dissenting.

In the last half century the United States, along with many, perhaps most, other nations of the world, has moved far toward becoming a welfare state, that is, a nation that for one reason or another taxes its most affluent people to help support, feed, clothe, and shelter its less fortunate citizens. The result is that today more than nine million men, women, and children in the United States receive some kind of state or federally financed public assistance in the form of allowances or gratuities, generally paid them periodically, usually by the week, month, or quarter. Since these gratuities are paid on the basis of need, the list of recipients is not static, and some people go off the lists and others are added from time to time. These ever-changing lists put a constant administrative burden on government and it certainly could not have reasonably anticipated that this burden would include the additional procedural expense imposed by the Court today.

The dilemma of the ever-increasing poor in the midst of constantly growing affluence presses upon us and must inevitably be met within the framework of our democratic constitutional government if our system is to survive as such.

. . . .

The more than a million names on the relief rolls in New York, and the more than nine million names on the rolls of all the 50 States were not put there at random. The names are there because state welfare officials believed that those people were eligible for assistance. Probably in the officials' haste to make out the lists many names were put there erroneously in order to alleviate immediate suffering, and undoubtedly some people are drawing relief who are not entitled under the law to do so. Doubtless some draw relief checks from time to time who know they are not eligible, either because they are not actually in need or for some other reason. Many of those who thus draw undeserved gratuities are without sufficient property to enable the government to collect back from them any money they wrongfully receive. But the Court today holds that it would violate the Due Process Clause of the Fourteenth Amendment to stop paying those people weekly or monthly allowances unless the government first affords them a full "evidentiary hearing" even though welfare officials are persuaded that the recipients are not rightfully entitled to receive a penny under the law. In other words, although some recipients might be on the lists for payment wholly because of deliberate fraud on their part, the Court holds that the government is helpless and must continue, until after an evidentiary hearing, to pay money that it does not owe, never has owed, and never could owe. I do not believe there is any provision in our Constitution that should thus paralyze the government's efforts to protect itself against making payments to people who are not entitled to them.

Particularly do I not think that the Fourteenth Amendment should be given such an unnecessarily broad construction. That Amendment came into being primarily to protect Negroes from discrimination, and while some of its language can and does protect others, all know that the chief purpose behind it was to protect ex-slaves. Cf. *Adamson* v. *California,* 332 U. S. 46, 71-72, and n. 5 (1947) (dissenting opinion). The Court, however, relies upon the Fourteenth Amendment and in effect says that failure of the government to pay a promised charitable instalment to an individual deprives that individual of *his own property,* in violation of the Due Process Clause of the Fourteenth Amendment. It somewhat strains credulity to say that the government's promise of charity to an individual is property belonging to that individual when the government denies that the individual is honestly entitled to receive such a payment.

. . . Today's balancing act requires a "pre-termination evidentiary hearing," yet there is nothing that indicates what tomorrow's balance will be. Although the majority attempts to bolster its decision with limited quotations from prior cases, it is obvious that today's result does not depend on the language of the Constitution itself or the principles of other decisions, but solely on the collective judgment of the majority as to what would be a fair and humane procedure in this case.

This decision is thus only another variant of the view often expressed by some members of this Court that the Due Process Clause forbids any conduct that a majority of the Court believes "unfair," "indecent" or "shocking to their consciences." See, *e.g., Rochin* v. *California,* 342 U. S. 165, 172 (1952). Neither these words nor any like them appear anywhere in the Due Process Clause. If they did, they would leave the majority of Justices free to hold any conduct unconstitutional that they should conclude on their own to be unfair or shocking to them. Had the drafters of the Due Process Clause meant to leave judges such ambulatory power to declare laws unconstitutional, the chief value of a written constitution, as the Founders saw it, would have been lost. . . .

The procedure required today as a matter of constitutional law finds no precedent in our legal system. Reduced to its simplest terms, the problem in this case is similar to that frequently encountered when two parties have an ongoing legal relationship that requires one party to make periodic payments to the other. Often the situation arises where the party "owing" the money stops paying it and justifies his conduct by arguing that the recipient is not legally entitled to payment. The recipient can, of course, disagree and go to court to compel payment. But I know of no situation in our legal system in which the person alleged to owe money to another is required by law to continue making payments to a judgment-proof claimant without the benefit of any security or bond to insure that these payments can be recovered if he wins his legal argument. Yet today's decision in no way obligates the welfare recipient to pay back any benefits wrongfully received during the pre-termination evidentiary hearings or post any bond, and in all "fairness" it could not do so. These recipients are by definition too poor to post a bond or to repay the benefits that, as the majority assumes, must be spent as received to insure survival.

The Court apparently feels that this decision will benefit the poor and needy. In my judgment the eventual result will be just the opposite. While today's decision requires only an administrative, evidentiary hearing, the inevitable logic of the approach taken will lead to constitutionally imposed, time-consuming delays of a full adversary process of administrative and judicial review. In the next case the welfare recipients are bound to argue that cutting off benefits before judicial review of the agency's decision is also a denial of due process. Since, by hypothesis, termination of aid at that point may still "deprive an *eligible* recipient of the very means by which to live while he waits," *ante,* at 264, I would be surprised if the weighing process did not compel the conclusion that termination without full judicial review would be unconscionable. After all, at each step, as the majority seems to feel, the issue is only one of weighing the government's pocketbook against the actual survival of the recipient, and surely that balance must always tip in favor of the individual. Similarly today's decision requires only the opportunity to have the benefit of counsel at the administrative hearing, but it is difficult to believe that the same reasoning process would not require the appointment of counsel, for otherwise the right to counsel is a meaningless one since these people are too poor to hire their own advocates. Cf. *Gideon* v. *Wainwright,* 372 U. S. 335, 344 (1963). Thus the end result of today's decision may well be that the government, once it decides to give welfare benefits, cannot reverse that decision until the recipient has had the benefits of full administrative and judicial review, including, of course, the opportunity to present his case to this Court. Since this process will usually entail a delay of several years, the inevitable result of such a constitutionally imposed burden will be that the government will not put a claimant on the rolls initially until it has made an exhaustive investigation to determine his eligibility. While this Court will perhaps have insured that no needy person will be taken off the rolls without a full "due process" proceeding, it will also have insured that many will never get on the rolls, or at least that they will remain destitute during the lengthy proceedings followed to determine initial eligibility.

For the foregoing reasons I dissent from the Court's holding. The operation of a welfare state is a new experiment for our Nation. For this reason, among others, I feel that new experiments in carrying out a welfare program should not be frozen into our constitutional structure. They should be left, as are other legislative determinations, to the Congress and the legislatures that the people elect to make our laws.

[Dissenting opinions of Chief Justice Burger and Justice Stewart are omitted.]

NOTES AND QUESTIONS

1. It might be instructive to compare Continental European decisions dealing with denial of government benefits. *See, e.g., Sonaglia,* Ch. 6, § B.2.a., *supra,* and Decision of July 24, 1963, of the *Bundesverfassungsgericht,* § A.1.b ., *supra.* In deciding constitutional issues concerning the right to a fair hearing, is the "right-privilege" problem of the *Goldberg* case even discussed? Can you explain why the right to a fair hearing in connection with denials of government benefits has been a more contentious issue in the United States?

2. The Court's decision in *Goldberg* is premised on the conclusion that there is a statutory "entitlement" to welfare benefits. It is necessary to balance competing considerations in order to decide the nature of the required hearing. (Notice Justice Black's caustic characterization of the balancing process as a "balancing act.") Once an "entitlement" is found, however, due process will require some hearing procedure in connection with withdrawal of the "entitlement." For example, in *Goss* v. *Lopez,* 419 U.S. 565 (1975), the Court held that even temporary suspension from a public school required a hearing. (The four dissenters argued that a hearing should be required only where an individual suffers "severe detriment or grievous loss." For the majority however, the "balancing act" was relevant only to decide the nature of the required hearing — in *Goss,* little more than an opportunity for the student to tell his side of the story to an official who has informed him of the nature of his offense.)

3. If the requirement of a hearing does not turn on whether the individual has suffered a "severe" or "grievous" detriment, nor on a balance of competing considerations, does that mean that some hearing is required in connection with any government decision denying a benefit? Would it mean, for example, that the decision of a public school to buy its supplies from a new source would require that the stationer who formerly sold to the school be given a hearing?

For understandable reasons, the Court has stopped short of announcing a general principle that there must be a hearing in connection with any decision withdrawing a government benefit. S2

BISHOP v. WOOD

Supreme Court of the United States
426 U.S. 341, 96 S. Ct. 2074, 48 L. Ed. 2d 684 (1976)

MR. JUSTICE STEVENS delivered the opinion of the Court.

Acting on the recommendation of the Chief of Police, the City Manager of Marion, North Carolina, terminated petitioner's employment as a policeman without affording him a hearing to determine the sufficiency of the cause for his discharge. Petitioner brought suit contending that since a city ordinance classified him as a "permanent employee," he had a constitutional right to a pretermination hearing. During pretrial discovery petitioner was advised that his dismissal was based on a failure to follow certain orders, poor attendance at police training classes, causing low morale, and conduct unsuited to an officer. Petitioner and several other police officers filed affidavits essentially denying the truth of these charges. The District Court granted defendants' motion for summary judgment. The Court of Appeals affirmed and we granted certiorari, 423 U. S. 890.

The questions for us to decide are (1) whether petitioner's employment status was a property interest protected by the Due Process Clause of the Fourteenth Amendment and (2) assuming that the explanation for his discharge was false, whether that false explanation deprived him of an interest in liberty protected by that clause.

I

Petitioner was employed by the city of Marion as a probationary policeman on June 9, 1969. After six months he became a permanent employee. He was dismissed on March 31, 1972. He claims that he had either an express or an implied right to continued employment.

A city ordinance provides that a permanent employee may be discharged if he fails to perform work up to the standard of his classification, or if he is negligent, inefficient or unfit to perform his duties.[5] Petitioner first contends that even though the ordinance

---

[5] Article II, § 6, of the Personnel Ordinance of the city of Marion, reads as follows: *"Dismissal.* A permanent employee whose work is not satisfactory over a period of time shall be notified in what way his work is deficient and what he must do if his work is to be satisfactory. If a permanent employee fails to perform work up to the standard of the classification held, or continues to be negligent, inefficient, or unfit to perform his duties, he may be dismissed by the City Manager. Any discharged employee shall be given written notice of his discharge setting forth the effective date and reasons for his discharge if he shall request such a notice."

does not expressly so provide, it should be read to prohibit discharge for any other reason, and therefore to confer tenure on all permanent employees. In addition, he contends that his period of service, together with his "permanent" classification, gave him a sufficient expectancy of continued employment to constitute a protected property interest.

A property interest in employment can, of course, be created by ordinance, or by an implied contract.[6] In either case, however, the sufficiency of the claim of entitlement must be decided by reference to state law.[7] The North Carolina Supreme Court has held that an enforceable expectation of continued public employment in that State can exist only if the employer, by statute or contract, has actually granted some form of guarantee.... Whether such a guarantee has been given can be determined only by an examination of the particular statute or ordinance in question.

On its face the ordinance on which petitioner relies may fairly be read as conferring such a guarantee. However, such a reading is not the only possible interpretation; the ordinance may also be construed as granting no right to continued employment but merely conditioning an employee's removal on compliance with certain specified procedures.[8] We do not have any authoritative interpretation of this ordinance by a North Carolina state court. We do, however, have the opinion of the United States District Judge who, of course, sits in North Carolina and practiced law there for many years. Based on his understanding of state law, he concluded that petitioner "held his position at the will and pleasure of the city." [9]

---

[6] In *Perry* v. *Sindermann,* 408 U.S. 593, 601, the Court said that a "person's interest in a benefit is a 'property' interest for due process purposes if there are ... rules or mutually explicit understandings that support his claim of entitlement to the benefit and that he may invoke at a hearing."

[7] "Property interests, of course, are not created by the Constitution. Rather, they are created and their dimensions are defined by existing rules or understandings that stem from an independent source such as state law — rules or understandings that secure benefits and that support claims of entitlement to those benefits." *Board of Regents* v. *Roth,* 408 U. S. 564, 577.

[8] This is not the construction which six Members of this Court placed on the federal regulations involved in *Arnett* v. *Kennedy,* 416 U. S. 134. In that case the Court concluded that because the employee could only be discharged for cause, he had a property interest which was entitled to constitutional protection. In this case, a holding that as a matter of state law the employee "held his position at the will and pleasure of the city" necessarily establishes that he had *no* property interest. The Court's evaluation of the federal regulations involved in *Arnett* sheds no light on the problem presented by this case.

[9] "Under the law in North Carolina, nothing else appearing, a contract of employment which contains no provisions for the duration or termination of employment is terminable at the will of either party irrespective of the quality of performance by the other party. By statute, G. S. 115-142 (b), a County Board of

This construction of North Carolina law was upheld by the Court of Appeals for the Fourth Circuit, albeit by an equally divided Court. In comparable circumstances, the Court has accepted the interpretation of state law in which the District Court and the Court of Appeals have concurred even if an examination of the state law issue without such guidance might have justified a different conclusion.

In this case, as the District Court construed the ordinance, the City Manager's determination of the adequacy of the grounds for discharge is not subject to judicial review; the employee is merely given certain procedural rights which the District Court found not to have been violated in this case. The District Court's reading of the ordinance is tenable; it derives some support from a decision of the North Carolina Supreme Court . . .; and it was accepted by the Court of Appeals for the Fourth Circuit. These reasons are sufficient to foreclose our independent examination of the state law issue.

Under that view of the law, petitioner's discharge did not deprive him of a property interest protected by the Fourteenth Amendment.

II

Petitioner's claim that he has been deprived of liberty has two components. He contends that the reasons given for his discharge are so serious as to constitute a stigma that may severely damage his reputation in the community; in addition, he claims that those reasons were false.

In our appraisal of petitioner's claim we must accept his version of the facts since the District Court granted summary judgment against him. His evidence established that he was a competent police officer; that he was respected by his peers; that he made more arrests than any other officer on the force; that although he had been criticized for engaging in high speed pursuits, he had promptly complied with such criticism; and that he had a reasonable explanation for his imperfect attendance at police training sessions. We must therefore assume that his discharge was a mistake and based on incorrect information.

Education in North Carolina may terminate the employment of a teacher at the end of the school year without filing charges or giving its reasons for such termination, or granting the teacher an opportunity to be heard. *Still* v. *Lance,* 279 N. C., 254, 182 S. E. 2d 403 (1971).

"It is clear from Article II, Section 6, of the City's Personnel Ordinance, that the dismissal of an employee does not require a notice or hearing. Upon request of the discharged employee, he shall be given written notice of his discharge setting forth the effective date and the reasons for the discharge. It thus appears that both the city ordinance and the state law have been complied with.

"It further appears that the plaintiff held his position at the will and pleasure of the city."

In *Board of Regents* v. *Roth,* 408 U. S. 564, we recognized that the nonretention of an untenured college teacher might make him somewhat less attractive to other employers, but nevertheless concluded that it would stretch the concept too far "to suggest that a person is deprived of 'liberty' when he simply is not retained in one position but remains as free as before to seek another." *Id.,* at 575. This same conclusion applies to the discharge of a public employee whose position is terminable at the will of the employer when there is no public disclosure of the reasons for the discharge.

In this case the asserted reasons for the City Manager's decision were communicated orally to the petitioner in private and also were stated in writing in answer to interrogatories after this litigation commenced. Since the former communication was not made public, it cannot properly form the basis for a claim that petitioner's interest in his "good name, reputation, honesty, or integrity" [12] was thereby impaired. And since the latter communication was made in the course of a judicial proceeding which did not commence until after petitioner had suffered the injury for which he seeks redress, it surely cannot provide retroactive support for his claim. A contrary evaluation of either explanation would penalize forthright and truthful communication between employer and employee in the former instance, and between litigants in the latter.

Petitioner argues, however, that the reasons given for his discharge were false. Even so, the reasons stated to him in private had no different impact on his reputation than if they had been true. And the answers to his interrogatories, whether true or false, did not cause the discharge. The truth or falsity of the City Manager's statement determines whether or not his decision to discharge the petitioner was correct or prudent, but neither enhances nor diminishes petitioner's claim that his constitutionally protected interest in liberty has been impaired.[13] A contrary evaluation of his contention would enable every discharged employee to assert a constitutional claim merely by alleging that his former supervisor made a mistake.

The federal court is not the appropriate forum in which to review the multitude of personnel decisions that are made daily by public agencies.[14] We must accept the harsh fact that numerous individual

---

[12] See *Wisconsin* v. *Constantineau,* 400 U. S. 433, 437, and the discussion of the interest in reputation allied to employment in *Paul* v. *Davis,* 424 U. S. 693.

[13] Indeed, the impact on petitioner's constitutionally protected interest in liberty is no greater even if we assume that the City Manager deliberately lied. Such fact might conceivably provide the basis for a state law claim, the validity of which would be entirely unaffected by our analysis of the federal constitutional question.

[14] The cumulative impression created by the three dissenting opinions is that this holding represents a significant retreat from settled practice in the federal courts. The fact of the matter, however, is that the instances in which the federal judiciary has required a state agency to reinstate a discharged employee for failure to provide

mistakes are inevitable in the day-to-day administration of our affairs. The United States Constitution cannot feasibly be construed to require federal judicial review for every such error. In the absence of any claim that the public employer was motivated by a desire to curtail or to penalize the exercise of an employee's constitutionally protected rights, we must presume that official action was regular and, if erroneous, can best be corrected in other ways. The Due Process Clause of the Fourteenth Amendment is not a guarantee against incorrect or ill-advised personnel decisions.

The judgment is affirmed.

Mr. Justice BRENNAN, with whom Mr. Justice MARSHALL concurs, dissenting.

. . . .

I also fully concur in the dissenting opinions of MR. JUSTICE WHITE and MR. JUSTICE BLACKMUN, which forcefully demonstrate the Court's error in holding that petitioner was not deprived of "property" without due process of law. I would only add that the strained reading of the local ordinance, which the Court deems to be "tenable," . . . cannot be dispositive of the existence *vel non* of petitioner's "property" interest. There is certainly a federal dimension to the definition of "property" in the Federal Constitution; cases such as *Board of Regents* v. *Roth, supra,* held merely that "property" interests encompass those to which a person has "a legitimate claim of entitlement," . . . and *can* arise from "existing rules or understandings" that derive from "an independent source *such as* state law." *Ibid.* (emphasis supplied). But certainly, at least before a state law is definitively construed as not securing a "property" interest, the relevant inquiry is whether it was objectively reasonable for the employee to believe he could rely on continued employment. . . ("It is a purpose of the ancient institution of property to protect those claims upon which people rely in their daily lives, reliance that must not be arbitrarily determined."). At a mininum, this would require in this case an analysis of the common practices utilized and the expectations generated by respondents, and the manner in which the local ordinance would reasonably be

----

a pretermination hearing are extremely rare. The reason is clear. For unless we were to adopt MR. JUSTICE BRENNAN's remarkably innovative suggestion that we develop a federal common law of property rights, or his equally far reaching view that almost every discharge implicates a constitutionally protected liberty interest, the ultimate control of state personnel relationships is, and will remain, with the States; they may grant or withhold tenure at their unfettered discretion. In this case, whether we accept or reject the construction of the ordinance adopted by the two lower courts, the power to change or clarify that ordinance will remain in the hands of the City Council of the city of Marion.

read by respondents' employees.[5] These disputed issues of fact are not meet for resolution, as they were, on summary judgment, and would thus at a minimum require a remand for further factual development in the district court.

These observations do not, of course, suggest that a "federal court is . . . the appropriate forum in which to review the multitude of personal decisions that are made daily by public agencies." . . . However, the federal courts *are* the appropriate forum for ensuring that the constitutional mandates of due process are followed by those agencies of government making personnel decisions that pervasively influence the lives of those affected thereby; the fundamental premise of the Due Process Clause is that those procedural safeguards will help the government avoid the "harsh fact" of "incorrect or ill-advised personnel decisions." . . . Petitioner seeks no more than that, and I believe that his "property" interest in continued employment and his "liberty" interest in his good name and reputation dictate that he be accorded procedural safeguards before those interests are deprived by arbitrary or capricious government action.

MR. JUSTICE WHITE, with whom MR. JUSTICE BRENNAN, MR. JUSTICE MARSHALL, and MR. JUSTICE BLACKMUN join, dissenting.

I dissent because the decision of the majority rests upon a proposition which was squarely addressed and in my view correctly rejected by six Members of this Court in *Arnett* v. *Kennedy,* 416 U. S. 134 (1974).

Petitioner Bishop was a permanent employee of the Police Department of the City of Marion, N. C. The city ordinance applicable to him provides:

> *"Dismissal.* A permanent employee whose work is not satisfactory over a period of time shall be notifed in what way his work is deficient and what he must do if his work is to be satisfactory. *If* a permanent employee fails to perform work up to the standard of the classification held, or continues to be negligent, inefficient, or unfit to perform his duties, he may be dismissed by the City Manager. Any discharged employee shall

---

[5] For example, petitioner was hired for a "probationary" period of six months, after which he became a "permanent" employee. No reason appears on the record for this distinction, other than the logical assumption, confirmed by a reasonable reading of the local ordinance, that after completion of the former period, an employee may only be discharged for "cause." As to respondents' personnel practices, it is important to note that in a department which currently employs 17 persons, petitioner's was the only discharge, for cause or otherwise, during the period of over three years from the time of his hiring until the time of pretrial discovery.

be given written notice of his discharge setting forth the effective date and reasons for his discharge if he shall request such a notice." (Emphasis added.)

The second sentence of this ordinance plainly conditions petitioner's dismissal on cause — *i. e.,* failure to perform up to standard, negligence, inefficiency, or unfitness to perform the job. The District Court below did not otherwise construe this portion of the ordinance. In the only part of its opinion rejecting petitioner's claim that the ordinance gave him a property interest in his job, the District Court said, in an opinion predating this Court's decision in *Arnett* v. *Kennedy, supra,*

> "It is clear from Article II, Section 6, of the City's Personnel Ordinance, that the dismissal of an employee does not require a notice or hearing. Upon request of the discharged employee, he shall be given written notice of his discharge setting forth the effective date and the reasons for the discharge. It thus appears that both the city ordinance and the state law have been complied with."

Thus in concluding that petitioner had no "property interest" in his job entitling him to a hearing on discharge and that he held his position "at the will and pleasure of the city," the District Court relied on the fact that the ordinance described its own *procedures* for determining cause which procedures did not include a hearing. The majority purports ... to read the District Court's opinion as construing the ordinance *not* to condition dismissal on cause, and, if this is what the majority means, its reading of the District Court's opinion is clearly erroneous for the reasons just stated. However, later in its opinion the majority appears to eschew this construction of the District Court's opinion and of the ordinance. In the concluding paragraph of its discussion of petitioner's property interest, the majority holds that since neither the ordinance nor state law provides for a hearing, or any kind of review of the City Manager's dismissal decision, petitioner had no enforceable property interest in his job. The majority concludes:

> "In this case, as the District Court construed the ordinance, the City Manager's *determination of the adequacy of the grounds for discharge* is not subject to judicial review; the employee is merely given certain procedural rights which the District Court found not to have been violated in this case. The District Court's reading of the ordinance is tenable;. . ." (Emphasis added.)

The majority thus implicitly concedes that the ordinance supplies the "grounds" for discharge and that the City Manager must determine them to be "adequate" before he may fire an employee. The majority's holding that petitioner had no property interest in his

job in spite of the unequivocal language in the city ordinance that
he may be dismissed only for certain kinds of cause rests, then, on
the fact that state law provides no *procedures* for assuring that the
City Manager dismiss him only for cause. The right to his job
apparently given by the first two sentences of the ordinance is thus
redefined, according to the majority, by the procedures provided for
in the third sentence and as redefined is infringed only if the
procedures are not followed.

This is precisely the reasoning which was embraced by only three
and expressly rejected by six Members of this Court in *Arnett* v.
Kennedy, supra. There a federal employee had "a statutory
expectancy that he not be removed other than for 'such cause as will
promote the efficiency of the service.'" *Arnett* v. *Kennedy,* at
151-152 (opinion of MR. JUSTICE REHNQUIST). The three Justices
whose views were rejected by a majority of the Court went on to say

> "But the very sections of the statute which granted him that
> right ... expressly provided also for the procedure by which
> 'cause' was to be determined and expressly omitted the
> procedural guarantees which appellee insists are mandated by
> the Constitution. Only by bifurcating the very sentence of the Act
> of Congress which conferred upon appellee the right not to be
> removed save for cause could it be said that he had an expectancy
> of that substantive right without the procedural limitations which
> Congress attached to it. ..." *Id.,* at 152. (Opinion of MR. JUSTICE
> REHNQUIST.)

The three Justices went on:

> "Here the property interest which appellee had in his
> employment was itself conditioned by the procedural limitations
> which had accompanied the grant of that interest. ..." *Id.,* at
> 155. (Opinion of MR. JUSTICE REHNQUIST.)

Accordingly they concluded that the Constitution imposed no
independent procedural requirements.

This view was rejected by MR. JUSTICE POWELL in an opinion joined
by MR. JUSTICE BLACKMUN.

> "The plurality opinion evidently reasons that the nature of
> appellee's interest in continued federal employment is
> necessarily defined and limited by the statutory procedures for
> discharge and that the constitutional guarantee of procedural
> due process accords to appellee no procedural protections
> against arbitrary or erroneous discharge other than those
> expressly provided in the statute. The plurality would thus
> conclude that the statute governing federal employment
> determines not only the nature of appellee's property interest,
> but also the extent of the procedural protections to which he may

lay claim. It seems to me that this approach is incompatible with the principles laid down in *Roth* and *Sindermann.* Indeed, it would lead directly to the conclusion that whatever the nature of an individual's statutorily created property interest, deprivation of that interest could be accomplished without notice or a hearing at any time. This view misconceives the origin of the right to procedural due process. That right is conferred, *not by legislative grace, but by constitutional guarantee.* While the legislature may elect not to confer a property interest in federal employment, it may not constitutionally authorize the deprivation of such an interest, once conferred, without appropriate procedural safeguards...." *Id.,* at 166-167. (Emphasis added.)

I, too, disagreed with the view stated in MR. JUSTICE REHNQUIST'S opinion:

"I differ basically with the plurality's view that 'where the grant of a substantive right is inextricably intertwined with the limitations on the procedures which are to be employed in determining that right, a litigant in the position of appellee must take the bitter with the sweet,' and that 'the property interest which appellee had in his employment was itself conditioned by the procedural limitations which had accompanied the grant of that interest.' *Ante,* at 153-154, 155. The rationale of this position quickly leads to the conclusion that even though the statute requires cause for discharge, the requisites of due process could equally have been satisfied had the law dispensed with any hearing at all, whether pretermination or post-termination." *Id.,* at 177-178.

The view was also rejected by MR. JUSTICE MARSHALL in an opinion joined by MR. JUSTICE BRENNAN and MR. JUSTICE DOUGLAS in which it was correctly observed:

"Accordingly, a majority of the Court rejects MR. JUSTICE REHNQUIST's argument that because appellee's entitlement arose from statute, it could be conditioned on a statutory limitation of procedural due process protections, an approach which would render such protection inapplicable to the deprivation of any statutory benefit — any 'privilege' extended by Government — where a statute prescribed a termination procedure, no matter how arbitrary or unfair. It would amount to nothing less than a return, albeit in somewhat different verbal garb, to the thoroughly discredited distinction between rights and privileges which once seemed to govern the applicability of procedural due process." *Id.,* at 211.

The views now expressed by the majority are thus squarely

contrary to the views expressed by a majority of the Justices in *Arnett.* As MR. JUSTICE POWELL suggested in *Arnett,* they are also "incompatible with the principles laid down in *Roth* and *Sindermann.*" 416 U. S., at 166. I would not so soon depart from these cases nor from the views expressed by a majority in *Arnett.* The ordinance plainly grants petitioner a right to his job unless there is cause to fire him. Having granted him such a right it is the Federal Constitution,[3] not state law, which determines the process to be applied in connection with any state decision to deprive him of it.

MR. JUSTICE BLACKMUN, with whom MR. JUSTICE BRENNAN joins, dissenting.

I join MR. JUSTICE WHITE's dissent for I agree that the Court appears to be adopting a legal principle which specifically was rejected by a majority of the Justices of this Court in *Arnett* v. *Kennedy,* 416 U. S. 134 (1974).

I also feel, however, that *Still* v. *Lance,* 279 N. C. 254, 182 S. E. 2d 403 (1971), the only North Carolina case cited by the Court and by the District Court, is by no means the authoritative holding on state law that the Court, . . . seems to think it is. In *Still* the Supreme Court of North Carolina considered a statute that contained no "for cause" standard for failure to renew a teacher's contract at the *end* of a school year. In holding that this provision did not create a continued expectation of employment, the North Carolina court noted that it "does not limit the right of the employer board to terminate the employment of a teacher at the end of a school year to a specified cause or circumstance."

. . . This provision, the court observed, stood in sharp contrast with another provision of the statute relating to termination of employment *during* the school year and providing that when "it shall have been determined that the services of an employee are not

---

[3] The majority intimates in n. 8 that the views of the three plurality Justices in *Arnett* v. *Kennedy* were rejected because the other six Justices disagreed on the question of how the federal *statute* involved in that case should be construed. This is incorrect. All Justices agreed on the meaning of the statute. As the remarks of the six Justices quoted above indicate, it was the constitutional significance of the statute on which the six disagreed with the plurality.

Similarly, here, I do not disagree with the majority of the courts below on the meaning of the state law. If I did, I might be inclined to defer to the judgments of the two lower courts. The state law says that petitioner may be dismissed by the City Manager only for certain kinds of cause and then provides that he will receive notice and an explanation, but no hearing and no review. I agree that as a matter of state law petitioner has no remedy no matter how arbitrarily or erroneously the City Manager has acted. This is what the lower courts say the statute means. I differ with those courts and the majority only with respect to the constitutional significance of an unambiguous state law. A majority of the Justices in *Arnett* v. *Kennedy, supra,* stood on the proposition that the Constitutiton requires procedures *not* required by state law when the state conditions dismissal on "cause."

acceptable for the remainder of a current school year" (emphasis added), *ibid.,* notice and hearing were required.

The Marion ordinance in the present case contains a "for cause" standard for dismissal and, it seems to me, is like that portion of the statute construed in *Still* pertaining to termination of employment during the year. As such, it plainly does not subject an employee to termination at the will and pleasure of the municipality, but, instead, creates a proper expectation of continued employment so long as he performs his work satisfactorily. At this point, the Federal Constitution steps in and requires that appropriate procedures be followed before the employee may be deprived of his property interest.

NOTES AND QUESTIONS

1. Would a general requirement that all non-probationary government employees be given an adversary hearing prior to discharge be a net gain for good government? Professor Gerald Frug argues that it would not.*

> [P]rocedural protections ... restrict the government's ability to enforce a standard of job performance. Incompetence is generally assumed to be sufficient "cause" for termination. But the procedures that must be followed to establish incompetence make such terminations extremely unlikely. The problem of adequately defining a standard of competence, particularly in the higher-level and more important jobs, the uncertainty about the kind of evidence needed to prove a violation of that standard, the unpleasant nature of a formal confrontation between people with a personal, employer-employee relationship, and the supervisor's view that he, not the employee, will be put on trial — together with the natural reluctance to fire anyone in any event — combine to prevent legitimate discharges for incompetence. The result is that the level of competence in government declines.

Do you agree that hearing requirements for discharge of public employees causes a lower level of job performance in civil service positions? If that's the case, would you still argue that the injury to the employee in loss of employment is so drastic that adversary hearings should still be required *before* discharge?

2. After *Bishop* v. *Wood,* can a carefully drawn statute avoid a constitutional right for a hearing in the discharge of any public employee? Is that a necessary consequence of having the

---

* Frug, *Does the Constitution Prevent the Discharge of Civil Service Employees?* 124 U. PA. L. REV. 942, 946 (1976).

constitutional right to a hearing depend on whether *statutory* law gave the employee an entitlement to his job? If the government is free to give job security to public employees, and free not to give any job security at all, why should the government not be equally free to give job security without procedural protections? Once a legislature has seen fit to give an employee *some* job security, is it then required to provide an adversary hearing in connection with discharge or discipline of the employee? Does the Court's opinion in *Bishop* answer the last question asked?

3. The Achilles' heel of the constitutional right of public employees to fair procedures is the concept that the "entitlement" to public employment rests entirely on statute and not the Constitution. Does that mark a return to the old right-privilege distinction in other areas? Would it be possible for a legislature to redefine "entitlements" to welfare and public education so as to deny any right of a hearing to welfare recipients and public school pupils?

4. Role and Participation of Public Prosecutor

THE PATAKI-DUNSHIRN CASES

PATAKI v. AUSTRIA; DUNSHIRN v. AUSTRIA

Committee of Ministers of the Council of Europe, Resolution of
September 16, 1963
[1963] 6 Y.B. Eur. Conv. on Human Rights 714

A.

Summary

By letter dated August 30, 1959, Mr. Franz Pataki lodged an application with the European Commission of Human Rights against the Austrian Government. Mr. Pataki was convicted in 1959 on charges of theft and sentenced to three years' imprisonment. The prosecution appealed against the decision and on appeal, the sentence was increased to six years' imprisonment. Mr. Pataki complained the Convention was violated because he was not given a fair hearing and in particular, only the representative of the Public Prosecutor was present at, and heard by, the Court of Appeal.

On December 19, 1960, the Commission declared the application admissible in part* and on March 15, 1961, it joined the case with that of Dunshirn against Austria (No. 789/60).

By letter dated July 1, 1960, Mr. Dunshirn lodged an application with the Commission directed against the Austrian Government. He had been convicted in February, 1960 on several charges of larceny

---

* For the text of the decision on admissibility *see* Decision of Dec. 19, 1960, [1960] Y.B. Eur. Conv. on Human Rights 356-70 (Eur. Comm. of Human Rights).

and sentenced to fourteen months' imprisonment. The prosecution appealed against the decision and, on appeal, the sentence was increased to thirty months' imprisonment. Mr. Dunshirn complained that the Convention had been violated — in particular, art. 6 guaranteeing a fair hearing — as only the representative of the Public Prosecutor had been present at, and heard by, the Court of Appeal.

On March 15, 1961, the Commission declared this application admissible * and joined it with that of *Pataki v. Austria* (No. 596/59).

A Sub-Commission was set up to establish the facts of these cases and to try to reach a friendly settlement. No friendly settlement was reached and, on March 28, 1963, the Commission adopted its report in which it expressed the opinion that the proceedings conducted in the present cases on the basis of section 294, para. 3, of the Austrian Code of Criminal Procedure were not in conformity with the Convention.

In April 1963 a Federal Act on the reopening of appeal proceedings in criminal cases was promulgated in Austria. This Act provided a new remedy for persons whose applications had been declared admissible by the European Commission of Human Rights — including MM. Pataki and Dunshirn. They were given an opportunity to apply within a period of six months from the entry into force of the Act for the reopening of the proceedings before the Austrian Courts. After adopting its Report, the Commission took cognisance of the new Act and proposed that "no further action should be taken in the present cases."

The Commission's report was transmitted to the Committee of Ministers of the Council of Europe and the Austrian Government on May 6, 1963. Neither the Commission nor the Austrian Government brought these cases before the Court and, therefore, it was for the Committee of Ministers to decide, in accordance with art. 32 of the Convention, "whether there had been a violation of the Convention."

On September 16, 1963, the Committee of Ministers, by Resolution (63) DH 2, took account of the amendment made to Austrian legislation by the Federal Law of March 27, 1963, expressed its satisfaction with the measures introduced to ensure the full application of the Convention and decided that no further action was required in the present cases.

Extracts from the Report of the Commission and the text of the Resolution of the Committee of Ministers follow.

. . . .

---

* For the text of the decision on admissibility *see Dunshirn v. Austria,* [1961] Y.B. EUR. CONV. ON HUMAN RIGHTS 186-96 (Eur. Comm. of Human Rights).

B.

Report of the Commission

. . . .

The Law

Although the facts of the present case differ essentially from the facts of the *Ofner* and *Hopfinger* cases, the legal principles involved are the same in the two groups of cases. In the report adopted by the Commission on November 23, 1962, concerning the *Ofner* and *Hopfinger* cases, the legal problem was defined in the following terms, which the Commission reproduces as relevant also to the present cases:

"The legal problem at issue relates to the right of defence which the Convention guarantees to anyone charged with a criminal offence. The Applicants have invoked art. 6, para. 3, subpara. (c), according to which the right to defend himself is one of the minimum rights which every accused shall enjoy, and also the more general provision of art. 6, para. 1, which guarantees the right to a fair trial.

"Concerning this principle of a fair trial, and its relation to the minimum rights laid down in para. 3 of the article, the Commission has expressed the following opinion in a previous case:

" 'Art. 6 of the Convention does not define the notion of a fair trial in a criminal case. Para. 3 of the article enumerates certain specific rights which constitute essential elements of that general notion, and para. 2 may be considered to add another element. The words 'minimum rights', however, clearly indicate that the five rights specifically enumerated in para. 3 are not exhaustive, and that a trial may not conform to the general standard of a 'fair trial', even if the minimum rights guaranteed by para. 3 — and also the right set forth in para. 2 — have been respected.' (Report of March 15, 1961, in case 343/57, para. 52, *Nielsen v. Denmark.)*

"In the present cases the problem is whether the notion of a 'fair trial' embodies any right relating to the defence beyond and above the minimum rights laid down in para. 3. The Commission is of the opinion that what is generally called 'the equality of arms', that is the procedural equality of the accused with the Public Prosecutor, is an inherent element of a 'fair trial'. Whether such equality has its legal basis in para. 3 depends upon the interpretation of subparas. (b) ('to have adequate time and facilities for the preparation of his defence') and (c) ('to defend himself in person or through legal assistance'). The Commission need not express a definite opinion on this question, since in any case it is beyond doubt that the wider and general provision of a fair trial, contained in para. 1 of art. 6, embodies the notion 'equality of arms'."

In the present cases, the problem is whether the presence of the Public Prosecutor, without the presence of the accused or his counsel, at the session of the Court of Appeal when the case was heard and decided in conformity with section 294, para. 3, of the Code of Criminal Procedure, constituted an inequality in the representation of the parties, which is incompatible with the provisions of the Convention.

It is not possible to establish with certainty whether the Public Prosecutor has taken an active part in the deliberations of the Court. No records of the deliberations were kept. Even on the assumption, however, that the Public Prosecutor did not play an active role at this stage of the proceedings, the very fact that he was present and thereby had an opportunity of influencing the members of the Court, without the accused or his counsel having any similar opportunity or any possibility of contesting any statements made by the Prosecutor, constitutes an inequality which, in the opinion of the Commission, is incompatible with the notion of a fair trial.

The Commission therefore reaches the conclusion that the proceedings conducted in the present cases on the basis of section 294, para. 3, of the Code of Criminal Procedure, as it was then worded, were not in conformity with the Convention.

Revision of the Austrian Legislation During the Examination of the Cases by the Commission

Following negotiations, ... the Minister of Justice on June 26, 1962, submitted a Bill to the Austrian Parliament for the modification of certain sections of the Code of Criminal Procedure. ...

The explanatory observations which accompany the text of the proposed new rules refer to the cases pending before the European Commission. They also state that the proposed detailed amendments to the existing Code of Criminal Procedure are based on the principle that proceedings in appeal cases no longer shall be a unilateral non-public procedure on the basis of documents, but a bilateral procedure taking place in a public session.

Article II of the Bill contained certain transitory provisions according to which *inter alia,* where the European Commission had declared an application admissible or where appeal proceedings had taken place in non-public session within a period of six months preceding the coming into force of the new law, appeal proceedings already concluded could be resumed according to the new rules at the request of the Applicant, being the convicted person, or his legal representative.

On July 20, 1962, the Sub-Commission was informed, however, that art. II had not been adopted by the Austrian Parliament. Certain members of the Parliament had apparently taken the position that a provision of such an extraordinary character which introduced a certain retroactive effect, albeit in favor of the accused, required more careful consideration than could be given to it at this late stage of the parliamentary session. Consequently, only art. 1 of the Bill, containing the new rules applicable to future cases, was adopted, and this article came into force as of September 1, 1962.

Art. II of the Bill was adopted in a modified form by Parliament on March 26, 1963.

By the adoption of this Law, a new remedy has been made available to the applicants, and they are now entitled to have their cases re-examined by the Austrian tribunals under a procedure which will not give rise to the objections which the Commission has expressed concerning the previous proceedings.

Proposals of the Commission

In these circumstances the Commission wishes to avail itself of its right under art. 31, para. 3, of the Convention and to propose that the Committee of Ministers *take note* of this report, *express* its appreciation of the legislative measures adopted in Austria with a view to giving full effect to the Convention on Human Rights, and decide that no further action should be taken in the present cases.

C,

DECISION OF THE COMMITTEE OF MINISTERS

RESOLUTION (63) DH 2

Relating to the cases *Pataki* (Application No. 596/59) and *Dunshirn* (Application No. 789/60) adopted by the Ministers' Deputies on September 16, 1963.

The Committee of Ministers,

. . . .

Agreeing with the reasoning of the Commission;

Voting in accordance with the provisions of art. 32, para. 1, of the Convention;

Maintains the joinder of the cases of Franz Pataki (No. 596/59) and Johann Dunshirn (No. 789/60);

Takes Note of the Report of the Commission;

Taking Account of the amendment made to the Austrian legislation by the said Federal Law of March 27, 1963;

Expressing its satisfaction at the legislative measures introduced by the Austrian Government to ensure the full application of the Convention on Human Rights,

Decides that no further action is required in the present cases.

THE DELCOURT CASE

European Court of Human Rights, Decision of January 17, 1970
[1970] Y.B. EUR. CONV. ON HUMAN RIGHTS 1100

[THE FACTS:]

1. The Delcourt case was referred to the Court by the European Commission of Human Rights (hereinafter referred to as "the Commission"). The case has its origin in an Application lodged with the Commission under Article 25 of the Convention on 20th December 1965 by a Belgian national, Emile Delcourt, against the Kingdom of Belgium.

. . . .

9. The purpose of the Commission's request is to obtain a decision from the Court as to whether the facts of the case do or do not disclose a violation by the Kingdom of Belgium of the obligations binding on it under Article 6, para. 1, of the Convention.

. . . .

11. Emile Delcourt, a Belgian citizen, born on 28th December 1924, and a company director, has his residence at Waterloo. At the time of lodging his Application with the Commission (20th December 1965), he was imprisoned in the central gaol at Louvain.

12. Proceedings having been instituted against him by the Procureur du Roi at Bruges for obtaining money by menaces, fraud and fraudulent conversion, the Applicant was arrested on 23rd November 1963 and subsequently charged with a number of offences of fraud, fraudulent conversion, forgery and uttering forged documents, issuing uncovered cheques and fraudulent bills as well as obtaining credit by false pretences.

On 21st September 1964, he was found guilty by the Bruges Court of Summary Jurisdiction on thirty-six out of forty-one counts and sentenced to a year's imprisonment and a fine of two thousand Belgian francs.

On 17th March 1965, the Court of Appeal in Ghent modified this judgment against which both Delcourt and the prosecution had appealed on 25th and 26th September 1964. It found all the charges to be established including those on which Delcourt had been acquitted at first instance, stressed the seriousness of the offences and referred to his previous convictions. It accordingly increased his principal sentence to five years' imprisonment and further decided that on serving his sentence he should be "placed at the disposal of the Government" for ten years thus granting an application by the prosecution which had been rejected by the Bruges Court.

On 17th and 23rd March 1965, the Applicant appealed to the Court of Cassation against the judgment of the Court of Appeal and against that of the Court at Bruges. He lodged a memorial on 20th May 1965. The Procureur général's department (parquet) at the

Court of Appeal did not avail itself of its right to file a counter-memorial. A public hearing took place before the second chamber of the Court of Cassation on 21st June 1965; the Applicant himself was present at that hearing but not his counsel. The Court of Cassation heard the report of Judge De Bersaques, its rapporteur, and then the submissions of the Avocat général, Mr. Dumon, to the effect that the two appeals should be dismissed. In its judgment delivered the same day, after deliberations held in private the Court dismissed the two appeals.

. . . [Before the Commission, the Applicant] protested his innocence and alleged the violation of Articles 5, 6, 7 and 14 of the Convention; he presented numerous complaints almost all of which were declared inadmissible by the Commission on 7th February and 6th April 1967. On this last date, however, the Commission accepted one complaint which related to the question whether the presence of a member of the Procureur général's department at the deliberations of the Court of Cassation was compatible with the principle of "equality of arms" and hence with Article 6, paragraph (1), of the Convention.

In fact, the Avocat général, Mr. Dumon, was present at the Court's deliberations in accordance with Article 39 of the Prince Sovereign's Decree of 15th March 1815 which provides ". . . in cassation proceedings the Procureur général has the right to be present, without voting, when the Court retires to consider its decision". It may be observed that this Decree has recently been replaced by certain provisions of the new Judicial Code (Act of 10th October 1967) which was not yet in force when the Belgian Court of Cassation dismissed Delcourt's appeals. The above-mentioned provision of the 1815 Decree has been re-enacted in substance, in Article 1109 of this Code.

. . . .

[The Applicant maintained that this was] a violation of the rights of the defence and, particularly, of the principle of "equality of arms," as it was defined in the opinions given by the Commission in the Ofner, Hopfinger, Pataki and Dunshirn cases (Applications Nos. 524/59, 617/59, 596/59 and 789/60, Yearbook of the Convention, Vol. 6, pp. 696 to 706 and 730 to 732).

. . . .

16. On the failure of the attempt made by the Sub-Commission to arrange a friendly settlement, the plenary Commission drew up a Report as required under Article 31 of the Convention. This Report was adopted on 1st October 1968 and transmitted to the Committee of Ministers of the Council of Europe on 5th December 1968. The Commission expressed therein, by seven votes against six, the opinion that Article 6, para. 1, of the Convention was not violated in the present case. Two members of the majority expressed a joint

concurring opinion and the six members forming the minority expressed their dissent in a joint opinion.

. . . .

THE LAW

20. In its decision of 6th April 1967, the Commission declared the Application of Delcourt to be admissible on one point only, that is, whether the participation of a member of the Procureur général's department at the deliberations of the Court of Cassation in Belgium, on 21st June 1965, violated the rights and freedoms guaranteed by the Convention.

. . . .

21. Only one provision of the Convention requires examination for the purpose of deciding the present case. This is Article 6 (1) which provides that "in the determination of his civil rights and obligations or of any criminal charge against him, everyone is entitled to a fair and public hearing within a reasonable time by an independent and impartial tribunal established by law."

[The Court rejected the argument of the Belgian government that, since the Belgian Court of Cassation merely supervises the validity of judgments of lower courts, it does not actually make a "determination" of a "criminal charge" within the meaning of Art. 6 (1).]

Article 6 (1) of the Convention does not, it is true, compel the Contracting States to set up courts of appeal or of cassation. Nevertheless, a State which does institute such courts is required to ensure that persons amenable to the law shall enjoy before these courts the fundamental guarantees contained in Article 6. . . . There would be a danger that serious consequences might ensue if the opposite view were adopted; the Principal Delegate of the Commission rightly pointed to those consequences and the Court cannot overlook them. In a democratic society within the meaning of the Convention, the right to a fair administration of justice holds such a prominent place that a restrictive interpretation of Article 6 (1) would not correspond to the aim and the purpose of that provision (see, *mutatis mutandis,* the Wemhoff judgment of 27th June 1968, "As to the Law" paragraph 8).

26. Therefore, Article 6 (1) is indeed applicable to proceedings in cassation. The way in which it applies must, however, clearly depend on the special features of such proceedings. Thus, in order to determine whether Delcourt has been a victim of a violation of Article 6, it is necessary to examine what are, both in law and in practice, the functions exercised in a case of this kind by the Belgian Court of Cassation and by the Procureur général's department attached to that Court.

II. *As to the principal complaint of the Applicant*

27. The Applicant complains in the first place of the fact that a member of the Procureur général's department attached to the Court of Cassation, having made his submissions in open court, took part in its deliberations on 21st June 1965. It is beyond doubt that this participation was in conformity with the legislation in force in Belguim at that time; for under Article 39 of the Prince Sovereign's Decree of 15th March 1815 "in proceedings in cassation, the Procureur général (had) the right to be present, but without voting, when the Court (retired) to consider its decision". The Court is therefore called upon to judge, in the first place, the compatibility of Article 39 of the Decree of 15th March 1815 with Article 6 (1) of the Convention.

28. In the course of their respective submissions, the Commission and the Government referred mainly to the principle known as "equality of arms". The Court, however, will examine the problem by reference to the whole of paragraph (1) of Article 6. The principle of equality of arms does not exhaust the contents of this paragraph; it is only one feature of the wider concept of fair trial by an independent and impartial tribunal (see Neumeister judgment of 27th June 1968, "As to the Law" paragraph 22).

. . . .

In contrast to the Procureur général's department at the courts below, the Procureur général's department at the Belgian Court of Cassation does not ordinarily conduct public prosecutions, nor does it bring cases before that court, nor does it either have the character of respondent and it "cannot," therefore, "be considered as a party" (Article 37 of the Decree of 15th March 1815). This situation only changes in certain exceptional matters which are irrelevant to the present case, and in those instances the Procureur général's department at the Court of Cassation is not present at the deliberations of the judges of the court.

Yet it does not, however, necessarily follow from what precedes that Delcourt's complaints are unfounded. The Court must therefore make a careful examination of the real position and functions of the Procureur général's department attached to the Court of Cassation.

30. A series of elements allows one to understand the point of view of the Applicant and the opinion of the minority of the Commission.

First, the clear distinction which must be drawn, according to the Belgian Government, between the Procureur général's department at the Court of Cassation and the Procureur général's department at the lower courts, does not always appear very evident from the legislative texts. The same names, such as Procureur général's department (ministère public), are used to designate different institutions — which easily causes confusion. Moreover, the departments attached to the courts of first instance, of appeal and of cassation seem to constitute, in certain aspects, one single corps. Thus, Section 154 of the Act of 18th June 1869 (replaced recently by Article 400 of the 1967 Judicial Code) provides that the Procureur général at the Court of Cassation "shall exercise supervision over the Procureurs généraux attached to the courts of appeal," and it is only an examination of the practice which reveals that this supervision does not involve any power to intervene in the conduct of given cases but merely to give general opinions on matters of doctrine.

On a superficial glance at the situation, one might go so far as to wonder if the above-mentioned distinction really reflects the true position. The Procureur général's department at the Court of Cassation sometimes acts as the moving party; the task, for example, falls to it sometimes to institute a prosecution or disciplinary proceedings against judges (see also Article 90 of the Constitution concerning the indictment of ministers on impeachment). Furthermore, its members are sometimes recruited from among the members of the Procureur général's department at the courts below. Therefore, some litigants may quite naturally be inclined to view as an adversary a Procureur général or an Avocat général who submits that their appeals in cassation should be dismissed. They may be all the more inclined to do so when they find themselves deprived of any real debate before the highest court because the Procureur général's department at the Court of Appeal only very rarely makes use of the right of reply — in any event restricted — which the law confers on it in proceedings in cassation. And one may imagine that such litigants can have a feeling of inequality if, after hearing a member of the Procureur général's department at the Court of Cassation make, in open court, final submissions unfavourable to their pleas, they see him withdraw with the judges to attend the deliberations held in the privacy of chambers.

On this last point, Belgian legislation may well appear at first sight to be "unusual" . . . and it does not seem to have any equivalent today in the other member States of the Council of Europe, at least in criminal cases. It may be noted, moreover, that the Avocat général at the Court of Justice of the European Communities, even though there are analogies between his functions and those of the Procureur général at the Belgian Court of Cassation, does not take part in the deliberations.

31. The preceding considerations . . . do not, however, amount to proof of a violation of the right to a fair hearing. . . .

32. First, it is established that the Procureur général's department at the Court of Cassation functions wholly independently of the Minister of Justice, save in the exceptional matters which are irrelevant to this case. Thus, the Minister has no power to compel the Procureur général to make his submissions one way or the other,

while he has the power to direct the institution of prosecutions by the Procureur général's departments attached to the courts of first instance and appeal.

Furthermore, as has already been observed, the Procureur general at the Court of Cassation exercises supervision over the officers of the Procureur général's departments at the courts of first instance and appeal only in regard to matters of doctrine and does not give them injunctions or instructions. Thus, he is not entitled to instigate, or prevent the institution of, a prosecution before the lower courts or to intervene at any stage in the conduct of a case already brought before them, or to order the Procureur général's department at a court of appeal to lodge or withdraw an appeal in cassation.

33. Nor is the Procureur général at the Court of Cassation the virtual adversary of the accused whose convictions or acquittal may lead to an appeal in cassation; nor does he become their actual adversary when he submits in open court that their arguments should not be accepted. No doubt it is equally true that the officers of the Procureur général's department at the courts of first instance and appeal do not have the character of public accusers; indeed, Article 4 of Section VIII of the Decree of 16th-24th August 1790 so states *expressis verbis*. They also are bound to serve the public interest in all objectivity and, in particular, to ensure the observance of the laws concerned with public order; and they are to be considered parties only within the formal procedural meaning of the term. Their task, however, is in no way to be confused in criminal matters with that of the Procureur général's department at the Court of Cassation. Their task, in effect, is, before all else, to investigate and prosecute criminal offences in order to protect the safety of society (see, for example, Articles 22 and 271 of the Code of Criminal Procedure). The Procureur général's department at the Court of Cassation, on the other hand, upholds a different interest, that which is concerned with the observance by the judges of the law and not with the establishment of the guilt or innocence of the accused.

Incidentally, the Procureur général attached to the Court of Cassation exercises in civil matters functions close to those which he exercises in criminal matters. Yet no-one could ever seriously suggest that he becomes the opponent of a litigant with whose case his submissions do not agree.

34. Admittedly, even in the absence of a prosecuting party, a trial would not be fair if it took place in such conditions as to put the accused unfairly at a disadvantage. A close examination of the legislation in issue as it is applied in practice does not, however, disclose any such result. The Procureur général's department at the Court of Cassation is, in a word, an adjunct and an adviser of the Court; it discharges a function of a quasi-judicial nature. By the opinions which it gives according to its legal conscience, it assists the

Court to supervise the lawfulness of the decision attacked and to ensure the uniformity of judicial precedent.

Examination of the facts shows that these considerations are not abstract or theoretical but are indeed real and actual. The statistics cited at the hearing on 30th September 1969 are very striking on this point: they show that the Procureur général's department at the Court of Cassation frequently either submits that appeals in cassation against a decision of acquittal brought by the Procureur général's department at the courts of first instance or appeal should be dismissed or an appeal by a convicted person should be allowed, or even raises, *ex officio,* grounds which a convicted person has not relied on, has put forward out of time or has not formulated with sufficient clarity.

35. Nor could the independence and impartiality of the Court of Cassation itself be adversely affected by the presence of a member of the Procureur général's department at its deliberations once it has been shown that the Procureur général himself is independent and impartial.

36. One last point is that the system now challenged dates back for more than a century and a half. While it is true that the long standing of a national legal rule cannot justify a failure to comply with the present requirements of international law, it may under certain conditions provide supporting evidence that there has been no such failure. The Court is of opinion that this is the case here. In this connection, the Court notes that on two occasions a parliament chosen in free elections has deliberately decided to maintain the system, the first time unchanged (preparatory work to the Act of 19th April 1949), the second time in substance and after studying the question in the context of the Convention (preparation of the new Judicial Code). Furthermore, the propriety and fairness of the rule laid down in Article 39 of the Decree of 15th March 1815 and then in Article 1109 of the 1967 Judicial Code — as it operates in practice — appears never to have been put in question by the legal profession or public opinion in Belgium. This wide measure of agreement would be impossible to explain if the independence and impartiality of the men on whose shoulders fell the administration of this institution at the Court of Cassation were doubted in Belgium, if the worth of their contribution to the body of decisions of the highest court were disputed or if their participation at the deliberations of the judges had been thought in any single case to open the door to unfairness or abuse.

37. The Court therefore arrives at the conclusion that the system provided for in Article 39 of the Decree of 15th March 1815 as applied in practice was not incompatible with Article 6 (1) of the Convention.

III. *As to the "new complaints" of the Applicant*

... [T]he Court considers that it would be unduly formalistic and therefore unjustified not to take account of these elements in the case.

41. The Applicant's "new complaints" must, on the other hand, be rejected as ill-founded. The fact that the Procureur général's department at the Court of Cassation expresses its opinion at the end of the hearing, without having communicated it in advance to the parties, is explained by the very nature of its task as already described by the Court in pronouncing upon Delcourt's principal complaint. Article 6 of the Convention does not require, even by implication, that an accused should have the possibility of replying to the purely legal submissions of an independent official attached to the highest court in Belgium as its assistant and adviser.

. . . .

FOR THESE REASONS, THE COURT

Holds, unanimously, that in the present case there has been no breach of Article 6 (1) of the Convention.

NOTES AND QUESTIONS

1. Note the statement in the *Delcourt* decision that "no one could ever seriously suggest" that participation by the *Procureur général* in civil cases involves his acting as an adversary opponent of the party with whose submissions he disagrees. Would that still be true if the government were a party or had an interest in the outcome of the appeal?

2. The *Delcourt* decision concludes that the objectivity and impartiality of the Procureur général is "not abstract or theoretical but ... real and actual." Is that demonstrated to your satisfaction by statistics which indicate he opposes the government's position in some criminal appeals or raises points favorable to the accused? In the United States, the Solicitor General, who normally handles the government's side in cases before the United States Supreme Court, not infrequently "confesses error," arguing to the Court that the government's position in the lower courts was erroneous, and that the government should lose on the appeal. If that were to happen often enough, would it convince you that there would be no objection to the Solicitor General's participation in the Court's deliberations in cases where he did defend the government's position?

Would such participation by the Solicitor General violate the United States Constitution? Compare *Gerstein* v. *Pugh,* 420 U.S. 103 (1975), in which the Court held unconstitutional a Florida law which permitted criminal prosecution without a prior preliminary hearing or grand jury indictment. Florida argued that the decision by the prosecutor whether or not to file the criminal charge was equivalent to a preliminary hearing — that is, that the prosecutor did not file the criminal charge unless he made an independent determination that there was probable cause for a criminal prosecution. The Court responded that a prosecutor's determination of probable cause was not a substitute for a judge's determination of that issue, since due process of law required a determination of probable cause by someone independent of both police and prosecution.

3. What is the significance of the fact that the Belgian procedure under attack in *Delcourt* dates back to the early nineteenth century? Are you able to judge, from the opinion of the court, whether the Procureur général's department in fact operates with the objectivity and impartiality attributed to it?

4. In a case from the Netherlands, the Commission found a complaint similar to that in *Delcourt* to be inadmissible. *X* v. *The Netherlands,* [1970] Y.B. EUR. CONV. ON HUMAN RIGHTS 516 (Eur. Comm. of Human Rights). The applicant had been convicted of a criminal offense. Dutch procedure allowed the Procureur général to submit his conclusions to Holland's Supreme Court at a court session wherein no lawyer represented the defendant. (Unlike the Belgian procedure, the Procureur général is not present during deliberations of the court.) The Commission's decision was based on the *Delcourt* case. Does that decision foreclose the possibility of arguing that the Procureur général in a particular country is not as impartial as the European Court of Human Rights believed the Belgian Procureur général to be?

5. In Italy, the *Pubblico ministero* has a dual role, similar to the Procureur général, as advocate and officer of the Court. For example, under art. 380 of the Code of Civil Procedure, in cases before the *Corte di Cassazione* he must intervene to express his opinion on questions of law at issue on the appeal. He may argue orally in open court, and, until recently, participated, without a vote, in judicial deliberation in chambers. The *Corte di Cassazione* refused to submit the issue of the validity of this procedure to the *Corte Costituzionale* ruling the challenge "manifestly unfounded." Decision of Oct. 4, 1969, Corte cass., [1969] 92 Foro It. I, 2754; [1970] 122 Giur. Ital. I, 15 ("*Aristia*").

In 1972, however, the *Corte Costituzionale* held invalid another provision permitting the *Pubblico ministero* to be present, without a vote, during judicial deliberation. Decision of Feb. 17, 1972, Corte cost., [1972] 17 Giur. Cost. 113; [1972] 35 Rac. uff. corte cost. 151; [1972] 95 Foro It. I, 568. In disciplinary proceedings against lawyers, hearings are held by the *Consiglio nationale forense* (equivalent to state bar associations in the United States). By statute, the *Pubblico ministero* was entitled to be present during deliberations of the *Consiglio,* while the attorney subject to discipline and his counsel were excluded. The court found it impossible to reconcile the presence of the *Pubblico ministero* with the right of defense contained in art. 24 of the Constitution.

On the basis of the 1972 *Corte Costituzionale* decision, the decision of the *Corte di Cassazione* in *Aristia* might have been limited to permitting participation by the *Pubblico ministero* to those cases where he does not have the status of a party. A narrower distinction was possible, however, since proceedings before the *Consiglio* involved deliberations of the tribunal on diputed issues of fact, while the deliberations of the *Corte di Cassazione* were limited to abstract issues of law. In 1974, however, the *Corte Costituzionale* held art. 380 of the Code of Civil Procedure unconstitutional insofar as it allowed the *Pubblico ministero* to be present during deliberation even of such appeals in which he was, or had standing to be, a party rather than a mere advisor to the court. Decision of Jan. 14, 1974, Corte cost., [1974] 19 Giur. Cost. 8; [1974] 40 Rac. uff. corte cost. 17; [1974] 97 Foro It. I, 287; [1974] 126 Giur. Ital. I, 1016.

The most recent change in the role of the Italian *Pubblico ministero* came from the legislature. The Statute of August 8, 1977 abolishes the participation of the public prosecutor in the deliberations of the *Corte di Cassazione.* The change was not constitutionally mandated, however, but simply a matter of the legislature deciding to end the practice.

B. NOTICE

1. Italy

LODI

Corte costituzionale, Decision of July 6, 1965, No. 57
[1965] 10 Giur. Cost. 717; [1965] 22 Rac. uff. corte cost. 63
[1965] 88 Foro It. I, 1330

[FACTS: The *ordinanza* which submitted the question of constitutionality to the court does not state the particular fact situation. The case involves a challenge to the provision of art. 173 permitting filing of notice to *renitenti.*

[The Italian criminal process can function even if the accused is not at the disposition of the court. Thus, if a defendant has not been apprehended or refuses to present himself for the various stages of the *istruzione* or trial (*dibattimento*), the proceeding will begin and continue without him. There are, however, no default judgments in criminal cases: the *Pubblico ministero* must still face the counsel for the defendant* (appointed *ex officio* by the court) and present his

---

* In Italy, as in Germany and in other civil law countries, no one can be tried in a criminal matter without being represented by counsel; if the accused does not retain a lawyer, the court must appoint one for him. Counsel must be paid by the accused, unless he applies for and qualifies for legal aid. *See* Ch. 10, § A.3.b., *infra.*

case to the judge (who has substantial inquisitorial powers). If there is insufficient evidence to convict the accused, he will be acquitted.

[The general rule is that the accused must be notified personally of the proceeding and of the most important acts which are performed in the course of the proceeding. If, however, the accused cannot be located after a diligent search (*irreperibilità*), art. 170 of the Code of Criminal Procedure provides that notice of the criminal charge may be placed on file with the court clerk and a conclusive presumption of notice is thus established.

[Article 173 of the Code of Criminal Procedure extends the standards established by art. 170 to criminal defendants who have escaped from jail (*evasi*), to those who have not been apprehended (*latitanti*), and to those who fail, without good cause, to appear for questioning (*renitenti*).]

Opinion

According to the *ordinanza* of the *Tribunale* of Brescia the right of defense guaranteed by art. 24 of the Constitution would be violated by the application [to the *renitenti*] of art. 173 of the Code of Criminal Procedure. . . .

This article presupposes voluntary behavior on the part of the accused, who, having received proper notice of the warrant or court order to present himself for questioning, does not do so, thus refusing implicitly to advance his defense. The challenged norm must be examined with this legal implication in mind.

The challenge is well grounded.

The norm in question has the character of a penalty for the procedural behavior of the accused. By being present in his domicile, and not appearing for questioning, he does not enjoy the right of receiving notice of procedural acts in the form provided in art. 169 of the Code of Criminal Procedure (personal notice to the defendant) only because he has not obeyed the order of the court to present himself for interrogation. This article substitutes, without sufficient reason, notification by deposit of the judicial acts with the clerk, for the form of notification provided for by art. 169 of the Code of Criminal Procedure. Notification by deposit does not give the same certainty of knowledge on the part of the accused for whom such notice is intended, and, moreover, such deposit with the clerk normally provides only a legal presumption of knowledge. This constitutes an unreasonable diminution of the guarantee of the right of defense.

For the *evasi* and *latitanti*, notification executed according to art. 170 of the Code of Criminal Procedure does not act as an unreasonable limitation of any right since they have placed the court in a position in which it must, by necessity, resort to this form of notification. The same cannot be said of the *renitenti.*

Notice is a necessary instrument of a fair hearing, indispensable for the preparation of an effective defense. We cannot say that this fundamental need has been fulfilled when, despite the possibility of real and effective notice to the accused, there is in use a form of notification which establishes only a legal presumption of knowledge, and, in reality, is a very ineffective means of informing the accused of the charge against him.

Therefore, the challenged norm, which, with excessive severity, prescribes notice [by deposit with the clerk]. . . limits the guarantee of the right of defense, in that it does not give the accused an adequate opportunity to contest the charge made against him. The challenged provision is thus contrary to art. 24 of the Constitution. . . .

NOTES

1. In the *Perdomini* case (Decision of June 9, 1967, Corte cost., [1967] 12 Giur. Cost. 759; [1967] 90 Foro It. I, 1362), the challenged provision of the Code of Criminal Procedure dealt with notice to accused persons residing outside of the country. Notice was held insufficient under the guarantee of the right of defense because no provision was made for suspension or delay of the proceeding to give the accused sufficient time to elect a domicile in Italy and prepare an effective defense. The Court recognized that the election of domicile by the accused should not be allowed to unduly delay or negatively influence the course of the proceeding since it is an act which is exclusively within the control of the accused. The Court emphasized, however, that notice is not merely a formality, but is intended to provide the accused with the opportunity to exercise his right of defense.

2. In 1972 the *Corte Costituzionale* again seized an opportunity to reaffirm that notice is more than a mere formality. The Code of Criminal Procedure had provided that, under certain circumstances, notice by mail was effective when sent rather than when the letter was received. In its Decision of May 4, 1972, Corte cost., [1972] 17 Giur. Cost. 1061; [1972] 35 Rac. uff. corte cost. 515; [1972] 95 Foro It. I; 1137; [1972] 124 Giur. Ital. I, 1549, the Court held that this violated defendant's constitutional right of defense.

3. While the system of notification in criminal proceedings has produced considerable litigation before the *Corte Costituzionale* the system of civil notification has produced little constitutional litigation.

4. In Germany the guarantee of the right to be heard, set forth in art. 103 of the Basic Law, requires, as in Italy, that a person involved in a case be given effective notice of the commencement of the proceeding and of the acts which are performed in the course of such a proceeding. In exceptional cases, the German Code of Civil Procedure provides for notification by posting in a public place. There is a presumption of knowledge on the part of the interested party after the passage of a specific period of time (which is rather short). If the prescribed requirements for such a procedure are not strictly applied, however, there can be a violation of the constitutional right to a fair hearing. For example, see the decision of the Constitutional Court of June 13, 1952, BVerfGE 332, 347, where it was decided that "if organs of the state power compel a person to leave the country . . . a later notification by posting gives to the party only the appearance of a possibility to defend himself. . . . In truth he is deprived of his constitutional right to a fair hearing (*rechtliches Gehör*)."

2. United States

a. Civil Cases

ROBINSON v. HANRAHAN

Supreme Court of the United States

409 U.S. 38, 93 S. Ct. 30, 34 L. Ed. 2d 47 (1972)

PER CURIAM.

On June 16, 1970, appellant was arrested on a charge of armed robbery and, immediately thereafter, the State of Illinois instituted forfeiture proceedings against appellant's automobile pursuant to the Illinois vehicle forfeiture statute.

Appellant was held in custody in the Cook County jail from June 16, 1970, to October 7, 1970, awaiting trial. Nevertheless, the State mailed notice of the pending forfeiture proceedings, not to the jail facility, but to appellant's home address as listed in the records of the Secretary of State. It is undisputed that appellant, who remained in custody throughout the forfeiture proceedings, did not receive such notice until his release. After an *ex parte* hearing on August 19, 1970, the circuit court of Cook County ordered the forfeiture and sale of appellant's vehicle.

Upon learning of the forfeiture after his release, appellant filed a motion for rehearing, requesting that the order of forfeiture be set aside because the manner of notice did not comport with the requirements of the Due Process Clause of the Fourteenth Amendment. The circuit court of Cook County denied the motion. On appeal, the Supreme Court of Illinois, three justices dissenting, held that, in light of the *in rem* nature of the proceedings, substituted service as utilized by the State did not deny appellant due process of law. *People ex rel. Hanrahan* v. *One 1965 Oldsmobile*, 52 Ill. 2d 37, 284 N. E. 2d 646 (1972). We cannot agree.

In *Mullane* v. *Central Hanover Bank & Trust Co.*, 339 U. S. 306 (1950), after commenting on the vagueness of the classifications "*in rem,* or more indefinitely *quasi in rem,* or more vaguely still, 'in the nature of a proceeding *in rem,*'" this Court held that "the requirements of the Fourteenth Amendment to the Federal Constitution do not depend upon a classification for which the standards are so elusive and confused generally and which, being primarily for state courts to define, may and do vary from state to state." *Id.,* at 312. "An elementary and fundamental requirement of due process in any proceeding which is to be accorded finality is notice reasonably calculated, under all the circumstances, to apprise interested parties of the pendency of the action and afford them an opportunity to present their objections." *Id.,* at 314. More specifically, *Mullane* held that notice by publication is not sufficient with respect to an individual whose name and address are known or easily ascertainable. Similarly, in *Covey* v. *Town of Somers,* 351 U. S. 141 (1956), we held that, in the context of a foreclosure action by the town, notice by mailing, posting, and publication was inadequate where the individual involved was known by the town to be an incompetent without the protection of a guardian.

In the instant case, the State knew that appellant was not at the address to which the notice was mailed and, moreover, knew also that appellant could not get to that address since he was at that very time confined in the Cook County jail. Under these circumstances, it cannot be said that the State made any effort to provide notice which was "reasonable calculated" to apprise appellant of the pendency of the forfeiture proceedings. Accordingly, we grant the motion for leave to proceed *in forma pauperis,* reverse the judgment of the Supreme Court of Illinois, and remand for further proceedings not inconsistent with this opinion.

NOTES AND QUESTIONS

1. Suppose that, in an eviction action, the process server makes no effort to locate the tenant, and submits a false affidavit that the tenant was personally served. Does the default judgment against the tenant violate due process? *Velasquez* v. *Thompson,* 321 F.Supp. 34 (S.D.N.Y. 1970), *aff'd,* 451 F.2d 202 (2d Cir. 1971).

2. Suppose, in an eviction action, process is served in English on a tenant who speaks only Spanish by a marshall who speaks only English. The tenant does not understand the notice. Does the default judgment against the tenant violate due process? *Commonwealth* v. *Olivo,* 337 N.E.2d 904 (Mass. 1975). Consider the practice in

California state courts of having process forms printed with information in both English and Spanish.

3. The hypothetical situation in Note 2 has become particularly relevant in Germany where there is a population of several million foreign laborers, many of whom have little or no knowledge of German. In a recent case decided by the Constitutional Court, an Italian worker had received in the mail an order to pay a fine as a result of having driven an automobile which was not fit for use in traffic. The order was accompanied by a standard description of ways in which the order could be challenged, as well as by a notice that a protest had to be lodged within one week or the order would become final. The Italian worker missed the deadline because he could not understand the information sent with the order, both of which were printed only in German. His motion to be allowed to proceed as though he had met the deadline was denied by the *Amtsgericht* on the grounds that he should have found someone to translate the information for him. The *Landgericht* affirmed.

On appeal the Constitutional Court reversed, holding that a person who receives notice in a language he cannot understand must be treated as though he had no notice at all. The Court also said, however, that the petitioner had no constitutional right to notice in his native tongue, but simply that his rights under arts. 19(IV) and 103 would be infringed if he were held to a one week deadline after receiving notice which he could not understand. Decision of July 4, 1976, 1976 NEUE JURISTISCHE WOCHENSCHRIFT, Heft 25, at 1021.

b. Criminal Cases

TAYLOR v. UNITED STATES

Supreme Court of the United States

414 U.S. 17, 94 S. Ct. 194, 38 L. Ed. 2d 174 (1973)

PER CURIAM.

On the first day of his trial on four counts of selling cocaine . . . petitioner failed to return for the afternoon session. He had been present at the expiration of the morning session when the court announced that the lunch recess would last until 2 p. m., and he had been told by his attorney to return to the courtroom at that time. The judge recessed the trial until the following morning, but petitioner still did not appear. His wife testified that she had left the courtroom the previous day with petitioner after the morning session; that they had separated after sharing a taxicab to Roxbury; that he had not appeared ill; and, finally, that she had not heard from him since. The trial judge then denied a motion for mistrial by defense counsel, who asserted that the jurors' minds would be tained by petitioner's absence and that continuation of the trial in his absence deprived him of his Sixth Amendment right to confront witnesses against him. Relying upon Fed. Rule Crim. Proc. 43,[1] which expressly provides that a defendant's voluntary absence "shall not prevent continuing the trial," the court found that petitioner had absented himself voluntarily from the proceedings.

Throughout the remainder of the trial, the court admonished the jury that no inference of guilt could be drawn from petitioner's absence. Petitioner was found guilty on all four counts. Following his subsequent arrest, he was sentenced to the statutory five-year minimum. The Court of Appeals affirmed the conviction, 478 F. 2d 681 (CA1 1973), and we now grant the motion for leave to proceed *in forma pauperis* and the petition for certiorari and affirm the judgment of the Court of Appeals.

There is no challenge to the trial court's conclusion that petitioner's absence from the trial was voluntary, and no claim that the continuation of the trial was not authorized by Rule 43. Nor are we persuaded that Rule 43 is unconstitutional or that petitioner was deprived of any constitutional rights in the circumstances before us. Rule 43 has remained unchanged since the adoption of the Federal Rules of Criminal Procedure in 1945; and with respect to the consequences of the defendant's voluntary absence from trial, it reflects the long-standing rule recognized by this Court in *Diaz* v. *United States,* 223 U.S. 442, 455 (1912):

> "[W]here the offense is not capital and the accused is not in custody, the prevailing rule has been, that if, after the trial has begun in his presence, he voluntarily absents himself, this does not nullify what has been done or prevent the completion of the trial, but, on the contrary, operates as a waiver of his right to be present and leaves the court free to proceed with the trial in like manner and with like effect as if he were present." (Citations omitted.)

Under this rule, the District Court and the Court of Appeals correctly rejected petitioner's claims.

Petitioner, however, insists that his mere voluntary absence from his trial cannot be construed as an effective waiver, that is, "an intentional relinquishment or abandonment of a known right or privilege," *Johnson* v. *Zerbst,* 304 U.S. 458, 464 (1938), unless it

---

[1] Rule 43 provides, in pertinent part:

"The defendant shall be present at the arraignment, at every stage of the trial including the impaneling of the jury and the return of the verdict, and at the imposition of sentence, except as otherwise provided by these rules. In prosecutions for offenses not punishable by death, the defendant's voluntary absence after the trial has been commenced in his presence shall not prevent continuing the trial to and including the return of the verdict."

is demonstrated that he knew or had been expressly warned by the trial court not only that he had a right to be present but also that the trial would continue in his absence and thereby effectively foreclose his right to testify and to confront personally the witnesses against him.

Like the Court of Appeals, we cannot accept this position. Petitioner had no right to interrupt the trial by his voluntary absence, as he implicitly concedes by urging only that he should have been warned that no such right existed and that the trial would proceed in his absence. The right at issue is the right to be present, and the question becomes whether that right was effectively waived by his voluntary absence. Consistent with Rule 43 and *Diaz,* we conclude that it was.

It is wholly incredible to suggest that petitioner, who was at liberty on bail, had attended the opening session of his trial, and had a duty to be present at the trial, see *Stack* v *Boyle,* 342 U.S. 1, 4-5 (1951), entertained any doubts about his right to be present at every stage of his trial. It seems equally incredible to us, as it did to the Court of Appeals, "that a defendant who flees from a courtroom in the midst of a trial — where judge, jury, witnesses and lawyers are present and ready to continue — would not know that as a consequence the trial could continue in his absence." 478 F. 2d, at 691. Here the Court of Appeals noted that when petitioner was questioned at sentencing regarding his flight, he never contended that he was unaware that a consequence of his flight would be a continuation of the trial without him. Moreover, no issue of the voluntariness of his disappearance was ever raised. As was recently noted, "there can be no doubt whatever that the governmental prerogative to proceed with a trial may not be defeated by conduct of the accused that prevents the trial from going forward." *Illinois* v. *Allen,* 397 U.S. 337, 349 (1970) (BRENNAN, J., concurring). Under the circumstances present here, the Court of Appeals properly applied Rule 43 and affirmed the judgment of conviction.

Affirmed.

NOTES AND QUESTIONS

1. There are no cases in the United States dealing with notice to criminal defendants who have not been apprehended. That is because there is no provision made in the United States for trial in absentia of fugitives who manage to flee before initial apprehension. As we have seen, in civil law countries, provision is made for criminal trial in absentia of fugitives, and the only constitutional issue is the adequacy of notice.

Is this difference simply conceptual? In the nineteenth century in the United States, theories of judicial jurisdiction were grounded entirely on concepts of physical territorial power. In civil cases, this meant that the defendant had to be served with process while he was in the territorial jurisdiction of the court. *Pennoyer* v. *Neff,* 95 U.S. 714 (1877). Of course, in civil cases, the territorial theory of court jurisdiction has given way to a theory which permits assertion of jurisdiction if the defendant has minimum contacts with the jurisdiction. *International Shoe Co.* v. *Washington,* 326 U.S. 310 (1945). Once minimum contact is seen as the basis for jurisdiction, the function of service of process is seen as notification, and notice must be reasonably calculated to reach the defendant, under the *Mullane* decision cited in the *Robinson* case.

In civil law countries, the *International Shoe-Mullane* approach is used in both civil and criminal cases. But, in the United States, the older territorial view still governs criminal cases — physical apprehension of the suspect is required prior to the criminal trial. Thus, since criminal trials do not commence without prior physical apprehension, there are obviously no issues in criminal cases about lack of notice that charges have been filed.

If the difference is more than conceptual, is it a difference in basic constitutional values, such as the defendant's right to be personally present at his trial? Does it reflect a different — more adversary — structure and conception of the criminal process in the United States?

2. The 1912 *Diaz* case was an appeal from a Phillipine conviction for noncapital homicide. (Diaz had been unable to attend his trial on two occasions and had wired the judge to proceed without him.) Does the reference to noncapital cases in the *Diaz* dictum quoted by the Court in *Taylor* state the outer limits of the rule? Rule 43 of the Federal Rules of Criminal Procedure was amended in 1974 to eliminate reference to a distinction between capital and noncapital cases.

3. By its terms, Rule 43 applies only to the case where the defendant voluntarily absents himself after trial has commenced. If a criminal defendant has been arrested and arraigned, would it violate the Constitution to conduct a trial in absentia where the defendant absents himself before the trial has begun? Lower federal courts have concluded that it would not. (A leading case is *United States* v. *Tortora,* 464 F.2d 1202 (2d Cir.), *cert. denied,* 409 U.S. 1063 (1972). In *Tacon* v. *Arizona,* 410 U.S. 351 (1973), the Supreme Court granted certiorari to determine whether a state court criminal trial could be held in absentia where the defendant lacked the funds to return for trial. The writ was dismissed as improvidently granted because the issue had not been presented to the state courts. Justices Douglas, Brennan and Marshall, dissenting, concluded that the petitioner had not knowingly waived his right to be present at the trial.

4. Given the emphasis on "waiver" in these cases, would it be possible to try a defendant in absentia, upon adequate notice, if he fled the jurisdiction prior to arrest and arraignment? Are there advantages to the civil law system which permits the criminal trial of a fugitive criminal suspect to proceed in his absence? How can the eventual sentence be enforced after trial in absentia? Suppose a businessman, or even a Congressman, refused to leave his Caribbean resort to face fraud charges in New York. Would it be desirable to try him in absentia? How about a fugitive heiress wanted for bank robbery?

Chapter 8

JUDICIAL INDEPENDENCE

Like the right of action, the right to an impartial judge, free from improper influence, is embodied in the Italian and German Constitutions and in the European Convention on Human Rights.

Article 101, para. 2 of the Italian Constitution provides that "Judges are subject only to the law." Article 104, para. 1 establishes that "[t]he judiciary is an autonomous order independent of any other power." Article 107, paras. 1 and 2, further provides that

> Judges shall be irremovable. They shall not be discharged or suspended, or transferred to other offices or functions except following a decision of the Superior Council of the Judiciary,* taken either with their consent or for the reasons and with the guarantees of defense laid down by the law on the judicial organization.

Finally, art. 108, para. 2 adds:

> The law will ensure the independence of judges of special jurisdictions, of the office of the Public Prosecutor attached to them, and of any others who take part in the administration of justice.

In the Federal Republic of Germany, the principles are contained in arts. 20(2) and 97 of the Constitution:

> Article 20 . . .
> (2) All state authority emanates from the people. It shall be exercised by the people by means of elections and voting and by separate legislative, executive, and judicial organs.

> Article 97.
> (1) The judges shall be independent and subject only to the law.
> (2) Judges appointed on a tenured, full-time basis to an established post cannot, against their will, be dismissed, or

---

* Two thirds of the members of the Superior Council of the Judiciary are elected by all the regular judges from among the ranks of the judiciary, and one third is elected by Parliament from among law professors and lawyers with no less than fifteen years of practice. The President of the Republic presides over the Superior Council. Its main role is described as the "self-government" of the judiciary, including judicial appointments, promotions, transfers, and disciplinary sanctions. Italian Constitution, arts. 104-105.

permanently or temporarily suspended from office, or transferred to another post, or retired before the expiration of their term of office except by virtue of a judicial decision and only on the grounds and in the form provided for by law. Legislation may set age limits for the retirement of judges appointed for life. In the event of changes in the structure of the courts or their areas of jurisdiction, judges may be transferred to another court or removed from their office, provided they retain their full salary.

Under the European Convention, art. 6 guarantees a right "to a fair hearing . . . by an independent and impartial tribunal."

A. INDEPENDENCE FROM EXTERNAL CONTROL OF SALARY AND TENURE

United States Federal Judges

PALMORE v. UNITED STATES

Supreme Court of the United States
411 U.S. 389, 93 S. Ct. 1670, 36 L. Ed. 2d 342 (1973)

MR. JUSTICE WHITE delivered the opinion of the Court.

. . . [T]his case requires us to decide whether a defendant charged with a felony under the District of Columbia Code may be tried by a judge who does not have protection with respect to tenure and salary under Art. III of the Constitution. We hold that under its Art. I, § 8, cl. 17, power to legislate for the District of Columbia, Congress may provide for trying local criminal cases before judges who, in accordance with the District of Columbia Code, are not accorded life tenure and protection against reduction in salary. In this respect, the position of the District of Columbia defendant is similar to that of the citizen of any of the 50 States when charged with violation of a state criminal law: Neither has a federal constitutional right to be tried before judges with tenure and salary guarantees.

. . . Palmore was arrested and later charged with the felony of carrying an unregistered pistol in the District of Columbia after having been convicted of a felony, in violation of the District of Columbia Code, § 22-3204 (1967). He was tried and found guilty in the Superior Court of the District of Columbia.

Under Title I of the District of Columbia Court Reform and Criminal Procedure Act of 1970,[2] . . . the judges of the Superior

---

[2] Before passage of the District of Columbia Court Reform and Criminal Procedure Act of 1970, the local court system consisted of one appellate court and

Court are appointed by the President and serve for terms of 15 years.[3]

Palmore moved to dismiss the indictment against him, urging that only a court "ordain [ed] and establish [ed]" in accordance with Art. III of the United States Constitution could constitutionally try him for a felony prosecution under the District of Columbia Code. He also moved to suppress the pistol as the fruit of an illegal search and seizure. The motions were denied in the Superior Court, and Palmore was convicted.

The District of Columbia Court of Appeals affirmed, concluding that under the plenary power to legislate for the District of Columbia, conferred by Art. I, § 8, cl. 17, of the Constitution, Congress had "constitutional power to proscribe certain criminal conduct only in the District and to select the appropriate court, whether it is created by virtue of article III or article I, to hear and determine these particular criminal cases within the District."

. . . .

---

three trial courts, two of which, the juvenile court and the tax court, were courts of special jurisdiction. The third trial court, the District of Columbia Court of General Sessions, was one of quite limited jurisdiction, its criminal jurisdiction consisting solely of that exercised concurrently with the United States District Court over misdemeanors and petty offenses. . . . The court's civil jurisdiction was restricted to cases where the amount in controversy did not exceed $10,000, and it had jurisdiction over cases involving title to real property only as part of a divorce action. . . .

The United States District Court for the District had concurrent jurisdiction with the Court of General Sessions over most of the criminal and civil matters handled by that court . . . and had exclusive jurisdiction over felony offenses, even though committed in violation of locally applicable laws. Thus, the District Court was filling the role of both a local and federal court.

Seeking to improve the performance of the court system, Congress, in Title I of the Reorganization Act, invested the local courts with jurisdiction equivalent to that exercised by state courts. . . . The three former trial courts were combined into the new Superior Court of the District of Columbia. . . which was vested, with a minor exception. . . with exclusive jurisdiction over all criminal cases, including felonies, brought under laws applicable exclusively to the District. Its civil jurisdiction reached all civil actions and any other matter at law or in equity, brought in the District of Columbia, except those in which exclusive jurisdiction was vested in the United States District Court. . . . The local appeals court, the District of Columbia Court of Appeals, would ultimately not be subject to review by the United States Court of Appeals . . . and was declared to be the "highest court of the District of Columbia" for purposes of further review by this Court.

In addition to the shift in jurisdiction, the number of local judges was increased, their tenure was lengthened from 10 to 15 years, and their salaries were increased and fixed at a percentage of that of judges of the United States courts. . . . The Reorganization Act established a Commission on Judicial Disabilities and Tenure to deal with suspension, retirement, or removal of local judges.

[3] The 15-year term is subject to the provision for mandatory retirement at age 70. D. C. Code Ann. § 11-1502. (Supp. V. 1972).

Art. I, § 8, cl. 17, of the Constitution provides that Congress shall have power "[t]o exercise exclusive Legislation in all Cases whatsoever, over" the District of Columbia. The power is plenary. Not only may statutes of Congress of otherwise nationwide application be applied to the District of Columbia, but Congress may also exercise all the police and regulatory powers which a state legislature or municipal government would have in legislating for state or local purposes. . . . It is apparent that the power of Congress under Clause 17 permits it to legislate for the District in a manner with respect to subjects that would exceed its powers, or at least would be very unusual, in the context of national legislation enacted under other powers delegated to it under Art. I, § 8. . . .

. . . . Palmore's argument is straightforward: Art. III vests the "judicial Power" of the United States in courts with judges holding office during good behavior and whose salary cannot be diminished; the "judicial Power" that these courts are to exercise "shall extend to all Cases, in Law and Equity, arising under this Constitution, the Laws of the United States, and Treaties made, or which shall be made, under their Authority . . ."; the District of Columbia Code, having been enacted by Congress, is a law of the United States; this prosecution for violation of § 22-3204 of the Code is therefore a case arising under the laws of the United States, involves an exercise of the "judicial Power" of the United States, and must therefore be tried by an Art. III judge.

This position ultimately rests on the proposition that an Art. III judge must preside over every proceeding in which a charge, claim, or defense is based on an Act of Congress or a law made under its authority. At the very least, it asserts that criminal offenses under the laws passed by Congress may not be prosecuted except in courts established pursuant to Art. III. In our view, however, there is no support for this view in either constitutional text or in constitutional history and practice.

. . . [T]hroughout our history, Congress has exercised its power under Art. IV to "make all needful Rules and Regulations respecting the Territory or other Property belonging to the United States" by creating territorial courts and manning them with judges appointed for a term of years. These courts have not been deemed subject to the strictures of Art. III, even though they characteristically enforced not only the civil and criminal laws of Congress applicable throughout the United States, but also the laws applicable only within the boundaries of the particular territory. Speaking for a unanimous Court in *American Ins. Co.* v. *Canter,* 1 Pet. 511 (1828), Mr. Chief Justice Marshall held that the territorial courts of Florida, although not Art. III courts, could hear and determine cases governed by the admiralty and maritime law that ordinarily could be heard only by Art. III judges. "[T]he same limitation does not extend to the territories. In legislating for them, Congress exercises the combined powers of the general, and of a state government." *Id.,* at 546. This has been the consistent view of this Court. Territorial courts, therefore, have regularly tried criminal cases arising under the general laws of Congress, as well as those brought under territorial laws.

There is another context in which criminal cases arising under federal statutes are tried, and defendants convicted, in non-Art. III courts. Under its Art. I, § 8, cl. 14, power "[t]o make Rules for the Government and Regulation of the land and naval Forces," Congress has declared certain behavior by members of the Armed Forces to be criminal and provided for the trial of such cases by court-martial proceedings in the military mode, not by courts ordained and established under Art. III. Within their proper sphere, courts-martial are constitutional instruments to carry out congressional and executive will. *Dynes* v. *Hoover,* 20 How. 65, 79, 82 (1857). The "exigencies of military discipline require the existence of a special system of military courts in which not all of the specific procedural protections deemed essential in Art. III trials need apply," *O'Callahan* v. *Parker,* 395 U.S. 258, 261 (1969); and "the Constitution does not provide life tenure for those performing judicial functions in military trials," *Toth* v. *Quarles,* 350 U.S. 11, 17 (1955).

"The same confluence of practical considerations that dictated the result in [*American Ins. Co.* v. *Canter, supra*], has governed the decision in later cases sanctioning the creation of other courts with judges of limited tenure," *Glidden Co.* v. *Zdanok,* 370 U. S. 530, 547 (1962), such as the Court of Private Land Claims, *United States* v. *Coe,* 155 U. S. 76, 85-86 (1894); the Choctaw and Chickasaw Citizenship Court, *Shephens* v. *Cherokee Nation,* 174 U.S. 445 (1899); *Ex parte Joins,* 191 U.S. 93 (1903); *Wallace* v. *Adams,* 204 U.S. 415 (1907); courts created in unincorporated districts outside the mainland, *Downes* v. *Bidwell,* 182 U.S. 244, 266-267 (1901); *Balzac* v. *Porto Rico,* 258 U.S., at 312-313, and the Consular Courts established by concessions from foreign countries, *In re Ross,* 140 U.S. 453, 464-465, 480 (1891).

. . . .

It is apparent that neither this Court nor Congress has read the Constitution as requiring every federal question arising under the federal law, or even every criminal prosecution for violating an Act of Congress, to be tried in an Art. III court before a judge enjoying lifetime tenure and protection against salary reduction. Rather, both Congress and this Court have recognized that state courts are appropriate forums in which federal questions and federal crimes may at times be tried; and that the requirements of Art. III, which are applicable where laws of national applicability and affairs of national concern are at stake, must in proper circumstances give way to accommodate plenary grants of power to Congress to legislate with respect to specialized areas having particularized needs and warranting distinctive treatment. Here, Congress reorganized the court system in the District of Columbia and established one set of courts in the District with Art. III characteristics and devoted to matters of national concern. It also created a wholly separate court system designed primarily to concern itself with local law and to serve as a local court system for a large metropolitan area.

. . . Congress, after careful consideration, determined that it preferred, and had the power to utilize, a local court system staffed by judges without lifetime tenure. Congress made a deliberate choice to create judgeships with terms of 15 years. . . and to subject judges in those positions to removal or suspension by a judicial commission under certain established circumstances. . . . It was thought that such a system would be more workable and efficient in administering and discharging the work of a multifaceted metropolitan court system.

In providing for fixed terms of office, Congress was cognizant of the fact that "virtually no State has provided" for tenure during good behavior . . . noting that 46 of the 50 States have not provided life tenure for trial judges who hear felony cases; . . . and the provisions of the Act, with respect to court administration and to judicial removal and suspension, were considered by some as a model for the States.

We do not discount the importance attached to the tenure and salary provisions of Art. III, but we conclude that Congress was not required to provide an Art. III court for the trial of criminal cases arising under its laws applicable only within the District of Columbia. Palmore's trial in the Superior Court was authorized by Congress' Art. I power to legislate for the District in all cases whatsoever. Palmore was no more disadvantaged and no more entitled to an Art. III judge than any other citizen of any of the 50 States who is tried for a strictly local crime. Nor did his trial by a nontenured judge deprive him of due process of law under the Fifth Amendment any more than the trial of the citizens of the various States for local crimes by judges without protection as to tenure deprives them of due process of law under the Fourteenth Amendment.

The judgment of the District of Columbia Court of Appeals is affirmed.

So ordered.

MR. JUSTICE DOUGLAS, dissenting.

. . . .

The judges of the court that convicted [Palmore]

— hold office for a term of fifteen years, not for life as do Art. III judges;

— unlike Art. III judges, their salaries are not protected from diminishment during their continuance in office;

— unlike Art. III judges, they can be removed from office by a five-member Commission [4] through less formidable means of procedure than impeachment. . . .

In other words, these Superior Court judges are not members of the independent judiciary which has been one of our proudest boasts, by reason of Art. III. The safeguards accorded Art. III judges were designed to protect litigants with unpopular or minority causes or litigants who belong to despised or suspect classes. The safeguards surround the judge and give him a measure of protection against the hostile press, the leftist or rightist demands of the party in power, the glowering looks of those in the top echelon in whose hands rest the power of reappointment.

In the Constitutional Convention of 1787 it was proposed that judges "may be removed by the Executive on the application by the Senate and House of Representatives." The proposal was defeated, only Connecticut voting for it. Wilson apparently expressed the common sentiment: "The Judges would be in a bad situation if made to depend on any gust of faction which might prevail in the two branches of our Government."

Without the independence granted and enjoyed by Art. III judges,

---

[4] A Commission on Judicial Disabilities and Tenure is established with the power "to suspend, retire, or remove" one of these judges. . . . The President names three members, the Commissioner of the District names one, and the Chief Judge of the District Court names the fifth. There are three alternate members. The President names the Chairman. . . . All members are appointed for a term of six years. . . . A judge must be removed if he has committed a felony and been finally convicted. . . . He shall be removed if the Commission finds

"(A) willful misconduct in office,

"(B) willful and persistent failure to perform judicial duties, or

"(C) any other conduct which is prejudicial to the administration of justice or which brings the judicial office into disrepute."

He shall be involuntarily retired if "(1) the Commission determines that the judge suffers from a mental or physical disability (including habitual intemperance) which is or is likely to become permanent and which prevents, or seriously interferes with, the proper performance of his judicial duties, and (2) the Commission files in the District of Columbia Court of Appeals an order of involuntary retirement and the order is affirmed on appeal or the time within which an appeal may be taken from the order has expired."

a federal judge could more easily become the tool of a ravenous Executive Branch.

. . . .

The legislative history of the District of Columbia Court Reform and Criminal Procedure Act of 1970 makes abundantly clear that one main purpose was the creation of some political leverage over Superior Court judges. As the Senate Report states:

> [T]he committee . . . sought a tenure provision that would combine the attractiveness of the federal system with the opportunity for some review of the judge's work.
>
> . . . .
>
> "At present, the only means available to rid the local bench of a sick or venal judge is through the process of impeachment by the House of Representatives and trial by the U. S. Senate. To believe that the Congress at this time in our history has the time to police the local judiciary through the impeachment process is just not realistic. That process has not even proven viable when the conduct of Federal, good-behavior tenure judges is drawn into question."

. . . .

Much is made of the fact that many States (about three-fourths of them) have their judges at all levels elected by the people. That was one of the basic Jacksonian principles. But the principle governing federal judges is strongly opposed. Hamilton stated the proposition in No. 79 of the Federalist (J. Cooke ed. 1961):

> "Next to permanency in office, nothing can contribute more to the independence of the judges than a fixed provision for their support. The remark made in relation to the president, is equally applicable here. In the general course of human nature, *a power over a man's subsistence amounts to a power over his will*. . . ."

That theory is opposed to the Jacksonian philosophy concerning election of state judges. But the present statutory scheme for control over Superior Court judges is even opposed to the Jacksonian theory. In the District of Columbia the people do not elect these Art. I judges. Nor do they "recall" them as is done in some States. The Superior Court judges are named by the President and confirmed by the Senate and they are removable by a commission appointed by the President. The Superior Court judge has no opportunity to put his problems, his conduct, his behavior on the bench to the people. The gun of the commission is held at his head. All of the normal vices of a dependent, removable judiciary are accentuated in the District of Columbia.

. . . .

We take a great step backward today when we deprive our federal regime in the District of that judicial independence which helps insure fearless and evenhanded dispensation of justice. No federal court exercising Art. III judicial power should be made a minion of any cabal that from accidents of politics comes into the ascendancy as an overlord of the District of Columbia. That effort unhappily succeeds today and is in disregard of one of our most cherished constitutional provisions.

. . . .

Manipulated judiciaries are common across the world, especially in communist and fascist nations. The faith in freedom which we profess and which is opposed to those ideologies assumes today an ominous cast. It is ominous because it indirectly associates the causes of crime with the Bill of Rights rather than with the sociological factors of poverty caused by unemployment and disemployment, the abrasive political tactics used against minorities, the blight of narcotics and the like. Those who hold the gun at the heads of Superior Court judges can retaliate against those who respect the spirit of the Fourth Amendment and the Fifth Amendment and who stand firmly against the ancient practice of using the third degree to get confessions and who fervently believe that the end does not justify the means.

I would reverse the judgment below.

NOTES AND QUESTIONS

1. Would it be possible in the United States to transform quasi-judicial federal administrative agencies into specialized courts whose judges did not have lifetime tenure? Under the Court's rationale in *Palmore,* would it be possible for Congress to establish specialized courts, with judges holding office for limited terms, to handle litigation arising out of any federal statute? Would it be possible to dispense with courts entirely, and use federal administrative agencies with administrative "judges" of limited tenure, to litigate disputes, arising under federal laws, now litigated in ordinary federal courts?

2. The Court's opinion indicates that the Federal Constitution's provisions for tenure of federal judges have not been widely copied in state constitutions. Why not? Is tenure during good behavior only important for federal judges, given the kinds of cases on the federal court dockets? Or is this an issue which might be treated very differently today, even for United States Supreme Court Justices, if we were to start afresh?

3. Notice the provisions for removal of judges of the local D.C. courts. There have been serious legislative proposals to apply similar procedures to ordinary federal judges, who, until now, have been removable from office only through impeachment. Could the grounds for removal of D.C. judges be applied to ordinary federal judges? Whatever the appropriate grounds for removal, under the Constitution is impeachment by the House of Representatives and conviction by the Senate the only possible procedure for removal of ordinary federal judges?

4. In Germany, the Weimar Constitution of 1919 had guaranteed life tenure to judges. Under art. 97 of the Bonn Constitution, however, life tenure is not mandatory; instead, the period of service is left to the legislature. Nevertheless, ordinary legislation usually provides life tenure for professional judges. When a law provides a lesser tenure period, it must still be long enough to insure judicial independence. In the Decision of May 9, 1962 (14 BVerfGE 56, 71), the Constitutional Court held that a period of six years was not too short as to compromise the position of the judge, and in Decision of Nov. 24, 1964 (18 BVerfGE 241, 255), four years was held sufficient.

As for salary, the German Constitutional Court has emphasized that the principle of judicial independence comprehends a predetermined and stable income; from the requirement of stability is derived the idea that the economic treatment of the judges must be regulated in a general way by law and be placed beyond the discretion of the executive. (Promotions, however, are still to a great extent within the power of the executive and increases of salary are given upon promotion.) *See* the decision of the Constitutional Court of January 24, 1961 (12 BVerfGE 81, 88). In 1969, a majority of the Court rejected a claim that it was unconstitutional to tie judges' salaries to the salaries of civil service executive officials, and unanimously refused to consider a claim that the judges were entitled to a salary higher than that of corresponding civil servants. The Court decided that "so long as the judges' salaries are not clearly unsuitable, there is no . . . danger to their independence." (Decision of June 4, 1969, 26 BVerfGE 141.)

B. INFLUENCE BY THE EXECUTIVE

1. Italy

ALESSANDRO v. PRESIDENTE CONSIGLIO DEI MINISTRI

Corte costituzionale, Decision of June 3, 1966, No. 55
[1966] 11 Giur. Cost. 879; [1966] Rac. uff. corte cost. 483
[1966] 89 Foro It. I, 986

[FACTS: The *ordinanza* of the *Corte dei Conti* * — the court which submitted the question of constitutionality to the Constitutional Court — does not state the particular fact situation.]

OPINION

The constitutionality of the adjudicatory powers of the *Consigli di Prefettura* (Prefectural Councils)** over financial matters ... is challenged in light of the constitutional principles of independence and impartiality of the judge, the right of defense, and the concept of the natural judge.

The primary and fundamental objection is found in the second paragraph of art. 23 of the Consolidated Text. This section concerns the composition of the *Consiglio di Prefettura* when it adopts its judicial role in dealing with financial issues.

The rule stated therein presently provides that when acting as a court the body be composed of the prefect (or his representative), who is its president; two officials of the prefecture belonging to the same branch of the civil service and usually having the status of section directors; the director of accounting of the same prefecture; and the State's provincial director of accounting. All five members of the judicial body belong to the civil administration of the State, four to the interior administration and one to the treasury; all are hierarchically dependent on the executive power, which is competent to adopt measures relating to their careers, legal status, and transfers. Moreover, the agency relationship of the prefect to the government is a very pronounced one — the prefects are the principal operative instruments of the government in the local areas. The two officials from the interior administration are, in addition, directly responsible to the prefect (the president of the judicial body in question), who prepares the reports on which their promotion is based. The director of accounting is in a similar position of dependence.

---

* The *Corte dei Conti* is a special administrative court having jurisdiction over the financial liability of the state employees as well as pension claims. It sits as a five-judge panel.

** The *Consiglio di Prefettura* is a governmental organ of control of the local administration with, among other functions, some adjudicatory powers concerning the financial liability of the employees of the local entities.

There is no statute which regulates the composition of the *Consiglio di Prefettura* or the period of service of its members. Total or partial changes in the composition of this judicial organ, therefore, depend exclusively on the discretionary power of the central administration over the careers and transfers of officials. Moreover, the manner and time of rotation of the two officials of the career prefectorate are similarly conditioned on the free choice exercised by the prefect in the organization and supervision of his subordinates.

This being the legislation, the asserted unconstitutionality of the second paragraph of art. 23 cannot be denied. It is even more pronounced when the objective of the proceedings involved is considered. Financial liability proceedings as a check on the administration of the local departments, and those who manage the funds of such departments, serve as an indispensable instrument in guaranteeing the legality of their financial management.

These proceedings can influence the person and property of the agents of these departments and (what is more important) their directors. Of particular note among these are the directors of the territorial offices, some of whom are elected. If not conducted with absolute independence and impartiality, these proceedings can clearly exert a prejudicial influence in the area of local autonomy. That influence is strongest on the directors of the territorial offices, for a declaration of liability will result in their ineligibility for office. Moreover, an administrator who is a mayor, a president of the *Giunta provinciale* * or an assessor, and who is involved in a financial investigation, may be suspended until its completion. . . . The danger that such an organ, composed of officials who are dependent on the central government and empowered to adjudicate financial questions, represents to local autonomy is evident.

That part of the complaint concerning the second paragraph of art. 23, which points out the contrast between the rules regarding the composition of the *Consiglio di Prefettura* with the principle of judicial independence, is well grounded. That principle is embodied in the second paragraph of art. 108 of the Constitution, which assures independence to special courts, and in art. 101, second paragraph, which establishes that the judiciary is subject only to the law. Both articles would be diminished in those courts in which extra-legal factors were controlling. . . .

With reference to the other complaints contained in the *ordinanza,* the Court finds the following constitutional defects in the remaining

---

* The *Giunta Provinciale Amministrativa* is a governmental organ of control of the local administration. Its main function is the control of the decisions of Communes and Provinces. Before the decision of the Constitutional Court (*infra,* Note 1), it also acted as an administrative court of first instance in claims against local administrative entities.

rules of the Communal and Provincial Consolidated Text regarding the jurisdiction of the *Consiglio di Prefettura*:

Art. 260 is contrary to the principle of judicial impartiality, since proceedings against administrators are initiated and conducted by the *Consiglio di Prefettura* on its own initiative or at the bidding of the prefect-president, [who thus accumulates in himself the role of president of the council and] the administrative prosecuting function. (It should also be noted that the same article 260 contradicts the procedural rules regulating judicial bias and disqualification in civil, criminal, and administrative proceedings. . . .) Moreover, the discretionary nature of the power of the council and its prefect-president to initiate the proceeding (art. 260, second paragraph) can affect the equality of treatment of local administrators, even within the same department, as well as the impartiality of the judge. Clearly, given the subordination of all the body's members to the executive power, there is actual danger of discrimination, and particularly of political discrimination, without an opportunity for legal remedy.

Moreover, given the form of the proceeding, the lack of an adequate safeguard against the introduction of new evidence after the hearing of the private parties is contrary to the right of defense (art. 24, para. 2, of the Constitution). . . .

For the reasons stated above, para. 2 of art. 23 of the Communal and Provincial Consolidated Text is declared unconstitutional. . . .

NOTES

1. In its decision the *Corte Costituzionale* indicated its receptiveness to similar challenges to judicial powers exercised by administrative entities.

In response to this "invitation," another lower court challenged the *Giunta Provinciale Amministrativa. Dantonia* v. *Treso,* Corte Costituzionale, Decision of March 22, 1967, [1967] 12 Giur. Cost. 214; [1967] 25 Rac. uff. corte cost. 243; [1967] 90 Foro It. I, 681. As a consequence, the judicial competence of these bodies was similarly struck down.

The challenged members of the *Giunta* were "the prefect (or his representative), who heads the Committee, and two counsellors of the prefecture. . . . The two counsellors are designated at the beginning of each year by the prefect, and, in case of absence or other incapacitation, are replaced with an individual designated from among the same officials and in the same manner." The Court concluded: "From . . . the absolutely discretionary nature of both their appointment to, as well as their dismissal from, the judicial body — completely analogous to that of the *Consiglio di Prefettura* — it is clear that those officials, the majority of the members of the *Giunta* [composed of five members] are not independent of the executive, and that, moreover, two of them are in a position of strict subordination to the president of the body."

2. The criteria set forth by the *Corte Costituzionale* have been implemented by other decisions. Among the most important of these are the following: a) Decision of Apr. 3, 1969, [1969] 14 Giur. Cost. 971; [1969] 29 Rac. uff. corte cost. 543; [1969] 92 Foro It. I, 1036, finding a violation of the constitutional guarantee of impartiality in the judicial powers conferred on the *Intendente di Finanza* (a staff employee of the Ministry of Finance who had jurisdiction and power to prosecute delinquent taxpayers); b) Decision of July 9, 1970, [1970] 15 Giur. Cost. 1513; [1970] 32 Rac. uff. corte cost. 271; [1970] 93 Foro It. I, 1844, declaring unconstitutional Arts. 1238, 1242, 1243, 1246 and 1247 of the Navigation Code which allowed Harbor Masters (administrative officials of the Merchant Marine) to exercise some judicial functions.

3. The Decisions of February 6, 1969, [1969] 14 Giur. Cost. 36; [1969] 92 Foro It. I, 562, and February 10, 1969, [1969] 14 Giur. Cost. 61; [1969] 92 Foro It. I, 561, held that tax proceedings before city and provincial boards were administrative, rather than judicial, and that therefore members of the board were not governed by constitutional criteria of judicial independence. These judgments clearly reflected a desire not to disturb further the faltering system of administrative justice with another declaration of unconstitutionality. On the one hand, if the tax boards were courts they were incompatible with the requirement of judicial independence in art. 108 of the Constitution. On the other hand, a declaration of unconstitutionality would have brought disastrous results to both the boards themselves and the ordinary courts (in the form of a flood of proceedings from the then defunct boards). The Court held that the lack of independence was one of several clear signs that the power of the tax boards was essentially administrative rather than judicial. Thus, the boards survived, subject, however, to the full range of judicial control over administrative action guaranteed by art. 113 of the Italian Constitution. (If the boards acted judicially, and met constitutional criteria for judicial independence, no further judicial review would have been necessary.) Compare that result to the result in the German decision which follows.

2. Germany

DECISION OF NOVEMBER 9, 1955

Bundesverfassungsgericht
[1956] 4 BVerfGE 331

[FACTS: In 1949, in order to provide immediate assistance of an economic nature to aid in post-war reconstruction, the Economic Council of the United Economic Region, comprising roughly those areas occupied by the English and American forces, enacted the Immediate Assistance Act. The administration of the assistance provided for therein was designed to be implemented principally through two bodies — at the local level, the Immediate Assistance Agencies and, at the state (*Land*) level, the State Assistance Agencies — in addition to a central Main Office. Each of the local agencies was charged with the establishment of a Local Assistance Commission, to be headed by the director of the agency or his representative and further composed of two associate members elected for one-year terms by the county or town council. At the state level, analogous commissions — State Assistance Commissions for Appeals — were created, with the directors of the state agencies acting as their *ex officio* presidents, and two associate members elected by the state parliament for a period of one year. At the Main Office, a Division for Administrative Review was given the power of final review of claims presented to the subordinate commissions.

[While the Act declares (§ 69, para. 1) that the Local Assistance Commissions decide as administrative *agencies* according to the general directions of the president at the Main Office, § 69, para. 2, of the same Act states that the State Assistance Commissions for Appeals and the Division of Administrative Review decide as administrative *courts* and that their members are independent and subject only to the law. Para. 3 of the same section denies access to the ordinary courts.

[Requests for assistance are brought before the Local Assistance Commission. Appeals may be taken to the State Assistance Commissions in their capacity as special administrative courts. . . . Certain decisions of the State Assistance Commissions may then be brought to the Division for Administrative Review which examines only points of law.

[In the two proceedings with which the Court is presently concerned, the State Assistance Commissions rejected applications without permitting appeal to the Division for Administrative Review. Against these decisions, the applicants brought actions before the general administrative courts. The Administrative Court of Karlsruhe and the Superior Administrative Court of Hamburg considered themselves prevented by § 69, para. 2, from arriving at a decision on the merits. According to this provision, the State

Assistance Commissions are considered to be special administrative courts, and according to general procedural rules access to the general administrative courts is granted only if there is no particular administrative court competent to decide the question presented. In the view of the Karlsruhe and Hamburg courts, however, the organization of the State Assistance Commissions, as provided for in § 53 of the Act, does not conform to the requirements for a "court" as established in the Basic Law since these commissions act as adjudicatory bodies in the same matters in which their presidents have already participated in the making of the administrative decision in their capacity as directors of the State Assistance Agencies — that is, as ordinary administrative officials bound to directives. Therefore, in the opinion of the two courts, the State Assistance Commissions for Appeals cannot be considered impartial third parties. Both courts, therefore, considered that arts. 92 (on the exercise of judicial power by judges and courts) and 97 (independence of the judiciary) of the Basic Law had been violated. In addition, the Superior Administrative Court of Hamburg considered art. 20, para. 2, second sentence (on the separation of powers), to have been violated. In accordance with art. 100, para. 1, of the Basic Law, the courts suspended the proceeding pending before them and asked the Constitutional Court for a holding on the constitutionality of § 69, para. 2.]

[THE LAW]

. . . .

IV

The decisions of the State Assistance Commissions for Appeals deal with the question of whether the lower bodies charged with the administration of assistance as executive organs under the provisions of the Immediate Assistance Act, in their denial of such assistance, have violated the rights of the applicants. Against such decisions, an injured party must be granted, in accordance with art. 19, para. 4, of the Basic Law, *Rechtsweg,* that is access to the courts.

Access to the ordinary courts is expressly denied by § 69, para. 3. Access to the general administrative courts is, according to the respective procedural statutes of the various administrative courts, permitted only if there is no special administrative court within whose competence the matter falls. The question is whether the State Assistance Commissions for Appeals qualify as special administrative courts, with the consequence that access to other administrative courts is excluded. If this is not the case, then art. 19, para. 4, of the Basic Law would be violated. In such case, § 69, para. 2, would be null and the general administrative courts would have competence. . . .

1. The idea that the requisites, under which an institution can be considered as an ordinary or general administrative court, cannot be applied to special administrative courts is erroneous. The Basic Law comprehends a unitary concept of *Rechtsweg* and "court." It makes no distinction, with regard to the requisites imposed on a court, among the various branches of the judicial machinery. Practical exigencies may require the assignment of experts to the special administrative courts and the organization of these courts in a simpler fashion adapted to the particular branch of administration. Such exigencies, however, cannot avoid the fundamental requisites imposed on all courts.

2.a. Among these requisites, in any case, is that which requires that all members of the court be independent and subject only to the law. This *objective* independence applies to all judges — professional as well as lay judges — in accordance with art. 97, para. 1, of the Basic Law.

b. The *personal* independence of the professional judges (*Berufsrichter*) is accorded by art. 97, para. 2, of the Basic Law. According to this, "judges appointed on a tenured, full-time basis to an established post cannot, against their will, be dismissed, or permanently or temporarily suspended from office, or transferred to another post, or retired before the expiration of their term of office except by virtue of a judicial decision and only on the grounds and in the manner provided for by law. . . ." In this way the Basic Law differs in two essential points from the corresponding rule of the Weimar Constitution (art. 104). That rule concerned only the judges of "ordinary" (civil and criminal) jurisdictions, while art. 97, para. 2, concerns the professional judges of all five branches of the judiciary. Secondly, art. 97, para. 2, does not require, contrary to art. 104 of the Weimar Constitution, life tenure, but leaves this matter to the regulation of the legislative body. The constitutional protection of personal independence is no longer related to life tenure, but to professional assignment to a judicial position for a given period of service.

Art. 97, para. 2, does not expressly say where professional judges must be employed. It cannot be said, however, that a judge assumes personal independence in terms of the Basic Law simply by assignment to office in what is designated by the legislature as a court. The legislature which framed the Constitution took as a point of departure the concept that, when professional judges sit in the courts, they should have tenured, full-time appointments, and the use of probationary judges should take place only within the limits reasonably necessary to allow their training or for other strictly limited reasons.

Art. 97, para. 2, of the Basic Law denies status as a court to a panel when statutory provisions provide that one or more of its members are personally dependent officials who, during their period of service, may be transferred or suspended at any time without judicial proceeding.

Only this interpretation of art. 97, para. 2, of the Basic Law corresponds to the principles of the *Rechtsstaat*. First, it is feared that judges who are constantly endangered by recall feel themselves indirectly limited in their objective independence, and second, the citizen looks with lack of confidence on a court which is composed of judges who are substantially dependent on the executive. This is particularly true if the court must decide on administrative acts concerning that administrative agency which itself decides on the transfer or recall of the judges or exercises considerable influence over such transfer or recall.

c. In addition to freedom from directives, and the above-mentioned measures of institutionally guaranteed personal independence, it is essential to every judicial activity that it be conducted by an impartial third party. This idea is inseparably joined with the concepts of "judge" and "court." If the state or one of its agencies is a party to a proceeding, then in the final analysis there is no third party, but rather it is the state which sits in judgment of itself, as the administrative agencies and courts are both organs of the state. Therefore, the requirement of separation of powers, according to which the judicial function must be exercised by "separate" organs distinct from the legislative and executive powers (art. 20, para. 2, of the Basic Law) assumes, in this connection, a particular importance. Only if the courts are established as separate institutions independent of the executive can the judicial function stand, *through impartial judges,* against the state or its organs in the sense of art. 19, para. 4, of the Basic Law.

Certainly the Basic Law does not require a complete separation of the administrative from the judicial function, but rather allows certain overlappings. No problems exist with respect to the exercise by a judge of administrative duties involved in his official capacity, as traditionally occurs in ordinary jurisdictions even under the provisions of the Basic Law, since the character of the courts as separate organs of state power is not thereby prejudiced. The reconciliation of other overlappings of the courts and administrative agencies with the autonomous nature of the courts required by the Basic Law may, however, be doubted. In any case, given a court whose composition is regulated by statute and which includes personally dependent officials, if we add thereto the fact that these officials [have a dual role, as they] deal, as functionaries bound by directives, with the same matters upon which they are also called to decide as "independent" judges, then such a panel can no longer be considered as a "separate" organ of state power as required by the Basic Law. The official of the administrative body, who is bound by its directives, is, by the nature of things, himself a party. He cannot be transformed for certain matters from a representative of the executive into a representative of the judiciary merely by the utterance of the phrase that he is a judge not bound by directives. Such a mixture of administrative and judicial functions violates the principle of separation of powers in the sense of art. 20, para. 2, of the Basic Law in its very essence.

3. The rules of the Immediate Assistance Act do not grant to the presidents of the State Assistance Commissions for Appeals personal independence for their period of service. The president of such a commission cannot be considered an impartial third party.

The Immediate Assistance Act establishes that the director of the State Assistance Agency, or his representative, serves as president of the State Assistance Commission for Appeals ... but the period of service is not provided for therein, nor is there a guarantee of personal independence for the period of service. The president could, therefore, at any time be recalled or transferred because of supposedly undesirable "judicial" decisions. Personal independence, therefore, does not exist.

Objectively, the director of the State Assistance Agency, as well as his representative, is subject to the control of the Main Office. He must not only follow its directives himself, but must also pass them on to subordinate agencies. ... Such directives concern, among other things, the manner of evaluation of typical fact situations and the interpretation of general legal concepts contained in the Immediate Assistance Act. Where the president of the State Assistance Commission for Appeals disagrees with the opinion expressed in the directives, he must as a judge annul decisions of the Local Assistance Commission based on such directives, while, on the other hand, in his capacity as director of the State Assistance Agency, he is required to induce the subordinate bodies to follow the same directives. In such a situation a judicial decision is made extremely difficult for him. In fact, if as an administrative official, he had accepted the opinion of the superior agency, he could hardly come to a different opinion while serving in his capacity as judge.

The president of the State Assistance Commission for Appeals comes close, therefore, to acting as the judge who decides in his own cause. ...

. . . .

The State Assistance Commissions for Appeals are composed, in addition to the president, of two elected "honorary" associates. We do not need to examine whether these associate members meet the minimum standards of independence imposed for lay judges. This does not alter the fact that the State Assistance Commissions for Appeals are not courts in the sense of the Basic Law. ... The fact that even one member lacks the minimum measure of personal independence and impartiality according to the statutory rules is enough to deny the status of court to a panel.

. . . .

5. Therefore, the State Assistance Commissions for Appeals, as established by the Immediate Assistance Act, are not courts, but organs of internal control of the administration. . . . [They] do not conform to the requirements established for the courts by art. 20, para. 2, of the Basic Law (on the judicial functions of separate bodies) nor to the requirements of art. 97, para. 2 (personal independence of the judge). Since the qualification of the State Assistance Commissions for Appeals as special administrative courts denies access to the courts in the sense of the Basic Law, § 69, para. 2, of the Immediate Assistance Act is contrary to art. 19, para. 4, of the Basic Law and is therefore null.

NOTES AND QUESTIONS

1. What was the practical effect of the German decision? How did that differ from the effect of the Italian decisions? *See* Notes 2 and 3, *supra* § B.1.

2. The rationale of the principal case was confirmed by the Decision of Nov. 17, 1959 (10 BVerfGE 200). The Court invalidated a statute dealing with the jurisdiction of the "Courts of the Peace" of Baden-Württemberg, effectively abolishing these courts (of which there were more than 1400).

In Baden-Württemberg, the administration of justice had always been performed with less formality than in other parts of Germany. "Courts of the Peace" attempted to settle minor disputes in the community, and adjudicated civil controversies involving less than 150 German marks and minor criminal cases. There were two types of such courts: one was a collegial court, the other a single-judge court. The former was composed of the mayor, as president of the court, and two other members elected from the municipal council. In the single-judge form, the judge was chosen by the municipal council and was often the mayor.

The Constitutional Court declared that the "Courts of the Peace" did not meet the minimum standards of judicial independence which required separation of the judicial function from the public administration. The combination of administrative functionary and judge inevitably prejudiced the independence and the objectivity of the person in whom such functions were combined. The Court expressly recognized the value of lay participation in the administration of justice, noting that democratic life, particularly of small communities, may be enhanced by such participation. That value, however, was outweighed by the fundamental value of independence of the adjudicators in the administration of justice.

Following this decision, an attempt was made to preserve the tradition of informal justice by establishing courts composed of single judges elected for six year terms by the relevant town council, empowered only to decide minor property disputes between private persons. Any qualified member of the community, including the mayor, could be elected judge. A challenge to the independence of the judges of the new courts, called "Community Courts," proved unsuccessful, at least in part. Decision of the Constitutional Court of May 9, 1962 (14 BVerfGE 56). In reaching its decision the Court took note of the strong, local tradition favoring a speedy, informal type of justice. The Constitutional Court, however, did strike down one provision of the new law. Judges who were also employees or elected officials of the town were to end their terms as judges at the same time they left the service of the town administration. This feature was found to be invalid because it deprived those judges of independence from those who controlled their municipal employment.

3. United States

a. State Court Judges
WARD v. VILLAGE OF MONROEVILLE

Supreme Court of the United States
409 U.S. 57, 93 S. Ct. 80, 34 L. Ed. 2d 267 (1972)

Mr. Justice Brennan delivered the opinion of the Court.

Pursuant to Ohio Rev. Code Ann. § 1905.01 *et seq.* (1968), which authorizes mayors to sit as judges in cases of ordinance violations and certain traffic offenses, the Mayor of Monroeville, Ohio, convicted petitioner of two traffic offenses and fined him $50 on each. The Ohio Court of Appeals for Huron County, . . . and the Ohio Supreme Court, . . . three justices dissenting, sustained the conviction, rejecting petitioner's objection that trial before a mayor who also had responsibilities for revenue production and law enforcement denied him a trial before a disinterested and impartial judicial officer as guaranteed by the Due Process Clause of the Fourteenth Amendment.

The Mayor of Monroeville has wide executive powers and is the chief conservator of the peace. He is president of the village council, presides at all meetings, votes in case of a tie, accounts annually to the council respecting village finances, fills vacancies in village offices and has general overall supervision of village affairs. A major part of village income is derived from the fines, forfeitures, costs, and fees imposed by him in his mayor's court. Thus, in 1964 this income contributed $23,589.50 of total village revenues of $46,355.38; in 1965 it was $18,508.95 of $46,752.60; in 1966 it was $16,085 of

$43,585.13; in 1967 it was $20,060.65 of $53,931.43; and 1968 it was $23,439.42 of $52,995.95. This revenue was of such importance to the village that when legislation threatened its loss, the village retained a management consultant for advice upon the problem.

Conceding that "the revenue produced from a mayor's court provides a substantial portion of a municipality's funds," the Supreme Court of Ohio held nonetheless that "such fact does not mean that a mayor's impartiality is so diminished thereby that he cannot act in a disinterested fashion in a judicial capacity." ... We disagree with that conclusion. ...

The issue turns, as the Ohio court acknowledged, on whether the Mayor can be regarded as an impartial judge under the principles laid down by this Court in *Tumey* v. *Ohio,* 273 U. S. 510 (1927). There, convictions for prohibition law violations rendered by the Mayor of North College Hill, Ohio, were reversed when it appeared that, in addition to his regular salary, the Mayor received $696.35 from the fees and costs levied by him against alleged violators. This Court held that "it certainly violates the Fourteenth Amendment, and deprives a defendant in a criminal case of due process of law, to subject his liberty or property to the judgment of a court the judge of which has a direct, personal, substantial, pecuniary interest in reaching a conclusion against him in his case."

The fact that the mayor there shared directly in the fees and costs did not define the limits of the principle. Although "the mere union of the executive power and the judicial power in him can not be said to violate due process of law," ... the test is whether the mayor's situation is one "which would offer a possible temptation to the average man as a judge to forget the burden of proof required to convict the defendant, or which might lead him not to hold the balance nice, clear and true between the State and the accused ...." Plainly that "possible temptation" may also exist when the mayor's executive responsibilities for village finances may make him partisan to maintain the high level of contribution from the mayor's court. This, too, is a "situation in which an official perforce occupies two practically and seriously inconsistent positions, one partisan and the other judicial, [and] necessarily involves a lack of due process of law in the trial of defendants charged with crimes before him."

This situation is wholly unlike that in *Dugan* v. *Ohio,* 277 U. S. 61 (1928), which the Ohio Supreme Court deemed controlling here. There the Mayor of Xenia, Ohio, had judicial functions but only very limited executive authority. The city was governed by a commission of five members, including the Mayor, which exercised all legislative powers. A city manager, together with the commission, exercised all executive powers. In those circumstances, this Court held that the Mayor's relationship to the finances and financial policy of the city was too remote to warrant a presumption of bias toward conviction in prosecutions before him as judge.

. . . .

Respondent also argues that any unfairness at the trial level can be corrected on appeal and trial *de novo* in the County Court of Common Pleas. We disagree. This "procedural safeguard" does not guarantee a fair trial in the mayor's court; there is nothing to suggest that the incentive to convict would be diminished by the possibility of reversal on appeal. Nor, in any event, may the State's trial court procedure be deemed constitutionally acceptable simply because the State eventually offers a defendant an impartial adjudication. Petitioner is entitled to a neutral and detached judge in the first instance. Accordingly, the judgment of the Supreme Court of Ohio is reversed and the case is remanded for further proceedings not inconsistent with this opinion.

It is so ordered.

Mr. Justice White, with whom Mr. Justice Rehnquist joins, dissenting.

The Ohio mayor who judged this case had no direct financial stake in its outcome. *Tumey* v. *Ohio,* 273 U. S. 510 (1927), is therefore not controlling, and I would not extend it.

To justify striking down the Ohio system on its face, the Court must assume either that every mayor-judge in every case will disregard his oath and administer justice contrary to constitutional commands or that this will happen often enough to warrant the prophylactic, *per se* rule urged by petitioner. I can make neither assumption with respect to Ohio mayors nor with respect to similar officials in 16 other States. Hence, I would leave the due process matter to be decided on a case-by-case basis, a question which, as I understand the posture of this case, is not now before us. I would affirm the judgment.

NOTES AND QUESTIONS

1. Claims of judicial bias can come in many forms — previous involvement in the case, relationship of the judge to a party or counsel, personal antagonism to a party, etc. Do the *Tumey* and *Ward* cases mean that routine issues of judicial disqualification become issues of due process of law under the Fourteenth Amendment? * (Note that, to the extent that issues of procedural fairness are translated into issues of due process, federal judges have the last word on when state judges should recuse themselves.)

---

* Note also, *In re Murchison,* 349 U.S. 133 (1955), which is discussed in the case of *Withrow* v. *Larkin,* reproduced below.

2. Do *Tumey* and *Ward* establish a narrower constitutional rule than the German decision of November 17, 1959, discussed in note 2 of the previous section of this chapter? If so, why? Would it make sense in the United States to further prohibit, by a constitutional rule, service by executive officials as state court judges?

b. Administrative Agencies

[W]e . . . recognize the importance of not imposing upon the States or the Federal Government in this developing field of law any procedural requirements beyond those demanded by rudimentary due process. . . . [T]he decisionmaker's conclusion . . . must rest solely on the legal rules and evidence adduced at the hearing. . . . And, of course, an impartial decision maker is essential. (Mr. Justice Brennan for the Court in *Goldberg* v. *Kelly,* 397 U.S. 254, 267, 271 [1970].)

WITHROW v. LARKIN

Supreme Court of the United States
421 U.S. 35, 95 S. Ct. 1456, 13 L. Ed. 2d 712 (1975)

MR. JUSTICE WHITE delivered the opinion of the Court.

. . . .

I

Appellee, a resident of Michigan and licensed to practice medicine there, obtained a Wisconsin license in August 1971 under a reciprocity agreement between Michigan and Wisconsin governing medical licensing. His practice in Wisconsin consisted of performing abortions at an office in Milwaukee. On June 20, 1973, the Board sent to appellee a notice that it would hold an investigative hearing on July 12, 1973, under Wis. Stat. Ann. § 488.17 to determine whether he had engaged in certain proscribed acts. The hearing would be closed to the public, although appellee and his attorney could attend. They would not, however, be permitted to cross-examine witnesses. Based upon the evidence presented at the hearing, the Board would decide "whether to warn or reprimand if it finds such practice and whether to institute criminal action or action to revoke license if probable cause therefor exists under criminal or revocation statutes."

On July 6, 1973, appellee filed his complaint in this action under 42 U. S. C. § 1983 seeking preliminary and permanent injunctive relief and a temporary restraining order preventing the Board from investigating him and from conducting the investigative hearing. The District Court denied the motion for a temporary restraining order.

. . . .

The Board proceeded with its investigative hearing on July 12 and 13, 1973; numerous witnesses testified and appellee's counsel was present throughout the proceedings. Appellee's counsel was subsequently informed that appellee could, if he wished, appear before the Board to explain any of the evidence which had been presented.

On September 18, 1973, the Board sent to appellee a notice that a "contested hearing" would be held on October 4, 1973, to determine whether appellee had engaged in certain prohibited acts and that based upon the evidence adduced at the hearing the Board would determine whether his license would be suspended temporarily under Wis. Stat. § 448.18(7). Appellee moved for a restraining order against the contested hearing. The District Court granted the motion on October 1, 1973. Because the Board had moved from purely investigative proceedings to a hearing aimed at deciding whether suspension of appellee's license was appropriate, the District Court concluded that a substantial federal question had arisen, namely, whether the authority given to appellants both "to investigate physicians and present charges [and] to rule on those charges and impose punishment, at least to the extent of reprimanding or temporarily suspending" violated appellee's due process rights.

. . . .

On November 19, 1973, the three-judge District Court found (with an opinion following on December 21, 1973) that § 448.18(7) was unconstitutional as a violation of due process guarantees and enjoined the Board from enforcing it.

. . . .

III

The District Court framed the constitutional issue, which it addressed as being whether "for the board temporarily to suspend Dr. Larkin's license at its own contested hearing on charges evolving from its own investigation would constitute a denial to him of his rights to procedural due process." [13] . . .

. . . .

Concededly, a "fair trial in a fair tribunal is a basic requirement of due process." *In re Murchison,* 349 U. S. 133, 136 (1955). This applies to administrative agencies which adjudicate as well as to courts. *Gibson* v. *Berryhill,* 411 U. S. 564, 579 (1973). Not only is

---

[13] After the District Court made its decision, the Board altered its procedures. It now assigns each new case to one of the members for investigation, and the remainder of the Board has no contact with the investigative process. That change, designed to accommodate the Board's procedures to the District Court's decision, does not affect this case.

a biased decisionmaker constitutionally unacceptable but "our system of law has always endeavored to prevent even the probability of unfairness." *In re Murchison, supra,* at 136; cf. *Tumey* v. *Ohio,* 273 U. S. 510, 532 (1927). In pursuit of this end, various situations have been identified in which experience teaches that the probability of actual bias on the part of the judge or decisionmaker is too high to be constitutionally tolerable. Among these cases are those in which the adjudicator has a pecuniary interest in the outcome and in which he has been the target of personal abuse or criticism from the party before him.

The contention that the combination of investigative and adjudicative functions necessarily creates an unconstitutional risk of bias in administrative adjudication has a much more difficult burden of persuasion to carry. It must overcome a presumption of honesty and integrity in those serving as adjudicators; and it must convince that, under a realistic appraisal of psychological tendencies and human weakness, conferring investigative and adjudicative powers on the same individuals poses such a risk of actual bias or prejudgment that the practice must be forbidden if the guarantee of due process is to be adequately implemented.

Very similar claims have been squarely rejected in prior decisions of this Court. In *FTC* v. *Cement Institute,* 333 U. S. 683 (1948), the Commission had instituted proceedings concerning the respondents' multiple basing-point delivered-price system. It was demanded that the Commission members disqualify themselves because long before the Commission had filed its complaint it had investigated the parties and reported to Congress and to the President, and its members had testified before congressional committees concerning the legality of such a pricing system. At least some of the members had disclosed their opinion that the system was illegal. The issue of bias was brought here and confronted "on the assumption that such an opinion had been formed by the entire membership of the Commission as a result of its prior official investigations." *Id.,* at 700.

The Court rejected the claim, saying:

> "[T]he fact that the Commission had entertained such views as the result of its prior *ex parte* investigations did not necessarily mean that the minds of its members were irrevocably closed on the subject of the respondents' basing point practices. Here, in contrast to the Commission's investigations, members of the cement industry were legally authorized participants in the hearings. They produced evidence — volumes of it. They were free to point out to the Commission by testimony, by cross-examination of witnesses, and by arguments, conditions of the trade practices under attack which they though kept these practices within the range of legally permissible business activities." *Id.,* at 701.

In specific response to a due process argument, the Court asserted:

"No decision of this Court would require us to hold that it would be a violation of procedural due process for a judge to sit in a case after he had expressed an opinion as to whether certain types of conduct were prohibited by law. In fact, judges frequently try the same case more than once and decide identical issues each time, although these issues involve questions both of law and fact. Certainly, the Federal Trade Commission cannot possibly be under stronger constitutional compulsions in this respect than a court." *Id.*, at 702-703 (footnote omitted).

This Court has also ruled that a hearing examiner who has recommended findings of fact after rejecting certain evidence as not being probative was not disqualified to preside at further hearings that were required when reviewing courts held that the evidence had been erroneously excluded. *NLRB* v. *Donnelly Garment Co.,* 330 U.S. 219, 236-237 (1947). The Court of Appeals had decided that the examiner should not again sit because it would be unfair to require the parties to try "issues of fact to those who may have prejudged them. . . ." 151 F. 2d 854, 870 (CA8 1945). But this Court unanimously reversed, saying:

"Certainly it is not the rule of judicial administration that, statutory requirements apart . . . a judge is disqualified from sitting in a retrial because he was reversed on earlier rulings. We find no warrant for imposing upon administrative agencies a stiffer rule, whereby examiners would be disentitled to sit because they ruled strongly against a party in the first hearing." *Donnelly Garment Co., supra,* at 236-237.

More recently we have sustained against due process objection a system in which a Social Security examiner has responsibility for developing the facts and making a decision as to disability claims, and observed that the challenge to this combination of functions "assumes too much and would bring down too many procedures designed, and working well, for a governmental structure of great and growing complexity." *Richardson* v. *Perales,* 402 U. S. 389, 410 (1971).[16]

---

[16] The decisions of the courts of appeals touching upon this question of bias arising from a combination of functions are also instructive. In *Pangburn* v. *CAB,* 311 F. 2d 349 (CA1 1962), the Board had the responsibility of making an accident report and also reviewing the decision of a trial examiner that the pilot involved in the accident should have his airline transport pilot rating suspended. The pilot claimed that his right to procedural due process had been violated by the fact that the Board was not an impartial tribunal in deciding his appeal from the trial examiner's decision since it had previously issued its accident report finding pilot error to be the probable cause of the crash. The Court of Appeals found the Board's procedures to be constitutionally permissible:

That is not to say that there is nothing to the argument that those who have investigated should not then adjudicate. The issue is substantial, it is not new, and legislators and others concerned with the operations of administrative agencies have given much attention to whether and to what extent distinctive administrative functions should be performed by the same persons. No single answer has been reached. Indeed, the growth, variety, and complexity of the administrative processes have made any one solution highly unlikely. Within the Federal Government itself, Congress has addressed the issue in several different ways, providing for varying degrees of separation from complete separation of functions to virtually none at all. For the generality of agencies, Congress has been content with § 5 of the Administrative Procedure Act, 5 U. S. C. § 554 (d), which provides that no employee engaged in investigating or prosecuting may also participate or advise in the adjudicating function, but which also expressly exempts from this prohibition "the agency or a member or members of the body comprising the agency." [18]

"[W]e cannot say that the mere fact that a tribunal has had contact with a particular factual complex in a prior hearing, or indeed has taken a public position on the facts, is enough to place that tribunal under a constitutional inhibition to pass upon the facts in a subsequent hearing. We believe that more is required. Particularly is this so in the instant case where the Board's prior contact with the case resulted from its following the Congressional mandate to investigate and report the probable cause of all civil air accidents." *Id.,* at 358.

Those cases in which due process violations have been found are characterized by factors not present in the record before us in this litigation, and we need not pass upon their validity. In *American Cyanimid Co.* v. *FTC,* 363 F. 2d 757 (CA6 1966), one of the commissioners had previously served actively as counsel for a Senate subcommittee investigating many of the same facts and issues before the Commission for consideration. In *Texaco, Inc.* v. *FTC,* 118 U. S. App. D. C. 366, 336 F. 2d 754 (1964), vacated on other grounds, 381 U. S. 739 (1965), the court found that a speech made by a commissioner clearly indicated that he had already to some extent reached a decision as to matters pending before the Commission. See also *Cinderella Career & Finishing Schools, Inc.* v. *FTC,* 138 U. S. App. D. C. 152, 158-161, 425 F. 2d 583, 589-592 (1970). *Amos Treat & Co.* v. *SEC,* 113 U. S. App. D. C. 100, 306 F. 2d 260 (1962), presented a situation in which one of the members of the Commission had previously participated as an employee in the investigation of charges pending before the Commission. In *Trans World Airlines* v. *CAB,* 102 U. S. App. D. C. 391, 254 F. 2d 90 (1958), a commissioner had signed a brief in behalf of one of the parties in the proceedings prior to assuming membership on the Board.

[18] The statute provides in pertinent part:

"An employee or agent engaged in the performance of investigative or prosecuting functions for an agency in a case may not, in that or a factually related case, participate or advise in the decision, recommended decision, or agency review pursuant to section 557 of this title, except as witness or counsel in public proceedings. This subsection does not apply —

"(A) in determing applications for initial licenses;

"(B) to proceedings involving the validity or application of rates, facilities, or practices of public utilities or carriers; or

"(C) to the agency or a member or members of the body comprising the agency."

It is not surprising, therefore, to find that "[t]he case law, both federal and state, generally rejects the idea that the combination [of] judging [and] investigating functions is a denial of due process . . . ." 2 K. Davis, Administrative Law Treatise § 13.02, p. 175 (1958). Similarly, our cases, although they reflect the substance of the problem, offer no support for the bald proposition applied in this case by the District Court that agency members who participate in an investigation are disqualified from adjudicating. The incredible variety of administrative mechanisms in this country will not yield to any single organizing principle.

Appellee relies heavily on *In re Murchison, supra,* in which a state judge, empowered under state law to sit as a "one-man grand jury" and to compel witnesses to testify before him in secret about possible crimes, charged two such witnesses with criminal contempt, one for perjury and the other for refusing to answer certain questions, and then himself tried and convicted them. This Court found the procedure to be a denial of due process of law not only because the judge in effect became part of the prosecution and assumed an adversary position, but also because as a judge, passing on guilt or innocence, he very likely relied on "his own personal knowledge and impression of what had occurred in the grand jury room," an impression that "could not be tested by adequate cross-examination." 349 U. S., at 138.[19]

Plainly enough, *Murchison* has not been understood to stand for the broad rule that the members of an administrative agency may not investigate the facts, institute proceedings, and then make the necessary adjudications. The court did not purport to question the *Cement Institute* case, *supra,* or the Administrative Procedure Act and did not lay down any general principle that a judge before whom an alleged contempt is committed may not bring and preside over the ensuing contempt proceedings. The accepted rule is to the contrary. . . .

Nor is there anything in this case that comes within the strictures of *Murchison.* When the Board instituted its investigative procedures, it stated only that it would investigate whether proscribed conduct had occurred. Later in noticing the adversary hearing, it asserted only that it would determine if violations had been committed which would warrant suspension of appellee's license. Without doubt, the Board then anticipated that the proceeding would eventuate in an adjudication of the issue; but there

---

[19] Appellee also relies upon statements made by the Court in *Pickering* v. *Board of Education,* 391 U.S., at 578-579, n. 2. In that case, however, unlike the present one, "the trier of fact was the same body that was also both the victim of appellant's statements and the prosecutor that brought the charges aimed at securing his dismissal." *Ibid.* In any event, the Court did not analyze the question raised by this case because the appellant in *Pickering* had not raised a due process contention in the state proceedings.

was no more evidence of bias or the risk of bias or prejudgment than inhered in the very fact that the Board had investigated and would now adjudicate. Of course, we should be alert to the possibilities of bias that may lurk in the way particular procedures actually work in practice. The processes utilized by the Board, however, do not in themselves contain an unacceptable risk of bias. The investigative proceeding had been closed to the public, but appellee and his counsel were permitted to be present throughout; counsel actually attended the hearings and knew the facts presented to the Board. No specific foundation has been presented for suspecting that the Board had been prejudiced by its investigation or would be disabled from hearing and deciding on the basis of the evidence to be presented at the contested hearing. The mere exposure to evidence presented in nonadversary investigative procedures is insufficient in itself to impugn the fairness of the Board members at a later adversary hearing. Without a showing to the contrary, state administrators "are assumed to be men of conscience and intellectual discipline, capable of judging a particular controversy fairly on the basis of its own circumstances." *United States* v. *Morgan,* 313 U. S. 409, 421 (1941).

We are of the view, therefore, that the District Court was in error when it entered the restraining order against the Board's contested hearing. . . .

IV

. . . .

Judges repeatedly issue arrest warrants on the basis that there is probable cause to believe that a crime has been committed and that the person named in the warrant has committed it. Judges also preside at preliminary hearings where they must decide whether the evidence is sufficient to hold a defendant for trial. Neither of these pretrial involvements has been thought to raise any constitutional barrier against the judge's presiding over the criminal trial and, if the trial is without a jury, against making the necessary determination of guilt or innocence. Nor has it been thought that a judge is disqualified from presiding over injunction proceedings because he has initially assessed the facts in issuing or denying a temporary restraining order or a preliminary injunction. It is also very typical for the members of administrative agencies to receive the results of investigations, to approve the filing of charges or formal complaints instituting enforcement proceedings, and then to participate in the ensuing hearings. This mode of procedure does not violate the Administrative Procedure Act, and it does not violate due process of law.[24] We should also remember that it is not contrary to due

---

[24] "The Act does not and probably should not forbid the combination with judging of instituting proceedings, negotiating settlements, or testifying. What

process to allow judges and administrators who have had their initial decisions reversed on appeal to confront and decide the same questions a second time around.

. . . .

[J]ust as there is no logical inconsistency between a finding of probable cause and an acquittal in a criminal proceeding, there is no incompatibility between the agency filing a complaint based on probable cause and a subsequent decision, when all the evidence is in, that there has been no violation of the statute. Here, if the Board now proceeded after an adversary hearing to determine that appellee's license to practice should not be temporarily suspended, it would not implicitly be admitting error in its prior finding of probable cause. Its position most probably would merely reflect the benefit of a more complete view of the evidence afforded by an adversary hearing.

The initial charge or determination of probable cause and the ultimate adjudication have different bases and purposes. The fact that the same agency makes them in tandem and that they relate to the same issues does not result in a procedural due process violation. Clearly, if the initial view of the facts based on the evidence derived from nonadversarial processes as a practical or legal matter foreclosed fair and effective consideration at a subsequent adversary hearing leading to ultimate decision, a substantial due process question would be raised. But in our view, that is not this case.[25]

That the combination of investigative and adjudicative functions does not, without more, constitute a due process violation, does not, of course, preclude a court from determining from the special facts and circumstances present in the case before it that the risk of unfairness is intolerably high.

The judgment of the District Court is reversed and the case is remanded to that court for further proceedings consistent with this opinion.

So ordered.

---

heads of agencies do in approving the institution of proceedings is much like what judges do in ruling on demurrers or motions to dismiss. When the same examiner conducts a pre-hearing conference and then presides at the hearing, the harm, if any, is slight, and it probably goes more to impairment of effectiveness in mediation than to contamination of judging. If deciding officers may consult staff specialists who have not testified, they should be allowed to consult those who have testified; the need here is not for protection against contamination but is assurance of appropriate opportunity to meet what is considered." 2 K. Davis, Administrative Law Treatise § 13.11, p. 249 (1958).

[25] Quite apart from precedents and considerations concerning the constitutionality of a combination of functions in one agency, the District Court rested its decision upon *Gagnon* v. *Scarpelli,* 411 U. S. 778 (1973), and *Morrissey* v. *Brewer,* 408 U. S. 471 (1972). These decisions, however, pose a very different question. Each held that when review of an initial decision is mandated, the decisionmaker must be other than the one who made the decision under review.

NOTES AND QUESTIONS

1. Does Justice White's opinion rest on the rationale that administrative agencies are very different from courts, and that due process standards of judicial impartiality should not apply to an endless variety of administrative adjudication? Or, is it based on the rationale that due process requirements of impartiality for administrative agencies are no different than those applicable to courts?

2. Notice the reference, in footnote 16 of the opinion, to lower court cases which found due process violations in an administrative decisionmaker's lack of impartiality. While the Court distinguishes these cases, it is also quite careful not to "pass upon their validity." In light of the Court's rationale, however, are any of these decisions reliable precedents on the issue of constitutional requirements for impartiality?

3. The Court's discussion of the Administrative Procedure Act demonstrates that there has been increasing concern with separating the functions of prosecution and decision, at least at lower levels within administrative agencies. To the extent that requiring separation of functions represents a judgment that this is required by rudimentary notions of fairness, are there nevertheless good reasons not to incorporate those notions into constitutional norms? Are there reasons for more stringent constitutional rules concerning separation of functions within European administrative courts than those concerning separation of functions within administrative agencies in the United States?

4. In footnote 25, the Court distinguishes cases which require that an administrative decisionmaker be someone other than the person whose decision is being reviewed. *Goldberg* required that a fair hearing for welfare recipients whose benefits had been terminated be conducted by someone other than the caseworker who made the initial decision to terminate benefits. *Gagnon* and *Morrissey* required that probation and parole hearings be conducted by someone other than the probation or parole officer who had made the initial decision to revoke probation or parole. Can the fair hearing required by due process ever be held by administrators reviewing the correctness of their own decision? Could a public school board which had decided to fire a tenured teacher constitutionally preside at the teacher's hearing? *See Pickering* v. *Board of Education,* 391 U.S. 563, 578-79, n. 2 (1968) (cited in footnote 19 of *Withrow*). *Cf. Goss* v. *Lopez,* 419 U.S. 565 (1975) (temporary suspension of public school pupil). Should *Larkin* have been permitted to prove that the Michigan medical licensing board had, in fact, prejudged his case?

Gagnon, supra, at 785-786; *Morrissey, supra,* at 485-486; see also *Goldberg* v. *Kelly,* 397 U.S. 254, 271 (1970). Allowing a decisionmaker to review and evaluate his own prior decisions raises problems that are not present here. Under the controlling statutes, the Board is at no point called upon to review its own prior decisions.

C. INDEPENDENCE FROM IMPROPER INFLUENCE BY THE PARTIES TO THE LITIGATION AND BY INTEREST GROUPS

(X v. AUSTRIA)

European Commission of Human Rights, Decision of August 4, 1960
[1960] 3 Y.B. Eur. Conv. on Human Rights 288

THE FACTS: The Applicant is an Austrian citizen and a barrister-at-law. . . .

On July 10, 1959, in accordance with art. 19 of the Austrian Judicial Organisation Act, . . . the Applicant, who was party to a divorce suit against his wife, entered a challenge *propter affectum* against the judge appointed to hear the case. . . .

In support of his challenge the Applicant put forward a number of grounds all of which were based on the difference between the judge's attitude towards himself and his wife. He stated, in particular, that after the hearing of June 2, 1959 — which incidentally did not bring the proceedings to an end — and when everyone had left the Court, the judge remained behind with the Applicant's wife and spoke with her, whereas a few days earlier he had refused to speak with the Applicant who was anxious to draw his attention "to the opinions expressed in the legal textbooks and to the relevant case law."

The Applicant, in support of his right of challenge *propter affectum,* referred both to art. 19 of the above-mentioned Act and art. 6 of the Convention on Human Rights and Fundamental Freedoms which provides that "everyone is entitled to a fair and public hearing within a reasonable time by an independent and impartial tribunal established by law."

The Applicant's challenge was rejected by the Civil Court of . . . Province in its decision of July 21, 1959. The Tribunal stated:

— that, inasmuch as the grounds for challenge referred to events prior to the hearing of June 2, 1959, at which the Applicant appeared although without making any reference to the said grounds, the plea must be rejected in accordance with art. 21, para. 2, of the Austrian Judicial Organisation Act which provides that the right of challenge *propter affectum* cannot be exercised as long as the party concerned continues to take part in the hearing;

— that the other reasons put forward by the Applicant, and in particular the conversation of the judge with the Applicant's wife after the hearing, did not constitute sufficient grounds for challenge. Finally the Court stated that there was no reason to suppose that the judge was influenced in his decision by "personal considerations."

The Applicant appealed from the decision of July 21, 1959. He reiterated and indeed supplemented the list of grounds for challenge indicated in his initial plea. He also pointed out that, by virtue of the entry into force of the Convention (notably art. 6), art. 21, para. 2, of the above-mentioned Austrian Act had been modified and that, in consequence, his challenge *propter affectum* was no longer subject to certain conditions. The lower Court was therefore wrong in introducing the time factor as ground for rejecting one part of his application.

In its decision of August 18, 1959, the Provincial Court of Appeal ... held that the said art. 21, para. 2, was in no way inconsistent with art. 6 of the Convention. It pointed out in particular that "the two reservations (made by Austria) expressly prevented any interpretation to the effect that Austrian laws should be modified in the light of art. 6 of the Convention." * For the rest the Court adopted all the reasons of the Court of first instance.

In his Application, Mr. X. maintains that the Convention, which has become an integral part of Austrian law and the provisions of which are "unconditional," has been violated in this case. He emphasises that the divorce proceedings have been going on for more than a year and a half. He asks the Commission to find that "the Convention had been violated in his case";

Whereas the Applicant complains that his right "to a fair hearing ... by an independent and impartial tribunal" guaranteed by art. 6 of the Convention, has been violated in his case; whereas in his view this violation has resulted from the rejection, by application of art. 21, para. 2, of the Austrian Judicial Organisation Act, of the grounds for challenge based on events prior to the hearing of June 2, 1959, and the rejection, as insufficient to justify challenging the judge, of the grounds relating to events subsequent to the above-mentioned hearing of June 2, 1959.

THE LAW

In regard to the first ground;

Whereas, inasmuch as the Applicant in support of his challenge referred to events prior to the hearing of June 2, 1959, his claim was rejected in accordance with art. 21, para. 2, of the Austrian Judicial Organisation Act; whereas the said article provides substantially that the right of challenge *propter affectum* does not apply when the allegedly injured party continues to take part in the hearing; whereas, therefore, the issue is whether or not art. 21, para. 2, is compatible

---

* Article 64 of the Convention provides:

"1. Any State may, when signing this Convention or when depositing its instrument of ratification, make a reservation in respect of any particular provision of the Convention to the extent that any law then in force in its territory is not in conformity with the provision. Reservations of a general character shall not be permitted under this Article.
2. Any reservation made under this Article shall contain a brief statement of the law concerned."

with art. 6, para. 1, of the Convention, which guarantees to all litigants the right to be heard by an impartial tribunal; whereas the limitation of the right of challenge *propter affectum* provided for by the said art. 21, para. 2, does not appear to the Commission to be contrary to art. 6, para. 1, of the Convention; whereas the intention of the Austrian legislator in imposing such a limitation was to prevent the course of law being constantly interrupted by interlocutory judgments; whereas the said limitation was likewise justified by reason of the implicit renunciation by the interested party of his right of challenge in regard to facts which might reasonably be considered to be established, in that without objecting to them, he continued to take part in the hearing; whereas, moreover, the examination of the file shows that by rejecting the challenge entered by the Applicant, the Austrian Tribunals were not applying art. 21, para. 2, of the Austrian Judicial Organisation Act in a manner contrary to the Convention, in particular art. 6, para. 1; and whereas therefore this part of the Application must be rejected as manifestly ill-founded in accordance with art. 27, para. 2, of the Convention;

In regard to the second ground:

Whereas, inasmuch as the Applicant supports his Application with grounds based on events subsequent to the hearing of June 2, 1959, his plea was rejected as ill-founded; whereas in the opinion of the Commission the facts as submitted by the Applicant in particular the judge's conversation in private with the Applicant's wife, are not sufficient to justify the presumption that the Court was no longer impartial; whereas, in other words, the Applicant has failed to submit sufficient factual elements to enable the Commission to find *prima facie* evidence of the partiality of the Court hearing his case; whereas it follows that the Application must be rejected ... as manifestly ill-founded in accordance with art. 27, para. 2, of the Convention;

Now therefore the Commission
DECLARES THIS APPLICATION INADMISSIBLE.

NOTES AND QUESTIONS

1. Accepting the right of the member states to regulate diverse aspects of their own procedures, does the limitation imposed by art. 21, para. 2, of the Austrian Judicial Organisation Act appear justifiable in view of its purpose? Is it too severe? While a single act of the judge may be insufficient basis for disqualification, should it be the basis for disqualification when there is a series of similar acts? If so, should not disqualification be based on the judge's comportment throughout the entire proceeding?

2. Does the Commission indicate that if sufficient evidence of personal bias had been adduced, the application would have been

admissible? Would that kind of personal bias in a judge presiding in a divorce case in the United States be a violation of due process? *See* note 1 following *Ward* v. *Village of Monroeville, supra* § B.3.a.

3. A challenge in the German Constitutional Court to the German Social Courts argued both influence by a lay organization and by a party to the action. Each division is composed, as a tribunal of first instance, of one professional judge who acts as president, and two lay judges selected by the government from lists prepared by professional, service, labor, or other "interested" organizations. One of the two lay judges must be chosen from the list provided by an organization "interested" on behalf of the plaintiff and the other from the list provided by an organization "interested" on behalf of the defendant.

In a controversy between a physician who was participating in the government health insurance program and his own professional organization, both lay judges were physicians selected (for four year terms) from the list prepared by the defendant professional organization since that organization was the "interested" organization both for itself and for physicians involved in controversies in matters of social assistance. The plaintiff-physician challenged the independence of these physician-judges on the ground that the two lay judges were chosen from a list prepared by an organization which really represented his adversary in the controversy.

The Court rejected this challenge (Decision of Dec. 17, 1969, 27 BVerfGE 312) because, *inter alia,* (1) these judges have expertise in this type of problem; (2) there was no indication that the judge would act in a biased manner; and (3) the defendant always has an opportunity to challenge the judge for lack of impartiality. Are there good grounds to distinguish the organization's representatives here from the civil servant in the State Assistance Commission case, *supra* § B.2? Is there more or less pressure brought to bear on their decisions?

4. In *Calibeo et al.* v. *President of the Council of Ministers, Corte Costituzionale,* Decision of Dec. 20, 1962, [1962] 7 Giur. Cost. 1451; [1962] 15 Rac. uff. corte cost. 199; [1963] 86 Foro It. I, 11, special divisions of the ordinary courts organized to deal with agriculture disputes were found to be unconstitutional in their composition. The "experts," who in essence acted as lay judges, lacked the independence required of the judiciary under arts. 102 and 108 of the Constitution. Each "expert" had to be selected from two names furnished by their professional associations, thus giving these bodies the power to influence the composition of the divisions. Moreover, the associations had the power to require the substitution of the "experts" at any time.

After this judgment the legislature revised the procedure for choosing "expert" members of the tribunals. The law of March 2, 1963, No. 320, [1963] Legislazione Italiana I, 1061, provides that each field office of the agricultural department, with the advice of the appropriate labor unions and the competent associations of agricultural professionals, will prepare a directory of those local persons they think qualified. Thereafter, the Chief Judge of the relevant Court of Appeal authenticates the relevant directory and chooses eight names for each agricultural division from which two experts as well as two substitute experts will be chosen. This final choice is made by lot. The *Corte Costituzionale* has rejected a constitutional challenge to both the manner of selection established by this law and to the independence of the experts selected according to its terms. Decision of Apr. 2, 1970, [1970] 15 Giur. Cost. 595.

5. In the United States, issues concerning media coverage of criminal trials are viewed as representing a conflict between constitutional guarantees of a free press and of a fair trial. (The considerable developments in this field of American constitutional law are, however, beyond the scope of this book. *See, e.g., Nebraska Press Ass'n* v. *Stuart,* 427 U.S. 539 (1976).) Similar problems have arisen in Europe and, in some cases, have been viewed as an issue of independence of the judiciary. In the *Fundres* case — Application No. 788160 (*Austria* v. *Italy*), European Commission of Human Rights, Decision of January 11, 1961, [1961] 4 Y.B. Eur. Conv. on Human Rights 116, defendants of German ethnic origin were tried in an Italian court for murder of an Italian official. The court in Trent, a region ethnically divided between Italian and German speaking people, had four Italian speaking lay members and two who were German speaking. The Commission concluded that the Italian speaking lay members had been subjected to improper influence by a combination of coverage of the trial in the Italian press, political tension, and improper argument by the public prosecutor and by civil parties to the case.

Chapter 9

THE "NATURAL JUDGE"

The right to be heard by a "natural" or "lawful" judge is a fundamental concept in continental Europe, and it is, accordingly, specifically guaranteed in the post-war constitutions. Article 25, para. 1, of the Italian Constitution assures that "no one shall be denied the right to be tried by his natural judge pre-established by statute." Article 101, para. 1, of the Bonn Constitution provides: "Extraordinary courts shall be inadmissible. No one may be removed from the jurisdiction of his lawful judge."

These provisions may be used for a variety of purposes. However, this chapter will focus on the right to adjudication before a court and judge predetermined by a general rule of law. This is also the concern of the final clause of art. 6, para. 1, first sentence, of the European Convention on Human Rights:

> In the determination of his civil rights and obligations or of any criminal charge against him, everyone is entitled to a fair and public hearing ... by an independent and impartial tribunal *established by law.* [Emphasis added.]

Although there is no explicit "natural judge" provision in the French Constitution, the *Conseil Constitutionnel* has interpreted the general equality clause of the Constitution to include a natural judge requirement. *See* Decision of July 23, 1975, *infra* § B.3. This demonstrates the basic nature of the natural judge concept in continental legal systems. That concept, however, is almost unknown in American and English jurisprudence. As you read the European decisions in this Chapter, consider what reasons explain the absence, in the United States, of a principle of procedural fairness considered to be central and fundamental in continental Europe.

A. DISCRETION IN THE CHOICE OF THE COURT

The principal requirement of the natural judge concept is that adjudication must proceed in a court predetermined by law.

The *Corte Costituzionale* addressed this aspect in *Pepe,* Decision of July 7, 1962; [1962] 7 Giur. Cost. 959; [1962] 15 Rac. uff. corte cost. 51; [1962] 85 Foro It. I, 1217; [1962] 114 Giur. Ital. I, 1409. Article 30 of the Code of Criminal Procedure gave the public prosecutor discretionary power to remove a proceeding from the *Tribunale* * to the *Pretura* ** when, in his opinion, not subject to review, extenuating circumstances existed which would reduce the appropriate sanction sufficiently to bring it within the competence of the *Pretura.* The court held that the discretionary power possessed by the Public Prosecutor would serve to deprive the accused of his "natural and lawfully appointed judge." The court pointed out that, although the concept of the "natural judge" appears to serve essentially the same function as the provision in art. 102 of the Constitution (which precludes the appointment of extraordinary or special judges), it has a different purpose. Article 102 was created to prohibit extraordinary (*ad hoc*) courts. The natural judge concept of art. 25, however, prohibits the abuses which might follow from *a posteriori* court selection.

However, in Germany the Constitutional Court upheld a statute which allowed the public prosecutor to transfer the trial of certain crimes from the *Amtsgericht* *** to the *Landgericht* *** if the prosecutor determined that the crime charged was of "particular importance." Decision of March 19, 1959, 9 BVerfGE 223. The Court, in holding that the criterion of particular importance of the crime was "sufficiently precise" and subject to review by the criminal judge, concluded that transfer did not depend on a discretionary act of the public prosecutor.

NOTES AND QUESTIONS

1. Do the Italian and German decisions both permit transfer of a case to another court if the standard of decision is "sufficiently precise"? (Consider, also, *Casoli, infra* § C.) If so, can you decide whether the Italian and German cases are consistent in their application of that standard? The German statute allowed greater judicial review of the prosecutor's decision of choice of tribunal than did the Italian statute. Would that justify a different criterion for the degree of allowable imprecision? Note that in the Italian case the discretion rested solely in the public prosecutor, whereas in Germany the judge may review the decision.

2. In a decision rendered on May 5, 1967, No. 56,**** the *Corte Costituzionale* again dealt with the "natural judge" concept. In that case, the defendant in a criminal proceeding challenged a legislative enactment that reshuffled the territorial jurisdiction boundaries of certain courts. The law provided that after September 1, 1964, all

---

* On the *Tribunale, see Carabba,* Ch. 6, § C.1., *supra.*

** On the *Pretura, see Stroppa,* Ch. 6, § B.2.a., *supra.*

*** On the *Amtsgericht* and *Landgericht, see* Ch. 7, § A.2., *supra.*

**** Decision Of May 5, 1967, Corte cost., [1967] 12 Giru. Cost. 654; [1967] 25 Rac. uff. corte cost. 405; [1967] 19 Giur. Ital. I, 732.

cases would be transferred to and decided by the court competent under the new law. Criminal and civil cases in the trial phase were excepted from the transfer requirement. The *ordinanza* of the lower court, however, argued that art. 25, para. 1 of the Constitution required that all pending cases be decided by the court that was competent at the time when charges had been filed. The *Corte Costituzionale* rejected the argument that venue could never be changed once a proceeding had begun without depriving the defendant of his "natural judge." The Court reasoned that the phrase "natural judge pre-established by law" in art. 25, para. 1, requires that the competent judge be determined by a legislative act which was not designed to choose particular judges for particular cases. The challenged statute changed court territorial boundaries as part of a general reform of venue and thus was not an *ad hoc* attempt to influence judicial selection.

3. As the *Corte Costituzionale* indicated, the ideal of the natural judge concept is that the court be predetermined by general statutory rules. However, as the German decision of March 19, 1959, demonstrates, it is not necessary that the court be chosen automatically by a statutory rule. Another example is the German decision of January 16, 1957,* where the Constitutional Court affirmed that ". . . it does not violate art. 101, para. 1, second sentence of the Basic Law that in the case of concurrent competence of two organs of the judiciary — one being regional and the other federal — the legislature entrusts, on the basis of specific objective criteria, to one of these organs the power to decide on the question of competence and thus determine which of the two organs will be the lawful judge. . . ."

4. The case last mentioned deals with the permissible discretion of a court to assign a case for trial. Would it be appropriate to require less precision in the objectivity of the criteria for assignment when assignment is made by a court rather than the public prosecutor? Consider the decision of the German Constitutional Court of Oct. 25, 1966, 20 BVerfGE 336, 345-46. Under the Code of Criminal Procedure, the court of last appeal had discretion to choose the lower court to which a case should be remanded. After noting that there would be some cases where it would be inappropriate to remand the case to the court which originally decided it, and whose decision was being reversed, the Court noted: "A normative determination of the alternate court would not be within the purpose of the regulation. The court of appeal must, in the interest of a just decision, have a greater ambit of choice." Even if one concedes that it might be difficult to spell out the criteria for deciding whether to remand to the original court or not, is it really necessary for the appellate court

---

* Decision of Jan. 16, 1957, 6 BVerfGE 45, 52.

to have complete discretion to remand to whichever court it chooses? The Constitutional Court stated that there would be a violation of art. 101 if the appellate court acted "in an arbitrary fashion." What would be the criteria for deciding when the choice of a particular court on remand is "arbitrary"? *Cf.* Note 1, § C., *infra.*

B. DISCRETION IN COMPOSITION OF THE JUDICIAL PANEL

1. Italy

DEPAOLI

Corte costituzionale, Decision of December 13, 1963, No. 156
[1963] 8 Giur. Cost. 1567; [1963] 18 Rac. uff. corte cost. 295
[1964] 87 Foro It. I, 16

FACTS

... [T]he Pretore of Bordighera certified to this Court questions concerning the constitutionality of art. 101 of the *ordinamento giudiziario** in that part in which it provides that a *Pretore* ... of another judicial district may be designated, by a decree of the Chief Justice of the Court of Appeal, to temporarily fill the office of a *Pretore* who is absent or otherwise incapacitated. The statute in question was thought to violate the "natural judge" provision of art. 25 ... of the Constitution because it might allow particular judges to be selected to hear particular cases.

In fact, the judge below ... was assigned by a decree of the Chief Justice of the Court of Appeal of Genoa, to the *Pretura* of Bordighera to sit two consecutive days a week for a two-month period. He felt that it was his duty to raise the question of constitutionality because a later declaration of the unconstitutionality of art. 101 would have rendered the criminal proceeding before him null and void.

. . . .

OPINION

. . . .

The Court does not share the constitutional doubts raised by the *Pretore* of Bordighera. It should be observed that art. 25, para. 1 of the Constitution according to which no one shall be denied the right to his natural and lawfully appointed judge ... means, on the one hand, that the competence of judges must be determined by a general rule, and that rule departed from only in cases of exceptional necessity, and even then only with adequate safeguards (see

*Royal Decree of Jan. 30, 1941, No. 12 on the *ordinamento giudiziario,* the law relating to the organization of the judiciary.

Constitutional Court, Decision No. 88 of 1962, and Nos. 59, 110, 122 and 130 of 1963). It also means that no appointment should ever be made with any single proceeding in mind (in fact, "plans for the division of labor" concerning the assignment of judges to each division within a composite judicial organ are prescribed by law and prepared at the beginning of every year). On the other hand, however, this rule does not and, in fact, could not without sacrificing the continuity and efficiency of the judicial function, prevent the filling of vacancies by means of permanent or temporary appointments. . . .

Therefore, the temporary "assignment" of a *Pretore* . . . to perform the function of an absent or otherwise incapacitated *Pretore* . . . cannot be said to violate the right not to be deprived of a natural judge, guaranteed to all by the first paragraph of art. 25 of the Constitution.

NOTE AND QUESTIONS

Is *Depaoli* consistent with *Pepe, supra* § A.? Are there reasons to be less concerned with discretion to choose the particular judge rather than the tribunal? Are there reasons to be less concerned with discretion exercised by judges rather than discretion exercised by the public prosecutor? Are there, finally, reasons to be less concerned with discretion which has no particular proceeding in mind? No later Italian decision has held discretion in composition of the judicial panel to be unconstitutional.

2. Germany

DECISION OF MARCH 20, 1956

Bundesverfassungsgericht
[1956] 4 BVerfGE 412

OPINION

A.

1. The petitioner was sentenced to a term of one year in prison and a fine of 10,000 DM, or an additional 100 days of imprisonment in lieu of the fine, by the Criminal Chamber of the *Landgericht* of Munich. On *Revision** the Federal Court annulled this decision and remanded the case for a new trial. On the basis of the new decision the petitioner was sentenced to one year's imprisonment. On a new appeal the petitioner claimed, *inter alia,* that he had been deprived

---

*Revision is an appeal on a point of law which, under a complicated system, can be brought as to any judgment of a criminal court. In cases where the *Landgericht* is the court of first instance, revision is the only possible appeal, bringing the case before the Federal Court (*Bundesgerichtshof*).

of his lawful judge because (*a*) certain members of the court, Dr. R and Dr. O, did not participate in the decision, and (*b*) the date of the trial was determined by Dr. L who was not competent to make the determination and who was influenced by Dr. M, the director of the *Landgericht*, who had been disqualified in the case. As a result of this determination Dr. R and Dr. O were excluded from participation.

The Federal Court rejected the appeal on the ground that the court which had made the decision was properly composed and that the petitioner had not been deprived of his lawful judge. . . .

. . . .

2. Against this decision the petitioner brought a *Verfassungsbeschwerde* claiming a violation of art. 101, para. 1, second sentence, of the Basic Law.

. . . .

B.

I. The decision [of the Federal Constitutional Court] is based on the following legal considerations:

1) The rule (of art. 101, para. 1, second sentence, of the Basic Law) that "no one shall be deprived of his lawful judge," like the guarantee of the independence of the courts, should preclude the interference of extraneous individuals in the administration of justice and protect the confidence of the litigants and the public in general in the impartiality and objectivity of the courts. The prohibition against extraordinary courts [explicitly stated in the first sentence of the same article], which is historically joined to this, serves to insure respect for the preceding rule. Since these rules in essence effectuate the idea of *Rechtsstaat* in the sphere of the judicial system, they were introduced in most of the constitutions of the *Länder* of the 19th century and given the status of constitutional rules. Article 105 of the Weimar Constitution continued this process. In the measures which have refined the principles of *Rechtsstaat* and the separation of powers, the rules concerning the lawful judge have been perfected. The law concerning the organization of the judiciary, the procedural laws and the plans for division of labor within the courts determine the territorial and material competence of the courts . . . and the composition of the individual divisions, chambers, and senates. If originally the principle of the lawful judge was primarily externally directed, especially against any form of *Kabinettsjustiz* [judicial activity through organs informally constituted and controlled by the executive], now the same principle is extended in its protective function to insure that no one is deprived, through internal measures of the judicial system, of the lawful judge in his cause.

2) This, however, does not mean that art. 101, para. 1, second sentence, of the Basic Law in every case is violated where someone other than the "lawful judge" sits. If the judicial measure, which has as its result that a judge different from the "lawful judge" sits, is based merely on a procedural error, there is no violation of that article. How "procedural errors" are distinguished from "deprivation of the lawful judge" can be left open, since a procedural error is, in any case, excluded when there is the interference of a person or agency which is outside of the judiciary. The same must hold true for persons who are within the judicial system, who generally or for a particular case cannot exercise a judicial function — for example, a disqualified judge.

3) Such persons can interfere in the administration of justice in violation of the Basic Law either directly, through the exercise of judicial functions, or indirectly, through influence in the content of judicial activities, by means of their authority. Only if art. 101, para. 1, second sentence, of the Basic Law protects against this also, does it fulfill its safeguarding function.

4) The pertinent provision of the Basic Law applies not only to the deciding judge, but also to the judge who determines the date of the trial. It follows from this that competence and personal composition of the courts is regulated by law and by the plan for the division of labor, not only for the decision itself, but also for the preliminary judicial activities. In any case, a defect in the determination of the date affects the decision only if the decision is based upon the defect, i.e. if there is a causal relationship between the procedural defect and the decision.

According to consistent judicial interpretation, such a relationship, resulting in the annulment of a decision through violation of essential procedural rules, exists when there is the possibility that the procedural error has influenced the content of the decision. . . . [Therefore] a violation of art. 101, para. 1, second sentence, of the Basic Law by the determination of a date leads to the annulment of the decision when it is possible that the judgment has been influenced by that violation. This possibility, because of the importance of the composition of the court in the determination of the decision, cannot be excluded if it occurs that through a correct determination of the date the court would have been differently composed.

II. Considering these principles the decision enacted against the petitioner by the *Landgericht* of Munich is contrary to art. 101, para. 1, second sentence, of the Basic Law since:

1) it is apparent that the determination of the date of the trial was decisively influenced by the disqualified president of the Criminal Chamber, the director of the *Landgericht,* Dr. M;

2) the possibility cannot be excluded that the court in the trial of the petitioner would have been differently composed without the interference of the disqualified judge.

. . . .

III. The decision of the *Landgericht* of Munich is annulled as contrary to art. 101, para. 1, second sentence, of the Basic Law. This annulment extends necessarily to the decision of the Federal Court since its decision confirms that of the *Landgericht*. . . .

According to § 95, para. 2, of the statute which regulates the Federal Constitutional Court, the cause is remanded to the *Landgericht* of Augsburg. The competent court in the sense of this provision is any court which has competence over the subject matter. Territorial competence is not relevant in this case, as it is not in the case in which the Federal Court, having quashed a lower court decision, assigns the case to a new court on remand.

NOTES AND QUESTIONS

1. Because the Constitutional Court is limited to deciding contentions of constitutional violation, it must distinguish between mere "errors in procedure" which are within the competence of the ordinary courts, and procedural errors of constitutional dimension. The problem is similar to United States Supreme Court review of fair procedure in criminal cases in State courts, where the Court has the power to review only those procedural errors which violate the United States Constitution. (*See, e.g., Faretta* v. *California, infra* Ch. 10, § A.3.a.) With reference to the natural judge problem, "mere" errors in applying statutes which fix the competence of particular courts or determine venue do not violate the German Constitution, but it is not clear when misapplication of statutory guidelines goes so far as to violate the natural judge principle in the constitution. Later decisions of the German Constitutional Court have continued to leave open the question of the distinction between "procedural errors" and constitutional violations in the selection of the natural judge. In cases like the principal case, should the distinction turn on the motives with which the error was made? On possible, if not actual, motives?

2. Notice that *Revision* permits either prosecutor or defendant to appeal a criminal court judgment on a point of law. In the United States, would permitting the *prosecutor* to appeal a criminal judgment on issues of law violate the principle of double jeopardy? (*Compare Palko* v. *Connecticut,* 302 U.S. 319 (1937) (state prosecutor's appeal of acquittal on issues of law does not violate 14th Amendment because protection against double jeopardy is not a requirement of due process) *with Benton* v. *Maryland,* 395 U.S. 784

(1969) (overruling *Palko* on the question whether protection against double jeopardy is a requirement of due process).)

DECISION OF MARCH 24, 1964

Bundesverfassungsgericht
[1965] 17 BVerfGE 294

OPINION

A.

1. The four petitioners were parties in three different civil suits which were decided in the last instance by the *Landgericht* of Mosbach. The petitioners K and M had presented, against the decisions concerning them, requests for nullification on the ground that the court in the former proceedings was improperly composed. These requests were rejected by the *Landgericht* of Mosbach. The petitioners Paul and Anna W had requested legal aid to present their appeal for nullification. This request was also rejected by the *Landgericht* of Mosbach. The petitions were submitted on different occasions.

The three constitutional petitions present the same claim, which is that the above-mentioned decisions of the *Landgericht* of Mosbach were based on a constitutional error since the court had been formed in a manner contrary to art. 101, para. 1, second sentence, of the Basic Law. They claim that the *Landgericht* of Mosbach lacks a division of labor from which it may be determined which judge is competent for anticipated civil litigation.

2. The *Landgericht* of Mosbach in the years 1962 and 1963 included the president, the director, five associate judges, and one probationary judge — in all, eight judges. During the same years, according to the plan for the division of labor, two civil and two criminal chambers were instituted.* The president of the 1st civil chamber was the *Landgericht* president, the president of the 2nd civil chamber and the 1st criminal chamber was the director of the *Landgericht,* the president of the 2nd criminal chamber was an associate judge. All of the associate judges and the probationary judge were assigned as ordinary members to the 1st civil chamber, the 2nd civil chamber, and the 1st criminal chamber. The same judges, with the exception of the oldest in time of service and the probationary judge, were assigned as ordinary members to the 2nd criminal chamber. Both civil chambers and the 1st criminal chamber were composed each of a president and six members. The 2nd

---

* Three judges, including the president, sit in each civil chamber. The "small" criminal chamber consists of one professional judge and two lay judges; the "large" criminal chamber, of three professional judges assisted by two lay judges in grave cases (*Schwurgericht*).

criminal chamber was composed of an associate judge as president and three other members.

. . . .

B.

The constitutional petitions are admissible and well-founded:

1. Article 101, para. 1, second sentence, of the Basic Law requires that the lawful judge in a specific case be unequivocally determined by means of a general norm. "Lawful judge" in the sense of this rule is not only the court as an organized entity or as an adjudicatory body before which the trial takes place and individual cases are decided, but also the individual judge who is called to present the decision in the particular case. This follows from the purpose of the provisions of art. 101, para. 1, second sentence, of the Basic Law.

Article 101, para. 1, second sentence, of the Basic Law insures against the danger that justice may be exposed, through manipulation of the judicial organs, to improper interference. In particular, it insures against the danger that influence on the result of a decision would be exercised in a specific case through *ad hoc* appointment of the judge responsible for the decision. It does not matter from which side the manipulation is exercised. The individual has a right that the litigation to which he is a party be decided by its lawful judge.

From the function of art. 101, para. 1, second sentence, of the Basic Law, it follows that the regulations which serve in the determination of the lawful judge must indicate in advance in as unequivocal a fashion as possible what court, what panel [within the court], and what judge will be called to decide a particular case.

The multiplicity of jurisdictions and courts, the diversity of organization of such courts, the different sizes of the courts, the variation in number of judges, the difference in amount of work, and the variation in amount of work within a single court, make it impossible to fix in the statutes all the rules concerning the lawful judge. The statutory provisions must therefore be supplemented by a plan for the division of labor to be made yearly by the *Praesidium* of the court in complete independence. In this regard it is necessary that the judge called to decide in anticipated proceedings be established in the most precise and unequivocal way possible.

This qualification "as precisely as possible" is necessary since the number of panels, the number of judges, the amount of work, and the efficiency of the judges vary. Moreover, retirements, sickness, vacations, and change of one or more judges must be taken into account. Only in cases where the inexactitude of the statute and the plan for the division of labor in determining the judge in the particular case results from such elements are these rules constitutional. In these cases, the lawful judge in the particular case must be determined on the basis of proper and objective considerations.

The plan for the division of labor must not, in accordance with the Basic Law, leave any avoidable discretion in the determination of the proper judge, or unnecessary uncertainty in the determination of the lawful judge. However, special circumstances, in particular the amount of work of the court, and the requirements and best equalization of judicial workloads within the court, may require the assignment of certain judges to more than one chamber or senate as ordinary members.

2. The plan for the division of labor of the *Landgericht* of Mosbach for the year 1963 . . . is contrary to the above-mentioned principles.

The appointment of judges as ordinary members of more than one chamber can be accomplished only where it is necessary, with respect to the aforementioned principles, in order to properly constitute each chamber. It is sufficient that the five associate members of the *Landgericht* of Mosbach and the probationary judge were assigned respectively to two different chambers as ordinary members. According to the plan for the division of labor for 1963, however, four of the judges were assigned concurrently to four chambers as ordinary members and two concurrently to three chambers as ordinary members. Insofar as the four judges are ordinary members of four chambers concurrently, they are in reality not in any way distributed among the panels, but are omnicompetent. It is not clear in advance which judge will be called to decide in a given proceeding. That such a plan is unsustainable results from the fact that it does not allow a sensible rule for the substitution of judges who are unable to appear, if the second criminal chamber, to which two of the judges do not belong, is not considered.

The plan leads necessarily to an unconstitutional organization of the chamber which made the challenged decision. The unconstitutionality consists in the fact that the regulation offers in itself the opportunity for arbitrary manipulation whether or not, in the specific case, there has actually been an arbitrary exercise of power. What constitutional limits exist regarding the overfilling of a panel in a particular case do not need to be determined here. In any case, a chamber is not composed in a manner consistent with art. 101, para. 1, second sentence, of the Basic Law if the number of its ordinary members allows that two differently constituted panels can sit or that the president can form three panels, each with different associates.

The argument that the selected division of labor takes into account the fact that a small *Landgericht* must be able to employ judges in each chamber in order to best balance its workload cannot prevail against the constitutional command that the lawful judge must be determined as precisely as possible by the plan for the division of labor. Moreover, that argument is objectively improper. In general, on the basis of court statistics of preceding years, the probable workload for the year can be determined. The appointment of judges to the various chambers can be based on this. . . .

The challenged decisions were made by a chamber which was unconstitutionally composed as a consequence of the plan for division of labor. They were not made by the lawful judge. Therefore they must be annulled. . . .

NOTES AND QUESTIONS

1. In Germany the division of labor in the courts has been so structured that the judge who will sit in a court on any given day can be determined in advance. This has been done because the "lawful judge" requirement was construed in the principal case to prohibit discretion in assigning particular judges to particular cases. A danger of "judge shopping" similar to forum shopping is, however, inherent in a system in which the individual judges are publicly identifiable in advance. A number of devices have been adopted to minimize this danger, such as a system of alphabetical determination based on the first letter of the names of the parties, or the "file number" of the complaints.

In its plan for division of labor each court has freedom to select appropriate criteria for the distribution of cases among the judges. But according to the decision of the Federal Court, 40 *Bundesgerichtshof in Zivilsachen* 91, a plan to divide cases among different sections of the court according to the order in which the cases are filed for appeal is impermissible if it gives the clerk an opportunity to influence the assignment of specific cases to specific chambers. Is the question whether a particular plan provides unnecessary risks of judge shopping a question of constitutional law?

2. The Constitutional Court Decision of April 16, 1969 (25 BVerfGE 336) dealt with the appointment of the investigatory judge by the President of the *Bundesgerichtshof.* In Germany the initial judicial stage in a criminal proceeding is the determination whether there is sufficient evidence to go to trial. This decision was largely in the hands of the investigatory judge who commanded a pivotal position in the criminal process. In certain important cases, including alleged crimes of a political nature, the investigatory judge was appointed by the President of the *Bundesgerichtshof,* pursuant to § 186 of the Code of Criminal Procedure.* At the time of this case, § 186 read as follows:

The President of the *Bundesgerichtshof* will choose the

─────────

* Strafprozessordnung [StPO] § 186 (W. Ger.) (1967).

investigatory judge ... from among the members of the
Bundesgerichtshof.

The President of the *Bundesgerichtshof* may also choose any
judge of any German court as the investigatory judge or as that
judge's representative for any part of the judicial work.

In practice, the President of the *Bundesgerichtshof* named a group
of judges, from which he would choose investigatory judges. The
President, however, had discretion in selecting the investigatory
judge for each case. The petitioner claimed that his investigatory
judge was illegally appointed, because the unlimited discretion given
by § 186 violated art. 101, para. 1, sentence 2, of the Basic Law.

The Constitutional Court disagreed, reasoning as follows:*

Arbitrary discretion in the choice of the judge competent for a
particular case can be entrusted not even to an independent
member of the judiciary. If literally interpreted and applied,
§ 186, paras. 1 and 2, of the Code of Criminal Procedure would
not conform to this requirement. ... However, the rule of § 186
of the Code of Criminal Procedure is not unconstitutional
because it does not "require" that the investigatory judge be
appointed *ad hoc* and *ad personam,* but also "allows" the
appointment to be done in a constitutional fashion. ...

The President of the *Bundesgerichtshof* did in fact establish
a plan for the appointment of the investigatory judge which
satisfies the requirements of art. 101, para. 1, sentence 2, of the
Basic Law. ...

Even if this plan leaves a certain area of discretion with the
President, it is not necessarily unconstitutional because the
discretion and the consequent possibility of choice are very
limited; furthermore, the choice is always made by the judiciary
[rather than the executive].

Is this decision irreconcilable with the holding in the principal case,
that the Constitution "requires that the lawful judge in a specific case
be unequivocally determined by means of a general norm"? Should
the court have held § 186 unconstitutional "on its face" because it
did not mandate sufficient standards for choice of the investigatory
judge in a particular case? Would the question whether there was too
much discretion in choice of the investigatory judge be different if
the investigatory judge also presided at the trial? (After the decision,
the institution of judicial investigation was abolished. Investigations
are now handled by the public prosecutor, with judges confined to
determining guilt and imposing sentence.)

3. Notwithstanding the wording in *Depaoli, supra* § B.1., most
Italian decisions do not go as far as the German decisions in

---

* Decision of Apr. 16, 1969, 25 BVerfGE 336, 348-50.

requiring that, in addition to the court, even the individual members of the court be predetermined by law. Can you think of reasons why the German cases might impose a more stringent standard than the Italian cases?

3. France

DECISION OF JULY 23, 1975

Conseil Constitutionnel
[1975] J.O. 7533

The *Conseil constitutionnel,*

Convened on June 30, 1975 by Messrs. . . . senators, according to the provisions of Article 61 of the Constitution for the purpose of passing judgment on the Law [*loi*] modifying and supplementing certain rules of penal procedure, as adopted by Parliament;

Having referred to the Constitution;

Having referred to the *ordonnance* of November 7, 1958 (*loi organique* on the *Conseil constitutionnel*), notably Chapter 2 of Title 2 of said *ordonnance*;

Having referred to the Code of Penal Procedure, notably Articles 398 and 398-1, as amended by Law [*loi*] of December 29, 1972;

Having heard the report by the reporting Justice;

Considering that the *Conseil constitutionnel* has been lawfully convened by 69 senators, according to Article 61 of the Constitution, for the purpose of ruling on the Law [*loi*] bringing modification of and addition to certain provisions of penal procedure, especially the text modifying Articles 398 and 398-1 of the Code of Penal Procedure;

Considering that the new provisions of Article 398-1 of the Code of Penal Procedure would allow the presiding judge of the *tribunal de grande instance,* in all matters appertaining to the jurisdiction of the *tribunal correctionnel,* with the exception of misdemeanors concerning the press [*délits de presse*], to decide in discretionary manner and without any possibility of appeal whether said *tribunal* shall be composed of three judges, according to the rule laid down by Article 398 of the Code of Penal Procedure, or of a single judge exercising the powers conferred on the presiding judge [of the *tribunal*];

Considering that cases of the same type could thus be judged by a *tribunal collégial* [a three-judge court] or by a single judge, according to the decision of the presiding judge of that jurisdiction;

Considering that by conferring such power, Article 6 of the Law which is under the scrutiny of this *Conseil constitutionnel,* inasmuch as it modifies Article 388-1 of the Code of Penal Procedure, challenges the principle of equality before the law (especially since we are here dealing with a penal law), a principle proclaimed in the Declaration of the Rights of Man of 1789 and solemnly reaffirmed by the Preamble of the Constitution;

Considering, in fact, that this principle precludes the possibility that citizens in a similar situation, prosecuted for the same infractions, should be judged by courts of different composition;

Considering, finally, that Article 34 of the Constitution, which preserves to the *loi* [Parliament] the task of establishing the rules of Penal Procedure, prohibits that the legislator, in such fundamental area as that concerning the rights and liberties of the citizens, confide to another authority the exercise, in the conditions set out above, of the powers indicated by Article 6 of the Law [*loi*] under the scrutiny of this Constitutional Council;

Considering that these legislative provisions therefore must be declared unconstitutional;

Considering, moreover, that these provisions are inseparable from those of the same Article 6, first paragraph, of the Law under consideration, which abrogate the last three paragraphs of Article 398 of the Code of Penal Procedure;

Considering that, at present, it is unnecessary for this Constitutional Council to rule on the question of constitutionality with respect to the other provisions of the Law referred to its scrutiny;

We hold:

1. The provisions of Article 6 of the Law modifying and adding to certain provisions of the Code of Penal Procedure are declared unconstitutional, inasmuch as, on the one hand, they abrogate the last three paragraphs of Article 398 of the Code of Penal Procedure and, on the other hand, they abrogate and replace the provisions of Article 398-1 of this Code;

2. The present decision shall be published in the *Journal Officiel* of the French Republic;

Deliberated by the *Conseil constitutionnel* on July 23, 1975.

NOTES AND QUESTIONS

1. Although the natural judge concept probably originated in France, there is, as the decision of the *Conseil Constitutionnel*

indicates, no explicit natural judge provision in the French Constitution. Do you find it strange that the decision is premised on a denial of the principle of equality? Compare the *Conseil Constitutionnel* decision of December 27, 1973, discussed in Ch. 3, § C.3.d. (In that case, limiting the right to contest an administrative tax assessment to lower income taxpayers was held to violate the principle of equality before the law.) In *Pepe, supra* § A., an argument that prosecutorial discretion in the choice of the trial court was a denial of equality was expressly rejected by the *Corte Constituzionale.*

2. Will the right-to-equality approach taken by the *Conseil Constitutionnel* generally replicate the principle of the natural judge as it has been developed in the German and Italian constitutional courts? Does it go further than that and suggest that all official discretion is unconstitutional if that discretion is not sufficiently defined? Or, is the opinion limited to discretion in enforcement of the criminal law? In the United States, for example, unguided prosecutorial discretion in deciding whether or not to prosecute an individual for violating the criminal law is commonplace, and a basic feature of the criminal justice system. By contrast, on much of the Continent (including Germany and Italy), in theory prosecutors have no discretion, and it is their *duty* to prosecute any person if a probable violation of the law is brought to their attention. Can you suggest reasons why Continental law has traditionally sought to outlaw any role for discretion in administering the laws, and why the scope of permissible discretion in the United States is so different?

3. Does that different view of the dangers of official discretion explain a total absence of the natural judge concept in constitutional law in the United States? Can you think of instances of result-oriented choice of a court or judge to try a particular case in the United States which ought to be deterred by a constitutional rule?

C. CHANGES OF VENUE NECESSITATED BY CONFLICTING CONSTITUTIONAL VALUES

CASOLI

Corte costituzionale, Decision of May 3, 1963, No. 50
[1963] 8 Giur. Cost. 471; [1963] 16 Rac. uff. corte cost. 335
[1963] 86 Foro It. I, 857

[FACTS: The declaration of unconstitutionality by the Court in *Pepe, supra,* may well have occasioned this challenge to art. 55 of the Code of Criminal Procedure which was brought the following year.

[The article in question provides for removal, by the *Corte di Cassazione,* of a proceeding from one court to another, upon the request of the Public Prosecutor * of the *Corte di Appello*** or the *Corte di Cassazione* where there exists (a) a potential danger to public order, or (b) cause to believe that the fairness of the proceeding may be prejudiced through intimidation or other influence (*legittimo sospetto*). It also provides for such removal at the request of the accused in criminal proceedings, but only in the latter instance (*legittimo sospetto*).

[The question arose when the Public Prosecutor of the *Corte di Appello* of Bologna invoked art. 55 in order to remove the proceeding against one Alfredo Casoli to a different *Corte di Assise. ***

[Given the local environment, the character of the offense with which Casoli was charged, and this man's personal and political influence in the community, the request was granted. The court cited the well-founded probability of pressure on the lay judges in the original court as well as upon the witnesses who might appear before it.

[The removal was challenged by the accused Casoli on the basis that the article under whose authority it was implemented was unconstitutional. In answering the attack, the *Avvocatura dello Stato* **** asserted that the article in question was fashioned to deal with instances wherein the judge normally invested with the competence to try a given matter is for some reason unfit. Where unfitness exists, such a judge cannot be considered to be the natural, lawfully determined judge. Each organ of a similar level of competence in the area of criminal jurisdiction then becomes potentially the lawful court in which the proceeding may take place. In such a situation it is merely a matter of determining the competence of a different judge chosen from among those who are potentially lawful. The *Avvocatura* argued that the same grounds which authorize the removal demonstrate the impossibility of judicial predetermination in these cases and urged against an excessively rigorous interpretation of art. 25 of the Constitution.]

---

* In Italy the Public Prosecutor is a member of the judiciary subject to the guarantees of art. 108 of the Constitution. As such he exercises a wider range of duties than would his American counterpart.

** The *Corte di Appello* is the normal court of second instance in cases originating in the *Tribunale.* It sits in three-judge panels.

*** The *Corti di Assise* hear the most serious criminal cases. These courts are now organized as specialized sections of the *Tribunali.* The *Corte di Assise* sits with a panel of two ordinary judges and six laymen acting as "popular" judges.

**** *See Carabba,* Ch. 6, § C.1., *supra,* for a description of the *Avvocatura dello Stato.*

OPINION

The question raised by the *ordinanza* requires an examination of art. 55 of the Code of Criminal Procedure, to determine if it contravenes the precepts of art. 25, para. 1, of the Constitution. Specifically, the Court must decide whether it is unconstitutional to give the *Corte di Cassazione* the power of removing the case to another court in instances where such removal is felt necessary for serious reasons of public order or to preclude any influence or intimidation of the court.

The *ordinanza* under consideration makes reference to decision No. 88 of 1962 of this Court which specifies that according to art. 25, para. 1, of the Constitution, "the natural judge" is the judge pre-established by law, *i.e.,* the judge whose competence is previously determined for cases which have not yet occurred. That decision declared unconstitutional art. 30 of the Code of Criminal Procedure and other articles of analogous content because they were irreconcilable with the concept of the "natural judge." Those articles left to the discretion of the Public Prosecutor the determination of the competent court judge.

According to the *ordinanza,* the doubt concerning the constitutionality of art. 55 derives from the fact that this article grants to the *Corte di Cassazione* the discretion to designate a different judge from the one originally established by the law.

The challenge is groundless.

The challenged rule, both from the procedural point of view and from its rationale, appears to be qualitatively different from that rule already examined by this Court. Therefore, to decide the question now raised it is necessary to turn to other principles, also sanctioned by the Constitution, which co-exist . . . with those already announced in the earlier decision.

From the procedural point of view, it must be noted that the power to change venue, for the reasons provided in art. 30 (and in the other articles declared unconstitutional), was within the absolute discretion of the Public Prosecutor, whenever he found, through provisional examination, extenuating circumstances for which the presumed sanction would be within the competence of the court to which the proceeding was to be transferred by him.

In the removal authorized by art. 55, on the other hand, the change of venue depends absolutely and exclusively on the objective ascertainment of facts based upon the results of a special proceeding initiated by the Public Prosecutor, or also (in the case of *legittimo sospetto*) by the accused. The final decision in this proceeding is made by the supreme organ of ordinary adjudication governing competence, *i.e.,* the *Corte di Cassazione.* Furthermore, although the legislative text uses the word "can," this does not mean that the *Corte di Cassazione* has discretionary power to effect such transfers. On the contrary, such a measure clearly constitutes the expression of the ordinary power-duty of judges to decide questions on the basis of verification and evaluation of the facts presented by the parties in the particular case, in relation to an abstract hypothetical fact situation anticipated by statute.

Moreover, the proper interpretation of art. 55 would place particular importance on the serious exigencies which the institution of removal, established by that article, is intended to satisfy. These exigencies, in the same manner as the prohibition against the denial of a natural, lawfully-appointed judge, are the expression of important constitutional principles, namely, independence and hence impartiality of the judicial organ and the protection of the right of defense. This further accentuates the difference between art. 55 and those previously declared unconstitutional.

This Court, with decision No. 108 of 1962, affirmed the fundamental and deeply-rooted importance of independence within the judicial function. Independence is guaranteed by the Constitution through the various provisions concerning the organs of ordinary adjudication (arts. 101, 104, 105 and 107), as well as in the special courts (art. 108).

It is certain, in fact, that the lack or the diminution of such guarantees cannot but seriously hinder the administration of justice, diverting it from its fundamental purpose, in which is inherent the very life of the State.

As it stands, the challenged provision . . . tends precisely to avoid that condition where popular unrest or other external factors can interfere with the criminal process, affecting the objectivity of the court and the proper application of the law.

If a situation such as that anticipated by art. 55 exists in the place of the proceeding; if there is manifested a reasonable danger, as in the instant case, of a grave disturbance to public tranquillity and peaceful existence of the citizenry with danger to personal security; or if through direct or indirect means, the participants in the proceeding are threatened with violence in an attempt to influence the development or the result of the proceeding; it is clear that it is not merely suitable, but essential that the proceeding take place before a judge different from the one originally established by law. The designation of such a judge is by practical necessity demanded of the judicial system.

In consequence of the considerations presented, the challenged article cannot be found to be contrary to the precepts contained in art. 25, para. 1, of the Constitution. . . .

NOTES AND QUESTIONS

1. As part of a proposed program for procedural reform, the *Pretore* of Firenze, Marco Ramat, in an article in *Il Ponte* of January 31, 1969, discussed the issue of *legittimo sospetto*:

> Aside from all the discussion still open on the question of constitutionality, what is most pressing is that the designation of the judge to whom the case is transferred (*i.e.*, the judge *ad quem*) does not remain in the mere discretion of the *Corte di Cassazione*. . . .
>
> It would seem necessary, therefore, that the judge in the jurisdiction to which the *Corte di Cassazione* assigns the proceeding be in some manner predetermined by law. This could be accomplished by transferral automatically provided for from one jurisdiction to another according to a table approved by law (for example, from Rome to Florence, from Florence to Bologna and so forth); alternatively and perhaps preferably, a restricted group of courts "of remand" provided by law could be established for particular areas with assignment by chance on a case-by-case basis in proceedings affected by *legittimo sospetto*. For example, from Milan, the case might be removed to Turin, Genoa, or Venice, and chance would say to which of the three predesignated areas it would be assigned.

Would limitations on the choice of the transferee court, analogous to those discussed above, be required by the Italian Constitution?

2. While it is difficult to find any analogue to the natural judge concept in the constitutional law of the United States, it is not uncommon to have venue rules for criminal law cases which are embodied in state constitutions as well as the United States Constitution. Even prior to adoption of the Bill of Rights, Article III, § 2, cl. 3 of the Constitution provided that "[t]he Trial of all crimes . . . shall be by Jury; and such Trial shall be held in the State where the said Crimes shall have been committed. . . ." The Sixth Amendment provides a constitutional right to "trial, by an impartial jury of the State and district wherein the crime shall have been committed, which district shall have been previously ascertained by law. . . ." Where the defendant's conduct and its effects occur in a single district, these provisions obviously operate to curtail a federal prosecutor's discretion as to the territorial jurisdiction within which to file criminal charges, although they do not speak to discretion in choice of the judge to preside at the trial. On the other hand, the "crime committed" formula can provide a wide choice of venue in complex conspiratorial crimes covering several states, crimes involving use of the mails and facilities of interstate commerce, etc. *See* Abrams, *Conspiracy and Multi-Venue in Federal Criminal*

Prosecutions: The Crime Committed Formula, 9 U.C.L.A. L. REV. 751 (1962). If the defendant publishes a magazine and mails it in California to Tennessee, for example, nothing in Article III or the Sixth Amendment forbids giving the federal prosecutor the choice of prosecuting an obscenity case in California or Tennessee.

3. Suppose that the defendant is a police officer in a Southern State who murdered a civil rights worker. After state officials fail to prosecute him, he is charged with the murder as a federal crime in a federal court. Would it violate Article III and the Sixth Amendment to permit the prosecutor to move for a change of venue to another state and another district on the ground that local citizens applaud the murder and are unlikely to convict the defendant? Was the primary concern of the Sixth Amendment, in requiring a jury drawn from the district where the crime was committed, to limit prosecutorial discretion, or to protect the jury's potential role in nullifying prosecution of unpopular federal crimes? Can the absence of a natural *judge* concept in all English legal systems be explained by the greater traditional role of the *jury* as finder of fact in criminal cases and suits at common law?

Chapter 10

RIGHT TO COUNSEL

A. CRIMINAL CASES

1. Preface: The Criminal Process in Civil Law Countries

a. *Comparison of English and Continental Criminal Procedure* *

On this occasion I propose to deal with the administration of the criminal law in England and in France, but necessarily only with the procedure applicable to the most serious crimes. It is a subject I approach with some reluctance: mainly because I am firmly persuaded that the English system is, in this particular, greatly superior to the French. I have previously suggested that it is desirable that a comparative lawyer should show, if possible, a partiality in favor of the foreign system: in this instance I fear that I have no such bias. . . .

Recent cases

What are the points on which there is today an outcry in France? First the unconscionable time during which a person charged with crime is kept in jail *before* trial — remanded in custody is the more euphemistic phrase in English. It should be noted that this imprisonment — détention préventive — is *lawful* as much in England as in France; but its *duration* in France may be, and often is, inordinate by any standard. In the case of Gaston Dominici, for example, recently convicted of the murder of Sir Jack Drummond and his wife and daughter (which murder was done on August 4, 1952), the accused, having often been previously interrogated, was finally charged and arrested on November 16, 1953; but he was actually tried only in November, 1954, and he was kept in prison for the whole year between the day of his arrest and the day of his trial. Marguerite Marty, who was charged with the murder of her cousin by administering to her an overdose of a sleeping draught and who was acquitted after a spectacular trial at Perpignan this year, was kept

---

* Excerpted from Hamson, *The Prosecution of the Accused — English and French Legal Methods,* 1955 CRIM. L. REV. 272. Reprinted with permission of Sweet and Maxwell Ltd., London.

in prison during the whole period of the fourteen months which
elapsed between the day of her arrest and the day of trial, though
the circumstances of the murder with which she was charged were
relatively simple, the motive alleged being that she was the mistress
of her cousin's husband. The most striking case on this point is that
of Marie Besnard, which is still unconcluded. This unhappy woman
was charged with the murder of a number of her relations by the
administration of arsenic. She was kept in jail for a period of over
four years before her first trial. In spite of that delay, her case as
presented to the court of trial was in such a state of confusion that
that court ordered une instruction supplémentaire — a repreparation
of the case — though mercifully releasing her on bail. At the retrial,
which itself was delayed, the second court again ordered a further
inquiry. Her case has not yet received final judgment five years after
she had been charged. Her spirit as well as her health has been
broken by a treatment which though lawful is unjustifiable upon any
view, whether she be finally found guilty or, as is almost certain, not
guilty.

The second criticism made generally in France, and recently with
particular vehemence, is concerned with the manner in which
confessions are procured — or the attempt is made to procure
confessions — from persons suspected of crime. Criticism is
especially directed against confessions obtained by the police *before*
the suspect is brought in front of the juge d'instruction and formally
charged, though in the case of Marie Besnard, at all events, the
pressure by the police was continued after she had been formally
charged. To put it bluntly, the French police are accused of behaving
not only oppressively but sometimes brutally. It certainly looks as if
Marguerite Marty, whom I have already mentioned, had been
maltreated before she was formally charged. . . . For our purposes
actual misbehaviour by the police is comparatively unimportant,
provided that such misbehaviour is recognised to be, as it is in
France, contrary to law. The question which is of importance is
whether the existing system encourages in the police a course of
conduct which easily and frequently declines into illegal
misbehaviour and whether for the misbehaviour which occurs a
prompt and effective remedy is provided. . . .

The third main ground of criticism of the French system by the
French themselves concerns the conduct in court of the final trial. . . .
[F]rench opinion is disturbed by the insufficient and apparently
muddled manner in which evidence, and especially perhaps expert
evidence, is presented to the court of trial. Certainly that
presentation seems to an English observer deficient. It is felt in
France that confusion results and that in the resulting confusion the
task of the jury — if jury it is — becomes unreasonably difficult and
even impossible. . . .

It is probably the mal-presentation of the evidence which is largely responsible for the numerous reforms, proposed and made in the past and now again brought forward, on the subject of the constitution and the function of the jury. Originally a body of twelve, expressly modelled on the English example and responsible, after deliberation among themselves alone, for a verdict (though by a majority) only upon the fact, they have now after many modifications been reduced to seven and become more lay assessors than a jury, since they sit and deliberate with the three judges of the court and pass not only upon the facts but also upon the sentence. . . .

To an English observer . . . the reform which is alleged to be desired may be obtainable only, if at all, by the destruction of the institution which it is proposed to reform; and the institution itself seems to be cherished more than the results of the reform. . . . [I]n France the accepted method of prosecuting criminals seems actually to be more prized, despite some of its necessary occasional defects, than any substituted method which would be adequate to eradicate those same defects against which there is now so clamorous a complaint. The substituted method, it may well be believed, would arouse more objection than it would appease.

English and French Methods Contrasted

The inquiry

In what then consists the real character of this accepted method, and upon what points does it present an instructive contrast to the English method? It is scarcely helpful to use the trite diagnosis that the French process is inquisitorial and the English accusatorial: first because we are not told what is the essential element in the process called inquisitorial which is offensive — the right and the duty of the *court* to inquire (if that is inquisitorial) is a most valuable and useful part of the French *administrative* process; secondly because it is questionable whether the French criminal process is predominantly inquisitorial in any precise sense — indeed most probably its defects are due mainly to its hybrid character; thirdly because it is hard to see how any criminal system could today be administered without a duty to inquire being cast upon some organised body, and it seems to me evident enough that such a duty is in England cast upon the police.

It is not the power or duty to inquire which makes a difference between systems: it may be the nature or character of the inquiry judged appropriate or fair which does. It is, I think, by the difference of their notions of what constitutes a fair or appropriate inquiry that the French and the English systems most differ. I trust that I do not unduly exaggerate when I suggest that in France it would be thought more than unfair, it would be thought most grossly improper, if the inquiry were conducted *ex parte* — without the presence of the person principally interested, the person, that is, against whom there were reasonable grounds of suspicion that he had committed the offense. The object of the traditional French process was not only to put the inquiry into the hands of a competent official — the juge d'instruction — but to draw the suspect in at the earliest possible opportunity. The presence of the suspect is not regarded as an imposition upon the suspect but rather as an important right of his. That an official should be allowed to gather together evidence against a citizen and to construct a case against him without his knowledge and without a right in him to make representations to that official and to put forward his own view of the situation from the start — that would generally be judged in France to be monstrous.

The suspect is brought into the French process at a point much earlier than that at which he is brought into the English process. In principle in France the inquiry proper — that of the juge d'instruction — starts *after* the suspect has been brought in: in England in principle the inquiry is concluded *before* the appearance of the prisoner in front of the magistrates. The magistrates in England do not conduct an inquiry: they hear the results of an inquiry which has been conducted. And indeed they are markedly restive if the police are not ready to produce those results by way of evidence very rapidly after the first appearance of the accused, especially if the police require the remand of the accused in custody. But if the magistrate has himself to conduct an inquiry and if it is judged right that the suspect should participate in that inquiry from the start, evidently the suspect will be a great deal longer before the magistrate; and in a grave case where there are reasonable grounds for suspicion, almost inevitably the suspect will during the inquiry be remanded in custody. This seems to me to be of the necessity of the case once it is admitted that the suspect should participate in the inquiry. And it is almost a necessary consequence, human nature being what it is, that if the suspect *is* in custody by order of the magistrate conducting the inquiry the urgency of concluding that inquiry, which may be complex and difficult, will to that magistrate appear to be greatly diminished.

Representation by counsel

On the classical French view, because the juge d'instruction's process was an inquiry merely and not a trial, there was no room in his process for the presence of counsel. On that view, it was as sensible to have counsel injected into the instruction as it would be to require the suspect's solicitor to be attached to the C.I.D. inspector in England. But in 1897 in France because of public outcry — which was no more unjustified than it is now — counsel *was* introduced into the instruction. The suspect brought before the juge d'instruction must now, at his first appearance, be informed of his right to nominate counsel and, if he has none to nominate, he must be provided with one at his request. The juge d'instruction cannot address any question to the suspect except in presence of his counsel, and must twenty-four hours before any such questioning make available to counsel the whole of the file in which is recorded all the juge d'instruction's material concerning the case. Counsel has the right freely to communicate with the suspect at any time, whether or not the suspect is in custody.

Again it seems to me that if this kind of fetter is to be put upon an inquiry, especially if the view is maintained that an inquiry must be conducted with the participation of the suspect, it will be necessarily be found that the process is extremely imperfect as an inquiry and likely to become very protracted. That undoubtedly is the French police view: inquiry by the juge d'instruction after the law of 1897 is in their opinion — and surely justifiably — hopeless as a police inquiry. And again, almost as a necessary consequence, we observe the growth in France of the enquête officieuse — the unofficial inquiry — by the police, outside the instruction: into which enquête, while the major French premise of the participation of the suspect remains, the suspect is almost of necessity again drawn. The growth of this enquête officieuse is further promoted by the constant delegation to the police by the juge d'instruction of such of his duties as he *lawfully* can delegate. The suggestion now mooted in France of injecting counsel into the enquête officieuse itself seems to me calculated to make confusion yet worse confounded.

Effect of the inquiry

Many further consequences flow from this participation of the suspect in the inquiry, of which I may note two. First, the attention of the prosecution is, again almost necessarily, centered upon the suspect. . . . [B]ut this centring of the attention upon the suspect is, at any rate in the English view, unhealthy. At an interrogation which I happened to attend it certainly could not have been suggested that the juge d'instruction bullied the suspect into talking: indeed the opposite was the difficulty — to restrain him from interminable speech. But the dialogue between the two necessarily amounted to a cross-examination; and when the person is believed to be guilty the distinction between a cross-examination of this kind and the attempt to procure an admission seems to me metaphysical. The French process of inquiry appears to be principally concerned with the attempt to obtain an admission of the truth of the charge from a person reasonably believed to be guilty; confession is self-evidently, surely, the most proper result of a properly conducted instruction which does not end in a discharge. It cannot be a matter of great surprise if in the hands of persons less meticulous and less

well-trained than are the juges d'instruction, in Paris at any rate, such
an examination should relatively easily degenerate into an attempt
improperly to extort a confession.

The preliminary examination in France does not result in a finding
of guilty — in the case of a committal for trial the juge d'instruction
concludes *only* that a case sufficient to warrant the *trial* of the suspect
has been made out; and at the trial the prisoner continues, as much
in France as in England, to be presumed innocent until the contrary
is proved. Yet because the inquiry in France is one in which the
suspect has officially participated and has been heard and during
which he may have actually admitted the offense, the committal by
itself is there a good deal more probative of his guilt than is the
English preliminary hearing, where the magistrate normally takes
cognisance only of the *ex parte* evidence collected by the police by
its own process and for its own purposes and where the prisoner
often enters only a formal plea of not guilty and reserves his defence.
Moreover the whole of the material of the preliminary hearing,
including the police procès verbaux of the enquête officieuse, is
consigned in writing in the file, the dossier, which goes forward with
the prisoner to the court of trial and which stands as an enormous
weight against him. The dossier lies on the desk in front of the
president of the court of trial, and indeed seems to preside over the
court more than the president himself.

The dossier

It is the continuity of this dossier which may account for the horror
felt in France at the notion that the preliminary examination might
be conducted without the participation of the person now on trial:
it is of great importance that *his* version of the circumstances should
be introduced into the fatal file at the earliest possible opportunity.
It is certainly this dossier which gives to the English observer the false
impression that the prisoner at his trial in France is presumed guilty.
And it is this dossier, I think, which produces the confusion at the
trial which the French critics reprobate. At the French criminal trial
oral evidence is orally adduced; but the evidence so adduced is not
self-contained and complete in the English sense. It is not rehearsed
anew, now once and for all, entire and in its only original form. It
gives the impression of being excerpts only — fragmentary and
imperfect excerpts — from a story more fully and more carefully told
in the dossier. . . .

[T]he English observer should not conclude that the obvious
remedy is . . . to introduce into France the circumstances of an
English trial. I suspect that it would be repugnant to the French sense
of justice and propriety to propose that the inquiry by the juge
d'instruction should be jettisoned and that the guilt or innocence of
the accused should be allowed finally to depend on what may seem

to the French to be, and what in France might well be, the extremely fortuitous outcome of that markedly gladiatorial, and in any event highly peculiar, enterprise which in England we call a trial. On the contrary, the most promising line of reform in France — a line which is indeed proposed by the more perspicacious there — may well lie in the attempt to make more careful, more exact and more effective that very inquiry by the juge d'instruction which to us seems the obstacle and the anomaly.

[T]he capital contrasts which I select between the French and the English criminal systems are these two. First, that we think it right and fair that the preliminary inquiry into crime should be conducted by the police alone, acting *ex parte* as they may be advised, and in principle without the participation of the suspect. The suspect is in England entitled wholly to dissociate himself from the preliminary inquiry: he need have nothing to do with the police unless and until they arrest him on a charge clearly formulated at the time of his arrest. At that moment he must be cautioned in a form which certainly entitles him, and in practice is taken to advise him, to keep quiet. This silence he is entitled to preserve, and in practice often does preserve, before the magistrate before whom he must by the police promptly be produced. The duty of the magistrate is merely to hear the *ex parte* evidence of the police and to decide whether that evidence so produced, usually without disclosure of the nature of the defence, is sufficient to warrant the committal of that prisoner for trial. And to trial in England the prisoner if committed goes, retaining intact if he so chooses what we regard as the very high privilege of an entire silence; at the trial, before a jury, after the previous disclosure of the prosecution's evidence, once and for all to defend himself as he may be advised. The second contrast is this: that our trial is wholly self-contained and depends exclusively and entirely upon the oral evidence then adduced. Nothing can be carried from the inquiry into the trial except over the remarkable hurdle of the rules of evidence; and everything which is so carried is as manifest to the public as it is to the jury. It is by the matter thus manifestly produced and by that matter alone that the guilt or innocence of the prisoner is with us finally determined.

b. Length of the Criminal Process in Civil Law Countries

THE WEMHOFF-NEUMEISTER CASES *

European Court of Human Rights, Judgments of June 27, 1968
[1968] 11 Y.B. EUR. CONV. ON HUMAN RIGHTS 796

[FACTS: Both petitions involved the same issue. Wemhoff, charged with various sorts of fraud, was held in detention from November 9,

---

* The facts of these two cases have been consolidated. The judgments, which were rendered separately by the Court, are set out below.

1961, until April 7, 1965, when a verdict was finally handed down by the court of first instance. All appeals for release on bail pending the trial, and, after the latter had begun, pending the verdict, had been refused by the West German courts which claimed that the defendant's release would involve a risk that he would attempt to destroy crucial evidence or would attempt to escape.

[Neumeister, also accused of fraud, was held in detention between February 24, 1961, to May 12 of the same year, and, later, from July 12, 1962, until September 16, 1964. All appeals for release on reasonable bail were refused, the Austrian authorities claiming that the defendant might escape if released pending the decision in the case. Neumeister was finally released on bail in 1964, but as of the date of this decision (June 27, 1968), the court of first instance had not yet reached a verdict.

[Both Wemhoff and Neumeister claimed violations of art. 5, para. 3 ("Everyone arrested or detained . . . shall be entitled to trial within a reasonable time or to release pending trial. Release may be conditioned by guarantees to appear for trial.") and of art. 6, para. 1 ("[E]veryone is entitled to a fair and public hearing within a reasonable time by an independent and impartial tribunal established by law").

[In both cases, the arguments turned on the definition of "reasonable time" as used in the two articles cited above.]

THE WEMHOFF CASE *

. . . .

THE LAW

. . . .

To understand the precise scope of the provision in question it must be set in its context.

Art. 5, which begins with an affirmation of the right of everyone to liberty and security of person, goes on to specify the situations and conditions in which derogations from this principle may be made, in particular with a view to the maintenance of public order, which requires that offences shall be punished. It is thus mainly in the light of the fact of the detention of the person being prosecuted that national courts, possibly followed by the European Court, must determine whether the time that has elapsed, for whatever reason, before judgment is passed on the accused has at some stage exceeded a reasonable limit, that is to say imposed a greater sacrifice than could, in the circumstances of the case, reasonably be expected of a person presumed to be innocent.

---

* [1968] 11 Y.B. EUR. CONV. ON HUMAN RIGHTS 796.

In other words it is the provisional detention of accused persons which must not, according to art. 5, para. 3, be prolonged beyond a reasonable time. This is, moreover, the interpretation given to the text by both the German Government and the Commission. . . .

With a view to reducing the risk and the extent of such differences and as a measure of intellectual discipline, as the President of the Commission put it in his address to the Court, the Commission has devised an approach which consists in defining a set of seven criteria whose application is said to be suitable for arriving at an assessment, whether favorable or otherwise, of the length of the detention imposed. The examination of the various aspects of the case in the light of these criteria is supposed to produce an evaluation of its features as a whole; the relative importance of each criterion may vary according to the circumstances of the case.

The Court does not feel able to adopt this method. Before being referred to the organs set up under the Convention to ensure the observance of the engagements undertaken therein by the High Contracting Parties, cases of alleged violation of art. 5, para. 3, must have been the subject of domestic remedies and therefore of reasoned decisions by national judicial authorities. It is for them to mention the circumstances which led them, in the general interest, to consider it necessary to detain a person suspected of an offence but not convicted. Likewise, such a person must, when exercising his remedies have invoked the reasons which tend to refute the conclusions drawn by the authorities from the facts established by them, as well as other circumstances which told in favor of his release.

It is in the light of these points that the Court must judge whether the reasons given by the national authorities to justify continued detention are relevant and sufficient to show that detention was not unreasonably prolonged and contrary to art. 5, para. 3, of the Convention. . . .

[The Court, by a vote of six to one, determined that there was no violation of art. 5, para. 3, in the case of Wemhoff. The exceptional length of the investigation and of the trial were justified by the exceptional complexity of the case and by other causes that were impossible to avoid.]

The Court is of opinion that the precise aim of this provision in criminal matters is to ensure that accused persons do not have to lie under a charge for too long and that the charge is determined.

There is therefore no doubt that the period to be taken into consideration in applying this provision lasts at least until acquittal or conviction, even if this decision is reached on appeal. There is furthermore no reason why the protection given to the persons concerned against the delays of the courts should end at the first hearing in a trial: unwarranted adjournments or excessive delays on the part of trial courts are also to be feared. . . .

[The Court unanimously decided that there was no violation of art. 6, para. 1.]

INDIVIDUAL DISSENTING OPINION OF JUDGE ZEKIA
(RE: ART. 5, PARA. 3)

Wemhoff, the Applicant, was arrested and kept in custody without interruption for three years and five months until the conclusion of his trial on April 7, 1965. . . .

The crux of the case is . . . the ascertainment of the extent of the "reasonable time" specified in art. 5, para. 3, in relation to the facts and accompanying circumstances of the case we are dealing with.

. . . .

It may not be difficult to arrive at a uniformity of thought or practice on such matters in a particular country or in countries where the provisions dealing with relevant points (arrest, detention, investigation, etc.) of the criminal procedure are substantially the same. But it is very difficult in a court or courts at international level to form consensus of judicial opinion on demarcating the bounds of reasonableness, even roughly, which art. 5, para. 3, contemplates. However, in the course of time this might become possible.

The legal system of a country, governing the provisions of the criminal law and procedure relating to pre-trial proceedings — such as preliminary enquiries, investigation and arraignment — as well as the presentation of a case to the court and the power of the court itself in reopening investigations, has a lot to do with the time taken in the conclusion of a trial. In a country where the common law system is followed the time taken in bringing the accused before a trial court and having him tried is relatively much shorter than the time needed for such a trial under the continental system.

In the former case it is the police and the prosecution who conduct the enquiries and collect the evidence. They present the case to a court either for trial or — in indictable offences — for preliminary enquiries for the purpose of committal before the assizes. Under the latter system the investigation is carried out by a judge and the trial of the accused is started after judicial investigations are closed and after the decision is taken for remitting the case before trial.

Under the common law system after a person has been charged he is not bound to say anything or assist the prosecution in any way in the investigation, unless after he is duly cautioned he elects to say something. In the continental system interrogation and confrontation of the man in custody is a normal procedural feature and the case is prepared during his detention.

While in the former system sufficient evidence to build up a prima facie case against the suspected person is normally expected to be available before he is charged and is taken into custody, in the latter case, i.e., continental system, it appears that the availability of such evidence at an early stage is not essential. Information to the satisfaction of the judicial officials seems to be sufficient for the arrest and detention of a suspect.

As a consequence of these basic divergences inherent in the two systems, suspected persons are, as a rule, kept in detention considerably longer on the continent than in the case of those in England or other countries where the system of common law prevails.

If in England you keep an accused person — even in an exceptionally difficult case — over six months without having been brought before a trial court, the repercussions caused not only among the judicial circles but also on the public would be great. A Writ of Habeas Corpus would certainly lie if the man is not committed for trial before the next assizes which periodically sits three times a year. What about if you keep an unconvicted person for three years and over? Surely this will be described as shocking.

My point is not to draw a comparison between the common law and continental systems governing criminal procedure. These systems being different in nature, one accusatorial and the other inquisitorial, may as a result cause a suspected person to be kept longer or shorter in accordance with the prevailing system in the country he lives in. My intention is neither to touch on the merits or demerits of either system. My digression from the track is to emphasise the fact that, if in England, a Member of the Council of Europe, the concept of "reasonable time" regarding the period of detention of an unconvicted person awaiting his trial does not allow us to stretch the time beyond six months even in an exceptionally difficult and complicated case, could we say that in the continent in a similar case, the period of detention might be six times longer and yet it could be considered as reasonable and therefore compatible with the Convention?

The Convention has aimed at setting a common standard as to the right to liberty and safety of persons for the people living in the territories of the member States of the Council of Europe. The difference of standards therefore in such countries cannot be substantially a great one. Coming from a country where the system of common law obtains,* I might unwittingly have been influenced by this system.

---

* Cyprus.

THE NEUMEISTER CASE *

The Law

[The European Court of Human Rights decided the Neumeister case, on reasoning similar to that in *Wemhoff.* A violation of art. 5, para. 3, was found, consisting in the refusal of the Austrian courts to accept Neumeister's offers to provide bail. The amount of bail demanded by the lower courts was not fixed by reference to the sum required to assure his appearance for trial, but rather was determined by reference to the amount the defendant was alleged to have obtained by fraud. No violation was found, however, in connection with Neumeister's claim that his case was not decided within a reasonable time.]

. . . .

[A]n examination . . . of the activities of the Investigating Judge between July 12, 1962, and the close of the investigation on November 4, 1963 . . . gives rise to serious disquiet. Not only was there during those fifteen months . . . no interrogation of Neumeister nor any confrontation of any importance with the other accused person whose statements are said to have caused the Applicant's second arrest, but between June 24, 1963, and September 18 of the same year, the Judge did not interrogate any of the numerous co-accused or any witness, nor did he proceed to any other measure of investigation.

Lastly, it is indeed disappointing that the trial was not able to commence before November 9, 1964, that is a year after the closing of the investigation, and even more disappointing that, following such a long investigation the trial court was compelled, after sitting for several months, to order further investigations which were not all caused by the statements of the accused Huber, who had remained silent until the trial.

The Court does not however consider these various facts sufficient to warrant the conclusion that the reasonable time laid down in art. 6, para. 1, of the Convention was exceeded in the present case.

It is beyond doubt that the Neumeister case was of extraordinary complexity. . . . It is, for example, not possible to hold the Austrian judicial authorities responsible for the difficulties they encountered abroad in obtaining the execution of their numerous letters rogatory. . . . The need to wait for replies probably explains the delay in closing the investigation, despite the fact that no further measures of investigation remained to be conducted in Austria.

The course of the investigation would probably have been accelerated had the Applicant's case been severed from those of his

---

* [1968] 11 Y.B. Eur. Conv. on Human Rights 812.

co-accused, but nothing suggests that such a severance would here have been compatible with the good administration of justice. . . .

It should moreover be pointed out that a concern for speed cannot dispense those judges who in the system of criminal procedure in force on the continent of Europe are responsible for the investigation or the conduct of the trial from taking every measure likely to throw light on the truth or falsehood of the charges.

Finally, it is obvious that the delays in opening and reopening the hearing were in large part caused by the need to give legal representatives of the parties and also the judges sitting on the case time to acquaint themselves with the case record, which comprised twenty-one volumes of about five hundred pages each as well as a large number of other documents. . . .

[Judge Zekia dissented from this portion of the Neumeister case.]

NOTES

1. Questions concerning reasonable time have been before the Court of Human Rights in other cases, including the following two, both concerning Austria: *Stögmüller,* [1969] Y.B. Eur. Conv. on Human Rights 364, and *Matznetter,* [1969] Y.B. Eur. Conv. on Human Rights 406. The Court held that there had been a violation of art. 5, para. 3, of the Convention in Stögmüller's case because his detention for two years pending trial on charges of fraud had exceeded a "reasonable time" since there was no danger that the offense would be repeated. In Matznetter's case, on the other hand, the Court found (by a vote of 5-2) that art. 5, para. 3, had not been violated. Because of the exceptional complexity of the case a detention of two years, one month, twenty-three days was justified. In the *Stögmüller* case the Court observed that it is impossible to translate the concept of reasonable time into a fixed number of days, weeks, months or years. The Court noted that each case must be tested in relation to the seriousness of the offense, the grounds stated by the judicial authorities to justify the detention, and other factual considerations. This evaluation must always be weighed, however, in the light of the fact that prolongation of detention is a serious departure from the presumption of innocence and respect for individual liberty.

2. There have been legislative responses to the problem of prolonged detention during the European criminal process. For example, both Germany and Italy have placed outer limits on the period of permitted detention. (Germany, Law of Dec. 19, 1964; Italy, Code of Criminal Procedure, arts. 272 and 275, as amended in 1970 and 1974.)

c. *Role of the Public Prosecutor*

BERTETT

Corte costituzionale, Decision of December 10, 1970, No. 190
[1970] 15 Giur. Cost. 2179; [1970] 32 Rac. uff. corte cost. 671
[1971] 94 Foro It. I, 8

FACTS

In the course of a criminal proceeding pending before the Tribunal of Rome, the attorney for the defendant made a motion to be present, on an equal footing with the Public Prosecutor, at the interrogation of the defendant, one Luigi Bertett. After the denial of this motion, that attorney challenged the constitutionality of art. 303 of the Code of Criminal Procedure in light of art. 24 of the Constitution: according to the defense's argument, the principle of equality between prosecution and defense, implicit in the constitutional norm, clashes with art. 303 which allows the Public Prosecutor to assist in the acts of the *istruzione* (as well as to make observations and motions) while it does not provide for the presence or the assistance of the defense attorney.

. . . .

In considering the argument, this Court has extended its examination to include art. 304-*bis,* first para. which denies the defense attorney the right to assist in the interrogation of the defendant. . . . Thus . . . the Court jointly considered the constitutionality of art. 303 and art. 304-*bis* in relation to art. 24 of the Constitution.

OPINION

. . . As a preliminary matter, it is necessary to ascertain whether the role of the Public Prosecutor and that of the defense attorney are similar enough to allow a fair comparison of their respective authority.

It should be recognized immediately that the Public Prosecutor cannot, strictly speaking, be considered a party in the traditional sense. He is a member of the judiciary and, as such, independent from the other branches of government. In this position he seeks to safeguard the general observance of the law rather than any specific interests. The Public Prosecutor [does not necessarily act against the interest of the defendant; his duty also includes] . . . examinations that may demonstrate the innocence of the defendant, . . . requests that the charges be dropped (*decreto di archiviazione*), and requests for the acquittal of the defendant. The special position of the Public Prosecutor, however, does not allow us to conclude that he is on an equal footing with the judge. . . . In practice, when it is the criminal responsibility of the defendant that is in dispute . . . , there are two opposing adversaries — the Public Prosecutor and the defendant. The clear contrast between the interests which they are each promoting justifies the conclusion that, before the judge, both must be considered parties. . . .

It should be emphasized, however, that this conclusion does not mean that the powers of the Public Prosecutor must always be equal to those of the defense. The unique institutional position and the function assigned to the Public Prosecutor by the Constitution itself can justify disparate treatment, but can do so only when a reasonable justification can be found in the nature of the function or the institutional position of the public Prosecutor.

Once it has been ascertained that the Public Prosecutor and the defendant are each adversaries, it is necessary to consider that . . . the right of defense is assured only to the extent that the defendant has the opportunity to participate in an effective adversary debate, which opportunity he is not likely to have without the aid of an attorney. . . .

One should bear in mind, however, that art. 24, second para. of the Constitution, in guaranteeing the right of defense in "every stage and phase of the proceeding" does not necessarily mean that the right to an attorney and the right to adversary debate must attach at every moment and in every step of the proceeding. On the other hand, at each step it is necessary to ascertain if the absence of the defense attorney, and the consequently attenuated adversary debate, deprive the defendant of the constitutional right of defense. Therefore, in reference to the present problem we must determine whether the interrogation of the accused, seen in the light of the entire *istruzione*, is so important that the absence of the defense attorney and the presence of the Public Prosecutor cause a serious infringement of the right of defense.

The Court holds that it must give an affirmative response to this query. Indeed, the fundamental importance of the interrogation of the accused has already been recognized several times by this Court (see e.g., this Court's decision No. 109, 1970) . . . [in that it is the basic tool] for the gathering of proof of innocence or guilt. . . .

The fact that the defendant is exposed to the observations, accusations, and arguments of the Public Prosecutor at a critical act without being assisted by an attorney to advise him of the necessity for appropriate defensive explanations, cannot help but seriously infringe the right of defense. And this is true notwithstanding the privilege against self-incrimination reaffirmed by law No. 932, of Dec. 5, 1969. The legislature itself has provided for some defensive intervention during the interrogation; indeed . . . , the transcripts of the interrogation must be filed with the clerk of the court within five days of its occurrence so that the defense attorney may view them and make motions; furthermore, art. 8 of the same law prohibits the use of statements given by the suspect before the appointment of the defense attorney. Nevertheless these legislative innovations, even if they demonstrate that the law has already pointed out the need for some protection, are clearly insufficient to afford effective protection. According to the rule still in force, the Public Prosecutor intervenes at the beginning of the interrogation while the defense attorney can intervene only after the interrogation has been completed, transcribed and filed. Moreover, art. 304-*quarter,* fifth para., of the Code of Criminal Procedure authorizes the judge, possibly even at the request of the Public Prosecutor, to order a delay in the filing of the transcripts; consequently, the intervention of the defense attorney can be delayed for a noteworthy period of time even beyond the completion of the interrogation. This gravely curtails the right of defense especially when the defense attorney, dealing with the matter of the defendant's detention, is constrained to ignore, in detail, both the charges brought against his client and the defenses already put forth by that client in the interrogation, in order to attempt to obtain the defendant's release from custody. Thus, the attorney is forced to make this attempt without being able to evaluate fully the defensive arguments that can be useful to get the defendant released.

The Court holds that such disparity of treatment between the Public Prosecutor and the defense of the accused — which, it bears repeating, can in some cases be extremely prejudicial — cannot be justified in light of the Constitution.

. . . It appears from the government report accompanying the 1955 reform that the exclusion of defense attorneys from the interrogation was . . . [justified] "in order to permit the defendant to respond to the questions with the greatest possible frankness — without the worry or the influence of a third party's presence." These reasons, in as much as they imply a complete distrust in the work of the defense attorney, conflict with the constitutional precepts implied by the right of defense. Rather than hindering or opposing justice, the presence of the attorney harmonizes perfectly with the ends sought by the judicial process. While it should be emphasized that the law authorizes the judge to repress any illegitimate interference, there is no reason to suppose that the motions and observations of the defense attorney will worry or influence the defendant any more than the activity and presence of the Public Prosecutor.

On the contrary it is reasonable to believe that equality of the disputants will not only guarantee the right of defense, but will also aid the judge, in exercising his delicate function. Moreover, one should not underestimate the likelihood that the presence and the assistance of the defense attorney will confer greater reliability on the results of the interrogation, even for those results that are unfavorable to the defendant. Thus, it must be admitted that, in so far as it relates to the interrogation, adversary debate is useful to the administration of justice.

. . . .

For all of these reasons, art. 304-*bis*, first para. of the Code of Criminal Procedure must be declared unconstitutional in that part in which it denies the right of the defendant to be assisted by an attorney at the interrogation.

NOTE

Compare *Bertett* with the decisions of the Ministers of the Council of Europe in the *Pataki* and *Dunshirn* cases, Ch. 7, § A.4., *supra.*

2. Right to Counsel in Pretrial Investigation

a. Italy

The present Code of Criminal Procedure in Italy was enacted in 1931, under the fascist regime. The criminal proceeding was envisioned as having two stages, the *istruzione* or fact-finding and proof-gathering stage, and the *dibattimento* or trial. There are two types of *istruzione*, the *istruzione sommaria* and the *istruzione formale.* The *istruzione sommaria* is performed by the Public Prosecutor. This proceeding is applicable in cases where the accused has been caught in the act of committing the crime, has confessed, has committed the crime while under arrest, detention or internment as a measure of security, and in cases in which evidence of the crime is clear. In the *istruzione formale*, on the other hand, the proof-gathering is conducted by an ordinary judge and the whole proceeding is subject to much stricter procedural controls. Article 304 of the Code granted the right to counsel only in the *istruzione formale*, but did not provide counsel during every investigative act performed during that stage.

In 1955, in an effort to reconcile the philosophies of the Code of Criminal Procedure of 1931 and the liberal, republican Constitution of 1948, an extensive reform of the Code was undertaken by the legislature. Among the changes introduced by this reform were arts. 304-*bis*, 304-*ter*, and 304-*quater*. These provisions stated that the counsel for the defendant had the right to be present at the various stages of the *istruzione formale,* such as confrontations (*confronti*), expert testimony (*perizie*), searches (*perquisizioni*), and lineups (*ricognizioni personali*). Defense counsel was also entitled to inspect and copy documents pertaining to the case, such as transcripts of the defendant's interrogation.

Article 392 of the Code of Criminal Procedure provides that the "standards, established for the *istruzione formale* shall be observed in the *istruzione sommaria* in those cases in which they are applicable." From 1955 until 1958 lower courts in Italy differed concerning whether or not arts. 304-*bis, -ter,* and -*quater* were also applicable to the *istruzione sommaria.* The *Corte di Cassazione* concluded that the provisions were not "applicable" because their application would destroy the distinction between the *istruzione sommaria* and the *istruzione formale.*

In 1965 the constitutionality of the phrase in art. 392, "in those cases in whch they are applicable," was attacked as contrary to art. 24, para. 2, of the Constitution which grants the right of defense "at every stage and phase" of a criminal proceeding.

In the *Venieri* case, Decision of June 26, 1965, Corte cost., [1965] 10 Giur. cost. 699; [1965] 22 Rac. uff. corte cost. 39; [1965] 88 Foro It. I, 1160, the *Corte Costituzionale* declared the phrase in question unconstitutional insofar as it made possible a denial of the extension of the guarantees of the *istruzione formale* to the *istruzione sommaria.*

AMADUCCI ET AL.

Corte costituzionale, Decision July 5, 1968, No. 86
[1968] 13 Giur. Cost. 1430; [1968] 28 Rac. uff. corte cost. 77
[1968] 91 Foro It. I, 1681

[At the time of this decision, in cases of urgency or where the accused was discovered in the commission of the crime, art. 225 of the Code of Criminal Procedure gave the judicial police the power to undertake preliminary investigations such as questioning the suspect and taking unsworn statements of witnesses. "[W]herever possible" these investigations had to be conducted according to the standards established for the *istruzione formale.*

[Article 392 of the Code of Criminal Procedure provided that the "standards, established for the *istruzione formale* shall be observed in the *istruzione sommaria* in those cases in which they are applicable."

[Article 232 allowed the Public Prosecutor to proceed with an investigation either himself or through use of the judicial police before requesting *istruzione formale* or initiating an *istruzione sommaria.*

[Article 395 applied in those cases in which the Public Prosecutor decided there was a lack of probable cause and requested a dismissal of the case. It required that the accused be interrogated if the dismissal was based on insufficient evidence or was in the form of a pardon or amnesty. The purpose of the interrogation was to allow the accused to present evidence which would absolve him of the crime.]

. . . .

According to the lower court's *ordinanze* ... [many scholars believe that] the standards relating to the *istruzione* are applicable to preliminary investigations as well. On the other hand, ... the courts have universally interpreted these rules to exclude such applicability ... despite the fact that acts of the judicial police are a part of the phases and stages of the proceeding in which the right of defense is constitutionally guaranteed. Furthermore, the statement of the accused may be taken in this preliminary investigation; and this may well be the most "critical" of the entire proceeding.

The judge of Bologna ... concluded that the "suspect" should always be able to defend himself before the authority of the police for two reasons: first, because evidence taken in this preliminary stage will inevitably affect the outcome of the proceeding, and second, because this is in accordance with the principle that no one shall be a witness against himself (*nemo tenetur edere contra se*) ....

OPINION

The three ordinances propose substantially the same question of constitutionality. Therefore these ordinances can be dealt with in a single proceeding.

Article 232 of the Code of Criminal Procedure is challenged because it allows the Public Prosecutor to perform necessary investigative acts, without providing the guarantees required in the *istruzione* by arts. 304 through 304-*quater* of the Code of Criminal Procedure.

It deals with the preliminary investigation which the Public Prosecutor makes immediately after the *notitia criminis* [i.e., when he first knows of the crime] and which precedes the true and proper *istruzione*, formal or summary. This investigation is ostensibly limited to the gathering of circumstantial proof or the taking of summary testimony; but it frequently consists of typical acts of *istruzione* (identification, examinations, confrontations, searches) during which evidence is taken that may be utilized directly against the defendant in the later course of the proceeding.

These acts, although of a provisional nature, do not differ substantially from those which take place in the true and proper *istruzione* and therefore can lead the trial along lines from which it will be difficult later to escape. It is enough to think of inspections which are not easily conducted a second time, investigations made in an atmosphere of anxiety to discover the guilty individual rapidly, and interrogations conducted feverishly in a climate of alarm caused by the crime. The manner in which the inquiries are made, the tools which the investigator is constrained to use, the absence of true participation on the part of the suspect (if there is one) and his counsel, can irreparably compromise the outcome of the proceeding. On the other hand if these same acts were accomplished in the course of *istruzione formale*, they would nearly all take place in the presence of the party's counsel. Moreover the documents, including the transcripts of interrogations, in which the progress of the investigations as well as the conclusions drawn therefrom were recorded, would be filed with the clerk. Thus they would be available to the accused in accordance with the requirements of a full exercise of the right of defense. Finally we must mention that the same rules govern the *istruzione sommaria* by virtue of our decision in [the *Venieri* case].

The difference between the *istruzione sommaria* which offers the suspect the guarantees provided in arts. 304-*bis* through 304-*quater*, and a proceeding which ignores these guarantees, is not justified in respect to art. 24, para. 2, of the Constitution. First of all, the difference is not justified by the urgency of the gathering of evidence since the challenged rule is also applied in cases in which no such urgency exists and, at any rate, such a situation is provided for in art. 304-*ter*. Secondly, it is not justified by the nature of the investigatory proceedings, given that they do not differ from that of *istruzione*; nor are they justified by their alleged estrangement from the true and proper proceeding, a very formalistic reason which is moreover contradicted by the participation of a member of the judiciary, i.e., the Public Prosecutor, in such acts.

In addition, the power conferred by art. 232 on the Public Prosecutor to complete his case in the preparatory phase instead of during the *istruzione* (where evidence is frequently difficult to gather) accentuates the unconstitutionality of the challenged rule. The breadth of the right of defense, which is guaranteed by the Constitution at every phase and stage of the proceeding, must not depend on the mere discretion of the investigator inclined, by the nature of his function, to enlarge somewhat the preliminary phase in relation to that of the *istruzione*. It is exactly this of which the *ordinanza* warns.

The reasons for the partial unconstitutionality of art. 232 also render unconstitutional, in part, another of the challenged rules, that is art. 225 which, in certain cases, allows the accomplishment of true and proper acts of *istruzione* at the initiative of the officials of the judicial police.

Here the gravity of the undertaking, unrequested by the Public Prosecutor, has been justified on grounds of flagrancy or urgency; no violation of the right of defense was thought to exist in the face of the obligation to observe the rules of *istruzione formale* and to transmit all acts to the Public Prosecutor. Reality brings us to a different conclusion.

Because of the tension between the delicacy of the functions, the desire to discover the guilty parties rapidly. . . , the fear (natural in this type of situation) of not finding or of losing evidence, and the difficulty of strict control on the part of the Public Prosecutor, . . . the concept of urgency or flagrancy is in practice, frequently enlarged. Despite contrary legislative intent, the right of defense is sacrificed to sometimes insubstantial exigencies that can be dealt with by the framework provided for in the *istruzione*, which can and often does reconcile the exercise of the right of defense with the proceeding's absolute needs, including even urgency.

Moreover, according to the challenged norm the guarantees of the *istruzione* may be extended to the preliminary inquiries only "wherever possible," in other words, practically at the discretion of the judicial police. And, as a matter of fact, reasons of urgency are usually advanced as the justification for having denied proper application of arts. 304-*bis*, -*ter* and -*quater* of the Code of Criminal Procedure. . . . There is no doubt that this is contrary to art. 24 of the Constitution. . . .

It is not correct to attempt to avoid the constitutional objection by pointing to the fact that these activities, which take place before the formal proceeding is initiated, would be outside of "every phase and stage" of the proceeding. On the contrary, the reasons given for limiting the activities of the Public Prosecutor apply with greater force to the activities of the judicial police. Their activities are not foreign to the proceeding, but consist of preliminary inquiries which will have a bearing on the eventual decision.

On the other hand, the declaration of unconstitutionality of part of art. 225 does not preclude the judicial police from undertaking the necessary inquiries in emergencies. It only imposes limitations [*i.e.*, the observance of the guarantees of defense] on inquiries which have the same content as acts of the *istruzione* and are to be used in the proceeding. In this connection the judge will control, in the preliminary phase also, the application of art. 390, which provides for judicial appointment of counsel where the suspect does not select his own. In any case, even if this requires the frequent intervention of the court, the inconvenience, looking at the experience of other countries, would not be excessive. The right of defense, in a legal system which establishes a presumption of innocence until the accused is found guilty in a proper court of law, is worth the sacrifice of a large measure of expediency in the conduct of investigations. . . .

NOTES AND QUESTIONS

1. The *Aliprandi* case, Decision of Dec. 3, 1969, Corte cost., [1969] 14 Giur. Cost. 2249; [1969] 30 Rac. uff. corte cost. 529; [1970] 93 Foro It. I, 10, involved two joined cases concerning technical operations by the police. In one case, the police had conducted a

scientific examination of sequestered wine. In the other case, the police had conducted laboratory analysis of a substance suspected to be hashish. The *Corte Costituzionale* held that the requirements of arts. 304-*bis*, -*ter* and -*quater* applied to all acts of the judicial police during the preliminary phase of criminal investigation, if those acts are the same as those that would be performed in the *istruzione.* Does it make sense to require that the accused's counsel be present while a blood sample is taken from him? While the blood sample is being analyzed by a laboratory technician?

2. A few days after the *Aliprandi* decision, the Italian Parliament passed a bill reforming several articles of the Code of Criminal Procedure to conform the Code to the principles of that decision. Among other things, the Law of Dec. 5, 1969, No. 932, stated that "during the preliminary investigations the rules of the *istruzione formale* must be observed."

3. Professor Paolo Barile noted immediately after the *Amaducci* case: *

> This important decision strikes a blow at the ambiguity of the so-called "preliminary investigations," undertaken by the Public Prosecutor and the judicial police in a stage of pre-*istruzione*, "behind the backs" of the citizens in a certain sense; that is, before the charge is brought. Until now, the criminal procedure has allowed the magistrate and the police not only to obtain physical evidence and collect summary information, but also to engage in acts typical of the *istruzione* (interrogation, investigation, confrontation of witnesses, searches and seizures) the results of which are to be directly used in a later stage of the proceeding. All this was undertaken without the participation of counsel, but above all, without comprehension of the importance of such acts on the part of the protagonists, who perhaps later found themselves in the position of the accused. The *Corte Costituzionale*, in a dramatic portrayal of this preliminary phase, emphasized the irreparable consequences which can follow an investigation which cannot be repeated, an identification "made in an atmosphere of anxiety to discover the guilty individual rapidly," "interrogation feverishly conducted in a climate of alarm caused by the crime" . . . and above all, pointed out that it is unconstitutional to allow the Public Prosecutor wide discretion between conducting preliminary inquiries and initiating the *istruzione*. If he would use the former, he must assure the possible accused the right of defense from the first moment. The same applies in cases in which the judicial police act because of the flagrancy of the crime or urgency of gathering proof or of preserving evidence. In such cases it is not necessary

---

* P. Barile, *I diritti dell'imputato,* in L'ESPRESSO, July 14, 1968.

that the police be precluded from undertaking investigations, but they must not be permitted to accomplish "true and proper acts of *istruzione* as are used in the proceeding." . . .

On this point the thinking of the Court seems to draw on those modern and democratic elements of the decisions of the Supreme Court of the United States. The "accusatory" system is in fact entering into our practice; the rules of "due process" are being adapted by us in the sense of insuring a fair hearing to all . . . , assuring the effectiveness of the right of defense.

4. Professor Barile argues that the *Amaducci* decision draws on decisions of the United States Supreme Court. Do you think that, in requiring counsel for the accused during the police investigation stage of a criminal case, the *Corte Costituzionale* is following the decisions of the United States Supreme Court? Is *Amaducci* the "Italian *Miranda*" decision? (*Miranda* v. *Arizona*, 384 U.S. 436 (1966) deals with the defendant's right to counsel during police investigation.) Consider the materials in the next section.

b. United States

UNITED STATES v. ASH

Supreme Court of the United States
413 U.S. 300, 93 S. Ct. 2568, 37 L. Ed. 2d 619 (1973)

MR. JUSTICE BLACKMUN delivered the opinion of the Court.

In this case the Court is called upon to decide whether the Sixth Amendment grants an accused the right to have counsel present whenever the Government conducts a post-indictment photographic display, containing a picture of the accused, for the purpose of allowing a witness to attempt an identification of the offender.

I

On the morning of August 26, 1965, a man with a stocking mask entered a bank in Washington, D. C., and began waving a pistol. He ordered an employee to hang up the telephone and instructed all others present not to move. Seconds later a second man, also wearing a stocking mask, entered the bank, scooped up money from tellers' drawers into a bag, and left. The gunman followed, and both men escaped through an alley. The robbery lasted three or four minutes.

A Government informer, Clarence McFarland, told authorities that he had discussed the robbery with Charles J. Ash, Jr., the respondent here. Acting on this information, an FBI agent, in February 1966, showed five black-and-white mug shots of Negro males of generally the same age, height, and weight, one of which was of Ash, to four witnesses. All four made uncertain identifications of Ash's picture.

At this time Ash was not in custody and had not been charged. On April 1, 1966, an indictment was returned charging Ash and a codefendant, John L. Bailey, in five counts related to this bank robbery.

Trial was finally set for May 1968, almost three years after the crime. In preparing for trial, the prosecutor decided to use a photographic display to determine whether the witnesses he planned to call would be able to make in-court identifications. Shortly before the trial, an FBI agent and the prosecutor showed five color photographs to the four witnesses who previously had tentatively identified the black-and-white photograph of Ash. Three of the witnesses selected the picture of Ash, but one was unable to make any selection. None of the witnesses selected the picture of Bailey which was in the group. This post-indictment [3] identification provides the basis for respondent Ash's claim that he was denied the right to counsel at a "critical stage" of the prosecution.

. . . .

II

. . . .

In *Powell* v. *Alabama,* 287 U. S. 45, 60-66 (1932), the Court discussed the English common-law rule that severely limited the right of a person accused of a felony to consult with counsel at trial. The Court examined colonial constitutions and statutes and noted that "in at least twelve of the thirteen colonies the rule of the English common law, in the respect now under consideration, had been definitely rejected and the right to counsel fully recognized in all criminal prosecutions, save that in one or two instances the right was limited to capital offenses or to the more serious crimes." The Sixth Amendment counsel guarantee, thus, was derived from colonial statutes and constitutional provisions designed to reject the English common-law rule.

Apparently several concerns contributed to this rejection at the very time when countless other aspects of the common law were being imported. One consideration was the inherent irrationality of the English limitation. Since the rule was limited to felony proceedings, the result, absurd and illogical, was that an accused misdemeanant could rely fully on counsel, but the accused felon, in theory at least, could consult counsel only on legal questions that the accused proposed to the court. English writers were appropriately critical of this inconsistency.

---

[3] Respondent Ash does not assert a right to counsel at the black-and-white photograhic display in February 1966 because he recognizes that *Kirby* v. *Illinois,* 406 U. S. 682 (1972), forecloses application of the Sixth Amendment to events before the initiation of adversary criminal proceedings.

A concern of more lasting importance was the recognition and awareness that an unaided layman had little skill in arguing the law or in coping with an intricate procedural system. The function of counsel as a guide through complex legal technicalities long has been recognized by this Court.... The Court frequently has interpreted the Sixth Amendment to assure that the "guiding hand of counsel" is available to those in need of its assistance.

Another factor contributing to the colonial recognition of the accused's right to counsel was the adoption of the institution of the public prosecutor from the Continental inquisitorial system.... Thus, an additional motivation for the American rule was a desire to minimize the imbalance in the adversary system that otherwise resulted with the creation of a professional prosecuting official....

This historical background suggests that the core purpose of the counsel guarantee was to assure "Assistance" at trial, when the accused was confronted with both the intricacies of the law and the advocacy of the public prosecutor. Later developments have led this Court to recognize that "Assistance" would be less than meaningful if it were limited to the formal trial itself.

This extension of the right to counsel to events before trial has resulted from changing patterns of criminal procedure and investigation that have tended to generate pretrial events that might appropriately be considered to be parts of the trial itself. At these newly emerging and significant events, the accused was confronted, just as at trial, by the procedural system, or by his expert adversary, or by both. In [*United States* v.] *Wade* [388 U.S. 218 (1967)], the Court explained the process of expanding the counsel guarantee to these confrontations:

> "When the Bill of Rights was adopted, there were no organized police forces as we know them today. The accused confronted the prosecutor and the witnesses against him, and the evidence was marshalled, largely at the trial itself. In contrast, today's law enforcement machinery involves critical confrontations of the accused by the prosecution at pretrial proceedings where the results might well settle the accused's fate and reduce the trial itself to a mere formality. In recognition of these realities of modern criminal prosecution, our cases have construed the Sixth Amendment guarantee to apply to 'critical' stages of the proceedings."

. . . .

The function of counsel in rendering "Assistance" continued at the lineup under consideration in *Wade* and its companion cases. Although the accused was not confronted there with legal questions, the lineup offered opportunities for prosecuting authorities to take advantage of the accused. Counsel was seen by the Court as being more sensitive to, and aware of, suggestive influences than the accused himself, and as better able to reconstruct the events at trial. Counsel present at lineup would be able to remove disabilities of the accused in precisely the same fashion that counsel compensated for the disabilities of the layman at trial. Thus, the Court mentioned that the accused's memory might be dimmed by "emotional tension," that the accused's credibility at trial would be diminished by his status as defendant, and that the accused might be unable to present his version effectively without giving up his privilege against compulsory self-incrimination. It was in order to compensate for these deficiencies that the Court found the need for the assistance of counsel.

III

. . . .

After the Court in *Wade* held that a lineup constituted a trial-like confrontation requiring counsel, a more difficult issue remained in the case for consideration. The same changes in law enforcement that led to lineups and pretrial hearings also generated other events at which the accused was confronted by the prosecution. The Government had argued in *Wade* that if counsel was required at a lineup, the same forceful considerations would mandate counsel at other preparatory steps in the "gathering of the prosecution's evidence," such as, for particular example, the taking of fingerprints or blood samples.

The Court concluded that there were differences. Rather than distinguishing these situations from the lineup in terms of the need for counsel to assure an equal confrontation at the time, the Court recognized that there were times when the subsequent trial would cure a one-sided confrontation between prosecuting authorities and the uncounseled defendant. In other words, such stages were not "critical." Referring to fingerprints, hair, clothing, and other blood samples, the Court explained:

> "Knowledge of the techniques of science and technology is sufficiently available, and the variables in techniques few enough, that the accused has the opportunity for a meaningful confrontation of the Government's case at trial through the ordinary processes of cross-examination of the Government's expert witnesses and the presentation of the evidence of his own experts."

The structure of *Wade,* viewed in light of the careful limitation of the Court's language to "confrontations," makes it clear that lack of scientific precision and inability to reconstruct an event are not the tests for requiring counsel in the first instance. These are, instead, the tests to determine whether confrontation with counsel at trial can serve as a substitute for counsel at the pretrial confrontation. If accurate reconstruction is possible, the risks inherent in any confrontation still remain, but the opportunity to cure defects at trial causes the confrontation to cease to be "critical." . . . Judge Friendly, writing for the Second Circuit in *United States* v. *Bennett,* 409 F. 2d 888 (1969), recognized that the "criticality" test of *Wade,* if applied outside the confrontation context, would result in drastic expansion of the right to counsel:

> "None of the classical analyses of the assistance to be given by counsel, Justice Sutherland's in Powell v. Alabama . . . and Justice Black's in Johnson v. Zerbst . . . and Gideon v. Wainwright . . . suggests that counsel must be present when the prosecution is interrogating witnesses in the defendant's absence even when, as here, the defendant is under arrest; counsel is rather to be provided to prevent the defendant himself from falling into traps devised by a lawyer on the other side and to see to it that all available defenses are proffered. Many other aspects of the prosecution's interviews with a victim or a witness to a crime afford just as much opportunity for undue suggestion as the display of photographs; so, too, do the defense's interviews, notably with alibi witnesses." . . .

IV

A substantial departure from the historical test would be necessary if the Sixth Amendment were interpreted to give Ash a right to counsel at the photographic identification in this case. Since the accused himself is not present at the time of the photographic display, and asserts no right to be present, . . . no possibility arises that the accused might be misled by his lack of familiarity with the law or overpowered by his professional adversary. Similarly, the counsel guarantee would not be used to produce equality in a trial-like adversary confrontation. Rather, the guarantee was used by the Court of Appeals to produce confrontation at an event that previously was not analogous to an adversary trial.

Even if we were willing to view the counsel guarantee in broad terms as a generalized protection of the adversary process, we would be unwilling to go so far as to extend the right to a portion of the prosecutor's trial-preparation interviews with witnesses. . . . The traditional counterbalance in the American adversary system for these interviews arises from the equal ability of defense counsel to seek and interview witnesses himself.

That adversary mechanism remains as effective for a photographic display as for other parts of pretrial interviews. No greater limitations are placed on defense counsel in constructing displays, seeking witnesses, and conducting photographic identifications than those applicable to the prosecution. . . .

The argument has been advanced that requiring counsel might compel the police to observe more scientific procedures or might encourage them to utilize corporeal rather than photographic displays. This Court has recognized that improved procedures can minimize the dangers of suggestion. . . . Commentators have also proposed more accurate techniques.

Pretrial photographic identifications, however, are hardly unique in offering possibilities for the actions of the prosecutor unfairly to prejudice the accused. Evidence favorable to the accused may be withheld; testimony of witnesses may be manipulated; the results of laboratory tests may be contrived. In many ways the prosecutor, by accident or by design, may improperly subvert the trial. The primary safeguard against abuses of this kind is the ethical responsibility of the prosecutor, who, as so often has been said, may "strike hard blows" but not "foul ones." If that safeguard fails, review remains available under due process standards. These same safeguards apply to misuse of photographs.

We are not persuaded that the risks inherent in the use of photographic displays are so pernicious that an extraordinary system of safeguards is required.

We hold, then, that the Sixth Amendment does not grant the right to counsel at photographic displays conducted by the Government for the purpose of allowing a witness to attempt an identification of the offender. . . .

Reversed and remanded.

Mr. Justice Stewart, concurring in the judgment.
. . . .

The Court held, [in *Wade*] that counsel was required at a lineup, primarily as an observer, to ensure that defense counsel could effectively confront the prosecution's evidence at trial. Attuned to the possibilities of suggestive influences, a lawyer could see any unfairness at a lineup, question the witnesses about it at trial, and effectively reconstruct what had gone on for the benefit of the jury or trial judge.*

---

* I do not read *Wade* as requiring counsel because a lineup is a "trial-type" situation, nor do I understand that the Court required the presence of an attorney because of the advice or assistance he could give to his client at the lineup itself. Rather, I had thought the reasoning of *Wade* was that the right to counsel is essentially a protection for the defendant at trial, and that counsel is necessary at a lineup in order to ensure a meaningful confrontation and the effective assistance of counsel at trial.

A photographic identification is quite different from a lineup, for there are substantially fewer possibilities of impermissible suggestion when photographs are used, and those unfair influences can be readily reconstructed at trial. . . .

Preparing witnesses for trial by checking their identification testimony against a photographic display is little different, in my view, from the prosecutor's other interviews with the victim or other witnesses before trial. See *United States* v. *Bennett,* 409 F. 2d 888, 900. While these procedures can be improperly conducted, the possibility of irretrievable prejudice is remote, since any unfairness that does occur can usually be flushed out at trial through cross-examination of the prosecution witnesses. The presence of defense counsel at such pretrial preparatory sessions is neither appropriate nor necessary under our adversary system of justice "to preserve the defendant's basic right to a fair trial as affected by his right meaningfully to cross-examine the witnesses against him and to have effective assistance of counsel at the trial itself." *United States* v. *Wade, supra,* at 227.

MR. JUSTICE BRENNAN, with whom MR. JUSTICE DOUGLAS and MR. JUSTICE MARSHALL join, dissenting.

. . . To the extent that misidentification may be attributable to a witness' faulty memory or perception, or inadequate opportunity for detailed observation during the crime, the risks are obviously as great at a photographic display as at a lineup. But "[b]ecause of the inherent limitations of photography, which presents its subject in two dimensions rather than the three dimensions of reality, . . . a photographic identification, even when properly obtained, is clearly inferior to a properly obtained corporeal identification." Indeed, noting "the hazards of initial identification by photograph," we have expressly recognized that "a corporeal identification . . . is normally more accurate" than a photographic identification. Thus, in this sense at least, the dangers of misidentification are even greater at a photographic display than at a lineup.

Moreover, as in the lineup situation, the possibilities for impermissible suggestion in the context of a photographic display are manifold.

. . . .

Moreover, as with lineups, the defense can "seldom reconstruct" at trial the mode and manner of photographic identification. . . .

Finally, and *unlike* the lineup situation, the accused himself is not even present at the photographic identification, thereby reducing the likelihood that irregularities in the procedures will ever come to light.

. . . .

Ironically, the Court does not seriously challenge the proposition that presence of counsel at a pretrial photographic display is essential

to preserve the accused's right to a fair trial on the issue of identification. Rather, in what I can only characterize a triumph of form over substance, the Court seeks to justify its result by engrafting a wholly unprecedented — and wholly unsupportable — limitation on the Sixth Amendment right of "the accused . . . to have the Assistance of Counsel for his defence." Although apparently conceding that the right to counsel attaches, not only at the trial itself, but at all "critical stages" of the prosecution . . . the Court holds today that, in order to be deemed "critical," the particular "stage of the prosecution" under consideration must, at the very least, involve the physical "presence of the accused," at a "trial-like confrontation" with the Government, at which the accused requires the "guiding hand of counsel." According to the Court a pretrial photographic identification does not, of course, meet these criteria.
    . . . .

[C]ontrary to the suggestion of the Court, the conclusion in *Wade* that a pretrial lineup is a "critical stage" of the prosecution did not in any sense turn on the fact that a lineup involves the physical "presence of the accused" at a "trial-like confrontation" with the Government. And that conclusion most certainly did not turn on the notion that presence of counsel was necessary so that counsel could offer legal advice or "guidance" to the accused at the lineup. On the contrary, *Wade* envisioned counsel's function at the lineup to be primarily that of a trained observer, able to detect the existence of any suggestive influences and capable of understanding the legal implications of the events that transpire. Having witnessed the proceedings, counsel would then be in a position effectively to reconstruct at trial any unfairness that occurred at the lineup, thereby preserving the accused's fundamental right to a fair trial on the issue of identification.

There is something ironic about the Court's conclusion today that a pretrial lineup identification is a "critical stage" of the prosecution because counsel's presence can help to compensate for the accused's deficiencies as an observer, but that a pretrial photographic identification is not a "critical stage" of the prosecution because the accused is not able to observe at all. In my view, there simply is no meaningful difference, in terms of the need for attendance of counsel, between corporeal and photographic identifications. And applying established and well-reasoned Sixth Amendment principles, I can only conclude that a pretrial photographic display, like a pretrial lineup, is a "critical stage" of the prosecution at which the accused is constitutionally entitled to the presence of counsel.

NOTES AND QUESTIONS

1. Is *Ash* consistent with *Miranda* v. *Arizona,* 384 U.S. 436 (1966)? (Recall that the "Miranda warning," required to be given before interrogation, informs the accused that he has a constitutional right to counsel prior to interrogation, and counsel will be furnished to him if he lacks funds.) *Kirby* v. *Illinois,* 406 U.S. 682 (1972), held that the right to counsel did not arise prior to the formal initiation of criminal proceedings. (Thus, in *Kirby,* there was no right to counsel in a lineup conducted prior to formal criminal charge.) Distinguishing *Miranda,* Mr. Justice Stewart's opinion for the Court noted that Miranda's right to counsel "was not to vindicate the constitutional right to counsel as such," but was designed to guarantee against violation of the privilege against self-incrimination.

2. Whether the right to counsel during police interrogation is premised on the Fifth Amendment or the Sixth Amendment, was it ever more than a fiction? Empirical studies indicate that the mere giving of the "Miranda warning" has had little impact on police interrogation practices. *See* Project, *Interrogations in New Haven: The Impact of Miranda,* 76 YALE L.J. 1519 (1967); O. STEPHENS, THE SUPREME COURT AND CONFESSIONS OF GUILT, 168-200 (1973). The thesis of the *Miranda* decision was, in part, that the decision of a person in custody to incriminate himself could not be voluntary unless made with the guidance of counsel. Should that not logically require that the decision to waive the right to counsel also be on the advice of counsel? For additional discussion of the *Miranda* rule, *see infra,* Ch. 11, § B.1.d.

3. Unlike *Miranda, United States* v. *Wade,* 388 U.S. 218 (1967), is premised on the right to counsel "as such." What is the role of the accused's counsel at a post-indictment lineup? Is he simply a witness?

4. After *Kirby* and *Ash,* is the accused entitled to be represented by counsel at any investigatory proceeding other than police interrogation, and a lineup following the formal criminal charge? Should the court have extended the right to counsel to all pretrial investigations by the police and prosecutor which could be characterized as a "critical stage" in the prosecution? Would that be infeasible, as Judge Friendly argued? Would it have been inconsistent with the adversary role of the prosecution?

3. Right to Counsel at Criminal Trial

a. United States

GIDEON v. WAINWRIGHT

Supreme Court of the United States
372 U.S. 335, 83 S. Ct. 792, 9 L. Ed. 2d 799 (1963)

MR. JUSTICE BLACK delivered the opinion of the Court.

Petitioner was charged in a Florida state court with having broken and entered a poolroom with intent to commit a misdemeanor. This offense is a felony under Florida law. Appearing in court without funds and without a lawyer, petitioner asked the court to appoint counsel for him, whereupon the following colloquy took place:

> "The COURT: Mr. Gideon, I am sorry, but I cannot appoint Counsel to represent you in this case. Under the laws of the State of Florida, the only time the Court can appoint Counsel to represent a Defendant is when that person is charged with a capital offense. I am sorry, but I will have to deny your request to appoint Counsel to defend you in this case.
>
> "The DEFENDANT: The United States Supreme Court says I am entitled to be represented by Counsel."

Put to trial before a jury, Gideon conducted his defense about as well as could be expected from a layman. He made an opening statement to the jury, cross-examined the State's witnesses, presented witnesses in his own defense, declined to testify himself, and made a short argument "emphasizing his innocence to the charge contained in the Information filed in this case." The jury returned a verdict of guilty, and petitioner was sentenced to serve five years in the state prison. Later, petitioner filed in the Florida Supreme Court this habeas corpus petition attacking his conviction and sentence on the ground that the trial court's refusal to appoint counsel for him denied him rights "guaranteed by the Constitution and the Bill of Rights by the United States Government." [1] Treating the petition for habeas corpus as properly before it, the State Supreme Court, "upon consideration thereof " but without an opinion, denied all relief. Since 1942, when *Betts* v. *Brady,* 316 U. S. 455, was decided by a divided Court, the problem of a defendant's federal constitutional right to counsel in a state court has been a continuing source of controversy and litigation in both state and federal courts. To give this problem another review here, we granted certiorari. 370 U. S. 908. Since Gideon was proceeding *in forma pauperis,* we appointed counsel to represent him and requested both sides to discuss in their

---

[1] Later in the petition for habeas corpus, signed and apparently prepared by petitioner himself, he stated, "I, Clarence Earl Gideon, claim that I was denied the rights of the 4th, 5th and 14th amendments of the Bill of Rights."

briefs and oral arguments the following: "Should this Court's holding in *Betts* v. *Brady,* 316 U. S. 455, be reconsidered?"

I.

The facts upon which Betts claimed that he had been unconstitutionally denied the right to have counsel appointed to assist him are strikingly like the facts upon which Gideon here bases his federal constitutional claim. Betts was indicted for robbery in a Maryland state court. On arraignment, he told the trial judge of his lack of funds to hire a lawyer and asked the court to appoint one for him. Betts was advised that it was not the practice in that county to appoint counsel for indigent defendants except in murder and rape cases. He then pleaded not guilty, had witnesses summoned, cross-examined the State's witnesses, examined his own, and chose not to testify himself. He was found guilty by the judge, sitting without a jury, and sentenced to eight years in prison. Like Gideon, Betts sought release by habeas corpus, alleging that he had been denied the right to assistance of counsel in violation of the Fourteenth Amendment. Betts was denied any relief, and on review this Court affirmed. It was held that a refusal to appoint counsel for an indigent defendant charged with a felony did not necessarily violate the Due Process Clause of the Fourteenth Amendment, which for reasons given the Court deemed to be the only applicable federal constitutional provision. The Court said:

> "Asserted denial [of due process] is to be tested by an appraisal of the totality of facts in a given case. That which may, in one setting, constitute a denial of fundamental fairness, shocking to the universal sense of justice, may, in other circumstances, and in the light of other considerations, fall short of such denial." 316 U.S., at 462.

Treating due process as "a concept less rigid and more fluid than those envisaged in other specific and particular provisions of the Bill of Rights," the Court held that refusal to appoint counsel under the particular facts and circumstances in the *Betts* case was not so "offensive to the common and fundamental ideas of fairness" as to amount to a denial of due process. Since the facts and circumstances of the two cases are so nearly indistinguishable, we think the *Betts* v. *Brady* holding if left standing would require us to reject Gideon's claim that the Constitution guarantees him the assistance of counsel. Upon full reconsideration we conclude that *Betts* v. *Brady* should be overruled.

II.

The Sixth Amendment provides, "In all criminal prosecutions, the accused shall enjoy the right . . . to have the Assistance of Counsel for his defence." We have construed this to mean that in federal courts counsel must be provided for defendants unable to employ counsel unless the right is competently and intelligently waived.[3] Betts argued that this right is extended to indigent defendants in state courts by the Fourteenth Amendment. In response the Court stated that, while the Sixth Amendment laid down "no rule for the conduct of the States, the question recurs whether the constraint laid by the Amendment upon the national courts expresses a rule so fundamental and essential to a fair trial, and so, to due process of law, that it is made obligatory upon the States by the Fourteenth Amendment." 316 U. S., at 465. In order to decide whether the Sixth Amendment's guarantee of counsel is of this fundamental nature, the Court in *Betts* set out and considered "[r]elevant data on the subject . . . afforded by constitutional and statutory provisions subsisting in the colonies and the States prior to the inclusion of the Bill of Rights in the national Constitution, and in the constitutional, legislative, and judicial history of the States to the present date." 316 U. S., at 465. On the basis of this historical data the Court concluded that "appointment of counsel is not a fundamental right, essential to a fair trial." 316 U. S., at 471. It was for this reason the *Betts* Court refused to accept the contention that the Sixth Amendment's guarantee of counsel for indigent federal defendants was extended to or, in the words of that Court, "made obligatory upon the States by the Fourteenth Amendment." Plainly, had the Court concluded that appointment of counsel for an indigent criminal defendant was "a fundamental right, essential to a fair trial," it would have held that the Fourteenth Amendment requires appointment of counsel in a state court, just as the Sixth Amendment requires in a federal court.

We think the Court in *Betts* had ample precedent for acknowledging that those guarantees of the Bill of Rights which are fundamental safeguards of liberty immune from federal abridgment are equally protected against state invasion by the Due Process Clause of the Fourteenth Amendment. This same principle was recognized, explained, and applied in *Powell* v. *Alabama,* 287 U. S. 45 (1932), a case upholding the right of counsel, where the Court held that despite sweeping language to the contrary in *Hurtado* v. *California,* 110 U. S. 516 (1884), the Fourteenth Amendment "embraced" those " 'fundamental principles of liberty and justice which lie at the base of all our civil and political institutions,' " even though they had been "specifically dealt with in another part of the federal Constitution." 287 U. S., at 67. In many cases other than

---

[3] *Johnson* v. *Zerbst,* 304 U. S. 458 (1938).

Powell and *Betts*, this Court has looked to the fundamental nature of original Bill of Rights guarantees to decide whether the Fourteenth Amendment makes them obligatory on the States. . . .

We accept *Betts* v. *Brady*'s assumption, based as it was on our prior cases, that a provision of the Bill of Rights which is "fundamental and essential to a fair trial" is made obligatory upon the States by the Fourteenth Amendment. We think the Court in *Betts* was wrong, however, in concluding that the Sixth Amendment's guarantee of counsel is not one of these fundamental rights. Ten years before *Betts* v. *Brady,* this Court, after full consideration of all the historical data examined in *Betts,* had unequivocally declared that "the right to the aid of counsel is of this fundamental character." *Powell* v. *Alabama,* 287 U. S. 45, 68 (1932). While the Court at the close of its *Powell* opinion did by its language, as this Court frequently does, limit its holding to the particular facts and circumstances of that case, its conclusions about the fundamental nature of the right to counsel are unmistakable.

. . . *Betts* v. *Brady* made an abrupt break with . . . well-considered precedents. In returning to these old precedents, sounder we believe than the new, we but restore constitutional principles established to achieve a fair system of justice. Not only these precedents but also reason and reflection require us to recognize that in our adversary system of criminal justice, any person haled into court, who is too poor to hire a lawyer, cannot be assured a fair trial unless counsel is provided for him. This seems to us to be an obvious truth. Governments, both state and federal, quite properly spend vast sums of money to establish machinery to try defendants accused of crime. Lawyers to prosecute are everywhere deemed essential to protect the public's interest in an orderly society. Similarly, there are few defendants charged with crime, few indeed, who fail to hire the best lawyers they can get to prepare and present their defenses. That government hires lawyers to prosecute and defendants who have the money hire lawyers to defend are the strongest indications of the widespread belief that lawyers in criminal courts are necessities, not luxuries. The right of one charged with crime to counsel may not be deemed fundamental and essential to fair trials in some countries, but it is in ours. From the very beginning, our state and national constitutions and laws have laid great emphasis on procedural and substantive safeguards designed to assure fair trials before impartial tribunals in which every defendant stands equal before the law. This noble ideal cannot be realized if the poor man charged with crime has to face his accusers without a lawyer to assist him. A defendant's need for a lawyer is nowhere better stated than in the moving words of Mr. Justice Sutherland in *Powell* v. *Alabama:*

> "The right to be heard would be, in many cases, of little avail if it did not comprehend the right to be heard by counsel. Even

the intelligent and educated layman has small and sometimes no skill in the science of law. If charged with crime, he is incapable, generally, of determining for himself whether the indictment is good or bad. He is unfamiliar with the rules of evidence. Left without the aid of counsel he may be put on trial without a proper charge, and convicted upon incompetent evidence, or evidence irrelevant to the issue or otherwise inadmissible. He lacks both the skill and knowledge adequately to prepare his defense, even though he have a perfect one. He requires the guiding hand of counsel at every step in the proceedings against him. Without it, though he be not guilty, he faces the danger of conviction because he does not know how to establish his innocence." 287 U. S., at 68-69.

The Court in *Betts* v. *Brady* departed from the sound wisdom upon which the Court's holding in *Powell* v. *Alabama* rested. Florida, supported by two other States, has asked that *Betts* v. *Brady* be left intact. Twenty-two States, as friends of the Court, argue that *Betts* was "an anachronism when handed down" and that it should now be overruled. We agree.

The judgment is reversed and the cause is remanded to the Supreme Court of Florida for further action not inconsistent with this opinion.

Reversed.

MR. JUSTICE CLARK, concurring in the result.

In *Bute* v. *Illinois,* 333 U. S. 640 (1948), this Court found no special circumstances requiring the appointment of counsel but stated that "if these charges had been capital charges, the court would have been required, both by the state statute and the decisions of this Court interpreting the Fourteenth Amendment, to take some such steps." *Id.,* at 674. . . .

I must conclude . . . that the Constitution makes no distinction between capital and noncapital cases. The Fourteenth Amendment requires due process of law for the deprival of "liberty" just as for deprival of "life," and there cannot constitutionally be a difference in the quality of the process based merely upon a supposed difference in the sanction involved. How can the Fourteenth Amendment tolerate a procedure which it condemns in capital cases on the ground that deprival of liberty may be less onerous than deprival of life — a value judgment not universally accepted — or that only the latter deprival is irrevocable? I can find no acceptable rationalization for such a result, and I therefore concur in the judgment of the Court.

MR. JUSTICE HARLAN, concurring.

I agree that *Betts* v. *Brady* should be overruled, but consider it entitled to a more respectful burial than has been accorded, at least on the part of those of us who were not on the Court when that case was decided.

I cannot subscribe to the view that *Betts* v. *Brady* represented "an abrupt break with . . . well-considered precedents." . . .

The principles declared in *Powell* and in *Betts,* however, have had a troubled journey throughout the years that have followed first the one case and then the other. . . .

In noncapital cases, the "special circumstances" rule has continued to exist in form while its substance has been substantially and steadily eroded. In the first decade after *Betts,* there were cases in which the Court found special circumstances to be lacking, but usually by a sharply divided vote. However, no such decision has been cited to us, and I have found none, after . . . 1950. At the same time, there have been not a few cases in which special circumstances were found in little or nothing more than the "complexity" of the legal questions presented, although those questions were often of only routine difficulty. The Court has come to recognize, in other words, that the mere existence of a serious criminal charge constituted in itself special circumstances requiring the services of counsel at trial. In truth the *Betts* v. *Brady* rule is no longer a reality. . . .

NOTES AND QUESTIONS

1. *Johnson* v. *Zerbst,* 304 U.S. 458 (1938) held that the Sixth Amendment's guarantee of right to counsel required the appointment of counsel to represent an indigent criminal defendant. At issue in *Gideon* v. *Wainwright* was the question whether the Sixth Amendment, as interpreted in *Johnson* v. *Zerbst,* applied to state criminal trials. Justice Black, then in his first term as a Supreme Court Justice, also wrote the opinion in *Johnson* v. *Zerbst.* That opinion cited history for the proposition that "the average defendant does not have the professional legal skill to protect himself when brought before a tribunal with power to take his life or liberty, wherein the prosecution is represented by experienced and learned counsel." But, as to the right to appointed counsel, he referred to the "humane policy of the modern criminal law. . . ." Justice Black has been noted for arguing that the Bill of Rights has a fixed historical meaning. At the time the Sixth Amendment was adopted, did it require that indigents be furnished appointed counsel in criminal cases? If not, what reason was there to interpret it, 150 years later, to require that the poor be furnished lawyers at state expense?

2. Did the seeds of the destruction of the doctrine of *Betts* v. *Brady* lie, as suggested by Justice Harlan, in the inability to draw the line at the point where "special circumstances" required the appointment of counsel in non-capital criminal cases? That issue was always difficult to determine after the completion of the trial. Theoretically, the issue was whether the accused had been denied a fair trial by the absence of counsel. It was impossible to say, however, what new issues might have been injected into the trial if counsel had been appointed. It was doubly difficult to decide, before the trial began, whether counsel should be appointed. In any event, the line eventually drawn under *Gideon* does have the virtue of simplicity and administrability — counsel must be furnished in any criminal case if the accused is to be incarcerated for any period of time. *Argersinger* v. *Hamlin,* 407 U.S. 25 (1972) (Prior to *Gideon* v. *Wainwright,* all but three states had extended the right to appointed counsel to all felony cases. *Argersinger,* however, required a change in practice in many states — providing appointed counsel in non-felony cases involving a sentence of incarceration. Justice Powell, concurring in *Argersinger,* argued that, in minor criminal cases, the right to appointed counsel should be determined on a case-by-case basis, depending on whether counsel was necessary to insure a fair trial.)

FARETTA v. CALIFORNIA

Supreme Court of the United States
422 U.S. 806, 95 S. Ct. 2525, 45 L. Ed. 2d 562 (1975)

MR. JUSTICE STEWART delivered the opinion of the Court.

The Sixth and Fourteenth Amendments of our Constitution guarantee that a person brought to trial in any state or federal court must be afforded the right to the assistance of counsel before he can be validly convicted and punished by imprisonment. This clear constitutional rule has emerged from a series of cases decided here over the last 50 years. The question before us now is whether a defendant in a state criminal trial has a constitutional right to proceed *without* counsel when he voluntarily and intelligently elects to do so. Stated another way, the question is whether a State may constitutionally hail a person into its criminal courts and there force a lawyer upon him, even when he insists that he wants to conduct his own defense. It is not an easy question, but we have concluded that a State may not constitutionally do so.

I

Anthony Faretta was charged with grand theft in an information filed in the Superior Court of Los Angeles County, California. At the arraignment, the Superior Court Judge assigned to preside at the trial appointed the public defender to represent Faretta. Well before the date of trial, however, Faretta requested that he be permitted to represent himself. Questioning by the judge revealed that Faretta had once represented himself in a criminal prosecution, that he had a high school education, and that he did not want to be represented by the public defender because he believed that that office was "very loaded down with . . . a heavy case load." The judge responded that he believed Faretta was "making a mistake" and emphasized that in further proceedings Faretta would receive no special favors. Nevertheless, after establishing that Faretta wanted to represent himself and did not want a lawyer, the judge, in a "preliminary ruling," accepted Faretta's waiver of the assistance of counsel. The judge indicated, however, that he might reverse this ruling if it later appeared that Faretta was unable adequately to represent himself.

Several weeks thereafter, but still prior to trial, the judge *sua sponte* held a hearing to inquire into Faretta's ability to conduct his own defense, and questioned him specifically about both the hearsay rule and the state law governing the challenge of potential jurors. After consideration of Faretta's answers, and observations of his demeanor, the judge ruled that Faretta had not made an intelligent and knowing waiver of his right to the assistance of counsel, and also ruled that Faretta had no constitutional right to conduct his own defense. The judge accordingly reversed his earlier ruling permitting self-representation and again appointed the public defender to represent Faretta. Faretta's subsequent request for leave to act as co-counsel was rejected, as were his efforts to make certain motions on his own behalf.[5] Throughout the subsequent trial, the judge required that Faretta's defense be conducted only through the appointed lawyer from the public defender's office. At the conclusion of the trial, the jury found Faretta guilty as charged, and the judge sentenced him to prison.

The California Court of Appeal, relying upon a then recent California Supreme Court decision that had expressly decided the issue, affirmed the trial judge's ruling that Faretta had no federal or state constitutional right to represent himself. . . .[8]

---

[5] Faretta also urged without success that he was entitled to counsel of his choice, and three times moved for the appointment of a lawyer other than the public defender. These motions, too, were denied.

[8] The California courts' conclusion that Faretta had no constitutional right to represent himself was made in the context of the following not unusual rules of California criminal procedure: An indigent criminal defendant has no right to appointed counsel of his choice. . . . The appointed counsel manages the lawsuit and has the final say in all but a few matters of trial strategy. . . . A California conviction will not be reversed on grounds of ineffective assistance of counsel except in the extreme case where the quality of representation was so poor as to render the trial a "farce and a sham." . . .

II

In the federal courts, the right of self-representation has been protected by statute since the beginnings of our Nation. . . .

This Court's past recognition of the right of self-representation, the federal court authority holding the right to be of constitutional dimension, and the state constitutions pointing to the right's fundamental nature form a consensus not easily ignored. "[T]he fact that a path is a beaten one," Mr. Justice Jackson once observed, "is a persuasive reason for following it." We confront here a nearly universal conviction, on the part of our people as well as our courts, that forcing a lawyer upon an unwilling defendant is contrary to his basic right to defend himself if he truly wants to do so.

III

This consensus is soundly premised. The right of self-representation finds support in the structure of the Sixth Amendment, as well as in the English and colonial jurisprudence from which the Amendment emerged.

A

The Sixth Amendment includes a compact statement of the rights necessary to a full defense:

> "In all criminal prosecutions, the accused shall enjoy the right . . . to be informed of the nature and cause of the accusation; to be confronted with the witnesses against him; to have compulsory process for obtaining witnesses in his favor, and to have the Assistance of Counsel for his defence."

. . . The rights to notice, confrontation, and compulsory process, when taken together, guarantee that a criminal charge may be answered in a manner now considered fundamental to the fair administration of American justice — through the calling and interrogation of favorable witnesses, the cross-examination of adverse witnesses, and the orderly introduction of evidence. In short, the Amendment constitutionalizes the right in an adversary criminal trial to make a defense as we know it. . . .

The Sixth Amendment does not provide merely that a defense shall be made for the accused; it grants to the accused personally the right to make his defense. It is the accused, not counsel, who must be "informed of the nature and cause of the accusation," who must be "confronted with witnesses against him," and who must be accorded "compulsory process for obtaining witnesses in his favor." Although not stated in the Amendment in so many words, the right to self-representation — to make one's own defense personally — is thus necessarily implied by the structure of the Amendment. The right to defend is given directly to the accused; for it is he who suffers the consequences if the defense fails.

The counsel provision supplements this design. It speaks of the "assistance" of counsel, and an assistant, however expert, is still an assistant. The language and spirit of the Sixth Amendment contemplate that counsel, like the other defense tools guaranteed by the Amendment, shall be an aid to a willing defendant — not an organ of the State interposed between an unwilling defendant and his right to defend himself personally. To thrust counsel upon the accused, against his considered wish, thus violates the logic of the Amendment. In such a case, counsel is not an assistant, but a master; and the right to make a defense is stripped of the personal character upon which the Amendment insists. It is true that when a defendant chooses to have a lawyer manage and present his case, law and tradition may allocate to the counsel the power to make binding decisions of trial strategy in many areas. . . . This allocation can only be justified, however, by the defendant's consent, at the outset, to accept counsel as his representative. An unwanted counsel "represents" the defendant only through a tenuous and unacceptable legal fiction. Unless the accused has acquiesced in such representation, the defense presented is not the defense guaranteed him by the Constitution, for, in a very real sense, it is not *his* defense.

. . . .

IV

There can be no blinking the fact that the right of an accused to conduct his own defense seems to cut against the grain of this Court's decisions holding that the Constitution requires that no accused can be convicted and imprisoned unless he has been accorded the right to the assistance of counsel. . . .

But it is one thing to hold that every defendant, rich or poor, has the right to the assistance of counsel, and quite another to say that a State may compel a defendant to accept a lawyer he does not want. The value of state-appointed counsel was not unappreciated by the Founders, yet the notion of compulsory counsel was utterly foreign to them. And whatever else may be said of those who wrote the Bill of Rights, surely there can be no doubt that they understood the inestimable worth of free choice.

It is undeniable that in most criminal prosecutions defendants could better defend with counsel's guidance than by their own unskilled efforts. But where the defendant will not voluntarily accept representation by counsel, the potential advantage of a lawyer's training and experience can be realized, if at all, only imperfectly.

To force a lawyer on a defendant can only lead him to believe that the law contrives against him. Moreover, it is not inconceivable that in some rare instances, the defendant might in fact present his case more effectively by conducting his own defense. Personal liberties are not rooted in the law of averages. . . .[46]

V

When an accused manages his own defense, he relinquishes, as a purely factual matter, many of the traditional benefits associated with the right to counsel. For this reason, in order to represent himself, the accused must "knowingly and intelligently" forego those relinquished benefits. . . . Although a defendant need not himself have the skill and experience of a lawyer in order competently and intelligently to choose self-representation, he should be made aware of the dangers and disadvantages of self-representation.

. . . Faretta was literate, competent, and understanding, and . . . he was voluntarily exercising his informed free will. . . . We need make no assessment of how well or poorly Faretta had mastered the intricacies of the hearsay rule and the California code provisions that govern challenges of potential jurors on *voir dire*. For his technical legal knowledge, as such, was not relevant to an assessment of his knowing exercise of the right to defend himself.

. . . .

Judgment vacated and case remanded.

MR. CHIEF JUSTICE BURGER, with whom MR. JUSTICE BLACKMUN and MR. JUSTICE REHNQUIST join, dissenting.

This case . . . is another example of the judicial tendency to constitutionalize what is thought "good." That effort fails on its own terms here, because there is nothing desirable or useful in permitting every accused person, even the most uneducated and inexperienced, to insist upon conducting his own defense to criminal charges. Moreover, there is no constitutional basis for the Court's holding and

---

[46] We are told that many criminal defendants representing themselves may use the courtroom for deliberate disruption of their trials. But the right of self-representation has been recognized from our beginnings by federal law and by most of the States, and no such result has thereby occurred. Moreover, the trial judge may terminate self-representation by a defendant who deliberately engages in serious and obstructionist misconduct. . . . Of course, a State may — even over objection by the accused — appoint a "standby counsel" to aid the accused if and when the accused requests help, and to be available to represent the accused in the event that termination of the defendant's self-representation is necessary. . . .

The right of self-representation is not a license to abuse the dignity of the courtroom. Neither is it a license not to comply with relevant rules of procedural and substantive law. Thus, whatever else may or may not be open to him on appeal, a defendant who elects to represent himself cannot thereafter complain that the quality of his own defense amounted to a denial of "effective assistance of counsel."

it can only add to the problems of an already malfunctioning criminal justice system. I therefore dissent. . . .

In short, both the "spirit and the logic" of the Sixth Amendment are that every person accused of crime shall receive the fullest possible defense; in the vast majority of cases this command can be honored only by means of the expressly-guaranteed right to counsel, and the trial judge is in the best position to determine whether the accused is capable of conducting his defense. . . .

It hardly needs repeating that courts at all levels are already handicapped by the unsupplied demand for competent advocates, with the result that it often takes far longer to complete a given case than experienced counsel would require. If we were to assume that there will be widespread exercise of the newly-discovered constitutional right to self-representation, it would almost certainly follow that there will be added congestion in the courts and that the quality of justice will suffer. . . .

MR. JUSTICE BLACKMUN, with whom THE CHIEF JUSTICE and MR. JUSTICE REHNQUIST join, dissenting.

Today the Court holds that the Sixth Amendment guarantees to every defendant in a state criminal trial the right to proceed without counsel whenever he elects to do so. I find no textual support for this conclusion in the language of the Sixth Amendment. I find the historical evidence relied upon by the Court to be unpersuasive, especially in light of the recent history of criminal procedure. Finally, I fear that the right to self-representation constitutionalized today frequently will cause procedural confusion without advancing any significant strategic interest of the defendant. I therefore dissent.

. . . .

In conclusion, I note briefly the procedural problems that, I suspect, today's decision will visit upon trial courts in the future. Although the Court indicates that a *pro se* defendant necessarily waives any claim he might otherwise make of ineffective assistance of counsel . . . the opinion leaves open a host of other procedural questions. Must every defendant be advised of his right to proceed *pro se*? If so, when must that notice be given? Since the right to assistance of counsel and the right to self-representation are mutually exclusive, how is the waiver of each right to be measured? If a defendant has elected to exercise his right to proceed *pro se,* does he still have a constitutional right to assistance of standby counsel? How soon in the criminal proceeding must a defendant decide between proceeding by counsel or *pro se*? Must he be allowed to switch in mid-trial? May a violation of the right to self-representation ever be harmless error? Must the trial court treat the *pro se* defendant differently than it would professional counsel? I assume that many of these questions will be answered with finality in due course. Many of them, however, such as the standards of waiver and the treatment of the *pro se* defendant, will haunt the trial of every defendant who elects to exercise his right to self-representation. The procedural problems spawned by an absolute right to self-representation will far outweigh whatever tactical advantage the defendant may feel he has gained by electing to represent himself.

If there is any truth to the old proverb that "One who is his own lawyer has a fool for a client," the Court by its opinion today now bestows a *constitutional* right on one to make a fool of himself.

b. Continental Europe

The traditional rule of the Civil Law is that a criminal case cannot proceed without counsel (exceptions are limited to minor offenses). Since the defendant *must* be represented by counsel, it is obvious that the right to retain paid counsel is never in issue. For the same reason, the issues of the *Gideon* and *Faretta* cases, in the previous section, cannot arise. Obviously, if the defendant cannot afford counsel to represent him, counsel must still be furnished. And, no matter the defendant's wishes, he has no right to represent himself.

Although the presence of counsel at the criminal trial is a foregone conclusion in continental Europe, the problem of appointed counsel for defendants in criminal trials may raise two kinds of issues: whether an indigent defendant may choose appointed counsel, if counsel is paid by the state; whether compensation paid appointed counsel is adequate. With reference to the second issue, methods of paying counsel fees differ. In Germany, appointed counsel is paid by the state. In Italy, it is an "honorific duty" for counsel to serve without pay. In 1972, France switched from the Italian to the German system.

(i) Choice of Appointed Counsel

DECISION OF DECEMBER 16, 1958

Bundesverfassungsgericht
[1959] 9 BVerfGE 36

I.

The petitioner was sentenced by the criminal chamber of the *Landgericht* of Oldenburg . . . to three months' imprisonment as a result of his membership in a secret and criminal organization. . . . The appeal of the petitioner to the *Bundesgerichtshof* . . . has been rejected as manifestly unfounded.

In the proceeding before the criminal chamber the petitioner requested that Attorney K of Oldenburg be assigned to represent him as court-appointed attorney. This application was rejected by the acting president of the chamber, who instead assigned Attorney C of Osnabrück. As motivation for this assignment he indicated, on the basis of determinations made by the court, that Attorney K could offer no assurance that he would conduct the defense in a proper manner and in the interests of the accused since he held a position of confidence within the illegal organization *Freie Deutsche Jugend* [the official East German youth organization]. As counsel for the *FDJ* in a series of proceedings of a similar nature, he did not properly represent the interests of the individuals accused, but subordinated himself to the directives of the organization. It did not seem proper [to the president of the chamber] to assign an attorney who would follow the directives of the *FDJ* and who, in addition, at the cost of the State, would use the proceeding to foster the unconstitutional activities of the *FDJ*.

The Criminal Senate of the *Oberlandesgericht* of Oldenburg rejected the appeal, accepting the motivation of the lower court. In addition, the Criminal Senate remarked that the assignment of the Osnabrück attorney was proper in that the Criminal Chamber intended that the proceeding take place in Osnabrück, the place of residence of the petitioner.

A new application of the petitioner, requesting that Attorney K be appointed as his attorney, was rejected at the beginning of the trial with the motivation that the accused had already been assigned Attorney C as his attorney, and no grounds existed which would justify a lack of confidence on the part of the accused in the court-appointed attorney.

The petitioner asserts that his rights under arts. 1, 2, 3, 5, 11, 24, 25, and 33 of the Basic Law as well as art. 6, para. 3c of the European Convention on the Protection of Human Rights and Fundamental Freedoms were violated since the assignment of Attorney K as his attorney was denied and Attorney C was imposed upon him as his court-appointed attorney.

With the constitutional petition (*Verfassungsbeschwerde*) he challenges, therefore, the decision on the choice of the court-appointed attorney as well as the decision of the *Bundesgerichtshof* which affirmed the sentence imposed by the court of first instance (3 months imprisonment).

II.

In a criminal proceeding the court-appointed attorney, according to § 142, para. 1, of the Criminal Code, must be chosen by the president of the court, within his reasoned discretion, and, if possible, from the roll of attorneys admitted to practice before the court of the judicial district. According to the rule, the accused has no right to have an attorney of his own selection as his appointed counsel. It does not appear that this rule is contrary to the Basic Law. In the appointment of counsel we are dealing with a measure of public welfare in which, if possible, the wishes of the accused should certainly be taken into account, but in which the decision remains with the State.

As a rule, unless there are contrary reasons, the assigned counsel should be one who has the confidence of the accused. According to the will of the legislature, through the assignment of counsel, the accused should obtain substantially the same legal protection as an accused who has retained an attorney at his own expense.

Since the legal norm cannot be constitutionally attacked, the challenged decisions can only be examined in this regard if the courts in the exercise of their assigned discretion act unconstitutionally. This is not the case here. As the extensive analysis relating to the choice of counsel, apparent in the documents of the proceeding, demonstrates, the president of the Criminal Chamber assigned another attorney to the petitioner instead of the proposed attorney who enjoyed his particular political confidence, in the petitioner's own interest as well as in the interest of a proper defense. This decision as well as the motivation given by the *Oberlandesgericht* is not based on improper considerations and there does not appear to have been an abuse of the discretion granted to the court in the choice of counsel. Therefore, there is no violation of the prohibition against arbitrary acts of art. 3, para. 1, of the Basic Law.

All other claims of the petitioner are obviously unfounded as well. This is particularly true in relation to the right expressed in art. 6, para. 3c, of the Convention on the Protection of Human Rights and Fundamental Freedoms, since the protection accorded by that article does not go beyond that of German law. Therefore, the court leaves open the question of whether or not a constitutional petition can be based on a violation of the Convention.

III.

The constitutional petition must be rejected according to § 24 of the Law of the Federal Constitutional Court as manifestly unfounded.

NOTES AND QUESTIONS

1. If the defendant had been able to afford retained counsel, the criminal courts could not have overruled defendant's choice of counsel because of doubt that he would represent the defendant in an improper manner or would disrupt orderly trial proceedings. Are you persuaded that, when counsel is paid by the state, the expenditure of state funds provides an appropriate state interest which justifies control over defendant's choice of counsel?

2. Even if the defendant's constitutional right to choice of appointed counsel is limited, in practice the defendant's request that a particular lawyer represent him is often honored in Germany, although the actual appointment is within the judge's discretion. Moreover, the indigent has the right to reject an appointment by the court if he does not trust the appointed lawyers and the court determines that the mistrust is "reasonable." In the United States, the indigent's choice of counsel to represent him is much more limited. Defendant has no constitutional right to choice of appointed counsel. More significant, in practice, whether counsel is provided by a public defender office or court appointment, the defendant's choice of counsel is seldom honored. It was a major argument in the *Faretta* case, in the previous section (see note 5 in the *Faretta* case opinion) that the defendant ought to be entitled to represent himself because he had no choice of counsel to represent him. Does it make sense to permit a defendant to represent himself because he has no right to choose counsel who will follow particular trial strategies? Would it make more sense to develop a constitutional right, even if a limited right, to choice of counsel?

(ii) Compensation of Appointed Counsel

(a) Italy

The method of compensating appointed counsel in continental Europe is determined by the general laws governing legal aid. In Italy, a basic distinction is drawn between civil and criminal cases as to eligibility for legal aid. In civil cases, a party must meet two criteria — poverty and reasonable probability of success. In criminal cases, the only criterion is poverty. Legal aid, however, is still administered in Italy in accordance with a royal decree of 1923, which makes no provision for payment of appointed counsel in either civil or criminal cases. Members of the legal profession have an "honorific duty" to represent persons who meet the criteria for legal aid. In a civil suit, an attorney may have some hope of compensation if his client prevails, since attorney's fees are awarded the prevailing party by his losing adversary. Ironically, even this gambler's chance of being compensated is absent if an attorney is representing a defendant in a criminal case.

In 1964, the constitutionality of the approach of the 1923 law to compensation of appointed counsel was presented to the *Corte Costituzionale.* Disciplinary proceedings had been brought against an appointed attorney, who was accused of inadequately representing the defendant in a criminal case. The defendant's lawyer challenged the constitutionality of provisions of the Code of Criminal Procedure which required appointed counsel to serve when appointed, and provided for suspension of the attorney who refused to serve without justification. These provisions were claimed to conflict with arts. 24, para. 3, and 35, para. 1, of the Constitution, which provide:

> Article 24 (3) The indigents are entitled, through special institutions, to proper means for action or defense at all levels of jurisdiction.
> Article 35 (1) The Republic safeguards labor in all its forms and methods of execution.

The *Corte Costituzionale* found the challenge unfounded. Decision of Dec. 22, 1964, Corte cost., [1964] 9 Giur. Cost. 1163; [1964] 20 Rac. uff. corte cost. 373; [1965] 88 Foro It. I, 158. The court concluded that the requirement of providing legal assistance to indigents was a responsibility of the legal profession, and the challenged provisions of the Code of Criminal Procedure did not, thus, impinge on the free exercise of the legal profession. With reference to art. 24, the court's opinion contained this significant dictum (*id.* at 1175):

> A different question, not concerning constitutionality, is that of the adequacy of the system of administration of legal aid to fulfill the constitutional guarantee. *De lege ferenda* and from a point of view of legislative policy it is possible to hope for a different and better system for the defense of the poor; but from that need for a different body of law which better corresponds to the purpose of art. 24 of the Constitution it is not proper to infer the unconstitutionality of the means now existing, which are directed to the same general end. To consider, in theory, such means as insufficient, or of minimal efficiency, with respect to the scope expressed in the Constitution, is not to say that they are unconstitutional, and to deprive thereby the poor of even that assistance which they now have.

In 1970, however, the court rejected a challenge to the entire Italian system of legal aid, holding that, although the system of unpaid representation was ineffective, it met the minimal constitutional obligation of providing an "institution" for the purpose of providing legal aid, as required by art. 24, para. 3. Decision of June 16, 1970, No. 97, Corte cost., [1970] 15 Giur. Cost. 1150; [1970] 32 Rac. uff. corte cost. 103; [1970] 93 Foro It. I, 1848; [1970] 122 Giur. Ital. I, 1378. The question of the effectiveness of the Italian legal aid system in civil cases will be addressed below, § B.2.b.ii. However ineffective the Italian legal aid system has been in civil cases, would you guess that the poor are better or worse represented in criminal cases?

(b) European Convention on Human Rights

GUSSENBAUER v. AUSTRIA

European Commission of Human Rights
[1972] Y.B. Eur. Conv. on Human Rights 558

[Under the Austrian legal aid system, the government paid the Austrian Bar Association an annual fixed lump sum to pay for representation of indigents. The total sum represents one fourth to one third of the amount which would be paid to lawyers if they were paid for indigent representation at the official legal tariff. The Bar Association does not, however, pay the appropriation to appointed attorneys for their work, but uses the money to pay pensions to poor retired lawyers.]

The applicant . . . complains that by decision of the Viennese Bar Committee of 20 August 1970 he was chosen to act as an ex-officio counsel for Mrs. R.H., who was charged with theft. On the opening of the trial, on 22 September 1970, the applicant was orally appointed by the Regional Court of Vienna as an ex-officio counsel, but the written decision was sent to him as late as 16 November 1970. He attended the trial for three days and acted as counsel for Mrs. R.H. Owing to this he could not personally plead on these days for several of his private clients, and a substitute had to deal with them. This caused him costs which were not, however, according to the Austrian established case-law refunded to him. The applicant did not request the Judges' Chamber under Article 43 of the Code of Penal Procedure to release him from the obligation to act as an ex-officio counsel for Mrs. R.H.

The applicant indicates that he had no remedy at his disposal according to Austrian law and that in any event such a remedy would not have been effective since the written decision charging him with the duty to defend Mrs. R.H. was served on him almost two months after the trial.

The applicant alleges that the obligation to act as an ex-officio counsel under the Austrian legal aid system constitutes forced labour under Art. 4 of the Convention, and violated the Convention. In this respect he indicates that by the above decision of the Vienna Regional Court he was forced to defend Mrs. R.H. without any remuneration. He further alleges that none of the exceptions which justify forced labour under para. 3 of Art. 4 existed in the present case. In particular he emphasises that the work he was required to do did not form "part of normal civic obligations" within the meaning of Art. 4 (3) (d) of the Convention, since other comparable legal professions had no such obligations under the law. In this respect he also alleges a violation of Art. 14 of the Convention.

The applicant alleges a violation of Art. 1 of the Protocol No. 1, since he had to work without remuneration and without compensation for the actual costs which he incurred.

SUBMISSIONS OF THE PARTIES

As regards the exhaustion of domestic remedies

The *respondent Government* submit that the applicant has failed to exhaust the remedies available to him under the Austrian Code of Penal Procedure. They indicate in this respect that he did not request his release as ex-officio counsel from the Judges' Chamber. . . .

The *applicant* replies that, in a formal sense, no appeal lies against a decision of the president of a jury of the Regional Court, by which someone is appointed ex-officio counsel. . . .

As to the violation of Art. 4 of the Convention

The *respondent Government* submit that the professional duty of lawyers to assume the defence of poor parties in criminal or civil proceedings does not constitute forced or compulsory labour under Art. 4 of the Convention.

In this respect they refer to various Conventions of the International Labour Organisation on this subject, and in particular to Convention No. 29 concerning Forced or Compulsory Labour, adopted in 1930. Art. 2, line 1 of this Convention gives, according to them, a tentative definition of forced or compulsory labour. The Government submit that on the basis of this definition, and in the light of other ILO Conventions, the concept of forced or compulsory labour is not only characterised by non-voluntary work exacted under the menace of penalty but also contains the elements of arbitrariness, discrimination, economic and political suppression and exploitation.

Another definition is also submitted according to which forced or compulsory labour means the absence of freedom to work as a system.

. . . .

In this respect [the Government] submit that the essential element of compulsory labour, namely the enforcement of the labour concerned, is lacking, since the fulfilment of this professional duty cannot be directly or indirectly enforced by the State, and any refusal to carry out this obligation merely entails disciplinary sanctions or consequences under civil law. It is further stated that any lawyer, by voluntarily choosing this profession, accepts the obligation to act as an ex-officio counsel, and that consequently this is a consequence of his own free decision.

The Government also submit that the obligation to act as a counsel under the legal aid system does not restrict counsel's personal freedom to work, nor is it discriminatory and arbitrary, nor does it exploit counsel. It is submitted that this system has an objective justification, namely to ensure proper administration of justice and fair proceedings as required under Art. 6 of the Convention and that the obligations resulting from it are operational requirements governing the exercise of a certain profession. In this respect reference is made to other similar obligations of other professions.

The Government are further of the opinion that, even assuming that these obligations of lawyers under the legal aid system constituted forced or compulsory labour, they would be covered by Art. 4 (3) (d) of the Convention. This provision allows such labour if it forms part of normal civic obligations of the person concerned. In this regard they submit that the duty to act as an ex-officio counsel is in the interest of public welfare and concerns equally every lawyer, and is a typical professional duty. Such duties are, according to the Government, imposed similarly on other professions and therefore concern equally every citizen without any undue differentiation.

The *applicant* . . . is of the opinion that, by having imposed on him the duty to carry out the defence of Mrs. R.H., he was subjected to compulsory labour. In this respect he refers to the structure of Art. 4 of the Convention and in particular to para. (3) thereof, which exhaustively lists the kind of compulsory labour which is allowed under this article. He indicates that, for example, the service of a military character mentioned in Art. 4 (3) (b) would not qualify as compulsory labour under the criteria set forth by the respondent Government and that, consequently, it would not have been necessary to include this sub-paragraph if the notion of forced or compulsory labour in para. (2) had the meaning the Government gave it.

With reference to the respondent Government's argument about the definition of the concept of forced or compulsory labour as contained in Convention No. 29 of ILO, the applicant submits that the criteria set forth in this Convention, if applied to the present situation, show that he has been forced to do compulsory labour. According to this Convention "all work or service which is exacted from any person under the menace of a penalty and for which the said person has not offered himself voluntarily" constitutes compulsory labour.

He submits that the respondent Government, by imposing the duty on lawyers to carry out ex-officio defences without payment, exploit this particular profession and discriminate against it. The applicant also submits that it is incorrect that, as the Government alleges, they neither directly nor indirectly force the lawyer concerned to act according to his duties under the legal aid system. He indicates in this respect that he was subject to the full scale of disciplinary sanctions which can be imposed on lawyers who fail to carry out their professional obligations. . . .

As regards the number of cases which an average lawyer has to take before the courts in Austria under the legal aid system, the applicant indicates that this varies: in smaller towns, where only few counsel are practising, it amounts to almost 60 a year, whereas in Vienna it is limited to approximately 4 to 6.

The applicant also refutes the Government's argument that he had, by choosing the legal profession, accepted the obligation to act unpaid under the legal aid system. In this respect the applicant states that this obligation is imposed on the legal profession in a discriminatory way, since counsel are the only legal practitioners who are forced to work unpaid: that court experts and interpreters are fully paid by the State for their services. According to the applicant, this shows that this obligation, which is restricted to the legal profession, is not work which forms part of normal civic obligations under Art. 4 (3) (d).

As to the alleged interference with the applicant's right to property under Art. 1 of Protocol No. 1.

The *respondent Government* admit implicitly that there was an interference with the applicant's right to property but submit that this interference was in the public interest because only in this way could the proper administration of justice be ensured according to the principles laid down in the Convention. The Government also indicate that this obligation of lawyers is enshrined in the national Austrian legislation and that, therefore, the formal requirement of Art. 1 of the Protocol is fulfilled. With respect to the lump-sum paid to the Bar Association, it is stated that this corresponds approximately to one-third of the costs otherwise to be paid under the official tariff and that the distribution of this sum is left, under the Ministry's supervision, to the Bar Association. This uses it for charitable assistance to members of the Bar, or to their descendants and widows.

The applicant replies that indeed this system of legal aid is in violation of Art. 1 of the Protocol. He indicates that the lump-sum paid by the Government should be increased 3½ times to a sum of 49 million Austrian schillings a year.

THE LAW

1. . . . The respondent Government has objected that this complaint does not involve the responsibility of the Austrian State

as the applicant was chosen to act in the criminal proceedings concerned by the Committee of the Bar, being an organ of an institution which enjoyed self-government under Austrian law and for which, consequently, the Austrian State could not be held responsible under the Convention. . . .

[Because] the applicant's appointment was made by the Vienna Regional Court for which the Austrian State is, of course, fully responsible for the purposes of Art. 25 of the Convention, the Commission does not need to deal with the question whether or not the acts of an organ of a self-governing institution, as is the Bar Association under Austrian law, might, in principle, entail the responsibility of the Austrian State under Art. 25 of the Convention.

2. The respondent Government has further objected that the applicant has not exhausted his remedies under Austrian law and that he has, therefore, not complied with the requirements under Art. 26 of the Convention.

. . . The Commission, in this respect, is of the opinion that counsel's possibility under the above Article to request his release from his obligations as a legal aid counsel, constitutes a remedy which theoretically might provide an effective and sufficient means of redressing the alleged wrong which is the subject of the applicant's present complaint. . . . [A]ccording to the above rules of international law, the exhaustion of a given remedy ceases to be necessary, if the applicant can show that in the particular circumstances this remedy was unlikely to be effective and adequate in regard to the grievances in question.

. . . In this respect the Commission noted the applicant's explanation that the established practice of the Austrian courts when applying the above Article of the Code of Penal Procedure was only to release legal aid counsel who proved that they were sick or that they were confronted with a conflict of interests, insofar as they were already representing other parties whose interests were opposed to those of the person for whose defence they had been appointed by the court. The Commission further noted that the established court practice was not to reimburse any clerical expenses of a legal aid counsel. . . . [T]he Commission is of the opinion that the applicant has clearly shown that the above remedy, although theoretically capable of constituting a remedy, does not in reality offer any chance of redressing the damage alleged, and therefore need not be exhausted.

In the opinion of the Commission the applicant has, consequently, complied with the exigencies of Art. 26 of the Convention and his application cannot be rejected under Art. 27 (3) of the Convention for non-exhaustion of domestic remedies.

3. The Commission next had regard to the substance of the applicant's complaints under Arts. 4 and 14 of the Convention, and

Art. 1 of Protocol No. 1. It finds that, in the light of the submissions of the parties, these complaints raise issues of a complex nature not only under the above Art. 4, but also under the other Articles just mentioned, and that they could, therefore, not be declared inadmissible as being manifestly ill-founded.

For these reasons the Commission

DECLARES THIS APPLICATION AS A WHOLE ADMISSIBLE.

GUSSENBAUER v. AUSTRIA

European Commission of Human Rights
[1972] Y.B. Eur. Conv. on Human Rights 448

. . . .

THE LAW

1. The applicant has complained that he was compelled to perform compulsory labour when called upon, under the Austrian legal aid scheme, to act as an unpaid defence counsel on behalf of a person who was the subject of criminal proceedings and who lacked the financial means himself to pay for counsel. He alleges that thereby the Austrian Government has violated Art. 4 of the Convention which guarantees that "No one shall be required to perform forced or compulsory labour," and Art. 14 of the Convention as well as Art. 1 of Protocol No. 1.

2. On 22 March 1972 the Commission declared admissible application No. 4897/71 lodged by the same applicant. In that application he complained in exactly the same way that on another occasion he was called upon to act under the Austrian legal aid scheme and thereby compelled to perform compulsory labour. The Commission then was of the opinion that this complaint raised issues of a complex nature under Arts. 4 and 14 of the Convention, and under Art. 1 of Protocol No. 1, and that the application could, therefore, not be declared inadmissible as being manifestly ill-founded. In the proceedings relating to that application the respondent Government had invoked Art. 26 of the Convention and submitted that the applicant had not exhausted the domestic remedies available to him since he had failed to request from the Regional Court, in accordance with Art. 43 (1) of the Austrian Code of Penal Procedure, his release from the duties concerned. The Commission, however, found that the applicant had clearly shown that this remedy, although theoretically capable of constituting a remedy, did not in reality offer any chance of redressing the damage alleged. The Commission therefore found that, having regard to the provision in Art. 26 that remedies must be exhausted "according to the general rules of international law" the remedy referred to was

not one that need be exhausted in order to satisfy the terms of Art. 26.

3. In the present case the applicant has indeed availed himself of this remedy, but without success: the Court decided that the applicant's request for release could not be granted since the mere allegation that his appointment as legal aid counsel constituted compulsory labour contrary to the guarantees of Art. 4 of the Convention was not a valid reason for such release under Art. 43 of the above Code. The Commission consequently notes that no question under Art. 26 of the Convention arises in the present application.

4. The Commission, having regard to the fact that the applicant's present application raises issues which are identical with those raised by the applicant's first application, is therefore of the opinion that the present application can equally not be declared inadmissible as being manifestly ill-founded as it raises the same complex questions under Arts. 4 and 14 of the Convention, as well as under Art. 1 of Protocol No. 1.

5. The Commission consequently decides now to declare this application admissible without inviting the parties to submit written observations on admissibility and provided that the respondent Government does not require to make oral explanations on the question of admissibility (1).

For these reasons, the Commission

DECLARES THIS APPLICATION ADMISSIBLE AND JOINS IT TO APPLICATION NO. 4897/71.

NOTES AND QUESTIONS

1. Before a final decision by the Committee of Ministers, Gussenbauer settled his case with the Austrian government under art. 28(b) of the Convention. *See* [1975] 18 Y.B. EUR. CONV. ON HUMAN RIGHTS. The 1974 ANNUAL REVIEW, EUR. COMM. OF HUMAN RIGHTS 27 reported the following:

> Under the terms of the friendly settlement concluded in October 1974, the Austrian Government reimbursed [Gussenbauer] for the costs incurred during the proceedings before the Commission. In approving the settlement, the Commission took note of a statement by the Government to the effect that when ratifying the regulations of the various Austrian Bar Associations, it would make sure that provision was made for a fair distribution of legal aid cases between Counsels.

Gussenbauer also brought a similar case before the Constitutional Court of Austria. (*See* § B.2.b.ii, *infra.*)

2. Why do you suppose Gussenbauer settled? Why did he bring the suit in the first place? Is it odd that he would seek a fairer

distribution of legal aid cases, considering that he was practicing in Vienna, where the burden on lawyers was least? Is it odd, too, that the issue in these cases is phrased in terms of lawyers' rights, rather than the rights of clients? Would clients be better represented if the annual appropriation were increased but lawyers were still unpaid for appointed representation?

4. Right to Counsel in Criminal Appeals

a. *European Convention on Human Rights*

DUNSHIRN v. AUSTRIA *

European Commission of Human Rights
[1961] Y.B. Eur. Conv. on Human Rights 186

THE FACTS

Whereas the facts of the case may be summarised as follows:
The Applicant is an Austrian citizen born in 1931.

On February 19, 1960, the Applicant was convicted by the Regional Court (*Landesgericht*) of Vienna on diverse charges of larceny; the Court took into consideration certain extenuating circumstances, including *inter alia,* the fact that the Applicant had made restitution to his victims of 90% of the amount of money which he had stolen from them, and sentenced the Applicant to fourteen months' imprisonment with the additional penalty of "sleeping hard" four times a year.

The Applicant accepted this sentence upon his lawyers' advice.

It appears that the Applicant had previous convictions and that shortly before his last conviction he had been released on probation from a labour institution two years before the expiration of his sentence. This release was subject to the condition that in the event of the Applicant being convicted of a further offence he would have to complete the full term in the labour institution. . . .

The Applicant states that his lawyer made no representation as to the amount of his sentence but that the Public Prosecutor appealed from the decision of the Regional Court of Vienna to the Court of Appeal in Vienna. On April 13, 1960, the Court of Appeal, after hearing the Public Prosecutor *in camera* but without hearing the Applicant or his lawyer, stated that it did not accept the existence of extenuating circumstances and increased the Applicant's sentence from fourteen months to thirty months.

The Applicant states that the increase of his sentence has resulted in his having to serve two years in a labour institution and he alleges

---

* For the decision of the Committee of Ministers on the merits of this and the *Pataki* case, *see* Ch. 7, § A.4., *supra.*

that the Court of Appeal in effect increased his sentence from fourteen months to fifty-four months.

The Applicant states that no further appeal is available to him either in respect of the original conviction or as to the increase of his sentence.

Whereas the Applicant now asks for a reduction of the sentence imposed upon him by the Court of Appeal on the grounds that it was rendered in his absence and without his being heard on the question of its increase.

Whereas the Applicant alleges violations of the Convention.

. . . .

THE LAW

Whereas art. 6, para. 1, of the Convention provides *inter alia*:

"In the determination . . . of any criminal charge against him everyone is entitled to a fair . . . hearing . . ." and whereas art. 6, para. 3 (c) provides:

"Everyone charged with a criminal offence has the following minimum rights: . . . to defend himself in person or through legal assistance of his own choosing. . . ."

Whereas section 294 of the Austrian Code of Criminal Procedure provides:

"1. The appeal shall be lodged with the Court of first instance within the time-limit specified in section 284. . . .

"2. . . . Notice of appeal, containing the grounds therefor, or the appellant's memorial lodged within the prescribed time-limit, shall be communicated to the other party with the intimation that he may submit his rejoinder within fourteen days.

"3. After the rejoinder has been submitted, or after expiration of the prescribed time-limit therefor, all the documents in the case shall be laid before the Court of second instance which, sitting *in camera,* shall give judgment on the appeal after hearing the Public Prosecutor."

Whereas the Applicant alleges that the requirements of art. 6 of the Convention were not complied with in his case in that when the Court of Appeal heard the appeal neither he nor his lawyer was present although the Public Prosecutor was heard;

Whereas the Respondent Government submitted that . . . the appeal was justified in substance as the extenuating circumstances mentioned in the judgment of the Regional Court were less significant than the particularly aggravating circumstances constituted by the recidivist character of the offence; that the Applicant, who was represented by Counsel before the Regional Court, did not appeal his sentence but later instructed his Counsel, to whom the Public Prosecutor's appeal had been communicated under section 294, para. 2, of the Code of Criminal Procedure, to file a counter-memorial in which he asked for the appeal to be dismissed but did not attempt to refute the arguments by the Prosecution; that, in accordance with section 294, para. 3, of the Code of Criminal Procedure, the decision of the Court of Appeal was taken after the hearing of the Public Prosecutor *in camera;* that the hearing of the Public Prosecutor can in no way prejudice the accused as no facts can be raised other than those known to the parties from the documents in the case, and, further, the Court of Appeal is bound, under section 3 of the Code of Criminal Procedure, to take into consideration *ex officio* all elements favourable or unfavourable to the accused regardless of whether they have been referred to by either party; that the Chief Public Prosecutor has accordingly no possibility to influence the Court of Appeal and in fact, in the present case, entered into no details but simply asked that the appeal be upheld; that, as the Respondent Government has observed in regard to the similar Application lodged against it by Franz Pataki (*No. 596/59*), the Court of Appeal thus takes cognisance of the accused's objections to the Public Prosecutor's appeal and the two parties are then on an equal footing; that the defendant enjoys an advantage over the Public Prosecutor as, unlike the latter, he is not required to be objective and, moreover, has the chance that unjustified grounds of appeal advanced by subordinate public prosecutors may be withdrawn; that, in this respect, it is not correct, as was alleged by Pataki, that "there has never yet been a single case in which the Chief Public Prosecutor has withdrawn, in favour of the convicted person, an appeal for a heavier sentence;" that, in fact, at least ten per cent of criminal appeals by public prosecutors are withdrawn by the Chief Public Prosecutor; that in accordance with section 294, para. 3, of the Code of Criminal Procedure, the Chief Public Prosecutor at the Court of Appeal is bound to lodge a plea of nullity "in the interest of the law" in regard to any decision which appears to be contrary to the law and which is to the prejudice of the accused; that, if the Court of Appeal finds that there has been such a violation of the law to the prejudice of the accused, it quashes the decision concerned; that, if it finds, however, that there has been a violation of the law to the advantage of the convicted person, it records its finding but the decision concerned remains valid; that the action of the Public Prosecutor in criminal appeal proceedings can accordingly never be against the interests of the accused and even may be to his advantage; that in the present case the Court of Appeal, in strict compliance with all the rules of procedure laid down for its observance, upheld the Public Prosecutor's appeal and increased the Applicant's sentence to two and a half years' imprisonment with one day of "sleeping hard" every three months; that the grounds stated by the Court of Appeal were that the extenuating circumstances carried little weight while the reversion to crime by the Applicant during a period of probation following his conditional release from a labour institution constituted an aggravating circumstance; that the hearing of the Public Prosecutor in the present case in no way prejudiced the rights of the accused to defend himself within the meaning of art. 6 of the Convention;

Whereas the Commission has also *ex officio* taken note of the observations of the Respondent Government in the *Application (No. 596/59)* of Franz Pataki against the Respondent Government;. . . .

Whereas in the present case a preliminary examination of the information and arguments submitted to the Commission by the Parties does not enable it to determine here and now whether the facts of the complaint that the procedure followed by the Court of Appeal violated the Convention exclude any possibility of such violation; whereas, moreover, to carry the preliminary examination of the complaint beyond the point which it has now reached by pursuing the matter further, whether in written or oral proceedings, would necessarily entail going fully into the merits of the case; whereas it follows that the Applicant's complaint in regard to the procedure followed by the Court of Appeal in dealing with the appeal in his case cannot be regarded as manifestly ill-founded within the meaning of art. 27, para. 2, of the Convention, and cannot be declared inadmissible on that ground;

For these reasons, and without in any way prejudging the merits of the case the Commission

DECLARES ADMISSIBLE AND ACCEPTS THE APPLICATION.
NOTE

From *Dunshirn* and other cases dealing with the same problem one may derive the principle that though the contracting states are not required to provide a double level of jurisdiction, where appeals are permitted the fair trial principles of art. 6 — including the right to counsel — must be adhered to at the appellate level also. In fact the laws of most European countries provide that counsel *must* be appointed for criminal appeals if the defendant does not retain counsel himself.

X v. FEDERAL REPUBLIC OF GERMANY

European Commission of Human Rights
[1961] Y.B. Eur. Conv. on Human Rights 296

THE FACTS

[The applicant is a German litigant who had lodged a constitutional appeal (*Verfassungsbeschwerde*) with the German Constitutional

---

* [1960] Y.B. Eur. Conv. on Human Rights 356 (Eur. Comm. of Human Rights); [1960] Y.B. Eur. Conv. on Human Rights 322 (Eur. Comm. of Human Rights); [1960] Y.B. Eur. Conv. on Human Rights 370 (Eur. Comm. of Human Rights).

Court.] He . . . alleges a violation of art. 6 of the Convention on the ground that he was not given the opportunity to submit additional arguments to the Federal Constitutional Court after he had been informed officially by a judge of the Court that his constitutional appeal appeared unfounded.

. . . .

The Law

. . . .

Whereas, with regard to the Applicant's complaint of an alleged violation of art. 6 of the Convention on the ground that he was not given an opportunity to submit additional arguments to the Federal Constitutional Court after he had been informed officially by a Judge of the Court that his constitutional appeal appeared unfounded, it is to be observed that no clause of the Convention obliges a High Contracting Party to allow its citizens access to a Constitutional Court as well as to the normal courts of appeal; and whereas if a High Contracting Party sets up a Supreme Constitutional Court, as has been done by the Federal Republic of Germany, it is entitled to lay down its own regulations regarding the right of appeal to that Court; whereas in the Act setting up the Federal Constitutional Court the Federal Republic laid down certain rules defining the circumstances in which a constitutional appeal could be lodged with that Court, and whereas art. 91 (a) of the said Act provides that any constitutional appeal to the Court shall be examined by a bench of three judges, to determine whether it complies with the requirements for bringing a case before the Court; whereas, consequently, in the present case, the function of the aforesaid three judges was not to hear the case, but solely to decide whether the requirements for lodging a constitutional appeal with the Court had been fulfilled; whereas such a decision does not relate to "the determination of civil rights and obligations" or to "any criminal charge" against the Applicant, within the meaning of art. 6 of the Convention; whereas, therefore, the bench of three judges appointed to decide whether the Applicant was entitled to appeal to the Federal Constitutional Court did not constitute a tribunal to which the terms of art. 6 of the Convention apply; whereas it follows that the Application, insofar as it concerns the proceedings before the Federal Constitutional Court, is manifestly ill-founded and must be rejected in accordance with art. 27, para. 2, of the Convention;

Whereas, moreover, an examination of the other aspects of the case as it has been submitted, including an examination made by the Commission *ex officio*, does not disclose any appearance of a violation of the rights and freedoms set forth in the Convention; and whereas it follows that the Application in its entirety is manifestly ill-founded and must be rejected in accordance with art. 27, para. 2, of the Convention;

Now, therefore, the Commission,
DECLARES THIS APPLICATION INADMISSIBLE.

NOTES AND QUESTIONS

1. The problem of the *Verfassungsbeschwerde* has been similarly treated in a number of other decisions of the Commission wherein the procedure involved in constitutional recourse was challenged. [1958-59] Y.B. EUR. CONV. ON HUMAN RIGHTS 386 (Eur. Comm. of Human Rights); [1958-59] Y.B. EUR. CONV. ON HUMAN RIGHTS 39 (Eur. Comm. of Human Rights); [1960] Y.B. EUR. CONV. ON HUMAN RIGHTS 254 (Eur. Comm. of Human Rights); *A. and B. X.* v. *Federal Republic of Germany,* [1961] Y.B. EUR. CONV. ON HUMAN RIGHTS 286 (Eur. Comm. of Human Rights).

2. Because of the large number of *Verfassungsbeschwerde* brought in the first few years after the introduction of this device in 1951, an amendment was introduced establishing a three judge committee which exercises a type of "certiorari" function with regard to the petitions submitted to the court. This committee is, in German law, not a separate tribunal, but a subsection of the Constitutional Court. At the time the instant case was brought before the Commission, its competence extended to an examination as to whether the formal requirements for acceptance had been met and, in addition, whether the claim was or was not "manifestly unfounded." Is it true, then, as the decision of the Commission seems to indicate, that there is no "determination" in the report of the committee with regard to the civil rights of the petitioner in the sense required by the article? Would not the ascertainment of whether the case was or was not "manifestly unfounded" involve an investigation of the merits?

3. If one rejects the argument that the decision whether a constitutional claim is unfounded does not constitute a decision on the merits, can the *reasoning* in this case be reconciled with that in the *Dunshirn* case? Note particularly the argument that Germany did not have to provide appeal to a constitutional court, and, having allowed the appeal, could then provide a more limited hearing. Should it have been relevant that, in the *Dunshirn* case, the procedure involved an appeal by the prosecution rather than the defendant? Can the cases be reconciled on the ground that there is no issue in the principal case as to the adversary's right to appear in the absence of the applicant? Would the reasoning of the principal case permit the denial of counsel to assist in filing a constitutional appeal with the Constitutional Court?

4. What effect would a different result have had on the German judicial system? Should pragmatism be a factor in the determination of constitutional justice? *Cf. Faretta* v. *California, supra* § A.3.a. (Chief Justice Burger, dissenting).

b. United States

ROSS v. MOFFITT

Supreme Court of the United States
417 U.S. 600, 94 S. Ct. 2437, 41 L. Ed. 2d 341 (1974)

MR. JUSTICE REHNQUIST delivered the opinion of the Court.

We are asked in this case to decide whether *Douglas* v. *California,* 372 U.S. 353 (1963), which requires appointment of counsel for indigent state defendants on their first appeal as of right, should be extended to require counsel for discretionary state appeals and for applications for review in this Court. The Court of Appeals for the Fourth Circuit held that such appointment was required by the Due Process and Equal Protection Clauses of the Fourteenth Amendment.

I

. . . .

The Court of Appeals [for the Fourth Circuit held] that respondent was entitled to the assistance of counsel at state expense both on his petition for review in the North Carolina Supreme Court and on his petition for certiorari to this Court. Reviewing the procedures of the North Carolina appellate system and the possible benefits that counsel would provide for indigents seeking review in that system, the court stated:

> "As long as the state provides such procedures and allows other convicted felons to seek access to the higher court with the help of retained counsel, there is a marked absence of fairness in denying an indigent the assistance of counsel as he seeks access to the same court."

This principle was held equally applicable to petitions for certiorari to this Court. For, said the Court of Appeals, "[t]he same concepts of fairness and equality, which require counsel in a first appeal of right, require counsel in other and subsequent discretionary appeals."

. . . For the reasons hereafter stated we reverse the Court of Appeals.

II

This Court, in the past 20 years, has given extensive consideration to the rights of indigent persons on appeal. In *Griffin* v. *Illinois,* 351 U. S. 12 (1956), the first of the pertinent cases, the Court had before it an Illinois rule allowing a convicted criminal defendant to present claims of trial error to the Supreme Court of Illinois only if he procured a transcript of the testimony adduced at his trial. No exception was made for the indigent defendant, and thus one who was unable to pay the cost of obtaining such a transcript was precluded from obtaining appellate review of asserted trial error. Mr. Justice Frankfurter, who cast the deciding vote, said in his concurring opinion:

> ". . . Illinois has decreed that only defendants who can afford to pay for the stenographic minutes of a trial may have trial errors reviewed on appeal by the Illinois Supreme Court."

The Court in *Griffin* held that this discrimination violated the Fourteenth Amendment.

Succeeding cases invalidated similar financial barriers to the appellate process, at the same time reaffirming the traditional principle that a State is not obliged to provide any appeal at all for criminal defendants. *McKane* v. *Durston,* 153 U. S. 684 (1894). The cases encompassed a variety of circumstances but all had a common theme. For example, *Lane* v. *Brown,* 372 U. S. 477 (1963), involved an Indiana provision declaring that only a public defender could obtain a free transcript of a hearing on a *coram nobis* application. If the public defender declined to request one, the indigent prisoner seeking to appeal had no recourse. In *Draper* v. *Washington,* 372 U. S. 487 (1963), the State permitted an indigent to obtain a free transcript of the trial at which he was convicted only if he satisfied the trial judge that his contentions on appeal would not be frivolous. The appealing defendant was in effect bound by the trial court's conclusions in seeking to review the determination of frivolousness, since no transcript or its equivalent was made available to him. In *Smith* v. *Bennett,* 365 U. S. 708 (1961), Iowa had required a filing fee in order to process a state habeas corpus application by a convicted defendant, and in *Burns* v. *Ohio,* 360 U. S. 252 (1959), the State of Ohio required a $20 filing fee in order to move the Supreme Court of Ohio for leave to appeal from a judgment of the Ohio Court of Appeals affirming a criminal conviction. Each of these state-imposed financial barriers to the adjudication of a criminal defendant's appeal was held to violate the Fourteenth Amendment.

The decisions discussed above stand for the proposition that a State cannot arbitrarily cut off appeal rights for indigents while leaving open avenues of appeal for more affluent persons. In *Douglas*

v. *California,* 372 U. S. 353 (1963), however, a case decided the same day as *Lane, supra,* and *Draper, supra,* the Court departed somewhat from the limited doctrine of the transcript and fee cases and undertook an examination of whether an indigent's access to the appellate system was adequate. The Court in *Douglas* concluded that a State does not fulfill its responsibility toward indigent defendants merely by waiving its own requirements that a convicted defendant procure a transcript or pay a fee in order to appeal, and held that the State must go further and provide counsel for the indigent on his first appeal as of right. It is this decision we are asked to extend today.

. . . .

This Court held unconstitutional California's requirement that counsel on appeal would be appointed for an indigent only if the appellate court determined that such appointment would be helpful to the defendant or to the court itself. The Court noted that under this system an indigent's case was initially reviewed on the merits without the benefit of any organization or argument by counsel. By contrast, persons of greater means were not faced with the preliminary "*ex parte* examination of the record," *id.,* at 356, but had their arguments presented to the court in fully briefed form. The Court noted, however, that its decision extended only to initial appeals as of right, and went on to say:

> "We need not now decide whether California would have to provide counsel for an indigent seeking a discretionary hearing from the California Supreme Court after the District Court of Appeal had sustained his conviction . . . or whether counsel must be appointed for an indigent seeking review of an appellate affirmance of his conviction in this Court by appeal as of right or by petition for a writ of certiorari which lies within the Court's discretion. But it is appropriate to observe that a State can, consistently with the Fourteenth Amendment, provide for differences so long as the result does not amount to a denial of due process or an 'invidious discrimination.' *Williamson* v. *Lee Optical Co.,* 348 U. S. 483, 489; *Griffin* v. *Illinois, supra,* p. 18. Absolute equality is not required; lines can be and are drawn and we often sustain them." *Id.,* at 356-357.

The precise rationale for the *Griffin* and *Douglas* lines of cases has never been explicitly stated, some support being derived from the Equal Protection Clause of the Fourteenth Amendment, and some from the Due Process Clause of that Amendment.[8] Neither Clause

---

[8] The Court of Appeals in this case, for example, examined both possible rationales, stating:
"If the holding [in *Douglas*] be grounded on the equal protection clause, inequality in the circumstances of these cases is as obvious as it was in the circumstances of

by itself provides an entirely satisfactory basis for the result reached, each depending on a different inquiry which emphasizes different factors. "Due process" emphasizes fairness between the State and the individual dealing with the State, regardless of how other individuals in the same situation may be treated. "Equal protection," on the other hand, emphasizes disparity in treatment by a State between classes of individuals whose situations are arguably indistinguishable. We will address these issues separately in the succeeding sections.

III

Recognition of the due process rationale in *Douglas* is found both in the Court's opinion and in the dissenting opinion of Mr. Justice Harlan. The Court in *Douglas* stated that "[w]hen an indigent is forced to run this gantlet of a preliminary showing of merit, the right to appeal does not comport with fair procedure." 372 U. S., at 357. Mr. Justice Harlan thought that the due process issue in *Douglas* was the only one worthy of extended consideration, remarking: "The real question in this case, I submit, and the only one that permits of satisfactory analysis, is whether or not the state rule, as applied in this case, is consistent with the requirements of fair procedure guaranteed by the Due Process Clause." *Id.,* at 363.

We do not believe that the Due Process Clause requires North Carolina to provide respondent with counsel on his discretionary appeal to the State Supreme Court. At the trial stage of a criminal proceeding, the right of an indigent defendant to counsel is fundamental and binding upon the States by virtue of the Sixth and Fourteenth Amendments. *Gideon* v. *Wainwright,* 372 U. S. 335 (1963). But there are significant differences between the trial and appellate stages of a criminal proceeding. The purpose of the trial stage from the State's point of view is to convert a criminal defendant from a person presumed innocent to one found guilty beyond a reasonable doubt. To accomplish this purpose, the State employs a prosecuting attorney who presents evidence to the court, challenges any witnesses offered by the defendant, argues rulings of the court, and makes direct arguments to the court and jury seeking to persuade them of the defendant's guilt. Under these circumstances "reason

---

Douglas. If the holding in *Douglas* were grounded on the due process clause, and Mr. Justice Harlan in dissent thought the discourse should have been in those terms, due process encompasses elements of equality. There simply cannot be due process of the law to a litigant deprived of all professional assistance when other litigants, similarly situated, are able to obtain professional assistance and to be benefited by it. The same concepts of fairness and equality, which require counsel in a first appeal of right, require counsel in other and subsequent discretionary appeals." 483 F. 2d, at 655.

and reflection require us to recognize that in our adversary system of criminal justice, any person haled into court, who is too poor to hire a lawyer, cannot be assured a fair trial unless counsel is provided for him." *Id.,* at 344.

By contrast, it is ordinarily the defendant, rather than the State, who initiates the appellate process, seeking not to fend off the efforts of the State's prosecutor but rather to overturn a finding of guilt made by a judge or jury below. The defendant needs an attorney on appeal not as a shield to protect him against being "haled into court" by the State and stripped of his presumption of innocence, but rather as a sword to upset the prior determination of guilt. This difference is significant for, while no one would agree that the State may simply dispense with the trial stage of proceedings without a criminal defendant's consent, it is clear that the State need not provide any appeal at all. *McKane* v. *Durston,* 153 U. S. 684 (1894). The fact that an appeal *has* been provided does not automatically mean that a State then acts unfairly by refusing to provide counsel to indigent defendants at every stage of the way. *Douglas* v. *California, supra.* Unfairness results only if indigents are singled out by the State and denied meaningful access to the appellate system because of their poverty. That question is more profitably considered under an equal protection analysis.

IV

Language invoking equal protection notions is prominent both in *Douglas* and in other cases treating the rights of indigents on appeal. The Court in *Douglas,* for example, stated:

> "[W]here the merits of *the one and only appeal* an indigent has as of right are decided without benefit of counsel, we think an unconstitutional line has been drawn between rich and poor." 372 U. S., at 357. (Emphasis in original.)
> . . . .

Despite the tendency of all rights "to declare themselves absolute to their logical extreme," there are obviously limits beyond which the equal protection analysis may not be pressed without doing violence to principles recognized in other decisions of this Court. The Fourteenth Amendment "does not require absolute equality or precisely equal advantages," *San Antonio Independent School District* v. *Rodriguez,* 411 U. S. 1, 24 (1973), nor does it require the State to "equalize economic conditions." *Griffin* v. *Illinois,* 351 U. S., at 23 (Frankfurter, J., concurring). It does require that the state appellate system be "free of unreasoned distinctions," . . . and that indigents have an adequate opportunity to present their claims fairly within the adversary system. . . . The State cannot adopt procedures which leave an indigent defendant "entirely cut off from any appeal at all," by virtue of his indigency, ... or extend to such indigent defendants merely a "meaningless ritual" while others in better economic circumstances have a "meaningful appeal."

The question is not one of absolutes, but one of degrees. In this case we do not believe that the Equal Protection Clause, when interpreted in the context of these cases, requires North Carolina to provide free counsel for indigent defendants seeking to take discretionary appeals to the North Carolina Supreme Court, or to file petitions for certiorari in this Court.

A. The North Carolina appellate system, as are the appellate systems of almost half the States, is multi-tiered, providing for both an intermediate Court of Appeals and a Supreme Court.

... North Carolina has followed the mandate of *Douglas* v. *California, supra,* and authorized appointment of counsel for a convicted defendant appealing to the intermediate Court of Appeals, but has not gone beyond *Douglas* to provide for appointment of counsel for a defendant who seeks either discretionary review in the Supreme Court of North Carolina or a writ of certiorari here.

B. ... We do not believe that it can be said, therefore, that a defendant in respondent's circumstances is denied meaningful access to the North Carolina Supreme Court simply because the State does not appoint counsel to aid him in seeking review in that court. At that stage he will have, at the very least, a transcript or other record of trial proceedings, a brief on his behalf in the Court of Appeals setting forth his claims of error, and in many cases an opinion by the Court of Appeals disposing of his case. These materials, supplemented by whatever submission respondent may make *pro se,* would appear to provide the Supreme Court of North Carolina with an adequate basis for its decision to grant or deny review.

... Once a defendant's claims of error are organized and presented in a lawyerlike fashion to the Court of Appeals, the justices of the Supreme Court of North Carolina who make the decision to grant or deny discretionary review should be able to ascertain whether his case satisfies the standards established by the legislature for such review.

This is not to say, of course, that a skilled lawyer, particularly one trained in the somewhat arcane art of preparing petitions for discretionary review, would not prove helpful to any litigant able to employ him. An indigent defendant seeking review in the Supreme Court of North Carolina is therefore somewhat handicapped in comparison with a wealthy defendant who has counsel assisting him in every conceivable manner at every stage in the proceeding. But both the opportunity to have counsel prepare an initial brief in the Court of Appeals and the nature of discretionary review in the Supreme Court of North Carolina make this relative handicap far less than the handicap borne by the indigent defendant denied counsel on his initial appeal as of right in *Douglas.* And the fact that a particular service might be of benefit to an indigent defendant does not mean that the service is constitutionally required. The duty of the State under our cases is not to duplicate the legal arsenal that may be privately retained by a criminal defendant in a continuing effort to reverse his conviction, but only to assure the indigent defendant an adequate opportunity to present his claims fairly in the context of the State's appellate process. We think respondent was given that opportunity under the existing North Carolina system.

V

Much of the discussion in the preceding section is equally relevant to the question of whether a State must provide counsel for a defendant seeking review of his conviction in this Court. . . . This Court's review, much like that of the Supreme Court of North Carolina, is discretionary and depends on numerous factors other than the perceived correctness of the judgment we are asked to review.

There is also a significant difference between the source of the right to seek discretionary review in the Supreme Court of North Carolina and the source of the right to seek discretionary review in this Court. The former is conferred by the statutes of the State of North Carolina, but the latter is granted by statute enacted by Congress. Thus the argument relied upon in the *Griffin* and *Douglas* cases, that the State having once created a right of appeal must give all persons an equal opportunity to enjoy the right, is by its terms inapplicable. The right to seek certiorari in this Court is not granted by any State, and exists by virtue of federal statute with or without the consent of the State whose judgment is sought to be reviewed.

The suggestion that a State is responsible for providing counsel to one petitioning this Court simply because it initiated the prosecution which led to the judgment sought to be reviewed is unsupported by either reason or authority. It would be quite as logical under the rationale of *Douglas* and *Griffin,* and indeed perhaps more so, to require that the Federal Government or this Court furnish and compensate counsel for petitioners who seek certiorari here to review state judgments of conviction. Yet this Court has followed a consistent policy of denying applications for appointment of counsel by persons seeking to file jurisdictional statements or petitions for certiorari in this Court. . . .

VI

We do not mean by this opinion to in any way discourage those States which have, as a matter of legislative choice, made counsel available to convicted defendants at all stages of judicial review. Some States which might well choose to do so as a matter of legislative policy may conceivably find that other claims for public funds within or without the criminal justice system preclude the implementation of such a policy at the present time. North Carolina, for example, while it does not provide counsel to indigent defendants seeking discretionary review on appeal, does provide counsel for indigent prisoners in several situations where such appointments are not required by any constitutional decision of this Court. Our reading of the Fourteenth Amendment leaves these choices to the State, and respondent was denied no right secured by the Federal Constitution when North Carolina refused to provide counsel to aid him in obtaining discretionary appellate review.

The judgment of the Court of Appeals' holding to the contrary is

Reversed.

MR. JUSTICE DOUGLAS, with whom MR. JUSTICE BRENNAN and MR. JUSTICE MARSHALL concur, dissenting.

I would affirm the judgment below because I am in agreement with the opinion of Chief Judge Haynsworth for a unanimous panel in the Court of Appeals.

... More familiar with the functioning of the North Carolina criminal justice system than are we, he concluded that "in the context of constitutional questions arising in criminal prosecutions, permissive review in the state's highest court may be predictably the most meaningful review the conviction will receive."

Chief Judge Haynsworth also correctly observed that the indigent defendant proceeding without counsel is at a substantial disadvantage relative to wealthy defendants represented by counsel when he is forced to fend for himself in seeking discretionary review from the State Supreme Court or from this Court. ... Furthermore, the lawyer who handled the first appeal in a case would be familiar with the facts and legal issues involved in the case. It would be a relatively easy matter for the attorney to apply his expertise in filing a petition for discretionary review to a higher court, or to advise his client that such a petition would have no chance of succeeding.

Douglas v. *California* was grounded on concepts of fairness and equality. The right to seek discretionary review is a substantial one, and one where a lawyer can be of significant assistance to an indigent defendant. It was correctly perceived below that the "same concepts of fairness and equality, which require counsel in a first appeal of right, require counsel in other and subsequent discretionary appeals."

NOTES AND QUESTIONS

1. *Griffin* v. *Illinois,* 351 U.S. 12 (1956), which held that indigent criminal defendants were entitled to free trial transcipts necessary to an appeal, was decided seven years before *Gideon* v. *Wainwright.* Some thought that the equal protection principle of *Griffin* would require the overruling of *Betts* v. *Brady.* Nevertheless, when *Betts* was overruled, the vehicle proved to be the Sixth Amendment's guarantee of right to counsel rather than the Fourteenth Amendment's Equal Protection Clause. *Douglas* v. *California,* 372 U.S. 353 (1963), was decided the very same day as *Gideon.* In contrast to *Gideon,* Justice Douglas' opinion in *Douglas* relied on the Equal Protection Clause. Why the difference in rationale? Would the Sixth Amendment provide a viable source for a right to counsel on appeal if there were no constitutional right to an appeal?

2. Since the rationale of *Douglas* turned on the unconstitutional discrimination between rich and poor, why did that opinion cautiously limit itself to the first criminal appeal as of right? Would it have been possible to implement the logical extension of the *Douglas* principle — furnishing criminal defendants counsel whenever the affluent had a right to representation by retained counsel? Would it have been possible to implement the *Griffin-Douglas* principle to furnish other necessities for trial or appeal (transcripts, expert witnesses, investigative services, etc.) which the affluent could afford?

3. In *Ross,* under the rationale of Judge Haynsworth's opinion for the Court of Appeals and Justice Douglas' dissent, why was the State obligated to furnish counsel in seeking review in the United States Supreme Court? If there were a constitutional right to appointed counsel in a federal court proceeding, should it not be the federal government which has the obligation to furnish the money?

4. If there were a right to appointed counsel in discretionary appeals, would there also be a right to appointed counsel for post-conviction proceedings, such as habeas corpus, in the state courts? For habeas corpus in a federal court for persons convicted of crime in the state courts?

5. Right to Counsel on Revocation of Parole or Probation

GAGNON v. SCARPELLI

Supreme Court of the United States
411 U.S. 778, 93 S. Ct. 1756, 36 L. Ed. 2d 656 (1973)

MR. JUSTICE POWELL delivered the opinion of the Court.

This case presents the related questions whether a previously sentenced probationer is entitled to a hearing when his probation is revoked and, if so, whether he is entitled to be represented by appointed counsel at such a hearing.

I

Respondent, Gerald Scarpelli, pleaded guilty in July 1965, to a charge of armed robbery in Wisconsin. The trial judge sentenced him to 15 years' imprisonment, but suspended the sentence and placed him on probation for seven years in the custody of the Wisconsin Department of Public Welfare (the Department).[1] . . .

On August 6, respondent was apprehended by Illinois police, who had surprised him and one Fred Kleckner, Jr., in the course of the burglary of a house. After being apprised of his constitutional rights, respondent admitted that he and Kleckner had broken into the house for the purpose of stealing merchandise or money, although he now asserts that his statement was made under duress and is false. Probation was revoked by the Wisconsin Department on September 1, without a hearing. The stated grounds for revocation were that:

> "1. [Scarpelli] has associated with known criminals, in direct violation of his probation regulations and his supervising agent's instructions;
> "2. [Scarpelli,] while associating with a known criminal, namely Fred Kleckner, Jr., was involved in, and arrested for, a burglary . . . in Deerfield, Illinois." App. 20.

On September 4, 1965, he was incarcerated in the Wisconsin State Reformatory at Green Bay to begin serving the 15 years to which he had been sentenced by the trial judge. At no time was he afforded a hearing.

Some three years later, on December 16, 1968, respondent applied for a writ of habeas corpus. . . . On the merits, the District Court held that revocation without a hearing and counsel was a denial of due process. . . . The Court of Appeals affirmed.

II

Two prior decisions set the bounds of our present inquiry. In *Mempa* v. *Rhay*, 389 U. S. 128 (1967), the Court held that a probationer is entitled to be represented by appointed counsel at a combined revocation and sentencing hearing. Reasoning that counsel is required "at every stage of a criminal proceeding where

---

[1] The Court's order placing respondent on probation provided, among other things, that "[i]n the event of his failure to meet the conditions of his probation he will stand committed under the sentence all ready [*sic*] imposed." . . . The agreement specifying the conditions of the probation, duly executed by respondent, obligated him to "make a sincere attempt to avoid all acts which are forbidden by law . . . ."

substantial rights of a criminal accused may be affected," *id.,* at 134, and that sentencing is one such stage, the Court concluded that counsel must be provided an indigent at sentencing even when it is accomplished as part of a subsequent probation revocation proceeding. But this line of reasoning does not require a hearing or counsel at the time of probation revocation in a case such as the present one, where the probationer was sentenced at the time of trial.

Of greater relevance is our decision last Term in *Morrissey* v. *Brewer,* 408 U. S. 471 (1972). There we held that the revocation of parole is not a part of a criminal prosecution.

. . . .

Even though the revocation of parole is not a part of the criminal prosecution, we held that the loss of liberty entailed is a serious deprivation requiring that the parolee be accorded due process. Specifically, we held that a parolee is entitled to two hearings, one a preliminary hearing at the time of his arrest and detention to determine whether there is probable cause to believe that he has committed a violation of his parole, and the other a somewhat more comprehensive hearing prior to the making of the final revocation decision.

Petitioner does not contend that there is any difference relevant to the guarantee of due process between the revocation of parole and the revocation of probation, nor do we perceive one. Probation revocation, like parole revocation, is not a stage of a criminal prosecution, but does result in a loss of liberty. Accordingly, we hold that a probationer, like a parolee, is entitled to a preliminary and a final revocation hearing, under the conditions specified in *Morrissey* v. *Brewer, supra.*

III

The second, and more difficult, question posed by this case is whether an indigent probationer or parolee has a due process right to be represented by appointed counsel at these hearings.[6] . . .

. . . *Morrissey* mandated preliminary and final revocation hearings. At the preliminary hearing, a probationer or parolee is entitled to notice of the alleged violations of probation or parole, an opportunity to appear and to present evidence in his own behalf, a conditional right to confront adverse witnesses, an independent

---

[6] In *Morrissey* v. *Brewer,* we left open the question "whether the parolee is entitled to the assistance of retained counsel or to appointed counsel if he is indigent." 408 U. S., at 489. Since respondent did not attempt to retain counsel but asked only for appointed counsel, we have no occasion to decide in this case whether a probationer or parolee has a right to be represented at a revocation hearing by retained counsel in situations other than those where the State would be obliged to furnish counsel for an indigent.

decisionmaker, and a written report of the hearing. . . . The final hearing is a less summary one because the decision under consideration is the ultimate decision to revoke rather than a mere determination of probable cause, but the "minimum requirements of due process" include very similar elements:

> "(a) written notice of the claimed violations of [probation or] parole; (b) disclosure to the [probationer or] parolee of evidence against him; (c) opportunity to be heard in person and to present witnesses and documentary evidence; (d) the right to confront and cross-examine adverse witnesses (unless the hearing officer specifically finds good cause for not allowing confrontation); (e) a 'neutral and detached' hearing body such as a traditional parole board, members of which need not be judicial officers or lawyers; and (f) a written statement by the factfinders as to the evidence relied on and reasons for revoking [probation or] parole." *Morrissey* v. *Brewer, supra,* at 489.

These requirements in themselves serve as substantial protection against ill-considered revocation, and petitioner argues that counsel need never be supplied. What this argument overlooks is that the effectiveness of the rights guaranteed by *Morrissey* may in some circumstances depend on the use of skills which the probationer or parolee is unlikely to possess. Despite the informal nature of the proceedings and the absence of technical rules of procedure or evidence, the unskilled or uneducated probationer or parolee may well have difficulty in presenting his version of a disputed set of facts where the presentation requires the examining or cross-examining of witnesses or the offering or dissecting of complex documentary evidence.

By the same token, we think that the Court of Appeals erred in accepting respondent's contention that the State is under a constitutional duty to provide counsel for indigents in all probation or parole revocation cases. While such a rule has the appeal of simplicity, it would impose direct costs and serious collateral disadvantages without regard to the need or the likelihood in a particular case for a constructive contribution by counsel. In most cases, the probationer or parolee has been convicted of committing another crime or has admitted the charges against him. And while in some cases he may have a justifiable excuse for the violation or a convincing reason why revocation is not the appropriate disposition, mitigating evidence of this kind is often not susceptible of proof or is so simple as not to require either investigation or exposition by counsel.

The introduction of counsel into a revocation proceeding will alter significantly the nature of the proceeding. If counsel is provided for the probationer or parolee, the State in turn will normally provide its own counsel; lawyers, by training and disposition, are advocates and bound by professional duty to present all available evidence and arguments in support of their clients' positions and to contest with vigor all adverse evidence and views. The role of the hearing body itself, aptly described in *Morrissey* as being "predictive and discretionary" as well as factfinding, may become more akin to that of a judge at a trial, and less attuned to the rehabilitative needs of the individual probationer or parolee. In the greater self-consciousness of its quasi-judicial role, the hearing body may be less tolerant of marginal deviant behavior and feel more pressure to reincarcerate than to continue nonpunitive rehabilitation. Certainly, the decisionmaking process will be prolonged, and the financial cost to the State — for appointed counsel, counsel for the State, a longer record, and the possibility of judicial review — will not be insubstantial.[11]

In some cases, these modifications in the nature of the revocation hearing must be endured and the costs borne because, as we have indicated above, the probationer's or parolee's version of a disputed issue can fairly be represented only by a trained advocate. But due process is not so rigid as to require that the significant interests in informality, flexibility, and economy must always be sacrificed.

In so concluding, we are of course aware that the case-by-case approach to the right to counsel in felony prosecutions adopted in *Betts* v. *Brady,* 316 U. S. 455 (1942), was later rejected in favor of a *per se* rule in *Gideon* v. *Wainwright,* 372 U. S. 335 (1963). . . . We do not, however, draw from *Gideon* and *Argersinger* the conclusion that a case-by-case approach to furnishing counsel is necessarily inadequate to protect constitutional rights asserted in varying types of proceedings: there are critical differences between criminal trials and probation or parole revocation hearings, and both society and the probationer or parolee have stakes in preserving these differences.

In a criminal trial, the State is represented by a prosecutor; formal rules of evidence are in force; a defendant enjoys a number of procedural rights which may be lost if not timely raised; and, in a jury trial, a defendant must make a presentation understandable to untrained jurors. In short, a criminal trial under our system is an adversary proceeding with its own unique characteristics. In a revocation hearing, on the other hand, the State is represented, not by a prosecutor, but by a parole officer with the orientation described above; formal procedures and rules of evidence are not employed;

---

[11] The scope of the practical problem which would be occasioned by a requirement of counsel in all revocation cases is suggested by the fact that in the mid-1960's there was an estimated average of 20,000 adult felony parole revocations and 108,000 adult probation revocations each year.

and the members of the hearing body are familiar with the problems and practice of probation or parole. The need for counsel at revocation hearings derives, not from the invariable attributes of those hearings, but rather from the peculiarities of particular cases.

The differences between a criminal trial and a revocation hearing do not dispose altogether of the argument that under a case-by-case approach there may be cases in which a lawyer would be useful but in which none would be appointed because an arguable defense would be uncovered only by a lawyer. Without denying that there is some force in this argument, we think it a sufficient answer that we deal here, not with the right of an accused to counsel in a criminal prosecution, but with the more limited due process right of one who is a probationer or parolee only because he has been convicted of a crime.[12]

We thus find no justification for a new inflexible constitutional rule with respect to the requirement of counsel. We think, rather, that the decision as to the need for counsel must be made on a case-by-case basis in the exercise of a sound discretion by the state authority charged with responsibility for administering the probation and parole system. Although the presence and participation of counsel will probably be both undesirable and constitutionally unnecessary in most revocation hearings, there will remain certain cases in which fundamental fairness — the touchstone of due process — will require that the State provide at its expense counsel for indigent probationers or parolees.

It is neither possible nor prudent to attempt to formulate a precise and detailed set of guidelines to be followed in determining when the providing of counsel is necessary to meet the applicable due process requirements. The facts and circumstances in preliminary and final hearings are susceptible of almost infinite variation, and a considerable discretion must be allowed the responsible agency in making the decision. Presumptively, it may be said that counsel should be provided in cases where, after being informed of his right to request counsel, the probationer or parolee makes such a request, based on a timely and colorable claim (i) that he has not committed the alleged violation of the conditions upon which he is at liberty; or (ii) that, even if the violation is a matter of public record or is uncontested, there are substantial reasons which justified or mitigated the violation and make revocation inappropriate, and that the reasons are complex or otherwise difficult to develop or present.

---

[12] Cf. *In re Gault,* 387 U. S. 1 (1967), establishing a juvenile's right to appointed counsel in a delinquency proceeding which, while denominated civil, was functionally akin to a criminal trial. A juvenile charged with violation of a generally applicable statute is differently situated from an already-convicted probationer or parolee, and is entitled to a higher degree of protection.

In passing on a request for the appointment of counsel, the responsible agency also should consider, especially in doubtful cases, whether the probationer appears to be capable of speaking effectively for himself. In every case in which a request for counsel at a preliminary or final hearing is refused, the grounds for refusal should be stated succinctly in the record.

IV

We return to the facts of the present case. Because respondent was not afforded either a preliminary hearing or a final hearing, the revocation of his probation did not meet the standards of due process prescribed in *Morrissey,* which we have here held applicable to probation revocations. Accordingly, respondent was entitled to a writ of habeas corpus. On remand, the District Court should allow the State an opportunity to conduct such a hearing. As to whether the State must provide counsel, respondent's admission to having committed another serious crime creates the very sort of situation in which counsel need not ordinarily be provided. But because of respondent's subsequent assertions regarding that admission, we conclude that the failure of the Department to provide respondent with the assistance of counsel should be re-examined in light of this opinion. The general guidelines outlined above should be applied in the first instance by those charged with conducting the revocation hearing.

Affirmed in part, reversed in part, and remanded.

Mr. Justice Douglas, dissenting in part.

I believe that due process requires the appointment of counsel in this case because of the claim that respondent's confession of the burglary was made under duress.

NOTES AND QUESTIONS

1. How does one explain the decision adopting a case-by-case standard for the right to counsel, in light of the experience with that policy under the rule of *Betts* v. *Brady?* How significant is the statistic showing the number of parole and probation revocations each year? Is that more significant than the "critical differences" between parole and probation revocation hearings on the one hand and criminal trials on the other?

2. If the state permits retained counsel at a probation or parole revocation hearing, will the Equal Protection Clause then require the furnishing of appointed counsel even in the absence of special circumstances? Alternatively, can it be argued that once the state permits retained counsel, it has decided to forego its interest in

informality and flexibility, and that due process then requires furnishing of appointed counsel? Does the decision in *Ross* v. *Moffitt, supra,* foreclose the arguments? (In *Wainwright* v. *Cottle,* 414 U.S. 895 (1973), Justices Douglas and Blackmun dissented from denial of certiorari in a case involving the issue.)

3. The European analogues of probation and parole are the "conditional sentence" (*e.g.,* Italian Criminal Code, arts. 163-69) and the "conditional liberation" from prison (*e.g.,* Italian Criminal Code, arts. 176, 177). However, the revocation of these requires a new judicial decision (*e.g.,* Italian criminal code, arts. 168, 177), usually based on the commission of a new crime for which there must be a new prosecution and sentence. This means that revocation can be effected only after a judicial hearing which includes the party's right (and duty) to be represented by counsel.

B. RIGHT TO COUNSEL IN CIVIL CASES

1. Right to Retain Counsel

We have already encountered in the civil law tradition that, in criminal cases, litigation as a rule cannot proceed without counsel on both sides. That tradition applies in civil cases as well. Article 82 of the Italian Code of Civil Procedure, for example, requires that parties be represented by counsel at all stages of the litigation. (Exceptions are made for some courts of inferior jurisdiction, where appearance through an attorney is optional.) Obviously, in a system that demands that litigation be conducted through lawyers, the issue of the right to retain counsel cannot arise.

As in small claims cases in the United States, there may be methods of dispute resolution where attorneys are barred from appearance. Those procedures, however, can raise serious questions whether a fair hearing is denied if the parties are required to proceed without a lawyer. A 1971 decision of the Italian *Corte Costituzionale,* for example, dealt with initial stages of a judicial proceeding for marital separation. The Code of Civil Procedure required the spouses to appear personally, before the President of the Tribunal, who was required to attempt to reconcile the parties. Failing reconciliation, the President was required to issue provisional orders regarding custody of the children, and financial and living arrangements. The *Corte Costituzionale* decided that the President must hear the parties' attorneys before issuing a provisional order, since that order may seriously affect personal and property rights of the parties. Decision of June 30, 1971, Corte cost., [1971] 16 Giur. Cost. 1672; [1971] 34 Rac. uff. corte cost. 345; [1971] 94 Foro It. I, 2132. Consider, in connection with the following case, whether all dispute resolution procedures which do not rest on the consent of the parties, and which involve dispositive orders affecting personal and property rights, require participation by lawyers.

X and Y v. FEDERAL REPUBLIC OF GERMANY

European Commission of Human Rights
[1962] Y.B. Eur. Conv. on Human Rights 158

THE FACTS

[The applicants are a workman and his attorney. The workman had instituted an action in a German labor court to recover compensation allegedly due him from a former employer. The workman executed a power of attorney to his lawyer to pursue the case in the labor court, but the labor court refused to permit the attorney to prosecute the action, under paragraph 11 of the German Act on Labor Courts of Sept. 3, 1953, which reads:

> Before the Labour Courts the parties may present their case themselves or be represented by representatives of trade unions or employers' unions or of an association of such unions when, according to statutes or special mandates, such persons are competent to represent and act for the Association, the union or its members and do not, in addition to this representation, practise as a lawyer, or, without being a lawyer, practise professionally for fees for taking cases before the Court; the same applies to representation by representatives of independent organisations of employees with social or professional objects. Lawyers are only admitted before the Labour Courts as representatives or counsel when it seems necessary for the safeguard of the rights of the parties. The President of the Labour Court shall decide on this question. If admission is refused the party concerned may request a decision from the chamber of the Labour Court. This decision is final. If the value of the matters in dispute is not less than 300 DM, lawyers are admitted as representatives.

> The parties must be represented before the Regional Labour Courts and the Federal Labour Court by lawyers; and a lawyer admitted to the bar of a German court is entitled to be a representative. . . .

It was argued before the labor court that the workman's scanty knowledge of law did not permit him to plead his case adequately, and that his present work made it impossible for him to attend court hearings. The lawyer further claimed that Article 11 interfered with his right to act as legal representative, and that the provision permitting appearances by trade union representatives would force workers to join unions. These arguments were rejected by the labor court, which held that the plaintiff was absent without excuse, and entered judgment for the defendant by default, requiring the plaintiff to pay costs. A constitutional recourse was then brought before the Constitutional Court which rejected it as being manifestly ill-founded. Before the Commission, it was claimed that refusing the workman the right to be represented by a lawyer denied him a fair hearing.]

THE LAW

Whereas art. 6, para. 1, of the Convention provides that "in the determination of his civil rights and obligations . . . everyone is entitled to a fair and public hearing . . .", whereas the action introduced by the first Applicant, Mr. X, for obtaining compensation for loss of holidays and pay during illness was clearly an action to determine that Applicant's civil rights; whereas the question arises whether or not the refusal by the Labour Court to accept his representation by a lawyer constituted a violation of the provision of a "fair hearing" within the meaning of art. 6; whereas this principle cannot be determined *in abstracto* but must be considered in the light of the special circumstances of each case;

Whereas, when a case does not give rise to any serious legal dispute but only necessitates a correct establishment of the facts, the barring of the parties from the right to be represented or assisted by practising lawyers in the procedure cannot be held to constitute a denial of a fair hearing;

Whereas it is clear that the action introduced by the first Applicant, which concerned a sum of less than 100 DM, did not involve legal issues making it necessary for him to be represented or assisted by a lawyer;

Whereas it is to be noted that para. 11 of the Act on Labour Courts provides that, in cases where the value of the matters in dispute is less than 300 DM, lawyers shall only be admitted before the Labour Courts as representatives or as counsel when it seems necessary for the safeguard of the rights of the parties;

Whereas the first Applicant, when he consulted the second Applicant, who was a lawyer, must have been informed of the Rules laid down in para. 11 of the Act on Labour Courts; whereas he must thus have been fully aware of the risk to which he exposed himself by insisting upon being represented by a lawyer, even after the refusal by the Court of . . . 1960, and by failing to appear in person, or by some representative other than a lawyer, at the sessions of the Court to which he was duly summoned;

Whereas it follows that the proceedings before the Labour Court did not in the present case violate the principle of "fair hearing" within the meaning of art. 6, para. 1, of the Convention; whereas the

Application lodged by the first Applicant is manifestly ill-founded and must be rejected in accordance with art. 27, para. 2, of the Convention.

. . . .

Now therefore the Commission
DECLARES THIS APPLICATION INADMISSIBLE.

NOTES AND QUESTIONS

1. The rule that the right to be represented by retained counsel depends upon the "special circumstances" of each case bears an analytical resemblance to the rule which governed the right to appointed counsel in criminal cases in the United States prior to *Gideon* v. *Wainwright* (§ A.3.a., *supra*), and still governs the right to be represented by counsel in cases of parole or probation revocation (*Gagnon* v. *Scarpelli,* § A.5., *supra*). We have already seen that one of the difficulties with the "special circumstances" rule is the difficulty of ascertaining in each case whether there are such circumstances as will require assistance of counsel. Does the Commission's decision involve a similar case-by-case decision-making process? Will all decisions by the labor court that, in a particular case, representation by counsel was not "necessary for the safeguard of the parties," be subject to review by the Commission?

2. Notice that the Commission gives two reasons why representation by counsel was unnecessary. Would either of those reasons be sufficient, in the absence of the other? Specifically, can representation by counsel be denied in small cases which involve complex legal issues? Or, can representation by counsel be denied in larger cases which involve only issues of fact? The American experience with the "special circumstances" rule may be instructive in judging the soundness of the Commission's conclusion that it is not a denial of a fair hearing to require a non-lawyer to develop the facts. *Betts* v. *Brady,* 316 U.S. 455 (1942), which announced the special circumstances rule, involved a defendant who had been convicted of robbery. The Court concluded that there were no special circumstances requiring assistance of counsel because the only issue was identity of the robber, and the truth or falsity of defendant's alibi. On the other hand, Betts was only identified by the robbery victim when he was shown in a one man lineup while wearing clothing identical to that worn by the robber. In cross-examining the prosecution witness, Betts never made the obvious point that the witness had identified the clothing and not him, and that the clothing was not his but had been furnished by the police! See Kamisar, *The Right to Counsel and the Fourteenth Amendment,* 30 U. Chi. L. Rev. 1, 42-56 (1962). Of course, American criminal trials often present the adversary trial process at its most adversary. The experience with the rule of *Betts* v. *Brady* demonstrates that, in adversary trials, the assistance of trained counsel is often indispensable in presentation of "simple" issues of fact. Is that true of trial processes which are less adversary?

2. Right to Appointed Counsel

a. *Constitutional Entitlement*

(i) Europe

As previously indicated, the Italian Constitution contains a specific provision establishing a constitutional right to legal aid. Article 24, para. 3, provides "[d]estitute persons shall, by institutions created for that purpose, be assured the means to plead and defend themselves before any judicial jurisdiction." Other European constitutions do not contain an analogous provision, raising the issue whether more general provisions of the constitutions should be interpreted to include a constitutional guarantee of legal aid in civil cases.

DECISION OF JULY 9, 1952

Bundesgericht, Switzerland
[1952] 78 Entscheidungen des Schweizerisches Bundesgerichts (BGE) I 193*

[Facts: Plaintiff requested legal aid to appeal a trial court decision to the Cantonal Court of Appeal. That court rejected his request for legal aid, and plaintiff appealed that ruling directly to the Supreme Court.]

Opinion: This court has consistently affirmed that a party who is unable to afford the costs of a lawsuit without jeopardizing the livelihood of himself and his family and whose case is not unfounded, is entitled under the provisions of Article 4 of the Constitution (principle of equality)** to a right of judicial protection. This right means that the judge must consider his case, that the indigent litigant shall not be required to pay court costs in advance nor to post security for costs, and further that he is to be granted the assistance of a lawyer (without cost) in all cases where a lawyer is required for the adequate protection of his interests. This right of the indigent to judicial protection embraces every action to be taken during the proceeding of the first instance, unless the action is manifestly

---

* Translation reprinted from M. Cappelletti, J. Gordley, & E. Johnson, Jr., Toward Equal Justice: A Comparative Study of Legal Aid in Modern Societies, 704-06 (Giuffrè — Oceana 1975).

** Article 4 of the Constitution of the Swiss Confederation reads: "All Swiss are equal before the law. In Switzerland there is neither subjection or privilege of locality, birth, family, or person."

unfounded or inadmissible; and this right extends also to challenges against the judgment of the first instance.

. . . .

In the present case the right to judicial protection under the Federal Constitution is brought into question, since sec. 221 of the code of civil procedure of the Canton of Solothurn permits an appeal only if the appellant has paid the costs of the proceedings in the first instance as well as the fee required for filing the appeal. . . .

Ordinarily the Supreme Court would be able to question only whether the lower courts have applied the cantonal legal aid provisions in a manner which is manifestly unfair and arbitrary. However, since the Federal Constitution itself guarantees the right to legal aid, this Court is authorized to examine the facts adduced by the party and those ascertained in the proceeding of the first instance in order to determine whether the indigent's grounds for appeal are unfounded. Consequently, in the instant case the court can evaluate on its own whether the appeal is manifestly unfounded. It is true that this Court has stated that when reviewing a lower court's determination of indigency, it will only reverse for arbitrariness or manifest inconsistency with the facts. Nevertheless this Court remains entirely free to itself assess the indigent party's case anew when the issue is his probability of success.

According to recent decisions of this Court, a case must be considered to have no probability of success only when the probability of failure clearly prevails or when the case must be considered capricious. And merely because the chances of success are equivalent or slightly inferior to the chances of failure, the case must not be rejected as failing to demonstrate the requisite probability of success.

[The decision of the Court of Appeal was reversed.]

DECISION OF JUNE 6, 1967

Bundesverfassungsgericht
[1967] 22 BVerfGE 83

FACTS

The petitioners lost in the [civil] trial court. On August 20, 1963, within the time for appeal (four weeks), the petitioners requested legal aid for the appellate proceedings. The court of appeal granted the request in an order of June 26, 1964. The petitioners then had two weeks to request that their failure to appeal within the normal period be excused. However, they filed an appeal and made such a motion on July 14, after the expiration of the two week period, and the Court of Appeal dismissed the case. On final appeal to the Federal Court, this decision was affirmed. The Federal Court held that a double excuse for failure to meet a time limitation — i.e., a request to be excused from failing to make a timely motion to be excused from not taking a timely appeal — is not permitted. Against this decision, a *Verfassungsbeschwerde* was brought based upon an asserted violation of art. 3 of the Constitution (equality of all people).

OPINION

II

The *Verfassungsbeschwerde* is well founded. The decision of the Federal Court violates the basic right of the petitioners under art. 3.

1. In the area of legal protection, the general equality of people (art. 3) in conjunction with the principle of the social state (art. 20) requires us to adjust as much as possible the procedural status of the rich and the poor. A poor party must not be handicapped from adequately asserting and defending his rights against a rich party. . . . Due to their heavy caseload, the courts usually cannot make decisions upon requests for legal aid within the period to make an appeal, even when the requests are timely filed. . . . Therefore, the poor party is generally forced to request to be excused from not filing a timely appeal. The rich party, however, need do this only in extraordinary cases. Therefore, the disadvantage of the poor party is . . . that unlike the rich party, he is generally forced to combine the appeal with a request to be excused for the delay. Taking an overview of this situation, in the light of justice an adjustment of the procedural positions of rich and poor parties can only be achieved by a regulation that allows the poor party to bring an appeal with generally the same chances as the rich party, starting with the granting of legal aid . . . . Therefore, art. 3 and the principle of the social state forbid the denial of a double excuse.

NOTE AND QUESTIONS

Both the Swiss and German decisions base the constitutional right to legal aid, in whole or part, on a general constitutional right of equality. Can a principle of equality of rich and poor in the capacity to conduct civil litigation be limited to a requirement that the state furnish legal counsel to the poor? Would the acceptance of a similar general principle in the United States, under the Equal Protection Clause of the Fourteenth Amendment, require the states to furnish legal aid to poor civil litigants? Finally, if the right to legal aid turns on equality between rich and poor litigants, are the poor entitled to legal aid in any case where the rich are entitled to be represented by retained counsel? (As to the last question, *see* § B.2.b.(i) *infra.*)

(ii) United States

BODDIE v. CONNECTICUT

Supreme Court of the United States
401 U.S. 371, 91 S. Ct. 780, 28 L. Ed. 2d 113 (1971)

[The report of this case appears *supra* Ch. 6, § C.3.]

PAYNE v. SUPERIOR COURT

Supreme Court of California
17 Cal.3d 908, 132 Cal. Rptr. 405, 553 P. 2d 565 (1976)

Mosk, Associate Justice.

Few liberties in America have been more zealously guarded than the right to protect one's property in a court of law. This nation has long realized that none of our freedoms would be secure if any person could be deprived of his possessions without an opportunity to defend them " 'at a meaningful time and in a meaningful manner.' " ... In a variety of contexts, the right of access to the courts has been reaffirmed and strengthened throughout our 200-year history.

For one limited category of Californians, however, the right is more illusory than real. An indigent prisoner may be sued civilly by anyone in this state, but is unable to defend against that suit. Although a monetary judgment may pursue him for the rest of his life, ... he may not personally appear to prevent its original imposition. If he cannot afford counsel to appear as his surrogate, he will almost inevitably suffer a default judgment. One such prisoner, Torrey Wood Payne, asserts that this denial of access to the courts violates his rights to due process and equal protection of the law under the state and federal Constitutions. We agree with him in principle.

Payne (petitioner) was charged in a criminal complaint with stealing guard dogs from a business competitor, South Bay Sentry Dogs, Inc. A jury convicted him of receiving stolen property, while finding him not guilty of grand theft charges, and he was placed on three years' probation.

Shortly thereafter, South Bay filed a civil complaint against petitioner seeking damages arising from the theft of the guard dogs. The attorney who had represented petitioner in his criminal trial filed an answer in his behalf.

Several months later, petitioner's probation in the criminal case was revoked and he was sentenced to prison. Petitioner's attorney asked to be relieved as counsel and requested petitioner to sign a release form, as there was little likelihood that the attorney would be paid for services rendered in either the civil or the criminal case.

The civil case soon began its inexorable progress toward trial. Petitioner's request of the Department of Corrections to allow him to attend the civil trial was denied. In another letter, petitioner asked respondent court to dismiss the action against him because he had not received copies of the complaint, pointing out that he was incarcerated.

In petitioner's forced absence, a default judgment was entered against him for $24,722. One month later, petitioner sought a writ of error *coram nobis* in respondent court on the grounds that he had been denied permission to attend the trial and had been denied his right to counsel. Treating the petition as a motion to vacate a default judgment, the court rejected the request.

. . . .

We must decide not only whether petitioner was unconstitutionally deprived of his right of access to the courts, but if so, what the appropriate remedy should be.

. . . *In re McNally* (1956) 144 Cal.App.2d 531, 300 P.2d 869, ruled that a prisoner was entitled to engage paid counsel, reasoning that a prisoner's liability to be sued necessarily carries with it a right to defend.

The right to defend, however, has been tempered by judicial determination that a prisoner has no right to appear personally in court to protect his property. . . . [T]he issue is the propriety of depriving indigent prisoners of both those rights and thereby virtually denying their access to the courts.

The Fourteenth Amendment to the United States Constitution prohibits a state from depriving any person of property without due process of law. This mandate has been interpreted to require, at a minimum, that "absent a countervailing state interest of overriding significance, persons forced to settle their claims of right and duty through the judicial process must be given a meaningful opportunity to be heard." (*Boddie* v. *Connecticut* (1971) supra, 401 U.S. at p. 377. . . .) Thus, the United States Supreme Court has long recognized a constitutional right of access to the courts for all persons, including prisoners.

For the most part this access right has been related to review of criminal convictions, particularly by writs of habeas corpus. But . . . the due process right is much broader . . . .

In the landmark case of *Boddie* v. *Connecticut . . . supra, . . .* the Supreme Court ruled that indigents could not be forced to pay a filing fee in order to dissolve their marriage. . . .

Two subsequent Supreme Court decisions limited somewhat the scope of *Boddie,* but did not alter the impact of the decision on the rights of civil defendants. In *United States* v. *Kras* (1973) 409 U.S. 434, . . . the court found no constitutional infirmity in the requirement that an indigent debtor pay a $50 filing fee in order to obtain a discharge in bankruptcy. This decision was followed by *Ortwein* v. *Schwab* (1973) 410 U.S. 656, . . . in which the court upheld the validity of a $25 filing fee required for appellate review of an agency determination resulting in lower welfare payments for a poor person.

Each of the latter opinions carefully distinguished *Boddie* in two major respects. First, in both decisions the court reasoned that the underlying interest the indigent litigant was seeking to protect in court was not as constitutionally significant as the dissolution of marriage. . . .

In contrast, a defendant in a civil case seeks not merely the benefit of a statutory expectancy, but the protection of property he already owns or may own in the future. The distinction can be seen by hypothesizing legislative attempts to eliminate the rights involved in *Kras, Ortwein,* and the present case. Congress could permissibly repeal all bankruptcy laws; similarly, a state legislature is under no constitutional mandate to provide welfare payments. But absent a constitutional amendment, it is beyond question that neither Congress nor any state legislature could provide for extensive confiscation of private property without compensation. Thus the underlying right petitioner seeks to protect equals in constitutional significance the right to dissolve a marriage that was protected in *Boddie.*

The second major articulated distinction among the cases is that the indigents in *Kras* and *Ortwein,* unlike the couple in *Boddie,* were not compelled to rely solely on the courts to pursue their interests. . . .

It is evident, of course, that the petitioner in the present case has no alternative to the court system to protect his interests. Formally thrust into the judicial process, he may not, like the indigent debtor in *Kras,* informally settle his dispute. And unlike the plaintiff in *Ortwein,* he has no alternative opportunity to obtain an administrative hearing. In this respect, his position is identical to that of the indigents in *Boddie.* . . .

However, it is argued that unlike the inability to pay the filing fees in *Boddie,* petitioner's disabilities do not absolutely foreclose him from access to the courts. If a person cannot pay a filing fee, he manifestly cannot pursue his case in court; but the state maintains that indigent prisoners have alternative means of insuring that they will be heard. In order to ascertain the extent to which petitioner's access right has been infringed, it is necessary to examine the proposed alternatives.

First, it is suggested that prisoners, like other indigent civil litigants, may solicit free legal counsel. This possibility has been judicially recognized as an alternative to appointed counsel for ordinary civil litigants. In *Hunt* v. *Hackett* (1973) 36 Cal. App.3d 134, 111 Cal.Rptr. 456, the court, holding that indigent civil litigants do not have a right to appointed counsel, surmised that the result was not necessarily harsh. The court pointed to existing alternatives to appointed counsel, including services provided by legal aid societies, public defenders in some instances . . ., and California attorneys who have the ethical duty not to reject the cause of the defenseless or the oppressed.

But the indigent prisoner often lacks even the limited resources of his nonprisoner impoverished counterpart. . . . Shut off from most contacts with the world outside his prison, he is unlikely to have ready access to or even information about legal aid societies or attorneys willing to perform *pro bono* work. The problem is particularly acute in this state, where the "remoteness of many California penal institutions makes a personal visit to an inmate client a time-consuming undertaking" for counsel. . . .

. . .In California, a State Bar committee has found that "legal services to prison inmates . . . are completely unavailable on a systematic basis." . . . Petitioner's theoretical right to find his own voluntary counsel, accordingly, provides little realistic access to the courts.

. . . .

Similarly it benefits petitioner only minimally that he may obtain assistance from more experienced inmates, sometimes known as "jailhouse lawyers." . . . Whatever his legal expertise, usually limited to writ preparation, a jailhouse lawyer has no right to appear for petitioner in court.

In short, petitioner, as an indigent prisoner seeking to defend a civil suit, has a due process right of access to the courts which has been abridged. The state has the burden of demonstrating a compelling state interest to justify the infringement.

The denial of access also constitutes a prima facie equal protection violation. Indigent prisoners are denied access to the courts to defend a civil suit, while free persons and prisoners possessing the means to hire counsel retain an access right. As has been established, to be heard in court to defend one's property is a right of fundamental constitutional dimension; in order to justify granting the right to one group while denying it to another, the state must show a compelling state interest. . . .

Seeking to justify petitioner's deprivation, the state relies extensively on *Wood* v. *Superior Court* (1974), 36 Cal. App.3d 811, 112 Cal. Rptr. 157. The *Wood* court listed a number of state interests to rationalize the denial of the right of personal appearance. Some of them, if legitimate and applicable, arguably support the deprivation in the present case. The court reasoned, "First, the state cannot properly bear the cost of transporting the prisoner from the prison to the county where the trial is to occur, since the trip would be for the prisoner's private benefit, not the state's [citations]. Second, prison officials and others assigned to guard the prisoner during his transportation and at the trial would be exposed to danger and unnecessary risk [citation]. Third, a rule allowing prisoners to personally attend trials might lead to spurious and time-consuming lawsuits contrived to allow them to avoid confinement in their designated institutions. Finally, extended absences from the prison, hospital or treatment center might interfere with whatever program of rehabilitation, training or treatment the prisoner is taking." These purported interests must be explored. . . .

We question how substantially state costs would be increased if either remedy were adopted. By statute, a prisoner is already granted personal appearance rights in certain family disputes, probably the most common area of civil litigation for prisoners: when a proceeding is brought to terminate the parental rights of a prisoner, he has the right to appear; and a trial court may order his presence in any action in which his parental or marital rights are to be adjudicated. . . . As for the possibility of other kinds of actions against prisoners, the state has offered no empirical evidence on how often prisoners are sued. Notwithstanding the present case, we doubt that numerous plaintiffs will undergo the expense of litigation when the prospects for substantial recovery depend not only on victory on the merits of their cases but also on the possibility that indigent defendants will become adequately solvent after release from prison.

Nor do we find any merit whatever in the state's contention that appointment of counsel for prisoners will discourage settlement of cases. To the contrary: at present plaintiffs have no incentive to settle, as they may easily obtain default judgments; equalizing the litigation resources of the parties would likely motivate both litigants, acting through responsible counsel, to compromise the suit and to keep any damage recovery within realistic limits. It is cynical to suggest that the only incentive for a civil litigant to compromise is the expense of legal fees. If this were accurate, legal aid societies, other lawyers representing the poor, or even lawyers representing the state, would never settle a case — a demonstrably inaccurate supposition.[6] . . .

The second state interest advanced in *Wood* — protecting prison officials and the civil courts from the danger presented by prisoners — cannot justify denying the right of personal appearance *and* appointment of counsel. At most it supports the denial of a prisoner's right to appear. But even that proposition is debatable, for prisoners are now being regularly transported to criminal trials, as both defendants and witnesses, with a minimum of incidents. . . .

Third, the *Wood* court feared that prisoners would contrive suits against themselves in order to obtain a respite from confinement. But prisoners are far more likely to file frivolous suits as plaintiffs than they are to contrive opposition suits . . . .

. . . .

---

[6] The state also apparently assumes that if this court orders counsel appointed in certain cases, it will mandate that counsel be paid from public funds. We do not assert such power. If and how counsel will be compensated is for the Legislature to decide. Until that body determines that appointed counsel may be compensated from public funds in civil cases, attorneys must serve gratuitously in accordance with their statutory duty not to reject "the cause of the defenseless or the oppressed."

Finally, the *Wood* court's declaration that allowing a prisoner personal appearance rights might hinder rehabilitation efforts will not support the dual deprivation in question here. Although it might justify denying a prisoner an unlimited right of personal appearance in court, it does not justify a denial of the right to counsel.

. . . .

As no state interests can thus be advanced in support of the denial of access to the courts, we conclude that such unqualified deprivation constitutes a violation of petitioner's rights under the due process and equal protection clauses of both the state and federal Constitutions.

. . . .

We do not rule that appointment of counsel is an absolute right. . . . [B]efore appointing counsel for a defendant prisoner in a civil suit the trial court should determine first whether the prisoner is indigent. If he is indigent and the court decides that a continuance is not feasible, it should then ascertain whether the prisoner's interests are actually at stake in the suit and whether an attorney would be helpful to him under the circumstances of the case. . . .

In the present case petitioner's stake in the proceedings was undisputed, and if the court ascertained that petitioner was indigent it had no other course but to vacate the judgment and appoint counsel. Failure to do so is grounds for writ of mandate.

Finally, we emphasize the limits of our holding. We have not ruled that all indigents have a right to counsel in civil cases. Nor have we established that indigent prisoners who are plaintiffs in civil actions may secure appointed counsel or the right to appear personlly . . . .

Neither of those questions is before us, and we do not resolve them here. All we decide is that when a prisoner is threatened with a judicially sanctioned deprivation of his property, due process and equal protection require a meaningful opportunity to be heard. How that is to be achieved is to be determined by the exercise of discretion by the trial court.

. . . .

WRIGHT, C. J., and TOBRINER, and SULLIVAN, JJ., concur.

RICHARDSON, Associate Justice (dissenting).

I respectfully dissent.

While I have no quarrel with many of the generalities urged by the majority, I am unable to agree with their principal conclusion or the reasoning that leads to it. One can easily resonate to the abstract proposition that indigent prisoners should be afforded both counsel and full opportunity for a personal appearance at trial in the defense of *civil* suits filed against them. Yet the Legislature has not as yet seen fit to establish such procedures and in the absence of some constitutional compulsion applicable to civil actions the judicial function does not extend to this type of prison reform.

The practical difficulties presented by this case are far better resolved by action of the Legislature following that body's traditional study and debate.

. . . .

The majority's main premise, however, that indigent prisoners possess a general "right of access" in the sense that they are entitled to free legal representation or their personal presence in civil courts, either or both, is incorrect under existing decisions of this state. Prisoners in California enjoy only a limited statutory degree of "access" to the courts. . . . With respect to the asserted right to appointed counsel for prisoners in civil cases it is not accurate to say that prisoners are "deprived" of such a right, for under existing law even nonprisoner indigents have no abstract "right" to appointed counsel in ordinary civil matters. . . .

The majority note the anomaly created by their requirement that indigent prisoners defending civil cases receive appointed counsel and/or a personal appearance while the indigent nonprisoner is assured of no such benefit. Thus, the prisoner is elevated above the law-abiding citizen. The Legislature has never seen fit to effect this startling result, and for good reason. In its reluctance, thus far, to assure prisoners a "right" to counsel and presence in civil actions the Legislature need not ignore the fact that the reason for the prisoner's inability to attend trial is because of his intentional and wilful violation of the state's criminal laws and his subsequent conviction and confinement. Similarly, other adverse consequences follow from the prisoner's own conduct, self-induced. His constitutional right to travel, for example, is thereby inhibited. Part of the disparity between the remedies available to prisoner and nonprisoner indigents stems from the very nature of the criminal system. . . .

The majority's use of the term "right of access" to the courts, accordingly, must be understood in its proper perspective. Prisoners do have access to the courts. On the criminal side it is extensive. On the civil side it is much more limited. . . .

The commendable goals of affording all of our citizens, whether entirely indigent or not, prisoners and nonprisoners alike, access to adequate counsel in civil cases are gaining the attention of legislative bodies, federal and state; thus the creation of Legal Services Corporation, federally funded to make more available and accessible competent legal assistance in the civil areas. But the much needed impetus toward affording more adequate and more widely distributed legal representation in civil litigation, comes from a growing awareness of a demonstrable social need and legislative and professional policy decisions implementing it, not from any Fourteenth Amendment compulsion.

The majority rely upon *Boddie v. Connecticut* . . . as establishing a general right of free access to the civil courts in favor of all indigent persons including prisoners. *Boddie,* however, does not constitute authority for such a proposition. The *Boddie* court, on the contrary, implicitly limited the scope of its holding to actions brought *to dissolve a marriage.* . . . It seems obvious that if, as in *Ortwein* and *Kras,* an indigent may *constitutionally* be denied free access to the courts to challenge a welfare reduction on the one hand, or assert a bankruptcy on the other, a fortiori the state may decline to provide prisoners free, legal representation and physical presence in the defense of personal injury suits.

. . . .

At present the average indigent must face civil litigation bereft of counsel. His recourse, in propria persona, is to seek help where he can find it. This is often difficult. Two principal sources are available to him. One is the membership of the organized bar which, pro bono publico, may respond free of charge or expense to the historic and compelling professional call. . . : "Never to reject, for any consideration personal to himself, the cause of the defenseless or the oppressed." Far more frequently than is generally known or accepted the profession has favorably responded to this ethical mandate. The indigent civil litigant also has access to legal aid societies where help may be available. Indigent prisoners are physically more isolated than nonprisoner indigents, but they may by mail also seek legal assistance, request continuances, file pleadings, motions and other legal papers. Judging by the number of criminal petitions flowing with regularity into the California court system, I think it is reasonable to conclude that these inmate rights are fairly well known among those affected. . . .

Thus imprisonment does not totally deprive the indigent prisoner of all opportunity to reach the civil courts. Access is limited and does not achieve perfect equality with nonprisoners, which inequality is an incident of the prisoner's lawful confinement.

Other interesting questions remain unresolved by the majority's formulation, among them: What of the indigent *plaintiff* who, in propria persona, sues the indigent prisoner? Is he also entitled, because of due process and equal protection arguments, to court-appointed counsel to represent him free of charge in his civil action against the indigent prisoner who, under the majority's proposal, now has counsel? Who is to bear the cost of this additional increment of legal expense? Suppose the legal representation for either indigent nonprisoner plaintiff, or prisoner defendant is wholly inadequate or ineffective without an expert witness or extensive discovery? Is this to be afforded pro bono publico?

. . . .

I do not know, and neither apparently do the majority, whether the number of criminal indigent civil defendants who would be affected by the majority's holding is large or small. The majority "doubt" that it would be large, noting the absence of any empirical evidence. They may be right or wrong, but this uncertainty alone, in my view, suggests the need for legislative inquiry first to trace the dimensions of the problem on the basis of facts not speculation, and then carefully to weigh the various alternatives. This is the procedure which has been successfully followed in analogous situations. Thus, in meeting the need for representation of criminal indigents, the *Legislature* adopted . . . a carefully conceived plan for compensated representation. Similarly, when it became apparent that the appellate rights of the criminal indigents required consistent and adequate representation, again, the *Legislature* has very recently in the Government Code established the office of State Public Defender . . . and carefully defined its duties and powers.

In the final analysis the majority will mandate the rendition of free legal service by the bar to convicted criminals in civil cases, which professional service we have not as yet required be extended to law-abiding citizens. The majority concede that we cannot compel appropriation of monies, legislative or otherwise, for these services. This means that a large measure of *voluntary* cooperation will be required from the bar as to counsel. Similarly, depending upon the magnitude of the problem, law enforcement agencies are necessarily involved in any pronouncement, legislative or judicial, which requires the prisoner's personal presence. The cooperation of both affected groups is more likely to be achieved through their participation in legislative formulations in the traditional manner. A fair legislative solution of the problem of the indigent prisoner in civil actions doubtless will give appropriate consideration to the plight of the indigent *nonprisoner* and maintain a fair relationship between the two.

. . . .

McComb and Clark, JJ., concur.

NOTES AND QUESTIONS

1. Did the California Court in *Payne* convincingly distinguish the *Krass* and *Ortwein* cases? Does an indigent debtor really have a better opportunity to informally settle his dispute than an indigent prisoner defendant?

2. The *Boddie, Kras* and *Ortwein* cases all involved the issue of court filing fees. In terms of a potential right to appointed counsel

for indigents in civil cases, does it matter that *Kras* and *Ortwein* restricted *Boddie* rather than extending it? *Boddie* still requires the waiver of court filing fees in divorce cases. If an indigent is unable to maintain a divorce action because there are technical intricacies requiring representation by counsel, is there a constitutional right to appointed counsel? *

3. Even if the right to counsel in *criminal* cases extended further than it does (*see Ross* v. *Moffitt, supra* § A.4.b.), would there be additional problems in extending an equal protection right of appointed counsel to civil cases generally? In brief, lower courts have been unreceptive to a generalized right of appointed counsel for indigents in civil cases. Apart from *Payne,* those cases which have affirmed a limited right of counsel have involved civil proceedings which carry the threat of incarceration, and litigation between the state and a parent concerning the parent's right to custody of children. (On the latter issue, a leading case is *Danforth* v. *State Department of Health and Welfare,* 303 A.2d 794 (Me. 1973).) And notice that even *Payne* was a 4-3 decision, which carefully distinguished prisoner plaintiffs and regular civil defendants from prisoner defendants. What explains European constitutional law, which does not distinguish between the right to legal aid in criminal and civil cases? In terms of constitutional law, is the distinction between civil and criminal cases more tenable in the United States?

4. In criminal cases, the immediate sanction for denial of the right to counsel is reversal of a conviction. Does that suggest that a constitutional right to appointed counsel in civil cases should be limited to civil defendants since the right to counsel could be enforced by the simple, analogous process of reversing a judgment for plaintiff? (Moreover, the civil defendant, like the criminal defendant, has been involuntarily summoned into court.) Would not a distinction between plaintiffs and defendants be, in many cases, the result of irrelevant differences in circumstance? (For example, consider the case of the impoverished owner of a small farm. If he is in possession and being sued by his adversary in an action for

---

* Consider the opinion of Justice Black, dissenting from the denial of certiorari in *Meltzer* v. *C. Buck LeCraw & Co.,* 402 U.S. 954 (1971). In general, Justice Black, who dissented in *Boddie,* was now arguing for its extension on the ground that its logic could not be limited to waiver of filing fees in divorce cases. On the issue of right to counsel, he said:

> Finally, there cannot be meaningful access to the judicial process until every serious litigant is represented by competent counsel. Cf. *Gideon* v. *Wainwright; Douglas* v. *California.* Of course, not every litigant would be entitled to appointed counsel no matter how frivolous his claims might be. But the fundamental importance of legal representation in our system of adversary justice is beyond dispute. Since *Boddie* held that there must be meaningful access to civil courts in divorce cases, I can only conclude that *Boddie* necessitates the appointment of counsel for indigents in such cases.

ejectment, he is a defendant. Would his plight be much different if he were forcefully dispossessed and had to sue as a plaintiff to recover possession of his farm?) How would the right of a civil plaintiff to appointed counsel be enforced? Eventually, would federal courts have to require that the state courts create affirmative mechanisms and expend state funds to hire lawyers to represent the poor?

5. If there were a general right to assistance of counsel in civil cases, would it be a right to the *effective* assistance of counsel? Consider the following opinion dissenting from the denial of certiorari in *Sandoval* v. *Rankin,* 385 U.S. 901 (1966).

> MR. JUSTICE FORTAS, with whom MR. JUSTICE DOUGLAS joins, dissenting from the denial of certiorari.
>
> In my judgment, this petition presents important issues as to the scope of the requirement, derived from the Due Process Clause of the Fourteenth Amendment, that state courts in civil actions must afford to each litigant a "proper opportunity to present his evidence."
>
> Petitioners are illiterate indigents. They speak only Spanish. They and their five children have lived for many years on the meager homestead involved in this case. Petitioners executed a deed to the homestead. Respondent is assignee of this deed. Respondent brought this action and obtained a judgment confiming his title and possessory rights to the property under the deed. Petitioners seek review of the judgment of the Texas Court of Civil Appeals which affirmed this judgment.
>
> At the trial, petitioners were represented by a Legal Aid attorney. The trial was perfunctory. After judgment was entered for respondent, petitioners obtained new counsel who filed a timely motion for new trial. This motion alleged that petitioners had a good and sufficient defense to the action: namely, that the "deed" was in truth a mortgage given to secure a debt and that respondent took with notice of this fact. The motion alleged that this defense was not adduced at trial because of the default of petitioners' Legal Aid counsel.
>
> The trial court held an elaborate hearing on the motion for new trial. The Legal Aid lawyer who had represented petitioners at the trial testified candidly that he had not had adequate time to prepare the case, and that he was further handicapped by his inability to speak or understand Spanish.
>
> Petitioners' counsel in this Court urge that, in the circumstances of this case, the refusal of the trial court to grant the timely motion for a new trial deprived petitioners of their rights under the Fourteenth Amendment. I believe that we should grant the writ and rule upon the question so presented.

To some extent, a lawyer's client like a doctor's patient must suffer the consequences of his champion's mistakes. But there are limits; and the courts are and should be quick to relieve the client of his lawyer's default whenever that is feasible and does not result in unfairness to others.

Obviously, this principle applies to the defaults of lawyers made available to aid indigents. The measure of constitutional protection afforded citizens who are recipients of free legal services, whether provided by the State or by private charity, is not less than that available to those who pay their own way.

6. In the last decade, the United States has not been indifferent to the needs of the poor for legal services. Significant sums are spent on the federal, state and local levels to furnish legal services to the indigent. No one argues seriously that the needs of the poor for legal services are adequately met, however. Is it better that the issue of representation of the poor in civil cases be seen as a nonconstitutional issue of legislative policy rather than an issue of federal constitutional law? Consider the following statement of Justice Douglas dissenting from the denial of certiorari in *Williams* v. *Shaffer,* 385 U.S. 1037 (1967): *

The problem of housing for the poor is one of the most acute facing the Nation. The poor are relegated to ghettos and are beset by substandard housing at exorbitant rents. Because of their lack of bargaining power, the poor are made to accept onerous lease terms. Summary eviction proceedings are the order of the day. Default judgments in eviction proceedings are obtained with machine-gun rapidity, since the indigent cannot afford counsel to defend. Housing laws often have a built-in bias against the poor. Slumlords have a tight hold on the Nation. Lyford, The Airtight Cage (1966).³ And see Schorr, Slums and Social Insecurity (1964).

---

* The *Williams* case, which arose prior to *Boddie* v. *Connecticut,* involved the issue of a bond requirement for tenants in summary dispossession actions. After *Boddie,* if the tenant is indigent, would a requirement that a bond be posted in order to defend be constitutional? *See Lindsey* v. *Normet,* 405 U.S. 56 (1972).

³ "They have not the economic power to make themselves heard, and their official political representatives have built their power on the ghetto and are committed to its perpetuation. In New York City a vast, informal machinery funnels society's discipline and health problems in to the West Ninety-third Streets, and just about every sector of the establishment participates in running the machinery or lubricating it: slumlords who rent to the dead as well as the living provided they get a good price for it and have immunity from fire, building, health, and rent regulations; the city employee who collaborates in the arrangement; the welfare and health departments that go along because they have no other alternative; judges who tap the slumlord on the wrist on the rare occasions when he is brought into court. Approval of the system is given by business leaders who lead the fight against adequate welfare and

The plight of the poor is being somewhat ameliorated by federal and state programs (particularly the Neighborhood Legal Services under OEO) and by private organizations dedicated to the representation of indigents in civil matters. This Court of course does not sit to cure social ills that beset the country. But when we are faced with a statute that apparently violates the Equal Protection Clause by patently discriminating against the poor and thereby worsening their already sorry plight, we should address ourselves to it. I would grant certiorari.

Is Justice Douglas saying that the inability of the poor to obtain counsel to defend eviction actions is a "social ill" similar to nonenforcement of building and health codes?

7. The general structure of the United States Constitution, a product of the eighteenth and nineteenth centuries, is to provide constitutional protection of individual rights — rights the individual has to be free of enumerated government interference. Unlike many twentieth century constitutions, nothing explicit is said in the United States Constitution about social rights — rights to affirmative benefits each person can demand from government. A lively debate has centered around the question of the application of the Equal Protection Clause to various social rights. *See, e.g., Dandridge* v. *Williams,* 397 U.S. 471 (1970) (welfare); *San Antonio Independent School District* v. *Rodriguez,* 411 U.S. 1 (1973) (financing of public schools). Would it be appropriate to characterize the problem of furnishing counsel to indigents in civil cases as an issue of social rights while that of furnishing counsel to indigent criminal defendants is a matter of individual rights? Does it matter?

8. Consider finally the significance of the decision of the Italian *Corte Costituzionale* that, although the provision of legal aid through unpaid counsel was ineffective, there was no denial of the constitutional guarantee of legal aid. (Decision of June 16, 1970, No. 97, noted in § A.3.b.(ii), *supra.*) Is the Italian decision simply a result of the timidity of the Italian court in resolving complex constitutional issues, or does it suggest an inherent limitation of judicial power to enforce affirmative social rights? The next section of this chapter will deal, in part, with the effectiveness of the Italian legal aid system. Is the American system of legal aid in civil cases, which exists without

housing, prosperous financial institutions that refuse to lend money for private investment in slum rehabilitation; foundations that avoid any significant commitment to abolition of the slum; labor unions that have abandoned the low-paid worker and practice racial discrimination; and white and black political organizations that have a vested interest in segregation and race politics. When the slum is used as a concentration camp for the criminal and disabled, the virulence of all the diseases endemic in slum life is intensified." Lyford, *supra,* at xxi-xxii.

any constitutional guarantee, more effective after all than the Italian system, which is mandated by the constitution?

b. *Operation of Legal Aid Systems in Europe*

(i) Eligibility for Legal Aid

Of course, the basic precondition for receipt of legal aid is poverty. Unlike criminal cases, however, many countries are unwilling to furnish legal aid to the indigent civil litigant unless the applicant can also demonstrate a reasonable prospect of success and the "non-frivolous" character of his claim or defense.

DECISION OF JUNE 18, 1957

Bundesverfassungsgericht
[1957] 7 BVerfGE 53

[The state attorney brought an action against a minor child, challenging the child's legitimacy. The request of the child's guardian for legal aid was rejected. The trial court rejected the request on the ground that the defense lacked sufficient probability of success. The appeals court (*Oberlandesgericht*) affirmed the decision — but on a different ground. It did not reach the question whether there was sufficient probability of success in defense of the proceeding. It reasoned that, under the Code of Civil Procedure, in legitimacy proceedings the trial court was required, *ex officio,* to consider all relevant facts and take such evidence as is required to properly determine the child's status. Given the trial court's investigatory function, even a person with means would reasonably decide not to be represented by counsel; requesting legal aid in such proceedings was, therefore, "frivolous."]

Against this decision the *Verfassungsbeschwerde* has been presented asserting a violation of the right to a fair hearing (art. 103, para. 1, of the Basic Law).

OPINION

. . . This claim is well-founded.

The Federal Constitutional Court has earlier affirmed that it is not unconstitutional and, in particular, that it does not violate the principle of equality or the right to a fair hearing if § 114 of the Code of Civil Procedure makes the granting of legal aid, and the temporary gratuitous assignment of a lawyer, dependent on the fact that the assertion by a plaintiff of his legal right offers a sufficient probability of success and does not appear frivolous. . . . In the case of a defendant also, the application of [this standard] generally encounters no constitutional doubts.

Whether the courts apply or interpret the general laws correctly in their decisions is substantially not a matter for reexamination by the Constitutional Court. This is true also for decisions concerning the granting of legal aid. An exception to this rule must, however, exist if a court through interpretation of an indefinite legal concept involves considerations which injure the basic rights protected in the Constitution. In the present case the *Oberlandesgericht* in its interpretation of the indefinite legal concept of "frivolity" misunderstood the significance of the right to a fair hearing under art. 103, para. 1, of the Basic Law and thereby violated this right of the petitioner.

The challenged decision takes as its basic consideration that a party who does not request legal aid would, after appropriate evaluation of the circumstances, do without representation by counsel in the proceeding since the obligation of the court to clarify the fact situation in an *ex officio* manner would sufficiently assure a just and proper decision. This point of departure is obviously inapplicable for a *plaintiff.* [S]ince the challenge to legitimacy cannot be brought otherwise than in a formal proceeding [in which the assistance of counsel is mandatory], legal aid cannot be denied a poor plaintiff on the basis of frivolity. But also with regard to the *defendant,* this point of departure does not take into proper consideration the significance of the right to a fair hearing. Article 103, para. 1, of the Basic Law grants for all court proceedings a minimum of a fair hearing; particularly, all parties to the proceeding must have the possibility to be heard on all matters pertinent to the decision before it is made. This right is independent of the particular configuration taken by the proceeding as a result of the applicable procedural law. It applies also in proceedings in which the court fulfills an investigatory function. It cannot be expected of the parties that they would leave the formulation of a just decision to the courts on the basis of this official function alone. . . . Although the court must use its powers within its ambit of discretion, the right of the parties to request that further evidence be taken should not be considered superfluous. Requests for the taking of evidence as well as supporting material in proceedings before the *Landgericht* can be made only by a lawyer. . . . The conception on which the challenged decision is based results in the defendant becoming simply an object of the proceeding, while the law itself assigns to him the formal position of an autonomous party to the proceeding. In the decisions and the doctrine, therefore, the opinion that the concession of legal aid is unnecessary when the Court has the duty to determine the facts *ex officio* has justly been generally rejected.

. . . .

The challenged decision must therefore be annulled and the cause remanded to the *Oberlandesgericht.*

3. In the new decision the *Oberlandesgericht* must consider that the form of a legitimacy proceeding which requires a formal action against a child puts the child in the position of a defendant, giving him no possibility of avoiding the litigation. It can be left open if in this particular situation it is possible even to speak of frivolity where a child undergoes litigation into which he is forced in this manner. The question may also be raised whether it is possible to interpret § 114 *ZPO* in view of the Basic Law to require that, in cases such as this, examination of the probability of success be eliminated, since it is constitutionally doubtful that the law, on the one hand, would assign to a participant in the clarification of a question of status, with out his own initiative, the role of defendant, and on the other — if he is poor — impede him in his participation as a party on the basis that he does not have sufficient probability of success. This question naturally would only have arisen if the *Oberlandesgericht* had denied that the defendant had sufficient probability of success. Since the court did not examine this question the Federal Constitutional Court does not need to take a position on it at this time.

NOTES AND QUESTIONS

1. Does the nature of the proceeding involved in the principal case have anything to do with the decision? In the United States, over the last decade, a number of cases in the Supreme Court have struck down legal distinctions between the rights of legitimate and illegitimate children, as a violation of the Equal Protection Clause of the Fourteenth Amendment. For example, in *Trimble* v. *Gordon,* 430 U.S. 762 (1977), the Court invalidated a state law which prohibited inheritance by illegitimate children from their fathers through intestate succession. At the time the principal case was decided, an illegitimate child had no right under German law to inherit from or through his father, although his rights vis-à-vis his mother were the same as those of a legitimate child.

2. Suppose the *Oberlandesgericht* were now to decide that the petitioner's defense did not have sufficient probability of success, and again denied application for legal aid. Would the denial of legal aid constitute denial of a fair hearing? The Constitutional Court faced this question several years later in another illegitimacy case and held that it was not unconstitutional for the courts to consider the probability of success of the defense as a factor in deciding whether to grant legal aid. [1959] 9 BVerfGE 256.

STRUPPAT v. FEDERAL REPUBLIC OF GERMANY

European Commission of Human Rights
[1968] Y.B. Eur. Conv. on Human Rights 380

THE FACTS

[At the time of his application, the Applicant was incarcerated following his 1962 conviction for indecent assault on a minor child. In 1964, the victim of the assault brought a civil action against the Applicant before the *Landgericht* (Regional Court). Her representative was granted legal aid. The Applicant's request for legal aid was denied, however, on the ground that he had not shown that his defense had sufficient chance of success. An attorney, Dr. Y, had agreed to serve as the Applicant's counsel if legal aid was granted. The *Landgericht* invited Dr. Y to support the request for legal aid by substantiating the Applicant's defense to the civil proceeding. Dr. Y refused to do so, on the ground that he was unable to offer any assistance unless legal aid was granted.

[In its decision denying Applicant's legal aid, the *Landgericht* had referred to the criminal proceedings, and concluded that the Applicant could not succeed in defending against liability since his only asserted defense was that he was not the person who injured the child. It also pointed out that none of the Applicant's arguments referred to the amount of compensation claimed. Three appeals from the denial of legal aid were rejected. At the *Landgericht* hearing, the Applicant was present without counsel. Under German law, a person not represented by counsel in a civil action may not address the *Landgericht*, and is treated as if he failed to appear. Accordingly, the court granted judgment for 12,000 DM to the plaintiff by default. In the appellate court, an objection to the entry of the default judgment was rejected on the basis of a statute which provided that such objections must be lodged by counsel.]

THE LAW

As to art. 6, para. 1 of the Convention

Whereas art. 6, para. 1, of the Convention provides that, in the determination of his civil rights and obligations, everyone is entitled to a fair and public hearing by a tribunal established by law; whereas the Applicant submits that, his petition for free legal aid having been refused in the preliminary proceedings, his right to a fair and public hearing was violated in the main proceedings before the Regional Court when the Court determined the question of his liability and his resultant obligation to compensate the victim of the indecent assault of December 23, 1961; whereas the Government argues that the Applicant's right to a fair and public hearing was fully observed by the competent German courts in the course of the proceedings as a whole;

Whereas the Commission, in examining the Applicant's above complaint, has first had regard to its constant jurisprudence according to which the right to free legal aid in civil cases, as opposed to criminal cases, is not as such included among the rights and freedoms guaranteed by the Convention; whereas, in this respect, reference is made to the Commission's decision on the admissibility of Application No. 3011/67 (25 Collection of Decisions 70, 73-74);

Whereas, however, it follows from the text of its above decision that the Commission, when dealing with complaints concerning the refusal of free legal aid in civil proceedings, also considers the general clause of art. 6, para. 1, of the Convention in order to determine whether such refusal constituted, in the particular circumstances of the case, a violation of the right of the person concerned to be granted a fair hearing; whereas, indeed, the Commission also regards this further aspect when examining the issue of legal aid in criminal proceedings; and the Commission has previously held that the right to a fair hearing, both in civil and criminal proceedings, contemplates that everyone who is a party to such proceedings shall have a reasonable opportunity of presenting his case to the court under conditions which do not place him at a substantial disadvantage *vis-à-vis* his opponent; whereas, in this respect, the Commission refers to its decisions on the admissibility of Applications Nos. 434/58 and 1092/61, 2 YEARBOOK 354, 370, 372 and 5 YEARBOOK 210, and, further, to its reports, and the decisions of the Committee of Ministers, in the cases of *Ofner, Hopfinger, Pataki,* and *Dunshirn;*

Accordingly, with regard to the present complaint, the Commission is called upon to consider whether the specific circumstances of the proceedings against the Applicant amounted to a denial of his right to a fair hearing within the meaning of art. 6, para. 1; whereas, in this connection, it is not the task of the Commission to examine in general whether the relevant provisions of the German Code of Civil Procedure are in conformity with the Convention; whereas the question to be determined is solely whether the application of these provisions in the present case violated art. 6, para. 1; and whereas the Commission holds that this question cannot properly be determined on the basis of an isolated consideration of the main civil proceedings against the Applicant which led to the judgment by default of September 30, 1965, but that regard must be had to all the relevant proceedings;

Whereas, with respect to these proceedings, the Commission observes that the civil proceedings of which the Applicant complains were the sequel to the criminal proceedings against him in which he had been convicted and sentenced; whereas, following this conviction and sentence, the Applicant attempted on several occasions to obtain a retrial; and whereas he again contested the findings of the criminal courts when applying for free legal aid in the above civil proceedings against him;

Whereas it is true that the Applicant was not heard by the Regional Court in the main civil proceedings on September 30, 1965, when a judgment by default was given against him; whereas, however, it is clear, both from the decisions rendered by the criminal courts in the proceedings concerning his petitions for retrial and from the decisions of the civil courts regarding his petition for free legal aid, that the arguments submitted by the Applicant in the civil proceedings in his defence against the plaintiff's claim for compensation were carefully examined by these courts at two instances and found not to be sufficient to upset, or to put into doubt, the findings of the criminal courts that he had committed the assault in question; whereas, further, as to the amount of damages, the Applicant, although invited to do so, did not make any submissions on this point in the proceedings, concerning his petition for free legal aid;

Whereas, in conclusion, having regard to the proceedings as a whole, the Commission finds that the Applicant was accorded an adequate hearing by the courts before the civil judgment of September 30, 1965, was given against him; whereas, in particular, it does not appear that he was placed at such a disadvantage *vis-à-vis* the infant plaintiff as to have prejudiced him in the effective exercise of his defence against the plaintiff's claim; whereas, therefore, the Applicant's right to a fair hearing in the determination of his civil obligation to compensate the victim of his alleged assault was not violated in the proceedings concerned;

Whereas finally, the Commission has also considered the Applicant's further complaint under art. 6, para. 1, that he was not heard in public as to the child's claim for compensation; whereas, in this respect, the Commission notes that the main proceedings before the Regional Court were public; whereas, in particular, the judgment of September 30, 1965, was pronounced at a public session of the Court; whereas, in conclusion, the Commission, again having regard to the course of the proceedings as a whole, does not find that the Applicant's right to a public hearing was violated by the German courts;

As to art. 14 in conjunction with art. 6, para. 1, of the Convention

Whereas the Applicant also alleges a violation of art. 14 of the Convention, complaining that the Regional Court granted free legal aid only to the plaintiff and that consequently he himself, being equally without means to pay a barrister's fees, was not represented by counsel in the main proceedings before the Regional Court;

Whereas, according to art. 14, the enjoyment of the rights and freedoms set forth in the Convention shall be secured without any discrimination on the ground of property; whereas, in this respect, the Commission has already stated above that the right to free legal aid in civil cases is not as such guaranteed by the Convention; that, nevertheless, the refusal of such aid may be considered under the "fair hearing" clause of art. 6, para. 1; but that there was no violation of this clause in the present case; whereas, in particular, it is clear from the decisions of the German courts that the refusal of the Applicant's petition for free legal aid was not based on any consideration of property but solely on an appreciation of the prospects of his defence against the plaintiff's claim; whereas, therefore, the decisions concerned do not as such violate art. 14 of the Convention;

Whereas, finally, it is true that, as a result of the decisions refusing his petition for free legal aid on the ground that his defence failed to show a sufficient prospect of success, the Applicant, being without means to pay a barrister's fees, was prevented from pleading his case in the main proceedings before the Regional Court, while a person with sufficient means could have done so irrespective of the prospects of his case; whereas, however, the Commission holds that such inequality does not violate the Convention; whereas, indeed, it follows from art. 6, para. 3, sub-para. (c), that even in criminal proceedings, where a right to free legal aid is guaranteed by the Convention, this right is limited to cases "where the interests of justice so require;" whereas this limitation has also been held by the Commission to apply to its consideration under art. 6, para. 1, of complaints concerning the refusal of free legal aid in criminal cases; whereas, consequently, a reasonable limitation of the right to free legal aid in civil cases, which is itself not guaranteed by the Convention, can *a fortiori* not be regarded as violating the "fair hearing" clause of art. 6, para. 1; whereas, similarly, such reasonable limitation cannot be considered as being contrary to the provisions of art. 14; and whereas, in the present case, the limitation of the right to free legal aid under art. 114 of the German Code of Civil Procedure, which led to the above formal inequality, must nevertheless be considered reasonable;

Whereas, in conclusion, the Commission finds that an examination of the Applicant's complaints under arts. 6 and 14 does not disclose the appearance of a violation of the Convention; whereas it follows that the application is manifestly ill-founded within the meaning of art. 27, para. 2, of the Convention;

Now therefore the Commission
DECLARES THIS APPLICATION INADMISSIBLE.

NOTES AND QUESTIONS

1. The Commission has continued to state that, although legal aid in civil cases is not a right guaranteed, as such, by the Convention, denial of legal aid in a particular case can constitute denial of a fair hearing under art. 6 (1). The individual decisions, however, have generally sustained the denial of legal aid. For example, no denial of a fair hearing was found in *X* v. *Federal Republic of Germany,* [1969] 29 COLLECTION OF DECISIONS 15 (Eur. Comm. of Human Rights). The case is different from *Struppat* in that the applicant claimed as a defense in the civil case a new ground that had not been litigated in his prior criminal trial. His new defense was that he had not eaten properly in the two weeks prior to the crime, causing diminished responsibility. The German courts rejected the new defense as a basis for granting legal aid, on grounds that it was factually unlikely and contrary to the defendant's statements during his criminal trial.

2. The *Struppat* case was in the German courts several years after the decision of the German Constitutional Court of 1957, which precedes *Struppat* in this section. Does the 1957 decision suggest that there was reasonable probability of success in a constitutional petition directed by Struppat to the denial of legal aid in his case? Did Struppat neglect to petition the constitutional court because he had no lawyer to assist him, or to advise him of the merits of his constitutional claim? More generally, notice that he had no legal assistance in preparing his application for legal aid. Would he have been granted legal aid if he had raised an argument as to the amount of damages claimed by the plaintiff? Can we know whether his failure to contest the amount of damages was deliberate or was a result of the failure to be advised by counsel?

3. Notice Struppat's claim that it was a denial of equality to require him to proceed without a lawyer, when an affluent litigant would have been permitted to be represented. Does that argument seem particularly compelling to you, in light of German procedure which, in certain cases, prohibits the unrepresented litigant from making representations to the court? The Commission rejected that claim because the Convention contains no general guarantee of a right of equality, but only a guarantee of equality in those rights which are independently guaranteed by the Convention. Thus, the decision that there was no denial of a fair hearing under art. 6(1), determined that there was no discrimination in the enjoyment of a right guaranteed by the Convention. Would Struppat's equality argument, however, have succeeded if it had been presented to the German Constitutional Court? Consider the Decision of June 6, 1967, reproduced in § B.2.a.(i), *supra.* Consider, in particular, the Decision of January 22, 1959, which follows.

DECISION OF JANUARY 22, 1959

Bundesverfassungsgericht
[1959] 9 BVerfGE 124

In a proceeding before the Social Court, plaintiff's request for accident compensation was rejected. She appealed to the State Social Court and requested, at the same time, that counsel be appointed to assist her. The State Social Court rejected her request for legal aid, noting that in cases before the State Social Court, the statute does not provide for the appointment of counsel.

Petitioner's Constitutional complaint argues that there has been a violation of Arts. 3 and 103 (1) [of the Constitution]. She contends that in denying her the appointment of counsel without even considering the prospect of success of her claim, the court discriminated against her vis-à-vis indigent plaintiffs in other proceedings and plaintiffs before the Social Courts who have enough money to cover costs. Further, she argues that not appointing counsel violates the principle that parties in the same legal proceedings should be on equal footing with their opponents who in the case of the Social Courts are official organs represented by trained government counsel.

On the one hand, petitioner contends that the law of the Social Courts allows for the appointment of legal aid counsel. Alternatively, she maintains that the law itself is unconstitutional.

OPINION

[The Constitutional Court rejected the argument that the statute relating to the Social Courts permits the appointment of legal aid counsel.]

Assuming that the law of the Social Courts does not provide for the appointment of legal aid counsel, the question remains whether this law violates Art. 3 of the Constitution when considered in conjunction with Art. 103 (1).

. . . [T]he Court must consider the law of the Social Courts in light of the general principle of equality in Art. 3 (1). This provision does not mandate complete equality. It demands equality only when the question at hand is so important that equal treatment is required by a proper sense of justice. Such is not the case here.

Legal aid frees the indigent from court costs, fees and other expenses, and allows for the appointment of counsel. It is granted only where there is a sufficient probability of success. This distinction manifests the fact that legal aid cannot achieve complete equality among the parties. In fact, it merely permits the indigent to protect his rights in approximately the same way as do the rich. Justice requires no more than this. The indigent cannot demand appointment of counsel just because his opponent has a lawyer. Complete equality of means and of opportunity is impossible.

Moreover, just because the Code of Civil Procedure allows legal aid in certain types of proceedings does not mean that legal aid is required in all other legal proceedings. The question hinges on whether the nature of the proceeding protects the rights of the indigent party by affording him sufficient access to the court so that he is heard.

In proceedings where court costs and a lawyer are mandatory, the availability of legal aid is essential, assuming that there is a sufficient probability of success. If this was not the case, the indigent would be unreasonably hindered in, if not denied, his right to action and defense vis-à-vis a wealthier party. If legal aid was not granted by statute in such a case, it would violate Art. 3 (1) and Art. 103 (1) of the Constitution.

But, in the first and second instances of proceedings before the Social Courts, a lawyer is not required and there are no costs. Hence, there is no violation of the Constitution. Article 103 guarantees a right to be heard but not a right to be heard by means of a lawyer.

In addition, proceedings before the Social Courts can be readily distinguished from other legal proceedings in several ways. The fact situations are usually simple; one's opponent is bound to the truth; and the court makes its own evaluation of the facts. Moreover, the judge has the duty to explain to the parties the consequences of their pleadings and actions in court. In his decision, the judge has to advise the parties as to the available legal remedies. If requested to do so, the court clerk must aid the unrepresented party in writing his pleadings. Finally, the special rate schedule makes attorney's fees lower than usual.

[In view of the differences outlined above, the Court decided that the principle of equality was not violated by the failure to provide legal aid counsel in cases before the Social Courts.]

(ii) Mechanisms for Delivery of Legal Aid *

In European countries there are three typical approaches to the provision of legal aid — the *political*, the *charitable* and the *legal*. Under the political approach political parties, labor unions and other groups provide legal assistance as one of the services by which the allegiance of group members is maintained. Historically, the political approach was typical of ancient Rome; the patron (*patronus*) provided assistance to his "clients" (*clientes*) as a reward for their

---

*Adapted from Revised Summary, Report by M. Cappelletti to the Committee on Legal Aid in Developing Countries (I.L.C. Conference, New York, November, 1972).

political affiliation to him. The charitable approach is typical of Christianity and the Middle Ages; legal aid was given as a charitable, but not legal, obligation. Of course, both in ancient Rome and the Middle Ages, deviant institutions can be found, but they are sporadic and usually of short duration. An example is a salaried "public defender" which was introduced for a short period under the Roman Empire and reintroduced from time to time in some parts of Europe in the Middle Ages.

Under the legal approach legal aid and advice are offered as a right of the individual. A French statute of 1851 embodies this concept. Italy's statute dates from 1865, Germany's from 1877 and Spain's from 1881. These statutes placed on the private lawyer a duty to provide legal services to the poor gratuitously. Actually these provisions may be viewed as a hybrid of the legal and charitable approaches. Because no compensation was paid to lawyers, these provisions did not work effectively — they provided poor justice for the poor. This approach reflected the prevailing laissez-faire philosophy of the period, with its desire to minimize the extent to which the state need become involved in affirmative action.

The twentieth century has witnessed a reform movement in the provision of legal services to the poor, involving an enshrinement of the legal approach in pure form. Germany, under the Weimar Constitution, provided by statute that the state had to pay for services rendered by lawyers to the poor. England has a series of acts which have established legal aid as a right. The most important English statute is the Legal Aid and Advice Act of 1949; the most recent, the Legal Assistance and Advice Act of 27 July 1972. France has also established a reformed system of legal services to the poor as of 3 January 1972, based on the principle of state compensation to lawyers appointed to handle legal aid cases. A Senate bill was approved in 1971 by the Italian Senate but it has not yet been adopted by both branches of Parliament. These reform schemes have certain common characteristics: they provide for compensation by the state for services rendered by private practitioners. Some provide total compensation; others are based on special fee schedules for legal aid cases or on a percentage of the normal fee. There is no provision for public salaried lawyers in any of these systems, except in the 1972 English Act. Possibly the most important distinguishing characteristic of these programs is that they rely on the private practicing profession for the delivery of legal aid to the poor. The lawyers can be chosen by the party litigant himself (England and the Italian bill), by the judge (Germany), or by the chairman of the local bar (France). Provisions are made for people who can afford to pay part of the cost. Eligibility requirements are determined in a number of ways: by the judge in Germany, by a mixed group of the bar, judges and government representatives in France, and by legal aid committees composed of local lawyers in England. As has been proved in England and Germany, these new schemes are able to serve a much larger number of civil and criminal cases than have been served under the hybrid 19th-Century solution, which did not provide for compensation for the legal-aid lawyer. Legal aid of this latter type reaches very few potential poor litigants. For instance, legal aid is provided in only 1 percent of all civil cases in Italy and, before the 1972 reform, 6 percent in France. In Germany, by contrast, legal aid is provided in approximately 18 percent of all civil cases. On the criminal side a larger volume of cases have been handled, but the service has been perfunctory at best due to the absence of effective compensation of the lawyers involved. There is a weakness, however, in the reformed Continental systems in that they do not provide for effective legal advice; this service is frequently left to the voluntary, charitable action of private lawyers and the bar.

The experience gained in Europe and the United States indicates that the gratuitous model — based on uncompensated or only nominally compensated work by private practioners — is a trap which has not worked well anywhere and which realistically cannot be expected to work well in the future in almost any conceivable setting. The 20th-Century "Judicare" model, on the other hand, to work effectively, requires a large and influential legal profession. It is not suited to an in-depth attack on poverty nor to societies with a sharp lack of cultural, social, and geographic homogeneity between the rich and poor. This is so because the judicare system requires the poor to be able to act to a greater degree on their own initiative. Thus the "Judicare" model has proven workable in some European societies, whereas it might prove unworkable elsewhere. In its turn, the "Neighborhood Legal Services" model, used since 1965 in the United States, requires a large degree of freedom from government bureaucratic control, and governmental consensus about the desirability of attacking poverty at public expense. Also, it is a model less suited to countries in which law reform is not possible through court decisions or to countries in which the courts are more inclined to kill progress rather than promote it. Therefore, one may be forced to conclude that most developing countries lack the basic premises for either a "Judicare" system (because of lack of a large legal profession and minimal homogeneity) or a "Neighborhood" system (lacking the necessary degree of freedom from bureaucratic control, etc.). This pessimistic conclusion could even be enhanced on the basis of Max Weber's theory that industrial development was furthered in England by the sad fact that the courts were closed to the economically weaker groups in society; it may be that equal justice can be achieved only at the price of a more rapid rate of economic development. If this pessimism is justified, then the better way to deal with the problems of the poor in developing countries would be to adopt a broader conception of legal aid than is inherent in mere courtroom representation. Law must be de-aggrandized and larger access to justice must be sought through a much broader range of devices — including informal models of proceedings, out-of-court methods of dispute resolution and changes in the substantive law.

NOTES AND QUESTIONS

1. The most recent approach to delivering legal aid has occurred in Sweden and Quebec, Canada, where the "Judicare" and "staff attorney" models have been combined. The client thus has the option of turning to either one — the private bar or a government staff attorney. This combination is clearly the trend now, in an attempt to realize the advantages of both: the Judicare approach embodies a greater degree of certainty and less danger of arbitrariness in granting legal aid, while the staff attorney system more consciously attempts to break the cycle of poverty through use of the legal system, since it is more concerned with reaching out to the poor and with community legal education.

2. How did the California Supreme Court in *Payne, supra* § B.2.a.ii., handle the problem of delivering the new right it announced? *See* footnote 6 of the opinion. Is this a system of "honorific duty"? What alternatives did the Court have?

DECISION OF DECEMBER 19, 1972

Verfassungsgerichtshof (Constitutional Court of Austria)
Suppl. (*Beilage*) [Feb. 1973] Österreichisches Anwaltsblatt *

[Gussenbauer, who mounted similar complaints related to criminal cases before the European Commission of Human Rights (*see* § A.3.b.(ii)(b), *supra*), and requested annulment of two appointments as legal aid counsel in civil cases. In the Austrian Constitutional Court, he again argued that his appointment constituted forced labor in violation of art. 4 (2) of the Convention, which has the force of constitutional law in Austria. He also alleged that his appointment denied the guarantee of equality of all citizens before the law, provided by art. 7 of the Austrian Constitution. The Constitutional Court concluded that, under the Austrian Code of Civil Procedure, legal aid counsel were required to serve without compensation, and were not entitled to collect fees out of the lump sum appropriated by the Austrian Government to the Bar Association.]

*Translation from M. Cappelletti, J. Gordley, & E. Johnson, Jr., Toward Equal Justice: A Comparative Study of Legal Aid in Modern Societies 721-25 (Giuffrè — Oceana 1975).

The Constitutional Court holds that a provision through which a lawyer is compelled to furnish legal services without compensation embodies an unequal treatment of the lawyers *vis-à-vis* other professionals which cannot be reasonably justified. Through such a provision the lawyers are placed in an inferior position relative to all other professionals, because the other professionals must act without compensation only in known emergencies or in cases falling within the duty of all professional groups to act for the benefit of the general public. For such discriminatory treatment, no sufficient justification has been provided in this proceeding. To be sure, the government pointed out that in its opinion the professional situation of the lawyer is different from that of other professions because the lawyer is "an organ of the administration of justice" and, as such, the system gives him a monopoly over legal representation and advice which has significant economic advantages. But, even if this proposition is true, it does not justify the obligation of the attorney to serve without compensation since there are other professions which enjoy similar monopolies without the attendant obligation to serve without compensation (e.g., the druggist and the doctor). Thus, the government's allusion to the professional duty connected with certain professions is unsound because in other professions the duty does not carry with it an obligation to serve without pay. Therefore, Sec. 66, para. 2 and Sec. 67 [of the Code of Civil Procedure] contradict the principle of equality because they require the lawyer to represent the poor without compensation.

This conclusion is not changed by the fact that the State paid the Bar Association a lump sum in 1970 and 1971 according to federal law No. 191 (1969) for the uncompensated services provided by lawyers in its lists who acted as legal aid counsel in criminal and civil proceedings. Through such payment the state provided a dividend for the lawyers who served without compensation.

. . . .

However, the statute under consideration cannot justify the fact that the legal aid attorney must serve without compensation. . . . This follows from the fact that the duty of the State to pay a lump sum to the Bar Association was established for only two years, and thus the Bar Association has no certain and lasting claim to the money. Moreover, the amount of the lump sum was unreasonably low; the federal government itself conceded that it covered only about 1/3 of the established fees for those who furnished services for the poor.

CONCLUSION: Sec. 66, para. 2 and Sec. 67 of the Code of Civil Procedure are annulled as unconstitutional.

The annulment is effective as of 30 November 1973.

Earlier legal determinations are no longer in force.

The President is ordered to make the annulment known without delay in the state law journals.

NOTES AND QUESTION

1. Notice the prospective character of the Austrian decision rendered on December 19, 1972, to become effective only as of November 30, 1973. (*See* Ch. 4, §§ C.3. and C.4, *supra.*)

2. The legislative response to the decision of the Austrian Constitutional Court came on November 8, 1973. It was twofold: the standards for admissibility to legal aid were changed, and the lump sum paid to the Bar Association was raised from 14 million to 32 million Austrian schillings (from approximately $700,000 to approximately $1,600,000). No substantial change was made, however, in the system of distribution of this fund. Do these changes alleviate the constitional objections of the Constitutional Court?

Chapter 11

ILLEGALLY OBTAINED EVIDENCE

A. INTRODUCTION

In the nineteenth century, in both common law and civil law nations, the major development in the field of evidence was the elimination of binding, rigid rules of admission and evaluation of evidence. In the twentieth century, the principal evidentiary development has been the exclusion of evidence obtained through illegal means. In the United States, *Weeks* v. *United States,* 232 U.S. 383 (1914) and *Gouled* v. *United States,* 255 U.S. 298 (1921) initiated the rule excluding tangible physical evidence seized in violation of the Fourth Amendment. *Mapp* v. *Ohio,* 367 U.S. 643 (1961) held that rule applicable to the states. A similar trend is apparent in post-World War II Europe, especially in Italy and Germany, and also in Japan.

These different themes of the nineteenth and twentieth centuries are not as antagonistic as they appear. The reforms of the nineteenth century eliminated rules which were intended to determine the manner or method of finding the truth in civil and criminal litigation. For example, testimony of interested witnesses had been inadmissible because it was believed to be unreliable; testimony of citizens of lesser status, like women or commoners, had been given less weight than that of the elite segments of society. This was a formalistic, *a priori* methodology of ascertaining facts, typical of scholastic thinking predominant in the Middle Ages. Thus the abolition of these rules in modern societies is easy to understand. The modern approach is inductive and concrete, and not based on *a priori,* rigidly applied abstract assumptions in actual cases.

The twentieth century, on the other hand, introduced rules to protect extrinsic values, especially fundamental, constitutional values. Evidence is excluded, not because it is unreliable, but because it was obtained in violation of constitutional rights, and despite the fact that some of the excluded evidence is probative of facts critical to the litigation. To understand this development, one must ascertain its rationale. What fundamental values are involved? Are those values absolute or relative? Are the asserted values really promoted by the exclusion of reliable evidence? These are the basic issues underlying

493

the current debate over the utility and proper scope of the exclusionary rule.

B. CRIMINAL CASES

1. Exclusionary Rule

a. Italy

The principal provisions of the Italian Constitution concerning illegal seizure of evidence are arts. 13-15.*

Article 13

Personal liberty shall be inviolable.

There shall be no form of detention, inspection, or search of the person, nor any other restriction whatsoever of personal liberty, except by an order, wherein the reasons are stated, of the judicial authorities, and only in cases and in the manner prescribed by law.

In exceptional cases of necessity and urgency, expressly provided for by law, the police authorities may take provisional measures, of which the judicial authorities must be notified within forty-eight hours. If the judicial authorities do not confirm their validity within forty-eight hours, such measures shall be considered as revoked and of no effect.

Physical and moral violence against persons placed under any form of detention shall be punished.

The law shall establish the maximum periods for which persons may be kept in custody before trial.

Article 14

The home is inviolable.

No inspection, search, or seizures shall be carried out therein, except in the cases and in the manner established by law in accordance with the guarantees prescribed for the protection of personal liberty.

Investigations and inspections carried out for the purpose of public health and safety, or for economic or fiscal reasons, shall be regulated by special legislation.

Article 15

Freedom and secrecy of correspondence and of every other form of communication shall be inviolable.

They may be limited only by an order, wherein the reasons are

---

*Article 21 deals with searches and seizures regarding the press.

stated, of the judicial authorities under the guarantees established by law.

EGIDI

Corte di Cassazione, Decision of December 14, 1957
1 RIVISTA ITALIANA DI DIRITTO E PROCEDURA PENALE 564 (1958)

[The appellant, Lionello Egidi, was detained by the police as the principal suspect in the disappearance of a female child. He was later released and then upon the discovery of the child's body, again taken into custody on the afternoon of March 3, 1951. He was subjected to repeated questioning by the police, during which he denied any part in the murder of the child, although he was unable to provide an alibi for the period of time in question. During this period he was also questioned by the Public Prosecutor, who, he was told, was only another police official. Again, before this "police official," he maintained his innocence. On the seventh day of his detention, the police placed two agents in the cell in which he was being held, their purpose being to gain his confidence by appearing to be fellow prisoners and then frighten him into making a confession by describing the brutal treatment which he would receive if he did not confess. These "prisoners" explained that the confession was not important because it would be a simple matter to subsequently retract it before the court. That same day, March 10, he confessed to having beaten the child to death. This confession was made, shortly before midnight, to officials of the police. The same Public Prosecutor who had earlier questioned him was immediately summoned, and Egidi repeated his confession to that official at 12:50 a.m. on the morning of March 11. Beyond all this, a later physical examination showed that the appellant had suffered physical mistreatment during that week of detention.

[Since the version of the murder presented in the confession did not conform with the findings of the autopsy (the child having died of knife wounds), an attempt was made to get Egidi to alter this confession. Under the influence of the same police agents Egidi did this, but on March 14 while being interrogated again by the Public Prosecutor, he retracted his confession and manifested surprise that it had been made before a magistrate, having been told that his confession was being made only to police officials. Thereafter, he continuously maintained his innocence.

[Egidi was convicted of murder by the *Tribunale* of Rome, the conviction being sustained by the Court of Appeal. The Court of Cassation annulled the decision and remanded the case to the Court of Appeal of Florence saying that the confession was not supported by the evidence, and that the trial judge failed to exercise proper control over the circumstances under which the confession was obtained. While the Court of Cassation readily recognized the confession's lack of reliability, it refused to dismiss the confession itself as a procedural nullity even though the confession was made after the legal period of detention had elapsed.* Despite the defense's argument that detention after the legal maximum invalidated all subsequent acts, the Court held:]

> ... The acts, which took place (albeit only in part) after the seventh day of detention cannot be said to be a nullity. Even though the illegal protraction of the detention beyond the legal period may result in the application of disciplinary sanctions against the officials of the judicial police and possibly even in a criminal action, it does not result in the nullity of the procedural acts.

NOTES AND QUESTIONS

1. The *Egidi* case is representative of continental law, which draws no precise distinctions between illegally seized tangible evidence and illegally obtained confessions. As we will see, the law in the United States has drawn that distinction, and has been more complex. (*See* § B.1.d.(ii), *infra.*)

2. Some later statements by Italian courts are contrary to the dictum in the *Egidi* case. On October 10, 1967, the *Tribunale* of Imperia acquitted an accused when the only evidence against her had been illegally obtained. ([1969] 74 GIUSTIZIA PENALE 363.) The defendant was charged with possession of an illegal weapon, which had been found in a search authorized by an invalid search warrant. And, in the Decision of Dec. 2, 1970, No. 175, Corte cost., [1970] 15 Giur. Cost. 2101; [1970] 32 Rac. uff. corte cost. 589; [1970] 93 Foro It. I, 2985, the *Corte Costituzionale* stated the following, in dictum: "The principle that the judge is allowed to freely evaluate the evidence according to his experience presupposes that it does not involve evidence forbidden by law."

3. Does the language of arts. 13-15 of the Italian Constitution require exclusion of evidence obtained in violation of those articles? Do those articles, in any event, impliedly require that evidence obtained by their violation be excluded? And what of the violation of statutes designed to implement the same constitutional values? **

---

*Article 238 of the Code of Criminal Procedure, in the text in force at the time of the case, allowed for pretrial detention of suspects by order of the judicial police under certain circumstances. Within 48 hours of the initial detention, the arresting police officials in compliance with art. 13 of the Constitution were obliged to notify the Public Prosecutor who, within another 48 hours, could confirm the detention order for a maximum total duration of seven days.

** Note the analogy of art. 238 of the Italian Code of Criminal Procedure to common provisions of American statutes which require the police to bring the

MARAZZANI ET AL. v. PRESIDENTE CONSIGLIO DEI MINISTRI
Corte Costituzionale, Decision of April 6, 1973 No. 34
[1973] 18 Giur. Cost. 316; [1973] 37 Rac. uff. corte cost. 245
[1973] 96 Foro It. I, 953

[FACTS: Defendants were suspected of operating a house of prostitution. The police obtained a court-authorized wiretap to confirm the suspicion and introduced evidence at trial based on the wiretap. The constitutionality of the wiretap was referred to the Constitutional Court.]

OPINION

1. The *Tribunale* of Bolzano has raised the issue of constitutionality of the last paragraph of art. 226 of the Code of Criminal Procedure, which permits the police, during preliminary investigations (prior to the *istruzione* stage of the proceeding) to wiretap, listen in on, or prevent phone calls, provided that the competent judge authorizes these acts by reasoned decree (*decreto motivato*).

According to the *Tribunale*, this provision conflicts with arts. 15 and 24 of the Constitution: the wiretapping of conversations of people suspected of having committed a crime violates their right not to answer the questions of investigating officials (art. 78 of the Code of Criminal Procedure as amended. . .).

2. The issue of the constitutionality of art. 226 in reference to art. 15 of the Constitution is not well-founded. Article 15, in fact, proclaims in the first paragraph the inviolability of the freedom and secrecy of correspondence and of any other form of communication, but explicitly states in the second paragraph that "[they] may be limited only by reasoned decree of the judge under the guarantees provided by law." Two distinct interests are therefore protected by this constitutional provision, i.e., the interest inherent in the freedom and secrecy of communications, recognized as inherent in the rights of personality held inviolable by art. 2 of the Constitution, [and] the interest connected with the need for preventing and repressing crimes, another value protected by the Constitution.

In our legal system the limitation of the right to privacy of phone communications is not entrusted to the police, but to the judge. It is to the latter that the law gives the power of ordering the wiretapping, and the limits of this power emerge clearly in the law itself. The request for a wiretap has to be evaluated by the judge with extreme caution — the judge must balance two constitutional interests so as not to unduly sacrifice the right of privacy to the need

---

accused before a magistrate for arraignment within a brief period of time — usually 48 hours. In the past, such provisions were often ignored as the police held a suspect incommunicado for lengthy questioning. *See* § B.1.d.(iii), *infra*.

for effective repression of crime. It is therefore necessary for the judge to ascertain whether the wiretapping is really necessary for the administration of justice and whether it can be reasonably believed that the wiretapping will produce positive results for the investigation.

The judge must show that he has used his power correctly by stating adequate and specific reasons for his order. [He must also establish] time limits for the wiretap and state his reasons for any further extension.

Satisfaction of constitutional requirements does, however, necessitate more than simply a statement of the reasons for the judicial wiretap order. They include: a) guarantees that the necessary technical devices will only be used for the specifically authorized wiretap and within the limits of the authorization, and b) guarantees that there is some control over the legitimacy of the order of the judge, and limits established on the use of the information collected through the wiretap at trial.

. . . .

From what we have said, it follows that the present regulation of wiretapping is not contrary to art. 15 of the Constitution. . . . This provision would be violated if wiretaps obtained without the previous and reasoned permission of the judge, were used as evidence against the interested party. In such a case, a right which the Constitution guarantees as inviolable would be seriously infringed.

This Court must emphasize the principle that acts violating the fundamental rights of man cannot provide the basis [for setting the machinery of justice in motion] against the person who has suffered those unconstitutional acts. However, the Court holds that such a serious infringement of constitutional rights does not take place [in cases such as this], since procedural law contains no rule, in the field of wiretapping, which reduces or hampers the effectiveness of that principle. On the contrary, this effectiveness is strengthened and made concrete by recent statutory provisions such as the last part of art. 304 of the Code of Criminal Procedure. [Once it was established that the right to] appointed counsel before interrogation is part of the right of defense (Const., art. 24), the legislature — giving content to a principle already inherent in the legal system — excluded the use in evidence of statements made by the accused before the appointment of counsel.

3. The second issue raised is also unfounded. There is no conflict between art. 226, last para. of the Code of Criminal Procedure and art. 24, para. 2 of the Constitution.

[The right to silence now granted to the accused as part of his right of defense (art. 24)] is not applicable here, since that right does not extend to the preliminary wiretap investigations before the *istruzione* stage of the proceeding.

The guarantee of the right to silence is a recent qualification of the right of defense proclaimed by the Constitution and only concerns interrogation of the accused; that is, when the latter is directly confronted by the inquiring authority. Obviously, its purpose is to strengthen the freedom of the accused, to raise him from the state of psychological awe in which he might find himself while facing the inquiring authority, and to shield him from possible pressure.

A totally different situation is that of statements or admissions made spontaneously by a suspected person during a phone call wiretapped upon the order of the judge during an investigation prior to the *istruzione* stage of the proceeding. In this case, the person does not directly face the authority, is not forced by it to answer, and cannot undergo any kind of pressure. Thus the person is in a situation in which the guarantee of the right to silence, as it is recognized by our Code, is meaningless and cannot apply.

NOTES AND QUESTIONS

1. What is the holding of the *Marazzani* decision? Is exclusion of evidence illegally obtained by the police now a constitutional requirement, or is the Court's discussion of this merely dicta? Consider the potential effects of the Law of April 8, 1974, No. 98, passed after *Marazzani* was decided. Article 226 *quinquies* of the new law states that "[o]n pain of irremediable nullity, to be officially noted at all stages. . . of the proceedings, no account may be taken of [telephone and telecommunication] interceptions effectuated beyond the cases permitted by law or carried out other than in conformity with the prescriptions laid down by law. . . ." Is this statutory provision merely a restatement of the constitutional requirement? Or does it establish a stricter standard for police and prosecutorial behavior? Does the new law prohibit a judge from applying the rule of proportionality to a case, restricting him to deciding only the question of whether the evidence was legally obtained and excluding it if it was not?

2. If *Marazzani* requires the exclusion of illegally obtained evidence, what is the reason for its exclusion? Is it to deter police activity which violates the Constitution? Is it, instead, to protect the "integrity" of judicial proceedings from the use of evidence obtained in violation of the Constitution?

3. The Court's last point, that wiretapping the accused is not a violation of the accused's right to silence, is in accord with American law that intercepting the accused's conversations does not violate the privilege against self-incrimination. (In the United States, wiretapping is subject to the Fourth Amendment's prohibitions on unreasonable search and seizure. *Katz* v. *United States,* 389 U.S. 347 (1967).) Suppose, however, that conversations of the accused were wiretapped after the *istruzione* stage of the criminal proceeding had begun? (Is that feasible? *See* Ch. 10, § A.2., *supra.*) *Compare Massiah* v. *United States,* 377 U.S. 201 (1964). While defendant was released on bail pending trial, a codefendant engaged him in an incriminating conversation. Unknown to the defendant, his codefendant was cooperating with the prosecution, and relayed the conversation to authorities through a hidden transmitter. The Court held that the intercepted conversation must be excluded as a violation of Massiah's right to counsel.

b. Germany

Basic Law of the Federal Republic of Germany

Article 2(1)

Everyone shall have the right to the free development of his personality insofar as he does not violate the rights of others or offend against the constitutional order or the moral code.

Article 10

(1) Privacy of post and telecommunications shall be inviolable.
(2) This right may be restricted only pursuant to a law. Such a law may lay down that the person affected shall not be informed of any such restriction if it serves to protect the free democratic basic order or the existence or security of the Federation or a *Land*, and that recourse to the courts shall be replaced by a review of the case by bodies appointed by Parliament.

Article 13

(1) The home shall be inviolable.
(2) Searches may be ordered only by a judge or, in the event of danger in delay, by other organs as provided by law and may be carried out only in the form prescribed by law.

DECISION OF FEBRUARY 21, 1964

Bundesgerichtshof (Criminal Chamber)

[1964] Neue Juristische Wochenschrift 1139

Opinion

The accused had been convicted of perjury. She was a teacher in a county elementary school where the married teacher M was also employed. He lived in quarters provided by the school. The accused had a room on the floor above in the same building. After a while, as the *Landgericht* ascertained, an intimate relationship developed between the accused and M. Around Easter of 1956 M was assigned as principal of another school and ... moved there. The accused often visited the family of M there. She also often met with M alone. Initially he was interested in her from the aspect of educational matters since she lacked experience in this area. The accused had, in addition, joined a union for young teachers of which M had been the director since 1956. He was also a member of the commission which conducted the second-level teachers' examination, which she passed in 1959.

The accused had, since her school days, made almost daily notations of happenings which to her seemed important, even including intimate matters, but in the latter case her notations were made in shorthand. In the years between 1954 and 1958 she yearly filled an appointment book with notes, which she entered daily or almost daily.

On a summer vacation in 1957 the accused began an intimate relationship with a designer, Mr. V, which she continued until June 1959. He often visited her and spent the night with her. At the end of October, 1957, V found her appointment books from 1954 to 1957 as well as fifteen letters from M. ... . He took these books and letters in order that he could later completely decipher them and use them to reproach the accused. A reconciliation took place, however, and the intimate relationship resumed until June of 1959. The accused knew that V had taken the letters and diaries. ... Upon the severance of the relationship she asked V that they be returned. He refused at that time. The accused, consequently, employed an attorney to demand their return. The exchange of letters [between the attorney and V] came into the hands of V's wife. She took the letters and appointment books to use in a contemplated divorce action. The V's, however, reconciled. Mrs. V directed in August of 1959 a request ... to the *Amstgericht* in S, enclosing the letters and diaries in order that these "sealed packages with evidentiary documents be held for a period of 10 years by the state attorney."

From the *Amtsgericht* the letters and diaries were transferred to the office of the public prosecutor both according to the request of Mrs. V and on her express suspicion of the existence of a crime of unchastity with a subordinate. The public prosecutor brought an action against M on the ground of unchastity. In the pretrial proceeding the accused refused to testify as to her relations with M. In a disciplinary proceeding against him, however, she made some statements. In the trial of M before the *Landgericht* of S she was called to give testimony, admonished to tell the truth, and warned of the importance of the oath and the criminal penalties which could result from giving false or misleading testimony. After having been informed of her right to refuse according to § 55 of the Code of

Criminal Procedure,* she gave testimony. Later she was again examined and at this time was sworn. Her statement . . . consisted substantially in that the diary notations did not always correspond with facts, as she expressed also her wishes and dreams therein . . . . If the diaries give the impression that she had had sexual relations with M, such impression would not correspond to reality. The sexual intentions of which she had written were only the product of her fantasies . . . . M had visited her home only in an official capacity and on no occasion when she was in bed. The notations regarding sexual relations referred to V.

M was absolved of guilt. The Criminal Chamber on the basis of the accused's statement was convinced that no sexual relations had existed between her and M and that the diary notations regarding sexual relations concerned her relationship with V.

. . . .

[The *Bundesgerichtshof* continues, stating that the accused was then tried and convicted of perjury in connection with the testimony she had presented regarding the diary notations. The lower court motivated its holding on a reexamination of the diaries and the inconsistencies between her statements and the notations they contained. The court was faced *inter alia* with the problem of the admissibility of the diaries and letters as evidence. It held that they were admissible notwithstanding that the notations they contained were intended solely for the accused and that they expressed strictly personal and private feelings. It considered that the use of these in evidence would violate no fundamental right.]

. . . .

The appeal asserts that the diary notations pertain to the privacy of the accused and may not be used in evidence against her will.

This claim is well-founded. In examining whether, and to what extent, there exists a constitutional prohibition against the use of private notations in evidence, we must start with the analogous considerations found in previous decisions of this Court on the use in evidence of tape recordings. . . .

Articles 1 and 2 of the Basic Law grant inviolability of human dignity and the right to free development of personality as basic values of the legal order. They bind the state, its agencies, and the citizen in private legal relations. . . . The legal protection conferred by the general right of personality accords to the citizen in the sphere of his personality the freedom and self-determination essential for the development of personality. On this legal ground this Court has decided that, as a general rule, whoever records a conversation

---

* Under § 55 a witness has a right to refuse to testify when there is a danger that he might incriminate himself.

without the consent of the participants violates the constitutionally guaranteed right to personality which protects one's privacy. In oral conversation the particular personality of each speaker finds its expression. Everyone has the right to speak freely without the sensation of mistrust or suspicion. A substantial violation of the right to the development of personality would take place if every participant had to fear that without his knowledge a tape recording was being made of his words. The particular unrepeatable atmosphere of the conversation could not be retained and concomitantly there would exist mistrust and suspicion. The possibility, as a part of human nature, of exchanging one's thought with others in a confidential fashion would be intolerably hindered. Through the uncritical use of technical devices there can occur great damage to human relations. . . .

These principles apply most strongly when someone records opinions, thoughts or experiences for himself not wanting them to come to the knowledge of others, with rare exceptions determined by the recorder himself.

Notations of an intimate character are not usually intended for the knowledge of other people. If the author were to fear that they would be read or used against his will, this would substantially limit the free development of his personality. Everyone must be free to record for himself sensations as he likes without the feeling that such notations will be used in an unauthorized way. . . . It can be, for example, that someone through such written annotations is trying to form a sort of internal communication or resolve personal tensions. This need can occur when one has no opportunity for other company.

The notations of the accused by their content could have been intended in this way. In this and similar cases a legally protectable need for nonutilization in a criminal proceeding of such intimate papers must be recognized under prerequisites which must be more clearly defined by this Court. The legal value of privacy, its recognition and protection are growing. . . .

A further question is to what extent and under what legal requirements such a sphere of protection, which contains a constitutional prohibition against the utilization of evidence, must be recognized in a criminal proceeding, insofar as the interested party does not consent to the use of personal notations in evidence. It must be taken into consideration that the purpose of the clarification and investigation of criminal acts is certainly a matter of extreme importance, but it is not and cannot be always and under all circumstances the predominant interest of the State. . . .

The particular importance of the protection of human dignity and the right to the free development of one's personality as granted by the Basic Law is demonstrated by the fact that in the existing law prohibitions against the evaluation of certain evidence are explicitly established. Otherwise, the guarantees of fundamental rights would be prejudiced. . . . The aforementioned articles of the Basic Law by themselves provide a corrective effect upon the ordinary law, in particular with regard to the law of criminal procedure which is correctly considered as "applied constitutional law" (*angewandtes Verfassungsrecht*). . . . Since the State must respect and protect human dignity and the free development of personality, a prohibition of the utilization of notations of the type mentioned, in the sense that such notations cannot be used without the consent of the party, must be recognized to a certain extent. . . . With regard to the afore-mentioned intimate notations the personality can be protected properly only if a prohibition of their utilization is recognized independently of the fact that these notations came into the possession of the public prosecutor through a State act or a private act. In such cases no type of interference in the privacy of the person is permissible, no matter in what fashion the notations came into the possession of the authorities against the will of their author.

Such a prohibition however is justified only insofar as it concerns expressions which by their content must be considered as manifestations of the personality of the author. In the case where we deal with diaries of a very personal nature this is quite obvious. However, where a criminal makes notations about his crimes and victims. . . , or a foreign agent about his espionage activities, there is no room for protection of the personality. The development, not the degeneration, of the personality, is protected by the fundamental rights. Also commercial notations and others which refer simply to nonpersonal circumstances (*Vorgänge äusserer Art*) might not fall within this prohibition. There may be cases in which this essential distinction can cause difficulties. The problem of distinguishing must often be solved in legal matters. . . .

The need for a prohibition against utilization can be ascertained, moreover, only after a careful weighing of the personal, con-stitutionally guaranteed interests in the protection of one's privacy on one hand, and the interest of the State in the prosecution of criminal justice on the other. . . . The principle of proportionality in the determination of the admissibility of measures of criminal prosecution has been developed and is quite clear in the decisions of the Federal Constitutional Court. This principle applies generally in criminal proceedings. Further, in the tape recorder decision of 1958, the Civil Chamber of this *Bundesgerichtshof* stated that the interference in the right of personality through illegal tape recordings has no legal consequence under certain circumstances, such as legitimate defense or prosecution of higher legitimate interests. The same could apply where the use of such notations provides the only means whereby the accused can contest the accusation. In such case the higher interest must be determined, whether priority should be given to the fundamental right to privacy or to the public and private interest in the exculpation of the innocent. Here, not only the interest of the State in the clarification of criminal acts and that of the individual in maintaining his privacy are counterposed, but also important is that of the accused not to be unjustly convicted. . . . In any case the balancing must be made in considering the interest in criminal prosecution in the light of the importance of the fundamental rights, whereby the gravity of the crime committed, as far as it can be determined, must be taken into consideration.

From the fact that the accused allowed V to keep the notations and letters it is not to be assumed that she gave up her right to the protection of personality. She believed that V would allow no one access to these papers. In fact he hid them. As soon as her relationship with V ended she immediately asked for the return of the diaries and letters. They came to public knowledge only through the behavior of V's wife. Therefore it is impossible to say the accused had renounced the protection of personality. This is true even though the accused made statements against the accusations on the basis of her diaries. She had no legal experience. She did not know the importance of the particular fundamental rights as they apply in this case. . . . The significance of the basic rights has not as yet come to have sufficiently deep meaning for the general public.

On the basis of the determinations of the instant proceeding, it does not appear that the crime involved is so serious that sacrifice of the right of the accused to privacy should be made. . . .

. . . .

The decision must therefore be annulled. The *Landgericht* in the new trial may not use the diaries as evidence. Nor can their content be used in other ways, such as through examination of individuals who have knowledge of such content.

NOTES AND QUESTIONS

1. The Bonn Constitution contains no explicit provisions regulating police techniques in the acquisition of evidence, nor, obviously, any provision requiring exclusion of evidence obtained unlawfully by the police. There are provisions of the Constitution which provide for the privacy of correspondence (art. 10) and inviolability of the home (art. 13). There are, in addition, guarantees of the dignity of man (art. 1) and of personal liberty (art. 2). What constitutional articles are the basis for the decision in the principal case? Would those articles form the basis for exclusion of unlawfully seized evidence generally? Would the court's rationale, coupled with other provisions of the Bonn Constitution, support a general rule excluding all unlawfully seized evidence?

2. There are, of course, statutory rules which regulate police searches and seizures and interrogations. German decisions have tended to admit evidence obtained in violation of these statutory rules, unless the statute explicitly requires exclusion of evidence obtained in its violation. (Such an explicit provision appears in § 136a of the Code of Criminal Procedure, which regulates police methods of interrogation.)

3. You have, no doubt, noticed that the unlawful seizure of evidence in this case resulted from the conduct of private persons, rather than of the police. What would be the result in the United States if evidence unlawfully seized by private persons was utilized by the district attorney in a criminal case? (*See* § C.3., *infra.*)

4. The principal case discusses the doctrine of "proportionality," which is applied in Germany when a rule generally requires exclusion of unlawfully obtained evidence. One example of the application of this doctrine is in the decision of the Federal Constitutional Court of November 14, 1969 ([1970] 2 *Neue Juristische Wochenschrift*, Heft 4, p. II). A criminal action was suspended on grounds that the accused was too aged and infirm. An order of the Court of Appeal of Karlsruhe, that the accused submit to a physical examination to determine his capacity to be tried, was challenged in the Constitutional Court as an invasion of privacy. The challenge was rejected on the basis of the principle of proportionality.

5. In the case last discussed, proportionality required weighing the interest of the accused to be free from involuntary physical examination, and the interest of the state in resolution of the criminal charge against the accused. Although never labelled as a special doctrine of proportionality, the constitutional rules controlling police practices are often developed by American courts through balancing competing interests of the individual and the government. The balancing process, of course, determines whether particular challenged police practices are lawful or not. Does the European concept of proportionality simply mean that, in deciding whether evidence was obtained in an unlawful manner, competing interests will be balanced? Or does the doctrine go further and provide that, even if the evidence was obtained unlawfully, competing interests may require that it be used as evidence? What if the accused in the principal case had been charged with murder, rather than perjury, and the evidence in the diaries had been crucial to determine her guilt?

6. What does the German Court mean when it says that "[t]he development, not the degeneration, of the personality is protected by the fundamental rights"? Do you see any dangers in such a statement?

7. For a discussion of proportionality in the context of the law of the United States, *see* § B.1.d., *infra.* For further discussion of the German concept of proportionality, *see* § C.2., *infra.*

c. European Convention on Human Rights

SCHEICHELBAUER v. AUSTRIA

European Commission of Human Rights, Decision of October 3, 1969

30 COLLECTION OF DECISIONS 1

THE FACTS

[The Applicant, an Austrian lawyer, was convicted on several counts of fraud, breach of trust and assault. He had with the aid of one M. defrauded D. of the sum of 316,000 shillings in a complex real estate mortgage arrangement.

[The police first began investigating M. who confessed to the swindle. The Applicant then sought to contact M. and a meeting was arranged. With the aid of police agent K., who knew of the forthcoming meeting, a microphone and radio transmitter were used to record the meeting. However, the meeting failed to take place when the Applicant become suspicious.

[At a later time, a meeting took place between M. and the Applicant in the latter's office. This time the meeting was recorded with equipment procured without police aid; agents K. and L., however, were present in the apartment where the recording was made. The recording was deposited with a notary.

[Later, during the trial, the prosecutor asked the court to listen to the recording. The Applicant objected. The court, however, did hear the tape, and admitted it into evidence.]

THE LAW

The present decision refers to the only complaint of the Applicant that the Commission had not declared inadmissible in its partial decision of July 19, 1968,* namely the complaint based on the tape

---

* In Section 9 of that decision (Decision of July 19, 1968, [1969] 28 COLLECTION OF DECISIONS 43, 48) the Commission stated:

It appears from the judgment . . . that the [Austrian] Court considered in detail the question whether the tape-recording of the conversation between the Applicant and M. on . . . September 1962, which was made without the Applicant's knowledge, could be put in evidence at the hearing. The Court found that the recording . . . [was] admissible in evidence under the Code of Criminal Procedure for the following reasons:

The Code of Criminal Procedure did not contain an exhaustive list of the kinds of admissible evidence but on the contrary any type of evidence likely to assist in the search for truth was admissible. The fact that the recording of the meeting on September 18, 1962, between the Applicant and M. and on the utilization of this recording as a means of proof before the . . . Court of Vienna.

The examination of the dossier gives rise to serious indicia that some agents of the Austrian judicial police, in the exercise of their duties, had lent assistance to the recording in question. It is true that the Government has maintained that the recording was carried out by private parties and that the presence of the police was for no other end than the protection of M.; however, at the hearing of the Commission on October 2, 1969, Doctor Okresek, counsel for the Government, stated that on September 18, 1962, the date of the recording, agent K. was already entrusted with the conduct of the investigation directed against the Applicant, an investigation begun in the Spring of 1962. On the other hand, the Court had utilized the controversial tape as a means of proof, in spite of the protests of the Applicant. The Court could not ignore the circumstances under which this recording was carried out and — more particularly — it could not ignore that a problem arose regarding the respect, on the part of the public authority, for the privacy of the Applicant.

The Application . . . has been consolidated into a single complaint, namely the violation of the right to a fair hearing in the sense of art. 6 of the Convention because of the utilization on the part of the Court of a recording carried out under the circumstances in this case. . . .

Although art. 27, para. 2, of the Convention, obliges the Commission to declare "inadmissible" individual applications that are found to be "manifestly ill-founded," it does not grant the Commission the authority to reject, in the stage of examination of their admissibility, applications whose ill-foundedness is not evident. . . . The problems that arise here show themselves to be sufficiently

---

Court listened to the tape recording had caused the Applicant to make a partial confession. It had also made it possible to verify the truth of the statements by his co-accused M. . . . Moreover, recent decisions had approved the use of tape-recordings in criminal proceedings.

The Court stated that . . . the recording did not amount to an improper procedure on the part of the police. . . .

The Court found that the recording of . . . September, 1962, was made exclusively by private persons (M. and two other persons) and that the two policemen, K. and L., were only present in the room where the recording was made in order to protect M. if necessary. . . .

The Court recalled the protective nature of criminal law (*Schutzrecht*). After carefully weighing the conflicting interests, i.e., the interest of the population in the discovery of crime and protection against criminals on the one hand and the rights of the defense of a person suspected of several crimes, as in the present case, the Court gave greater weight to the investigation of the true facts (*materielle Wahrheit*) and the protection of the public. . . .

complex so that their solution requires an examination of the merits of the case. . . .

Now therefore the Commission
DECLARES THE APPLICATION ADMISSIBLE.

NOTES AND QUESTIONS

1. The *Scheichelbauer* case was referred to the Committee of Ministers, which arrived at the following conclusion:

> Whereas the Commission on 19 July 1968, rejected certain parts of the application as being inadmissible and on 3 October 1969 declared admissible the applicant's complaint alleging violation of the right to a fair trial within the meaning of Article 6 of the Convention owing to the use of the recording on a magnetic tape of a conversation between the applicant and his co-defendant as evidence before the Vienna Regional Criminal Court;
>
> Whereas the Commission during its examination of the merits of the case considered that the Commission was not required in the present case to decide the question whether the tape recordings of a private conversation unbeknown to the participants, or one of them, constitutes in principle an interference with privacy; the problem before the Commission was only whether the use by the Austrian court of the recording in evidence constituted a violation in the present case of the applicant's right to a fair hearing within the meaning of Article 6(1) of the Convention;
>
> . . . .
>
> Whereas the Commission also considered the further allegation of the applicant that if the use of the tape recording as evidence was contrary to the Convention, there was also a violation of Article 13, since, according to him, the Code of Criminal Procedure made no provision for appeal in such cases;
>
> Agreeing with the opinion expressed by the Commission in accordance with Article 31, paragraph 1 of the Convention [the Committee of Ministers concludes]:
>
> (a) by seven votes to four, that in this case there was no violation of Article 6(1) of the Convention;
>
> (b) by six votes to five that since the applicant's rights under other articles of the Convention had not been violated in this case, Article 13 had not been violated;
>
> Voting in accordance with the provisions of Article 32, paragraph 1 of the Convention;
>
> Decides that in this case there was no violation of the

Convention for the Protection of Human Rights and Fundamental Freedoms.
Resolution DH(71)3 of Nov. 12, 1971, [1971] Y.B. Eur. Conv. on Human Rights 902, 904-06 (Committee of Ministers' Deputies).

Does the decision of the Committee of Ministers mean that the Convention does not require exclusion of unlawfully obtained evidence?

2. Would the evidence in the *Scheichelbauer* case have been admitted in a criminal trial in the United States? Would a decision that there had been no violation of the Fourth Amendment because the search was purely private be plausible? *Compare Stapleton* v. *Superior Court,* 70 Cal.2d 97, 447 P.2d 967 (1968) (police participated in planning and execution of arrest by agents of a credit card company; evidence excluded).

3. A more basic issue, even if the search is treated as perpetrated by the government, is the problem of monitoring conversations with consent of one party. In *On Lee* v. *United States,* 343 U.S. 747 (1952), the defendant made incriminating statements to an old acquaintance. Unknown to the defendant, his acquaintance was an undercover agent "wired for sound" with a transmitter broadcasting to a narcotics agent stationed outside. The Court sustained the admission of the evidence. The *On Lee* case, however, was decided when the prevailing rule was that evidence obtained by electronic eavesdropping violated the Fourth Amendment only when there was an illegal physical intrusion onto property. In 1967, the Court held that unreasonable electronic eavesdropping violated the Fourth Amendment. *Katz* v. *United States,* 389 U.S. 347 (1967). In *United States* v. *White,* 401 U.S. 745 (1971), however, a majority of the Court appeared to reaffirm the *On Lee* case. Justice White's plurality opinion stated "[i]f the law gives no protection to the wrongdoer whose trusted accomplice is or becomes a police agent, neither should it protect him when that same agent has recorded or transmitted the conversations which are later offered in evidence. . . ." Justice Harlan, dissenting, disagreed:

> The impact of the practice . . . must . . . [undermine] . . . that confidence and sense of security in dealing with one another that is characteristic of individual relationships between citizens in a free society. . . . Much off-hand exchange is easily forgotten and one may count on the obscurity of his remarks, . . . the . . . limited audience, and the likelihood that the listener will either overlook or forget what is said . . . . All these values are sacrificed by a rule of law that permits official monitoring of private discourse limited only by the need to locate a willing assistant.

What is at issue in cases like *Scheichelbauer* and *On Lee*? Is it the loss of privacy in government listening to private conversations? Is it the loss of privacy when ephemeral remarks are accurately recorded?

d. United States

(i) Tangible Physical Evidence

STONE v. POWELL

Supreme Court of the United States

428 U.S. 465, 96 S. Ct. 3037, 49 L.Ed.2d 1067 (1976)

MR. JUSTICE POWELL delivered the opinion of the Court.

Respondents in these cases were convicted of criminal offenses in state courts, and their convictions were affirmed on appeal. The prosecution in each case relied upon evidence obtained by searches and seizures alleged by respondents to have been unlawful. Each respondent subsequently sought relief in a federal district court by filing a petition for a writ of federal habeas corpus under 28 U.S.C. § 2254. The question presented is whether a federal court should consider, in ruling on a petition for habeas corpus relief filed by a state prisoner, a claim that evidence obtained by an unconstitutional search or seizure was introduced at his trial, when he has previously been afforded an opportunity for full and fair litigation of his claim in the state courts. The issue is of considerable importance to the administration of criminal justice.

. . . .

II

. . . .

Prior to the Court's decision in *Kaufman* v. *United States,* 394 U.S. 217 (1969), a substantial majority of the federal courts of appeals had concluded that collateral review of search-and-seizure claims was inappropriate on motions filed by federal prisoners under 28 U.S.C. § 2255, the modern post-conviction procedure available to federal prisoners in lieu of habeas corpus. The primary rationale advanced in support of those decisions was that Fourth Amendment violations are different in kind from denials of Fifth or Sixth Amendment rights in that claims of illegal search and seizure do not "impugn the integrity of the fact-finding process or challenge evidence as inherently unreliable; rather, the exclusion of illegally seized evidence is simply a prophylactic device intended generally to deter Fourth Amendment violations by law enforcement officers."

Kaufman rejected this rationale and held that search-and-seizure claims are cognizable in § 2255 proceedings. The Court noted that "the federal habeas remedy extends to state prisoners alleging that unconstitutionally obtained evidence was admitted against them at trial," and concluded, as a matter of statutory construction, that there was no basis for restricting "access by federal prisoners with illegal search-and-seizure claims to federal collateral remedies, while placing no similar restriction on access by state prisoners," . . . .

The discussion in *Kaufman* of the scope of federal habeas corpus rests on the view that the effectuation of the Fourth Amendment, as applied to the States through the Fourteenth Amendment, requires the granting of habeas corpus relief when a prisoner has been convicted in state court on the basis of evidence obtained in an illegal search or seizure since those Amendments were held in *Mapp* v. *Ohio,* 367 U. S. 643 (1961), to require exclusion of such evidence at trial and reversal of conviction upon direct review. Upon examination, we conclude, in light of the nature and purpose of the Fourth Amendment exclusionary rule, that this view is unjustified. We hold, therefore, that where the State has provided an opportunity for full and fair litigation of a Fourth Amendment claim, the Constitution does not require that a state prisoner be granted federal habeas corpus relief on the ground that evidence obtained in an unconstitutional search or seizure was introduced at his trial.[17]

III

. . . .

The exclusionary rule was a judicially created means of effectuating the rights secured by the Fourth Amendment. Prior to the Court's decisions in *Weeks* v. *United States,* 232 U. S. 383 (1914), and *Gouled* v. *United States,* 255 U.S. 298 (1921), there existed no barrier to the introduction in criminal trials of evidence obtained in violation of the Amendment. In *Weeks* the Court held that the defendant could petition before trial for the return of property secured through an illegal search or seizure conducted by federal authorities. In *Gouled* the Court held broadly that such evidence could not be introduced in a federal prosecution.

Thirty-five years after *Weeks* the Court held in *Wolf* v. *Colorado,* 338 U. S. 25 (1949), that the right to be free from arbitrary intrusion by the police that is protected by the Fourth Amendment is "implicit

---

[17] We find it unnecessary to consider the other issues concerning the exclusionary rule, or the statutory scope of the habeas corpus statute, raised by the parties. These include, principally, whether in view of the purpose of the rule, it should be applied on a *per se* basis without regard to the nature of the constitutional claim or the circumstances of the police action.

in 'the concept of ordered liberty' and as such enforceable against the States through the [Fourteenth Amendment] Due Process Clause." The Court concluded, however, that the *Weeks* exclusionary rule would not be imposed upon the States as "an essential ingredient of that right." The full force of *Wolf* was eroded in subsequent decisions, and a little more than a decade later the exclusionary rule was held applicable to the States in *Mapp* v. *Ohio,* 367 U. S. 643 (1961).

Decisions prior to *Mapp* advanced two principal reasons for application of the rule in federal trials. The Court in *Elkins* [v. *United States,* 364 U.S. 206 (1960)] for example, in the context of its special supervisory role over the lower federal courts, referred to the "imperative of judicial integrity," suggesting that exclusion of illegally seized evidence prevents contamination of the judicial process. But even in that context a more pragmatic ground was emphasized:

> "The rule is calculated to prevent, not to repair. Its purpose is to deter — to compel respect for the constitutional guaranty in the only effectively available way — by removing the incentive to disregard it."

The *Mapp* majority justified the application of the rule to the States on several grounds, but relied principally upon the belief that exclusion would deter future unlawful police conduct.

Although our decisions often have alluded to the "imperative of judicial integrity," *e. g., United States* v. *Peltier,* 422 U. S. 531, 536-539 (1975), they demonstrate the limited role of this justification in the determination whether to apply the rule in a particular context. Logically extended, this justification would require that courts exclude unconstitutionally seized evidence despite lack of objection by the defendant, or even over his assent. It also would require abandonment of the standing limitations on who may object to the introduction of unconstitutionally seized evidence, and retreat from the proposition that judicial proceedings need not abate when the defendant's person is unconstitutionally seized. Similarly, the interest in promoting judicial integrity does not prevent the use of illegally seized evidence in grand jury proceedings. *United States* v. *Calandra,* 414 U. S. 338 (1974). Nor does it require that the trial court exclude such evidence from use for impeachment of a defendant, even though its introduction is certain to result in convictions in some cases. *Walder* v. *United States,* 347 U. S. 62 (1954). The teaching of these cases is clear. While courts, of course, must ever be concerned with preserving the integrity of the judicial process, this concern has limited force as a justification for the exclusion of highly probative evidence. The force of this justification becomes minimal where federal habeas corpus relief is sought by a prisoner who previously has been afforded the opportunity for full and fair consideration of his search-and-seizure claim at trial and on direct review.

The primary justification for the exclusionary rule then is the deterrence of police conduct that violates Fourth Amendment rights. Post-*Mapp* decisions have established that the rule is not a personal constitutional right. It is not calculated to redress the injury to the privacy of the victim of the search or seizure, for any "[r]eparation comes too late." *Linkletter* v. *Walker,* 381 U. S. 618, 637 (1965). Instead,

> "the rule is a judicially created remedy designed to safeguard Fourth Amendment rights generally through its deterrent effect. . . ." *United States* v. *Calandra, supra,* at 348.

[D]espite the broad deterrent purpose of the exclusionary rule, it has never been interpreted to proscribe the introduction of illegally seized evidence in all proceedings or against all persons. As in the case of any remedial device, "the application of the rule has been restricted to those areas where its remedial objectives are thought most efficaciously served." *United States* v. *Calandra, supra.*[24] Thus, our refusal to extend the exclusionary rule to grand jury proceedings was based on a balancing of the potential injury to the historic role and function of the grand jury by such extension against the potential contribution to the effectuation of the Fourth Amendment through deterrence of police misconduct:

> "Any incremental deterrent effect which might be achieved by extending the rule to grand jury proceedings is uncertain at best. Whatever deterrence of police misconduct may result from the exclusion of illegally seized evidence from criminal trials, it is unrealistic to assume that the application of the rule to grand jury proceedings would significantly further that goal. Such an extension would deter only police investigation consciously directed toward the discovery of evidence solely for use in a grand jury investigation. . . .
>
> "We therefore decline to embrace a view that would achieve

---

[24] As Professor Amsterdam has observed:

"The rule is unsupportable as reparation or compensatory dispensation to the injured criminal; its sole rational justification is the experience of its indispensibility in 'exert[ing] general legal pressures to secure obedience to the Fourth Amendment on the part of . . . law-enforcing officers.' As it serves this function, the rule is a needed, but grudgingly [*sic*] taken, medicament; no more should be swallowed than is needed to combat the disease. Granted that so many criminals must go free as will deter the constables from blundering, pursuance of this policy of liberation beyond the confines of necessity inflicts gratuitous harm on the public interest . . . ." Amsterdam, Search, Seizure, and Section 2255: A Comment, 112 U. Pa. L. Rev. 378, 388-389 (1964) (footnotes omitted).

a speculative and undoubtedly minimal advance in the deterrence of police misconduct at the expense of substantially impeding the role of the grand jury."

The same pragmatic analysis of the exclusionary rule's usefulness in a particular context was evident earlier in *Walder* v. *United States, supra,* where the Court permitted the Government to use unlawfully seized evidence to impeach the credibility of a defendant who had testified broadly in his own defense. . . .

The balancing process at work in these cases also finds expression in the standing requirement. Standing to invoke the exclusionary rule has been found to exist only when the Government attempts to use illegally obtained evidence to incriminate the victim of the illegal search. The standing requirement is premised on the view that the "additional benefits of extending the rule" to defendants other than the victim of the search or seizure are outweighed by the "further enroachment [*sic*] upon the public interest in prosecuting those accused of crime and having them acquitted or convicted on the basis of all the evidence which exposes the truth."

We turn now to the specific question presented by these cases. . . .

The costs of applying the exclusionary rule even at trial and on direct review are well known: the focus of the trial, and the attention of the participants therein, is diverted from the ultimate question of guilt or innocence that should be the central concern in a criminal proceeding. Moreover, the physical evidence sought to be excluded is typically reliable and often the most probative information bearing on the guilt or innocence of the defendant. . . . Application of the rule thus deflects the truthfinding process and often frees the guilty. The disparity in particular cases between the error committed by the police officer and the windfall afforded a guilty defendant by application of the rule is contrary to the idea of proportionality that is essential to the concept of justice.[29] Thus, although the rule is thought to deter unlawful police activity in part through the nurturing of respect for Fourth Amendment values, if applied indiscriminately it may well have the opposite effect of generating disrespect for the law and administration of justice. These long-recognized costs of the rule persist when a criminal conviction is sought to be overturned on collateral review on the ground that

---

[29] Many of the proposals for modification of the scope of the exclusionary rule recognize at least implicitly the role of proportionality in the criminal justice system and the potential value of establishing a direct relationship between the nature of the violation and the decision whether to invoke the rule. See A. L. I., A Model Code of Pre-arraignment Procedure, May 20, 1975, § 290.2, at 181-183 ("substantial violations"); H. Friendly, Benchmarks 260-262 (1967) (even at trial, exclusion should be limited to "the fruit of activity intentionally or flagrantly illegal."); [8 J. WIGMORE, EVIDENCE § 2184a, pp. 52-53].

a search-and-seizure claim was erroneously rejected by two or more tiers of state courts.

Evidence obtained by police officers in violation of the Fourth Amendment is excluded at trial in the hope that the frequency of future violations will decrease. Despite the absence of supportive empirical evidence, we have assumed that the immediate effect of exclusion will be to discourage law enforcement officials from violating the Fourth Amendment by removing the incentive to disregard it. More importantly, over the long term, this demonstration that our society attaches serious consequences to violation of constitutional rights is thought to encourage those who formulate law enforcement policies, and the officers who implement them, to incorporate Fourth Amendment ideals into their value system.

We adhere to the view that these considerations support the implementation of the exclusionary rule at trial and its enforcement on direct appeal of state court convictions. But the additional contribution, if any, of the consideration of search-and-seizure claims of state prisoners on collateral review is small in relation to the costs. . . . Even if one rationally could assume that some additional incremental deterrent effect would be present in isolated cases, the resulting advance of the legitimate goal of furthering Fourth Amendment rights would be outweighed by the acknowledged costs to other values vital to a rational system of criminal justice.

In sum, we conclude that where the State has provided an opportunity for full and fair litigation of a Fourth Amendment claim, a state prisoner may not be granted federal habeas corpus relief on the ground that evidence obtained in an unconstitutional search or seizure was introduced at his trial. In this context the contribution of the exclusionary rule, if any, to the effectuation of the Fourth Amendment is minimal and the substantial societal costs of application of the rule persist with special force.

Accordingly, the judgments of the Courts of Appeals are

Reversed.

———————

MR. CHIEF JUSTICE BURGER, concurring.

I concur in the Court's opinion. By way of dictum, and somewhat hesitantly, the Court notes that the holding in this case leaves undisturbed the exclusionary rule as applied to criminal trials. For reasons stated in my dissent in *Bivens* v. *Six Unknown Named Federal Agents,* 403 U. S. 388, 441 (1971), it seems clear to me that the exclusionary rule has been operative long enough to demonstrate its flaws. The time has come to modify its reach, even if it is retained for a small and limited category of cases.

Over the years, the strains imposed by reality, in terms of the costs to society and the bizarre miscarriages of justice that have been experienced because of the exclusion of reliable evidence when the "constable blunders", have led the Court to vacillate as to the rationale for deliberate exclusion of truth from the factfinding process. The rhetoric has varied with the rationale to the point where the rule has become a doctrinaire result in search of validating reasons.

. . . .

. . . The rule is based on the hope that events in the courtroom or appellate chambers, long after the crucial acts took place, will somehow modify the way in which policemen conduct themselves. A more clumsy, less direct means of imposing sanctions is difficult to imagine, particularly since the issue whether the policeman did indeed run afoul of the Fourth Amendment is often not resolved until years after the event.

Despite this anomaly, the exclusionary rule now rests upon its purported tendency to deter police misconduct, . . . although, as we know, the rule has long been applied to wholly good-faith mistakes and to purely technical deficiencies in warrants. Other rhetorical generalizations, including the "imperative of judicial integrity," have not withstood analysis as more and more critical appraisals of the rule's operation have appeared. Indeed, settled rules demonstrate that the "judicial integrity" rationalization is fatally flawed. . . . [A]s one scholar has correctly observed:

> "[I]t is difficult to accept the proposition that the exclusion of improperly obtained evidence is necessary for 'judicial integrity' when no such rule is observed in other common law jurisdictions such as England and Canada, whose courts are otherwise regarded as models of judicial decorum and fairness."

Despite its avowed deterrent objective, proof is lacking that the exclusionary rule, a purely judge-created device based on "hard cases," serves the purpose of deterrence. Notwithstanding Herculean efforts, no empirical study has been able to demonstrate that the rule does in fact have any deterrent effect. In the face of dwindling support for the rule some would go so far as to extend it to *civil* cases.

To vindicate the continued existence of this judge-made rule, it is incumbent upon those who seek its retention — and surely its *extension* — to demonstrate that it serves its declared deterrent purpose and to show that the results outweigh the rule's heavy costs to rational enforcement of the criminal law. The burden rightly rests upon those who ask society to ignore trustworthy evidence of guilt, at the expense of setting obviously guilty criminals free to ply their trade.

In my view, it is an abdication of judicial responsibility to exact such exorbitant costs from society purely on the basis of speculative and unsubstantiated assumptions. Judge Henry Friendly has observed:

> "[T]he same authority that empowered the Court to supplement the [fourth] amendment by the exclusionary rule a hundred and twenty-five years after its adoption, likewise allows it to modify that rule as the 'lessons of experience' may teach." Friendly, The Bill of Rights as a Code of Criminal Procedure, 53 Cal. L. Rev. 929, 952-953 (1965).

In *Bivens,* I suggested that, despite its grave shortcomings, the rule need not be totally abandoned until some meaningful alternative could be developed to protect innocent persons aggrieved by police misconduct. With the passage of time, it now appears that the continued existence of the rule, as presently implemented, inhibits the development of rational alternatives. The reason is quite simple: incentives for developing new procedures or remedies will remain minimal or nonexistent so long as the exclusionary rule is retained in its present form.

It can no longer be assumed that other branches of government will act while judges cling to this Draconian, discredited device in its present absolutist form. Legislatures are unlikely to create statutory alternatives, or impose direct sanctions on errant police officers or on the public treasury by way of tort actions, so long as persons who commit serious crimes continue to reap the enormous and undeserved benefits of the exclusionary rule. And of course, by definition the direct beneficiaries of this rule can be none but persons guilty of crimes. With this extraordinary "remedy" for Fourth Amendment violations, however slight, inadvertent or technical, legislatures might assume that nothing more should be done, even though a grave defect of the exclusionary rule is that it offers no relief whatever to victims of overzealous police work who never appear in court. And even if legislatures were inclined to experiment with alternative remedies, they have no assurance that the judicially created rule will be abolished or even modified in response to such legislative innovations. The unhappy result, as I see it, is that alternatives will inevitably be stymied by rigid adherence on our part to the exclusionary rule. I venture to predict that overruling this judicially contrived doctrine — or limiting its scope to egregious, bad-faith conduct — would inspire a surge of activity toward providing some kind of statutory remedy for persons injured by police mistakes or misconduct.

. . . .

MR. JUSTICE BRENNAN, with whom MR. JUSTICE MARSHALL concurs, dissenting.

The Court today holds "that where the State has provided an opportunity for full and fair litigation of a Fourth Amendment claim, a state prisoner may not be granted federal habeas corpus relief on the ground that evidence obtained in an unconstitutional search or seizure was introduced at his trial." To be sure, my Brethren are hostile to the continued vitality of the exclusionary rule as part and parcel of the Fourth Amendment's prohibition of unreasonable searches and seizures. But these cases, despite the veil of Fourth Amendment terminology employed by the Court, plainly do not involve any question of the right of a defendant to have evidence excluded from use against him in his criminal trial when that evidence was seized in contravention of rights ostensibly secured by the Fourth and Fourteenth Amendments. Rather, they involve the question of the availability of a *federal forum* for vindicating those federally guaranteed rights. Today's holding portends substantial evisceration of federal habeas corpus jurisdiction, and I dissent.

. . . .

The Court, focusing on Fourth Amendment rights argues that habeas relief for non-"guilt-related" constitutional claims is not mandated because such claims do not affect the "basic justice" of a defendant's detention; this is presumably because the "ultimate goal" of the criminal justice system is "truth and justice."

This denigration of constitutional guarantees and *constitutionally mandated procedures,* relegated by the Court to the status of mere utilitarian tools, must appall citizens taught to expect judicial respect and support for their constitutional rights. Even if punishment of the "guilty" were society's highest value — and procedural safeguards denigrated to this end — in a constitution that a majority of the members of this Court would prefer, that is not the ordering of priorities under the Constitution forged by the Framers, and this Court's sworn duty is to uphold that Constitution and not to frame its own. The procedural safeguards mandated in the Framers' Constitution are not admonitions to be tolerated only to the extent they serve functional purposes that ensure that the "guilty" are punished and the "innocent" freed; rather, every guarantee enshrined in the Constitution, our basic charter and the guarantor of our most precious liberties, is by it endowed with an independent vitality and value, and this Court is not free to curtail those constitutional guarantees even to punish the most obviously guilty. Particular constitutional rights that do not affect the fairness of fact-finding procedures cannot for that reason be denied at the trial itself. What possible justification then can there be for denying vindication of such rights on federal habeas when state courts do deny those rights at trial?

. . . .

MR. JUSTICE WHITE, dissenting.

For many of the reasons stated by Mr. Justice BRENNAN, I cannot agree that the writ of habeas corpus should be any less available to those convicted of state crimes where they allege Fourth Amendment violations than where other constitutional issues are presented to the federal court . . . .

I feel constrained to say, however, that I would join four or more other Justices in substantially limiting the reach of the exclusionary rule as presently administered under the Fourth Amendment in federal and state criminal trials.

Whether I would have joined the Court's opinion in *Mapp* v. *Ohio,* had I then been a Member of the Court, I do not know. But as time went on after coming to this bench, I became convinced that both *Weeks* v. *United States* and *Mapp* v. *Ohio* had overshot their mark insofar as they aimed to deter lawless action by law enforcement personnel and that in many of its applications the exclusionary rule was not advancing that aim in the slightest and that in this respect it was a senseless obstacle to arriving at the truth in many criminal trials.

. . . I would overrule neither *Weeks* v. *United States* nor *Mapp* v. *Ohio.* I am nevertheless of the view that the rule should be substantially modified so as to prevent its application in those many circumstances where the evidence at issue was seized by an officer acting in the good-faith belief that his conduct comported with existing law and having reasonable grounds for this belief. These are recurring situations; and recurringly evidence is excluded without any realistic expectation that its exclusion will contribute in the slightest to the purposes of the rule, even though the trial will be seriously affected or the indictment dismissed.

An officer sworn to uphold the law and to apprehend those who break it inevitably must make judgments regarding probable cause to arrest: is there reasonable ground to believe that a crime has been committed and that a particular suspect has committed it? Sometimes the historical facts are disputed or are otherwise in doubt. In other situations the facts may be clear so far as they are known, yet the question of probable cause remain. In still others there are special worries about the reliability of secondhand information such as that coming from informants. In any of these situations, which occur repeatedly, when the officer is convinced that he has probable cause to arrest he will very likely make the arrest. Except in emergencies, it is probable that his colleagues or superiors will participate in the decision, and it may be that the officer will secure a warrant, although warrantless arrests on probable cause are not forbidden by the Constitution or by state law. Making the arrest in such circumstances is precisely what the community expects the police officer to do. Neither officers nor judges issuing arrest warrants need delay apprehension of the suspect until unquestioned proof against him has accumulated. The officer may be shirking his duty if he does so.

In most of these situations, it is hoped that the officer's judgment will be correct; but experience tells us that there will be those occasions where the trial or appellate court will disagree on the issue of probable cause, no matter how reasonable the grounds for arrest appeared to the officer and though reasonable men could easily differ on the question. . . .

In these situations, excluding the evidence will not further the ends of the exclusionary rule in any appreciable way; for it is painfully apparent that in each of them the officer is acting as a reasonable officer would and should act in similar circumstances. Excluding the evidence can in no way affect his future conduct unless it is to make him less willing to do his duty. It is true that in such cases the courts have ultimately determined that in their view the officer was mistaken; but it is also true that in making constitutional judgments under the general language used in some parts of our Constitution, including the Fourth Amendment, there is much room for disagreement among judges, each of whom is convinced that both he and his colleagues are reasonable men. Surely when this Court divides five to four on issues of probable cause, it is not tenable to conclude that the officer was at fault or acted unreasonably in making the arrest.

When law enforcement personnel have acted mistakenly, but in good faith and on reasonable grounds, and yet the evidence they have seized is later excluded, the exclusion can have no deterrent effect. The officers, if they do their duty, will act in similar fashion in similar circumstances in the future; and the only consequence of the rule as presently administered is that unimpeachable and probative evidence is kept from the trier of fact and the truth-finding function of proceedings is substantially impaired or a trial totally aborted.

Admitting the evidence in such circumstances does not render judges participants in Fourth Amendment violations. The violation, if there was one, has already occurred and the evidence is at hand. Furthermore, there has been only mistaken, but unintentional and faultless, conduct by enforcement officers. Exclusion of the evidence does not cure the invasion of the defendant's rights which he has already suffered. . . .

He is not at all recompensed for the invasion by merely getting his property back. It is often contraband and stolen property to which he is not entitled to in any event. He has been charged with crime and is seeking to have probative evidence against him excluded, although often it is the instrumentality of the crime. There is very little equity in the defendant's side in these circumstances. The exclusionary rule, a judicial construct, seriously shortchanges the public interest as presently applied. I would modify it accordingly.

NOTES AND QUESTIONS

1. A number of recent Supreme Court decisions have relied upon the deterrent function of the exclusionary rule as the rationale for refusing to apply it. Among them are: *United States* v. *Calandra,* 414 U.S. 338 (1974) (introduction of illegally seized evidence before grand jury); *United States* v. *Peltier,* 422 U.S. 531 (1975) (retroactivity of decision that warrantless automobile searches near border violate Fourth Amendment); *United States* v. *Janis,* 428 U.S. 433 (1976) (introduction of evidence illegally seized by State officers in federal civil tax assessment proceeding). Justice Brennan, dissenting in all these cases, has argued that deterring illegal police activity is only one reason for the exclusionary rule, and that the rationale of maintaining the integrity of the judicial process is an important goal of the exclusionary rule. He made this argument at greatest length in the *Calandra* case, where he said, in part:

> The commands of the Fourth Amendment are, of course, directed solely to public officials. Necessarily, therefore, only official violations of those commands could have created the evil that threatened to make the Amendment a dead letter. But curtailment of the evil, if a consideration at all, was at best only a hoped-for effect of the exclusionary rule, not its ultimate objective. Indeed, there is no evidence that the possible deterrent effect of the rule was given any attention by the judges chiefly responsible for its formulation. Their concern as guardians of the Bill of Rights was to fashion an enforcement tool to give content and meaning to the Fourth Amendment's guarantees. They thus bore out James Madison's prediction in his address to the First Congress on June 8, 1789:
>
>> If they [the rights] are incorporated into the Constitution, independent tribunals of justice will consider themselves in a peculiar manner the guardians of those rights; they will be an impenetrable bulwark against every assumption of power in the Legislative or Executive; they will be naturally led to resist every encroachment upon rights expressly stipulated for in the Constitution by the declaration of rights. 1 Annals of Cong. 439 (1789).
>
> Since, however, those judges were without power to direct or control the conduct of law enforcement officers, the enforcement

tool had necessarily to be one capable of administration by judges. The exclusionary rule, if not perfect, accomplished the twin goals of enabling the judiciary to avoid the taint of partnership in official lawlessness and of assuring the people — all potential victims of unlawful government conduct — that the government would not profit from its lawless behavior, thus minimizing the risk of seriously undermining popular trust in government.

That these considerations, not the rule's possible deterrent effect, were uppermost in the minds of the framers of the rule clearly emerges from the decision which fashioned it:

> The effect of the Fourth Amendment is to put the courts of the United States and Federal officials, in the exercise of their power and authority, under limitations and restraints as to the exercise of such power and authority, and to forever secure the people, their persons, houses, papers and effects against all unreasonable searches and seizures under the guise of law. . . . The tendency of those who execute the criminal laws of the country to obtain conviction by means of unlawful seizures . . . *should find no sanction in the judgments of the courts which are charged at all times with the support of the Constitution and to which people of all conditions have a right to appeal for the maintenance of such fundamental rights. . . .*
>
> . . . .
>
> This protection is equally extended to the action of the Government and officers of the law acting under it. . . . *To sanction such proceedings would be to affirm by judicial decision a manifest neglect if not an open defiance of the prohibitions of the Constitution, intended for the protection of the people against such unauthorized action. Weeks* v. *United States,* 232 U. S. 383, 391-392, 394 (1914) (emphasis added).

Mr. Justice Brandeis and Mr. Justice Holmes added their enormous influence to these precepts in their notable dissents in *Olmstead* v. *United States,* 277 U. S. 438 (1928). Mr. Justice Brandeis said:

> In a government of laws, existence of the government will be imperilled if it fails to observe the law scrupulously. Our Government is the potent, the omnipresent teacher. For good or for ill, it teaches the whole people by its example. Crime is contagious. If the Government becomes a lawbreaker, it breeds contempt for law; it invites every man to become a law unto himself; it invites anarchy. *Id.,* at 485.

And Mr. Justice Holmes said:

> [W]e must consider the two objects of desire, both of which we cannot have, and make up our minds which to choose. It is desirable that criminals should be detected, and to that end that all available evidence should be used. It also is desirable that the Government should not itself foster and pay for other crimes, when they are the means by which the evidence is to be obtained. . . . We have to choose, and for my part I think it a less evil that some criminals should escape than that the Government should play an ignoble part.
>
> . . . If the existing code does not permit district attorneys to have a hand in such dirty business it does not permit the judge to allow such iniquities to succeed. *Id.,* at 470.

To be sure, the exclusionary rule does not "provide that illegally seized evidence is inadmissible against anyone for any purpose." *Alderman* v. *United States,* 394 U. S. 165, 175 (1969). But clearly there is a crucial distinction between withholding its cover from individuals whose Fourth Amendment rights have not been violated — as has been done in the "standing" cases, . . . and withdrawing its cover from persons whose Fourth Amendment rights have in fact been abridged.

. . . .

. . . I am left with the uneasy feeling that today's decision may signal that a majority of my colleagues have positioned themselves to reopen the door still further and abandon altogether the exclusionary rule in search-and-seizure cases; for surely they cannot believe that application of the exclusionary rule at trial furthers the goal of deterrence, but that its application in grand jury proceedings will not "significantly" do so. Unless we are to shut our eyes to the evidence that crosses our desks every day, we must concede that official lawlessness has not abated and that no empirical data distinguishes trials from grand jury proceedings. I thus fear that when next we confront a case of a conviction rested on illegally seized evidence, today's decision will be invoked to sustain the conclusion in that case also, that "it is unrealistic to assume" that application of the rule at trial would "significantly further" the goal of deterrence — though, if the police are presently undeterred, it is difficult to see how removal of the sanction of exclusion will induce more lawful official conduct. [*United States* v. *Calandra,* 414 U. S. 338, 356-61, 364-66.]

2. How crucial is the debate over the reason for the exclusionary rule? Does it control the result in *Stone* v. *Powell* and the cases mentioned at the beginning of the previous note? For example, could one accept the argument that deterrence is the primary goal of the exclusionary rule, and yet conclude that all those cases were wrongly decided?

3. While the Court's opinion in *Stone* states continuing adherence to application of the exclusionary rule in criminal trials, note 17 carefully leaves open the question raised by Justice White's dissent. Among the most prominent proposals for introduction of a rule of proportionality is the American Law Institute's Model Code of Pre-arraignment Procedure, cited in note 29 of Justice Powell's opinion. Is the debate over the purpose of the exclusionary rule relevant to this issue?

(ii) Confessions

BREWER v. WILLIAMS

Supreme Court of the United States
430 U.S. 387, 97 S. Ct. 1232, 51 L. Ed. 2d 424
rehearing denied, 431 U.S. 925, 97 S. Ct. 2200, 53 L. Ed. 2d 240 (1977)

MR. JUSTICE STEWART delivered the opinion of the Court.

An Iowa trial jury found the respondent, Robert Williams, guilty of murder. The judgment of conviction was affirmed in the Iowa Supreme Court by a closely divided vote. In a subsequent habeas corpus proceeding a federal district court ruled that under the United States Constitution Williams is entitled to a new trial, and a divided Court of Appeals for the Eighth Circuit agreed. The question before us is whether the District Court and the Court of Appeals were wrong.

On the afternoon of December 24, 1968, a 10-year-old girl named Pamela Powers went with her family to the YMCA in Des Moines, Iowa, to watch a wrestling tournament in which her brother was participating. When she failed to return from a trip to the washroom, a search for her began. The search was unsuccessful.

Robert Williams, who had recently escaped from a mental hospital, was a resident of the YMCA. Soon after the girl's disappearance Williams was seen in the YMCA lobby carrying some clothing and a large bundle wrapped in a blanket. He obtained help from a 14-year-old boy in opening the street door of the YMCA and the door to his automobile parked outside. When Williams placed the bundle in the front seat of his car the boy "saw two legs in it and they were skinny and white." Before anyone could see what was in the bundle Williams drove away. His abandoned car was found the following day in Davenport, Iowa, roughly 160 miles east of Des Moines. A warrant was then issued in Des Moines for his arrest on a charge of abduction.

On the morning of December 26, a Des Moines lawyer named

Henry McKnight went to the Des Moines police station and informed the officers present that he had just received a long distance call from Williams, and that he had advised Williams to turn himself in to the Davenport police. Williams did surrender that morning to the police in Davenport, and they booked him on the charge specified in the arrest warrant and gave him the warnings required by *Miranda* v. *Arizona,* 384 U. S. 436. . . . The Davenport police then telephoned their counterparts in Des Moines to inform them that Williams had surrendered. McKnight, the lawyer, was still at the Des Moines police headquarters, and Williams conversed with McKnight on the telephone. In the presence of the Des Moines Chief of Police and a Police Detective named Leaming, McKnight advised Williams that Des Moines police officers would be driving to Davenport to pick him up, that the officers would not interrogate him or mistreat him, and that Williams was not to talk to the officers about Pamela Powers until after consulting with McKnight upon his return to Des Moines. As a result of these conversations, it was agreed between McKnight and the Des Moines police officials that Detective Leaming and a fellow officer would drive to Davenport to pick up Williams, that they would bring him directly back to Des Moines, and that they would not question him during the trip.

In the meantime Williams was arraigned before a judge in Davenport on the outstanding arrest warrant. The judge advised him of his *Miranda* rights and committed him to jail. Before leaving the courtroom, Williams conferred with a lawyer named Kelly, who advised him not to make any statements until consulting with McKnight back in Des Moines.

Detective Leaming and his fellow officer arrived in Davenport about noon to pick up Williams and return him to Des Moines. Soon after their arrival they met with Williams and Kelly, who, they understood, was acting as Williams' lawyer. Detective Leaming repeated the *Miranda* warnings, and told Williams:

> ". . . we both know that you're being represented here by Mr. Kelly and you're being represented by Mr. McKnight in Des Moines, and . . . I want you to remember this because we'll be visiting between here and Des Moines."

Williams then conferred again with Kelly alone, and after this conference Kelly reiterated to Detective Leaming that Williams was not to be questioned about the disappearance of Pamela Powers until after he had consulted with McKnight back in Des Moines. When Leaming expressed some reservations, Kelly firmly stated that the agreement with McKnight was to be carried out — that there was to be no interrogation of Williams during the automobile journey to Des Moines. Kelly was denied permission to ride in the police car back to Des Moines with Williams and the two officers.

The two Detectives, with Williams in their charge, then set out on the 160-mile drive. At no time during the trip did Williams express a willingness to be interrogated in the absence of an attorney. Instead, he stated several times that "[w]hen I get to Des Moines and see Mr. McKnight, I am going to tell you the whole story." Detective Leaming knew that Williams was a former mental patient, and knew also that he was deeply religious.

The Detective and his prisoner soon embarked on a wide-ranging conversation covering a variety of topics, including the subject of religion. Then, not long after leaving Davenport and reaching the interstate highway, Detective Leaming delivered what has been referred to in the briefs and oral arguments as the "Christian burial speech." Addressing Williams as "Reverend," the Detective said:

> "I want to give you something to think about while we're traveling down the road. . . . Number one, I want you to observe the weather conditions, it's raining, it's sleeting, it's freezing, driving is very treacherous, visibility is poor, it's going to be dark early this evening. They are predicting several inches of snow for tonight, and I feel that you yourself are the only person that knows where this little girl's body is, that you yourself have only been there once, and if you get a snow on top of it you yourself may be unable to find it. And, since we will be going right past the area on the way into Des Moines, I feel that we could stop and locate the body, that the parents of this little girl should be entitled to a Christian burial for the little girl who was snatched away from them on Christmas Eve and murdered. And I feel we should stop and locate it on the way in rather than waiting until morning and trying to come back out after a snow storm and possibly not being able to find it at all."

Williams asked Detective Leaming why he thought their route to Des Moines would be taking them past the girl's body, and Leaming responded that he knew the body was in the area of Mitchellville — a town they would be passing on the way to Des Moines. Leaming then stated: "I do not want you to answer me. I don't want to discuss it further. Just think about it as we're riding down the road."

As the car approached Grinnell, a town approximately 100 miles west of Davenport, Williams asked whether the police had found the victim's shoes. When Detective Leaming replied that he was unsure, Williams directed the officers to a service station where he said he had left the shoes; a search for them proved unsuccessful. As they continued towards Des Moines, Williams asked whether the police had found the blanket, and directed the officers to a rest area where he said he had disposed of the blanket. Nothing was found. The car continued towards Des Moines, and as it approached Mitchellville,

Williams said that he would show the officers where the body was. He then directed the police to the body of Pamela Powers.

. . . .

[T]here is no need to review in this case the doctrine of *Miranda* v. *Arizona, supra,* a doctrine designed to secure the constitutional privilege against compulsory self-incrmination. It is equally unnecessary to evaluate the ruling of the District Court that Williams' self-incriminating statements were, indeed, involuntarily made. For it is clear that the judgment before us must in any event be affirmed upon the ground that Williams was deprived of a different constitutional right — the right to the assistance of counsel.

. . . .

There can be no doubt in the present case that judicial proceedings had been initiated against Williams before the start of the automobile ride from Davenport to Des Moines. A warrant had been issued for his arrest, he had been arraigned on that warrant before a judge in a Davenport courtroom, and he had been committed by the court to confinement in jail. The State does not contend otherwise.

There can be no serious doubt, either, that Detective Leaming deliberately and designedly set out to elicit information from Williams just as surely as — and perhaps more effectively than — if he had formally interrogated him. Detective Leaming was fully aware before departing for Des Moines that Williams was being represented in Davenport by Kelly and in Des Moines by McKnight. Yet he purposely sought during Williams' isolation from his lawyers to obtain as much incriminating information as possible. . . .

. . . .

The Iowa courts recognized that Williams had been denied the constitutional right to the assistance of counsel. They held, however, that he had waived that right during the course of the automobile trip from Davenport to Des Moines. . . .

. . . .

The District Court and the Court of Appeals were also correct in their understanding of the proper standard to be applied in determining the question of waiver as a matter of federal constitutional law — that it was incumbent upon the State to prove "an intentional relinquishment or abandonment of a known right or privilege." . . .

We conclude, finally that the Court of Appeals was correct in holding that, judged by these standards, the record in this case falls far short of sustaining the State's burden. It is true that Williams had been informed of and appeared to understand his right to counsel.

But waiver requires not merely comprehension but relinquishment, and Williams' consistent reliance upon the advice of counsel in dealing with the authorities refutes any suggestion that he waived that right. . . .

Despite Williams' express and implicit assertions of his right to counsel, Detective Leaming proceeded to elicit incriminating statements from Williams. Leaming did not preface this effort by telling Williams that he had a right to the presence of a lawyer, and made no effort at all to ascertain whether Williams wished to relinquish that right. The circumstances of record in this case thus provide no reasonable basis for finding that Williams waived his right to the assistance of counsel.

The Court of Appeals did not hold, nor do we, that under the circumstances of this case Williams *could not,* without notice to counsel, have waived his rights under the Sixth and Fourteenth Amendments. It only held, as do we, that he did not.

The crime of which Williams was convicted was senseless and brutal, calling for swift and energetic action by the police to apprehend the perpetrator and gather evidence with which he could be convicted. No mission of law enforcement officials is more important. Yet "[d]isinterested zeal for the public good does not assure either wisdom or right in the methods it pursues." *Haley* v. *Ohio,* 332 U. S. 596, 605 (Frankfurter, J., concurring in the judgment). Although we do not lightly affirm the issuance of a writ of habeas corpus in this case, so clear a violation of the Sixth and Fourteenth Amendments as here occurred cannot be condoned. The pressures on state executive and judicial officers charged with the administration of the criminal law are great, especially when the crime is murder and the victim a small child. But it is precisely the predictability of those pressures that makes imperative a resolute loyalty to the guarantees that the Constitution extends to us all.

The judgment of the Court of Appeals is affirmed.

It is so ordered.

Mr. Justice Marshall, concurring.

I concur wholeheartedly in my Brother Stewart's opinion for the Court, but add these words in light of the dissenting opinions filed today. The dissenters have, I believe, lost sight of the fundamental constitutional backbone of our criminal law. They seem to think that Detective Leaming's actions were perfectly proper, indeed laudable, examples of "good police work." In my view, good police work is something far different from catching the criminal at any price. It is equally important that the police, as guardians of the law, fulfill their responsibility to obey its commands scrupulously. For "in the end life and liberty can be as much endangered from illegal methods used to convict those thought to be criminals as from the actual criminals themselves." *Spano* v. *New York,* 360 U. S. 315, 320-321.

. . . If Williams is to go free — and given the ingenuity of Iowa prosecutors on retrial or in a civil commitment proceeding, I doubt very much that there is any chance a dangerous criminal will be loosed on the streets, the blood-curdling cries of the dissents notwithstanding — it will hardly be because he deserves it. It will be because Detective Leaming, knowing full well that he risked reversal of Williams' conviction, intentionally denied Williams the right of *every* American under the Sixth Amendment to have the protective shield of a lawyer between himself and the awesome power of the State.

I think it appropriate here to recall not Justice Cardozo's opinion in the *Defore* case, see opinion of THE CHIEF JUSTICE, but rather the closing words of Justice Brandeis' great dissent in *Olmstead* v. *United States,* 277 U.S. 438, 471, 485 (1928).

> "In a government of laws, existence of the government will be imperilled if it fails to observe the law scrupulously. Our Government is the potent, the omnipresent teacher. For good or for ill, it teaches the whole people by its example. Crime is contagious. If the Government becomes a lawbreaker, it breeds contempt for law; it invites every man to become a law unto himself; it invites anarchy. To declare that in the administration of the criminal law the end justifies the means — to declare that the Government may commit crimes in order to secure the conviction of a private criminal — would bring terrible retribution. Against that pernicious doctrine this Court should resolutely set its face."

MR. JUSTICE POWELL, concurring.

As the dissenting opinion of THE CHIEF JUSTICE sharply illustrates, resolution of the issues in this case turns primarily on one's perception of the facts. . . .

The critical factual issue is whether there had been a voluntary waiver, and this turns in large part upon whether there was interrogation. . . .

I join the opinion of the Court which also finds that the efforts of Detective Leaming "to elicit information from Williams," as conceded by counsel for the State at oral argument, were a skillful and effective form of interrogation. Moreover, the entire setting was conducive to the psychological coercion that was successfully exploited.

In discussing the exclusionary rule, the dissenting opinion of THE CHIEF JUSTICE refers to *Stone* v. *Powell,* 428 U.S. 465 (1976) decided last Term. In that case, we held that a federal court need not apply the exclusionary rule on habeas corpus review of a Fourth Amendment claim absent a showing that the state prisoner was denied an opportunity for a full and fair litigation of that claim at trial and on direct review. The applicability of the rationale of *Stone* in the Fifth and Sixth Amendment context raises a number of unresolved issues. Many Fifth and Sixth Amendment claims arise in the context of challenges to the fairness of a trial or to the integrity of the factfinding process. In contrast, Fourth Amendment claims uniformly involve evidence that is "typically reliable and often the most probative information bearing on the guilt or innocence of the defendant." Whether the rationale of *Stone* should be applied to those Fifth and Sixth Amendment claims or classes of claims that more closely parallel claims under the Fourth Amendment is a question as to which I intimate no view, and which should be resolved only after the implications of such a ruling have been fully explored.

MR. JUSTICE STEVENS, concurring.

. . . .

Underlying the surface issues in this case is the question whether a fugitive from justice can rely on his lawyer's advice given in connection with a decision to surrender voluntarily. . . . If, in the long run, we are seriously concerned about the individual's effective representation by counsel, the State cannot be permitted to dishonor its promise to this lawyer.

MR. CHIEF JUSTICE BURGER, dissenting.

The result in this case ought to be intolerable in any society which purports to call itself an organized society. It continues the Court — by the narrowest margin — on the much-criticized course of punishing the public for the mistakes and misdeeds of law enforcement officers, instead of punishing the officer directly, if in fact he is guilty of wrongdoing. It mechanically and blindly keeps reliable evidence from juries whether the claimed constitutional violation involves gross police misconduct or honest human error.

Williams is guilty of the savage murder of a small child; no member of the Court contends he is not. While in custody, and after no fewer than *five* warnings of his rights to silence and to counsel, he led police to the concealed body of his victim. The Court concedes Williams was not threatened or coerced and that he spoke and acted voluntarily and with full awareness of his constitutional rights. In the face of all this, the Court now holds that because Williams was prompted by the detective's statement — not interrogation but a statement — the jury must not be told how the police found the body.

Today's holding fulfills Justice Cardozo's grim prophecy that someday some court might carry the exclusionary rule to the absurd extent that its operative effect would exclude evidence relating to the body of a murder victim because of the means by which it was found.[1] In so ruling the Court regresses to playing a grisly game of "hide and seek," once more exalting the sporting theory of criminal justice which has been experiencing a decline in our jurisprudence.

. . . .

The Exclusionary Rule Should Not be Applied to Non-egregious Police Conduct

Even if there was no waiver, and assuming a technical violation occurred, the Court errs gravely in mechanically applying the exclusionary rule without considering whether that draconian judicial doctrine should be invoked in these circumstances, or indeed whether any of its conceivable goals will be furthered by its application here.

The obvious flaws of the exclusionary rule as a judicial remedy are familiar. . . .

Accordingly, unlawfully obtained evidence is not automatically excluded from the factfinding process in all circumstances. In a variety of contexts we inquire whether application of the rule will promote its objectives sufficiently to justify the enormous cost it imposes on society. . . .

This is, of course, the familiar balancing process applicable to cases in which important competing interests are at stake. It is a recognition, albeit belated, that "the policies behind the exclusionary rule are not absolute," *Stone* v. *Powell*, 428 U. S. at 465 (1976). . . .

Against this background, it is striking that the Court fails even to consider whether the benefits secured by application of the exclusionary rule in this case outweigh its obvious social costs. Perhaps the failure is due to the fact that this case arises not under the Fourth Amendment, but under *Miranda* v. *Arizona* . . ., and the Sixth Amendment right to counsel. The Court apparently perceives the function of the exclusionary rule to be so different in these varying contexts that it must be mechanically and uncritically applied in all cases arising outside the Fourth Amendment.

But this is demonstrably not the case where police conduct collides with *Miranda*'s procedural safeguards rather than with the Fifth Amendment privilege against compulsory self-incrimination. Involuntary and coerced admissions are suppressed because of the inherent unreliability of a confession wrung from an unwilling suspect by threats, brutality, or other coercion.

---

[1] "The criminal is to go free because the constable has blundered. . . . A room is searched against the law, and the body of a murdered man is found. . . . The privacy of the home has been infringed, and the murderer goes free." *People* v. *Defore,* 242 N.Y. 13, 21, 23-24, 150 N.E. 585, 587, 588 (1926).

But use of Williams' disclosures and their fruits carries no risk whatever of unreliability, for the body was found where he said it would be found. Moreover, since the Court makes no issue of voluntariness, no dangers are posed to individual dignity or free will. *Miranda*'s safeguards are premised on presumed unreliability long associated with confessions extorted by brutality or threats; they are not personal constitutional rights, but are simply judicially created prophylactic measures. . . .

Thus, in cases where incriminating disclosures are voluntarily made without coercion, and hence not violative of the Fifth Amendment, but are obtained in violation of one of the *Miranda* prophylaxis, suppression is no longer automatic. Rather, we weigh the deterrent effect on unlawful police conduct, together with the normative Fifth Amendment justifications for suppression, against "the strong interest under any system of justice of making available to the trier of fact all concededly relevant and trustworthy evidence which either party seeks to adduce. . . . We also 'must consider society's interest in the effective prosecution of criminals. . . .' " *Michigan* v. *Tucker,* 417 U.S., at 450. . . . This individualized consideration or balancing process with respect to the exclusionary sanction is possible in this case, as in others, because Williams' incriminating disclosures are not infected with any element of compulsion the Fifth Amendment forbids; nor, as noted earlier, does this evidence pose any danger of unreliability to the factfinding process. In short, there is no reason to exclude this evidence.

. . . .

. . . In this case, where the evidence of how the child's body was found is of unquestioned reliability, and since the Court accepts Williams' disclosures as voluntary and uncoerced, there is no issue either of fairness or evidentiary reliability to justify suppression of truth. It appears suppression is mandated here for no other reason than the Court's general impression that it may have a beneficial effect on future police conduct; indeed, the Court fails to say even that much in defense of its holding.

Thus, whether considered under *Miranda* or the Sixth Amendment, there is no more reason to exclude the evidence in this case than there was in *Stone* v. *Powell.*

MR. JUSTICE WHITE, with whom MR. JUSTICE BLACKMUN and MR. JUSTICE REHNQUIST join, dissenting.

The respondent in this case killed a 10-year-old child. The majority sets aside his conviction, holding that certain statements of unquestioned reliability were unconstitutionally obtained from him, and under the circumstances probably makes it impossible to retry him. Because there is nothing in the Constitution or in our previous cases which requires the Court's action, I dissent.

. . . .

. . . The majority simply finds that no waiver was *proved* in this case. I disagree. That respondent knew of his right not to say anything to the officers without advice and presence of counsel is established on this record to a moral certainty. He was advised of the right by three officials of the State — telling at least one that he understood the right — and by two lawyers. Finally, he further demonstrated his knowledge of the right by informing the police that he would tell them the story in the presence of McKnight when they arrived in Des Moines. The issue in this case, then, is whether respondent relinquished that right intentionally.

. . . .

The majority's contrary conclusion seems to rest on the fact that respondent "asserted" his right to counsel by retaining and consulting with one lawyer and by consulting with another. How this supports the conclusion that respondent's later relinquishment of his right not to talk in the absence of counsel was unintentional is a mystery. The fact that respondent consulted with counsel on the question whether he should talk to the police in counsel's absence makes his later decision to talk in counsel's absence *better* informed and, if anything, more intelligent.

. . . .

. . . The police did nothing "wrong," let alone anything "unconstitutional." To anyone not lost in the intricacies of the prophylactic rules of *Miranda* v. *Arizona, supra,* the result in this case seems utterly senseless; and . . . the statements made by respondent were properly admitted. In light of these considerations, the majority's protest that the result in this case is justified by a "clear violation" of the Sixth and Fourteenth Amendments has a distressing hollow ring. I respectfully dissent.

MR. JUSTICE BLACKMUN, with whom MR. JUSTICE WHITE and MR. JUSTICE REHNQUIST join, dissenting.

The State of Iowa, and 21 States and others, as *amici curiae,* strongly urge that this Court's procedural (as distinguished from constitutional) ruling in *Miranda* v. *Arizona,* 384 U.S. 436 (1966), be re-examined and overruled. I, however, agree with the Court that this is not now the case in which that issue need be considered.

. . . .

First, the police did not deliberately seek to isolate Williams from his lawyers so as to deprive him of the assistance of counsel. . . .

Second, Leaming's purpose was not solely to obtain incriminating evidence. . . .

Third, not every attempt to elicit information should be regarded as "tantamount to interrogation," ... I am not persuaded that Leaming's observations and comments, made as the police car traversed the snowy and slippery miles between Davenport and Des Moines that winter afternoon, were an interrogation, direct or subtle, of Williams. . . .

... When there is no interrogation, such statements should be admissible as long as they are truly voluntary.

. . . .

... This was a brutal, tragic, and heinous crime inflicted upon a young girl on the afternoon of the day before Christmas. With the exclusionary rule operating as the Court effectuates it, the decision today probably means that, as a practical matter, no new trial will be possible at this date eight years after the crime, and that this respondent necessarily will go free. That, of course, is not the standard by which a case of this kind strictly is to be judged. But, as Judge Webster in dissent below observed, 509 F.2d, at 237, placing the case in sensible and proper perspective: "The evidence of Williams' guilt was overwhelming. No challenge is made to the reliability of the fact-finding process." I am in full agreement with that observation.

NOTES AND QUESTIONS

1. Prior to *Mapp* v. *Ohio*, 367 U.S. 643 (1961), state courts were free to admit evidence obtained by illegal searches and seizures. At the same time, however, use by a State court of a "coerced" confession to obtain a criminal conviction was a violation of the Due Process Clause of the Fourteenth Amendment. At the outset, the dichotomy was easily explained. The earliest cases concerned confessions obtained by physical brutality or such extreme psychological pressure that the confessions were of dubious reliability. The first case, *Brown* v. *Mississippi*, 297 U.S. 278 (1936), involved aggravated torture. Later cases recognized that prolonged questioning, incommunicado detention, and psychological pressure could have all the characteristics of torture. *Chambers* v. *Florida*, 309 U.S. 227 (1940). Thus, the confession cases were cases where the confessions admitted into evidence were of doubtful veracity, and effectively denied the accused a fair trial in open court. On the other hand, illegally seized physical evidence *was* reliable, and its admission into evidence did not compromise the fact-finding process of the trial.

2. The tension between the two rules — one for confessions and another for tangible evidence — began as later confession cases focused less on potentially unreliable confessions, and more on the

police methods used to produce confessions. As the Court stated in *Rogers* v. *Richmond,* 365 U.S. 534, 541-42 (1961), involuntary confessions were excluded:

> not because such confessions are unlikely to be true but because the methods used to extract them offend an underlying principle in the enforcement of our criminal law: that ours is an accusatorial ... system — a system in which the State must establish guilt by evidence independently and freely secured and may not by coercion prove its charge against an accused out of his own mouth.

Thus, if the State was required to exclude reliable confessions because the evidence was obtained in violation of the Constitution, why was the State not required to exclude tangible evidence obtained in violation of the Constitution? Finally, with the *Mapp* decision in 1961, the tension between the confession and physical evidence cases was relieved.

3. A new anomaly soon appeared, however, in the separate rules for confessions and physical evidence. All tangible physical evidence obtained by unconstitutional police methods was excluded under the *Mapp* rule. Not all confessions were excluded if they were produced by police questioning during incommunicado, and often illegal, detention. The confession was excluded only if it was "involuntary." Critics argued that basing the admissibility of confession on a case-by-case determination of whether the particular confession was voluntary had two defects: the entire process of incommunicado detention and questioning was coercive, and violated the "underlying principle" announced in *Rogers* v. *Richmond;* case-by-case decision did not produce sufficient guidance as to the forms of police interrogation which were lawful and the forms which violated the Constitution. Thus, it was argued, a more prophylactic rule was necessary in determining the admissibility of confessions obtained by pretrial police interrogation.

4. One potential prophylactic rule was the so-called *McNabb-Mallory* rule, announced in *McNabb* v. *United States,* 318 U.S. 332 (1943) and reaffirmed in *Mallory* v. *United States,* 354 U.S. 449 (1957). The rule was a non-constitutional rule, and required by the Supreme Court only in federal criminal trials. (Indeed, the rule was repealed by a federal statute. 18 U.S.C. § 3501 (c) [1970].) The rule required the exclusion of all confessions obtained during periods of unlawful detention. The *McNabb-Mallory* rule, however, did not prove to be the source of the new rule for state criminal trials, which focused instead on the Sixth Amendment guarantee of right to counsel and the Fifth Amendment's privilege against self-incrimination.

5. *Escobedo* v. *Illinois,* 378 U.S. 478 (1964) involved questioning of a suspect while his retained counsel was repeatedly, and unlawfully, denied permission to speak to his client. The Court's 5-4 majority required exclusion of the confession because Escobedo had been denied his Sixth Amendment right to consult with his lawyer. Two years later, the Court faced the much more common situation of the unrepresented criminal suspect subjected to questioning by the police. The famous decision in *Miranda* v. *Arizona,* 384 U.S. 436 (1966) imposes two requirements: first, an elaborate set of warnings by the police that the accused has a right to consult with an attorney and a right to remain silent; second, a requirement that, once the accused indicates he wishes to remain silent, "interrogation must cease."

6. It has been questioned whether the *Miranda* warnings have had more than a formal impact on previous police interrogation techniques. *See* Ch. 10, § A.2.b., n. 2, *supra.* Where, however, the accused manifests his desire to remain silent, the *Miranda* requirement that interrogation cease, can be a significant limitation on police interrogation.

7. Prior to its decision, the *Brewer* case was thought to involve possible reconsideration of *Miranda*'s second rule. The *Miranda* case, itself, was decided by a vote of 5-4, and several members of the Court that decided *Brewer* were known to be out of sympathy with the *Miranda* decision. The State, in *Brewer,* specifically argued that the *Miranda* rule should be substantially modified or abolished altogether. How was it possible for the Court's majority to affirm the exclusion of Williams' confession without reaffirming the *Miranda* rule itself ? Should it have made a difference if Williams had not been represented by counsel, but had indicated that he did not want to answer police questions?

8. Criticisms of the exclusionary rule have often combined two different elements — criticism of exclusion of reliable evidence, and criticism of the restriction on police conduct which the rule enforces. Are the dissents arguing that the primary reason that Williams' confession should be admitted is that the police behavior was appropriate and not in violation of the Constitution? Or is the primary concern that, even if the police conduct was unlawful, exclusion of a reliable, corroborated confession is too high a price to pay?

9. If the Court were to abandon the *Escobedo* and *Miranda* rules, and return to the prior law that only an involuntary confession must be excluded from evidence, what would be the result in the *Brewer* case? If the confession was truly involuntary, should it nevertheless be admitted into evidence if it is reliable, and a person guilty of a serious crime is likely to go free because of the unavailability of other evidence? Would it be appropriate to apply a rule of proportionality to admit some confessions obtained by physical torture, or by constant questioning during a week of illegal detention in-communicado?

10. If the police in *Brewer* v. *Williams* are not allowed to testify as to the *manner* in which they found the victim's body, may they nevertheless testify that the body was found? *See* § B.2. which follows.

2. Fruit of the Poisonous Tree

a. *United States*

SILVERTHORNE LUMBER CO. v. UNITED STATES
Supreme Court of the United States
251 U.S. 385, 40 S. Ct. 182, 64 L. Ed. 319 (1920)

MR. JUSTICE HOLMES delivered the opinion of the Court.

This is a writ of error brought to reverse a judgment of the District Court fining the Silverthorne Lumber Company two hundred and fifty dollars for contempt of court and ordering Frederick W. Silverthorne to be imprisoned until he should purge himself of a similar contempt. The contempt in question was a refusal to obey subpoenas and an order of Court to produce books and documents of the company before the grand jury to be used in regard to alleged violation of the statutes of the United States by the said Silverthorne and his father. One ground of the refusal was that the order of the Court infringed the rights of the parties under the Fourth Amendment of the Constitution of the United States.

The facts are simple. An indictment upon a single specific charge having been brought against the two Silverthornes mentioned, they both were arrested at their homes early in the morning of February 25, and were detained in custody a number of hours. While they were thus detained representatives of the Department of Justice and the United States marshal without a shadow of authority went to the office of their company and made a clean sweep of all the books, papers and documents found there. All the employés [*sic*] were taken or directed to go to the office of the District Attorney of the United States to which also the books, &c., were taken at once. An application was made as soon as might be to the District Court for a return of what thus had been taken unlawfully. It was opposed by the District Attorney so far as he had found evidence against the plaintiffs in error, and it was stated that the evidence so obtained was before the grand jury.

. . . Photographs and copies of material papers were made and a new indictment was framed based upon the knowledge thus obtained. The District Court ordered a return of the originals but impounded the photographs and copies. Subpoenas to produce the originals then were served and on the refusal of the plaintiffs in error to produce them the Court made an order that the subpoenas should be complied with, although it had found that all the papers had been seized in violation of the parties' constitutional rights. The refusal to obey this order is the contempt alleged. The Government now, while in form repudiating and condemning the illegal seizure, seeks to maintain its right to avail itself of the knowledge obtained by that means which otherwise it would not have had.

The proposition could not be presented more nakedly. It is that although of course its seizure was an outrage which the Government now regrets, it may study the papers before it returns them, copy them, and then may use the knowldge that it has gained to call upon the owners in a more regular form to produce them; that the protection of the Constitution covers the physical possession but not any advantages that the Government can gain over the object of its pursuit by doing the forbidden act. *Weeks* v. *United States,* 232 U.S. 383, to be sure, had established that laying the papers directly before the grand jury was unwarranted, but it is taken to mean only that two steps are required instead of one. In our opinion such is not the law. It reduces the Fourth Amendment to a form of words. The essence of a provision forbidding the acquisition of evidence in a certain way is that not merely evidence so acquired shall not be used before the Court but that it shall not be used at all. Of course this does not mean that the facts thus obtained become sacred and inaccessible. If knowledge of them is gained from an independent source they may be proved like any others, but the knowledge gained by the Government's own wrong cannot be used by it in the way proposed. . . .

NOTES

1. *Nardone* v. *United States,* 308 U.S. 338 (1939), was decided long before the Court held that electronic eavesdropping was within the purview of the Fourth Amendment. In the previous case of *Nardone* v. *United States,* 302 U.S. 379 (1937), the Court had decided that federal courts must exclude wiretap evidence under the Federal Communications Act of 1934. In the 1939 *Nardone* case, the Court extended the doctrine of the *Silverthorne Lumber* case to evidence excluded under the Communications Act. Moreover, in stating that the accused must be given the opportunity to prove that the case against him was "a fruit of the poisonous tree," Justice Frankfurter's opinion for the Court coined the phrase that has indelibly marked this area of the law.

2. The fruit of the poisonous tree doctrine has been applied in a wide variety of contexts. In *Wong Sun* v. *United States,* 371 U.S. 471 (1963), incriminating statements by the accused which "derived immediately" from an unlawful entry and search were excluded. In *Harrison* v. *United States,* 392 U.S. 219 (1968), a coerced confession had been improperly introduced at the defendant's prior criminal trial. This also required, at a later trial, that defendant's damaging admissions from the witness stand at the prior trial be excluded since he would not have taken the stand except to try to contradict the inadmissible confession. *Davis* v. *Mississippi,* 394 U.S. 721 (1969), required exclusion of the defendant's fingerprints which were obtained through his unlawful detention. *United States* v. *Wade,* 388 U.S. 218 (1967) required exclusion of a witness' testimony identifying the accused in open court if that identification was "tainted" by the witness first identifying the accused in an illegal, suggestive lineup.

3. More recent cases have been concerned with setting limits to the outer edges of the fruit of the poisonous tree doctrine. *Michigan* v. *Tucker,* 417 U.S. 433 (1974) involved a confession inadmissible under the *Miranda* rule, although the interrogation took place prior to the time the *Miranda* case was decided. The Court decided that other evidence which was the "fruit" of the inadmissible confession could be used in evidence, since the police acted in "complete good faith." Significantly, the Court reserved the question whether the "poisonous tree" doctrine would be extended, in any case, to fruits of confessions obtained in violation of the *Miranda* rule. In *United States* v. *Calandra,* 414 U.S. 338 (1971), the Court decided that grand jury witnesses could be required to answer questions, even if the questions were based on evidence obtained by an illegal search and seizure.

4. Whatever its limits, the fruit of the poisonous tree doctrine has been a characteristic of American law for over half a century. As the following case shows, however, the applicability of the doctrine is still being examined in Continental Europe.

b. Italy

PALAZZOLI

Tribunale of Rome, Decision of April 28, 1969
[1969] Giustizia Penale III 631

[FACTS: Palazzoli was tried for exploiting and inducing Livia Di Siena into prostitution. The Public Prosecutor, at the request of the police, had given a decree authorizing the monitoring of Ms. Di Siena's telephone, and the conversations had been recorded. After she was confronted with the recorded conversations, she admitted them and confirmed the contents of the transcripts.

[At the outset of the trial, the counsel for the accused brought exception, asserting the nullity of the decree under which the Public Prosecutor authorized the telephone wiretap.

[The initial decree authorizing the wiretap stated simply that the Public Prosecutor "finds it necessary for reasons of criminal justice" to monitor the telephone, and authorized the monitoring for fifteen days. Two additional decrees, extending the monitoring for fifteen days each, simply contained the statement: "authorized."]

OPINION

[The *Tribunale* found the exception well grounded, and declared that the decree authorizing the monitoring was a nullity. Under art. 339 of the Code of Criminal Procedure, the Public Prosecutor acts as a judicial officer in entering a decree authorizing the police to monitor telephones, and must provide a "well grounded decree." In addition, art. 111 of the Constitution requires that in all judicial decisions, grounds (*motivazione*) must be stated. The *Tribunale* concluded that the stated grounds in the decree were inadequate, and thus required that transcripts of the telephone calls be removed from the transcript of the proceeding.]

The statement of the grounds which have determined the emanation of a judicial decision . . . must be made by the same person who pronounces the decision. The argument of the prosecution that the "authorizations" of the *Procuratore della Repubblica* (Public Prosecutor), made at the bottom of the requests of the police, could be considered grounded *per relationem,* that is through the fiction that the reasons presented by the police for the monitoring are therein included, is without basis.

The tendency to approve the requests of the police without due consideration is obviously dangerous. Such action risks nullifying the constitutional guarantee of giving the grounds and reasons of the decrees which authorize telephone monitoring. . . . The result would be inordinately great power vested in the police organs.

This Court must, moreover, underline that in the instant case we are dealing not with a single decree of the Public Prosecutor, but with three distinct decrees which prolonged the period of the telephonic monitoring, each of which required a new, autonomous, and independent evaluation of the circumstances which would induce the sacrifice of the freedom of individual communication to the defense of the community. . . .

Finally, we must add that this Court cannot be concerned with the alternatives of "saving the case" ["salvare il processo" — i.e., the evidentiary results of the proceeding], as is said in legal jargon, or of censuring the clear defects of the decrees authorizing the monitoring, for the simple reason that before the law the judge has no other alternative than to observe it faithfully and fully. The judge is the servant of the law.

In this particular case, however, since the magistrate diligently interrogated Miss Di Siena and Mr. Palazzoli about the content of the salient telephone conversations which they then verified, it follows that the evidence, thus independently gathered in a proper procedural fashion, though the same as the illegally intercepted communications, is fully valid. . . .

NOTES AND QUESTIONS

1. Would *Palazzoli* be decided the same way by a court in the United States? Note, first, that the requirement for *motivazione* for the decree is consistent with the requirement in the United States that the police affidavits which furnish the basis for a magistrate's issuance of the search warrant contain the facts which establish probable cause to issue the warrant. *Spinelli* v. *United States,* 393 U.S. 410 (1969). There is no constitutional requirement that the warrant re-recite those facts, however. Is a requirement that the Public Prosecutor's decree recite the *motivazione* for his decision formalism, or does it make it more likely that "due consideration" will be given before police requests for telephone monitoring are approved? On the other hand, in the United States, a search warrant must be issued by a judicial officer and, under the Constitution, a search warrant issued by the district attorney would be a nullity. *Coolidge* v. *New Hampshire,* 403 U.S. 443 (1971). How do you explain the Italian law, which treats the Public Prosecutor's decree as a judicial order?

2. In the United States, no matter how unlawful the telephone monitoring, Palazzoli would not be permitted to challenge admission of the evidence against him unless he had "standing" to do so. Generally, this means that the defendant cannot challenge unlawful police conduct, even if it produces evidence against him, if the conduct invaded only the rights of third parties. Thus, if Palazzoli was not a party to the intercepted telephone messages and did not own the telephone or the premises on which it was located, he would lack standing to object to admission of the telephone conversations. *Alderman* v. *United States,* 394 U.S. 165 (1969).

3. In the United States, fine points of causation can be involved in applying the fruit of the poisonous tree doctrine. Assuming that the telephone interception was unlawful, and that the defendant had standing to challenge it, would the prosecution be permitted to introduce the telephone messages by having a participant confirm that the transcript of them was accurate? Would the prosecution be permitted to ask Livia Di Siena questions about her activities if particular questions were prompted by the contents of the intercepted messages? Would the prosecution be forbidden to use Livia Di Siena as a witness at all, if her identity was discovered only

because the telephone was tapped? Would the prosecution be forbidden to prosecute Palazzoli at all, if the crime for which he was charged was first brought to the prosecution's attention by the intercepted messages? Does the Italian court implicitly reject the fruit of the poisonous tree doctrine because of these difficulties, or is its opinion simply an example of formalism in reasoning?

4. Even if one rejects the fruit of the poisonous tree doctrine, are some of its ramifications inevitable in applying the exclusionary rule? If there is a rule excluding unlawfully obtained evidence, can the police be allowed to introduce copies of unlawfully seized documents? Can they be allowed to testify as to the identity and nature of illegally seized objects if the objects themselves cannot be introduced in evidence? With particular reference to the *Palazzoli* case, can the prosecutor be allowed to introduce the transcript of unlawfully recorded telephone messages if a participant verifies their accuracy?

Consider the law of Germany. In 1968, the Federal Supreme Court decided, in two cases, that evidence obtained as a result of impermissible questioning of the accused can be admitted into evidence. H. Jeschek, *Principles of German Criminal Procedure in Comparison with American Law,* 56 VA. L. REV. 239, 246 (1970). Compare, however, the final sentences of the Decision of the *Bundesgerichtshof* of February 21, 1964, which appears *supra,* § B.1.b. (The court stated that the diaries were inadmissible in evidence, and that their contents could not be "used in other ways, such as through examination of individuals who have knowledge of their content.") Is this decision inconsistent with later rejection by the Federal Supreme Court of the doctrine of the fruit of the poisonous tree?

C. CIVIL CASES

1. Italy

VIGO v. FORMENTI

Corte di Appello of Milan, Decision of April 5, 1934
[1935] 12 RIVISTA DI DIRITTO PROCESSUALE CIVILE II 63

FACTS

On the night of the 7th of May 1932, Mario Formenti, resident on his own farm, Pezzolo dei Codazzi in the territory of Pieve Fissiraga, died in a Milan convalescent hospital where he had been taken following surgery.

He was unmarried and had no natural children, brothers, sisters, or living forebears.

On the morning of May 8, 1932, his cousin and friend, Guglielmo Vigo, believing himself to be the testamentary heir, went, without notifying the legal heirs, to the domicile of the deceased. He was accompanied by his nephews *Avvocato* Emilio and Dr. Alessandro Acerbi, and by a notary of Lodi, Bernardo Stabilini. Together they searched the house, looking for the will of the deceased. They opened the furnishings, went through drawers and made a thorough examination of the premises, including at one point the forcible opening of a locked cabinet. They did not, however, find the will. Instead they found money, bank books, account books, receipts, and various documents, among which were two notes in the handwriting of the deceased on cards bearing the words: "Mario Formenti — Pieve Fissiraga — Lodi."

The first read as follows: "Pezzolo dei Codazzi, December 30, 1929. I, the undersigned Mario Formenti, acknowledge indebtedness to my cousin, Guglielmo Vigo, in the amount of £.255,000 (two hundred fifty five thousand lire), which debt is secured by my property of Pezzolo.

"These sums were delivered to me in order to complete the purchase of Pezzolo, in which he is to participate in ownership. The dates when the sums were received are as follows. . . .

"Therefore, Guglielmo Vigo has a claim on my property of Pezzolo in the amount of £.255,000 (two hundred fifty five thousand lire). In witness of the above — Mario Formenti."

The second: "Pezzolo dei Codazzi, January 18, 1930.

"Dear Guglielmo, I the undersigned declare to have received from you on a number of occasions Italian lire in an amount totaling 270,000 (two hundred seventy thousand) to complete payment in the purchase of the farmstead of Pezzolo dei Codazzi located in the municipality of Pieve Fissiraga, and specifically. . . .

"As a result of this money, amounting to £.270,000 I have received, you have acquired part ownership in the Pezzolo property. In witness of the above — Mario Formenti."

These two notes and the bank books were placed in the possession of the notary Stabilini. The other documents were placed in a bag and retained by Vigo, who kept 3,312 lire found in the house and, also, the key, in order to continue his search. . . . The notary Stabilini also drew 6,000 lire from a savings account of the deceased and gave the money to Vigo to take care of funeral expenses.

. . . .

But at the end of May 1932, Mrs. Marcellina Formenti, maternal aunt of the deceased, having learned that no will existed, requested of the *Pretore* of Lodi that she be authorized, as a presumed heir, to inventory the hereditaments in accordance with the Code of Civil Procedure. The *Pretore,* on May 28, 1932, granted the authorization, designating the notary Guido Cassina of Milan to make the inventory. The inventory was begun on June 2, 1932. . . .

. . . .

Mrs. Formenti filed a formal complaint with the Public Prosecutor and a criminal proceeding was initiated against Vigo. The Public Prosecutor dismissed the charge on January 10, 1933, asserting that Vigo had acted with the conviction that he was the testamentary heir, and in the scope of searching for the will and caring for the hereditaments and documents pertaining to the inheritance he had acted in good faith.

. . . .

On July 9, 1932, Vigo brought a civil action before the *Tribunale* of Milan against Marcellina Formenti and Giuseppe, Carlotta and Anna De Paoli [who, in the meantime, had asserted rights of descent and distribution]. He alleged that the sum of 270,000 lire which he loaned to Mario Formenti was used to complete payment on the farmstead Pezzolo dei Codazzi, that Formenti had acknowledged his indebtedness in that amount, and that as a result of the acknowledged indebtedness there existed in Vigo the right of co-ownership of the farmstead. Vigo continued that, despite this, the defendants, as the legal heirs of Formenti, have refused either to recognize this co-ownership of the farmstead or to pay him the sum stated. The complaint asked that Vigo be declared co-owner of the farmstead Pezzolo dei Codazzi to the extent of £.270,000 or alternatively that the defendant be required to pay such sum with interest. . . .

Mrs. Formenti asked principally that the notary Stabilini and Vigo be ordered to deposit, with the clerk of the *Tribunale,* the originals of the notes of December 30, 1929, and January 18, 1930. . . .

With a decision of March 9, 1933, the *Tribunale* held for the defendants, ordering Vigo to pay costs.

Opinion

. . . This Court rejects Vigo's appeal. Mr. Vigo bases his claim on the loan agreements which he argues were concluded with Mario Formenti in November 1928 and December 1929. Certainly he must provide proof of such agreements. These however, cannot be proved by the documents in question, nor can they be ascertained through the means proposed by the plaintiff.

Vigo cannot use as evidence the two notes of December 30, 1929, and January 18, 1930. These notes were taken from the papers of the deceased Mario Formenti which belonged to the legal heirs. Thus we must conclude that these notes were illegally obtained. . . .

Although the Public Prosecutor dismissed the criminal charge against Vigo because the accused lacked the necessary element of criminal intent . . ., it does not necessarily follow that the appellant acted in accordance with the Civil Code.

Since there were legal heirs residing in a different place from that where the deceased resided, Vigo, as possibly having the right of succession, should have requested that the property be sealed, which is the only legal guarantee for the absent heirs. The notary Stabilini should have apprised him of the proper course of action, rather than joining him in the ransacking of the deceased's home.

Even overlooking the illegal search for the will and the failure to notify the legal heirs, there was no justification whatsoever for the appellant to take the papers and goods of the deceased into his personal possession and to represent himself as the testamentary heir.

In this manner the appellant deprived the legal heirs, to whom the right of possession passed without need of a physical taking of possession of the property of the deceased.

Therefore he cannot base his claim on the notes in question. Our law does not allow a party to force his opponent to produce documents which could serve as proof of the former's claims, unless the party in need of the documents is owner or co-owner of such documents. Acceptance of the two notes in evidence would allow a party to achieve in an illegal fashion that which he could not accomplish through licit activity.

In support of his claim Vigo cited some decisions . . . which held that correspondence between a wife and her correspondent intercepted by the husband in violation of the privacy of the mails, can constitute evidence of the wife's infidelity in a civil proceeding for separation. The husband, as head of the family, has a power of surveillance over his wife and has, moreover, the specific right to her fidelity, such right being protected by civil and criminal sanctions.

The husband cannot be denied the right to open and read his wife's correspondence if the purpose is to prevent improper behavior. Thus, such letters from or directed to the wife which prove her infidelity are admissible as evidence in a legal proceeding.

Though it is good that the husband, for the sake of discretion, respect the privacy of the mail belonging to his wife, this does not prevent him from legally intercepting her mail and using it as evidence where he has reasonable cause for suspicion.

Similarly, a parent cannot be denied the right to intercept correspondence of minor children and of using it in a legal proceeding in their interest. In such case the right is included in the exercise of parental control.

But none of this has anything to do with the illegal appropriation of notes belonging to another in order to use them as evidence to show the owner's indebtedness. There was no legal relationship between Vigo and Formenti which entitled him to possession of the documents in question.

In one of the decisions cited by Vigo, which contains the maxim *nomo ex delicto meliorem suam condicionem facere potest* (no one can profit by his own wrong), the Court observed that this maxim was to be rigorously observed in matters of obligation, though making an exception in the case of adultery.... Thus, according to the cases cited by Vigo himself, as well as according to unanimous doctrine, the maxim does not admit of exception in matters of obligation.

Concluding this part of its decision, this Court confirms that Vigo may not use as evidence the two notes in question....

QUESTIONS

Note the date of the *Vigo* case carefully. Does *Vigo* adopt an exclusionary rule for illegally seized evidence in civil cases decades before Italian courts, operating under a democratic constitution, adopted an exclusionary rule for criminal cases? Or, is the *Vigo* case simply an accidental combination of two formalistic procedural notions — a limited concept of discovery of the opponent's evidence, coupled with conceptions of property which are not surprising in a fascist state?

L. v. C.

Corte di Appello of Milan, Decision of July 9, 1971
[1972] 27 Foro Padano I, 193

[FACTS: In a separation action a husband (appellee) introduced a recording of his wife's phone call as evidence of adultery. This evidence was corroborated by the behavior of his wife (appellant) in the shop of the tradesman who supplied the recorder and by some witnesses. The *Tribunale* found the evidence insufficient to prove adultery but adequate to constitute an *injuria gravis* ("grave injury") to her husband. Appellant argues that the admission of this evidence violated her right to secrecy of private communications as established in art. 15 of the Italian Constitution and art. 616 of the Criminal Code.]

OPINION

The first problem [on which the Court must rule] concerns the use of the so-called "illegally obtained evidence." In criminal proceedings, the question has been resolved by Constitutional Court, Decision of December 2, 1970, No. 175 . . ., which determined that evidence illegally obtained cannot be used in a criminal proceeding. In civil proceedings, divergent scholarly opinion ought to be now settled that such evidence cannot be admitted, as stated by the Court of Cassation in its judgment of Feb. 8, 1935.

This solution conforms to arts. 13-15 of the Constitution, which guarantee the civil rights of citizens, including secrecy of correspondence and of any other form of communication.

Thus, it must be held that the admission of evidence obtained in violation of those rights is contrary to the Constitution. The decision of the judge to admit such evidence would therefore ratify an illegal act.

[The second problem is that] of the illegality of wiretapping by the husband of phone calls directed to his wife.

The *Tribunale* [found the wiretap] legitimate, since "the plaintiff did nothing illegal or contrary to the principles of the Constitution, because the recording device had been installed upon his request not on somebody else's telephone, but on his telephone, in his house, as he certainly had a right to do, though using the work of third persons."

This court does not fully agree with this reasoning. Article 15 of the Italian Constitution states that freedom and secrecy of correspondence and of any other form of communication are inviolable. Freedom and secrecy are therefore guaranteed to every person as against all others. Only the judge (see art. 226 of the Code of Criminal Procedure) can authorize a wiretap, and must state his reasons in issuing the relevant decree. Furthermore, [even] before the enactment of the Constitution, art. 616 of the [current] Criminal Code punished those who listen to phone calls not directed to them, and art. 617 punished "whoever" either listened to a phone call by fraudulent means, or had interrupted or prevented such a call.

Thus, the criminal law protects the secrecy of phone calls as against everyone, including the holder of the contract with the telephone company ["owner" of the phone]. ["Ownership"], therefore, does not give the right to listen in on phone calls either directed to or made by those who have been allowed to use the telephone.

In fact, it is also clear that [even relatives] are entitled to the secrecy of their phone calls.

The secrecy of phone calls receives a further protection within the wider "right to privacy." This Court has several times affirmed that certain rights recognized by specific statutory provisions are only particular expressions of that wider right. Among these rights are, for instance, the right to secrecy of phone calls (arts. 616-617, Crim. Code) and correspondence (arts. 616-620, Crim. Code); the use of one's name (art. 6, Civ. Code); the use of one's picture (art. 10, Civ. Code, integrated [into arts. 96-97 of the law of] copyright); copyright (art. 20, same law) and other rights protected by arts. 93-96 of the same law (the right to prevent the publication of personal and family memoirs, as well as of letters, without the consent of the author, or his heirs, and addressee); and the right of professionals to protect their client confidences (arts. 616-22, Crim. Code).

The "right to privacy," which protects the most intimate human sphere and which is one of the fundamental rights of man, has been explicitly recognized by the Law of 4 August 1955, No. 848, which ratified the European Convention for the Protection of Human Rights and Fundamental Freedoms, approved by the Council of Europe and signed in Rome on November 4, 1950.

Article 8 of the Convention states that "everyone has the right to respect for his private and family life, his home and his correspondence."

This provision ... therefore expressly recognizes the right to privacy. . . .

It is necessary, however, to mention that the right to privacy is not limitless. The Convention itself provides, in art. 8, para. 1, that it can be limited whenever it is necessary.

This provision legitimates, from the point of view of international law, the statutes restricting the right to privacy which have been or may be enacted by the member states in conformity with art. 8 of the Convention.

In this regard, art. 226 of the Code of Criminal Procedure has already been mentioned. It is intended to prevent crime and to protect basic rights and freedoms, and provides that judges can authorize police wiretaps. Article 51 of the Criminal Code likewise does not contravene the European Convention, though it can indirectly limit the right to secrecy of phone calls. Article 51 prevents punishment for crimes which are committed in order to exercise a right or to perform a duty imposed either by a legal norm or by a legitimate order of the public authority.

[Article 51] is also justified by art. 8, para. 1 of the Convention, whenever [it can be applied for such reasons as] the prevention of crime, the protection of morals, of rights and freedoms, i.e., those exigencies which most closely are involved in the present case.

That being stated, the spouse who wiretaps the other spouse's phone calls exercises some of the rights inherent in his *status* [as spouse] and therefore does not violate the rights and freedoms protected by art. 8 of the Convention. In particular no violation will be committed by the husband who, as the head of the family, watches, whenever it is necessary, over the moral conduct of his wife, either directly, or through third persons (e.g., private detectives), by monitoring her phone calls.

The sacrifice of the wife's "right to privacy" is justified here by the protection of rights recognized by the Convention as prevailing over that right. Indeed, the right to the spouse's faithfulness (art. 143, Civ. Code), the right to ask for the judicial separation for fault of the unfaithful spouse (Civ. Code arts. 150 & 141), the protection of the unity of the family, which is protected also by art. 29 of the Constitution — all belong to the "rights and freedoms" recognized by art. 8, para. 1 of the Convention; and their defense is also justified by the exigency of "protection of morals" mentioned in the same paragraph.

Since wiretapping is performed by husbands in the exercise of a right, which also entails duties and responsibilities, it is not punishable as a crime. Articles 616-617 of the Criminal Code do not apply because their operation in this case is stayed by the applicability of art. 51.

It remains to examine the problem of a possible conflict between the mentioned provisions and the Constitution.

Article 15 of the Constitution establishes that the freedom and secrecy of correspondence and of any other communication are inviolable. Article 29, however, after recognizing that "marriage is founded on the moral and legal equality of the spouses," adds that this foundation is subject to "the limits established by the law in order to guarantee the unity of the family."

Given the reference to these "limits," we cannot consider art. 144 Civil Code in conflict with the Constitution, when it attributes to the husband the quality of "head of the family" and the "potestà maritale" over the wife. It is also incontrovertible that the right/duty to mutual faithfulness (art. 143 Civ. Code) is fully compatible with the principle of moral and legal equality. In particular, the exemption clause provided for by art. 51 of the Criminal Code does not conflict with art. 15 of the Constitution, since it is implicitly legitimated by art. 29. The spouse violates the secrecy of the other spouse's phone calls in order to protect a right of his, recognized both by the Constitution and the Civil Code.

That in the case at hand, the husband has acted to protect that right, cannot be seriously contested.

The wife's behavior ... was such as to justify well-founded suspicions of her faithfulness, which were confirmed by the wiretapping, witnesses, and by the extra-judicial behavior of the party herself.

NOTES AND QUESTIONS

1. Contrast the rationale of the Court of Appeals of Milan in the principal case with that given thirty-seven years earlier by the same tribunal in the *Vigo* case. Note, particularly, the husband's rejected argument that his "ownership" of the telephone was a sufficient reason to monitor all calls on the instrument. Is the court's rationale for holding the particular wiretap lawful any more enlightened than

dicta in the *Vigo* case discussing the same issue? Is it an example of the doctrine of proportionality?

2. Note, finally, that both the *Vigo* case and the principal case involve not only civil litigation, but, more significantly, evidence obtained by private parties. Would the court's rationale for exclusion of the evidence in the principal case be applicable to the United States Constitution? (*See* § C.3., *infra.*)

2. Germany

DECISION OF MAY 20, 1958

Bundesgerichtshof (Civil Chamber)
[1958] NEUE JURISTISCHE WOCHENSCHRIFT 1344

OPINION*

The appellate court justly sustained a decision that the defendant through his secret tape recording of his conversation with the plaintiff had interfered in the plaintiff's right to the free development of his personality. The provisions of arts. 1 and 2 of the Basic Law, in which the inviolability of human dignity and the right of everyone to the free development of his personality are recognized as basic values of our legal order, bind not only the State and its organs but must also be applied in private legal relations. . . .

2. The legal protection accorded by the general right of personality attributes to the individual in his internal personal sphere the freedom and self-determination necessary for the development of his personality. To this also appertains the faculty of the individual to decide himself if his words are to be destined for the person with whom he is speaking, for a particular group, or for the public; in particular, if his words may be preserved by means of a recording device.

Certainly there can be cases in which a recording made without the consent of the interested party does not injure his right to personality. Since in commercial relations it is common practice to record telephone transmissions, orders, stock reports, etc. by acoustic devices instead of through stenographic means . . . the speaker can rarely be injured through this manner of recording his words. In the acoustical recording of simple news or communications the element of fixing an objective event so predominates that the relation to the speaker's personality is severed. . . .

A personal conversation which serves as an exchange of thoughts and opinions is another matter completely. . . .

---

* The *Neue Juristische Wochenschrift* omits the statement of the fact situation in this case.

In conversation with another individual, the particular personality of the speaker finds its expression; therefore, he has the right to conduct his speech freely and without feelings of mistrust and suspicion. . . . A sensible dialogue cannot take place without candor and without that improvisation peculiar to conversation. . . . If the participant in a conversation must fear that without his knowledge every expression of his speech, to include even the sound of his voice and its peculiarities and weaknesses, may be recorded, a grave curtailment of his development of personality exists. From this fear there would follow feelings of suspicion and mistrust. Confidential conversation with another person, typical of human nature, would no longer be possible. It must also be considered that the authorization to record one's speech depends on personal confidence, since with such recording its misuse is possible. The possessor of the recording can, through editing, alter the sense of the speech. He can determine when the speaker's voice is heard, and through the choice of certain segments can give the speech a different meaning when it is played back than that which it originally had. Finally, he can make the conversation accessible to persons by whom . . . the speaker did not intend it should be heard. Because of these possibilities the secret recording itself, and not just the playing back of such a recording, must be considered as illegal interference with one's privacy. . . . If in consideration of technical development one must accept that his speech may be overheard and fixed through recording devices, then the technical progress resulting from precise methods of recording speech will have been gained at the high cost of a loss of candor in human relations seriously impeding the development of the personality. The legal order which must protect the aforementioned values of the personality cannot tolerate the misuse of such a device. The relevant legal writings also support the view that even without special legislative rules the problem of the recording of a conversation must be considered a substantially illegal interference in the general right of personality.

This legal consideration does not mean that in commercial and legal relations the use of recording devices is completely forbidden. Whoever must conduct contractual negotiations or other important matters, and who feels that a subsequent written transcription would be imprecise and does not want to employ simultaneous written transcription or does not desire the presence of a third party, must then obtain the consent of the other participant in the conversation to make an acoustic recording. If he does not obtain this consent, he must accept the situation. Whether in public speeches or assemblies other principles apply need not be examined. Similarly in the present case we need not discuss the controversial question of whether or not in the taking of recorded testimony, especially in interrogation in criminal proceedings, the consent of the interested party is always necessary.

3. It must be admitted that limits exist to the general right of personality. Limitation applies as well to the right to determine whether one's spoken words may be transcribed. Legitimate defense and analogous situations may justify secret recording in a particular case, such as, for example, when oral threats are used for purposes of extortion. At any rate, in consideration of the importance of privacy and of the fact that a secret recording contains an element of deception and therefore of illegality, such limitations are possible only in exceptional cases. A solely private interest in retaining a record of the content of a conversation or in procuring evidence for later anticipated litigation is generally insufficient to justify such a serious interference with the privacy of the participant as occurs with the use of recording devices.

In the present case the defendant presented no justification for having made the secret recording. . . . The injury to the right of personality of the plaintiff continues as long as the unerased tape remains in the hands of the defendant. The interference in the privacy of the plaintiff exists as long as the defendant has the recording at his disposition and can therefore reproduce the voice of the plaintiff without his having any possibility of control.

Therefore, the defendant has been correctly ordered to erase the recordings.

QUESTION

Can one infer from the order to erase that the recordings would have been inadmissible as evidence? Compare the decision which follows.

DECISION OF JUNE 3, 1955

Kammergericht,* Berlin
[1956] NEUE JURISTISCHE WOCHENSCHRIFT 26

OPINION

The parties to the present controversy are divorced. About one year before the divorce proceedings the defendant, without the knowledge of the plaintiff, had recorded . . . statements which his wife had made in the course of marital controversies. These recordings were used as evidence in the divorce proceedings. The plaintiff asserts that the defendant in this way filled 72 tapes and

---

* A special traditional name for the Berlin equivalent of the *Oberlandesgericht*, or Court of Appeal.

played them for third parties to malign the plaintiff. The plaintiff asked that the defendant be required to turn over the tapes to the court in order that they might be erased. The defendant denies that he made use of the tapes in such a manner as to offend the plaintiff. He asserts that the statements of the plaintiff were taken only for use as evidence. The recordings would be necessary in a pending criminal proceeding and in another civil action initiated by the plaintiff. The *Landgericht* [trial court] found in the behavior of the defendant a violation of the plaintiff's dignity and granted the request of the plaintiff. Against this decision appeal has been presented.

The court recognizes that modern German law comprehends a general right to personality as a consequence of arts. 1 and 2 of the Basic Law. . . . It also accepts that the recording for reproduction of the expressions of an individual without his consent by tape recorder or other means represents a violation of the general right to personality. . . .

. . . [B]ut, at the same time the Court affirms that interference in the general right of personality is legal when, and only when, in the case of contrasting interests, after careful weighing of values and duties, it appears as absolutely necessary and represents in content, form and circumstances the only adequate means of accomplishing its intended purpose.

The purpose of the recording of the plaintiff's statements was to use them as evidence in a divorce proceeding. . . . This purpose . . . can be justified on evaluation of the values and duties involved. In marital proceedings it is difficult to obtain evidence of events which occur between the married couple while they are by themselves. The examination of the parties — as every judge knows from experience — as a means of determining the truth may be ineffective, and only rarely is adequate. If, therefore — as in the present case — the plaintiff repeatedly insulted the defendant and manifested the intention of denying this if questioned by the court, the recording is not illegal since as such it is adequate and necessary according to its form and the attendant circumstances to induce the plaintiff to make true statements in the proceeding.

However, the defendant cannot keep and use the tapes in an unlimited way. As soon as the recordings have served their purpose as evidence they must be erased. The violation of the general right of personality of the plaintiff cannot be allowed to continue indefinitely.

QUESTIONS

1. If the balancing required by the proportionality doctrine leads to this result in a civil case, when would it lead to exclusion of evidence in a criminal case? Does it depend on the egregiousness of the method of obtaining the evidence? The necessity for the particular evidence in the concrete case? Are these factors relevant to the theoretical bases for an exclusionary rule, or merely pragmatic compromises?

2. What is the effect of the following decision of the *Bundesgerichtshof* on this holding of the *Kammergericht*? How does the *Bundesgerichtshof* approach the issues raised in Question 1?

DECISION OF JUNE 19, 1970

Bundesgerichtshof (Civil Chamber)
[1970] NEUE JURISTISCHE WOCHENSCHRIFT 1848

[FACTS: The petitioner and his wife were married on August 31, 1965, but since October, 1966 they have lived separate lives though they still share the same household. The husband seeks a divorce according to § 43 of the Marriage Law (*Ehegesetz*) due to the improper behavior of his wife. The *Landgericht* rejected the husband's request for a divorce. On appeal, the *Oberlandesgericht* reversed the judgment of the *Landgericht* and granted the husband's request for a divorce. The wife sought Revision in the *Bundesgerichtshof* to annul the decision of the *Oberlandesgericht;* it was granted.]

OPINION

. . . .

1. The *Oberlandesgericht* considered the marriage broken due to the violation of § 43 of the Marriage Law. It found that the marriage had been irreparably damaged. The destruction of the marriage had been caused by the grave misbehavior of the wife. . . . One of the acts of misbehavior of the wife was that she had offended and insulted her husband by words and gestures in the period from February 17, 1968 to April 6, 1968 in their home where they were living together. . . .

2. The evidence of the insults and offenses of the wife to the husband is based on the testimony of the shoemaker K. During several nights the husband secretly brought K to a room to which the wife had no entry so that the husband could have a witness to her behavior. K observed the couple through two holes in the wall. . . . K could also hear what was spoken because of the thin walls in the house.

The *Oberlandesgericht* considered K a credible witness. Although they had some reservations about allowing K's testimony in as evidence, they admitted it nevertheless and considered it in making their decision. They felt that the intrusion into the privacy of the marriage as well as the violation of the general right to personality were not illegal since . . . the interference in the named rights was necessary considering the conflicting values and duties involved, and since the interference represented adequate and necessary means in order to reach a justified aim. The husband would not have been able to prove the nature of his wife's behavior by other means. They concluded that although a witness who works as an informer gets his knowledge in a morally reproachful way, this is insufficient to prohibit the use of his testimony.

The wife claims that the *Oberlandesgericht* could not use the testimony of this witness K. We agree.

To begin with, the husband acted illegally when he allowed the witness K to make observations of the behavior of the wife for this long period in their home. The law guarantees a personal sphere of privacy to the individual which is essential for the development of the personality, and a part of this sphere of privacy is the inviolability of the home (art. 13 of the Basic Law). As long as it is not justified by predominating public or private values, the interference in this personal sphere represents an injury of the general right to personality which is guaranteed in arts. 1 and 2 of the Basic Law.

Even if a divorce proceeding is pending and the husband needs evidence to use against his wife which he cannot get in any other way, nonetheless he cannot expose his wife in her own home to the continuous secret observation of an informer whom he wants to use as a witness in the divorce case. In this particular case the husband was not trying to convict his wife of grave crimes of which he suspected her; had he been, he perhaps would have been justified in observing her behavior and secretly listening to her speech even in her own home. Nor did a situation of absolute necessity for self-defense exist to justify his behavior. Rather, he simply wanted to have a person witness the behavior of the wife in her daily life with him so that he could prove her hateful manner toward him. That was entirely insufficient to justify such a serious intrusion into the wife's privacy such as occurred here. . . . In a previous decision of the *Bundesgerichtshof* [Decision of May 20, 1958, *supra*] it is stated that there is a violation of the privacy of the individual if someone secretly records conversations without the consent of the people conversing and that such interference generally cannot be justified by the desire of the person making the recording to get evidence for a potential litigation. The opinion of the *Kammergericht* [Decision of June 3, 1955, *supra*] that the secret recording of personal remarks of a married person in order to use them as evidence in a divorce proceeding could be justified in certain cases by considering the values and duties involved can be agreed to only in very special situations of necessity. Such necessity is not present when one desires to prove facts in a divorce proceeding which cannot be proven in any other way. The use of an informer in the home and in the internal marital sphere is no less grave than the employment of a secret recording device. Were married persons who have a troubled marriage to use such methods, every possibility of reconciliation would disappear and the marriage would be poisoned. The use of such methods would also be intolerable in the case in which a married person could count on winning an otherwise doubtful divorce proceeding by employing such methods. The secret use of an observer in the home of a married person cannot be put on the same level as the right of a married person under certain circumstances and for sufficient reasons of suspicion to use a detective outside the home to observe his spouse.

These considerations necessarily bring us to the conclusion that under the circumstances in this case, the testimony of hired informers in divorce proceedings is not admissible. . . . We must also consider the credibility of the testimony of a witness who observes married people, one of whom knows of the surveillance and prepares himself for it, while the other knows nothing. Such a witness could hardly perceive an objective picture of the relations of the married couple. . . .

If the court knows in advance that the proffered testimony was obtained in the above-described illegal manner, it must refuse to hear that testimony. If, after hearing the testimony, the court discovers that the testimony was illegally obtained, it must not consider such testimony in making its decision.

. . . .

QUESTIONS

1. Suppose a married person reasonably suspects that his spouse has committed "grave crimes" and uses an informer as here. Would the informer's testimony be admissible if the suspicions were, in fact, unfounded? Is the court saying that, under certain circumstances, the observations by an informer can be used in a divorce proceeding? How "grave" must the suspected crimes be, and how strong the suspicion?

2. Near the end of its opinion, the *Bundesgerichtshof* intimates that the use of testimony of a detective who observes the spouse outside the house is legitimate in certain circumstances and may be used in a divorce proceeding. Would the employment of a detective not interfere with the possible reconciliation of which the Court speaks, or does the employment of a detective outside the home serve a different function?

3. Compare this decision with the 1955 Decision of the *Kammergericht, supra.* How far do the two courts differ in weighing the principle of the right to personality against the individual's right to present evidence and the court's need to find the truth?

4. Note the last sentence of the principal case. Can a judge really "not consider such testimony" once he has heard it? Are judges more able than jurors to disregard crucial evidence once it has been heard? Should the fact that a judge has heard important testimony, later discovered to have been illegally obtained, be grounds for his disqualification?

3.　United States

SACKLER v. SACKLER

New York Court of Appeals
15 N.Y.2d 40, 203 N.E.2d 481 (1964)

DESMOND, Chief Judge.

Plaintiff husband was given a divorce judgment against his wife on a jury's verdict of adultery, and the Appellate Division agreed. The question of law on this appeal: should the proof as to the wife's guilt have been excluded from evidence because it was gotten by means of an illegal forcible entry into the wife's home by the husband and several private investigators employed by him? Agreeing with the Trial Justice and the Appellate Division, we hold that the evidence was admissible.

Nowhere, as all admit, is there any constitutional, statutory or decisional authority for rejecting otherwise valid evidence on such a ground. Our State's prohibitions against unreasonable search and seizures (N.Y.Const. art. I, § 12; Civil Rights Law, Consol.Laws, c. 6, § 8) do not have that purpose or effect (*People* v. *Defore,* 242 N.Y. 13, 23, 150 N.E. 585, 588 [1926].... The rule was and is that "Evidence is not excluded because the private litigant who offers it has gathered it by lawless force." [S]uccessive legislatures and constitutional revisers since *Defore*'s case have always refused to act favorably on proposals to bar from evidence proofs so obtained. The Supreme Court's decision of 1961 in *Mapp* v. *Ohio,* 367 U.S. 643, applying the Fourth Amendment is of course not controlling here or even applicable since its impact is on governmental seizures only and not on evidence illegally gathered by private persons. However, the argument is presented that the *Mapp* holding makes it logical and just that our court should announce a similar exclusionary rule as to evidence illegally gathered by private persons. The theory seems to run like this: before *Mapp,* the law of evidence in this State was the same as to all illegal searches whether governmental or not, that is, all evidence so produced was receivable. Now we are told that since evidence which is the fruit of illegal governmental incursions is banned, so, for uniformity's sake, should proof of similar character be refused acceptance when procured by illegal searches and under nongovernmental auspices. The argument goes too far and proves too much.

Fourth Amendment protections of privacy against unlawful searches and seizures have their origins in English law of the 17th Century and earlier. Never were those protections applicable to searches and seizures by any persons other than government officers and agents. Searches by "the government" only are covered, that is, "official acts and proceedings" and "invasions on the part of the government and its employes [*sic*] of the sanctity of a man's home and the privacies of life". . . .

The definitive holding that the Fourth Amendment has nothing to do with nongovernmental intrusions is in *Burdeau* v. *McDowell,* 256 U.S. 465 [1921], which has never been overruled in this respect. In *Burdeau* the court said flatly and finally that the Fourth Amendment's "origin and history clearly show that it was intended to be a restraint upon the activities of sovereign authority, and was not intended to be a limitation upon other than governmental agencies." Neither history, logic nor law give any support for the idea that uniform treatment should be given to governmental and private searches, and to the evidence disclosed by such searches.

With the supposed analogy to *Mapp* eliminated, no reason remains for holding inadmissible the evidence here presented. The basic rule is that all competent, substantial, credible and relevant evidence is to be available to the courts. The interests of justice will not be promoted by the announcement by the courts of new exclusions, since the process of investigating the truth in courts of justice is an indispensable function of society and since "judicial rules of evidence were never meant to be used as an indirect method of punishment" of trespassers and other lawless intruders (8 Wigmore, Evidence [McNaughton rev.], § 2183; *Commonwealth* v. *Dana,* 2 Metc. [43 Mass.] 329 [1841]). Any court is taking extreme measures when it refuses convincing evidence because of the way it was procured. Proof of guilt collected in raids by private detectives has been, pursuant to rules not heretofore questioned, the basis for thousands of divorce decrees in our State. And the New York Legislature, when it has found necessity for outlawing evidence because it was secured by particular unlawful means, has provided specific statutory prohibitions such as those against the use of proof gotten by illegal eavesdropping. Further dealings with the problem (absent controls imposed by the Federal or State Constitutions or supervening United States Supreme Court decisions) should be by the Legislature.

For further clarity, it should be noted that the question we are discussing is not as to whether evidence invalidly gotten by governmental people may be used in a civil litigation or whether evidence wrongfully obtained by private individuals may be used by the State in a criminal prosecution. The only question here is whether evidence gotten by persons not in government service may be rejected in a civil litigation, in the absence of constitutional or statutory compulsion for such rejection.

The judgment should be affirmed, without costs.

VAN VOORHIS, Judge (dissenting).

... When evidence illegally obtained is offered in evidence in court, that is done for the purpose of inducing official action by the courts, which appears to be contrary to the purpose served by the adjudication in *Mapp* v. *Ohio.* In either instance the product of the search cannot legally be utilized by the courts as an official branch of the State. . . .

BERGAN, Judge (dissenting).

Had the police intruded into the defendant's home in the same manner employed by plaintiff and his detectives, and found evidence of murder, the court would have suppressed the evidence on constitutional grounds. It is not possible to draw a fully logical difference on the question of admissibility between evidence wrongfully obtained by a private citizen and evidence wrongfully obtained by public authority. Indeed, since the motivation of public authority is the common good of the community and the motivation of the private citizen the advantage of his lawsuit, it might be supposed we would more readily suppress wrongfully taken evidence in the private suit than in the criminal action.

. . . .

If, instead of wrongfully entering her home, the plaintiff had obtained the evidence for his divorce suit by listening in on defendant's telephone line in violation of the eavesdropping statute (Penal Law, § 738), the court would exclude the evidence (CPLR 4506). It is true enough that the eavesdropping rule is of legislative origin, but the general rule of admissibility was fashioned judicially and the court has a responsibility to refashion it when it can be seen, as it now becomes obvious, that it is operating unfairly and out of balance.

We ought not hang on tenaciously to the remnant of an old rule out of sentiment or by reason of inertia. If we continue to sanction a duality of this kind in the practice it will develop into an ultimate procedural incongruity which in the end will have to be adjusted. We ought to deal with it now by making the change in the direction of consistency while the criminal practice is adapting itself to *Mapp.* The change in fundamental viewpoint and the approach to wrongfully obtained evidence have made our rule of admissibility in private cases inconsistent and discriminatory.

The judgment should be reversed.

NOTES AND QUESTIONS

1. Does the rationale of the majority in *Sackler* depend on the civil nature of the proceeding or on the identity of the party engaged in unlawful conduct? Courts have declined to exclude evidence in criminal cases, where the evidence was unlawfully obtained by private persons not acting in concert with or on behalf of the police. *Barnes* v. *United States,* 373 F.2d 517 (5th Cir. 1967). On the other hand, evidence has been excluded when the unlawful search was conducted by the police, and the evidence was sought to be introduced in quasi-criminal or civil enforcement actions brought by the government. *One 1958 Plymouth Sedan* v. *Pennsylvania,* 380 U.S. 693 (1965); *but cf. United States* v. *Janis,* 428 U.S. 433 (1976) (permitting introduction of evidence illegally seized by State officers in federal civil tax assessment proceeding).

2. Is the rule that evidence illegally seized by private parties is admissible in civil litigation supported simply by the fact that state and federal constitutions are applicable only to official searches and seizures? Can the desirability of the rule be judged simply by asking whether mere admission of the evidence by a court is "state action"? Would the evidence have been admissible in *Sackler* if it had been obtained in an illegal police raid? (*See Honeycutt* v. *Aetna Ins. Co.,* 510 F.2d 340 (7th Cir.), *cert. denied,* 421 U.S. 1011 (1975).)

3. Can the rule in *Sackler* be supported by the argument that private illegal searches are episodic and unlikely to be deterred by a rule excluding the evidence in civil litigation? At the time the *Sackler* case was decided, the grounds for divorce in New York were quite limited, and one may speculate that illegal conduct occurred routinely to obtain proof of a spouse's infidelity. Should that make a difference?

4. Can the rule in the *Sackler* case be supported, finally, by arguing that the integrity of the judicial process is less compromised by the introduction of the fruits of unlawful *private* conduct? Suppose that department store employees routinely spy on customers in changing rooms through one-way mirrors. In a criminal prosecution for shoplifting, should an employee's testimony as to what he saw through the mirror be admissible? *Cf. Burdeau* v. *McDowell,* 256 U.S. 465 (1921).

Chapter 12

CONSTITUTIONAL DECISIONS ON ABORTION

A. UNITED STATES

ROE v. WADE

Supreme Court of the United States
410 U.S. 113, 93 S. Ct. 705, 35 L. Ed. 2d 147 (1973)

MR. JUSTICE BLACKMUN delivered the opinion of the Court.

This Texas federal appeal and its Georgia companion, *Doe* v. *Bolton,* 410 U.S. 179, present constitutional challenges to state criminal abortion legislation. The Texas statutes under attack here are typical of those that have been in effect in many States for approximately a century. The Georgia statutes, in contrast, have a modern cast and are a legislative product that, to an extent at least, obviously reflects the influences of recent attitudinal change, of advancing medical knowledge and techniques, and of new thinking about an old issue.

We forthwith acknowledge our awareness of the sensitive and emotional nature of the abortion controversy, of the vigorous opposing views, even among physicians, and of the deep and seemingly absolute convictions that the subject inspires. One's philosophy, one's experiences, one's exposure to the raw edges of human existence, one's religious training, one's attitudes toward life and family and their values, and the moral standards one establishes and seeks to observe, are all likely to influence and to color one's thinking and conclusions about abortion.

In addition, population growth, pollution, poverty, and racial overtones tend to complicate and not to simplify the problem.

Our task, of course, is to resolve the issue by constitutional measurement, free of emotion and of predilection. We seek earnestly to do this, and, because we do, we have inquired into, and in this opinion place some emphasis upon, medical and medical-legal history and what that history reveals about man's attitudes toward the abortion procedure over the centuries. We bear in mind, too, Mr. Justice Holmes' admonition in his now-vindicated dissent in *Lochner* v. *New York,* 198 U.S. 45, 76 (1905):

"[The Constitution] is made for people of fundamentally differing views, and the accident of our finding certain opinions natural and familiar, or novel, and even shocking, ought not to conclude our judgment upon the question whether statutes embodying them conflict with the Constitution of the United States."

I

The Texas statutes that concern us here ... make it a crime to "procure an abortion," as therein defined, or to attempt one, except with respect to "an abortion procured or attempted by medical advice for the purpose of saving the life of the mother." Similar statutes are in existence in a majority of the States.

. . . .

II

Jane Roe, a single woman who was residing in Dallas County, Texas, instituted this federal action in March 1970 against the District Attorney of the county. She sought a declaratory judgment that the Texas criminal abortion statutes were unconstitutional on their face, and an injunction restraining the defendant from enforcing the statutes.

Roe alleged that she was unmarried and pregnant; that she wished to terminate her pregnancy by an abortion "performed by a competent, licensed physician, under safe, clinical conditions"; that she was unable to get a "legal" abortion in Texas because her life did not appear to be threatened by the continuation of her pregnancy; and that she could not afford to travel to another jurisdiction in order to secure a legal abortion under safe conditions. She claimed that the Texas statutes were unconstitutionally vague and that they abridged her right of personal privacy, protected by the First, Fourth, Fifth, Ninth, and Fourteenth Amendments. By an amendment to her complaint Roe purported to sue "on behalf of herself and all other women" similarly situated.

. . . .

V

The principal thrust of appellant's attack on the Texas statutes is that they improperly invade a right, said to be possessed by the pregnant woman, to choose to terminate her pregnancy. Appellant would discover this right in the concept of personal "liberty" embodied in the Fourteenth Amendment's Due Process Clause; or in personal, marital, familial, and sexual privacy said to be protected by the Bill of Rights or its penumbras, see *Griswold* v. *Connecticut,* 381 U.S. 479 (1965); *Eisenstadt* v. *Baird,* 405 U.S. 438 (1972); *id.,* at 460 (White, J., concurring in result); or among those rights reserved to the people by the Ninth Amendment, *Griswold* v. *Connecticut,* 381 U.S., at 486 (Goldberg, J., concurring). Before addressing this claim, we feel it desirable briefly to survey, in several aspects, the history of abortion, for such insight as that history may afford us, and then to examine the state purposes and interests behind the criminal abortion laws.

[The "brief" survey, omitted here, fills nearly 20 pages of the U.S. Reports.]

VII

Three reasons have been advanced to explain historically the enactment of criminal abortion laws in the 19th century and to justify their continued existence.

It has been argued occasionally that these laws were the product of a Victorian social concern to discourage illicit sexual conduct. Texas, however, does not advance this justification in the present case, and it appears that no court or commentator has taken the argument seriously. The appellants and *amici* contend, moreover, that this is not a proper state purpose at all and suggest that, if it were, the Texas statutes are overbroad in protecting it since the law fails to distinguish between married and unwed mothers.

A second reason is concerned with abortion as a medical procedure. When most criminal abortion laws were first enacted, the procedure was a hazardous one for the woman. This was particularly true prior to the development of antisepsis. Antiseptic techniques, of course, were based on discoveries by Lister, Pasteur, and others first announced in 1867, but were not generally accepted and employed until about the turn of the century. Abortion mortality was high. Even after 1900, and perhaps until as late as the development of antibiotics in the 1940's, standard modern techniques such as dilation and curettage were not nearly so safe as they are today. Thus, it has been argued that a State's real concern in enacting a criminal abortion law was to protect the pregnant woman, that is, to restrain her from submitting to a procedure that placed her life in serious jeopardy.

Modern medical techniques have altered this situation. Appellants and various *amici* refer to medical data indicating that abortion in early pregnancy, that is, prior to the end of the first trimester, although not without its risk, is now relatively safe. Mortality rates for women undergoing early abortions, where the procedure is legal, appear to be as low as or lower than the rates for normal childbirth. Consequently, any interest of the State in protecting the woman from an inherently hazardous procedure, except when it would be equally dangerous for her to forgo it, has largely disappeared. Of course, important state interests in the areas of health and medical standards do remain. The State has a legitimate interest in seeing to it that abortion, like any other medical procedure, is performed under circumstances that insure maximum safety for the patient. This interest obviously extends at least to the performing physician and his staff, to the facilities involved, to the availability of after-care, and to adequate provision for any complication or emergency that might arise. The prevalence of high mortality rates at illegal "abortion mills" strengthens, rather than weakens, the State's interest in regulating the conditions under which abortions are performed. Moreover, the risk to the woman increases as her pregnancy continues. Thus, the State retains a definite interest in protecting the woman's own health and safety when an abortion is proposed at a late stage of pregnancy.

The third reason is the State's interest — some phrase it in terms of duty — in protecting prenatal life. Some of the argument for this justification rests on the theory that a new human life is present from the moment of conception. The State's interest and general obligation to protect life then extends, it is argued, to prenatal life. Only when the life of the pregnant mother herself is at stake, balanced against the life she carries within her, should the interest of the embryo or fetus not prevail. Logically, of course, a legitimate state interest in this area need not stand or fall on acceptance of the belief that life begins at conception or at some other point prior to live birth. In assessing the State's interest, recognition may be given to the less rigid claim that as long as at least *potential* life is involved, the State may assert interests beyond the protection of the pregnant woman alone.

It is with these interests, and the weight to be attached to them, that this case is concerned.

VIII

The Constitution does not explicitly mention any right of privacy. In a line of decisions, however, going back perhaps as far as *Union Pacific R. Co.* v. *Botsford,* 141 U.S. 250, 251 (1891), the Court has recognized that a right of personal privacy, or a guarantee of certain areas or zones of privacy, does exist under the Constitution. In varying contexts, the Court or individual Justices have, indeed, found at least the roots of that right in the First Amendment, . . . in the Fourth and Fifth Amendments, . . . in the penumbras of the Bill of Rights, *Griswold* v. *Connecticut,* 381 U.S., at 484-485; in the Ninth Amendment, *id.,* at 486 (Goldberg, J., concurring); or in the concept of liberty guaranteed by the first section of the Fourteenth Amendment, see *Meyer* v. *Nebraska,* 262 U.S. 390, 399 (1923). These decisions make it clear that only personal rights that can be deemed "fundamental" or "implicit in the concept of ordered liberty," . . . are included in this guarantee of personal privacy. They also make it clear that the right has some extension to activities relating to marriage, procreation, contraception, family relationships, and child rearing and education. This right of privacy, whether it be founded in the Fourteenth Amendment's concept of personal liberty and restrictions upon state action, as we feel it is, or, as the District Court determined, in the Ninth Amendment's reservation of rights to the people, is broad enough to encompass a woman's decision whether or not to terminate her pregnancy. The detriment that the State would impose upon the pregnant woman by denying this choice altogether is apparent. Specific and direct harm medically diagnosable even in early pregnancy may be involved. Maternity, or additional offspring, may force upon the woman a distressful life and future. Psychological harm may be imminent. Mental and physical health may be taxed by child care. There is also the distress, for all concerned, associated with the unwanted child, and there is the problem of bringing a child into a family already unable, psychologically and otherwise, to care for it. In other cases, as in this one, the additional difficulties and continuing stigma of unwed motherhood may be involved. All these are factors the woman and her responsible physician necessarily will consider in consultation.

On the basis of elements such as these, appellant and some *amici* argue that the woman's right is absolute and that she is entitled to terminate her pregnancy at whatever time, in whatever way, and for whatever reason she alone chooses. With this we do not agree. Appellant's arguments that Texas either has no valid interest at all in regulating the abortion decision, or no interest strong enough to support any limitation upon the woman's sole determination, are unpersuasive. The Court's decisions recognizing a right of privacy also acknowledge that some state regulation in areas protected by that right is appropriate. As noted above, a State may properly assert important interests in safeguarding health, in maintaining medical standards, and in protecting potential life. At some point in pregnancy, these respective interests become sufficiently compelling to sustain regulation of the factors that govern the abortion decision. The privacy right involved, therefore, cannot be said to be absolute. In fact, it is not clear to us that the claim asserted by some *amici* that one has an unlimited right to do with one's body as one pleases bears a close relationship to the right of privacy previously articulated in the Court's decisions. . . .

We, therefore, conclude that the right of personal privacy includes the abortion decision, but that this right is not unqualified and must be considered against important state interests in regulation.

   . . . .

Where certain "fundamental rights" are involved, the Court has held that regulation limiting these rights may be justified only by a "compelling state interest," . . . and that legislative enactments must be narrowly drawn to express only the legitimate state interests at stake. . . .

IX

. . . .

A. The appellee and certain *amici* argue that the fetus is a "person" within the language and meaning of the Fourteenth Amendment. In support of this, they outline at length and in detail the well-known facts of fetal development. If this suggestion of personhood is established, the appellant's case, of course, collapses, for the fetus' right to life would then be guaranteed specifically by the Amendment. The appellant conceded as much on reargument. . . .

The Constitution does not define "person" in so many words. Section 1 of the Fourteenth Amendment contains three references to "person." The first, in defining "citizens," speaks of "persons born or naturalized in the United States." The word also appears both in the Due Process Clause and in the Equal Protection Clause. "Person" is used in other places in the Constitution: in the listing of qualifications for Representatives and Senators, Art. I, § 2, cl. 2, and § 3, cl. 3; in the Apportionment Clause, Art. I, § 2, cl. 3; in the Migration and Importation provision, Art. I, § 9, cl. 1; in the Emolument Clause, Art. I, § 9, cl. 8; in the Electors provisions, Art. II, § 1, cl. 2, and the superseded cl. 3; in the provision outlining qualifications for the office of President, Art. II, § 1, cl. 5; in the Extradition provisions, Art. IV, § 2, cl. 2, and the superseded Fugitive Slave Clause 3; and in the Fifth, Twelfth, 'and Twenty-second Amendments, as well as in §§ 2 and 3 of the Fourteenth Amendment. But in nearly all these instances, the use of the word is such that it has application only postnatally. None indicates, with any assurance, that it has any possible prenatal application.

All this, together with our observation, *supra,* that throughout the major portion of the 19th century prevailing legal abortion practices were far freer than they are today, persuades us that the word "person," as used in the Fourteenth Amendment, does not include the unborn. . . .

This conclusion, however, does not of itself fully answer the contentions raised by Texas, and we pass on to other considerations.

B. The pregnant woman cannot be isolated in her privacy. She carries an embryo and, later, a fetus, if one accepts the medical definitions of the developing young in the human uterus. . . .

Texas urges that, apart from the Fourteenth Amendment, life begins at conception and is present throughout pregnancy, and that, therefore, the State has a compelling interest in protecting that life from and after conception. We need not resolve the difficult question of when life begins. When those trained in the respective disciplines of medicine, philosophy, and theology are unable to arrive at any consensus, the judiciary, at this point in the development of man's knowledge, is not in a position to speculate as to the answer.

. . . .

In areas other than criminal abortion, the law has been reluctant to endorse any theory that life, as we recognize it, begins before live birth or to accord legal rights to the unborn except in narrowly defined situations and except when the rights are contingent upon live birth. . . .

In short, the unborn have never been recognized in the law as persons in the whole sense.

X

In view of all this, we do not agree that, by adopting one theory of life, Texas may override the rights of the pregnant woman that are at stake. We repeat, however, that the State does have an important and legitimate interest in preserving and protecting the health of the pregnant woman, whether she be a resident of the State or a nonresident who seeks medical consultation and treatment there, and that it has still *another* important and legitimate interest in protecting the potentiality of human life. These interests are separate and distinct. Each grows in substantiality as the woman approaches term and, at a point during pregnancy, each becomes "compelling."

With respect to the State's important and legitimate interest in the health of the mother, the "compelling" point, in the light of present medical knowledge, is at approximately the end of the first trimester. This is so because of the now-established medical fact . . . that until the end of the first trimester mortality in abortion may be less than mortality in normal childbirth. It follows that, from and after this point, a State may regulate the abortion procedure to the extent that the regulation reasonably relates to the preservation and protection of maternal health. Examples of permissible state regulation in this area are requirements as to the qualifications of the person who is to perform the abortion; as to the licensure of that person; as to the facility in which the procedure is to be performed, that is, whether it must be a hospital or may be a clinic or some other place of less-than-hospital status; as to the licensing of the facility; and the like.

This means, on the other hand, that, for the period of pregnancy prior to this "compelling" point, the attending physician, in consultation with his patient, is free to determine, without regulation by the State, that, in his medical judgment, the patient's pregnancy should be terminated. If that decision is reached, the judgment may be effectuated by an abortion free of interference by the State.

With respect to the State's important and legitimate interest in potential life, the "compelling" point is at viability. This is so because the fetus then presumably has the capability of meaningful life outside the mother's womb. State regulation protective of fetal life after viability thus has both logical and biological justifications. If the State is interested in protecting fetal life after viability, it may go so far as to proscribe abortion during that period, except when it is necessary to preserve the life or health of the mother.

Measured against these standards, Art. 1196 of the Texas Penal Code, in restricting legal abortions to those "procured or attempted by medical advice for the purpose of saving the life of the mother," sweeps too broadly. The statute makes no distinction between abortions performed early in pregnancy and those performed later, and it limits to a single reason, "saving" the mother's life, the legal justification for the procedure. The statute, therefore, cannot survive the constitutional attack made upon it here.

. . . .

XI

To summarize and to repeat:

1. A state criminal abortion statute of the current Texas type, that excepts from criminality only a *life-saving* procedure on behalf of the mother, without regard to pregnancy stage and without recognition of the other interests involved, is violative of the Due Process Clause of the Fourteenth Amendment.

(a) For the stage prior to approximately the end of the first trimester, the abortion decision and its effectuation must be left to the medical judgment of the pregnant woman's attending physician.

(b) For the stage subsequent to approximately the end of the first trimester, the State, in promoting its interest in the health of the mother, may, if it chooses, regulate the abortion procedure in ways that are reasonably related to maternal health.

(c) For the stage subsequent to viability, the State in promoting its interest in the potentiality of human life may, if it chooses, regulate, and even proscribe, abortion except where it is necessary, in appropriate medical judgment, for the preservation of the life or health of the mother.

. . . .

MR. JUSTICE STEWART, concurring.

. . . As Mr. Justice Black's opinion for the Court in [*Ferguson* v. *Skrupa,* 372 U.S. 726, 730 (1963)] put it: "We have returned to the original constitutional proposition that courts do not substitute their social and economic beliefs for the judgment of legislative bodies, who are elected to pass laws." *Id.,* at 730.

Barely two years later, in *Griswold* v. *Connecticut,* 381 U.S. 479, the Court held a Connecticut birth control law unconstitutional. In review of what had been so recently said in *Skrupa,* the Court's opinion in *Griswold* understandably did its best to avoid reliance on the Due Process Clause of the Fourteenth Amendment as the ground for decision. Yet, the Connecticut law did not violate any provision of the Bill of Rights, nor any other specific provision of the Constitution. So it was clear to me then, and it is equally clear to me now, that the *Griswold* decision can be rationally understood only as a holding that the Connecticut statute substantively invaded the "liberty" that is protected by the Due Process Clause of the Fourteenth Amendment. As so understood, *Griswold* stands as one in a long line of pre-*Skrupa* cases decided under the doctrine of substantive due process, and I now accept it as such.*

. . . .

Clearly, . . . the Court today is correct in holding that the right asserted by Jane Roe is embraced within the personal liberty protected by the Due Process Clause of the Fourteenth Amendment.

It is evident that the Texas abortion statute infringes that right directly. Indeed, it is difficult to imagine a more complete abridgment of a constitutional freedom than that worked by the inflexible criminal statute now in force in Texas. The question then becomes whether the state interests advanced to justify this abridgment can survive the "particularly careful scrutiny" that the Fourteenth Amendment here requires.

. . . I join the Court's opinion holding that that law is invalid under the Due Process Clause of the Fourteenth Amendment.

MR. JUSTICE REHNQUIST, dissenting.

The Court's opinion brings to the decision of this troubling question both extensive historical fact and a wealth of legal scholarship. While the opinion thus commands my respect, I find myself nonetheless in fundamental disagreement with those parts of it that invalidate the Texas statute in question, and therefore dissent.

. . . .

. . . I have difficulty in concluding, as the Court does, that the right of "privacy" is involved in this case. Texas, by the statute here

---

*Justice Stewart, along with Justice Black, dissented in the *Griswold* case.

challenged, bars the performance of a medical abortion by a licensed physician on a plaintiff such as Roe. A transaction resulting in an operation such as this is not "private" in the ordinary usage of that word. Nor is the "privacy" that the Court finds here even a distant relative of the freedom from searches and seizures protected by the Fourth Amendment to the Constitution, which the Court has referred to as embodying a right to privacy.

If the Court means by the term "privacy" no more than that the claim of a person to be free from unwanted state regulation of consensual transactions may be a form of "liberty" protected by the Fourteenth Amendment, there is no doubt that similar claims have been upheld in our earlier decisions on the basis of that liberty. I agree with the statement of MR. JUSTICE STEWART in his concurring opinion that the "liberty," against deprivation of which without due process the Fourteenth Amendment protects, embraces more than the rights found in the Bill of Rights. But that liberty is not guaranteed absolutely against deprivation, only against deprivation without due process of law. The test traditionally applied in the area of social and economic legislation is whether or not a law such as that challenged has a rational relation to a valid state objective. *Williamson* v. *Lee Optical Co.,* 348 U.S. 483 (1955). The Due Process Clause of the Fourteenth Amendment undoubtedly does place a limit, albeit a broad one, on legislative power to enact laws such as this. If the Texas statute were to prohibit an abortion even where the mother's life is in jeopardy, I have little doubt that such a statute would lack a rational relation to a valid state objective under the test stated in *Williamson, supra.* But the Court's sweeping invalidation of any restrictions on abortion during the first trimester is impossible to justify under that standard, and the conscious weighing of competing factors that the Court's opinion apparently substitutes for the established test is far more appropriate to a legislative judgment than to a judicial one.

. . . .

While the Court's opinion quotes from the dissent of Mr. Justice Holmes in *Lochner* v. *New York,* 198 U.S. 45, 74 (1905), the result it reaches is more closely attuned to the majority opinion of Mr. Justice Peckham in that case. As in *Lochner* and similar cases applying substantive due process standards to economic and social welfare legislation, the adoption of the compelling state interest standard will inevitably require this Court to examine the legislative policies and pass on the wisdom of these policies in the very process of deciding whether a particular state interest put forward may or may not be "compelling." The decision here to break pregnancy into three distinct terms and to outline the permissible restrictions the State may impose in each one, for example, partakes more of judicial legislation than it does of a determination of the intent of the drafters of the Fourteenth Amendment.

. . . .

MR. CHIEF JUSTICE BURGER, concurring.*

. . . .

I do not read the Court's holdings today as having the sweeping consequences attributed to them by the dissenting Justices; the dissenting views discount the reality that the vast majority of physicians observe the standards of their profession, and act only on the basis of carefully deliberated medical judgments relating to life and health. Plainly, the Court today rejects any claim that the Constitution requires abortions on demand.

MR. JUSTICE DOUGLAS, concurring.

While I join the opinion of the Court, I add a few words.

I

The questions presented in the present cases . . . involve the right of privacy, one aspect of which we considered in *Griswold* v. *Connecticut,* 381 U.S. 479, 484, when we held that various guarantees in the Bill of Rights create zones of privacy.

The *Griswold* case involved a law forbidding the use of contraceptives. We held that law as applied to married people unconstitutional:

> "We deal with a right of privacy older than the Bill of Rights — older than our political parties, older than our school system. Marriage is a coming together for better or for worse, hopefully enduring, and intimate to the degree of being sacred."

. . . .

The Ninth Amendment obviously does not create federally enforceable rights. It merely says, "The enumeration in the Constitution, of certain rights, shall not be construed to deny or disparage others retained by the people." But a catalogue of these rights includes customary, traditional, and time-honored rights, amenities, privileges, and immunities that come within the sweep of "the Blessings of Liberty" mentioned in the preamble to the Constitution. Many of them, in my view, come within the meaning of the term "liberty" as used in the Fourteenth Amendment.

---

* The concurring opinions of Chief Justice Burger and Justice Douglas, and the dissenting opinion of Justice White, are applicable to *Roe* v. *Wade,* and the companion case of *Doe* v. *Bolton.*

First is the autonomous control over the development and expression of one's intellect, interests, tastes, and personality.

These are rights protected by the First Amendment and, in my view, they are absolute, permitting of no exceptions. . . .

. . . .

Second is freedom of choice in the basic decisions of one's life respecting marriage, divorce, procreation, contraception, and the education and upbringing of children.

These rights, unlike those protected by the First Amendment, are subject to some control by the police power. . . .

. . . .

Third is the freedom to care for one's health and person, freedom from bodily restraint or compulsion, freedom to walk, stroll, or loaf.

These rights, though fundamental, are likewise subject to regulation on a showing of "compelling state interest." . . .

. . . .

. . . I am not prepared to hold that a State may equate, as Georgia has done, all phases of maturation preceding birth. We held in *Griswold* that the States may not preclude spouses from attempting to avoid the joinder of sperm and egg. If this is true, it is difficult to perceive any overriding public necessity which might attach precisely at the moment of conception. As Mr. Justice Clark has said:

> "To say that life is present at conception is to give recognition to the potential, rather than the actual. The unfertilized egg has life, and if fertilized, it takes on human proportions. But the law deals in reality, not obscurity — the known rather than the unknown. When sperm meets egg life may eventually form, but quite often it does not. The law does not deal in speculation. The phenomenon of life takes time to develop, and until it is actually present, it cannot be destroyed. Its interruption prior to formation would hardly be homicide, and as we have seen, society does not regard it as such. The rites of Baptism are not performed and death certificates are not required when a miscarriage occurs. No prosecutor has ever returned a murder indictment charging the taking of the life of a fetus. This would not be the case if the fetus constituted human life."

In summary, the enactment is overbroad. It is not closely correlated to the aim of preserving prenatal life. In fact, it permits its destruction in several cases, including pregnancies resulting from sex acts in which unmarried females are below the statutory age of consent. At the same time, however, the measure broadly proscribes aborting other pregnancies which may cause severe mental disorders. Additionally, the statute is overbroad because it equates the value of embryonic life immediately after conception with the worth of life immediately before birth.

. . . .

MR. JUSTICE WHITE, with whom MR. JUSTICE REHNQUIST joins, dissenting.

At the heart of the controversy in these cases are those recurring pregnancies that pose no danger whatsoever to the life or health of the mother but are, nevertheless, unwanted for any one or more of a variety of reasons — convenience, family planning, economics, dislike of children, the embarrassment of illegitimacy, etc. The common claim before us is that for any one of such reasons, or for no reason at all, and without asserting or claiming any threat to life or health, any woman is entitled to an abortion at her request if she is able to find a medical advisor willing to undertake the procedure. The Court for the most part sustains this position: . . .

With all due respect, I dissent. I find nothing in the language or history of the Constitution to support the Court's judgments. The Court simply fashions and announces a new constitutional right for pregnant women and, with scarcely any reason or authority for its action, invests that right with sufficient substance to override most existing state abortion statutes. The upshot is that the people and the legislatures of the 50 States are constitutionally disentitled to weigh the relative importance of the continued existence and development of the fetus, on the one hand, against a spectrum of possible impacts on the mother, on the other hand. As an exercise of raw judicial power, the Court perhaps has authority to do what it does today; but in my view its judgment is an improvident and extravagant exercise of the power of judicial review that the Constitution extends to this Court.

The Court apparently values the convenience of the pregnant woman more than the continued existence and development of the life or potential life that she carries. Whether or not I might agree with that marshaling of values, I can in no event join the Court's judgment because I find no constitutional warrant for imposing such an order of priorities on the people and legislatures of the States. In a sensitive area such as this, involving as it does issues over which reasonable men may easily and heatedly differ, I cannot accept the Court's exercise of its clear power of choice by interposing a constitutional barrier to state efforts to protect human life and by investing women and doctors with the constitutionally protected right to exterminate it. This issue, for the most part, should be left with the people and to the political processes the people have devised to govern their affairs.

NOTES

1. As indicated in the Court's opinion, *Roe* v. *Wade* involved a typical nineteenth century law which forbade abortion except when necessary to save the woman's life. The Georgia law involved in the companion case, *Doe* v. *Bolton,* 410 U.S. 179, *rehearing denied,* 410 U.S. 959 (1973), had been enacted in 1968 and was patterned after the Model Penal Code of the American Law Institute. The grounds for abortion permitted by the law went beyond danger to the woman's life, including in addition: danger of serious and permanent injury to the woman's health; likelihood that the fetus would be born with a permanent grave mental or physical defect; pregnancy resulting from forcible or statutory rape. The lower court had ruled that the statute too narrowly limited permissible abortions, and an appeal to the Supreme Court by the State had been dismissed for technical reasons. It was obvious, however, on the basis of the decision in *Roe* v. *Wade,* that the Georgia statute would not survive constitutional scrutiny. 410 U.S. at 187, n. 8.

2. At issue in *Doe* v. *Bolton* was plaintiffs' appeal from portions of the lower court decision which upheld numerous procedural requirements for obtaining a lawful abortion. Starting from the premise of *Roe* v. *Wade* that, during the first trimester "the abortion decision and its effectuation must be left to the medical judgment of the pregnant woman's attending physician," the Court invalidated requirements: that the abortion be performed in an accredited hospital; that the abortion be approved by the hospital staff abortion committee; and that the physician's judgment be confirmed by two other physicians. The Court also invalidated a requirement that the woman must be a resident of the State of Georgia. Three years later, the Court held unconstitutional requirements that abortion be consented to by the spouse of a married woman or by the parents of an unmarried woman under the age of 18. *Planned Parenthood of Missouri* v. *Danforth,* 428 U.S. 52 (1976).

3. One result of the political furor that followed *Roe* v. *Wade* was the introduction of proposed amendments to the Constitution. One proposed amendment would have overruled *Roe* v. *Wade* by stating that nothing in the Constitution shall be construed to bar any State from "allowing, regulating, or prohibiting the practice of abortion." H.R.J. Res. 96, 94th Cong., 1st Sess., 94 CONG. REC. 216 (1975). A more significant amendment, introduced by Senator Buckley of New York on behalf of the National Right to Life Committee would have provided that a fetus is a "person" as that term is used in the Fifth and Fourteenth Amendments, and that "no unborn person shall be deprived of life by any person" except when necessary to prevent the death of the mother. S. J. Res. 11, 94th Cong., 1st Sess., 94 CONG. REC. 687 (1975).

4. No decision of the United States Supreme Court interpreting the Bill of Rights (Amendments I-VIII) or the Fourteenth Amendment has ever been overturned by amending the Constitution, and knowledgeable observers do not expect that this will occur with reference to the abortion decisions. A more immediate political response, however, has occurred with reference to public assistance for the medically indigent. Federal, and many state, laws have provided that public medical assistance funds shall not be used for all, or for selected, abortions. The Supreme Court has decided that restrictions on expenditure of public funds for abortion are constitutional. *Maher* v. *Roe,* 432 U.S. 464 (1977). Justice Powell's opinion for the Court reasoned that *Roe* v. *Wade* established a woman's freedom from affirmative interference with her decision to terminate pregnancy, but left the State free to favor childbirth over abortion in the expenditure of public funds. Justices Blackmun, Brennan and Marshall, dissenting, argued that the decision was a major retreat from the decision in *Roe* v. *Wade,* and showed a "distressing insensitivity to the plight of impoverished pregnant women."

B. FRANCE

DECISION OF JANUARY 15, 1975

Conseil Constitutionnel
[1975] D.S. Jur. 529; [1975] A.J.D.A. 134

The *Conseil Constitutionnel* seized the 20th of December, 1974, by M.M. . . . under the terms provided by Article 61 of the Constitution, with the issue concerning the constitutionality of the text of the law adopted by Parliament relative to the voluntary interruption of pregnancy;

Considering the observations produced in support of this issue;

Considering the Constitution, and notably its Preamble;

Considering the *ôrdonnance* of November 7, 1958 (the organic law of the *Conseil Constitutionnel*), in particular Chapter II of Title II of the *ôrdonnance*;

Having heard the Reporter's report;

Considering that Article 61 of the Constitution does not confer on the *Conseil Constitutionnel* a general power of evaluation and decision identical to that of Parliament, but rather gives it competence solely to pronounce the conformity to the Constitution of the laws referred to its scrutiny;

Considering in the first place, that, according to the terms of Article 55 of the Constitution, "The treaties or [international] accords regularly ratified or approved have, from their publication, an authority superior to that of the laws, upon the reservation, for each accord or treaty, of its application by the other party";

Considering that, even though these provisions, under the conditions which they define, confer on treaties superiority over the laws, they neither prescribe nor imply that the respect of this superiority principle must be enforced within the framework of the control of the conformity of laws to the Constitution provided by Article 61;

Considering that, in effect, the decisions taken on the basis of Article 61 of the Constitution assume an absolute and definitive character, as is made clear by Article 62, which prevents the promulgation and application of all provisions once declared unconstitutional [by this *Conseil Constitutionnel*]; that, in contrast, the superiority of the treaties over the laws, which principle is posed by the aforementioned Article 55, has a character at the same time relative and contingent, since such superiority is limited to the scope of the application of the treaty and is subordinated to a condition of reciprocity, and the realization of this condition may vary according to the behavior of one or more of the signatory States at the time when one must judge the respect of the condition;

Considering that a law contrary to a treaty would thus not be, for that reason only, contrary to the Constitution;

Considering that, therefore, the control of the respect of the principle of Article 55 of the Constitution would not be exercisable under the framework of review provided by Article 61, by reason of the difference in nature of the two controls;

Considering that, under these conditions, it is not the task of this *Conseil Constitutionnel,* when it is seized [with issues of constitutionality] under the terms of Article 61 of the Constitution, to examine the conformity of a law to the provisions of a treaty or an international accord;

Considering, in the second place, that the law relative to the voluntary interruption of pregnancy respects the liberty of the persons who have recourse to or participate in an interruption of pregnancy, whether they do so in a situation of distress or for a therapeutic reason; that, therefore, that law does not infringe upon the principle of liberty posed by Article 2 of the Declaration of the Rights of Man and of the Citizen;

Considering that the law referred to this *Conseil Constitutionnel* does not authorize any violation of the principle of respect for every human being from the very commencement of life, a principle stated in Article 1, except in case of necessity and according to the conditions and limitations which it defines;

Considering that none of the provisions of the law are, as it now appears, contrary to the fundamental principles recognized by the laws of the Republic, nor do they disregard the principle stated in the Preamble of the Constitution of October 27, 1946, according to which the nation guarantees the protection of children's health, nor any of the other provisions given constitutional value by the same text;

Considering, in consequence, that the law relative to the voluntary interruption of pregnancy does not contradict any of the texts to which the Constitution of October 4, 1958 made reference in its Preamble, nor any of the articles of the Constitution itself;

Therefore [this *Conseil Constitutionnel*] DECIDES that:

1. The provisions of the law concerning the voluntary termination of pregnancy, referred to the *Conseil Constitutionnel*, are not contrary to the Constitution.
2. The present decision will be published in the Official Journal of the Republic.

NOTE *

The *Conseil Constitutionnel* handed down two bold decisions, in 1971 and 1973. It has now handed down, on January 15, 1975, a cautious decision. Opinion was not unanimous on the bold decisions: among those who approved the liberal inspiration of the decision of July 16, 1971 ** declaring unconstitutional the legislative restriction on the freedom of association, some were concerned, from the standpoint of legal technique, about the uncertainty of the effect of the recourse to the fundamental principles recognized by the laws of the Republic on the content of the rights guaranteed by the Constitution. And if the "little phrase" of the decision of November 28, 1973,*** giving the legislature the right to inflict prison sentences for minor infractions, received the approval of some writers, whose opinions are influential, it did not convince either the Council of State or the Court of Cassation.

The decision in which the *Conseil* has affirmed the constitutionality of the law concerning the voluntary termination of pregnancy, published in the Official Journal of January 18, has already aroused by its caution as much criticism as the previous ones by their boldness, even from those who basically approve the solution adopted. From a juridical point of view — the only one we should consider here — caution is revealed in regard to the two series of arguments put forward by the authors of the recourse. Asked to affirm the non-conformity of the law to Article 2 of the European Convention on Human Rights, the *Conseil* declared itself incompetent to give a ruling in this capacity. As for the confrontation

---

* [1975] A.J.D.A. 134, note by Professor J. Rivero of the University of Paris.
** For the text of this decision, *see* Ch. 3, § C.3.a., *supra*.
*** This decision appears at Ch. 3, § C.3.b., *supra*.

between the law and the constitutional texts in opposition to it, it remained strictly literal excluding any interpretation liable to be imputed to the personal options of the members of the Council in an issue which engaged and divided consciences at their deepest level.

It is this double caution — in regard to international law (I) and to the constitutional texts (II) — that we should like to analyze, and try to understand (III).

[Professor Rivero's comments on the *Conseil*'s treatment of the European Convention are translated and reprinted *supra,* Ch. 5, § C.1.]

II. The examination by the *Conseil* of the conformity of the law to the provisions of the Constitution invoked by the recourse requires fewer comments. But, though we can discern the confirmation (which is no longer daring) of past boldness, caution is revealed in the method of interpreting the texts invoked.

It has been established, at least since the decision of July 16, 1971, that the Preamble and the texts to which it refers — the Declaration of 1789, Preamble of 1946, and also "fundamental principles recognized by the laws of the Republic," with the factor of uncertainty affecting them — are an integral part of the Constitution, and are thereby binding on the legislature. The solution was clarified with the aid of various elements: the Preamble of 1946 by the decision of June 19, 1970, "fundamental principles" by that of July 16, 1971, the Declaration of Rights with the decision of December 27, 1963 (A.J.D.A. 1974, p. 246).

The decision of January 15 confirms and restates this fact. The *Conseil* examines successively the conformity of the text deferred to it to Articles 1 and 2 of the Declaration, to the "fundamental principles," and to the "provisions having constitutional value enacted by the Preamble to the Constitution of October 17, 1946." Thus, the constitutional value of the texts to which the Constitution of October 4, 1958 refers in its Preamble is confirmed once more, according to the synthetic formula with which the decision ends.

As to the method followed, its caution is in contrast to the much more flexible method which characterized former decisions. Is it this concern with precision which led the *Conseil,* in the grounds for its decision, to ignore one of the arguments which had been suggested in support of the solution it adopted? The argument was in fact surprising: it linked the constitutionality of the reform to the secularity of the state. The prohibition of abortion would only have been the sanction by the legislature of a religious rule decreed by the Catholic Church. Secularity demanded that an end be put to this situation. It is understandable that the *Conseil Constitutionnel* did not commit itself to this course. If they were to pursue this reasoning in fact, and consider unconstitutional, as being contrary to secularity, all the provisions of the Penal Code which establish as offenses acts the Church considers as sins, a large part of it would probably be emptied of its content. The prohibition of murder, theft, rape, all of them also condemned by the Decalogue, would not escape the censure of the guardians of secularity in this sense. Whether one likes it or not, at the base of our juridical system there is a judeo-christian ethic, born of the Old Testament and the Gospels. The Church — and one cannot hold this against it — remains more attached to it than does the civil society, which diverges from it on a number of points, as the law in point precisely demonstrates. But that is not sufficient reason to consider those that still coincide with it as an outrage against secularity.

The decision ignores this dubious area. However, it is not limited to a mere statement. From this point of view, comparison with prior decisions is striking: that of July 16, 1971 defines a fundamental principle and determines its content without giving reasons; that of November 28, 1973 does not see fit to indicate the reasoning which leads from the texts it invokes to the conclusion it draws from them. Here, the procedure is less imperious. The decision analyzes in some detail the essential provisions of the law. It compares them with the constitutional texts which may be invoked in this case — Article 2 of the Declaration of 1789, and the provision of the Preamble guaranteeing the protection of a child's health. It even gives the outline of arguments; the law is not contrary to the principle of freedom laid down in Article 2, since it imposes no obligation; it leaves everyone the responsibility for his acts, whether it be to "participate in or have recourse to a voluntary termination of pregnancy"; it is not contrary to the "principle of respect for every human being from the beginning of life" (which, we may note in passing, is not explicitly stated in any of the constitutional texts considered, although it is formulated in Article 2 of the European Declaration), since it bases the only violations it does admit on "necessity" strictly defined. Affirmation without argument only reappears in the penultimate consideration, concerning the derogations provided for by the law. The procedure as a whole nevertheless appears more concerned with justifications than that adopted in prior decisions.

But is it convincing? It would not have been impossible to censure the law from the texts in question. But, inasmuch as none of them obviously referred directly to the problem posed, which their authors had not for an instant envisaged, this result could only have been reached by way of a very free interpretation, inspired by a different position than that adopted by the legislature. The *Conseil* did not consider itself authorized to censure it on that subjective basis, however serious the issue, since judicial government begins precisely at the point where judges diverge from the letter of the constitutional texts, the respect for which they must ensure, to make them the receptacles of their own ideology, as opposed to that reflected in the law.

III. To ward off the specter of judicial government: this could well be the ultimate explanation for the decision of January 15 and the caution characterizing it, in the areas of the European Convention and the interpretation of constitutional texts. In the early commentaries, little attention was paid to the consideration with which it begins, which says that "Article 61 of the Constitution does not give the *Conseil Constitutionnel* a general power of evaluation and decision equal to that of Parliament, but only gives it the authority to pronounce on the conformity to the Constitution of laws deferred for its examination." One might say this is obvious. But why did the *Conseil* insist on formulating it at the head of a decision required to close a particularly serious debate, when it did not think to do so when called upon to exercise for the first time its authority as guardian of the Constitution with regard to the legislature, not in the area of procedure, but in the much more difficult area of protection of fundamental rights?

Any outside reply to such a question is obviously hazardous, since it is the institutional policy of the *Conseil* that is being questioned. Formerly, every time it was petitioned, it drew back from enlarging its field of action, behind the constitutional texts defining its authority to the point that many reproached it for confining itself too narrowly in the role of strict guardian of the limits in which the 1958 Constitution aimed to enclose legislative action, to the benefit of the executive. Yet this caution was justified: a new institution, breaking with a long tradition of absolute parliamentary sovereignty, and taking its place in a juridical environment little inclined to welcome it, had to stay modest in order to be accepted and to find its definitive place in our overall political and jurisdictional structures.

The decision of July 16, 1971 marks the end of this first stage: this time, the *Conseil* established itself not as the defender of executive prerogatives against Parliament, but as the guardian of constitutional freedoms against a coalition of the government and its parliamentary majority. The protection of freedoms by the control of legislative constitutionality became a fact. This immense progress, which opinion has not taken the full measure of, was confirmed in later years, and the constitutional reform of October 29, 1974, giving Parliament the right of referral — which has also been underestimated — gives a new dimension to the ground gained.

Once the control of constitutionality is a fact, once the possibility of applying it becomes much more frequent, the return to an initial caution is explained: for "government by judges," that is, the substitution for the will of Parliament of the will of an irresponsible group slipping its own options into the flexible frame of constitutional formulas, ceases to be a myth and becomes a possibility.

It is this possibility, and the legitimate fear it arouses among some excellent minds, that the decision of January 15 doubtless sought to set aside. Its opening consideration, referred to above, thus appears as the key to the explanation of both the *Conseil*'s concern not to enlarge the constitutional superlegality of the whole body of international acts passed by France, and of its refusal to interpret constitutional texts in terms of an ideological standpoint.

How can this desire for caution be faulted on principle? The insertion in the French legal environment of the control of legislative constitutionality, a logical and already traditional crowning of the rule of law in a number of free countries, is a too recent progression not to be fragile still. It is understandable that the body responsible for implanting it in our national life thought it opportune to protect it against hostile reactions, by forestalling any suspicion of judicial imperialism.

However, there is perhaps a contradiction between this purpose and the means serving it. The constitutional formulas guaranteeing our freedoms have the prestige of ancient or recent history on their side. But they were not made with a view to concrete application. The Declaration of 1789 — except on the precise point of "inviolable and sacred" property, in which it is manifestly outdated — is very elevated in the sphere of ideas, the Preamble of 1946 has the nebulous character of political compromises, and what can one say about the "fundamental principles recognized by the laws of the Republic" except that one finds there what one brings along, as in Spanish inns in the past? When the constitutional judge must compare with these texts laws elaborated with a view to concrete situations and precise problems, he is likely to find himself in a dilemma: he must either stand by the letter of the constitutional provisions, which do not supply a useful answer to the question posed, which would make control ineffective, or give them force by a necessarily subjective interpretation, and so expose himself to the reproach of arbitrariness. A constitutional control which is both useful for the protection of citizens and acceptable to Parliament implies that the judge can find a precise and sure basis in the texts for which he must ensure respect.

The European Convention is precise, much more so than the heterogeneous documents which recapitulate the Preamble to the Constitution. More easily than the latter, it could guide the proceedings of the *Conseil Constitutionnel* between the two dangers of ineffectiveness and judicial government. Caution set this aside. Caution should perhaps have meant referring to it in order to give an institution both necessary and perilous the foundation which is uneasily furnished by constitutional texts encumbered with history.[9]

NOTES AND QUESTIONS

1. Professor Rivero's note is nearly silent as to the major moral arguments put forth by anti-abortion and pro-abortion forces. Instead, he discusses the opinion as an example of judicial caution caused by the traditional French fear of judicial government. As we have seen (Chapter 3), that debate in France has focused on the question whether there should be any institution of judicial review. In the United States, a similar debate has focused on the question whether, in particular decisions, the Court was furthering its own set of values — values not reflected in the Constitution itself. That debate was most intense from the beginning of this century until the mid-1930's, when the Supreme Court read the Due Process Clauses of the Fifth and Fourteenth Amendments to impose its own notions of *laissez faire* economics. The watershed case in the development of "economic due process" was *Lochner* v. *New York,* 198 U.S. 45 (1905). The core of the criticism of that position, which was expressed in Justice Holmes' famous dissent (quoted in Justice Blackmun's opinion in *Roe* v. *Wade*) was that it was an abuse of judicial power to read the Due Process Clauses to reflect the judges' own conceptions of government policy. Despite the fact that economic due process disappeared from the American judicial stage over forty years ago, the ghost of *Lochner* continues to preside over the debate in cases involving personal liberty, rather than economic liberty. American scholars who agree with the decision in *Roe* v. *Wade* as a matter of legislative policy have disagreed whether the decision is a return to judicial activism of the *Lochner* era. *Compare* Ely, *The Wages of Crying Wolf: A Comment on Roe* v. *Wade,* 82

---

[9] This study was completed before the decision of the Constitutional Court of the Federal Republic of Germany affirming the unconstitutionality of the law liberalizing abortion became known. A comparison between the positions taken on the same problem by the judges of Karlsruhe and the *Conseil Constitutionnel* would be rash as long as the German decision is known only through the analyses given of it in the press. But we may still consider whether the contradiction between the two decisions does not confirm to a certain extent the above conclusions. The [German] Fundamental Law defines fundamental rights with a precision lacking in the French texts. Article 2, paragraph 2, recognizing everyone's "right to life and to corporal integrity" does not have an equivalent in the Preamble, and the Court believed itself to be bound by these terms. The apparently opposite comportments of the two High Jurisdictions is perhaps explained by the differences in the texts they have to apply, in regard to the precision with which each formulates fundamental rights.

YALE L.J. 920 (1973) *with* Tribe, *Forward: Toward a Model of Roles in the Due Process of Life and Law,* 87 HARV. L. REV. 1 (1973).

2. The American experience during the heyday of economic due process has had, and continues to have, a significant impact upon French thought. The catchphrase *"gouvernement des juges"* is taken from a 1921 book by Edouard Lambert, LE GOUVERNEMENT DES JUGES ET LA LUTTE CONTRE LA LÉGISLATION SOCIALE AUX ETATS-UNIS. Studying the role of the United States Supreme Court from 1883 to 1920, Lambert demonstrated that judges in modern democratic state were quite capable of behaving as had the French judges of the *ancien régime* to impose a conservative veto on progessive legislation. It has been argued that the force of Lambert's criticism would be attenuated if the French were aware of the demise of economic due process, and of contemporary use by the United States Supreme Court of substantive due process to protect important personal liberties. Given his emphasis on the issue of judicial activism, do you find it strange that Professor Rivero's comment does not make any comparison of the *Conseil Constitutionnel* decision with the activist decision of the United States Supreme Court in *Roe* v. *Wade*? If *Roe* v. *Wade* were interjected into the contemporary French debate over judicial review, would it support the argument that Lambert's 1921 criticism of the United States Supreme Court continues to be valid? Do you agree with Professor Rivero that the *Conseil Constitutionnel* decision represents unusual caution in constitutional interpretation, or is the decision simply the correct resolution of the issue, even for an activist court?

3. A number of attempts have been made to reformulate the issues in *Roe* v. *Wade,* in order to avoid the spectre of judges freely picking among conflicting values which are not reflected in the Constitution. An argument sometimes heard is that *Roe* v. *Wade* represents an application of a principle expressed in the First Amendment — the prohibition on government "establishment" of religion. The argument has been that restrictive abortion legislation is an outgrowth of efforts by particular religious groups to express their own views of religious morality and impose that morality on the entire population. Professor Rivero's comment mentions that the *Conseil Constitutionnel* did not respond to one of the arguments urged in support of the abortion law — that the law reflected the constitutional principle of the "secularity of the state." Professor Rivero explains why the *Conseil Constitutionnel* ignored that argument in support of its result. Does it suggest the weakness of the argument which might have led Justice Blackmun in *Roe* v. *Wade* to ignore a similar agrument which might have supported his result?

C. GERMANY

DECISION OF FEBRUARY 25, 1975

Bundesverfassungsgericht
[1975] 39 BVerfGE 1

[Prior to 1974, German penal law generally forbade all abortions. After decades of debate and controversy, on June 18, 1974, the "Fifth Statute to Reform the Criminal Law" made major changes in the criminal law respecting abortion.

[Section 218c made it a crime to terminate any pregnancy unless the woman had been counseled by a physician or counseling agency. The most controversial provision, § 218a, provided that there was no criminal penalty for abortion within the first twelve weeks after conception if the woman had been counseled as provided in § 218c. Section 218b permitted abortion after twelve weeks if there was expert certification that there was danger to the life of the woman or of grave injury to her health, or danger of irreversible damage to the unborn child.

[The Government of the *Land* Baden-Württemberg applied to the Constitutional Court for a provisional order staying the enforcement of § 218a, the "time-phase" rule permitting abortion within twelve weeks of conception. On June 21, 1974, the day the new law was promulgated, the Court issued the stay, but provided that abortions which had medical, eugenic or ethical indications should not be punishable. Thereafter, 193 members of the Federal Diet, and the governments of five Laender petitioned the Court for constitutional review of § 218a.]

[OPINION *]

. . . .

The question of the legal treatment of the termination of pregnancy has been discussed publicly for decades and from various points of view. In fact, this phenomenon of social life raises diverse problems of a biological nature, especially those of a human-genetic, anthropological, medical, psychological, social, sociopolitical and, not least, ethical and moral-theological type, which touch upon fundamental questions of human existence. It is the task of the legislator to evaluate these arguments which have been developed from different viewpoints and have many-sided interrelations with one another, to supplement them by specifically juridico-political considerations and by practical experience [gained] through the law in operation and, on this basis, to . . . decide in what manner the legal

---

* Abridgement of *The Abortion Decision of February 25, 1975, of the Federal Constitutional Court, Federal Republic of Germany* (E. Jann trans. 1975).

order is to react to this social process. The legal rule in the Fifth Statute to Reform the Criminal Law, which was arrived at after extraordinarily extensive preliminary work, may be examined by the Federal Constitutional Court solely from the viewpoint of whether it is compatible with the Basic Law as the supreme law in force in the Federal Republic. The weight and seriousness of the constitutional question becomes clear if one calls to mind that the protection of human life is involved here, a central value of every legal order. Any decision bearing on the scale and limits of legislative freedom to make decisions calls for a total view of the store of constitutional norms and of the order of values encompassed therein.

I.

1. Article 2, paragraph 2, sentence 1, of the Basic Law also protects the life developing within the mother's womb as an independent legal interest.

a) The categorical inclusion of the inherently self-evident right to life in the Basic Law — unlike the case of the Weimar Constitution — may be explained principally as a reaction to the "Destruction of Life Unworthy to Live," the "Final Solution," and "Liquidations" carried out by the National Socialist Regime as governmental measures. Article 2, paragraph 2, sentence 1, of the Basic Law implies, as does the repeal of the death penalty by Article 102 of the Basic Law, "an affirmation of the fundamental value of human life and of a State concept that puts itself into emphatic opposition to the views of a political regime for which the individual life had little significance and therefore which practiced unlimited abuse in the name of the arrogated right over life and death . . . of the citizen."

b) In interpreting Article 2, paragraph 2, sentence 1, of the Basic Law, one must proceed from its wording: "Everyone shall have the right to life. . . ." Life in the sense of the developmental existence of a human individual in any event begins, according to established biological-physiological findings, on the 14th day after conception. . . .

The development process thus begun is a continuous one which manifests no sharp caesuras and does not permit any precise delimitation of the various developmental stages of the human life. It does not end with birth either; the phenomena of consciousness specific to human personality, for instance, do not appear until some time after birth. Therefore the protection of Article 2, paragraph 2, sentence 1, of the Basic Law may not be limited either to the "completed" human being after birth nor to the independently viable *nasciturus*. The right to life is guaranteed to everyone who "lives;" no distinction can be made between individual stages of the developing life before birth or between prenatal and postnatal life.

c) In countering the objection that "everyone" in common parlance and in legal terminology generally denotes a "completed" human person, [and] that, therefore, a purely verbal interpretation militates against the inclusion of the prenatal life in the range of efficacy of Article 2, paragraph 2, sentence 1, of the Basic Law, it must be emphasized that in any event the sense and purpose of this constitutional provision require that the protection of life be also extended to the developing life. The safeguarding of human existence against transgressions of the State would be incomplete if it did not also comprise the preliminary phase of the "completed life," the prenatal life.

This extensive interpretation corresponds to the principle established in the case law of the Federal Constitutional Court "according to which, in cases of doubt, that interpretation is to be chosen which most strongly develops the juridical efficacy of the constitutional norm." . . .

d) The history of the origin of Article 2, paragraph 2, sentence 1, of the Basic Law also lends itself to the substantiation of this conclusion.

. . . .

The legislative history of Article 2, paragraph 2, sentence 1, of the Basic Law . . . suggests that the formulation of "everyone has the right to life" was also to include "nascent life." In any event, even less can be deduced from the documentation of record for the contrary view. On the other hand, it furnishes no clue as to the answer to the question of whether the prenatal life must be protected by the criminal law.

. . . .

. . . [W]e need not decide on the controversial question at issue in the present proceedings, as well as in case law and scientific literature, of whether the *nasciturus* itself is the bearer of basic rights or whether, because its capacity to exercise legal and constitutional rights is lacking, it is protected "only" by the objective norms of the Constitution in its right to life. According to established precedent of the Federal Constitutional Court, the constitutional norms contain not only an individual's subjective defensive rights against the State, but they also represent at the same time an objective order of values which serves as a basic constitutional decision for all areas of the law and provides guidelines and impulses for legislation, administration, and judicial practice. . . . Whether and, in the appropriate case, to what extent the State is constitutionally obligated to furnish protection for the developing life may therefore be deduced already from the objective-legal content of the constitutional norms.

II.

1. The obligation of the State to furnish protection is comprehensive. It prohibits not only — as a matter of course — direct governmental encroachments upon the developing life, but also commands the State to position itself in a protective and supportive role for this life, which means, above all, to safeguard it from illegal encroachments from others. The individual spheres of the legal order must take directional guidance from this commandment in accordance with their particular tasks. The higher the legal interest within the order of the values of the Constitution, the more seriously the State's obligation to furnish protection must be taken. The human life represents a supreme value within the constitutional order that needs no further justification; it is the vital basis of . . . human dignity and the prerequisite of all other basic rights.

2. The obligation of the State to take the developing life under its protection also exists in principle in regard to the mother. Undoubtedly the natural union of the prenatal life with the mother establishes a particular type of relationship for which there is no parallel in any other factual situation in life. Pregnancy belongs to the intimate sphere of the woman whose protection is constitutionally guaranteed by Article 2, paragraph 1, in conjunction with Article 1, paragraph 1, of the Basic Law. If the embryo were to be regarded only as a part of the maternal organism, the termination of pregnancy would also remain within the sphere of private life into which the legislator is barred from intruding. . . . Since the *nasciturus* is an independent human being under the protection of the Constitution, termination of pregnancy has a social dimension which makes it accessible to and in need of regulation by the State. The right of a woman to a free development of her personality which embraces freedom of action in its comprehensive meaning and thus also comprises the woman's responsibility to self to decide against parenthood, and the duties deriving therefrom may, it is true, also lay claim to recognition and protection. But this right is not given without limitation — the rights of others, the constitutional order, and moral law limit it. It can never comprise *a priori* the authority to intrude upon the protected legal sphere of another without justifiable . . . reason, not to mention destroying it [such sphere] along with a life, least of all when in the nature of things a special responsibility precisely for such life exists.

A compromise which both guarantees the protection of the life of the *nasciturus* and concedes to the pregnant woman the freedom of terminating the pregnancy is not possible because termination of pregnancy always means destruction of the prenatal life. . . .

3. Here there is revealed the basic position of the legal order demanded by the Constitution in relation to the termination of

pregnancy: The legal order may not constitute the woman's right of self-determination as the sole guideline for its regulation. The State must in principle proceed from a duty of bringing the pregnancy to term [and] therefore in principle consider its termination as a wrong. The disapproval of the termination of pregnancy must be clearly expressed in the legal order. The false impression must be avoided that termination of pregnancy involves the same social preeminence as say a trip to the physician for the purpose of healing an illness, or even that it involves a legally irrelevant alternative to contraception. Moreover, the State by postulating a legal vacuum cannot escape its responsibility by refraining from any valuation and leaving the decision to the individual's own responsibility.

III.

It is, first of all, incumbent upon the legislator to decide how the State is to fulfill its obligation to give effective protection to the developing life. He determines what protective measures he considers suited to the purpose and required in order to guarantee an effective protection of life.

1. ... It is therefore the State's task to employ, first of all, sociopolitical and welfare measures to safeguard the developing life. What can be done here and how the assistance measures are to be organized in detail are left in a large measure to the legislator and in general are removed from review by a constitutional court. . . .

2. The question of the extent to which the State is constitutionally obligated also to employ, for the protection of the prenatal life, the means of the criminal law as the most incisive weapon at his [the legislator's] disposal cannot be answered on the basis of a simplified formulation of the question of whether the State must punish certain acts. A total view is necessary. . . .

In principle, the legislator is not obligated to resort to the same penal measures to protect the prenatal life which he would consider expedient and required to safeguard the postnatal life. . . .

a) From time immemorial it has been the task of the criminal law to protect the elementary values of community life. . . .

[T]he employment of the criminal law to punish "acts of abortion" is undoubtedly legitimate; it is the law in force in most civilized states — under variously formulated conditions — and is particularly in accord with the German legal tradition. It also follows that we cannot forgo a clear legal designation of this process as a "wrong."

b) However, punishment should never be self-serving. Its employment is in principle subject to the decision of the legislator. There is nothing to stop him from expressing, with due regard for the above-indicated viewpoints, the constitutionally required legal disapproval of the termination of pregnancy in a manner other than by means of a penal sanction. The decisive point is whether the totality of the measures serving the protection of the prenatal life, whether they be classifiable as measures of the civil law [or] public law, particularly the social law or criminal law, in fact guarantee a protection corresponding to the importance of the legal interest to be safeguarded. In the extremé case, namely where the protection mandated by the Constitution cannot be achieved in any other way, the legislator may be obligated, for the purpose of protecting the developing life, to employ the means of the criminal law. . . . It then is not a matter of an "absolute" duty of punishing, but rather of a "relative" obligation to use the penal sanction [which obligation] arises from the awareness that all other means are inadequate.

. . . .

3. The obligation of the State to protect the developing life exists — as shown — with respect to the mother also. Here, however, the employment of the criminal law gives rise to special problems which result from the singular situation of the pregnant woman. The incisive effects of a pregnancy upon the physical and mental condition of the woman are immediately apparent and require no further exposition. They often signify a considerable change in the entire conduct of [her] life and a limitation of personal developmental potential. This burden is not always or fully compensated by the fact that the woman finds new fulfillment in her task as a mother and that the pregnant woman has a claim to assistance by the community (Art. 6, para. 4, of the Basic Law). Here grave, indeed life-threatening conflict situations may arise in individual cases. The right to life of the unborn may lead to a burden on the woman which substantially exceeds the measure normally connected with a pregnancy. The question arises of what she may be reasonably expected to bear, in other words, the question of whether the State, also in such cases, may, by means of the criminal law, enforce the bringing of the . . . pregnancy to term. Esteem for the prenatal life conflicts with the right of the woman not to be forced beyond reasonable expectations to sacrifice her own life's values in order to foster respect for that [other] legal interest. In such a conflict situation, which generally does not permit any unequivocal moral evaluation and in which a decision to terminate the pregnancy may achieve the level of a decision of conscience worthy of respect, the legislator is bound to show particular restraint. If in these cases he does not consider the conduct of the pregnant woman as deserving of punishment and forgoes the means of a criminal sanction, then it must always be accepted constitutionally as the result of a judgment incumbent upon the legislator.

In interpolating the criterion of what may reasonably be expected, circumstances must be eliminated which do not gravely burden the duty-bound person, since they represent a normal situation everyone must cope with. Rather, circumstances of extraordinary weight must exist which make it so difficult for the person concerned to fulfill one's duties that one may not equitably be expected to do so. They exist especially when the person concerned is precipitated into grave inner conflicts by fulfilling the duty. The resolution of such conflicts by a penal sanction does not generally appear appropriate . . ., since it exerts an external compulsion in a case where respect for the personality sphere of the human being presupposes full internal freedom of decision.

The continuation of pregnancy in particular appears to exceed reasonable expectations if it is shown that termination is necessary in order to "avert a danger to the life" of the pregnant woman "or the danger of a grave injury to her health." . . . In this case her own "right to life and physical inviolability" (Art. 2. para. 2, sentence 1, of the Basic Law) is at stake, the sacrificing of which cannot be expected of her for prenatal life. Beyond this the legislator is free to exempt the termination of pregnancy from penal sanction also in the case of other extraordinary burdens for the pregnant woman which, from the viewpoint of what may be [reasonably] expected of her, are similarly as oppressive as those given in Section 218b, clause 1. We may include here the cases of indications based on eugenic, ethical (criminological), and social [considerations] or urgent necessity [pointing] toward a termination of pregnancy which were contained in the Draft of the Federal Government submitted during the Sixth Federal Diet and were discussed publicly and in the course of the legislative proceedings. . . . The decisive point is that in all these cases another interest equally worthy of protection by the Constitution asserts itself with such urgency that the State's legal order cannot demand here that the pregnant woman under all circumstances concede preeminence to the right of the unborn.

Also the indication of a general necessity (social indication) may be included here. For the general social situation of the pregnant woman and of her family may bring forth conflicts of such gravity that sacrifices in favor of the prenatal life exceeding a certain measure cannot be exacted by the instrumentalities of the criminal law. In the regulation of this indication case, the legislator must circumscribe the factual elements not subject to punishment in such a manner that the gravity of the social conflict to be presumed here is clearly recognizable and that — viewing the matter from the standpoint of what may not [reasonably] be expected [of the parties involved] — congruence of this indication with other indication cases remains assured. If the legislator removes genuine cases of conflict of this type from the sphere of criminal law protection, he does not violate his duty to protect life. In these cases the State, moreover, may not content itself with merely examining whether, and, in the appropriate case certifying that, the legal prerequisites exist for an unpunishable termination of pregnancy. Rather, the State is also expected here to offer counseling and assistance for the purpose of admonishing the pregnant woman as to her fundamental duty to respect the right to life of the unborn, of encouraging her to continue the pregnancy, and of supporting her — particularly in cases of social need — with practical assistance measures.

In all other cases the termination of pregnancy remains a wrong deserving of punishment; for here the destruction of a legal interest of the highest order is subject to the discretion — unmotivated by any necessity — of a third party. If the legislator had wanted to dispense with the criminal sanction here, this would have been compatible with the protective command of Article 2, paragraph 2, sentence 1, of the Basic Law only under the condition that another equally effective legal sanction was at his disposal which permits one clearly to recognize the character of the act as a wrong (disapprobation by the legal order) and which prevents terminations of pregnancy as effectively as a penal provision.

D.

If one examines the contested time-phase rule of the Fifth Statute to Reform the Criminal Law in the light of these standards, one finds that the Law does not, to the required extent, do justice to the obligation derivable from Article 2, paragraph 2, sentence 1, in conjunction with Article 1, paragraph 1, of the Basic Law to effectively protect the developing life.

I.

It is true that the constitutional command to protect the developing life is first of all directed at the legislator. The Federal Constitutional Court, however, has the task to determine, in the exercise of the function assigned it by the Basic Law, whether the legislator has complied with this command. It is true that the Court must carefully respect the latitude accorded to the legislator in evaluating the factual situations subject to his regulation, the requisite prognosis, if any, and the choice of means. The Court may not take the place of the legislator; but it is its task to examine whether the legislator, within the framework of the possible choices at his disposal, has done what was required in order to avert dangers from the legal interest to be protected. This in principle also applies to the question of whether the legislator is obligated to resort to his most incisive measure, the criminal law, in which context, however, the examination may not extend to the individual modalities of punishment.

II.

It is generally recognized that Section 218 StGB [Criminal Code], heretofore in force, gave only inadequate protection to the developing life, precisely because it threatened undifferentiated punishment for almost all cases of termination of pregnancy. The recognition that there are cases in which the penal sanction is inappropriate finally led to a situation where cases truly deserving of punishment were no longer prosecuted with the required severity. In the case of this crime, there is the further fact that, due to the nature of the matter, clarification of the facts is often difficult. Admittedly, the statistics on the high percentage of undetected crimes in the case of terminations of pregnancy differ widely, and it may hardly be possible to establish reliable data by pertinent empirical investigations. In any event, the number of illegal terminations of pregnancy in the Federal Republic has been high. The existence of a generalized penal norm may have contributed to the fact that the State has failed to take other adequate measures for the protection of the developing life. . . . Basic to the Law is the concept that *the developing life is better protected by individual counseling of the pregnant woman than by a penal sanction which removes the person willing to submit to an abortion from any possible persuasive influence, which is wrong as a matter of criminal policy and, moreover, has proved to be ineffective.* The legislator drew the conclusion from this that the penal sanction for the first twelve weeks of the pregnancy should be completely abandoned under certain conditions and preventive counseling and instruction should be introduced in its stead.

It is constitutionally unobjectionable and to be approved when the legislator attempts to fulfill his duty of furnishing better protection for the prenatal life by preventive measures, including counseling, to reinforce the woman's responsibility to self. However, the regulation adopted meets with pervasive constitutional misgivings in several respects.

1. The legal disapproval of the termination of pregnancy demanded by the Constitution must clearly be in evidence in the subconstitutional legal order. Only such cases may be exempted from this [rule] — as already shown — in which the continuation of the woman's pregnancy cannot be [reasonably] expected of her also under the criterion of the value judgment made in Article 2, paragraph 2, sentence 1, of the Basic Law. This general expression of disapproval is not manifest in the provisions of the Fifth Statute to Reform the Criminal Law on termination of pregnancy within the first twelve weeks; for the Statute leaves it unclear whether, in the wake of the suspension of the penal clause by Section 218a StGB, the termination of pregnancy without an indication for it remains

right or wrong. . . . The planned overall regulation can . . . only be interpreted in the sense that the termination of pregnancy performed by a physician within the first twelve weeks is not illegal [and] therefore permitted (by law).

. . . There are many women who, even without having reasons for the termination which merit respect under the Constitution's order of values, from the very first have decided upon a termination of pregnancy and are not accessible to any counseling. . . . These women find themselves neither in a state of material necessity nor in a situation of grave mental conflict. They reject pregnancy because they are not willing to shoulder the sacrifice and the natural maternal duties connected with it. They may have serious reasons for their attitude toward the developing life; but these are not reasons which prevail before the command to protect human life. The woman may [reasonably] be expected to bear the pregnancy in the light of the above-stated principles. . . .

It is argued that, based on experience unpersuasible women mostly know how to escape punishment, so the penal sanction in any event amounts to lost motion. . . . At the same time, . . . the penal sanction prevents the saving of lives through the counseling of persuasible women; . . . . The legislator has no choice but to weigh one life against the other, namely, the life which could presumably be saved by a certain regulation of the abortion question as against the life which is presumably sacrificed by the same regulation; for the penal sanction also not only protects, but at the same time destroys prenatal life. . . .

a) This view, first of all, does not do justice to the essence and function of criminal law. The penal norm is in principle directed at all those who are subject to the law and obligates them in the same manner. It is true that the authorities charged with penal prosecution never succeed in practice in subjecting to punishment all perpetrators who violate the criminal law. The percentage amounts of undetected crimes vary according to different crimes. Undoubtedly they are especially substantial in the case of abortion offenses. But this should not lead one to forget the general preventive function of the criminal law. If one sees the mission of the criminal law as one of protecting particularly important legal interests and elementary values of the community, then precisely this function assumes great importance. The remote effects of a penal norm, which in its fundamental normative content ("abortion is punishable") has now existed for a very long time, are just as important as the visible reactions in the individual case. The mere existence of such a penal sanction exercises an influence upon the value concepts and the manner of conduct of the population. . . . If the threat of punishment is generally removed, citizens will necessarily get the impression that a termination of pregnancy is legally permissible in all cases and should therefore no longer be condemned for socioethical reasons also.

b) The lump-sum balancing of life against life which leads to the decriminalization of the destruction of the supposedly smaller number [of lives] in the . . . interest of the allegedly higher number is incompatible with the obligation of giving individual protection to every single actual life.

The principle has been developed in the case law of the Federal Constitutional Court that the unconstitutionality of a legal provision, which according to its structure and actual effects discriminates against a certain group of persons, cannot be disproved by pointing out that this provision or other provisions of the law favor another group of persons. Emphasizing the general tendency of the law as a whole to promote legal protection carries even less weight in this context. . . .

c) Moreover, no dependable factual basis exists for any "overall statistical assessment" — which, in principle, is to be rejected. Adequate clues are lacking for us to suppose that the number of terminations of pregnancy will be substantially smaller than under the legal regulation heretofore in force. . . .

3. The counseling and instruction of the pregnant woman provided for cannot — even viewed by itself — be considered suitable to promote a continuation of the pregnancy.

. . . .

b) Particularly questionable is the fact that the instruction concerning social assistance may be given by the same physician who is to perform the termination of pregnancy. . . .

. . . .

A further element that dims the prospect of success is the fact that the instruction and counseling may be directly followed by the termination of pregnancy. One cannot expect that, under these circumstances, the pregnant woman and her relatives will seriously come to terms with the adverse arguments presented to her in the counseling. . . .

For any woman resolved to terminate her pregnancy, it therefore is only a matter of finding a compliant physician; since he is permitted to carry out both the social as well as the medical counseling and finally also the operation, no serious attempt on his part may be expected to deflect the pregnant woman from her decision.

III.

In summation, the following is to be stated as regards the constitutional evaluation of the time-phase rule adopted in the Fifth Statute to Reform the Criminal Law:

. . . .

If the legislator views the undifferentiated penal sanction hitherto in force for the termination of pregnancy as a questionable means of protecting life, this, nevertheless, does not free him of the obligation of at least attempting to achieve better protection of life by a more differentiated penal regulation that subjects those cases to punishment in which there are constitutional objections to a termination of pregnancy. A clear delimitation of this group of cases from other cases in which the woman may not [reasonably] be expected to continue the pregnancy will increase the potential of the penal norm for developing legal consciousness. . . .

IV.

The regulation adopted in the Fifth Statute to Reform the Criminal Law is now and then defended by reference to the fact that, *in other democratic countries of the Western World, the penal provisions on termination of pregnancy have most recently been "liberalized" or "modernized" in a similar or even more extensive manner; this is an indication that the new rule at least corresponds to the general development of views on this subject and is not incompatible with fundamental socioethical and legal principles.*

These considerations cannot influence the decision to be made here. Aside from the fact that all these foreign regulations are strongly controversial in their own countries, the legal standards which apply to the actions of the legislator there differ substantially from those of the Federal Republic of Germany.

Fundamental to the Basic Law are principles of state organization which can be explained only by reference to the historical experience and the intellectual and moral settling of accounts with the preceding system of National Socialism. As a bulwark against the omnipotence of the totalitarian state, which arrogated unlimited dominion over all areas of social life and for which consideration for the life of the individual fundamentally amounted to nothing in the pursuit of its governmental objectives, the Basic Law has erected a value-oriented order which places the individual human being and his dignity at the center of all its determinations. . . .

The Federal Constitutional Court, to which the Constitution has given the mandate of standing guard over the observance by all state organs of its fundamental principles and, in the appropriate case, their enforcement, can only orient its decisions toward these principles in the development of which the Court itself has made a decisive contribution by its own precedents. In so doing, no derogatory judgment is made about other legal systems "which have not had these experiences with a system of injustice and which, on the basis of a different historical development [and] of different political realities and fundamental political philosophies, have not made such a decision for themselves."

E.

In accordance with all the above, Section 218a StGB of the Criminal Code in the Version of the Fifth Statute to Reform the Criminal Law is incompatible with Article 2, paragraph 2, sentence 1, in conjunction with Article 1, paragraph 1, of the Basic Law insofar as that Section also exempts termination of pregnancy from punishability when no reasons exist which, in accordance with the preceding statements, prevail under the scale of values of the Basic Law. . . .

There were no grounds to annul any other provisions of the Fifth Statute to Reform the Criminal Law.

Dissenting Opinion

of Judge RUPP-V. BRÜNNECK and Judge DR. SIMON*

The life of every single human being is, of course, a central value of the legal order. It is indisputable that the constitutional obligation to protect this life also encompasses its preliminary stage before birth. The discussions in the Parliament and before the Federal Constitutional Court did not involve the *Whether,* but only the *How* of this protection. The decision in this matter is the legislator's responsibility. Under no circumstances can it be deduced from the Constitution that the State is obliged to subject the termination of pregnancy to punishment at every stage. The legislator was as free to opt for counseling and the time-phase rule as he was for the indication solution.

Any contrary constitutional interpretation is incompatible with the freedom-oriented character of the constitutional norms and, in a measure fraught with consequences, transfers decisional competences to the Federal Constitutional Court. . . . Because of the very fact that every solution remains a patchwork, one should not raise constitutional objections over the fact that the German legislator — in harmony with the reforms in other Western civilized states — has given sociopolitical measures priority over largely ineffective penal sanctions. The Constitution nowhere prescribes a statutory "disapproval" of morally reprehensible conduct without regard to the protective effect such [disapproval] may actually have.

---

*Judge Haager also dissented, but without opinion.

A.

I.

The authority of the Federal Constitutional Court to annul decisions of the parliamentary legislator demands restraint in its use in order to avoid a dislocation of power among the constitutional organs. The command of judicial self-restraint, which has been termed the "life-giving elixir" of the judicial function of the Federal Constitutional Court, applies in particular when it is not a matter of warding off encroachments by governmental authority, but when the Court by way of constitutional control would issue directives for the positive development of the social order to the legislator who has a direct mandate from the people. It is here that the Federal Constitutional Court is not permitted to succumb to the temptation itself to assume the functions of the organ to be controlled unless, in the long run, the standing of constitutional jurisdiction is to be endangered.

1. The review petitioned for in these proceedings moves beyond the area of classical control by constitutional courts. The fundamental norms at the heart of our Constitution guarantee to the citizen in his relation to the State, as *defensive rights,* a sphere of free development of life on one's own responsibility. To this extent the classic function of the Federal Constitutional Court consists in the warding off of excessive encroachments by governmental power upon this sphere of freedom. . . .

In the present constitutional litigation, an examination is undertaken for the first time in reverse order to determine whether the State *must* punish, namely, whether the repeal of the penal sanction against the termination of pregnancy during the first three months of pregnancy is compatible with basic rights. It is obvious, however, that dispensing with punishment is the opposite of an encroachment by the State. . . .

Basic rights, in the sense of defensive rights, have a relatively clear recognizable content. . . . On the other hand, as a rule it is a highly complex question as to *how* a value decision may be realized by positive measures of the legislator. . . . The decision, which frequently presupposes compromises and is accomplished in a trial-and-error procedure, is the responsibility of the legislator directly mandated by the people in accordance with the fundamental rule of the separation of powers and democratic principles.

Because of the growing importance of ameliorative social measures for the effectuation of basic rights one may not also relinquish all control by constitutional courts in this area; it will possibly be one of the main tasks of the judiciary in the next decades to work out suitable instrumentalities which leave the legislator freedom in developing [this area]. As long as [such instrumentalities] are still lacking, there is danger that constitutional courts will not limit their control to the review of a decision made by the legislator but will replace it with another that the Court deems better. This danger exists to an increased degree in very controversial questions if — as in this case — the losing minority goes before the Federal Constitutional Court to attack a decision of the parliamentary majority made after long discussions. Without prejudice to the legitimate standing of the petitioners to have doubts as to constitutionality cleared up in this way, the Federal Constitutional Court here unexpectedly finds itself in the situation of being enlisted as a political arbitrator to make the choice between competing legislative proposals.

. . . It [the Court] may oppose the legislator only if he has completely disregarded a value decision or if the mode and method of its realization are obviously erroneous. On the contrary, the majority [of the Court] in effect charges the legislator, in spite of a supposed recognition of his freedom of creative endeavor, with having failed to put into effect a self-evident value decision in a manner they believe to be the best possible one. If that were to become the general criterion, the command of judicial self-restraint would have been abandoned.

. . . .

1. The Constitution, of course, presupposes that the State may also use its power of punishment to protect an orderly social life; but it is not the meaning of basic rights to require such a commitment, but rather to set limits on it. Thus the Supreme Court of the United States has even considered the punishment of terminations of pregnancy performed by a physician with the consent of the pregnant woman during the first third of the pregnancy as a violation of a constitutional right. It is true that this would be going too far according to German constitutional law. Under the freedom-oriented character of our Constitution, the legislator, however, is in need of a justification for punishing, but not for abstaining from punishment. . . .

2. Moreover, the *legislative history* of the Basic Law speaks against anyone who would infer from the basic right norms that he has a duty ⋅ to punish. . . .

. . . .

. . . The decisive disassociation from the totalitarian National Socialist State accomplished with the Basic Law commands rather, on the contrary, reticence in dealing with criminal punishment whose wrongful utilization has already caused infinite suffering in the history of mankind.

B.

Even if one were to assume, in agreement with the majority but contrary to our understanding, a constitutional obligation to punish, one cannot charge the legislator with an infringement of the Constitution. The reasoning of the majority encounters the following objectons — without there being any need for us to enter into every detail:

I.

. . . Insofar as the problem concerns the evaluation of the factual situation and the efficacy of intended measures, the Court must accept the legislator's conception unless it is proven obviously erroneous.

The reasoning in support of the judgment does not meet these requirements. It repeatedly becomes entangled in contradictions and in the end virtually shifts the burden of proof: The legislator is to be permitted to dispense with a penal sanction only if it is established beyond any doubt that the milder measures which he prefers are "at least" equally or even more effective.

1. . . .

According to the *view of the undersigned judge* [Rupp-v. Brünneck], the refusal of the pregnant woman to permit the fetus to develop into a human being within her body is, not only according to the natural feelings of the woman but also according to the law, something entirely different from the destruction of independently existing life. It is for this reason already that we may not in principle equate abortion in the first stage of pregnancy with murder or intentional killing. Even more so is it inappropriate, if not biased, to equate the time-phase solution with euthanasia or even "killing of the unworthy life" in order thus to disparage it — as has been done in the public discussions. The fact that an independently existing living being separable from the maternal organism does not come into being until after a longer development process suggests, or at least permits us to take into consideration, in any legal evaluation periodic caesuras which correspond to this development. . . .

The *undersigned judge* [Simon] is inclined to accord less legal importance to these further considerations of the relationship between the pregnant woman and her fetus. If however — on the basis of other reasons already stated or yet to be discussed — there are no objections to the legislator's repeal of the criminal sanction for the first three months of pregnancy, then he is proceeding in harmony with the subject matter if he takes the mentioned circumstances into account in his regulation.

2. Any examination of whether an obligation to punish is to be demanded *ultima ratio* for the protection of prenatal life in spite of

the stated particularities must proceed from the *social problem* which has induced the legislator [to enact] his regulation. . . .

The legislator . . . could not treat it as a matter of indifference that illegal terminations of pregnancy today still lead to injuries to health, and that not only in the cases of abortions by "quacks" and "female angel-makers," but to a greater degree also because, in the case of operations by physicians, the illegality prejudices the total commitment of modern [medical] resources and of the necessary [medical] auxiliary personnel or prevents the necessary post-operative care. A further abuse is to be found in the commercial exploitation, here and abroad, of women who are willing to undergo an abortion, and the social inequality connected therewith; women who are better-off can, especially by traveling into neighboring foreign countries, obtain an abortion by a physician much more easily than poorer or less shrewd women. . . .

b) Of particular importance for the legislator's decision in seeking out the best remedy for these conditions was the fact that the decision to undergo a termination of pregnancy regularly results from a conflict situation which is based upon varied motivations strongly influenced by the conditions of the individual case. . . .

3. In this entire situation, the "containment of the abortion epidemic" is not only a "sociopolitically desirable goal" but is also urgently required in the meaning of a better protection of life and for the reestablishment of the credibility of the legal order. In his efforts to solve this extremely difficult task, the legislator has exhaustively weighed all essential points of view. . . .

In adopting his solution, it was open to the legislator to proceed from the realization that, in view of the failure of the penal sanction, the suitable means for redress are to be sought in the social and societal areas, [and] that the decisive point is to make it easier, on the one hand, for the mother to carry the child to term by preventive psychological, sociopolitical, and societal-political measures of a supportive nature and, on the other, to strengthen her own willingness to decrease the number of unwanted pregnancies through better information on the possibilities of contraception. Obviously the majority was not in doubt either that such measures, viewed as a whole, are the most effective ones and most readily correspond to an effectuation of basic rights in the meaning of greater freedom and increased social justice.

. . . .

We do not deny that this counseling rule — as shown in the Judgment — still shows weaknesses. Insofar as these could not be eliminated by an interpretation of the law in conformity with the Constitution and by appropriate implementing regulations of the Laender, the constitutionally based exceptions should have been limited to these shortcomings and should not have questioned the time-phase and counseling rule in its total concept. And last but not least, the success of a counseling regulation substantially depends upon whether the woman being counseled can be offered or provided assistance which for her opens a way out of her difficulties. If this cannot be done, then the criminal law is nothing but an alibi for the lack of effective assistance; the responsibility and burden are merely shifted to the weakest members of society. The majority — in accord with existing case law — declares itself incapable to this extent of limiting the creative freedom of the legislator and prescribing for him an expansion of sociopreventive measures. But if judicial restraint applies here, then the Constitutional Court, above all, may not force the legislator to utilize the power to punish as the strongest governmental pressure device in order to compensate by a penal sanction for social dereliction of duty. This certainly does not reflect the function of the criminal law in a freedom-oriented social state.

4. Also the majority recognizes the legislative intent to preserve life by counseling as an "estimable goal" but considers — in agreement with the petitioners — the imposition of concomitant penal sanctions to be indispensable because doing away entirely with punishment leaves a "gap in the protection" in those cases in which the termination of pregnancy is not based on respectable grounds.

a) The suitability of penal sanctions for the intended protection of life, however, appears *a priori* as doubtful. . . .

The majority at the very outset fails to furnish the proof incumbent upon it that in the age of "abortion tourism" domestic penal provisions can be expected to favorably influence such women as are determined, even without plausible reason, to undergo an abortion. Such a result can be expected, if at all, only in a certain number of cases — especially those involving members of socially weaker groups. In the case of women who are easily persuaded, the ambivalent effect of penal sanctions manifests itself, among other things, in that it may provide, on the one hand, a certain support against the demands for abortion by the procreator or the family but, on the other, may increase the frequency of abortions by driving the pregnant woman into isolation, thus exposing her all the more to such pressures and impelling her to [undertake] rash acts.

. . . .

The legislator, therefore, found himself in the dilemma according to which, in his judgment, preventive counseling and repressive penal sanction to an extent mutually cancel each other in their effect on the protection of life. His idea of forfeiting the possible inhibiting effect of penal sanctions in a probably small number of cases in order perhaps to save other life in a larger number of cases cannot be disposed of by countering that *this is a "lump sum balancing of life against life," which is incompatible with the constitutional duty to furnish individual protection for every prenatal life.* In so arguing the majority closes its mind, in a manner difficult to understand, to the perception that it itself is doing the same thing for which it reproaches the legislator. For the majority itself, by force even of constitutional reasoning, holds the legislator to such a numerical computation in that it compels him, by demanding the maintenance of the penal provision, to leave the prenatal life unprotected which [otherwise] could have been saved by replacing the penal sanction with appropriate counseling.

II.

. . . .

Our basic objection is directed at the majority for not showing whence the requirement of disapproval as an independent obligation is to be constitutionally derived. In our view, the Constitution nowhere prescribes the use of the statutory law to show disapproval of ethically reprehensible conduct *per se* or such conduct worthy of punishment without giving consideration of the effect achieved thereby. In a pluralistic, ideologically neutral, and freedom-oriented democratic community it is up to social forces to establish attitudinal postulates. The State must practice reticence in this area; its task is to protect the legal interests guaranteed and recognized by the Constitution. The sole determinant in making the constitutional decision is whether the penal provision is compulsorily mandated in order to secure an effective protection of the developing life with due consideration of such interests of the woman as are worthy of protection.

III.

Identical or similar *reform provisions in many foreign countries* show that the German legislator's decision in favor of the time-phase and counseling rule derives neither from a morally or legally reprehensible basic attitude nor from obviously erroneous premises in the evaluation of the conditions of life. In Austria, France, Denmark, and Sweden, terminations of pregnancy, when performed by a physician with the consent of the pregnant woman within the first twelve (in France, ten) weeks of the pregnancy, is not punishable; in Great Britain and the Netherlands, the indication rule applies, which amounts to the same thing in its practical application. Some of these nations may take pride in an impressive constitutional tradition and none of them yield to the German Federal Republic in their unconditional respect for the life of every individual human being; some of them also have had historical experience with injustice as a system that is contemptuous of humanity. Their decisions required the coming to terms with the same legal and social problems as did those of the Federal Republic of Germany. Moreover, in all these nations there is in force the European Convention on Human Rights whose Article 2 in paragraph 1 ("Everyone's right to life shall be protected by law") comes close to the constitutional provision of Article 2, paragraph 2, sentence 1, of the Basic Law and as a whole may even be more comprehensive than the domestic German norm. The Austrian Constitutional Court of Justice has expressly stated that the time-phase solution is compatible with the Human Rights Convention, which in Austria enjoys constitutional rank.

IV.

In summary, it is therefore our view that the Constitution does not bar the legislator from dispensing with a penal sanction which in his unrefuted view is largely ineffective, inadequate, and even noxious. His attempt to overcome by more adequate means the increasingly obvious inability of the State and of society under present conditions to protect life may be imperfect; nevertheless, the attempt is more in accord with the spirit of the Basic Law than is the demand for punishment or disapproval.

NOTES AND QUESTIONS

1. On May 18, 1976, new abortion legislation was enacted permitting abortion in four specified areas. First, at any time, an abortion is permitted for medical reasons — to safeguard the life or prevent grave impairment of the physical or mental health of the woman. The medical reasons for the abortion, however, must be ascertained by a physician who is not performing the abortion. Second, within 22 weeks of conception, abortion is permitted for eugenic reasons — where the unborn child is already irreversibly damaged. Third, within twelve weeks of conception, abortion is permitted if the pregnancy resulted from rape. Fourth, and perhaps most interesting, abortions are permitted within twelve weeks of conception, for "social" reasons — in cases where the extreme plight of the woman is such that the continuation of the pregnancy cannot be demanded, and the situation cannot be ameliorated by other reasonable means.

With some exceptions for some medical abortions, the woman must be advised by both a physician and a counselor. Social insurance pays for counseling, and in the case of permitted abortion, for the abortion itself. There has been political controversy concerning efforts of some district administrators to forbid abortion in district hospitals.

One main feature of an opposition bill by anti-abortion forces was that the "social" reasons for abortion were omitted (the opposition bill also had stricter requirements for counseling). There has been criticism of the enacted legislation on the ground that the "social" indication for abortion is so open-ended that it can lead, in practice, to the abortions which the Constitutional Court had indicated were prevented by the Constitution. Note that the Constitutional Court stated that abortion may be permitted in cases where "extraordinary burdens for the pregnant woman ... are oppressive." If abortion legislation is enacted — as it was — to permit abortions under that principle, would it have been possible for the legislature to provide criteria which would meaningfully define permissible and impermissible abortions?

2. In the United States, abortion litigation has raised problems concerning case and controversy. The constitutional issue has seldom been presented in the context of a defense to a criminal charge, but has usually been raised in a suit for injunction or declaratory judgment. The problem in those suits has been whether the plaintiff had standing to raise the issue. In *Roe* v. *Wade,* a childless couple who feared the consequences of future pregnancy were held to lack standing; a pregnant single woman, however, did have standing although her pregnancy had obviously terminated long before the Supreme Court decided her case. In *Doe* v. *Bolton,* an indigent, married woman who had been denied an abortion under the requirements imposed by the Georgia statute, and physicians who might be prosecuted for ignoring those requirements, were also accorded standing. Would there have been a case or controversy if either suit had been brought by parties analogous to those in the German case? Would the issues presented have been any more abstract, or less well presented by adversary parties interested in the outcome? Are there other characteristics of the German case which would have made it unwise for the United States Supreme Court to entertain a suit framed in an analogous manner? Is it significant that judicial review in the United States is "decentralized"?

3. Of all the opinions surveyed thus far, the dissenting opinion in the German case is most "realist" in approach — in the sense that it relies extensively on difficulties of the law in action when abortion is generally made a criminal offense. Beyond the facts that there are large numbers of illegal abortions, and that many of those abortions are carried out under conditions gravely endangering the woman's life, the dissent points out that there has been a significant problem of discrimination against the poor — that "women who are better-off can, especially by travelling into neighboring foreign countries, obtain an abortion by a physician much more easily than poorer or less shrewd women." One attempt to explain *Roe* v. *Wade* has been that, although it is not mentioned in the opinion, significant restrictions on the availability of abortion discriminate against the poor. That argument, however, has been foreclosed by the 1977 decision permitting governments to exclude abortions from programs of medical aid to the indigent. *Maher* v. *Roe,* 432 U.S. 464 (1977), *supra* § A., note 4. Indeed, the combination of *Roe* v. *Wade,* which disables government from interfering with abortion by women who can afford the medical expense, and *Maher* v. *Roe,* which permits government to deny money for medical aid in procuring an abortion, may produce an even larger discrimination against those who are most indigent. Does the discrimination argument carry more force under the German Constitution which includes, as a constitutional requirement, the institution of the "social state"?

4. Consider carefully the arguments of the majority and the dissent in the German decision as to whether it is appropriate for courts to interpret the Constitution to require the legislature to enact affirmative laws, as opposed to interpreting the Constitution to negative an invalid law. In the United States, prior to *Roe* v. *Wade,* constitutional attacks were occasionally mounted on permissive abortion laws on the ground that they violated the fetus' constitutional right to life. *See* Louisell, *Abortion, The Practice of Medicine and the Due Process of Law,* 16 U.C.L.A. L. REV. 233 (1969). One difficulty with the argument in support of that position was the proposition that the constitutional right to life affirmatively required government to enact and enforce criminal laws forbidding abortion. As has been noted (Ch. 10, § B.2.a.(ii), *supra*), the basic structure of the United States Constitution is to define liberty in the form of restrictions on government power rather than in terms of affirmative obligations of government to protect social rights. It was precisely that distinction on which Justice Powell's opinion of the Court relied in *Maher* v. *Roe* to conclude that government had no constitutional obligation to finance abortions. Is the argument that government has an affirmative obligation to enact laws to protect values defined by the Constitution easier under the twentieth century Bonn Constitution?

Even where a Constitution affirmatively mandates an obligation of the legislature to pass particular laws, does the German decision indicate some of the difficulties involved in judicial enforcement of that mandate? Suppose that, in the United States, a constitutional amendment were enacted which provided that an unborn person shall not be deprived of life by any person. (*See* § A., note 3, *supra.*) If a legislature were to repeal existing laws against abortion, what judicial relief would be available? Suppose that a State without a criminal prohibition on abortion were to refuse to enact one. On the date it was handed down, what was the effect of the decision of the German Constitutional Court on the criminality of abortion?

5. Notice that the dissent relies tangentially on the holding of the United States Supreme Court in *Roe* v. *Wade.* Would it have been more appropriate for the dissent to rely on Justice White's dissent, which had criticized the *Roe* v. *Wade* majority for "an exercise of raw judicial power"? Of course, the majority decisions of the German and United States courts are poles apart in their resolution of the abortion controversy. Are they nevertheless very much alike with reference to the issue of the appropriate spheres of judicial activism?

Suppose that, prior to enactment of the revision of the penal code, a constitutional defense had been made to a prosecution for engaging in a "therapeutic" abortion. Would the same judges of the Constitutional Court have urged judicial activism and judicial restraint?

6. One defense for the Court's activism in *Roe* v. *Wade* is that it was a propitious time for a decision which reflected the views of the majority, insuring eventual public receptivity to the decision. *See* Miller & Barron, *The Supreme Court, the Adversary System, and the Flow of Information to the Justices: A Preliminary Inquiry,* 61 VA. L. REV. 1187 (1975). Is that true? Is it equally true of the German decision? Is a national legislature most likely not to reflect the views of the majority? (Note that the German decision involved, unlike the United States decision, the validity of a national act.) A German public opinion poll showed that, of those having an opinion (18 percent did not), 61 percent regretted the decision while 39 percent favored it. German Catholics endorsed the decision by a slender margin, while Protestants condemned it by more than two to one. *See The Abortion Decision of February 25, 1975 of the Federal Constitutional Court, Federal Republic of Germany* (E. Jann trans. 1975).

7. The German Constitutional Court decision was challenged by two German women before the European Commission of Human Rights, Application No. 6959/75, *Rosemarie Brüggemann and Adelhaid Scheuten* v. *Federal Republic of Germany.* On May 19, 1976, the Commission decided that:

THE LAW
1. The applicants complain that under the law in force in the Federal Republic of Germany concerning intentional interruption of pregnancy they must either renounce sexual intercourse or use contraceptive measures or run the risk of unwanted offspring.

They take the view that this is the result of the judgment of the Federal Constitutional Court of 25 February 1975 which declared Section 218 of the Criminal Code, as amended by the Fifth Criminal Law Reform Act, null and void.

This Section provided that abortion, performed in the first twelve weeks of pregnancy by a doctor and with the consent of the mother, shall not constitute a punishable offence. The Court made a provisional order pending the coming into force of a new statute.

2. In the meantime, the Federal Parliament has adopted a new amendment, the Fifteenth Criminal Law Reform Act, based on the decision of the Federal Constitutional Court. It is foreseen that this amendment will be promulgated and enter into force in June 1976.

Under Article 25 (1) of the Convention only the victim of an alleged violation of the Convention may bring an application.

When dealing with a application introduced in 1960 by a man who complained of a Norwegian statute permitting interruption of pregnancy under certain conditions, the Commission had held that the applicant, who declared that he acted in the interest of third persons, could not claim to be himself the victim of a violation of the Convention and that it could not examine in abstracto the compatibility of a statute with the Convention (Application No. 867/60, Coll. 6, p. 34).

. . . .

4. The applicants have not here claimed to be pregnant, or to have been refused an interruption of pregnancy, or to have been prosecuted for unlawful abortion.

However, they claim that pregnancy and its interruption are a part of private life, and that the legal regulation of abortion is an intervention in that private life.

5. The Commission considers that pregnancy and the interruption of pregnancy are part of private life, and also in certain circumstances of family life. It further considers that respect for private life "comprises also, to a certain degree, the right to establish and to develop relationships with other human beings, especially in the emotional field, for the development and fulfilment of one's own personality" (Decision on Application No. 6825/74, X against Iceland), and that therefore sexual life is also part of private life; and in particular that legal regulation of abortion is an intervention in private life which may or may not be justified under Article 8 (2).

Consequently the Commission concludes that the application is not incompatible with the Convention and that the applicants are entitled under Article 25 to claim to be victims of a breach of the Convention.

6. The situation of which the applicants complain was created by the judgment of the Federal Constitutional Court of 25 February 1975, against which there is no remedy under German law.

Assuming, however, that the six months' time-limit contained in Article 26 of the Convention is applicable to an application directed against a legislative situation resulting from a judgment of a constitutional jurisdiction, it can be noted that the present application was introduced on 24 March 1975, i.e. less than six months after the judgment concerned. It follows that the application cannot be rejected for one of the reasons mentioned in Articles 26 and 27 (3) of the Convention.

7. The Commission having examined the observations of the applicants and the respondent Government, finds that the application is not manifestly ill-founded, since it raises issues under Article 8 of the Convention and in particular the question whether the intervention in their private life, of which the applicants complain, is justifiable. These issues are of a complexity and importance which require a consideration of the application on its merits.

8. One of the applicants has also alleged a violation of Article 12 of the Convention in that being unmarried she could by unwanted motherhood suffer an interference with her chances to marry. The applicants have further invoked Article 9 which guarantees the freedom of thought conscience and religion, of Article 11 which guarantees the freedom of association, and Article 14 which prohibits discrimination in the enjoyment of the rights and freedoms set forth in the Convention.

Having decided to submit the application to an examination of the merits, the Commission did not find it necessary to decide upon these further allegations at the present stage.

For these reasons, the Commission
DECLARES THE APPLICATION ADMISSIBLE.

[1976] 19 YEARBOOK EUR. CONV. ON HUM. RTS. 382, 412-16.

In a press release dated April 5, 1978, the Council of Europe announced that the Committee of Ministers had reached a decision on the merits of the applications of Brüggemann and Scheuten. The release stated:

When examining the case, the European Commission of Human Rights retained only issues under Article 8 of the Convention (Right to respect of private life). It considered that not every regulation on the termination of an unwanted pregnancy constituted an interference with the right of respect for the private life of the mother. Article 8, paragraph 1, could not therefore be interpreted as meaning that pregnancy and its termination are, as a principle, solely a matter of the private life of the mother.

In its report the Commission had concluded that the legal rules in force in German law since the judgement of the Federal Constitutional Court of 25 February 1975 about which the

applicants had complained, did not interfere with their right to respect for their private life. The Committee of Ministers, agreeing with the opinion expressed by the Commission, has decided that there was no violation of the European Convention. In agreement with the Government of the Federal Republic of Germany, the report of the Commission will be made public.

8. Do you agree with the following comment by Professor Kommers?

Whereas American constitutionalism [as exemplified by *Roe v. Wade*] emphasizes a rugged individualism in the exercise of personal freedom, German constitutionalism [as exemplified by the Constitutional Court's decision on abortion] has a larger communitarian thrust with a corresponding limitation upon the exercise of political freedom. This difference between American and German constitutionalism is one of emphasis, yet important to an understanding of the varying constitutional policies of the two countries.

Kommers, *Abortion and Constitution: United States and West Germany,* 25 Am. J. Compar. L. 255, 280 (1977).

9. Professor Rivero's comment to the decision of the French *Conseil Constitutionnel,* in a footnote at the end, suggests that the German and French decisions may be explained, in their opposite results, by differences in the French and German constitutional texts. Professor Rivero stated that this was a tentative explanation since he had not yet read the German decision. After reading the two decisions, are there differences in the constitutional texts which, standing alone, would explain the disparate results?

How much does the German decision turn on the flat conclusion that life begins on the 14th day after conception? Justice Blackmun's opinion in *Roe* v. *Wade* states that it was unnecessary for the Court to resolve the question when life beings. Did the majority of the United States Supreme Court, after noting that it was impossible to resolve that question in medicine, philosophy or theology, nevertheless resolve it for purposes of the United States Constitution?

Finally, is the reference to the National Socialist experience, which forms a backdrop to the provisions of the Bonn Constitution, merely a makeweight or is it a persuasive reason for the decision? How does one account for the fact that the abortion laws in National Socialist Germany (as well as fascist Italy and Vichy France) made almost all abortions a crime?

D. ITALY

CARMOSINA ET AL.

Corte costituzionale, Decision of February 18, 1975, No. 27
[1975] 20 Giur. Const. 117; [1975] 43 Rac. uff. corte cost. 201
[1975] 98 Foro It. I, 515

[FACTS: In the course of a criminal abortion proceeding, the examining judge of the *Tribunale* of Milan raised the constitutionality of art. 546 of the penal code. That provision appears to prohibit all abortions. Article 54 of the penal code, however, qualifies art. 546 by permitting the defense of strict "necessity." According to the *ordinanza,* the constitutional problem arises because therapeutic abortions are permitted, under the necessity defense, only when grave harm is inevitable, or there is great danger of such harm. Thus, therapeutic abortions to spare the woman aggravation of preexisting physical problems remain a crime. The *ordinanza* suggests conflict with art. 31, second paragraph of the Constitution, which "protects motherhood, infancy and youth, favoring the institutions necessary for this purpose"; and with art. 32, first paragraph, which "protects health as a fundamental right of the individual and a fundamental interest of society."]

[OPINION:]

The *ordinanza* by the examining judge of the *Tribunale* of Milan raises a serious problem which is the subject of debate and legislative activity in many nations.

This is not the place to retell the legislative history of voluntary abortion as a crime, a history which is linked with the development of religious thought and with the evolution of moral philosophy as well as social, legal, political and demographic doctrines. Not punished in certain epochs, punished in others sometimes lightly, sometimes very severely, voluntary abortion was considered violative of disparate values, such as life, family order, common morality, and the growth of the population.

In the present penal code voluntary abortion is termed "crime against the integrity of the progeny" (book II, title X of the penal code). According to the background materials and the report to the King which accompanied the [1931] code, the value protected is "the demographic interest of the State." The preceding [pre-facist] code, on the other hand, considered abortion among the "crimes against the person," seemingly a fairer and more correct way of putting it.

The product of conception was from time to time held to be simply a part of the woman's body, the hope of a person, and a thing alive from the beginning, or after a more or less long period of gestation.

The Court holds that the protection of conception — which already figures prominently in the law (articles 320, 339, 687 of the civil code) — has constitutional foundation. Article 31, 2nd paragraph, of the Constitution, expressly imposes the "protection of motherhood" and, more generally, article 2 of the Constitution recognizes and guarantees the inviolable rights of man, among which must be placed, although with the particular characteristics unique to it, the legal situation of the foetus.

What has just been said — which in itself justifies legislative intervention resulting in penal sanctions — must however be accompanied by the further consideration that the constitutionally protected interest of the foetus may conflict with other values which are themselves constitutionally protected. Consequently, the law cannot place a total and absolute priority on the first interest, denying adequate protection to the others. Herein lies the reason why, in the opinion of the Court, the present criminal legislation concerning abortion is unconstitutional.

The *ordinanza* under consideration specifically challenges only that part of article 546 of the penal code, in reference to articles 31 and 32 of the Constitution, which prescribes punishment both for anyone who performs an abortion for a consenting woman, and for the woman herself, "even when it has been ascertained that there are pregnancy dangers to the physical well-being and to the psychological equilibrium of the pregnant woman, but without the occurrence of all the elements of 'necessity' prescribed in article 54 of the penal code."

Within this scope, the question is well-founded. The condition of the pregnant woman is particular in every way and does not receive adequate protection in a law of general character like article 54 [of the penal code], which requires not only the gravity and the absolute inevitability of harm or of danger, but also its imminence, whereas injury or danger resulting from continuation of a pregnancy may be foreseen, but is not always imminent.

Moreover, the exemption contained in article 54 [of the penal code] is based on the presupposed equivalence of the infringed value to another value which this very infringement was meant to safeguard. Yet, there is no equivalence between the right not only to life but also to health of one who — like the pregnant woman — is already a person, and the safeguard of an embryo which has yet to become a person.

The legislature appropriately prescribed that in some particular cases, in addition to the general cause of exemption from the criminal sanction foreseen by article 54 of the criminal code, other kinds of "necessity" may exempt from the criminal sanction (article 384 of the penal code). Not less worthy of consideration is the unique state of necessity of the pregnant woman in grave danger of compromising her health.

Therefore, it seems inevitable that part of article 546 of the penal code must be declared unconstitutional.

It should be added, however, that the exemption from any
punishment of anyone who, in the situation described above,
procures the abortion, and of the woman who consents, does not at
all exclude the requirement, already under present law, that the
operation should be performed in such a way as to save, when
possible, the life of the foetus. But this Court also holds that it is the
legislators' obligation to set up the necessary legislative safeguards
intended to forbid the procuring of an abortion without careful
ascertainment of the reality and gravity of injury or danger which
might happen to the mother as the result of the continuation of
pregnancy: therefore the lawfulness of abortion must be anchored
to a preceding evaluation of the existence of the conditions which
justify it. For these reasons the Constitutional Court declares the
unconstitutionality of that part of article 546 of the penal code which
does not recognize that pregnancy may be interrupted when further
development of the gestation could imply injury or danger which is
grave, medically ascertained in the manner indicated above, and not
otherwise avoidable, for the health of the mother.

NOTES AND QUESTIONS

1. One obvious similarity of the decisions of *Carmosina* and *Roe*
v. *Wade* is in their immediate results — the invalidation of restrictive
abortion laws. There is another striking similarity. In the United
States, women's groups consider the validity of restrictive abortion
laws to be a central issue of the rights of women. (In Germany, the
abortion decision was followed by a bombing of the Federal
Constitutional Court. A revolutionary women's group claimed
responsibility for the act. Jann, *supra,* at 130.) *Roe* v. *Wade*
conspicuously avoids treating the issue as a women's rights issue. So,
too, does the Italian Constitutional Court.

The United States Supreme Court has decided that laws which
discriminate against women on the basis of outmoded sexual
stereotypes violate the Equal Protection Clause of the Fourteenth
Amendment. *See, e.g., Craig* v. *Boren,* 429 U.S. 190 (1976). Would
that rationale have provided a viable alternative starting point for
decision in both *Carmosina* and *Roe* v. *Wade*? Would it have blunted
the criticism of *Roe* v. *Wade* as a case where the judges read their
own values into the Due Process Clause?

Interestingly, other cases which have involved the issue of
pregnancy in the United States have been analyzed as not involving
discrimination against women. *Cleveland Board of Education* v.
LaFleur, 414 U.S. 632 (1974) struck down a mandatory maternity
leave requirement under the Due Process Clause of the Fourteenth
Amendment, reasoning that the requirement was not rationally
related to the school's asserted interest of maintaining continuity of

instruction. The Court's opinion had no reference to the issue of discrimination against women, and did not refer to previous cases involving discrimination against women. More significant was *Geduldig* v. *Aiello,* 417 U.S. 484 (1974), which held that it was constitutional to exclude the expenses of normal pregnancy from a state disability insurance program. The Court's opinion reasoned that a distinction between pregnancy-related disabilities and other medical and accidental disabilities involved no distinction between the sexes. The distinction drawn was not between men and women, but between pregnant persons (all women) and nonpregnant persons (many of whom were women). Is that reasoning persuasive?

Can the moral and constitutional issues which surround the subject of abortion be resolved without considering the impact of those laws on women as opposed to men?

2. Is the Italian Constitutional Court's decision closer in its reasoning to that of the German Constitutional Court than to that of the United States Supreme Court? What is the Court's view on the issue of when life begins? What would be the decision of the Italian Court if a law similar to that struck down in Germany had been enacted in Italy? What was the immediate impact of the Italian decision? Was abortion no longer a crime, or could non-therapeutic abortions continue to be prosecuted?

After the decision of the *Corte Costituzionale* in *Carmosina,* a bill on abortion was introduced which, while formally affirming that abortion was not to be used as a method of birth control, and was to be used only to protect the woman's physical or mental health, was claimed by critics to be unconstitutional since it, in fact, permitted "free abortions." The bill passed the Italian Chamber of Deputies. The Senate, however, voted by a 2 vote majority not to take the bill up. As this is written, a similar bill is again pending in the Chamber of Deputies. Many observers conclude that any legislation which is enacted will be subjected to a national referendum.

3. The Italian decision brings to three the number of decisions with which you are familiar where a court has entered the thicket of vetoing legislative choices on the abortion issue on the basis of vague constitutional values. Do the three decisions, read together, enlighten your views on the perennial debate over judicial activism and restraint?

E. AUSTRIA

DECISION OF OCTOBER 11, 1974

Verfassungsgerichtshof*

[1974] ERKLAERUNGEN DES VERFASSUNGSGERICHTSHOFS 221

The application by the Salzburg provincial government to delete paragraph 97 (1) (1) of the Federal Law of 23 January 1974, BGBl.

---

* Constitutional Court of Austria.

no. 60, on legally punishable acts (Penal Code) on grounds of unconstitutionality is not accepted.

Grounds of Judgment:

I.1. The Federal Law of 23 January 1974 on legally punishable acts contained provisions relating to abortions. These provide that an abortion with the consent of the pregnant woman, or by the pregnant woman herself, . . . as well as an abortion without the consent of the pregnant woman are subject to penalty. The penalties apply both to the abortionist, whether acting with or without the consent of the pregnant woman, and also to the woman who terminates her own pregnancy or allows another to do so. Para. 97 (1) sets out the cases in which the acts made punishable by paragraph 96 are exempt from punishment. The introductory sentence and the first sub-paragraph of these provisions read as follows:

Para. 97 (1). An Act described in para. 96 is not punishable

1. If the abortion is carried out by a doctor within the first three months after conception, following medical consultation. . . .

On 15 March 1974, the Salzburg provincial government submitted an application . . . for the suspension of para. 97 (1) (1) Penal Code on grounds of unconstitutionality; it considers this provision of the law unconstitutional in several respects, since in its opinion it violates the fundamental right and civil right to life and the fundamental right to equality before the law. . . .

II. The Constitutional Court made the following considerations:

. . . .

(2) . . . a) The Salzburg provincial government argues that para. 97 (1) Penal Code infringes the fundamental and civil right to life "according to constitutional law not based on international treaties."

Neither the Constitution nor the laws, also to be considered here, which according to Article 149 (1) have the force of constitutional laws, explicitly contain the right to life as a constitutionally guaranteed right. However, the explicitly defined fundamental and civil rights (in these laws) presuppose this right. . . .

[The Salzburg provincial government maintains that] out of respect for the right to life, the legislator is obliged not to make any provisions which subject this right to arbitrary governmental or other intervention[; that t]his is a right of the unborn both if (as maintained) the latter is a human being in the legal sense, and if he is regarded as another "legal person." In the latter case this right to life would belong to the unborn as a holder of rights, as such a right by its nature would pertain to him.

b) Against this objection by the Salzburg provincial government, the catalogue of fundamental rights of the National Basic Law of 21 December 1867, on the general rights of citizens, which, according to Article 149 of the Constitution, has the force of a constitutional law, is imbued — as is understandable from its period of production — with the classical liberal idea of guaranteeing the individual protection against acts of force by the state. . . .

Regarding the content of para. 97 (1) (1) of the Penal Code . . . it need not be proved whether and in what circumstances the existence of a fundamental and civil right to life, not explicitly defined, can be deduced as an interpretation of the rights explicitly defined in the National Basic Law. Such a right to life could, according to the provisions contained in the National Basic Law for protecting the rights it incorporates, only have the effect of protecting the individual against attacks on his life by the state. However, the provisions of paras. 96 and 97 of the Penal Code do not concern an interference with life by the state.

Nor can a right to life guaranteeing protection from attacks other than by the state, be found in other constitutional provisions "not based on international treaties."

. . . .

If, however, the "constitutional law not based on international treaties" does not contain a right to life giving protection against other than state interference, then it is unnecessary to go into the arguments of the Salzburg provincial government as to whether such a right also applies to the unborn. For if the right does not exist, the question who is entitled to it does not arise.

Para. 97 (1) (1) of the Penal Code is therefore not unconstitutional for the reason that it infringes a constitutionally guaranteed right to life not based on international treaties.

3. a) The Salzburg provincial government argues further that para. 97 (1) (1) of the Penal Code infringes the fundamental and civil right to life "according to constitutional provisions based on international treaties." It regards the challenged regulation first of all as an infringement of Article 2 of the European Convention on Human Rights, which, as an internal law of the state, has constitutional rank.

The first sentence of para. 1 of Article 2, in the authentic English and French versions and in the official German translation, is as follows:

> Everyone's right to life shall be protected by law.
> Le droit de toute personne à la vie est protégé par la loi.
> Das Recht jedes Menschen auf das Leben wird gesetzlich geschützt.

The Salzburg provincial government submits that Article 2 (1) protects life and that the term "life" is to be taken as meaning biological and physical existence. It alleges that this is a purely natural concept designating simply the fact of being alive, that is, the bodily existence of human beings in contrast to the states of being "not-yet-alive" or "dead." This life is to be protected by the state. The way of guaranteeing this protection is a matter for the legislator. However, the legal protection must be of such a kind as to prevent, in the most effective possible manner, any interference with life. The penal law is a necessary and irreplaceable form of such protection.

The history of the development of Article 2 itself provides no information as to the interpretation to be given it.

The European Human Rights Commission has not yet given a clear decision on the substantive questions. The European Court of Human Rights has not yet been asked to consider the question at all.

. . . .

Art. 2 of the European Convention contains no definition of the life that it protects; the point in time at which this life begins is not laid down.

The opinions represented in the literature are divergent. A number of authors hold the view that Art. 2 does not refer to nascent life. . . . On the other hand, a number of other authors take the view that the right to life laid down in Art. 2 does embrace nascent life. . . .

. . . .

This range of views represented in the international literature indicates the problems of interpreting Art. 2.

In the interpretation of international treaties, the common will is in principle to be taken as a basis. When there is doubt this is to be taken as the common minimum, on which there is general agreement. . . .

The objects of the European Convention are — as expressed in its title and preamble — "Human Rights and Fundamental Freedoms" ("Menschenrechte und Grundfreiheiten," "Droits de l'Homme et Libertés fondamentales"). The right to life guaranteed by Art. 2 to "everyone" (. . . the corresponding term in the other authentic text is "toute personne") can therefore refer only to a human being's own life. The concept of a person in Art. 2, however, is independent of the concept of a person in the national legal systems. Those entitled have, according to Art. 2, the right to life even where according to the national legal system of a contracting state they do not have legal personality, or have it only in part. Otherwise, the protection of the right to life rooted in the Convention could be made ineffective by any contracting state, by withdrawing legal personality from those entitled by Art. 2. On the other hand the conclusion cannot be drawn from the fact of recognition of legal personality or of partial legal personality by a national legal system that this recognition is causally linked with the protection of Art. 2 of the Convention.

The first sentence of Art. 2 (1) ("Everyone's right to life shall be protected by law") leaves it an open question whether the protection of life thereby laid down refers to nascent human life as well as to the life of born persons.

A consideration of the whole text of Art. 2 in its context, however, does not seem to suggest that this provision also covers nascent life.

Exceptions to the protection of life (Art. 2(1), first sentence) are provided in respect of the killing of born human beings (Art. 2(1), second sentence, and Art. 2(2), Art. 15(2)). If the first sentence of Art. 2(1) were meant also to cover the protection of nascent life, then to that extent this protection would be unconditional. It would not however be consistent in laying down the right to life to allow the killing of already born persons in exceptional circumstances, but to exclude interference with nascent life even in specially justified cases. It must therefore to concluded from the structure of this legal norm that Art. 2 does not extend to nascent life. . . .

. . . .

5. a) The Salzburg provincial government adduces further that § 97 (1) (1) of the Penal Code infringes the fundamental right to equality before the law "as an essential constituent of the democratic principle" and "in accordance with constitutional law not based on international treaties."

The equality principle is alleged to constitute one of the fundamental pillars of any democratic polity. Without the principle of equality there could be no democratic state.

. . . .

It follows from the principle of equal treatment that no human being ought to be given an inferior position to another. There was no objective reason for giving nascent human life a better legal position than previously from a particular month of life onwards. It might very well be the case that the mother of the growing child would suffer less from the separation from her child at an early stage than at a later one, and that it would be safer for her from a medical point of view. Such considerations would, however, overlook the fact that from the child's standpoint there is no objective reason for its arbitrary killing at any stage of its life. Otherwise, the unborn child would count as a thing up to a certain age and beyond that age as a person. Unequal treatment by the criminal law of the unborn according to age would therefore mean an infringement of the constitutional rule of equality.

[In the view of the Salzburg provincial government,] § 97 (1) (1) of the Penal Code is unconstitutional because, by simple legal regulation, it inappropriately put the unborn up to the age of three

months in an inferior position by depriving them of the protection
of § 96 of the Penal Code.

The Salzburg provincial government alleged also that conception
and death were the beginning and end points of a biologically closed
entity whose being remained always the same. Accordingly, the
time-phase rule treated equal things completely unequally, by setting
a particular stage of this closed entity outside legal protection and
thereby partly protecting human life through the penal law and partly
removing this protection from it. Situations of conflict between the
interests of the pregnant woman and the fetus might arise and ought
to be resolved in the interests of the former. However, making
abortion free of punishment in this way would amount to placing a
higher value on any interest, even a whim, of the pregnant woman
than on the interest of the life of the unborn, even perhaps where
the woman's interests might be grounded solely in convenience or
financial advantage. In the view of the Salzburg provincial
government, such boundless over-valuation of the arbitrary will of
one side has no constitutional cover.

(b) Since — as the foregoing considerations . . . show — nascent
human life as such has no special constitutional protection, there is
also no constitutional prohibition on the legislator from protecting
the fetus by making abortion punishable. However, if the legislator
adopts provisions on abortion, he is bound by the constitutional
restrictions that otherwise apply to the content of every act of
legislation. It follows from the principle of equality that there is a
constitutional obligation on the legislator that, within the framework
of his legal policy objectives, which except in the case of excess are
not subject to review by the constitutional court, he adopt only such
rules as are objectively justified having regard to the matter to be
regulated. There would then be an infringement of the equality
principle if a law contained discriminations within one and the same
legal institution which could not be justified from corresponding
differences as to the facts.

The provisions of § 97 (1) (1) of the Penal Code contain an
exception from the criminal law protection laid down in para. 96
Penal Code relating to abortion with the consent of the pregnant
woman or by the pregnant woman herself. This exception means that
the abortion is treated differently by the criminal law depending on
whether it takes place within the first three months of the pregnancy
or thereafter. Abortion without punishment is subject to the sole
precondition that it be carried out by a doctor following prior
medical consultations.

Pregnancy consists in the development of human life in the womb.
In evaluating the rules on abortion from the point of view of the
equality principle, the decisive factor is not that throughout the
whole duration of the pregnancy both the mother's life and the

nascent human life constitute constant life, but that the natural biological entity of the "fetus in the womb" be evaluated according to whether it constituted one and the same thing throughout the duration of the pregnancy.

Since the nascent human life goes through a development while in the stage of "fetus in the womb," passing from a fertilized egg cell, which under natural conditions is unable to survive outside the womb to a human being able to survive outside the womb, these various developmental phases of the biological entity "fetus in the womb" do not necessarily represent "one and the same thing" in the sense of the constitutional principle of equality.

The legislator therefore has the possibility, as regards the criminal law, of treating abortion differently depending on the stage of development of the embryo in the womb, without infringing the equality principle.

In its statement on the time-phase rule contained in para. 97 (1) (1) Penal Code the Austrian government alleged that the different evaluation in the criminal law of abortion within the first three months after conception on the one hand, and after the expiration of this period on the other hand, takes account of the development that the fetus goes through during pregnancy. An undifferentiated treatment of abortion during the whole duration of pregnancy would mean, considering the object of discourse, that unequal things were being treated equally. Just as the life of a born human being is evaluated more highly than that of the unborn embryo, so the value of the unborn fetus could not be set equal in each stage of development. At the point which the time-phase rule chose as a division, namely the end of the third month of pregnancy, the development of the fetus is still far from the stage of extrauterine viability. If the embryo were already capable of life outside the womb, then the circumstance that it was still inside the womb could not be evaluated as so important that abortion could be left to the decision of the pregnant woman, while killing outside the womb would be treated as murder or infanticide at birth and subject to severe penalty. Such considerations were removed from the state by the time-phase rule.

The Legal Affairs Committee's report of 16 November 1973 contains the observation that for health reasons the attempt must be made to keep the medical danger involved in abortion as small as possible. It was largely undisputed in the medical literature that the danger of intervention, both as regards complications and as regards later consequences, increased considerably after the third month of pregnancy.

The Constitutional Court can leave aside the question whether an undifferentiated treatment of the termination of pregnancy during the whole duration of a pregnancy — as is apparently the opinion of the Federal government — would contradict the principle of equality. The issue here is only whether the regulation contained in the disputed legal provision can continue to exist when confronted with the equality principle. On the considerations given above, the limitation on punishability given in para. 97 (1) (1) Penal Code as against para. 96 Penal Code is not inappropriate.

But regardless of how this regulation may be evaluated from the point of view of legal policy — according to the religious, philosophical or even scientific position of the observer it may be rejected or approved — an impropriety that would infringe the principle of equality cannot be discovered in the rule.

It should be noted in this connection that the legal development in states with different constitutional structures has led to similar results.

. . . .

[The Court then summarily rejected the arguments that the challenged law is incompatible with the principles of a democratic society embodied in the Austrian Constitution. It further rejected arguments premised on Article 8 of the European Convention, which provides that "Everyone has the right to respect for his private and family life. . . ." The Court rejected the argument under Art. 8 as this Article does not "contain any obligation on the legislator to make disrespect for family life punishable" under the criminal law. The same rationale disposed of the challenge based on Article 12 of the European Convention, which says that both men and women have "the right to marry and to found a family."]

9. Since accordingly the objections raised by the Salzburg provincial government against the constitutionality of para. 97 (1) (1) Penal Code do not hold, the application to suspend this legal provision as unconstitutional should remain without effect.

QUESTIONS

1. Can the different decisions of the Austrian and German Constitutional Courts, on the issue whether there is an affirmative constitutional obligation to protect fetal life, be explained by differences in the texts of the relevant constitutional documents? By differences in the historical setting of those texts?

2. The five decisions in this chapter represent a wide divergence in results, views on the moral issues of the abortion controversy, and views on the propriety of judicial activism and restraint. Are there any generalizations, beyond the accident of the views on abortion of a majority of the judges of any particular court, which satisfactorily explain why different national courts have approached the problem in different ways?

Index

References are to page numbers.

A

C

I

J

L

I

J

L

V